SQL Server 2016 Developer's Guide

Build efficient database applications for your organization
with SQL Server 2016

Dejan Sarka
Miloš Radivojević
William Durkin

BIRMINGHAM - MUMBAI

SQL Server 2016 Developer's Guide

First published: March 2017

Production reference: 1150317

Published by Packt Publishing Ltd.
Livery Place
35 Livery Street
Birmingham
B3 2PB, UK.
ISBN 978-1-78646-534-4

www.packtpub.com

Credits

Authors

Dejan Sarka

Miloš Radivojević

William Durkin

Reviewer

Tomaž Kaštrun

Commissioning Editor

Amey Varangaonkar

Acquisition Editor

Vinay Argekar

Content Development Editor

Aishwarya Pandere

Technical Editor

Vivek Arora

Copy Editor

Vikrant Phadke

Project Coordinator

Nidhi Joshi

Proofreader

Safis Editing

Indexer

Tejal Daruwale Soni

Production Coordinator

Shraddha Falebhai

About the Authors

Dejan Sarka, MCT and SQL Server MVP, is an independent trainer and consultant who focuses on the development of database and business intelligence applications, located in Ljubljana, Slovenia. Besides his projects, he spends around half of his time on training and mentoring. He is the founder of the Slovenian SQL Server and .NET Users Group. Dejan is the main author and co-author of many books and courses about databases and SQL Server. He is a frequent speaker at many worldwide events.

I would like to thank everybody involved in this book, especially to my co-authors, Miloš and William, to the content development editor, Aishwarya, and to the technical editor, Vivek.

Miloš Radivojević is a database consultant in Vienna, Austria. He is a Data Platform MVP and specializes in SQL Server for application developers and performance and query tuning. Currently, he works as a principal database consultant in bwin (GVC Holdings)—the largest regulated online gaming company in the world. Miloš is a co-founder of PASS Austria. He is also a speaker at international conferences and speaks regularly at SQL Saturday events and PASS Austria meetings.

I would like to thank my co-authors, Dejan Sarka and William Durkin. It has been a pleasure and privilege working with you guys! It was also a pleasure to work with editors, Aishwarya Pandere and Vivek Arora, in the production of this book. I'd also like to thank, Tomaž Kaštrun, for his prompt and helpful review. Finally, I would like to thank my wife, Nataša, my daughter, Mila, and my son, Vasilije, for all their sacrifice, patience, and understanding while I worked on this book.

William Durkin is a DBA and data platform architect for CloudDBA. He uses his decade of experience with SQL Server to help multinational corporations achieve their data management goals. Born in the UK and now based in Germany, he has worked as a database developer and DBA on projects ranging from single-server installations, up to environments spanning five continents using a range of high-availability solutions. William is a regular speaker at conferences around the globe, a Data Platform MVP and is the chapter leader of a German PASS chapter.

I would like to thank, Dejan and Miloš, for involving me in this book, it has been a challenge but a lot of fun! I would also like to thank Aishwarya and Vivek, for their editorial support. Last but certainly not least, thanks to my wife, Birgit, and son Liam, for your support and patience.

About the Reviewer

Tomaž Kaštrun is a SQL Server developer and data analyst. He has more than 15 years of experience in business warehousing, development, ETL, database administration and query tuning. He also has more than 15 years of experience in the fields of data analysis, data mining, statistical research, and machine learning.

He is a Microsoft SQL Server MVP for data platforms and has been working with Microsoft SQL Server since version 2000.

Tomaž is a blogger, author of many articles, co-author of statistical analysis books, speaker at community and Microsoft events, and avid coffee drinker.

Thanks to the people who inspire me, the community, and the SQL family. Thank you, dear reader, for reading this. For endless inspiration, thank you Rubi.

www.PacktPub.com

For support files and downloads related to your book, please visit www.PacktPub.com.

Did you know that Packt offers eBook versions of every book published, with PDF and ePub files available? You can upgrade to the eBook version at www.PacktPub.com and as a print book customer, you are entitled to a discount on the eBook copy. Get in touch with us at service@packtpub.com for more details.

At www.PacktPub.com, you can also read a collection of free technical articles, sign up for a range of free newsletters and receive exclusive discounts and offers on Packt books and eBooks.

https://www.packtpub.com/mapt

Get the most in-demand software skills with Mapt. Mapt gives you full access to all Packt books and video courses, as well as industry-leading tools to help you plan your personal development and advance your career.

Why subscribe?

- Fully searchable across every book published by Packt
- Copy and paste, print, and bookmark content
- On demand and accessible via a web browser

Customer Feedback

Thanks for purchasing this Packt book. At Packt, quality is at the heart of our editorial process. To help us improve, please leave us an honest review on this book's Amazon page at https://www.amazon.com/dp/1786465345.

If you'd like to join our team of regular reviewers, you can e-mail us at customerreviews@packtpub.com. We award our regular reviewers with free eBooks and videos in exchange for their valuable feedback. Help us be relentless in improving our products!

Table of Contents

Preface

Microsoft SQL Server is developing faster than ever in its nearly 30 years history. The newest version, SQL Server 2016, brings many important new features. Some of these new features just extend or improve features that were introduced in the previous versions of SQL Server, and some of them open a completely new set of possibilities for a database developer.

This book prepares the readers for more advanced topics by starting with a quick introduction of SQL Server 2016's new features and a recapitulation of the possibilities database developers had already in the previous versions of SQL Server. Then, the new tools are introduced. The next part introduces small delights in the Transact-SQL language, then the book switches to a completely new technology inside SQL Server—JSON support. This is where the basic chapters finish, and the more complex chapters start. Stretch database, security enhancements, and temporal tables are medium-level topics. The last chapters of the book cover advanced topics, including Query Store, columnstore indexes, and In-Memory OLTP. The final two chapters introduce R and R support in SQL Server and show how to use the R language for data exploration and analysis beyond that which a developer can achieve with Transact-SQL.

By reading this book, you will explore all of the new features added to SQL Server 2016. You will be capable of identifying opportunities for using the In-Memory OLTP technology. You will learn how to use columnstore indexes to get significant storage and performance improvements for analytical applications. You will be able to extend database design by using temporal tables. You will exchange JSON data between applications and SQL Server in a more efficient way. For vary large tables with some historical data, you will be able to migrate the historical data transparently and securely to Microsoft Azure by using Stretch Database. You will tighten security by using the new security features to encrypt data or to get more granular control over access to rows in a table. You will be able to tune workload performance more efficiently than ever with Query Store. Finally, you will discover the potential of R integration with SQL Server.

What this book covers

Chapter 1, *Introduction to SQL Server 2016*, very covers briefly the most important features and enhancements, not only those for developers. We want to show the whole picture and point where things are moving on.

Chapter 2, *Review of SQL Server Features for Developers,* is a brief recapitulation of the features available for developers in previous versions of SQL Server and serves as a foundation for an explanation of the many new features in SQL Server 2016. Some best practices are covered as well.

Chapter 3, *SQL Server Tools,* helps you understand the changes in the release management of SQL Server tools and explores small and handy enhancements in SQL Server Management Studio (SSMS). It also introduces RStudio IDE, a very popular tool for developing R code, and briefly covers SQL Server Data Tools (SSDT), including the new R Tools for Visual Studio (RTVS), a plugin for Visual Studio, which enables you to develop R code in an IDE that is common and well-known among developers that use Microsoft products and languages.

Chapter 4, *Transact-SQL Enhancements*, explores small Transact-SQL enhancements: new functions and syntax extensions, ALTER TABLE improvements for online operations, and new query hints for query tuning.

Chapter 5, *JSON Support in SQL Server*, explores the JSON support built into SQL Server. This support should make it easier for applications to exchange JSON data with SQL Server.

Chapter 6, *Stretch Database,* helps you understand how to migrate historical or less accessed data transparently and securely to Microsoft Azure by using the Stretch Database (Stretch DB) feature.

Chapter 7, *Temporal Tables,* introduces support for system-versioned temporal tables based on the SQL:2011 standard. We'll explain how this implemented in SQL Server is and demonstrates some use cases for it (for example, a time-travel application).

Chapter 8, *Tightening the Security,* introduces three new security features. With Always Encrypted, SQL Server finally enables full data encryption. Row-level security on the other side restricts which data in a table can be seen by specific user. Dynamic data masking is a soft feature that limits sensitive data exposure by masking it to non-privileged users.

Chapter 9, *Query Store,* guides you through Query Store, and helps you to troubleshoot and fix performance problems that are related to execution plan changes.

Chapter 10, *Columnstore Indexes*, revises the columnar storage and then explores the huge improvements for columnstore indexes in SQL Server 2016: updateable nonclustered columnstore indexes, columnstore indexes on in-memory tables, and many other new features for operational analytics.

Chapter 11, *Introducing SQL Server In-Memory OLTP*, describes a feature introduced in SQL Server 2014 that is still underused: the In-Memory database engine, which provides significant performance gains for OLTP workloads.

Chapter 12, *In-Memory OLTP Improvements in SQL Server 2016*, describes all of the improvements of the In-Memory OLTP technology in SQL Server 2016, which extend the number of potential use cases and allow implementation with less development effort and risk.

Chapter 13, *Supporting R in SQL Server*, introduces R Services and the R language. It explains how SQL Server R Services combine the power and flexibility of the open source R language with enterprise-level tools for data storage and management, workflow development, and reporting and visualization.

Chapter 14, *Data Exploration and Predictive Modeling with R in SQL Server*, shows how you can use R for advanced data exploration and manipulation, and for statistical analysis and predictive modeling that is way beyond what is possible when using T-SQL language.

What you need for this book

In order to run all of the demo code in this book, you will need SQL Server 2016 Developer or Enterprise Edition. In addition, you will extensively use SQL Server Management Studio. You will also need the RStudio IDE and/or SQL Server Data Tools with R Tools for Visual Studio plug-in.

Who this book is for

This book is aimed at database developers and solution architects who plan to use new SQL Server 2016 features or simply want to know what is now available and which limitations from previous versions have been removed. An ideal book reader is an experienced SQL Server developer, familiar with features of SQL Server 2014, but this book can be read by anyone who has an interest in SQL Server 2016 and wants to understand its development capabilities.

Conventions

In this book, you will find a number of text styles that distinguish between different kinds of information. Here are some examples of these styles and an explanation of their meaning.

Code words in text, database table names, folder names, filenames, file extensions, pathnames, dummy URLs, user input, and Twitter handles are shown as follows: " One table has `varchar(5)` columns, which will be small enough to fit in the in-row storage."

A block of code is set as follows:

```
EXEC dbo.InsertSimpleOrder
@OrderId = 5, @OrderDate = '20160702', @Customer = N'CustA';
EXEC dbo.InsertSimpleOrderDetail
@OrderId = 5, @ProductId = 1, @Quantity = 50;
```

When we wish to draw your attention to a particular part of a code block, the relevant lines or items are set in bold:

```
ProductId INT NOT NULL CONSTRAINT PK_Product PRIMARY KEY,
    ProductName NVARCHAR(50) NOT NULL,
    Price MONEY NOT NULL,
    ValidFrom DATETIME2 GENERATED ALWAYS AS ROW START NOT NULL,
    ValidTo DATETIME2 GENERATED ALWAYS AS ROW END NOT NULL,
    PERIOD FOR SYSTEM_TIME (ValidFrom, ValidTo)
```

Any command-line input or output is written as follows:

```
SQL Server Execution Times:
CPU time = 1797 ms, elapsed time = 1821 ms.
```

New terms and **important words** are shown in bold. Words that you see on the screen, for example, in menus or dialog boxes, appear in the text like this:

 Warnings or important notes appear in a box like this.

 Tips and tricks appear like this.

Reader feedback

Feedback from our readers is always welcome. Let us know what you think about this book-what you liked or disliked. Reader feedback is important for us as it helps us develop titles that you will really get the most out of. To send us general feedback, simply e-mail feedback@packtpub.com, and mention the book's title in the subject of your message. If there is a topic that you have expertise in and you are interested in either writing or contributing to a book, see our author guide at www.packtpub.com/authors.

Customer support

Now that you are the proud owner of a Packt book, we have a number of things to help you to get the most from your purchase.

Downloading the example code

You can download the example code files for this book from your account at http://www.packtpub.com. If you purchased this book elsewhere, you can visit http://www.packtpub.com/support and register to have the files e-mailed directly to you.

You can download the code files by following these steps:

1. Log in or register to our website using your e-mail address and password.
2. Hover the mouse pointer on the **SUPPORT** tab at the top.
3. Click on **Code Downloads & Errata**.
4. Enter the name of the book in the **Search** box.
5. Select the book for which you're looking to download the code files.
6. Choose from the drop-down menu where you purchased this book from.
7. Click on **Code Download**.

Once the file is downloaded, please make sure that you unzip or extract the folder using the latest version of:

- WinRAR / 7-Zip for Windows
- Zipeg / iZip / UnRarX for Mac
- 7-Zip / PeaZip for Linux

The code bundle for the book is also hosted on GitHub at `https://github.com/PacktPublishing/SQL-Server-2016-Developers-Guide`. We also have other code bundles from our rich catalog of books and videos available at `https://github.com/PacktPublishing/`. Check them out!

Errata

Although we have taken every care to ensure the accuracy of our content, mistakes do happen. If you find a mistake in one of our books-maybe a mistake in the text or the code-we would be grateful if you could report this to us. By doing so, you can save other readers from frustration and help us improve subsequent versions of this book. If you find any errata, please report them by visiting `http://www.packtpub.com/submit-errata`, selecting your book, clicking on the **Errata Submission Form** link, and entering the details of your errata. Once your errata are verified, your submission will be accepted and the errata will be uploaded to our website or added to any list of existing errata under the Errata section of that title.

To view the previously submitted errata, go to `https://www.packtpub.com/books/content/support` and enter the name of the book in the search field. The required information will appear under the **Errata** section.

Piracy

Piracy of copyrighted material on the Internet is an ongoing problem across all media. At Packt, we take the protection of our copyright and licenses very seriously. If you come across any illegal copies of our works in any form on the Internet, please provide us with the location address or website name immediately so that we can pursue a remedy.

Please contact us at `copyright@packtpub.com` with a link to the suspected pirated material.

We appreciate your help in protecting our authors and our ability to bring you valuable content.

Questions

If you have a problem with any aspect of this book, you can contact us at `questions@packtpub.com`, and we will do our best to address the problem.

1
Introduction to SQL Server 2016

SQL Server is the main relational database management product from Microsoft. It has been around in one form or another since the late 1980s (developed in partnership with Sybase), but as a standalone Microsoft product since the early 1990s. During the last 20 years, SQL Server has changed and evolved, gaining newer features and functionality along the way.

The SQL Server we know today is based on what was arguably the most significant (r)evolutionary step in its history, with the release of SQL Server 2005. The changes that were introduced have allowed the versions that followed the 2005 release to take advantage of newer hardware and software improvements such as: 64-bit memory architecture, better multi-CPU and multi-core support, as concludes the overview of programming better alignment with the .NET framework, and many more modernizations in general system architecture.

The incremental changes introduced in each subsequent version of SQL Server have continued to improve upon this solid foundation. Fortunately, Microsoft have changed their release cycle for multiple products, including SQL Server, resulting in shorter timeframes between releases. This has, in part, been due to Microsoft's focus on their much reported "Mobile First, Cloud First" strategy. This strategy, together with the development of the cloud version of SQL Server "Azure SQL Database", has forced Microsoft into a drastically shorter release cycle. The advantage of this strategy is that we are no longer required to wait three to five years for a new release (and new features). There have been releases every two years since SQL Server 2012 was introduced, with multiple releases of Azure SQL Database in between the *real* versions.

While we can be pleased that we no longer need to wait for new releases, we are also at a distinct disadvantage. The rapid release of new versions and features leaves us developers with ever decreasing periods of time to get to grips with the shiny new features. Previously, versions had many years between releases, allowing us to build up a deeper knowledge and understanding of the available features before having to consume new information.

In this chapter, we will introduce what's new inside SQL Server 2016. We will outline features that are brand new in this release of the product and look at features that have been extended or improved upon.

We will be outlining new features in the following areas:

- Security
- Engine features
- Programming
- Business intelligence

Security

The last few years have provided frequent demonstrations of the importance of security in IT. Whether we consider the repercussions of recent, high profile data leaks, or the multiple cases of data theft by hacking. While no system is completely impenetrable, we should always consider how we can improve security in the systems we build. These considerations are wide-ranging and sometimes even dictated by rules, regulations, and laws. Microsoft has responded to the increased focus on security by delivering new features to assist developers and DBAs in their search for more secure systems. The security features in SQL Server 2016 have been designed to make improving the security of SQL Server based solutions even easier to implement.

Row Level Security

The first technology that has been introduced in SQL Server 2016 to address the need for increased and improved security is **Row Level Security (RLS)**. RLS provides the ability to control access to the rows in a table based on the user executing a query. With RLS it is possible to implement a filtering mechanism on any table in a database completely transparently to any external application or direct T-SQL access. The ability to implement such filtering without having to redesign a data access layer allows system administrators to control access to data at an even more granular level than before.

The fact that this control can be achieved without any application logic redesign makes this feature potentially even more attractive to certain use cases. RLS also makes it possible, in conjunction with the necessary auditing features, to lock down a SQL Server database so that even the traditional "god-mode" sysadmin cannot access the underlying data.

 Further details for Row Level Security can be found in `Chapter` `8`, *Tightening the Security.*

Dynamic Data Masking

The second security feature that we will be covering is **Dynamic Data Masking (DDM)**. DDM allows the system administrator to define column level data masking algorithms that prevent users from reading the sensitive content of columns, while still being able to query the rows themselves. This feature seems to have been initially aimed at allowing developers to work with a copy of production data without having the ability to actually *see* the underlying data. This can be particularly useful in environments where data protection laws are enforced (for example, credit card processing systems, medical record storage). The data masking occurs for unauthorized users at query runtime and does not affect the stored data of a table. This means that it is possible to mask a multi-terabyte database through a simple DDL statement, rather than resorting to the previous solution of physically masking the underlying data in the table we want to mask. The current implementation of DDM provides the ability to define a fixed set of functions to columns of a table, which will mask data when a masked table is queried. If a user has permission to view the masked data, then the masking function(s) are not run, whereas a user without those permissions will be provided with the data as seen through the defined masking functions.

 Further details for Dynamic Data Masking can be found in `Chapter` `8`, *Tightening the Security.*

Always Encrypted

The third major security feature to be introduced in SQL Server 2016 is Always Encrypted. Encryption with SQL Server was previously a (mainly) server-based solution. Databases were either protected with encryption at the database level (the entire database was encrypted) or at the column level (single columns had an encryption algorithm defined). While this encryption was and is fully functional and safe, crucial portions of the encryption process (for example, encryption certificates) are stored inside SQL Server. This effectively gave the owner of a SQL Server instance the potential ability to gain access to this encrypted data; if not directly, there was at least an increased surface area for a potential malicious access attempt. As more and more companies moved into hosted service and cloud solutions (for example, Microsoft Azure), the old encryption solutions no longer provided the required level of control and security. Always Encrypted was designed to bridge this security gap by removing the ability of an instance owner to gain access to the encryption components. The entirety of the encryption process was moved outside SQL Server and resides on the client-side. Previously, you could achieve a similar effect using a homebrew solution, but Always Encrypted provides a fully integrated encryption suite into both the .NET Framework and SQL Server. Whenever data is defined as requiring encryption, the data is encrypted within the .NET Framework and only sent to SQL Server after encryption has occurred. This means that a malicious user (or even system administrator) will only ever be able to access encrypted information should they attempt to query data stored via Always Encrypted.

 Further details for Always Encrypted can be found in `Chapter 8`, *Tightening the Security.*

This concludes the overview of the three main security enhancements inside SQL Server 2016. Microsoft has made some positive progress in this area. While no system is completely safe, and no single feature can provide an all-encompassing solution, each of these three features provide a further option in building up, or improving upon, any system's current security level. As mentioned for each feature, consult the dedicated chapter to explore how each feature functions and how they may be used in your environments.

Engine features

The engine features section is traditionally the most important, or interesting, for most DBAs or system administrators when a new version of SQL Server is released. However, there are also numerous engine feature improvements that have tangential meaning for developers too. So, if you are a developer, don't skip this section or you may miss some improvements that could save you some trouble later on!

Query Store

The Query Store is possibly the biggest new engine feature to come with the release of SQL Server 2016. DBAs and developers should be more than familiar with the situation of a query behaving reliably for a long period, which suddenly changed into a slow-running, resource-killing monster query. Some readers may identify the cause of the issue being the phenomenon "parameter sniffing" or similarly "stale statistics". Either way, when troubleshooting why an unchanging query suddenly becomes slow, knowing the query execution plan(s) that SQL Server has created and used can be very helpful. A major issue when investigating these types of problems is the transient nature of query plans and their execution statistics. This is where Query Store comes into play; SQL Server collects and permanently stores statistics on query compilation and execution on a per database basis. This information is then persisted inside each database that has Query Store enabled, allowing a DBA or developer to investigate performance issues after the fact. It is even possible to perform query regression analysis, providing an insight into how query execution plans change over a longer timeframe. This sort of insight was previously only possible via hand-written solutions or third-party monitoring solutions, which may still not allow the same insights as the Query Store does.

 Further details on Query Store can be found in Chapter 9, *Query Store.*

Live Query Statistics

When we are developing inside SQL Server, each developer creates a mental model of how data flows inside SQL Server. Microsoft has provided a multitude of ways to display this concept when working with query execution. The most obvious visual aid is the graphical execution plan. There are endless explanations in books, articles and training seminars which attempt to make reading these graphical representations easier. Depending upon how your mind works, these descriptions can help or hinder your ability to understand the data flow concepts: fully blocking iterators, pipeline iterators, semi-blocking iterators, nested loop joins, the list goes on. When we look at an actual graphical execution plan, we are seeing a representation of how SQL Server processed a query: which data retrieval methods were used, which join types were chosen to join multiple data sets, what sorting was required, and so on. However, this is a representation after the query has completed execution. Live Query Statistics offers us the ability to observe during query execution and identify how, when, and where data moves through the query plan. This live representation is a huge improvement in making the concepts behind query execution clearer and is a great tool to allow developers to better design their query and indexing strategies to improve query performance.

 Further details for Live Query Statistics can be found in `Chapter 3`, *SQL Server Tools*.

Stretch Database

Microsoft has worked on their "Mobile First, Cloud First" strategy a lot in the past few years. We have seen a huge investment in Azure, their cloud offering, with the line between on-premises IT and cloud-based IT being continually blurred. The features being released in the newest products from Microsoft continue this approach and SQL Server is taking steps to bridge the divide between running SQL Server as a fully on-premises solution and storing/processing relational data in the cloud. One big step in achieving this approach is the new Stretch Database feature with SQL Server 2016. Stretch Database allows a DBA to categorize the data inside a database, defining which data is "hot" (frequently accessed data) and which is "cold" (infrequently accessed data). This categorization allows Stretch Database to then move the "cold" data out of the on-premises database and into Azure cloud storage. The segmentation of data remains transparent to any user/application that queries the data which now resides in two different locations.

The idea behind this technology is to reduce storage requirements for the on-premises system by offloading large amounts of archive data onto cheaper, slower storage in the cloud. This reduction should then allow the smaller "hot" data to be placed on smaller capacity, higher performance storage. The benefit of Stretch Database is the fact that this separation of data requires no changes at the application or database query level. Stretch Database has been implemented to allow each company to also decide for themselves how data is defined as "hot" or "cold", providing maximum flexibility with minimal implementation overhead. This is a purely storage level change, which means the potential ROI of segmenting a database is quite large.

 Further details on Stretch Database can be found in Chapter 6, *Stretch Database.*

Database scoped configuration

Many DBAs who support multiple third-party applications running on SQL Server experience the difficulty of setting up their SQL Server instances according to the application requirements or best practices. Many third-party applications have prerequisites that dictate how the actual instance of SQL Server must be configured. A common occurrence is a requirement of configuring the "Max Degree of Parallelism" to force only one CPU to be used for query execution. As this is an instance-wide setting, this can affect all other databases/applications in a multi-tenant SQL Server instance (which is generally the case). With Database Scoped Configuration in SQL Server 2016 several previously instance level settings have been moved to a database level configuration option. This greatly improves multi-tenant SQL Server instances, as the decision, for example, how many CPUs can be used for query execution can be made at the database level, rather than for the entire instance. This allows DBAs to host databases with differing CPU usage requirements on the same instance, rather than having to either impact the entire instance with a setting or be forced to run multiple instances of SQL Server and possibly incur higher licensing costs.

Temporal Tables

There are many instances where DBAs or developers are required to implement a change tracking solution, allowing future analysis or assessment of data changes for certain business entities. A readily accessible example is the change history on a customer account in a CRM system. The options for implementing such a change tracking system are varied and each option has strengths and weaknesses. One such implementation that has been widely adopted is the use of triggers to capture data changes and store historical values in an archive table. Regardless of the implementation chosen, it was often cumbersome to develop and maintain these solutions. One of the challenges was incorporating table structure changes in the table being tracked. It was equally challenging creating solutions to allow for querying both the base table and the archive table belonging to it. The intelligence of deciding whether to query the live and/or archive data can require some complex query logic.

With the advent of Temporal Tables, this entire process has been simplified for both developers and DBAs. It is now possible to activate this "change tracking" on a table and push changes into an archive table with a simple change to a table's structure. Querying the base table and including a temporal attribute to the query is also a simple T-SQL syntax addition. As such, it is now possible for a developer to submit temporal analysis queries and SQL Server takes care of splitting the query between the live and archive data and returning the data in a single result set.

 Further details for Temporal Tables can be found in Chapter 7, *Temporal Tables*.

Columnstore indexes

Traditional data storage inside SQL Server has used the row-storage format, where the data for an entire row is stored together on the data pages inside the database. SQL Server 2012 introduced a new storage format: Columnstore. This format stores the data as columns rather than rows, combining the data from a single column and storing the data together on the data pages. This storage format provides the ability for massive compression of data, orders of magnitude better than traditional row-storage. Initially, only non-clustered columnstore indexes were possible. With SQL Server 2014 clustered columnstore indexes were introduced, expanding the usability of the feature greatly. Finally, with SQL Server 2016 updateable columnstore indexes and support for In-Memory columnstore indexes have been introduced. The potential performance improvements through these improvements are huge.

Further details on Columnstore Indexes can be found in `Chapter 10`, *Columnstore Indexes*.

This concludes the section outlining the engine features implemented in SQL Server 2016. Through Microsoft's heavy move into cloud computing and their Azure offerings, they have increased the need to improve their internal systems for themselves. Microsoft is famous for their "dogfooding" approach to using their own software to run their own business, and Azure is arguably their largest foray into this area. The main improvements in the database engine have been fueled by the need to improve their own ability to continue offering Azure database solutions and provide features to allow databases of differing sizes and loads to be hosted together.

Programming

The programming landscape of SQL Server has continued to improve in order to adopt newer technologies over the years. SQL Server 2016 is no exception to this: there have been some long awaited general improvements and also some rather revolutionary additions to the product that change the way SQL Server may be used in future projects. This section will outline what programming improvements have been included in SQL Server 2016.

Transact SQL enhancements

The last major improvements in the T-SQL language allowed for better processing of running totals and other similar window functions. This was already a boon and allowed developers to replace arcane cursors with high performance T-SQL. These improvements are never enough for the most performance-conscious developers among us, and as such there were still voices requesting further incorporation of the ANSI SQL standards into the T-SQL implementation.

Notable additions to the T-SQL syntax include the ability to finally split comma separated strings via a single function call `STRING_SPLIT()` instead of the previous "hacky" implementations using loops, functions, XML conversions or even the CLR.

The sensible opposing syntax for splitting strings is a function to aggregate values together: `STRING_AGG()` returns a set of values in a comma separated string. This replaces similarly "hacky" solutions using the XML data type or one of a multitude of looping solutions.

Each improvement in the T-SQL language further extends the toolbox that we as developers possess in order to manipulate data inside SQL Server.

 Further details on T-SQL Enhancements can be found in Chapter 4, *Transact-SQL Enhancements*.

JSON

It is quite common to meet developers outside the Microsoft stack who look down on products released from Redmond. Web developers in particular have been critical of the access to the latest data exchange structures, or rather lack of it. JSON has become the de facto data exchange method for the application development world. It is similar in structure to the previous "cool-kid" XML, but for reasons beyond the scope of this book, JSON has overtaken XML in general programming projects and is the expected payload for application and database communications. Microsoft has included JSON as a possible data exchange data type in SQL Server 2016 and provided a set of functions to accompany the data type.

 Further details on JSON can be found in Chapter 5, *JSON Support in SQL Server*.

In-Memory OLTP

In-Memory OLTP (codename Hekaton) was introduced in SQL Server 2014. The promise of ultra-high performance data processing inside SQL Server was a major feature when SQL Server 2014 was released. As expected with a newly implemented feature, there were a wide range of limitations in the initial release and this prevented many customers from being able to adopt the technology. With SQL Server 2016 a great number of these limitations have been either raised to a higher threshold or completely removed. In-Memory OLTP has received the required maturity and extension in its feature set to make it viable for prime production deployment. Chapter 11, *Introducing SQL Server In-Memory OLTP*, of this book will show an introduction to In-Memory OLTP, explaining how the technology works under the hood and how the initial release of the feature works in SQL Server 2014. Chapter 12, *In-Memory OLTP Improvements in SQL Server 2016*, will build on the introduction and explain how the feature has matured and improved with the release of SQL Server 2016.

Further details on In-Memory OLTP can be found in `Chapter 11`, *Introducing SQL Server In-Memory OLTP* and `Chapter 12`, *In-Memory OLTP Improvements in SQL Server 2016.*

SQL Server tools

Accessing or managing data inside SQL Server and developing data solutions are two separate disciplines, each with their own specific focus on SQL Server. As such, Microsoft has created two different tools, each tailored towards the processes and facets of these disciplines.

SQL Server Management Studio (SSMS), as the name suggests, is the main management interface between DBAs/Developers and SQL Server. The studio was originally released with SQL Server 2005 as a replacement and consolidation of the old Query Analyzer and Enterprise Manager tools. As with any non-revenue generating software, SSMS received less attention over the years than the database engine, with limitations and missing tooling for many of the newer features in SQL Server. With SQL Server 2016 the focus inside Microsoft has been shifted and SSMS has been de-coupled from the release cycle of SQL Server itself. This decoupling allows both SSMS and SQL Server to be developed without having to wait for each other or for release windows. New releases of SSMS are created on top of more recent versions of Visual Studio and have seen almost monthly update releases since SQL Server 2016 was released to the market.

SQL Server Data Tools (SSDT) is also an application based on the Visual Studio framework. SSDT is focused on the application/data development discipline. SSDT is much more closely aligned with Visual Studio in its structure and the features offered. This focus includes the ability to create entire database projects and solution files, an easier integration into source control systems, the ability to connect projects into automated build processes, and generally offering a developer-centric development environment with a familiarity with Visual Studio. It is possible to design and create solutions in SSDT for SQL Server using the Relational Engine, Analysis Services, Integration Services, Reporting Services, and of course, for Azure SQL Database.

 Further details for SQL Server Tools can be found in `Chapter 3`, *SQL Server Tools.*

This concludes the overview of programming enhancements inside SQL Server 2016. The improvements outlined are all solid evolutionary steps in their respective areas. New features are very welcome and allow us to achieve more, while requiring less effort on our side. The In-Memory OLTP enhancements are especially positive, as they now expand on the groundwork laid down in the release of SQL Server 2014. Read the respective chapters to gain a deeper insight into how these enhancements can help you.

Business intelligence

Business intelligence is a huge area of IT and has been a cornerstone of the SQL Server product since at least SQL Server 2005. As the market and technologies in the Business intelligence space improve, so must SQL Server. The advent of cloud-based data analysis systems as well as the recent buzz around "big data" are driving forces for all data platform providers and Microsoft is no exception here. While there are many enhancements in the Business intelligence portion of SQL Server 2016, we will be concentrating on the feature that has a wider audience than just data analysts: The R language in SQL Server.

R in SQL Server

Data analytics has been the hottest topic in IT for the past few years, with new niches being crowned as the pinnacle of information science almost as fast as technology can progress. However, IT does have a few resolute classics that have stood the test of time and are still in wide use. SQL (in its many permutations) is a language we are well aware of in the SQL Server world. Another such language is the succinctly titled **R**. The R language is a data mining, machine learning and statistical analysis language that has existed since 1993. Many professionals with titles such as data scientists, data analyst, or statistician have been using the R language and tools that belong in that domain ever since. Microsoft has identified that, although they may want all the world's data inside SQL Server, this is just not feasible or sensible. External data sources and languages such as R exist and need to be accessible in an integrated manner.

For this to work, Microsoft made the decision to purchase Revolution Analytics (a commercial entity producing the forked Revolution R) in 2015, which made it possible for them to integrate the language and server process into SQL Server 2016. This integration allows a *normal* T-SQL developer to interact with the extremely powerful R service in a native manner and allow more advanced data analysis to be performed on their data.

Further details on R in SQL Server can be found in `Chapter 13`, *Supporting R in SQL Server* and `Chapter 14`, *Data Exploration and Predictive Modeling with R in SQL Server*.

Release cycles

Microsoft has made a few major public-facing changes in the past five years. These changes include a departure from longer release cycles for their main products and a transition towards subscription-based services, for example, Office 365 and Azure services. The ideas surrounding continuous delivery and agile software development have also shaped the way that Microsoft has been delivering their flagship integrated development environment, Visual Studio, with new releases approximately every six months. This change in philosophy is now flowing into the development cycle of SQL Server. Due to the similarly constant release cycle of the cloud-version of SQL Server (Azure SQL Database), Microsoft wants to keep both the cloud and on-premises versions of the product as close to each other as possible. As such, it is not a surprise to see that the previous release cycle of every three to five years is being replaced by much shorter intervals. A clear example of this was that SQL Server 2016 released to the market in June of 2016, with a **Community Technology Preview (CTP)** of the next version of SQL Server being released in November of 2016. The wave of technology progress stops for no one. This is clearly true in the case of SQL Server!

Summary

In this introductory chapter, we have given you a brief outline of what lies ahead in this book. Each version of SQL Server has hundreds of improvements and enhancements, both through new features and through extensions of previous versions. The outlines for each chapter provide an insight into the main topics covered in this book and allow you to identify which areas you may like to dive in to and where to find them.

As we've already hinted, we need to get to work and learn about SQL Server 2016 before it's too late!

2
Review of SQL Server Features for Developers

Before delving into the new features in SQL Server 2016, let's have a quick recapitulation of the features of SQL Server for developers already available in the previous versions of SQL Server. Recapitulating the most important features will help you remember what you already have in your development toolbox and also understand the need and the benefits of the new or improved features in SQL Server 2016.

This chapter has a lot of code. As this is not a book for beginners, the intention of this chapter is not to teach you the basics of database development. It is rather a reminder of the many powerful and efficient **Transact-SQL (T-SQL)** and other elements included in SQL Server version 2014 and even earlier.

The recapitulation starts with the mighty T-SQL SELECT statement. Besides the basic clauses, advanced techniques such as window functions, common table expressions, and the APPLY operator are explained. Then, you will pass quickly through creating and altering database objects, including tables and programmable objects, such as triggers, views, user-defined functions, and stored procedures. You will also review data modification language statements. Of course, errors might appear, so you have to know how to handle them. In addition, data integrity rules might require that two or more statements are executed as an atomic, indivisible block. You can achieve this with the help of transactions.

Note that this chapter is not a comprehensive development guide.

The last section of this chapter deals with the parts of SQL Server Database Engine marketed with a common name: "Beyond Relational." This is nothing beyond the relational model—beyond relational is really just a marketing term. Nevertheless, you will review the following:

- How SQL Server supports spatial data
- How you can enhance the T-SQL language with **Common Language Runtime (CLR)** elements written in a .NET language, such as Visual C#
- How SQL Server supports XML data

The code in this chapter uses the `WideWorldImportersDW` demo database. In order to test the code, this database must be present in the SQL Server instance you are using for testing, and you must also have **SQL Server Management Studio (SSMS)** as the client tool.

This chapter will cover the following points:

- Core Transact-SQL SELECT statement elements
- Advanced SELECT techniques
- Data definition language statements
- Data modification language statements
- Triggers
- Data abstraction: views, functions, and stored procedures
- Error handling
- Using transactions
- Spatial data
- CLR integration
- XML support in SQL Server

The mighty Transact-SQL SELECT

You probably already know that the most important SQL statement is the mighty SELECT statement you use to retrieve data from your databases. Every database developer knows the basic clauses and their usage:

- `SELECT` to define the columns returned, or a projection of all table columns
- `FROM` to list the tables used in the query and how they are associated, or joined
- `WHERE` to filter the data to return only the rows that satisfy the condition in the predicate

- GROUP BY to define the groups over which the data is aggregated
- HAVING to filter the data after the grouping with conditions that refer to aggregations
- ORDER BY to sort the rows returned to the client application

Besides these basic clauses, SELECT offers a variety of advanced possibilities as well. These advanced techniques are unfortunately less exploited by developers, although they are really powerful and efficient. Therefore, I advise you to review them and potentially use them in your applications. The advanced query techniques presented here include:

- Queries inside queries, or shortly, subqueries
- Window functions
- The TOP and OFFSET...FETCH expressions
- The APPLY operator
- Common tables expressions (CTEs)

Core Transact-SQL SELECT statement elements

Let's start with the simplest concept of SQL that every Tom, Dick, and Harry is aware of! The simplest query to retrieve the data you can write includes the SELECT and the FROM clauses. In the SELECT clause, you can use the star (*) character, literally SELECT *, to denote that you need all columns from a table in the result set. The following code switches to the WideWorldImportersDW database context and selects all data from the Dimension.Customer table. Note that there are many versions of this demo database, so your results might vary.

```
USE WideWorldImportersDW;
SELECT *
FROM Dimension.Customer;
```

The code returns 403 rows, all customers with all columns.

 Using SELECT * is not recommended in production. Such queries can return an unexpected result when the table structure changes, and it's also not suitable for good optimization.

Better than using `SELECT *` is to explicitly list only the columns you need. This means you are returning only a *projection* on the table. The following example selects only four columns from the table:

```
SELECT [Customer Key], [WWI Customer ID],
  [Customer], [Buying Group]
FROM Dimension.Customer;
```

Here is the shortened result, limited to the first three rows only:

```
Customer Key WWI Customer ID Customer                      Buying Group
------------ --------------- ----------------------------- ------------
0            0               Unknown                       N/A
1            1               Tailspin Toys (Head Office)   Tailspin Toys
2            2               Tailspin Toys (Sylvanite, MT) Tailspin Toys
```

You can see that the column names in the `WideWorldImportersDW` database include spaces. Names that include spaces are called **delimited identifiers**. In order to make SQL Server properly understand them as column names, you must enclose delimited identifiers in square parentheses. However, if you prefer to have names without spaces, or if you use computed expressions in the column list, you can add *column aliases*. The following query completely returns the same data as the previous one, just with columns renamed with aliases to avoid delimited names:

```
SELECT [Customer Key] AS CustomerKey,
  [WWI Customer ID] AS CustomerId,
  [Customer],
  [Buying Group] AS BuyingGroup
FROM Dimension.Customer;
```

You might have noticed in the result set returned from the last two queries that there is also a row in the table for an unknown customer. You can *filter* this row with the `WHERE` clause:

```
SELECT [Customer Key] AS CustomerKey,
  [WWI Customer ID] AS CustomerId,
  [Customer],
  [Buying Group] AS BuyingGroup
FROM Dimension.Customer
WHERE [Customer Key] <> 0;
```

In a relational database, you typically have data spread across multiple tables. Each table represents a *set of entities* of the same kind, like the customers in the examples you have seen so far. In order to get meaningful result sets for the business your database supports, most of the time you need to retrieve data from multiple tables in the same query. You need to *join* two or more tables based on some conditions.

The most frequent kind of a join is the **inner join**. Rows returned are those for which the condition in the join predicate for the two tables joined evaluates to *true*. Note that in a relational database, you have three-valued logic, because there is always a possibility that a piece of data is unknown. You mark the unknown with the NULL keyword. A predicate can thus evaluate to true, false, or NULL. For an inner join, the order of the tables involved in the join is not important. In the following example, you can see the Fact.Sale table joined with an inner join to the Dimension.Customer table:

```
SELECT c.[Customer Key] AS CustomerKey,
    c.[WWI Customer ID] AS CustomerId,
    c.[Customer],
    c.[Buying Group] AS BuyingGroup,
    f.Quantity,
    f.[Total Excluding Tax] AS Amount,
    f.Profit
FROM Fact.Sale AS f
    INNER JOIN Dimension.Customer AS c
        ON f.[Customer Key] = c.[Customer Key];
```

In the query, you can see that *table aliases* are used. If a column's name is unique across all tables in the query, then you can use it without a table name. If not, you need to use the table name in front of the column, to avoid ambiguous column names, in the table.column format. In the previous query, the [Customer Key] column appears in both tables. Therefore, you need to precede this column name with the table name of its origin to avoid ambiguity. You can shorten two-part column names by using table aliases. You specify table aliases in the FROM clause. Once you specify table aliases, you must always use the aliases; you can't refer to the original table names in that query anymore. Note that a column name might be unique in the query at the moment when you write the query. However, later somebody could add a column with the same name in another table involved in the query. If the column name is not preceded by an alias or by the table name, you would get an error when executing the query because of the ambiguous column name. In order to make the code more stable and more readable, you should always use table aliases for each column in the query.

The preceding query returns 228,265 rows. It is always recommended to know at least approximately the number of rows your query should return. This number is the first control of the correctness of the result set, or put differently, whether the query is written logically correct. The query returns the unknown customer and the orders associated with this customer, or more precisely put, associated to this placeholder for an unknown customer. Of course, you can use the WHERE clause to filter the rows in a query that joins multiple tables, just as you use it for a single table query. The following query filters the unknown customer's rows:

```
SELECT c.[Customer Key] AS CustomerKey,
   c.[WWI Customer ID] AS CustomerId,
   c.[Customer],
   c.[Buying Group] AS BuyingGroup,
   f.Quantity,
   f.[Total Excluding Tax] AS Amount,
   f.Profit
FROM Fact.Sale AS f
   INNER JOIN Dimension.Customer AS c
     ON f.[Customer Key] = c.[Customer Key]
WHERE c.[Customer Key] <> 0;
```

The query returns 143,968 rows. You can see that a lot of sales are associated with the unknown customer.

Of course, the Fact.Sale table cannot be joined to the Dimension.Customer table only. The following query joins it to the Dimension.Date table. Again, the join performed is an inner join:

```
SELECT d.Date, f.[Total Excluding Tax],
   f.[Delivery Date Key]
FROM Fact.Sale AS f
   INNER JOIN Dimension.Date AS d
     ON f.[Delivery Date Key] = d.Date;
```

The query returns 227,981 rows. The query that joined the Fact.Sale table to the Dimension.Customer table returned 228,265 rows. It looks as if not all Fact.Sale table rows have a known delivery date; not all rows can match the Dimension.Date table rows. You can use an **outer join** to check this.

With an outer join, you preserve the rows from one or both tables, even if they don't have a match in the other table. The result set returned includes all of the matched rows like you get from an inner join plus the preserved rows. Within an outer join, the order of the tables involved in the join might be important. If you use LEFT OUTER JOIN, then the rows from the left table are preserved. If you use RIGHT OUTER JOIN, then the rows from the right table are preserved. Of course, in both cases, the order of the tables involved in the join is important. With FULL OUTER JOIN, you preserve the rows from both tables, and the order of the tables is not important. The following query preserves the rows from the Fact.Sale table, which is on the left-hand side of the join to the Dimension.Date table. In addition, the query *sorts* the result set by the invoice date descending using the ORDER BY clause:

```
SELECT d.Date, f.[Total Excluding Tax],
  f.[Delivery Date Key], f.[Invoice Date Key]
FROM Fact.Sale AS f
  LEFT OUTER JOIN Dimension.Date AS d
    ON f.[Delivery Date Key] = d.Date
ORDER BY f.[Invoice Date Key] DESC;
```

The query returns 228,265 rows. Here is the partial result of the query:

Date	Total Excluding Tax	Delivery Date Key	Invoice Date Key
NULL	180.00	NULL	2016-05-31
NULL	120.00	NULL	2016-05-31
NULL	160.00	NULL	2016-05-31
...	...	...	...
2016-05-31	2565.00	2016-05-31	2016-05-30
2016-05-31	88.80	2016-05-31	2016-05-30
2016-05-31	50.00	2016-05-31	2016-05-30

For the last invoice date (2016-05-31), the delivery date is NULL. The NULL in the Date column from the Dimension.Date table is there because the data from this table is unknown for the rows with an unknown delivery date in the Fact.Sale table.

Joining more than two tables is not tricky if all the joins are inner joins. The order of joins is not important. However, you might want to execute an outer join after all of the inner joins. If you don't control the join order with the outer joins, it might happen that a subsequent inner join filters out the preserved rows of an outer join. You can control the join order with parentheses. The following query joins the Fact.Sale table with an inner join to the Dimension.Customer, Dimension.City, Dimension.[Stock Item], and Dimension.Employee tables, and with a left outer join to the Dimension.Date table:

```
SELECT cu.[Customer Key] AS CustomerKey, cu.Customer,
  ci.[City Key] AS CityKey, ci.City,
  ci.[State Province] AS StateProvince, ci.[Sales Territory] AS
```

```
    SalesTeritory,
      d.Date, d.[Calendar Month Label] AS CalendarMonth,
      d.[Calendar Year] AS CalendarYear,
      s.[Stock Item Key] AS StockItemKey, s.[Stock Item] AS Product, s.Color,
      e.[Employee Key] AS EmployeeKey, e.Employee,
      f.Quantity, f.[Total Excluding Tax] AS TotalAmount, f.Profit
    FROM (Fact.Sale AS f
      INNER JOIN Dimension.Customer AS cu
        ON f.[Customer Key] = cu.[Customer Key]
      INNER JOIN Dimension.City AS ci
        ON f.[City Key] = ci.[City Key]
      INNER JOIN Dimension.[Stock Item] AS s
        ON f.[Stock Item Key] = s.[Stock Item Key]
      INNER JOIN Dimension.Employee AS e
        ON f.[Salesperson Key] = e.[Employee Key])
      LEFT OUTER JOIN Dimension.Date AS d
        ON f.[Delivery Date Key] = d.Date;
```

The query returns 228,265 rows. Note that with the usage of the parenthesis the order of joins is defined in the following way:

- Perform all inner joins, with an arbitrary order among them
- Execute the left outer join after all of the inner joins

So far, I have tacitly assumed that the Fact.Sale table has 228,265 rows, and that the previous query needed only one outer join of the Fact.Sale table with Dimension.Date to return all of the rows. It would be good to check this number in advance. You can check the number of rows by *aggregating* them using the COUNT(*) aggregate function. The following query introduces this function:

```
SELECT COUNT(*) AS SalesCount
FROM Fact.Sale;
```

Now you can be sure that the Fact.Sale table has exactly 228,265 rows.

Many times, you need to aggregate data in *groups*. This is the point where the GROUP BY clause becomes handy. The following query aggregates the sales data for each customer:

```
SELECT c.Customer,
  SUM(f.Quantity) AS TotalQuantity,
  SUM(f.[Total Excluding Tax]) AS TotalAmount,
  COUNT(*) AS InvoiceLinesCount
FROM Fact.Sale AS f
  INNER JOIN Dimension.Customer AS c
    ON f.[Customer Key] = c.[Customer Key]
WHERE c.[Customer Key] <> 0
```

```
GROUP BY c.Customer;
```

The query returns 402 rows, one for each known customer. In the SELECT clause, you can have only the columns used for grouping, or aggregated columns. You need to get a scalar, a single aggregated value for each row for each column not included in the GROUP BY list.

Sometimes, you need to *filter aggregated data*. For example, you might need to find only frequent customers, defined as customers with more than 400 rows in the Fact.Sale table. You can filter the result set on the aggregated data using the HAVING clause, as the following query shows:

```
SELECT c.Customer,
  SUM(f.Quantity) AS TotalQuantity,
  SUM(f.[Total Excluding Tax]) AS TotalAmount,
  COUNT(*) AS InvoiceLinesCount
FROM Fact.Sale AS f
  INNER JOIN Dimension.Customer AS c
    ON f.[Customer Key] = c.[Customer Key]
WHERE c.[Customer Key] <> 0
GROUP BY c.Customer
HAVING COUNT(*) > 400;
```

The query returns 45 rows for the 45 most frequent known customers. Note that you can't use column aliases from the SELECT clause in any other clause introduced in the previous query. The SELECT clause logically executes after all other clause from the query, and the aliases are not known yet. However, the ORDER BY clause executes after the SELECT clause, and therefore the columns aliases are already known and you can refer to them. The following query shows all of the basic SELECT statement clauses used together to aggregate the sales data over the known customers, filters the data to include the frequent customers only, and sorts the result set descending by the number of rows of each customer in the Fact.Sale table:

```
SELECT c.Customer,
  SUM(f.Quantity) AS TotalQuantity,
  SUM(f.[Total Excluding Tax]) AS TotalAmount,
  COUNT(*) AS InvoiceLinesCount
FROM Fact.Sale AS f
  INNER JOIN Dimension.Customer AS c
    ON f.[Customer Key] = c.[Customer Key]
WHERE c.[Customer Key] <> 0
GROUP BY c.Customer
HAVING COUNT(*) > 400
ORDER BY InvoiceLinesCount DESC;
```

The query returns 45 rows. Here is the shortened result set:

```
Customer                             TotalQuantity TotalAmount  SalesCount
------------------------------------ ------------- ------------ ----------
Tailspin Toys (Vidrine, LA)                  18899    340163.80        455
Tailspin Toys (North Crows Nest, IN) 17684           313999.50        443
Tailspin Toys (Tolna, ND)                    16240    294759.10        443
```

Advanced SELECT techniques

Aggregating data over the complete input rowset or aggregating in groups produces aggregated rows only—either one row for the whole input rowset or one row per group. Sometimes you need to return aggregates together with the detailed data. One way to achieve this is by using subqueries, queries inside queries.

The following query shows an example of using two subqueries in a single query. In the SELECT clause, a subquery calculates the sum of quantities for each customer. It returns a scalar value. The subquery refers to the customer key from the outer query. The subquery can't execute without the outer query. This is a **correlated subquery**. There is another subquery in the FROM clause that calculates the overall quantity for all customers. This query returns a table, though it is a table with a single row and single column. It is a **self-contained subquery**, independent of the outer query. A subquery in the FROM clause is also called a **derived table**.

Another type of join is used to add the overall total to each detail row. A **cross join** is a Cartesian product of two input rowsets—each row from one side is associated with every single row from the other side. No join condition is needed. A cross join can produce an unwanted huge result set. For example, if you cross join just 1,000 rows from the left of the join with 1,000 rows from the right, you get 1,000,000 rows in the output. Therefore, typically you'd want to avoid a cross join in production. However, in the example in the following query, 143,968 rows from the left-hand-side rows are cross-joined to a single row from the subquery, therefore producing 143,968 rows only. Effectively, this means that the overall total column is added to each detail row:

```
SELECT c.Customer,
  f.Quantity,
  (SELECT SUM(f1.Quantity) FROM Fact.Sale AS f1
   WHERE f1.[Customer Key] = c.[Customer Key]) AS TotalCustomerQuantity,
  f2.TotalQuantity
FROM (Fact.Sale AS f
  INNER JOIN Dimension.Customer AS c
    ON f.[Customer Key] = c.[Customer Key])
  CROSS JOIN
```

```
    (SELECT SUM(f2.Quantity) FROM Fact.Sale AS f2
     WHERE f2.[Customer Key] <> 0) AS f2(TotalQuantity)
WHERE c.[Customer Key] <> 0
ORDER BY c.Customer, f.Quantity DESC;
```

Here is the abbreviated output of the query:

```
Customer                        Quantity TotalCustomerQuantity TotalQuantity
------------------------------- -------- --------------------- -------------
Tailspin Toys (Absecon, NJ) 360          12415                 5667611
Tailspin Toys (Absecon, NJ) 324          12415                 5667611
Tailspin Toys (Absecon, NJ) 288          12415                 5667611
```

In the previous example, the correlated subquery in the SELECT clause has to logically execute once per row of the outer query. The query was partially optimized by moving the self-contained subquery for the overall total in the FROM clause, where it logically executes only once. Although SQL Server can often optimize correlated subqueries and convert them to joins, there also exists a much better and more efficient way to achieve the same result as the previous query returned. You can do this by using the **window functions**.

The following query uses the window aggregate function SUM to calculate the total over each customer and the overall total. The OVER clause defines the partitions, or the windows of the calculation. The first calculation is partitioned over each customer, meaning that the total quantity per customer is reset to zero for each new customer. The second calculation uses an OVER clause without specifying partitions, thus meaning the calculation is done over all input rowsets. This query produces exactly the same result as the previous one:

```
SELECT c.Customer,
  f.Quantity,
  SUM(f.Quantity)
   OVER(PARTITION BY c.Customer) AS TotalCustomerQuantity,
  SUM(f.Quantity)
   OVER() AS TotalQuantity
FROM Fact.Sale AS f
  INNER JOIN Dimension.Customer AS c
    ON f.[Customer Key] = c.[Customer Key]
WHERE c.[Customer Key] <> 0
ORDER BY c.Customer, f.Quantity DESC;
```

You can use many other functions for window calculations. For example, you can use the **ranking functions**, such as ROW_NUMBER(), to calculate some rank in the window or in the overall rowset. However, rank can be defined only over some order of the calculation. You can specify the order of the calculation in the ORDER BY sub-clause inside the OVER clause. Note that this ORDER BY clause defines only the logical order of the calculation, and not the order of the rows returned. A standalone outer ORDER BY clause at the end of the query defines the order of the result.

The following query calculates a sequential number, the row number of each row in the output, for each detail row of the input rowset. The row number is calculated once in partitions for each customer and once ever the whole input rowset. The logical order of calculation is over quantity descending, meaning that row number 1 gets the largest quantity, either the largest for each customer or the largest in the whole input rowset:

```
SELECT c.Customer,
  f.Quantity,
  ROW_NUMBER()
   OVER(PARTITION BY c.Customer
        ORDER BY f.Quantity DESC) AS CustomerOrderPosition,
  ROW_NUMBER()
   OVER(ORDER BY f.Quantity DESC) AS TotalOrderPosition
FROM Fact.Sale AS f
  INNER JOIN Dimension.Customer AS c
    ON f.[Customer Key] = c.[Customer Key]
WHERE c.[Customer Key] <> 0
ORDER BY c.Customer, f.Quantity DESC;
```

The query produces the following result, again abbreviated to a couple of rows only:

Customer	Quantity	CustomerOrderPosition	TotalOrderPosition
Tailspin Toys (Absecon, NJ)	360	1	129
Tailspin Toys (Absecon, NJ)	324	2	162
Tailspin Toys (Absecon, NJ)	288	3	374
...	...	...	...
Tailspin Toys (Aceitunas, PR)	288	1	392
Tailspin Toys (Aceitunas, PR)	250	4	1331
Tailspin Toys (Aceitunas, PR)	250	3	1315
Tailspin Toys (Aceitunas, PR)	250	2	1313
Tailspin Toys (Aceitunas, PR)	240	5	1478

Note the position, or the row number, for the second customer. The order does not appear completely correct—it is 1, 4, 3, 2, 5, and not 1, 2, 3, 4, 5, as you might expect. This is due to the repeating value for the second largest quantity—the quantity 250. The quantity is not unique, and thus the order is not deterministic. The order of the result is defined over the quantity and not over the row number. You can't know in advance which row will get which row number when the order of the calculation is not defined on unique values. Also, note that you might get a different order when you execute the same query on your SQL Server instance.

Window functions are useful for some advanced calculations, such as running totals and moving averages as well. However, the calculation of these values can't be performed over the complete partition. Additionally, you can frame the calculation to a subset of rows of each partition only.

The following query calculates the running total of the quantity per customer (the Q_RT column alias in the query) ordered by the sale key and framed differently for each row. The frame is defined from the first row in the partition to the current row. Therefore, the running total is calculated over one row for the first row, over two rows for the second row, and so on. Additionally, the query calculates the moving average of the quantity (the Q_MA column alias in the query) for the last three rows:

```
SELECT c.Customer,
  f.[Sale Key] AS SaleKey,
  f.Quantity,
  SUM(f.Quantity)
   OVER(PARTITION BY c.Customer
        ORDER BY [Sale Key]
      ROWS BETWEEN UNBOUNDED PRECEDING
                  AND CURRENT ROW) AS Q_RT,
  AVG(f.Quantity)
   OVER(PARTITION BY c.Customer
        ORDER BY [Sale Key]
      ROWS BETWEEN 2 PRECEDING
                  AND CURRENT ROW) AS Q_MA
FROM Fact.Sale AS f
  INNER JOIN Dimension.Customer AS c
    ON f.[Customer Key] = c.[Customer Key]
WHERE c.[Customer Key] <> 0
ORDER BY c.Customer, f.[Sale Key];
```

The query returns the following (abbreviated) result:

```
Customer                        SaleKey  Quantity    Q_RT         Q_MA
------------------------------- -------- ----------  -----------  ----------
Tailspin Toys (Absecon, NJ)     2869     216         216          216
Tailspin Toys (Absecon, NJ)     2870     2           218          109
Tailspin Toys (Absecon, NJ)     2871     2           220          73
```

Let's find the top three orders by quantity for the Tailspin Toys (Aceitunas, PR) customer! You can do this by using the OFFSET...FETCH clause after the ORDER BY clause, as the following query shows:

```
SELECT c.Customer,
    f.[Sale Key] AS SaleKey,
    f.Quantity
FROM Fact.Sale AS f
    INNER JOIN Dimension.Customer AS c
      ON f.[Customer Key] = c.[Customer Key]
WHERE c.Customer = N'Tailspin Toys (Aceitunas, PR)'
ORDER BY f.Quantity DESC
OFFSET 0 ROWS FETCH NEXT 3 ROWS ONLY;
```

This is the complete result of the query:

```
Customer                        SaleKey  Quantity
------------------------------- -------- --------
Tailspin Toys (Aceitunas, PR)   36964    288
Tailspin Toys (Aceitunas, PR)   126253   250
Tailspin Toys (Aceitunas, PR)   79272    250
```

But wait.... Didn't the second largest quantity, the value 250, repeat three times? Which two rows were selected in the output? Again, because the calculation is done over a non-unique column, the result is somehow non-deterministic. SQL Server offers another possibility, the TOP clause. You can specify TOP n WITH TIES, meaning you can get all the rows with ties on the last value in the output. However, this way you don't know the number of rows in the output in advance. The following query shows this approach:

```
SELECT TOP 3 WITH TIES
    c.Customer,
    f.[Sale Key] AS SaleKey,
    f.Quantity
FROM Fact.Sale AS f
    INNER JOIN Dimension.Customer AS c
      ON f.[Customer Key] = c.[Customer Key]
WHERE c.Customer = N'Tailspin Toys (Aceitunas, PR)'
ORDER BY f.Quantity DESC;
```

This is the complete result of the previous query—this time it is four rows:

```
Customer                         SaleKey  Quantity
------------------------------   -------  --------
Tailspin Toys (Aceitunas, PR)     36964      288
Tailspin Toys (Aceitunas, PR)    223106      250
Tailspin Toys (Aceitunas, PR)    126253      250
Tailspin Toys (Aceitunas, PR)     79272      250
```

The next task is to get the top three orders by quantity for each customer. You need to perform the calculation for each customer. The APPLY Transact-SQL operator comes in handy here. You use it in the FROM clause. You apply, or execute, a table expression defined on the right-hand side of the operator once for each row of the input rowset from the left side of the operator. There are two flavors of this operator. The CROSS APPLY version filters out the rows from the left rowset if the tabular expression on the right-hand side does not return any rows. The OUTER APPLY version preserves the row from the left-hand side, even if the tabular expression on the right-hand side does not return any rows, just as the LEFT OUTER JOIN does. Of course, columns for the preserved rows do not have known values from the right-hand side tabular expression. The following query uses the CROSS APPLY operator to calculate the top three orders by quantity for each customer that actually does have some orders:

```
SELECT c.Customer,
   t3.SaleKey, t3.Quantity
FROM Dimension.Customer AS c
  CROSS APPLY (SELECT TOP(3)
                 f.[Sale Key] AS SaleKey,
                 f.Quantity
                 FROM Fact.Sale AS f
                 WHERE f.[Customer Key] = c.[Customer Key]
                 ORDER BY f.Quantity DESC) AS t3
WHERE c.[Customer Key] <> 0
ORDER BY c.Customer, t3.Quantity DESC;
```

The following is the result of this query, shortened to the first nine rows:

```
Customer                           SaleKey  Quantity
---------------------------------- -------- --------
Tailspin Toys (Absecon, NJ)          5620     360
Tailspin Toys (Absecon, NJ)        114397     324
Tailspin Toys (Absecon, NJ)         82868     288
Tailspin Toys (Aceitunas, PR)       36964     288
Tailspin Toys (Aceitunas, PR)      126253     250
Tailspin Toys (Aceitunas, PR)       79272     250
Tailspin Toys (Airport Drive, MO)   43184     250
Tailspin Toys (Airport Drive, MO)   70842     240
Tailspin Toys (Airport Drive, MO)     630     225
```

For the final task in this section, assume that you need to calculate some statistics on the totals of customers' orders. You need to calculate the average total amount for all customers, the standard deviation of this total amount, and the average count of the total count of orders per customer. This means you need to calculate the totals over customers in advance, and then use the AVG() and STDEV() aggregate functions on these aggregates. You could do aggregations over customers in advance in a derived table. However, there is another way to achieve this. You can define the derived table in advance, in the WITH clause of the SELECT statement. Such a subquery is called a **common table expression**, or **CTE**.

CTEs are more readable than derived tables, and may also be more efficient. You could use the result of the same CTE multiple times in the outer query. If you use derived tables, then you need to define them multiple times if you want to use them multiple times in the outer query. The following query shows the usage of a CTE to calculate the average total amount for all customers, the standard deviation of this total amount, and the average count of total count of orders per customer:

```
WITH CustomerSalesCTE AS
(
SELECT c.Customer,
  SUM(f.[Total Excluding Tax]) AS TotalAmount,
  COUNT(*) AS InvoiceLinesCount
FROM Fact.Sale AS f
  INNER JOIN Dimension.Customer AS c
    ON f.[Customer Key] = c.[Customer Key]
WHERE c.[Customer Key] <> 0
GROUP BY c.Customer
)
SELECT ROUND(AVG(TotalAmount), 6) AS AvgAmountPerCustomer,
  ROUND(STDEV(TotalAmount), 6) AS StDevAmountPerCustomer,
  AVG(InvoiceLinesCount) AS AvgCountPerCustomer
FROM CustomerSalesCTE;
```

It returns the following result:

```
AvgAmountPerCustomer   StDevAmountPerCustomer  AvgCountPerCustomer
--------------------   ----------------------  -------------------
270479.217661          38586.082621            358
```

DDL, DML, and programmable objects

As a developer, you are often also responsible to create database objects. Of course, in an application, you also need to insert, update, and delete the data. In order to maintain **data integrity**, enforcing data complies with business rules, you need to implement constraints. In a quick review of the **data definition language** (DDL) and **data modification language** (DML) elements, the following statements are presented:

- CREATE for creating tables and programmatic objects
- ALTER to add constraints to a table
- DROP to drop an object
- INSERT to insert new data
- UPDATE to change existing data
- DELETE to delete the data

In a SQL Server database, you can also use programmatic objects. You can use triggers for advanced constraints or to maintain redundant data like aggregated data. You can use other programmatic objects for data abstraction, for an intermediate layer between the actual data and an application. The following programmatic objects are introduced here:

- Triggers
- Stored procedures
- Views
- User-defined functions

 It is worth mentioning again that this chapter is just a reminder of the features SQL Server gives to developers. Therefore, this section is not a comprehensive database logical and physical design guide.

Data definition language statements

Let's start with data definition language statements. The following code shows how to create a simple table. This table represents customers' orders. For this demonstration of DDL and DML statements, only a couple of columns are created in the table. The `OrderId` column uniquely identifies each row in this table, is a **primary key** for the table, as the `PRIMARY KEY` constraint specifies. Finally, the code checks whether a table with the name `SimpleOrders` already exists in the `dbo` schema, and drops it in such a case:

```
IF OBJECT_ID(N'dbo.SimpleOrders', N'U') IS NOT NULL
    DROP TABLE dbo.SimpleOrders;
CREATE TABLE dbo.SimpleOrders
(
  OrderId   INT       NOT NULL,
  OrderDate DATE      NOT NULL,
  Customer  NVARCHAR(5) NOT NULL,
  CONSTRAINT PK_SimpleOrders PRIMARY KEY (OrderId)
);
```

For further examples, another table is needed. The following code creates the `dbo.SimpleOrderDetails` table in a very similar way to how the previous table was created, by checking for existence and dropping it if it exists. The `OrderId` and `ProductId` columns form a composite primary key. In addition, a `CHECK` constraint on the `Quantity` column prevents inserts or updates of this column to the value zero:

```
IF OBJECT_ID(N'dbo.SimpleOrderDetails', N'U') IS NOT NULL
    DROP TABLE dbo.SimpleOrderDetails;
CREATE TABLE dbo.SimpleOrderDetails
(
  OrderId   INT NOT NULL,
  ProductId INT NOT NULL,
  Quantity  INT NOT NULL
   CHECK(Quantity <> 0),
  CONSTRAINT PK_SimpleOrderDetails
   PRIMARY KEY (OrderId, ProductId)
);
```

The previous two examples show how to add constraints when you create a table. It is always possible to add constraints later too, by using the ALTER TABLE statement. The tables created in the previous two examples are associated through a **foreign key**. The primary key of the dbo.SimpleOrders table is associating the order details in the dbo.SimpleOrderDetails table with their correspondent order. The code in the following example defines this association:

```
ALTER TABLE dbo.SimpleOrderDetails ADD CONSTRAINT FK_Details_Orders
FOREIGN KEY (OrderId) REFERENCES dbo.SimpleOrders(OrderId);
```

Data modification language statements

The two demo tables are empty at the moment. You add data to them with the INSERT statement. You specify the data values in the VALUES clause. You can insert more than one row in a single statement, as the following code shows by inserting two rows into the dbo.SimpleOrderDetails table in a single statement. You can omit the column names in the INSERT part. However, this is not good practice. Your insert depends on the order of the columns if you don't specify the column names explicitly. Imagine what could happen if somebody later changes the structure of the table. In the event of a bad outcome, the insert would fail. However, you would at least have the information that something went wrong. In an even worse outcome, the insert into the altered table could succeed. You could end up with the wrong data in the wrong columns without even noticing this problem:

```
INSERT INTO dbo.SimpleOrders
  (OrderId, OrderDate, Customer)
VALUES
  (1, '20160701', N'CustA');
INSERT INTO dbo.SimpleOrderDetails
  (OrderId, ProductId, Quantity)
VALUES
  (1, 7, 100),
  (1, 3, 200);
```

The following query checks the recently inserted data. As you probably expected, it returns two rows:

```
SELECT o.OrderId, o.OrderDate, o.Customer,
  od.ProductId, od.Quantity
FROM dbo.SimpleOrderDetails AS od
  INNER JOIN dbo.SimpleOrders AS o
    ON od.OrderId = o.OrderId
ORDER BY o.OrderId, od.ProductId;
```

Here is the result:

```
OrderId       OrderDate   Customer ProductId    Quantity
-----------   ----------- -------- ------------ --------
1             2016-07-01 CustA    3            200
1             2016-07-01 CustA    7            100
```

The next example shows how to update a row. It updates the Quantity column in the dbo.SimpleOrderDetails table for the order with OrderId equal to 1 and for the product with ProductId equal to 3.

```
UPDATE dbo.SimpleOrderDetails
   SET Quantity = 150
WHERE OrderId = 1
  AND ProductId = 3;
```

You can use the same SELECT statement to check the data, whether it has updated correctly, as introduced right after the inserts.

Frequently, you really need to check data right after a modification. For example, you might use the IDENTITY property or the SEQUENCE object to generate identification numbers automatically. When you insert an order, you need to check the generated value of the OrderId column to insert the correct value to the order details table. You can use the OUTPUT clause for this task, as the following code shows:

```
INSERT INTO dbo.SimpleOrders
  (OrderId, OrderDate, Customer)
OUTPUT inserted.*
VALUES
  (2, '20160701', N'CustB');
INSERT INTO dbo.SimpleOrderDetails
  (OrderId, ProductId, Quantity)
OUTPUT inserted.*
VALUES
  (2, 4, 200);
```

The output of the two inserts is as follows:

```
OrderId       OrderDate   Customer
-----------   ----------- --------
2             2016-07-01 CustB
OrderId       ProductId   Quantity
-----------   ----------- --------
2             4           200
```

Using triggers

The code for creating the `dbo.SimpleOrders` table doesn't check the order date value when inserting or updating the data. The following `INSERT` statement, for example, inserts an order with a pretty old and probably incorrect date.

```
INSERT INTO dbo.SimpleOrders
  (OrderId, OrderDate, Customer)
VALUES
  (3, '20100701', N'CustC');
```

You can check that the incorrect date is in the table with the following query:

```
SELECT o.OrderId, o.OrderDate, o.Customer
FROM dbo.SimpleOrders AS o
ORDER BY o.OrderId;
```

Of course, it would be possible to prevent inserting an order date too far in the past, or updating it to a value that is too old, with a check constraint. However, imagine that you don't want to just reject inserts and updates with an order date value in the past; imagine you need to correct the value to a predefined minimal value, for example, January 1st, 2016. You can achieve this with a trigger.

SQL Server supports two different kinds of DML triggers and one kind of DDL trigger. DML triggers can fire after or instead of a DML action, and DDL triggers can fire only after a DDL action. For a database developer, the after DML triggers are the most useful. As you already know, you can use them for advanced constraints, for maintaining redundant data, and more. A **database administrator (DBA)** might use DDL triggers to, for example, check and reject the inappropriate altering of an object and to make a view updateable, *instead of DML triggers*. Of course, often there is no such strict role separation in place. DDL and instead-of-DML triggers are not forbidden for database developers. Anyway, the following code shows a trigger created on the `dbo.SimpleOrders` table that fires after an `INSERT` or an `UPDATE` to this table. It checks the `OrderDate` column value. If the date is too far in the past, it replaces it with the default minimum value:

```
IF OBJECT_ID(N'trg_SimpleOrders_OrdereDate', N'TR') IS NOT NULL
   DROP TRIGGER trg_SimpleOrders_OrdereDate;
GO
CREATE TRIGGER trg_SimpleOrders_OrdereDate
 ON dbo.SimpleOrders AFTER INSERT, UPDATE
AS
 UPDATE dbo.SimpleOrders
    SET OrderDate = '20160101'
 WHERE OrderDate < '20160101';
```

Let's try to insert a low order date, and update an existing value to a value too far in the past:

```
INSERT INTO dbo.SimpleOrders
  (OrderId, OrderDate, Customer)
VALUES
  (4, '20100701', N'CustD');
UPDATE dbo.SimpleOrders
   SET OrderDate = '20110101'
 WHERE OrderId = 3;
```

You can check the data after the updates with the following query:

```
SELECT o.OrderId, o.OrderDate, o.Customer,
   od.ProductId, od.Quantity
FROM dbo.SimpleOrderDetails AS od
  RIGHT OUTER JOIN dbo.SimpleOrders AS o
    ON od.OrderId = o.OrderId
ORDER BY o.OrderId, od.ProductId;
```

Here is the result. As you can see, the trigger changed the incorrect dates to the predefined minimum date:

OrderId	OrderDate	Customer	ProductId	Quantity
1	2016-07-01	CustA	3	150
1	2016-07-01	CustA	7	100
2	2016-07-01	CustB	4	200
3	2016-01-01	CustC	NULL	NULL
4	2016-01-01	CustD	NULL	NULL

Note that the query used OUTER JOIN to include the orders without the details in the result set.

Data abstraction - views, functions, and stored procedures

A very good practice is to use SQL Server stored procedures for data modification and data retrieval. Stored procedures provide many benefits. Some of the benefits include:

- **Data abstraction**: Client applications don't need to work with the data directly, rather they call the stored procedures. The underlying schema might even get modified without an impact on an application as long as you change the stored procedures that work with the objects with modified schema appropriately.

- **Security**: Client applications can access data through stored procedures and other programmatic objects only. For example, even if an end user uses their own SQL Server Management Studio instead of the client application that the user should use, the user still cannot modify the data in an uncontrolled way directly in the tables.
- **Performance**: Stored procedures can reduce network traffic, because you can execute many statements inside the procedure within a single call to a stored procedure. In addition, SQL Server has a lot of work with optimization and compilation of the code an application is sending. SQL Server optimizes this by storing the optimized and compiled code in memory. The compiled execution plans for stored procedures are typically held longer in memory than the execution plans for ad hoc queries and thus get reused more frequently.
- **Usage**: Stored procedures accept input and can return output parameters, so they can be easily coded to serve multiple users.

The code in the following example creates a stored procedure to insert a row into the dbo.SimpleOrders table. The procedure accepts one input parameter for each column of the table:

```
IF OBJECT_ID(N'dbo.InsertSimpleOrder', N'P') IS NOT NULL
   DROP PROCEDURE dbo.InsertSimpleOrder;
GO
CREATE PROCEDURE dbo.InsertSimpleOrder
(@OrderId AS INT, @OrderDate AS DATE, @Customer AS NVARCHAR(5))
AS
INSERT INTO dbo.SimpleOrders
  (OrderId, OrderDate, Customer)
VALUES
  (@OrderId, @OrderDate, @Customer);
```

Here is a similar procedure for inserting data into the dbo.SimpleOrderDetails table:

```
IF OBJECT_ID(N'dbo.InsertSimpleOrderDetail', N'P') IS NOT NULL
   DROP PROCEDURE dbo.InsertSimpleOrderDetail;
GO
CREATE PROCEDURE dbo.InsertSimpleOrderDetail
(@OrderId AS INT, @ProductId AS INT, @Quantity AS INT)
AS
INSERT INTO dbo.SimpleOrderDetails
  (OrderId, ProductId, Quantity)
VALUES
  (@OrderId, @ProductId, @Quantity);
```

Let's test the procedures. In the first part, the two calls to the dbo.InsertSimpleOrder procedure insert two new orders:

```
EXEC dbo.InsertSimpleOrder
  @OrderId = 5, @OrderDate = '20160702', @Customer = N'CustA';
EXEC dbo.InsertSimpleOrderDetail
  @OrderId = 5, @ProductId = 1, @Quantity = 50;
```

The following code calls the dbo.InsertSimpleOrderDetail procedure four times to insert four order details rows:

```
EXEC dbo.InsertSimpleOrderDetail
  @OrderId = 2, @ProductId = 5, @Quantity = 150;
EXEC dbo.InsertSimpleOrderDetail
  @OrderId = 2, @ProductId = 6, @Quantity = 250;
EXEC dbo.InsertSimpleOrderDetail
  @OrderId = 1, @ProductId = 5, @Quantity = 50;
EXEC dbo.InsertSimpleOrderDetail
  @OrderId = 1, @ProductId = 6, @Quantity = 200;
```

The following query checks the state of the two tables after these calls:

```
SELECT o.OrderId, o.OrderDate, o.Customer,
  od.ProductId, od.Quantity
FROM dbo.SimpleOrderDetails AS od
  RIGHT OUTER JOIN dbo.SimpleOrders AS o
    ON od.OrderId = o.OrderId
ORDER BY o.OrderId, od.ProductId;
```

Here is the result after the inserts go through the stores procedures:

OrderId	OrderDate	Customer	ProductId	Quantity
1	2016-07-01	CustA	3	150
1	2016-07-01	CustA	5	50
1	2016-07-01	CustA	6	200
1	2016-07-01	CustA	7	100
2	2016-07-01	CustB	4	200
2	2016-07-01	CustB	5	150
2	2016-07-01	CustB	6	250
3	2016-01-01	CustC	NULL	NULL
4	2016-01-01	CustD	NULL	NULL
5	2016-07-02	CustA	1	50

You can see in the result of the previous query that there are still some orders without order details in your data. Although this might be unwanted, it could happen quite frequently. Your end users might need to quickly find orders without details many times. Instead of executing the same complex query over and over again, you can create a view which encapsulates this complex query. Besides simplifying the code, views are also useful for tightening security. Just like stored procedures, views are *securables* as well. A DBA can revoke direct access to tables from end users, and give them access to view only.

The following example creates a view that finds the orders without details. Note that a view in SQL Server can consist of a single SELECT statement only, and that it does not accept parameters:

```
CREATE VIEW dbo.OrdersWithoutDetails
AS
SELECT o.OrderId, o.OrderDate, o.Customer
FROM dbo.SimpleOrderDetails AS od
  RIGHT OUTER JOIN dbo.SimpleOrders AS o
    ON od.OrderId = o.OrderId
WHERE od.OrderId IS NULL;
```

Now the query that finds the orders without details becomes extremely simple—it just uses the view:

```
SELECT OrderId, OrderDate, Customer
FROM dbo.OrdersWithoutDetails;
```

Here is the result: the two orders without order details.

```
OrderId     OrderDate   Customer
----------- ----------- --------
3           2016-01-01  CustC
4           2016-01-01  CustD
```

If you need to parameterize a view, you have to use an **inline table-valued function** instead. Such a function serves as a parameterized view. SQL Server also supports **multi-statement table-valued functions** and **scalar functions**. The following example shows an inline table-valued function that retrieves top two order details ordered by quantity for an order, where the order ID is a parameter:

```
CREATE FUNCTION dbo.Top2OrderDetails
(@OrderId AS INT)
RETURNS TABLE
AS RETURN
SELECT TOP 2 ProductId, Quantity
FROM dbo.SimpleOrderDetails
WHERE OrderId = @OrderId
```

```
ORDER BY Quantity DESC;
```

The following example uses this function to retrieve the top two details for each order with the help of the APPLY operator:

```
SELECT o.OrderId, o.OrderDate, o.Customer,
  t2.ProductId, t2.Quantity
FROM dbo.SimpleOrders AS o
  OUTER APPLY dbo.Top2OrderDetails(o.OrderId) AS t2
ORDER BY o.OrderId, t2.Quantity DESC;
```

Note that another form of the APPLY operator is used, the OUTER APPLY. This form preserves the rows from the left table. As you can see from the following result, the query returns two rows for orders with two or more order details, one for orders with a single order detail, and one with NULL values in the place of the order detail columns for orders without order detail:

```
OrderId     OrderDate   Customer ProductId    Quantity
----------- ----------- -------- ------------ -----------
1           2016-07-01  CustA    6            200
1           2016-07-01  CustA    3            150
2           2016-07-01  CustB    6            250
2           2016-07-01  CustB    4            200
3           2016-01-01  CustC    NULL         NULL
4           2016-01-01  CustD    NULL         NULL
5           2016-07-02  CustA    1            50
```

Transactions and error handling

In a real-world application, errors always appear. Syntax or even logical errors may be in the code, the database design might be incorrect, there might even be a bug in the database management system you are using. Even if everything works correctly, you might get an error because the users insert wrong data. With Transact-SQL error handling you can catch such user errors and decide what to do upon them. Typically, you want to log the errors, inform the users about the errors, and sometimes even correct them in the error handling code.

Error handling for user errors works on the statement level. If you send SQL Server a batch of two or more statements and the error is in the last statement, the previous statements execute successfully. This might not be what you desire. Frequently, you need to execute a batch of statements as a unit, and fail all of the statements if one of the statements fails. You can achieve this by using transactions. In this section, you will learn about:

- Error handling
- Transaction management

Error handling

You can see there is a need for error handling by producing an error. The following code tries to insert an order and a detail row for this order:

```
EXEC dbo.InsertSimpleOrder
  @OrderId = 6, @OrderDate = '20160706', @Customer = N'CustE';
EXEC dbo.InsertSimpleOrderDetail
  @OrderId = 6, @ProductId = 2, @Quantity = 0;
```

In SQL Server Management Studio, you can see that an error occurred. You should get a message that the error 547 occurred, that the INSERT statement conflicted with the CHECK constraint. If you remember, in order details, only rows where the value for the quantity is not equal to zero are allowed. The error occurred in the second statement, in the call of the procedure that inserts an order detail. The procedure that inserted an order was executed without an error. Therefore, an order with an ID equal to six must be in the dbo.SimpleOrders table. The following code tries to insert order 6 again:

```
EXEC dbo.InsertSimpleOrder
  @OrderId = 6, @OrderDate = '20160706', @Customer = N'CustE';
```

Of course, another error occurred. This time it should be error 2627, a violation of the PRIMARY KEY constraint. The values of the OrderId column must be unique. Let's check the state of the data after these successful and unsuccessful inserts:

```
SELECT o.OrderId, o.OrderDate, o.Customer,
  od.ProductId, od.Quantity
FROM dbo.SimpleOrderDetails AS od
  RIGHT OUTER JOIN dbo.SimpleOrders AS o
    ON od.OrderId = o.OrderId
WHERE o.OrderId > 5
ORDER BY o.OrderId, od.ProductId;
```

The previous query checks only orders and their associated details where the order ID value is greater than five. The query returns the following result set:

```
OrderId      OrderDate  Customer ProductId    Quantity
-----------  ---------- -------- ------------ --------
6            2016-07-06 CustE    NULL         NULL
```

You can see that only the first insert of the order with the ID 6 succeeded. The second insert of an order with the same ID and the insert of the detail row for the order six did not succeed.

You start handling errors by enclosing the statements in the batch you are executing in the BEGIN TRY...END TRY block. You can catch the errors in the BEGIN CATCH...END CATCH block. The BEGIN CATCH statement must be immediately after the END TRY statement. The control of the execution is passed from the try part to the catch part immediately after the first error occurs.

In the catch part, you can decide how to handle the errors. If you want to log the data about the error or inform an end user about the details of the error, the following functions might be very handy:

- ERROR_NUMBER(): This function returns the number of the error.
- ERROR_SEVERITY(): It returns the severity level. The severity of the error indicates the type of problem encountered. Severity levels 11 to 16 can be corrected by the user.
- ERROR_STATE(): This function returns the error state number. Error state gives more details about a specific error. You might want to use this number together with the error number to search Microsoft knowledge base for the specific details of the error you encountered.
- ERROR_PROCEDURE(): It returns the name of the stored procedure or trigger where the error occurred, or NULL if the error did not occur within a stored procedure or trigger.
- ERROR_LINE(): It returns the line number at which the error occurred. This might be the line number in a routine if the error occurred within a stored procedure or trigger, or the line number in the batch.
- ERROR_MESSAGE(): This function returns the text of the error message.

The following code uses the `try...catch` block to handle possible errors in the batch of the statements, and returns the information of the error using the preceding mentioned functions. Note that the error happens in the first statement of the batch:

```
BEGIN TRY
 EXEC dbo.InsertSimpleOrder
  @OrderId = 6, @OrderDate = '20160706', @Customer = N'CustF';
 EXEC dbo.InsertSimpleOrderDetail
  @OrderId = 6, @ProductId = 2, @Quantity = 5;
END TRY
BEGIN CATCH
 SELECT ERROR_NUMBER() AS ErrorNumber,
   ERROR_MESSAGE() AS ErrorMessage,
   ERROR_LINE() as ErrorLine;
END CATCH
```

There was a violation of the PRIMARY KEY constraint again, because the code tried to insert an order with an ID of six again. The second statement would succeed if you executed it in its own batch, without error handling. However, because of the error handling, the control was passed to the catch block immediately after the error in the first statement, and the second statement never executed. You can check the data with the following query:

```
SELECT o.OrderId, o.OrderDate, o.Customer,
   od.ProductId, od.Quantity
FROM dbo.SimpleOrderDetails AS od
  RIGHT OUTER JOIN dbo.SimpleOrders AS o
    ON od.OrderId = o.OrderId
WHERE o.OrderId > 5
ORDER BY o.OrderId, od.ProductId;
```

The result set should be the same as the results set of the last check of the orders with an ID greater than five—a single order without details. The following code produces an error in the second statement:

```
BEGIN TRY
 EXEC dbo.InsertSimpleOrder
  @OrderId = 7, @OrderDate = '20160706', @Customer = N'CustF';
 EXEC dbo.InsertSimpleOrderDetail
  @OrderId = 7, @ProductId = 2, @Quantity = 0;
END TRY
BEGIN CATCH
 SELECT ERROR_NUMBER() AS ErrorNumber,
   ERROR_MESSAGE() AS ErrorMessage,
   ERROR_LINE() as ErrorLine;
END CATCH
```

You can see that the insert of the order detail violates the CHECK constraint for the quantity. If you check the data with the same query as the last two times again, you will see that there are orders with an ID of six and seven in the data, both without order details.

Using transactions

Your business logic might request that the insert of the first statement fails when the second statement fails. You might need to repeal the changes of the first statement on the failure of the second statement. You can define that a batch of statements executes as a unit by using transactions. The following code shows how to use transactions. Again, the second statement in the batch in the try block is the one that produces an error:

```
BEGIN TRY
 BEGIN TRANSACTION
  EXEC dbo.InsertSimpleOrder
   @OrderId = 8, @OrderDate = '20160706', @Customer = N'CustG';
  EXEC dbo.InsertSimpleOrderDetail
   @OrderId = 8, @ProductId = 2, @Quantity = 0;
 COMMIT TRANSACTION
END TRY
BEGIN CATCH
SELECT ERROR_NUMBER() AS ErrorNumber,
   ERROR_MESSAGE() AS ErrorMessage,
   ERROR_LINE() as ErrorLine;
 IF XACT_STATE() <> 0
   ROLLBACK TRANSACTION;
END CATCH
```

You can check the data again:

```
SELECT o.OrderId, o.OrderDate, o.Customer,
  od.ProductId, od.Quantity
FROM dbo.SimpleOrderDetails AS od
  RIGHT OUTER JOIN dbo.SimpleOrders AS o
    ON od.OrderId = o.OrderId
WHERE o.OrderId > 5
ORDER BY o.OrderId, od.ProductId;
```

Here is the result of the check:

OrderId	OrderDate	Customer	ProductId	Quantity
6	2016-07-06	CustE	NULL	NULL
7	2016-07-06	CustF	NULL	NULL

You can see that the order with the ID 8 does not exist in your data. Because the insert of the detail row for this order failed, the insert of the order was rolled back as well. Note that in the catch block, the XACT_STATE() function was used to check whether the transaction still exists. If the transaction was rolled back automatically by SQL Server, then the ROLLBACK TRANSACTION would produce a new error.

The following code drops the objects (incorrect order, due to object constraints) created for the explanation of the DDL and DML statements, programmatic objects, error handling, and transactions:

```
DROP FUNCTION dbo.Top2OrderDetails;
DROP VIEW dbo.OrdersWithoutDetails;
DROP PROCEDURE dbo.InsertSimpleOrderDetail;
DROP PROCEDURE dbo.InsertSimpleOrder;
DROP TABLE dbo.SimpleOrderDetails;
DROP TABLE dbo.SimpleOrders;
```

Beyond relational

Beyond relational is actually only a marketing term. The relational model, used in the relational database management system, is nowhere limited to specific data types or specific languages only. However, with the term "beyond relational," we typically mean specialized and complex data types that might include spatial and temporal data, XML or JSON data, and extending the capabilities of the Transact-SQL language with CLR languages such as Visual C#, or statistical languages such as R. SQL Server in versions before 2016 already supports some of the features mentioned. Here is a quick review of this support that includes:

- Spatial data
- CLR support
- XML data

Defining locations and shapes with Spatial Data

In modern applications, often you want to show your data on a map, using the physical location. You might also want to show the shape of the objects that your data describes. You can use spatial data for tasks like these. You can represent the objects with points, lines, or polygons. From simple shapes, you can create complex geometrical objects or geographical objects, for example, cities and roads. Spatial data appears in many contemporary databases. Acquiring spatial data has become quite simple with the **Global Positioning System** (**GPS**) and other technologies. In addition, many software packages and database management systems help you to work with spatial data. SQL Server supports two spatial data types, both implemented as .NET common language runtime data types, from version 2008:

- The geometry type represents data in a **Euclidean (flat) coordinate system**.
- The geography type represents data in a **round-earth coordinate system**.

We need two different spatial data types because of some important differences between them. These differences include units of measurement and orientation.

In the planar, or flat-earth, system, you define the units of measurements. The length of a distance and the surface of an area are given in the same unit of measurement as you use for the coordinates of your coordinate system. You, as the database developer, know what the coordinates mean and what the unit of measure is. In geometry, the distance between the points described with the coordinates (1, 3) and (4, 7) is 5 units regardless of the units used. You, as the database developer who created the database where you are storing this data, know the context. You know what these 5 units mean: 5 kilometers, or 5 inches.

When talking about locations on earth, coordinates are given in degrees of latitude and longitude. This is the round-earth, or ellipsoidal system. Lengths and areas are usually measured in the metric system, in meters and square meters. However, not everywhere in the world is the metric system used for spatial data. The **spatial reference identifier** (**SRID**) of the geography instance defines the unit of measure. Therefore, whenever measuring a distance or area in the ellipsoidal system, you should always quote the SRID used, which defines the units.

In the planar system, the ring orientation of a polygon is not an important factor. For example, a polygon described by the points ((0, 0), (10, 0), (0, 5), (0, 0)) is the same as a polygon described by ((0, 0), (5, 0), (0, 10), (0, 0)). You can always rotate the coordinates appropriately to get the same feeling of the orientation. However, in geography, the orientation is needed to completely describe a polygon. Just think of the equator, which divides the earth into two hemispheres. Is your spatial data describing the northern or southern hemisphere?

The Wide World Importers data warehouse includes city locations in the `Dimension.City` table. The following query retrieves it for cities in the main part of the USA:

```
SELECT City,
  [Sales Territory] AS SalesTerritory,
  Location AS LocationBinary,
  Location.ToString() AS LocationLongLat
FROM Dimension.City
WHERE [City Key] <> 0
  AND [Sales Territory] NOT IN
      (N'External', N'Far West');
```

Here is the partial result of the query.

```
City          SalesTerritory   LocationBinary           LocationLongLat
-----------   --------------   ----------------------   --------------------
Carrollton    Mideast          0xE6100000010C70...      POINT (-78.651695
42.1083969)
Carrollton    Southeast        0xE6100000010C88...      POINT (-76.5605078
36.9468152)
Carrollton    Great Lakes      0xE6100000010CDB...      POINT (-90.4070632
39.3022693)
```

You can see that the location is actually stored as a binary string. When you use the `ToString()` method of the location, you get the default string representation of the geographical point, which is the degrees of longitude and latitude.

In SSMS, you send the results of the previous query to a grid, in the results pane you get an additional representation for the spatial data. Click on the **Spatial results** tab, and you can see the points represented in the longitude-latitude coordinate system, as you can see in the following screenshot:

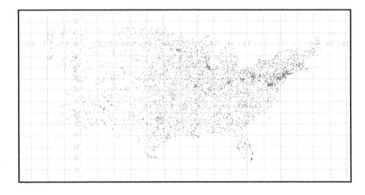

Figure 2.1: Spatial results showing customers' locations

If you executed the query, you might have noticed that the spatial data representation control in SSMS has some limitations. It can show only 5,000 objects. The result displays only the first 5,000 locations. Nevertheless, as you can see from the previous figure, this is enough to realize that these points form a contour of the main part of the USA. Therefore, the points represent the customers' locations for customers from USA.

The following query gives you the details, such as location and population, for Denver, Colorado:

```
SELECT [City Key] AS CityKey, City,
    [State Province] AS State,
    [Latest Recorded Population] AS Population,
    Location.ToString() AS LocationLongLat
FROM Dimension.City
WHERE [City Key] = 114129
    AND [Valid To] = '9999-12-31 23:59:59.9999999';
```

Spatial data types have many useful methods. For example, the STDistance() method returns the shortest line between two geography types. This is a close approximate to the geodesic distance, defined as the shortest route between two points on the Earth's surface. The following code calculates this distance between Denver, Colorado, and Seattle, Washington:

```
DECLARE @g AS GEOGRAPHY;
DECLARE @h AS GEOGRAPHY;
DECLARE @unit AS NVARCHAR(50);
SET @g = (SELECT Location FROM Dimension.City
          WHERE [City Key] = 114129);
SET @h = (SELECT Location FROM Dimension.City
          WHERE [City Key] = 108657);
SET @unit = (SELECT unit_of_measure
              FROM sys.spatial_reference_systems
              WHERE spatial_reference_id = @g.STSrid);
SELECT FORMAT(@g.STDistance(@h), 'N', 'en-us') AS Distance,
 @unit AS Unit;
```

The result of the previous batch is as follows:

```
Distance        Unit
-------------   ------
1,643,936.69    metre
```

Note that the code uses the sys.spatial_reference_system catalog view to get the unit of measure for the distance of the SRID used to store the geographical instances of data. The unit is meter. You can see that the distance between Denver, Colorado, and Seattle, Washington, is more than 1,600 kilometers.

The following query finds the major cities within a circle of 1,000 km around Denver, Colorado. Major cities are defined as those with a population larger than 200,000:

```
DECLARE @g AS GEOGRAPHY;
SET @g = (SELECT Location FROM Dimension.City
         WHERE [City Key] = 114129);
SELECT DISTINCT City,
  [State Province] AS State,
  FORMAT([Latest Recorded Population], '000,000') AS Population,
  FORMAT(@g.STDistance(Location), '000,000.00') AS Distance
FROM Dimension.City
WHERE Location.STIntersects(@g.STBuffer(1000000)) = 1
  AND [Latest Recorded Population] > 200000
  AND [City Key] <> 114129
  AND [Valid To] = '9999-12-31 23:59:59.9999999'
ORDER BY Distance;
```

Here is the result abbreviated to the 12 closest cities to Denver, Colorado:

```
City                State         Population   Distance
------------------  -----------   ----------   ----------
Aurora              Colorado      325,078      013,141.64
Colorado Springs    Colorado      416,427      101,487.28
Albuquerque         New Mexico    545,852      537,221.38
Wichita             Kansas        382,368      702,553.01
Lincoln             Nebraska      258,379      716,934.90
Lubbock             Texas         229,573      738,625.38
Omaha               Nebraska      408,958      784,842.10
Oklahoma City       Oklahoma      579,999      809,747.65
Tulsa               Oklahoma      391,906      882,203.51
El Paso             Texas         649,121      895,789.96
Kansas City         Missouri      459,787      898,397.45
Scottsdale          Arizona       217,385      926,980.71
```

There are many more useful methods and properties implemented in these two spatial data types. In addition, you can improve the performance of spatial queries with the help of specialized spatial indexes. Refer to the MSDN article *Spatial Data (SQL Server)* at https://msdn.microsoft.com/en-us/library/bb933790.aspx for more details on spatial data types, their methods, and spatial indexes.

CLR integration

You probably noticed that the two spatial data types are implemented as CLR data types. The spatial data types are shipped with SQL Server; therefore, Microsoft developers created them. However, you also can create your own CLR data types. SQL Server featured CLR inside the Database Engine for the first time in the 2005 version.

You can create the following CLR objects in a SQL Server database:

- User-defined functions
- Stored procedures
- Triggers
- User-defined aggregate functions
- User-defined data types

You can use CLR objects to extend the functionality of the Transact-SQL language. You should use CLR for objects that you can't create in Transact-SQL, like user-defined aggregates or user-defined data types. For objects that you can also create in Transact-SQL, like functions, stored procedures and triggers, you should use Transact-SQL to manipulate the data, and CLR only in the areas where CLR languages like Visual C# are faster than Transact-SQL, such as complex calculations, and string manipulations.

For example, Transact-SQL language includes only a fistful of aggregate functions. To describe a distribution of a continuous variable, in the **descriptive statistics** you use the first four population moments, namely the:

- Mean, or average value
- Standard deviation
- Skewness, or tailed-ness
- Kurtosis, or peaked-ness

Transact-SQL includes only aggregate functions for calculating the mean and the standard deviation. These two measures might be descriptors good enough to describe the regular normal, or Gaussian distribution, as this figure shows:

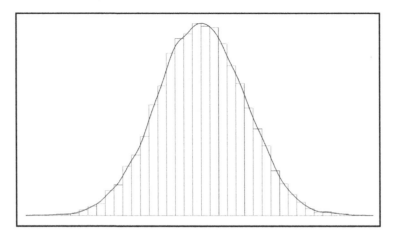

Figure 2.2: Normal or Gaussian distribution

However, a distribution in the real world might not follow the normal curve exactly. Often, it is skewed. A typical example is income, which is usually highly skewed to the right, known as a positive skew. The following figure shows a positively skewed distribution, where you have a long tail on the right side of the distribution:

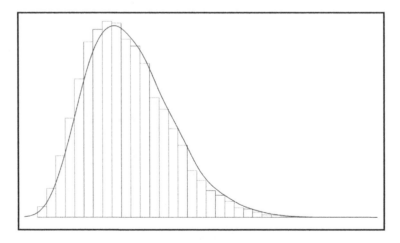

Figure 2.3: Positively skewed distribution

Here is the formula for skewness:

$$\text{Skew} = \frac{n}{(n-1)*(n-2)} * \sum_{i=1}^{n}\left(\frac{v_i - \mu}{\sigma}\right)^3$$

$n = number\ of\ cases$
$v_i = ith\ value$
$\mu = mean$
$\sigma = standard\ deviation$

The formula for skewness uses the mean value and the standard deviation in the formula. I don't want to calculate these values in advance. If I calculated these values in advance, I would need to scan through the data twice. I want to have a more efficient algorithm, an algorithm that will scan the data only once.

I use a bit of mathematics for this optimization. First, I expand the formula for the subtraction of the mean from the ith value on the third degree:

$$(v_i - \mu)^3 = v_i^3 - 3v_i^2\mu + 3v_i\mu^2 - \mu^3$$

Then I use the fact that the sum is distributive over the product, as shown in the formula for two values only:

$$3v_1\mu^2 + 3v_2\mu^2 = 3\mu^2(v_1 + v_2)$$

This formula can be generalized for all values:

$$\sum_{i=1}^{n}(3v_i\mu^2) = 3\mu^2\sum_{i=1}^{n}(v_i)$$

Of course, I can do the same mathematics for the remaining elements of the expanded formula for the subtraction and calculate all the aggregates I need with a single pass through the data, as shown in the following C# code for the user-defined aggregate function that calculates the skewness.

The first part of the code declares the namespaces used:

```
-- C# code for skewness
using System;
using System.Data;
using System.Data.SqlClient;
using System.Data.SqlTypes;
using Microsoft.SqlServer.Server;
```

You represent a **user-defined aggregate (UDA)** with a class or a structure in CLR. First, you decorate it with attributes that give some information about the UDA's behavior and information for the potential optimization of the queries that use it:

```
[Serializable]
[SqlUserDefinedAggregate(
    Format.Native,
    IsInvariantToDuplicates = false,
    IsInvariantToNulls = true,
    IsInvariantToOrder = true,
    IsNullIfEmpty = false)]
```

The next part of the code for the UDA defines the structure and internal variables used to hold the intermediate results for the elements of the calculation, as I explained in the formula reorganization:

```
public struct Skew
{
  private double rx;
  private double rx2;
  private double r2x;
  private double rx3;
  private double r3x2;
  private double r3x;
  private Int64 rn;
```

Structures or classes that represent UDAs must implement four methods. The Init() method initializes the internal variables:

```
  public void Init()
  {
    rx = 0;
    rx2 = 0;
    r2x = 0;
    rx3 = 0;
    r3x2 = 0;
    r3x = 0;
    rn = 0;
  }
```

The `Accumulate()` method does the actual work of aggregating:

```
public void Accumulate(SqlDouble inpVal)
{
  if (inpVal.IsNull)
  {
    return;
  }
  rx = rx + inpVal.Value;
  rx2 = rx2 + Math.Pow(inpVal.Value, 2);
  r2x = r2x + 2 * inpVal.Value;
  rx3 = rx3 + Math.Pow(inpVal.Value, 3);
  r3x2 = r3x2 + 3 * Math.Pow(inpVal.Value, 2);
  r3x = r3x + 3 * inpVal.Value;
  rn = rn + 1;
}
```

The `Merge()` method accepts another aggregate as the input. It merges two aggregates. Where do two or more aggregates come from? SQL Server might decide to execute the aggregating query in parallel, store the intermediate aggregate results internally, and then merge them by using the `Merge()` method:

```
public void Merge(Skew Group)
{
  this.rx = this.rx + Group.rx;
  this.rx2 = this.rx2 + Group.rx2;
  this.r2x = this.r2x + Group.r2x;
  this.rx3 = this.rx3 + Group.rx3;
  this.r3x2 = this.r3x2 + Group.r3x2;
  this.r3x = this.r3x + Group.r3x;
  this.rn = this.rn + Group.rn;
}
```

The `Terminate()` method does the final calculations and returns the aggregated value to the calling query. The return value type must be in compliance with SQL Server data types:

```
public SqlDouble Terminate()
{
  double myAvg = (rx / rn);
  double myStDev = Math.Pow((rx2 - r2x * myAvg + rn *
Math.Pow(myAvg, 2))
                    / (rn - 1), 1d / 2d);
  double mySkew = (rx3 - r3x2 * myAvg + r3x * Math.Pow(myAvg, 2)
                - rn * Math.Pow(myAvg, 3)) /
        Math.Pow(myStDev, 3) * rn / (rn - 1) / (rn - 2);
  return (SqlDouble)mySkew;
}
```

}

You can use the C# compiler to compile the code for the UDA. However, in the associated code for the book, a compiled assembly, the .dll file, is provided for your convenience. The code also includes the function that calculates the kurtosis; for the sake of brevity, this code is not explained in detail here.

In order to use CLR objects, you need to enable CLR for your instance. Then, you need to catalog, or deploy, the assembly in the database with the CREATE ASSEMBLY statement. Then, you create the aggregate functions with the CREATE AGGREGATE statement. The following code enables CLR, deploys the assembly provided with the book, and then creates the two aggregate functions. The code assumes that the assembly is stored in the C:SQL2016DevGuide folder:

```
EXEC sp_configure 'clr enabled', 1;
RECONFIGURE WITH OVERRIDE;

CREATE ASSEMBLY DescriptiveStatistics
FROM 'C:SQL2016DevGuideDescriptiveStatistics.dll'
WITH PERMISSION_SET = SAFE;

CREATE AGGREGATE dbo.Skew(@s float)
RETURNS float
EXTERNAL NAME DescriptiveStatistics.Skew;

CREATE AGGREGATE dbo.Kurt(@s float)
RETURNS float
EXTERNAL NAME DescriptiveStatistics.Kurt;
```

Once the assembly is cataloged and UDAs have been created, you can use them just like built-in aggregate functions. The following query calculates the four moments for the sum over customers of the amount ordered without tax. In a CTE, it calculates the sum of the amount per customer, and then in the outer query the average, the standard deviation, the skewness, and the kurtosis for this total:

```
WITH CustomerSalesCTE AS
(
SELECT c.Customer,
  SUM(f.[Total Excluding Tax]) AS TotalAmount
FROM Fact.Sale AS f
  INNER JOIN Dimension.Customer AS c
    ON f.[Customer Key] = c.[Customer Key]
WHERE c.[Customer Key] <> 0
GROUP BY c.Customer
)
SELECT ROUND(AVG(TotalAmount), 2) AS Average,
```

```
   ROUND(STDEV(TotalAmount), 2) AS StandardDeviation,
   ROUND(dbo.Skew(TotalAmount), 6) AS Skewness,
   ROUND(dbo.Kurt(TotalAmount), 6) AS Kurtosis
FROM CustomerSalesCTE;
```

Here is the result:

```
Average        StandardDeviation Skewness Kurtosis
-------------- ----------------- -------- ---------
270479.220000 38586.08          0.005943 -0.263897
```

After you have tested the UDAs, you can execute the following code to clean up your database, and potentially disable CLR. Note that you need to drop the UDAs before you drop the assembly:

```
DROP AGGREGATE dbo.Skew;
DROP AGGREGATE dbo.Kurt;
DROP ASSEMBLY DescriptiveStatistics;
/*
EXEC sp_configure 'clr enabled', 0;
RECONFIGURE WITH OVERRIDE;
*/
```

XML support in SQL Server

SQL Server in version 2005 also started to feature extended support for XML data inside the database engine, although some basic support was already included in version 2000. The support starts by generating XML data from tabular results. You can use the FOR XML clause of the SELECT statement for this task.

The following query generates an XML document from the regular tabular result set by using the FOR XML clause with AUTO option, to generate an element-centric XML instance, with namespace and inline schema included:

```
SELECT c.[Customer Key] AS CustomerKey,
   c.[WWI Customer ID] AS CustomerId,
   c.[Customer],
   c.[Buying Group] AS BuyingGroup,
   f.Quantity,
   f.[Total Excluding Tax] AS Amount,
   f.Profit
FROM Dimension.Customer AS c
   INNER JOIN Fact.Sale AS f
     ON c.[Customer Key] = f.[Customer Key]
WHERE c.[Customer Key] IN (127, 128)
```

```
FOR XML AUTO, ELEMENTS,
  ROOT('CustomersOrders'),
  XMLSCHEMA('CustomersOrdersSchema');
GO
```

Here is the partial result of this query. The first part of the result is the inline schema:

```
<CustomersOrders>
  <xsd:schema targetNamespace="CustomersOrdersSchema" ...
    <xsd:import namespace="http://schemas.microsoft.com/sqlserver
    /2004/sqltypes" ...
    <xsd:element name="c">
      <xsd:complexType>
        <xsd:sequence>
          <xsd:element name="CustomerKey" type="sqltypes:int" />
          <xsd:element name="CustomerId" type="sqltypes:int" />
          <xsd:element name="Customer">
            <xsd:simpleType>
              <xsd:restriction base="sqltypes:nvarchar" ...
                <xsd:maxLength value="100" />
              </xsd:restriction>
            </xsd:simpleType>
          </xsd:element>
          ...
        </xsd:sequence>
      </xsd:complexType>
    </xsd:element>
  </xsd:schema>
  <c xmlns="CustomersOrdersSchema">
    <CustomerKey>127</CustomerKey>
    <CustomerId>127</CustomerId>
    <Customer>Tailspin Toys (Point Roberts, WA)</Customer>
    <BuyingGroup>Tailspin Toys</BuyingGroup>
    <f>
      <Quantity>3</Quantity>
      <Amount>48.00</Amount>
      <Profit>31.50</Profit>
    </f>
    <f>
      <Quantity>9</Quantity>
      <Amount>2160.00</Amount>
      <Profit>1363.50</Profit>
    </f>
  </c>
  <c xmlns="CustomersOrdersSchema">
    <CustomerKey>128</CustomerKey>
    <CustomerId>128</CustomerId>
    <Customer>Tailspin Toys (East Portal, CO)</Customer>
```

```
    <BuyingGroup>Tailspin Toys</BuyingGroup>
    <f>
      <Quantity>84</Quantity>
      <Amount>420.00</Amount>
      <Profit>294.00</Profit>
    </f>
  </c>
  ...
</CustomersOrders>
```

You can also do the opposite process: convert XML to tables. Converting XML to relational tables is known as **shredding XML**. You can do this by using the nodes() method of the XML data type or with the OPENXML() rowset function.

Inside SQL Server, you can also query the XML data from Transact-SQL to find specific elements, attributes, or XML fragments. **XQuery** is a standard language for browsing XML instances and returning XML, and is supported inside XML data type methods.

You can store XML instances inside a SQL Server database in a column of the XML data type. An XML data type includes five methods that accept XQuery as a parameter. The methods support querying (the query() method), retrieving atomic values (the value() method), existence checks (the exist() method), modifying sections within the XML data (the modify() method), as opposed to overriding the whole thing and shredding XML data into multiple rows in a result set (the nodes() method).

The following code creates a variable of the XML data type to store an XML instance in it. Then, it uses the query() method to return XML fragments from the XML instance. This method accepts XQuery query as a parameter. The XQuery query uses the FLWOR expressions to define and shape the XML returned:

```
DECLARE @x AS XML;
SET @x = N'
<CustomersOrders>
  <Customer custid="1">
    <!-- Comment 111 -->
    <companyname>CustA</companyname>
    <Order orderid="1">
      <orderdate>2016-07-01T00:00:00</orderdate>
    </Order>
    <Order orderid="9">
      <orderdate>2016-07-03T00:00:00</orderdate>
    </Order>
    <Order orderid="12">
      <orderdate>2016-07-12T00:00:00</orderdate>
    </Order>
  </Customer>
```

```
  <Customer custid="2">
    <!-- Comment 222 -->
    <companyname>CustB</companyname>
    <Order orderid="3">
      <orderdate>2016-07-01T00:00:00</orderdate>
    </Order>
    <Order orderid="10">
      <orderdate>2016-07-05T00:00:00</orderdate>
    </Order>
  </Customer>
</CustomersOrders>';
SELECT @x.query('for $i in CustomersOrders/Customer/Order
                let $j := $i/orderdate
                where $i/@orderid < 10900
                order by ($j)[1]
                return
                <Order-orderid-element>
                 <orderid>{data($i/@orderid)}</orderid>
                 {$j}
                </Order-orderid-element>')
       AS [Filtered, sorted and reformatted orders with let clause];
```

Here is the result of the previous query:

```
<Order-orderid-element>
  <orderid>1</orderid>
  <orderdate>2016-07-01T00:00:00</orderdate>
</Order-orderid-element>
<Order-orderid-element>
  <orderid>3</orderid>
  <orderdate>2016-07-01T00:00:00</orderdate>
</Order-orderid-element>
<Order-orderid-element>
  <orderid>9</orderid>
  <orderdate>2016-07-03T00:00:00</orderdate>
</Order-orderid-element>
<Order-orderid-element>
  <orderid>10</orderid>
  <orderdate>2016-07-05T00:00:00</orderdate>
</Order-orderid-element>
<Order-orderid-element>
  <orderid>12</orderid>
  <orderdate>2016-07-12T00:00:00</orderdate>
</Order-orderid-element>
```

Summary

In this chapter, you got a review of the SQL Server features for developers that exist in the previous versions. You can see that this support goes well beyond basic SQL statements, and also beyond pure Transact-SQL.

The recapitulation in this chapter is also useful as an introduction to the new features in SQL Server 2016 covered in Chapter 4, *Transact-SQL Enhancements*, Chapter 5, *JSON Support in SQL Server*, Chapter 7, *Temporal Tables*, and Chapter 13, *Supporting R in SQL Server*.

3
SQL Server Tools

We as developers are accustomed to using **integrated development environments (IDEs)** in our software projects. Visual Studio has been a major player in the IDE space for many years, if not decades, and has allowed developers to use the latest software development processes to further improve quality and efficiency in software projects. Server management on the other hand, has generally been a second-class citizen for many products in the past. In general, this focus can be understood, if not agreed with. IDEs are tools that design and create software which can generate revenue for a business, whereas management tools generally only offer the benefit of some sort of cost savings, rather than direct revenue generation.

The SQL Server Tools of the past (pre-SQL 2005) were very much focused on fulfilling the requirements of being able to manage and query SQL Server instances and databases, but received no great investments in making the tools "comfortable", or even enjoyable to use. Advanced IDEs were firmly in the application development domain and application developers knew that databases were a storage system at best and therefore required no elegant tooling to work with them.

Luckily for us, the advent of SQL Server 2005, along with the release of the .NET Framework encouraged some people at Microsoft to invest a little more time and resources into providing an improved interface for both developers and DBAs for database and data management purposes. **SQL Server Management Studio (SSMS)** was born and unified the functionality of two legacy tools: Query Analyzer and Enterprise Manager. Anyone who has worked with SQL Server since the 2005 release will recognize the application regardless of whether they are using the 2005 release, or the latest 2016 build.

There have been several different names and releases of the second tool in this chapter: **SQL Server Data Tools** (**SSDT**), going back to SQL Server 2005/2008, when the tool was known as Visual Studio Database Projects (also known as Data Dude). The many incarnations of this tool since SQL Server 2005 have been focused on the development of database projects. SSDT has many of the tools and interfaces known to Visual Studio users and allows a seasoned Visual Studio user to quickly familiarize themselves with the tool. Particularly interesting is the improved ability to integrate database and business intelligence projects into source control, continuous integration and automated deployment processes.

In this chapter, we will be exploring:

- Changes in the release management of SQL Server tools (SSMS and SSDT)
- New SSMS features and enhancements
- Using live query statistics
- New developer tools for the R language

Installing and updating SQL Server tools

The very beginning of our journey with SQL Server starts with the installation process. In previous versions of SQL Server, the data management and development tools were delivered together with the SQL Server installation image. As such, if a developer wanted to install SSMS, the setup of SQL Server had to be used to facilitate the installation.

As of SQL Server 2016, Microsoft made the very smart decision to separate the management tools from the server installation. This is not only a separation of the installation medium, but also a separation of the release process. This separation means that both products can be developed and released without having to wait for the other team to be ready. Let's take a look at how this change affects us at installation time.

In the following screenshot, we see the **SQL Server Installation Center** screen. This is the first screen we will encounter when running the SQL Server setup.exe provided in the installation image. After choosing the **Installation** menu point on the left, we are confronted with the generic installation options of SQL Server, which have only minimally changed in the last releases. The second and third options presented on this screen are **Install SQL Server Management Tools** and **Install SQL Server Data Tools**. If we read the descriptions of these options, we note that both links will redirect us to the download page for either SSMS or SSDT. This is the first clear indication that the delivery of these tools has now been decoupled from the server installation.

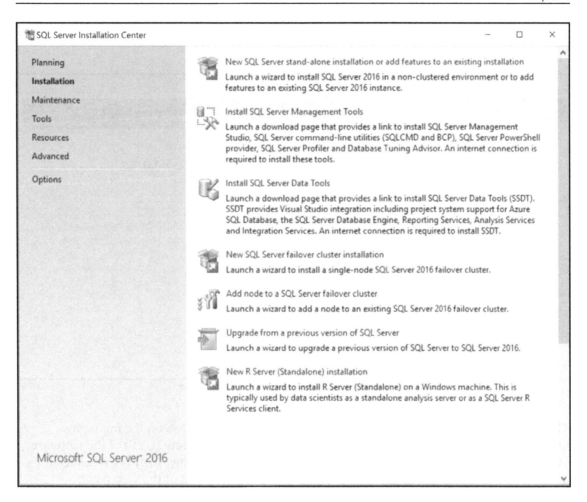

Figure 3.1: SQL Server Installation Center

After clicking on **Install SQL Server Management Studio**, you should be redirected to the download page, which should look like the following screenshot:

Figure 3.2: SQL Server Management Studio download page

The download page offers us the latest production version of SSMS on the main page, together with any beta versions or **community technology preview** (CTP) of the software. We are also able to see details of the current release, view and download previous releases, and find information on change logs and release notes on the left of the web page.

Figure 3.3: SQL Server Management Studio Setup Dialogue

After downloading the desired version of SSMS, we can run the installation just the same way as with previous versions of the tool. The next immediately noticeable difference to previous versions is the installation program itself. SSMS 2016 is based on Visual Studio 2015 Isolated Shell and as such, uses similar color schemes and iconography to Visual Studio 2015.

Once the installation has completed, we can start SSMS and are greeted with a similar starting screen to all previous versions of SSMS. The subtle differences in the application are exactly that, subtle. The splash screen at application start shows the SSMS is now "powered by Visual Studio"; otherwise there are no major indications that we are working in a tool based on Visual Studio. The interface may feel familiar, but the menus and options available are solely concentrated on working with SQL Server.

Previously, SQL Server and the SQL Server Tools were packaged together, leading to bug fixes and feature additions to the tools having to be bundled with **Cumulative Updates (CU)**, **Service Packs (SP)**, or general version releases of the SQL Server product. Through the decoupling of the applications SSMS and SSDT from SQL Server, we no longer have to wait for CUs, SPs, or version releases of SQL Server before we can receive the required/requested features and fixes for SSMS and SSDT. The SQL Server tools team has taken immediate advantage of this and has made regular releases to both SSMS and SSDT since the general release of SQL Server 2016. The initial release of SSMS 2016 was in June 2016 and there have been subsequent update releases in July 2016, August 2016, September 2016, and December 2016. Each release has included a range of bug fixes and feature additions and are much more rapidly deployable when compared to previous versions of SQL Server and SSMS.

A further advantage of the separation of the data tools from the server product is the reduced overhead of managing the installation and updating the tools in a network. The process of updating an already installed SSMS installation is demonstrated in *Figure 3.4* where we see that a **Check for Updates...** option has been included in the **Tools** menu of SSMS. Further to this, the separation of the tools as a standalone installer will reduce the administrative overhead in larger organizations where software is deployed using centralized management software. Where, previously, the larger ISO image of a SQL Server installation was required, now a smaller standalone installer is available for distribution.

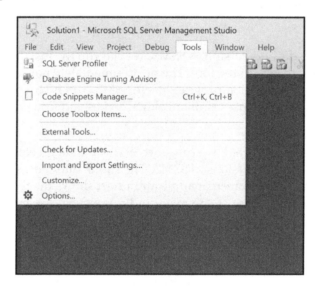

Figure 3.4: Check for Updates in SQL Server Management Studio

We also have the option to request that SSMS automatically checks for updates at application start. This will create a notification balloon message in Windows if a new version is available. A sample notification on a Windows 10 machine can be seen in the following screenshot:

Figure 3.5: Update notification for SQL Server Management Studio.

Once the update check has been opened, SSMS connects to the update systems of Microsoft and performs checks against the currently installed version and the latest downloadable release of the software. If updates have been found, these will be offered via the update mechanism, as shown in *Figure 3.6*. We are also able to decide whether the automated update check should be performed or not.

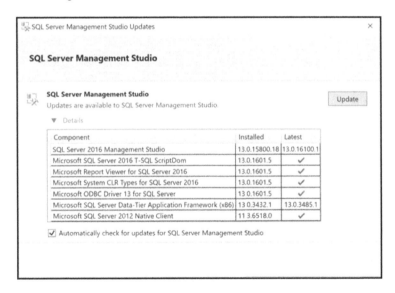

Figure 3.6: SQL Server Management Studio Update Checker

These enhancements to the install and update process are not mind-blowing, especially considering that these features have been available in other products for years or even decades. However, these are the first main improvements which have to do with the switch from a standalone application to an application based on the extremely successful Visual Studio framework.

New SSMS features and enhancements

As we saw with the installation process, there are already a few enhancements in the installation and updating process for SSMS. Through the migration of the SSMS application to the Visual Studio 2015 Isolated Shell, there are a number of additions into SSMS that will be familiar to application developers who use Visual Studio 2015 (or one of its derivatives). While some of these are simple improvements, these additions can be of help to many SQL developers who have been isolated inside SSMS 2016.

Autosave open tabs

The first improvement is the option to choose whether SSMS should prompt to save unsaved tabs when you decide to close SSMS. This is a simple change, but if you use SSMS to run many ad hoc queries and do not want to constantly close out and save each tab, this is now an option. The default is for SSMS to prompt when closing a window, but by unchecking the checkbox marked in *Figure 3.7*, you can force SSMS to silently close these windows.

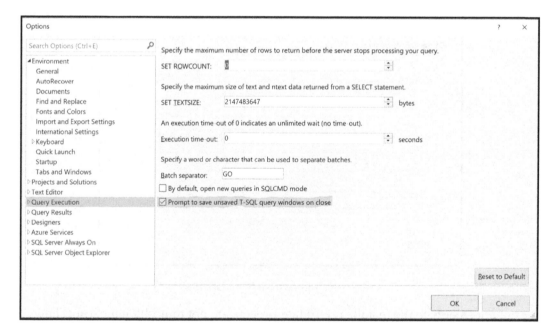

Figure 3.7: Options window in SQL Server Management Studio – prompt to save unsaved work

Searchable options

The next usability or productivity enhancement comes via the Visual Studio 2015 Isolated Shell features. The options menu inside Visual Studio, and SSMS, is jam-packed with features and functionalities that can be configured. Unfortunately, these options are so numerous that it can be difficult to navigate and find the option you are interested in. To aid us in the search for the settings we are interested in, we are now able to quickly search and filter in the options menu. The ability to quickly search through the options for settings via a text search without having to memorize where the settings are hidden is shown in *Figure 3.8*. Go to **Tools** | **Options** and you are then able to type your search string in the textbox in the top left of the options window. In *Figure 3.8*, the search term `execution` has been entered, filtering the results as the word is typed into the search form.

Figure 3.8: Options window – search/filter

Enhanced scroll bar

A further improvement that will be used on a much more regular basis is the enhanced scroll bar in the T-SQL editor tab. In *Figure 3.9* we can see an example of a T-SQL stored procedure that has been opened for editing.

```
ALTER PROCEDURE [Integration].[GetOrderUpdates]
   @LastCutoff datetime2(7),
   @NewCutoff datetime2(7)
   WITH EXECUTE AS OWNER
   AS
BEGIN
     SET NOCOUNT ON;
     SET XACT_ABORT ON;
     -- Added comment, not saved
     SELECT CAST(o.OrderDate AS date) AS [Order Date Key],
            CAST(ol.PickingCompletedWhen AS date) AS [Picked Date Key],
            o.OrderID AS [WWI Order ID],
            o.BackorderOrderID AS [WWI Backorder ID],
            ol.[Description],
            pt.PackageTypeName AS Package,
            ol.Quantity AS Quantity,
            ol.UnitPrice AS [Unit Price],
            ol.TaxRate AS [Tax Rate],
            ROUND(ol.Quantity * ol.UnitPrice, 2) AS [Total Excluding Tax],
            ROUND(ol.Quantity * ol.UnitPrice * ol.TaxRate / 100.0, 2) AS [Tax Amount],
            ROUND(ol.Quantity * ol.UnitPrice, 2) + ROUND(ol.Quantity * ol.UnitPrice * ol.TaxRate / 100.0, 2) AS [Total Including Tax],
            c.DeliveryCityID AS [WWI City ID],
            c.CustomerID AS [WWI Customer ID],
            ol.StockItemID AS [WWI Stock Item ID],
            o.SalespersonPersonID AS [WWI Salesperson ID],
            o.PickedByPersonID AS [WWI Picker ID],
            CASE WHEN ol.LastEditedWhen > o.LastEditedWhen THEN ol.LastEditedWhen ELSE o.LastEditedWhen END AS [Last Modified When]
```

Figure 3.9: SQL Server Management Studio Scroll bar enhancements

The main points to pay attention to are: the margin on the left-hand side of the screen and the scroll bar on the right-hand side of Management Studio. The enhancement here allows us to easily identify a few details in our script window.

- Green blocks show changes made in the editor have been saved to the file currently being edited
- Yellow blocks show changes that have not yet been saved
- Red blocks show code that is invalid or has syntax errors (native IntelliSense must be enabled for this feature to work)
- The blue marker on the scroll bar shows the location of the cursor

These subtle changes are further examples of the Visual Studio base providing us with further enhancements to make working inside SSMS easier. Knowing what code has been changed or is defective on a syntax level allows us to quickly navigate through our code inside SSMS.

Execution plan comparison

Refactoring and improving the performance of code is a regular occurrence in the working day of a developer. Being able to identify whether the refactoring of a particular query has helped improve an execution plan can sometimes be difficult. To help us identify plan changes, SSMS 2016 now offers the option to compare execution plans.

By saving the execution plan and the T-SQL of our initial query as a `.sqlplan` file, we can then run our redesigned query and compare the two plans. In *Figure 3.10*, we can see how to initiate a plan comparison.

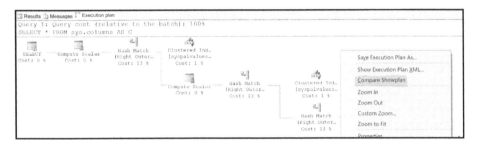

Figure 3.10: Activating a plan comparison session

Upon activation, we must choose which `.sqlplan` file we would like to use for the comparison session. The two execution plans are loaded into a separate **Showplan comparison** tab in SSMS and we can evaluate how the plans differ or how they are similar. In *Figure 3.11*, we see a plan comparison where there are only slight differences between the plans.

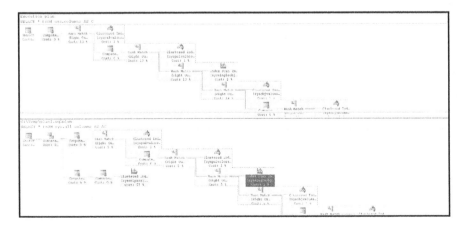

Figure 3.11: Showplan comparison tab

The nodes of the execution plans in *Figure 3.11* that are similar have a red background, while nodes that are different have a yellow background.

If we click the nodes inside one of the plans, the matching node in the comparison plan will be highlighted and we can then investigate how they are similar, and how they differ.

Once we have chosen the node in our execution plan, we will be able to view the properties of the node we wish to compare, similar to the details shown in *Figure 3.12*:

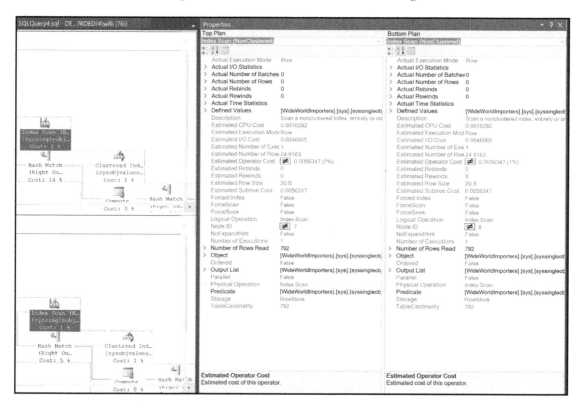

Figure 3.12: Showplan comparison – node properties

The properties tab clearly shows which parts of the node are different. In *Figure 3.12*, we can ignore the lower inequality, which is stating the Node ID is different, this will occur wherever our query has a slightly changed plan. Of interest in this case is the `Estimated Operator Cost` property, which is showing a difference. This example is very simple and the differences are minimal, but we are able to identify differences in a very similar plan with a few simple clicks. This sort of support is invaluable and a huge time saver, especially when plans are larger and more complex.

Live Query Statistics

Following on from the plan comparison feature, we have one of the more powerful features for a developer. **Live Query Statistics (LQS)** does exactly what the name says—it provides us with a live view of a query execution so that we can see exactly how data is flowing through the query plan. In previous versions of SQL Server and SSMS, we have been able to request a static graphical representation of a query execution plan. There have been multiple books, blogposts, videos, and training seminars designed and delivered to thousands of developers and DBAs around the world in an attempt to improve people's ability to understand these static execution plans. The ability of a developer to read and interpret the contents of these plans rests largely on these resources. With LQS, we have an additional tool at our disposal to be able to more easily identify how SQL Server is consuming and processing the T-SQL query that we have submitted to it. The special sauce in LQS is that we don't get a static graphical representation, but rather an animation of the execution. The execution plan is displayed in SSMS and the arrows between the plan nodes move to show the data flowing between the nodes. In *Figure 3.13*, we see how to activate LQS inside SSMS for a particular query tab.

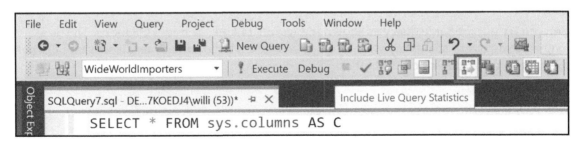

Figure 3.13: Activate Live Query Statistics

As Live Query Statistics shows a moving image, we are at a distinct disadvantage when trying to visualize it in a book! However, when we run a query with LQS activated, it is still possible to show an example of how LQS looks while running, as we can see in *Figure 3.14*.

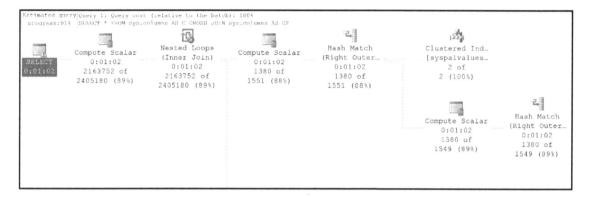

Figure 3.14: Live Query Statistics – Query execution

In *Figure 3.14*, we can see that the execution plan image that we are used to has been extended slightly. We now see a few extra details. Starting in the top left of this image, we see an estimated query progress in percent. As with anything to do with query execution and statistics, SQL Server is always working with estimations that are based on table and index statistics, which is a topic worthy of an entire book. We also see an execution time displayed below each node that is still actively processing data. Also below each node is a display of how many rows are still left to be processed (these are also based on estimations through statistics). Finally, we see the arrows connecting each node; solid lines are where execution has completed, dotted lines (which also move during execution), show where data is still flowing and being processed.

You can try out the same query as shown in *Figure 3.14* and see how LQS looks. This is a long-running query against `sys.objects` to produce a large enough result set that LQS has time to capture exhaustion information.

```
SELECT * FROM
          SYS.OBJECTS AS o1
CROSS JOIN sys.objects AS o2
CROSS JOIN sys.objects AS o3
```

This sample query should run long enough to allow LQS to display an animated query plan long enough to understand how LQS makes a query plan easier to understand. It should also be clear that LQS can only display a useful animation for queries that for run longer than a few seconds, as the animation only runs for the duration of the query.

This moving display of data flow allows us as developers to understand how SQL Server is processing our query. We are able to get a better insight into where execution is spending the most time and resources and also where we may need to consider re-writing a query or applying different indexing to achieve better results. LQS, coupled with query plan comparisons will allow us as developers to design better database solutions and better understand how SQL Server processes our queries. In particular, how SQL Server must wait for certain nodes in an execution plan to complete before continuing onto the next node.

However, we must not forget: running LQS, similar to running a trace, requires a certain set of permissions and also consumes resources on the server. We should approach our queries with LQS at the development stage and attempt to write optimal code before we deploy it into production. LQS should therefore be used primarily on your development work in a test environment and *not* in your production environment.

SQL Server Data Tools

As with the installation of SSMS, **SQL Server Data Tools** (**SSDT**) is also offered as a separate download. This can be found via the SQL Server setup screen shown at the beginning of the chapter. Clicking on **Install SQL Server Data Tools** will launch a web browser, directing to the download page for SSDT. This download page offers the latest stable build and also the latest release candidate of the next version of SSDT (with the usual warning of a release candidate not being production-ready). SSDT is delivered with the same Visual Studio Integrated Shell as SSMS, and can be installed as a standalone tool. However, SSDT is aimed at developers and the workflows associated with developing database solutions as a team member. This includes the processes of source control and the packaging of project deployments. With this in mind, it is also possible to install SSDT on a machine which has the full Visual Studio environment installed. Doing so will integrate SSDT into Visual Studio and incorporate the database development templates and workflows, allowing Visual Studio to remain the development environment, instead of adding a separate environment just for database development.

If Visual Studio is already installed, the SQL Server Data Tools Update can be installed from inside Visual Studio. To download and install this update, navigate to **Tools | Extensions and Updates** and select the node **Updates** on the left side of the **Extensions and Updates** modal window, as shown in the following screenshot:

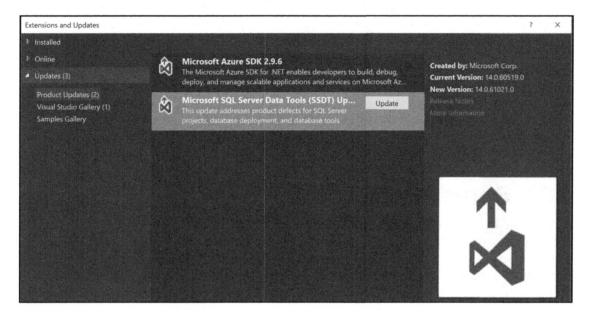

Figure 3.15 SSDT – Extensions and Updates

Once installed, SSDT (whether installed as a standalone tool or integrated into Visual Studio) provides four separate project templates to help jump-start development of SQL Server projects:

- **Relational databases**: This is a template designed for traditional relational database development and supports SQL Server versions from 2005 to 2016 (although SQL Server 2005 is now a deprecated version). SSDT also supports on-premises installations and Azure SQL Database projects (the Database as a Service solution hosted in Microsoft Azure). It is also possible to design queries (but not full projects) for Azure SQL Data Warehouse (the cloud-based data warehouse solution, hosted in Microsoft Azure).

- **Analysis Services models**: This template is designed to assist in the design and deployment of Analysis Services projects and supports SQL Server versions from 2008 to 2016.

- **Reporting Services reports** : This template is designed to assist in the design and deployment of Reporting Services projects and supports SQL Server versions 2008 until 2016.

- **Integration Services packages**: This template is designed to assist in the design and deployment of Integration Services projects and supports SQL Server versions from 2012 to 2016.

The template choice dictates what files and folders are automatically prepared at project creation time. Choosing **File | New Project** presents the new project dialogue shown in the following screenshot. There are two additions to the project type navigation tree. **Business Intelligence** groups **Analysis Services**, **Integration Services**, and **Reporting Services** projects together. The relational database project type is found under the **SQL Server** navigation node.

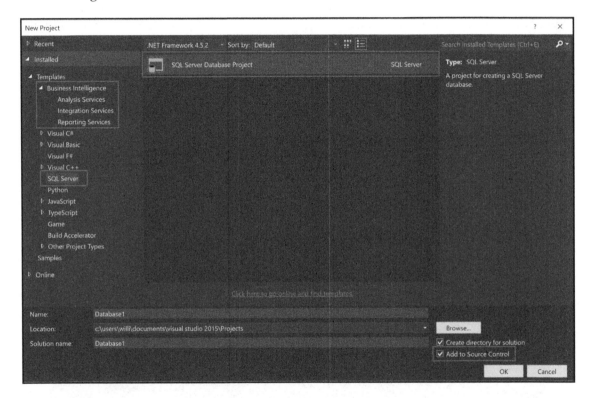

Figure 3.16: SSDT – New Project Dialogue

As shown in the preceding screenshot, a project folder is created and the option to add the project to a source control system is available. Visual Studio offers the option to natively access the source control system's Visual Studio Team Services (a hosted source control system from Microsoft) or alternatively to use a local source control system such as Git. Furthermore, source control systems can be added through the extensive extensions library offered through Visual Studio and can be accessed through the **Tools** | **Extensions and Updates** menu described earlier in this section.

Working with SSDT and the aforementioned templates should be familiar to any developer that has used Visual Studio before. Upon creating a project, the next step is to begin by adding new items (tables, view, stored procedures, and so on). The dialogue for this is filtered down to the project type and for a SQL Server database project, we have the option of creating items ranging from Application Roles to XML Schema Collections. Of note is the ability to create SQL CLR objects (C# based common language runtime objects), which provide the ability to create more complex calculations that are otherwise not possible (or perform poorly) in the T-SQL language.

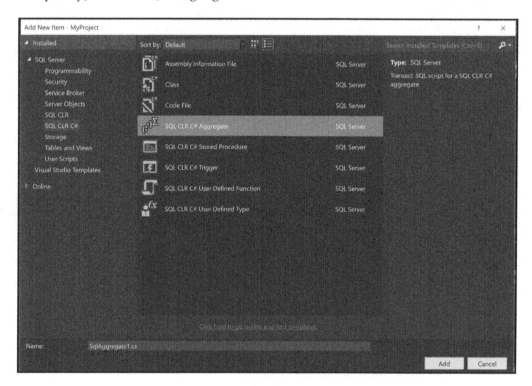

Figure 3.17: Add New SQL CLR C# Aggregate

The advantages of using SSDT over SSMS for developers is the focus on development workflows and the integrations in the program: source control integration, project structuring, and object templates. This developer focus is further strengthened through the possibility of connecting the source control system to a build system and the option to extend the build system to include **continuous integration/deployment (CI/CD)**. Both automated builds and CI/CD have become ubiquitous in applicationdevelopment circles in the past decade. This area has only seen limited support for database development until now, because databases also permanently store data. Now that application development environments have matured, the ability to introduce CI/CD to database projects has become a reality. Luckily, the foundation for CI/CD has long been laid for application development and so the work to implement CI/CD into a database project is greatly reduced. SSDT is therefore fully capable of integrating SQL Server database projects into a source control system *and* to extend those projects into automated build, test, and deployment workflows.

There are now a wealth of options to cover CI/CD in the SQL Server world. The tools TeamCity for continuous integration and Octopus Deploy are two products that have been proven to work well in conjunction with SSDT to provide a smooth process for CI/CD in SQL Server projects. An interesting and useful website to visit for more information on topics on SSDT is the Microsoft *SQL Server Data Tools Team Blog* at `https://blogs.msdn.microsoft.com/ssdt/`.

Tools for developing R code

As you probably already know, SQL Server 2016 brings support for the R language. Of course, you need to have a development tool for the R code. There is a free version of the **integrated development environment (IDE)** tool **RStudio IDE** that has been available for quite a long time. This is probably the most popular R tool. In addition, Microsoft developed **R Tools for Visual Studio (RTVS),** a plug-in for Visual Studio 2015, which enables you to develop R code in an IDE and is well-known among developers who use Microsoft products and languages.

In this section, you will learn about:

- RStudio IDE
- R Tools for Visual Studio

RStudio IDE

The first tool you get for writing and executing R code is the **R Console**. The console uses the greater than (>) sign as a prompt for the user. In the console, you write commands line by line, and execute them by pressing the *Enter* key. You have some limited editing capabilities in the console. For example, you can use the up and down arrow keys to retrieve the previous or the next command in the buffer. The following figure shows the console, with the demo() command executed, which opened an Explorer window with a list of demo packages.

Because R is a functional package, you close the R Console with the q() function call. Anyway, you probably want to use a nicer, graphical environment. Therefore, it is time to introduce the RStudio IDE.

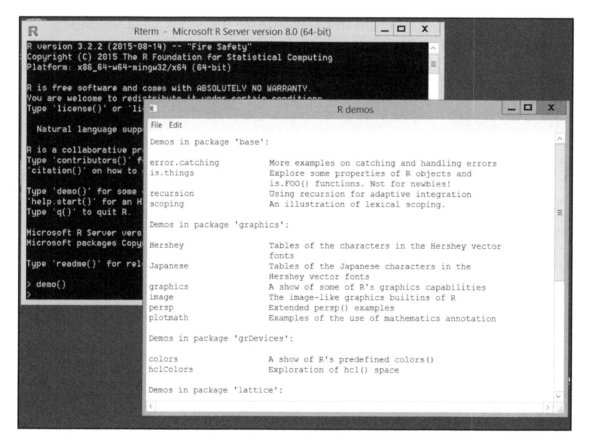

Figure 3.18: R Console

RStudio is a company that is dedicated to helping the R community with its products (https://www.rstudio.com/). Their most popular product is the RStudio IDE, or, as most R developers used to say, just RStudio. RStudio is available in open source and commercial editions, in both cases, for desktop computers or for servers. The open source desktop edition, which is described in this section, is very suitable for developing in R. Already, this edition has built in the majority of features needed for smooth and efficient coding. This edition is described in this section.

You can download the RStudio IDE from the RStudio company site. The IDE supports Windows, macOS, and Linux. Once you install it, you can open it through a desktop shortcut, which points to the C:Program FilesRStudiobinrstudio.exe file, if you used the defaults during installation.

RStudio screen is, by default, split into four panes when you open an R script file, as *Figure 3.19* shows. The open script file is showing the R script used for the demos in Chapter 13, *Supporting R in SQL Server*, of this book.

Figure 3.19: RStudio IDE

The bottom-left pane is the **Console** pane. It works similarly to the R Console command prompt utility shipped with the R engine. You can write statements and execute them one by one, by pressing the *Enter* key. However, in RStudio, you have many additional keyboard shortcuts available. One of the most important keyboard shortcuts is the *Tab* key, which provides you with the code complete option. You can press the *Tab* key nearly anywhere in the code. For example, if you press it when you are writing function arguments, it gives you a list of possible arguments, or, if you have already started to write the name of an object, all objects that start with the letters you have already written.

The top-left pane is the Source pane that is, by default, the settings used for the script. Writing R code line by line in a console is simple, but not very efficient for developing a script with thousands of lines. The **Source** pane does not execute your R code line by line. You highlight portions of your code and execute it by pressing the *Ctrl + Enter* keys.

The top-right pane is the **Environment** pane. It shows you the objects in your current environment, the objects currently loaded in memory. However, this pane has more than one function. You can see additional tabs at the top of the pane. By default, you see the **History** tab, the tab that leads you to the **History** pane where you can see the history of previous commands. The history goes beyond the commands in the current session, in the current console or script.

The bottom-right pane is also a multi-purpose pane. It includes the **Help** pane, **Plots** pane, **Files** pane, **Packages** pane, and **Viewer** pane by default. You can use the **Files** tab to check the files you saved in your RStudio account. With the help of the **Packages** tab, you can get a list of all R packages you have access to in the current session. The **Help** tab brings you, of course, to the R documentation and help system. You can use the **Viewer** tab to get to the **Viewer** pane, where you can see local web content that you can create with some graphical packages. The **Plots** pane shows you the plots you created by executing R code either in the **Console** or in the **Script** pane.

Figure 3.20 shows all four panes in action. You can see the usage of the *Tab* key in the **Source** pane to autocomplete the name of the dataset used in the plot () function. The dataset used is the iris dataset, a very well-known demo dataset in R. You can see the command echoed in the **Console** pane. The **Environment** pane shows details about the iris dataset that is loaded in memory. The **Plots** pane shows plots for all of the variables in the demo iris dataset.

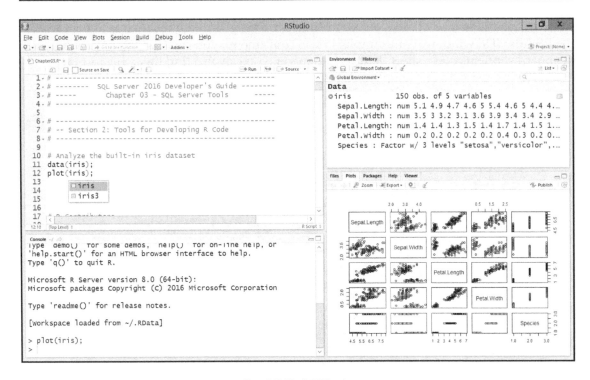

Figure 3.20: RStudio IDE in action

Note that you can enlarge the plot and save it in different graphical formats from the **Plots** pane.

There are literally dozens of keyboard shortcuts. It is impossible to memorize all of them. Nevertheless, you don't need to know all of the shortcuts before you start writing R code. You can always get a quick reference of the keyboard shortcuts by pressing the *Alt + Shift + K* keys at the same time. The **Keyboard Shortcut Quick Reference** cheat sheet appears, as *Figure 3.21* shows. You can get rid of this cheat sheet by pressing the *Esc* key.

Note that, although exhaustive, even this cheat sheet is not complete. In the top-right corner of the cheat sheet you can see a link to even more shortcuts. Finally, it is worth mentioning that you can modify the pre-defined shortcuts and replace them with your own.

You have access to many of the keyboard shortcut actions through the menus at the top of the RStudio IDE window. For example, in the **Tools** menu, you can find the link to the keyboard shortcuts cheat sheet. In the **Help** menu, you can also find links to various cheat sheets, for example, to the complete RStudio IDE cheat sheet, a PDF document you can download from the RStudio site, besides the help options you would usually expect.

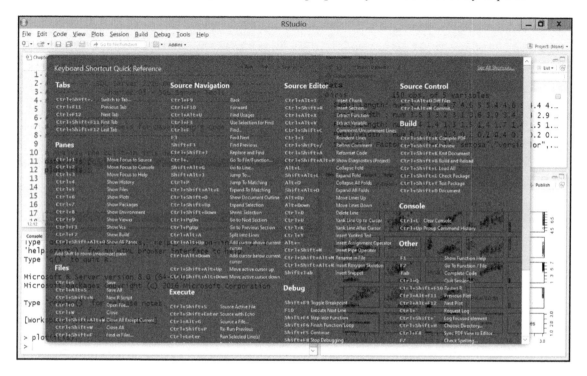

Figure 3.21: RStudio IDE keyboard shortcuts cheat sheet

R Tools for Visual Studio

Microsoft developed **R Tools for Visual Studio (RTVS)** for those developers who are used to developing code in the popular Microsoft's IDE, Visual Studio. You can download the tools from `https://www.visualstudio.com/vs/rtvs/`.

Once you install RTVS, you open the Visual Studio as you would open it for any other project. Of course, since **SQL Server Data Tools (SSDT)** is not a separate product, it is just another shortcut to the Visual Studio IDE. You can also open SSDT and get the R Tools menu besides other common Visual Studio menus.

With RTVS, you get most of the useful panes of the RStudio IDE. You get the **Source** pane, the **Console** pane, which is called **R Interactive** in RTVS, and the **Plots** pane. *Figure 3.22* shows the RTVS window with the **Source**, **R Interactive**, and the **Plots** pane open, showing the same plots for the variables from the iris demo dataset, as shown in *Figure 3.20* earlier in this section.

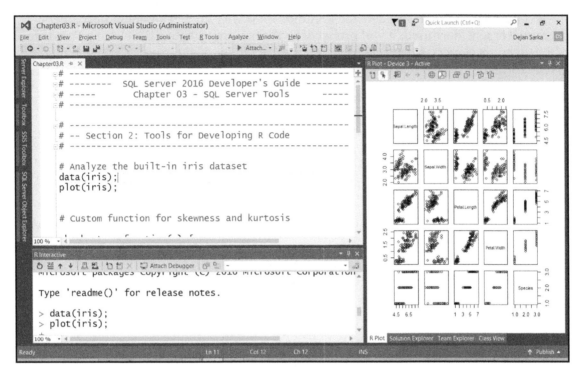

Figure 3.22: R Tools for Visual Studio

If you are familiar with the Visual Studio IDE, then you might want to test RTVS.

Summary

In this chapter, we have taken a look at the new additions in the developer toolset for SQL Server 2016. There have been some long-awaited improvements made, especially the separation of SQL Server Management Studio from the release cycle of SQL Server itself. Many developers are hoping that the release velocity of SSMS will remain as high as it has been in the months since the SQL Server 2016 release. Almost monthly releases mean we all have the chance to get extra features and bug fixes much more quickly than in previous years.

Some of the feature additions to SSMS are quite powerful and will allow us as developers to be more efficient. Live Query Statistics provide us with excellent insights into how our queries are *actually* processed, removing parts of the "guessing game" when trying to refactor or tune our queries.

For SQL Server developers, there are two new development environments for developing the R code. Of course, one of them, the RStudio IDE is well-known among R developers. Because it is so widely used, it will probably be the first choice when developing R code for SQL Server developers. Nevertheless, if you are used to the Visual Studio IDE, you might give R Tools for Visual Studio a try.

After this short excursion into the tools that are delivered with SQL Server 2016, we continue our journey through the new features and technologies in SQL Server 2016 in Chapter 4, *Transact-SQL Enhancements*.

4
Transact-SQL Enhancements

Each new SQL Server version brings numerous extensions and improvements to Transact-SQL language. Most of them are used to support newly added database engine features, but some of them address missing functionalities and limitations in previous versions. SQL Server 2016 comes up with many features that require extensions in Transact-SQL: temporal tables, JSON support, improvements for memory-optimized tables, columnstore tables and indexes, new security enhancements, and so on. They will be explored in detail in chapters dedicated to appropriate features.

This chapter covers *small* Transact-SQL features that can make developers' work more productive and enhancements that can increase the availability of database objects and enlarge the scope of existing functionalities, limited in the previous SQL Server versions.

This chapter is divided into the following three sections:

- New and enhanced Transact-SQL functions and expressions
- Enhanced DML and DDL statements
- New query hints

In the first section, you will see new out-of-the-box functions and expressions that allow developers string manipulations, compressions with the GZIP algorithm, and playing with session-scoped variables. In addition, the removal of restrictions or limitations of some functions makes them more interesting for usage in SQL Server 2016.

The further sections cover enhancements in data manipulation and data definition statements. The most important one will let you change the data type or other attributes of a table column, while the table remains available for querying and modifications. This is a very important feature for systems where continuous availability is required. You will also be aware of other improvements that let you perform some actions faster or with less written code.

Finally, there will be a demonstration on how to use newly added query hints to improve query execution and avoid problems caused by the Spool operator or inappropriate memory grants.

New and enhanced functions and expressions

SQL Server 2016 introduces several new functions that can help developers to be more productive and efficient. Additionally, by removing limitations in some existing functions, their scope of usage has been enlarged. Now, SQL Server contains more than 300 built-in functions. Here is the list of new or changed functions and expressions in SQL Server 2016:

- Two new string functions STRING_SPLIT and STRING_ESCAPE
- New date function and new expression DATEFDIFF_BIG and AT TIME ZONE
- Four new system functions COMPRESS, DECOMPRESS, SESSION_CONTEXT, and CURRENT_TRANSACTION_ID
- Enhancements in the cryptographic function HASHBYTES
- Four JSON-related functions ISSJON, JSON_VALUE, JSON_QUERY, JSON_MODIFY, and one new rowset function OPENJSON

STRING_SPLIT

Since SQL Server does not support arrays, when multiple values need to be send to it, developers use a list of values (usually comma-separated ones).

SQL Server 2008 introduced an excellent feature called **Table-Valued Parameters (TVP)**, which allows you to pack values in a table and transfer them to SQL Server in table format. On the server, stored procedures, or queries, use this parameter as a table variable and can leverage set-based operations to improve performance, compared to separate executions per single parameter value. Thus, from SQL Server 2008, it is strongly recommended to use TVP instead of a list of values in such cases.

However, lists of values as parameters for stored procedures are still widely used, mainly for the following two reasons:

- **Missing support for TVP in JDBC drivers**: Therefore, Java applications and services still have to use comma-separated lists or XML to transfer a list of values to SQL Server

- **Legacy code**: Significant amount of Transact-SQL code from the previous versions, where TVP was not supported

When a list of values is transferred to SQL Server as a stored procedure parameter in the stored procedure body, this list should be converted to a table. Until SQL Server 2016, there was no built-in function that could perform this action. Developers had to write **user-defined functions (UDF)** or play with the `FOR XML PATH` extension for that purpose. An excellent overview and performance comparison of the existing user-defined functions for converting a string to a table can be found in the article *Split strings the right way – or the next best way* written by Aaron Bertrand. This article is available at `http://sqlperformance.com/2012/07/t-sql-queries/split-strings`.

You might ask yourself why companies still have legacy code in production systems and why they don't migrate the old code so that they can use the benefits of new features and enhancements. For instance, why are old implementations with comma-separated lists not replaced by the recommended TVPs? The migration is an easy task. This is true, the migration steps are not complex and every developer can perform them. However, in a medium or large company, developers cannot decide what should be done. Their responsibility scope is related to *how* and not to *what*. Therefore, in such cases, the developer can suggest the migration to project managers or product owners and the decision about the priority of the action is made on the business side. To migrate a comma-separated list to TVP, you need to change not only the body of the stored procedures, but also its parameters, and its interface. You also need to change the data access layer, to touch the application code, unit tests, to compile the project, to deploy it. Even if your tests are fully automated, this is not a trivial effort. On the other hand, the migration does not bring significant improvements for customers. Nowadays, development processes are mostly based on the agile methodology and features mostly wanted and appreciated by customers have the highest priority. Therefore, such migration actions usually remain further down the to-do list, waiting for a miracle to happen.

Finally, the SQL Server development team added the `STRING_SPLIT` function into the latest release. This is a table-valued function and converts a delimited string into a single column table. The function accepts two input arguments:

- **String**: This is an expression of any nondeprecated string data type that needs to be split

- **Separator**: This is a single character used as a separator in the input string

Since it is a table-valued function, it returns a table. The returned table contains only one column with the `value` name and with a data type and length that are the same as that of the input string.

Here is an example showing how this function can be used to produce a three-row table for a comma-separated list as input. Execute this code:

```
USE tempdb;
SELECT value FROM STRING_SPLIT(N'Rapid Wien,Benfica Lisboa,Seattle
Seahawks',',');
```

The preceding query produces the following output:

```
value
-------------------
Rapid Wien
Benfica Lisboa
Seattle Seahawks
```

The actual execution plan for the preceding query looks as follows:

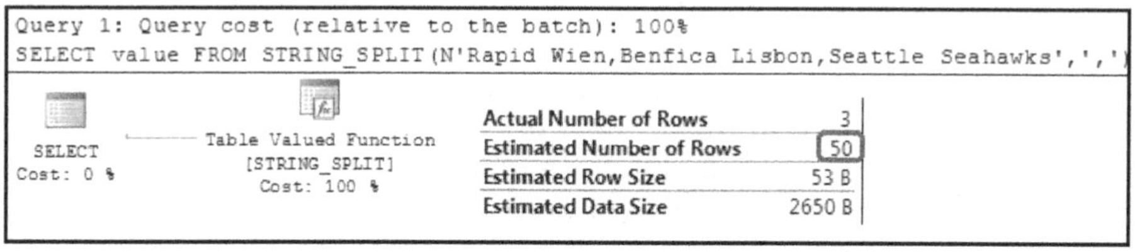

| Query 1: Query cost (relative to the batch): 100% |
| SELECT value FROM STRING_SPLIT(N'Rapid Wien,Benfica Lisbon,Seattle Seahawks',',') |

	Actual Number of Rows	3
Table Valued Function	Estimated Number of Rows	50
SELECT [STRING_SPLIT]	Estimated Row Size	53 B
Cost: 0 % Cost: 100 %	Estimated Data Size	2650 B

Figure 4.1: Estimated Number of Rows for the STRING_SPLIT function

Notice that, the **Estimated Number of Rows** is **50**. This is always the case with this function: the estimated output is 50 rows and it does not depend on the number of string elements. Even when you specify the `OPTION (RECOMPILE)` query hint, the estimation remains the same. In the case of user-defined table-valued functions, the estimated number of rows is 100.

As a table-valued function, `STRING_SPLIT` can be used not only in the `SELECT` clause, but also in `FROM`, `WHERE`, and wherever a table expression is supported. To demonstrate its usage, you will use the new SQL Server sample database `WideWorldImporters`. The database is available for download at
`https://github.com/Microsoft/sql-server-samples/releases/tag/wide-world-importe
rs-v1.0`. The following query extracts stock items having the `Super Value` tag in the `Tags` attribute:

```
USE WideWorldImporters;
SELECT StockItemID, StockItemName, Tags
FROM Warehouse.StockItems
WHERE '"Super Value"' IN (SELECT value FROM
STRING_SPLIT(REPLACE(REPLACE(Tags,'[',''), ']',''), ','));
```

This query produces the following result:

```
StockItemID  StockItemName                             Tags
-----------  ----------------------------------------  ----------------
150          Pack of 12 action figures (variety)       ["Super Value"]
151          Pack of 12 action figures (male)          ["Super Value"]
152          Pack of 12 action figures (female)        ["Super Value"]
```

The following code example demonstrates how this function can be used to return details about orders for IDs provided in a comma-separated list.

```
USE WideWorldImporters;
DECLARE @orderIds AS VARCHAR(100) = '1,3,7,8,9,11';
SELECT o.OrderID, o.CustomerID, o.OrderDate FROM Sales.Orders AS o
INNER JOIN STRING_SPLIT(@orderIds,',') AS x ON x.value= o.OrderID;
```

This produces the following output:

```
OrderID      CustomerID   OrderDate
-----------  -----------  ----------
1            832          2013-01-01
3            105          2013-01-01
7            575          2013-01-01
8            964          2013-01-01
9            77           2013-01-01
11           586          2013-01-01
```

Note that, since the function returns a column of string data type, there is an implicit conversion between the columns involved in the JOIN clause.

The function returns an empty table if the input string is not provided, as you can see in the next code example:

```
DECLARE @input AS NVARCHAR(20) = NULL;
SELECT * FROM STRING_SPLIT(@input,',');
```

This is the output produced by the preceding command:

```
value
--------
```

The STRING_SPLIT function requires that the database is in compatibility level 130. If this is not the case, you will get an error. The next code example demonstrates an attempt to use this function under compatibility level 120:

```
USE WideWorldImporters;
ALTER DATABASE WideWorldImporters SET COMPATIBILITY_LEVEL = 120;
GO
SELECT value FROM STRING_SPLIT('1,2,3',',');
/*Result:
Msg 208, Level 16, State 1, Line 65
Invalid object name 'STRING_SPLIT'.
*/
--back to the original compatibility level
ALTER DATABASE WideWorldImporters SET COMPATIBILITY_LEVEL = 130;
```

This is a handy function and will definitely have its use cases. However, as you will have already noticed, there are some limitations:

- **Single character separator**: The function accepts only a single character separator; if you had a separator with more characters, you would still need to write your own user-defined function.
- **Single output column**: The output is a single column table, without the position of the string element within the delimited string. Thus, you can only sort the output by the element name.
- **String data type**: When you use this function to delimit a string of numbers, although all the values in the output column are numbers, their data type is string and when you join them to numeric columns in other tables, data type conversion is required.

If these limitations are acceptable to you, you should use them in future developments. I would always suggest a built-in function rather than a user-defined one if they are similar from a performance point of view. It is always predeployed and available in all databases. Once again, take note that the database must be in the latest compatibility mode (130).

STRING_ESCAPE

The STRING_ESCAPE function is a scalar function and escapes special characters in input text according to the given formatting rules. It returns input text with escaped characters. The function accepts the following two input arguments:

- **Text**: This is an expression of any nondeprecated string data type

- **Type**: This must have the JSON value, since SQL Server 2016 currently supports only JSON as the formatting type

The return type of the function is nvarchar(max). The STRING_ESCAPE function is a deterministic function; it always returns the same result for the same input parameters.

 Data types text, ntext, and image are marked as deprecated features in SQL Server 2005. This means they can be removed in one of the next versions. The fact that they are still deprecated could mean that they will still be supported, because of legacy code. Microsoft does not want to take risks with actions that can cause damaging changes in customer applications. However, as you can see with these two functions, all new features, functions, and expressions that manipulate with strings don't accept these data types. This is an implicit way to force you to use the recommended data types varchar(max), nvarchar(max), and varbinary(max) instead of their deprecated counterparts.

JSON's escaping rules are defined in the ECMA 404 standard specification. *Table 4.1* provides the list of characters that must be escaped according to this specification and their JSON conform representation:

Special character	JSON conform character
Double quote	"
Backspace	\b
Solidus	\/
Reverse solidus	\\
Form feed	\f
Tabulation	\t
Carriage return	\r
New line	\n

Table 4.1: JSON escaping rules

In addition to this, all control characters with character codes in the range 0-31 need to be escaped, too. In JSON output, they are represented in the following format: \u<code>. Thus, the control character CHAR(0) is escaped as \u0000, while CHAR(31) is represented by \u001f.

The following several examples will be used to demonstrate how this function works. Suppose you need to escape the following string: a\bc/de"f. According to JSON's escaping rules, three characters should be escaped: back slash, solidus, and double quote. You can check it by calling the STRING_ESCAPE function for this string as the input argument:

```
SELECT STRING_ESCAPE('a\bc/de"f','JSON') AS escaped_input;
```

Here is the result returned by the function:

```
escaped_input
-------------
a\\bc\/de"f
```

The following example demonstrates the escape of the control characters with the code 0, 4, and 31:

```
SELECT
    STRING_ESCAPE(CHAR(0), 'JSON') AS escaped_char0,
    STRING_ESCAPE(CHAR(4), 'JSON') AS escaped_char4,
    STRING_ESCAPE(CHAR(31), 'JSON') AS escaped_char31;
```

This function call produces the following output:

```
escaped_char0      escaped_char4      escaped_char31
-------------      -------------      --------------
\u0000             \u0004             \u001f
```

The next example shows that the horizontal tab represented by the string and by the code is escaped with the same sequence:

```
SELECT
    STRING_ESCAPE(CHAR(9), 'JSON') AS escaped_tab1,
    STRING_ESCAPE('    ', 'JSON') AS escaped_tab2;
```

Both statements resulted in a \t sequence:

```
escaped_tab1      escaped_tab2
------------      --------------
\t                \t
```

The function returns a NULL value if the input string is not provided. To check this, run the following code:

```
DECLARE @input AS NVARCHAR(20) = NULL;
SELECT STRING_ESCAPE(@input, 'JSON') AS escaped_input;
```

You will get the expected result:

```
escaped_input
--------------
NULL
```

Escaping occurs both in the names of properties and in their values. Consider the following example, where one of the keys in the JSON input string contains a special character:

```
SELECT STRING_ESCAPE(N'key:1, i\d:4', 'JSON') AS escaped_input;
```

Here is the output:

```
escaped_input
---------------
key:1, i\\d:4
```

The STRING_ESCAPE function is internally used by the FOR JSON clause to automatically escape special characters and represents control characters in the JSON output. It can also be used for formatting paths, especially if you need to run it on UNIX systems (which is happening with R integration and SQL Server on Linux). Sometimes, a forward slash or backslash needs to be doubled, and this function is perfect when preparing code for Unix or CMD commands; a backslash needs to be doubled and converted to a forward slash. Unlike the STRING_SPLIT function, this function is available in a SQL Server 2016 database, even in old database compatibility levels.

COMPRESS

The COMPRESS function is a scalar function and compresses the input variable, column, or expression using the GZIP algorithm. The function accepts an expression, which can be either string or binary, but again, the deprecated data types text, ntext, and image are not supported.

The return type of the function is varbinary(max).

Use this function with wide text columns, especially when you do not plan to query them often. For large strings, the compression rate can be significant, particularly when the original string is an XML. Here is an example of significant compression. The example uses the output of the system Extended Event session system_health to check the compression rate when you use the COMPRESS function for the target_data column. Here is the code:

```
SELECT
  target_name,
  DATALENGTH(xet.target_data) AS original_size,
  DATALENGTH(COMPRESS(xet.target_data)) AS compressed_size,
  CAST((DATALENGTH(xet.target_data) -
DATALENGTH(COMPRESS(xet.target_data)))*100.0/DATALENGTH(xet.target_data) AS
DECIMAL(5,2)) AS compression_rate_in_percent
FROM sys.dm_xe_session_targets xet
INNER JOIN sys.dm_xe_sessions xe ON xe.address = xet.event_session_address
WHERE xe.name = 'system_health';
```

The following is the output generated by this query on my test server. You might get a different output, but similar results.

target_name	original_size	compressed_size	compression_rate_in_pct
ring_buffer	8386188	349846	95.83
event_file	410	235	42.68

You can see a quite impressive compression rate of 96%. On the other hand, the compressed representation of a short string can be even longer than the original. Consider the following example, where a short string with a size of 30 bytes is used as input:

```
DECLARE @input AS NVARCHAR(15) = N'SQL Server 2016';
SELECT @input AS input, DATALENGTH(@input) AS input_size, COMPRESS(@input)
AS compressed, DATALENGTH(COMPRESS(@input)) AS comp_size;
```

The result of this query (with abbreviated compressed value) is:

input	input_size	compressed	comp_size
SQL Server 2016	30	0x1F8B08000000000004000B660864F061	46

The COMPRESS function is not a replacement for row or page compression. It is invoked for a single expression and additional optimizations are not possible (exactly the same string tokens exist in some other row or column).

To compare compression rates for the Row and Page compression on one side and the compression by the COMPRESS function on the other side, I have created four clone tables of the system table sys.messages. I have left one uncompressed and have compressed the other three with ROW, PAGE, and COMPRESS functions respectively. The complete code for creating and populating tables, as well as for a comparison between compression methods, can be found in the code accompanying this book. *Figure 4.2* displays the result of this comparison:

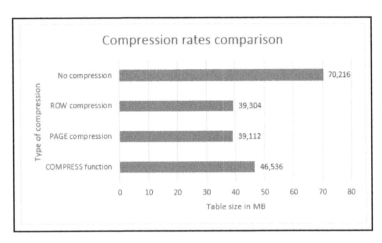

Figure 4.2: Compare compression rates between Row, Page, and Compress

You can see that (slightly) more compression can be achieved using Row and Page compression, but a notable compression is also obtained using the COMPRESS function.

Use this function when you want to save some storage space or to compress data that needs to be archived or logged and is thus rarely queried. Since it uses a common and well-known GZIP algorithm, you can compress/decompress data not only in SQL Server but also in client applications and tools communicating with SQL Server.

DECOMPRESS

The DECOMPRESS function decompresses the compressed input data in binary format (variable, column, or expression) using GZIP algorithm.

The return type of the function is varbinary(max). Yes, you read it right—the result of the decompression is still a varbinary data type and if you want to get the original data type, you need to cast the result explicitly.

Consider the following example, where the input string is first compressed and then decompressed with the same algorithm:

```
DECLARE @input AS NVARCHAR(100) = N'SQL Server 2016 Developer''s Guide';
SELECT DECOMPRESS(COMPRESS(@input));
```

Since the function DECOMPRESS is logically complementary to the COMPRESS function, you would expect to get the original input string as the result. The result is, however, in the binary format:

```
input
----------------------------------------------------------------------
0x530051004C0020005300650072007600650072002000320030003100360020004400650007
60065006C006F0070000650007200270073002000470075006900640006500
```

To get the input string back, you need to convert the result data type to the initial data type:

```
DECLARE @input AS NVARCHAR(100) = N'SQL Server 2016 Developer''s Guide';
SELECT CAST(DECOMPRESS(COMPRESS(@input)) AS NVARCHAR(100)) AS input;
```

Now, you will get the expected result:

```
input
----------------------------------
SQL Server 2016 Developer's Guide
```

 The input parameter for the DECOMPRESS function must have previously been with the GZIP algorithm compressed binary value. If you provide any other binary data, the function will return NULL.

Notice an interesting phenomenon if you miss the correct original type and cast to varchar instead of nvarchar:

```
DECLARE @input AS NVARCHAR(100) = N'SQL Server 2016 Developer''s Guide';
SELECT CAST(DECOMPRESS(COMPRESS(@input)) AS VARCHAR(100)) AS input;
```

When you use the **Results to Text** option to display query results, the following result is shown in SQL Server Management Studio:

```
input
--------------------------------------------------------------------
S Q L   S e r v e r   2 0 1 6   D e v e l o p e r ' s   G u i d e
```

However, when the **Results to Grid** option is your choice, the output looks different, as shown in *Figure 4.3*:

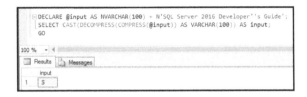

Figure 4.3: Side effect of an incorrect data type casting

Moreover, if you change the original type and cast to the Unicode data type, the result is very strange. When you swap the data types in the input string and the casted result, as shown here:

```
DECLARE @input AS VARCHAR(100) = N'SQL Server 2016 Developer''s Guide';
SELECT CAST(DECOMPRESS(COMPRESS(@input)) AS NVARCHAR(100)) AS input;
```

The output looks the same in all display modes, as shown here:

```
input
------------------------------
```

炃□敛癲牜(一)□″孜陬潭数(□昀摩e

As a comment on this bizarre behavior, keep in mind that it is always good to cast to the original data type and not to rely on the conversion internals.

CURRENT_TRANSACTION_ID

The CURRENT_TRANSACTION_ID function, as its name suggests, returns the transaction ID of the current transaction. The scope of the transaction is the current session. It has the same value as the transaction_id column in the dynamic management view sys.dm_tran_current_transaction. The function has no input arguments and the returned value is of type bigint.

Multiple calls of this function will result in different transaction numbers, since every single call is interpreted as an implicit transaction.

```
SELECT CURRENT_TRANSACTION_ID();
SELECT CURRENT_TRANSACTION_ID();
BEGIN TRAN
SELECT CURRENT_TRANSACTION_ID();
SELECT CURRENT_TRANSACTION_ID();
COMMIT
```

The result on my machine is (you will definitely get different numbers, but with the same pattern):

```
------------
921170382
921170383
921170384
921170384
```

There is also the SESSION_ID function, which returns the current session ID, but it works only in Azure SQL Data Warehouse and in Parallel Data Warehouse. When you call it in an on-premises instance of SQL Server 2016, instead of the current session ID, you will see the following error message:

```
Msg 195, Level 15, State 10, Line 1
'SESSION_ID' is not a recognized built-in function name.
```

You can use the CURRENT_TRANSACTION_ID function to check your transaction in active transactions as follows:

```
SELECT * FROM sys.dm_tran_active_transactions WHERE transaction_id =
CURRENT_TRANSACTION_ID();
```

SESSION_CONTEXT

Using and maintaining session variables or data within a user session in SQL Server is not so straightforward. With the SET CONTEXT_INFO statement, you can set a 128-bytes long binary value and you can read it with the CONTEXT_INFO function. However, having one single value within a scope of the session is a huge limitation. SQL Server 2016 brings more functionality for playing with session-scope-related data.

The SESSION_CONTEXT function returns the value of the specified key in the current session context. This value is previously set using the sys.sp_set_session_context procedure. It accepts the nvarchar data type as an input parameter. Interestingly, the function returns a value with the sql_variant data type.

Use the following code to set the value for the language key and then call the SESSION_CONTEXT function to read the value of the session key:

```
EXEC sys.sp_set_session_context @key = N'language', @value = N'German';
SELECT SESSION_CONTEXT(N'language');
```

The result of this action is shown as follows:

```
-------------
German
```

As mentioned earlier, the input data type must be `nvarchar`. An attempt to call the function with a different data type (including `varchar` and `nchar`!) ends up with an exception.

```
SELECT SESSION_CONTEXT('language');
```

You get the following message:

```
Msg 8116, Level 16, State 1, Line 51
Argument data type varchar is invalid for argument 1 of session_context
function.
```

The function argument does not need to be a literal; you can put it in a variable, as shown in the following code example:

```
DECLARE @lng AS NVARCHAR(50) = N'language';
SELECT SESSION_CONTEXT(@lng);
```

The size of the key cannot exceed 256 bytes and the limit for the total size of keys and values in the session context is 256 KB.

The system stored procedure `sys.sp_set_session_context` and the function `SESSION_CONTEXT` allow you to create and maintain session variables within SQL Server and overcome limitations from previous SQL Server versions. The `SESSION_CONTEXT` function is used as a part of the Row-Level Security feature, and it will be explored in more detail in `Chapter 8`, *Tightening the Security*.

DATEDIFF_BIG

The `DATEDIFF` function returns a number of time units crossed between two specified dates. The function accepts the following three input arguments:

- `datepart`: This is the time unit (`year`, `quarter`, `month`... `second`, `millisecond`, `microsecond`, and `nanosecond`)
- `startdate`: This is an expression of any date data type (`date`, `time`, `smalldatetime`, `datetime`, `datetime2`, and `datetimeoffset`)
- `enddate`: This is also an expression of any date data type (`date`, `time`, `smalldatetime`, `datetime`, `datetime2`, and `datetimeoffset`)

The return type of the function is `int`. This means that the maximum returned value is 2,147,483,647. Therefore, if you specify minor units (milliseconds, microseconds, or nanoseconds) as the first parameter of the function, you can get an overflow exception for huge date ranges. For instance, this function call will still work, as follows:

```
SELECT DATEDIFF(SECOND,'19480101','20160101') AS diff;
```

And it returns this result:

```
diff
-----------
2145916800
```

However, the following example will not work:

```
SELECT DATEDIFF(SECOND,'19470101','20160101') AS diff;
```

The result of this call is the following error message:

```
Msg 535, Level 16, State 0, Line 392
The datediff function resulted in an overflow. The number of dateparts
separating two date/time instances is too large. Try to use datediff with a
less precise datepart.
```

Due to the aforementioned data type limit, the maximal date difference that `DATEDIFF` can calculate for the `second` as date part is about 68 years. In *Table 4.2*, you can find the list of date part units and the maximum supported date difference for them.

Date part	Maximal supported date difference
Hour	250,000 years
Minute	4,086 years
Second	68 years
Millisecond	25 days
Microsecond	36 minutes
Nanosecond	2,14 seconds

Table 4.2: Maximal supported date difference per date part for the function DATEDIFF

In order to cover a greater date range for short date parts, the SQL Server development team has added a new function in SQL Server 2016 `DATEDIFF_BIG`.

It has exactly the same interface as DATEDIFF, the only difference is its return type—bigint. This means that the maximal returned value is 9,223,372,036,854,775,807. With this function, you will not get an overflow even when you specify a huge date range and choose a minor date part. The following code calculates the difference between the minimal and maximal value supported by the datetime2 data type in microseconds:

```
SELECT DATEDIFF_BIG(MICROSECOND,'010101','99991231 23:59:59.999999999') AS
diff;
```

The following is the very large number representing this difference:

```
diff
--------------------
252423993599999999
```

However, even with the DATEDIFF_BIG function, you can get an exception if you call it for the same dates and choose the date part nanosecond.

```
SELECT DATEDIFF_BIG(NANOSECOND,'010101','99991231 23:59:59.999999999') AS
diff;
```

The maximal value of the bigint data type is not enough to host this difference and to avoid an overflow:

```
Msg 535, Level 16, State 0, Line 419
The datediff_big function resulted in an overflow. The number of dateparts
separating two date/time instances is too large. Try to use datediff_big
with a less precise datepart.
```

Of course, the last two statements are listed just for demonstration purposes; I cannot imagine a reasonable use case where you will need to represent 10,000 years in microseconds or nanoseconds. Therefore, you can say that DATEDIFF_BIG meets all the reasonable requirements related to date difference calculations.

AT TIME ZONE

The AT TIME ZONE expression can be used to represent time in a given time zone. It converts an input date to the corresponding datetimeoffset value in the target time zone. It has the following two arguments:

- inputdate: This is an expression of the following date data types: smalldatetime, datetime, datetime2, and datetimeoffset.
- timezone: This is the name of the target time zone. The allowed zone names are listed in the sys.time_zone_info catalog view.

The return type of the expression is `datetimeoffset` in the target time zone.

Use the following code to display local UTC time, and the local time in New York and Vienna.

```
SELECT
  CONVERT(DATETIME, SYSDATETIMEOFFSET()) AS UTCTime,
  CONVERT(DATETIME, SYSDATETIMEOFFSET() AT TIME ZONE 'Eastern Standard
Time') AS NewYork_Local,
  CONVERT(DATETIME, SYSDATETIMEOFFSET() AT TIME ZONE 'Central European
Standard Time') AS Vienna_Local;
```

This query generates the following result:

```
UTCTime                 NewYork_Local           Vienna_Local
-------------------     -------------------     -------------------
2016-06-18 15:09:09.410 2016-06-18 10:09:09.410 2016-06-18 16:09:09.410
```

As mentioned earlier, the values supported for time zone can be found in a new system catalog `sys.time_zone_info`. This is exactly the same list as in the registry: `KEY_LOCAL_MACHINE\SOFTWARE\Microsoft\Windows NT\CurrentVersion\Time Zones`.

The target time zone does not need to be a literal; it can be wrapped in a variable and parameterized. The following code displays the time in four different time zones:

```
SELECT name, CONVERT(DATETIME, SYSDATETIMEOFFSET() AT TIME ZONE name) AS
local_time
FROM sys.time_zone_info
WHERE name IN (SELECT value FROM STRING_SPLIT('UTC,Eastern Standard
Time,Central European Standard Time,Russian Standard Time',','));
```

Note that another new function, `STRING_SPLIT`, is used in this query. The result of the previous query is as follows:

```
name                              local_time
--------------------------------  -----------------------
Eastern Standard Time             2016-06-18 11:10:46.257
UTC                               2016-06-18 15:10:46.257
Central European Standard Time    2016-06-18 17:10:46.257
Russian Standard Time             2016-06-18 18:10:46.257
```

By using AT TIME ZONE, you can convert a simple datetime value without a time zone offset to any time zone by using its name. What time is it in Seattle when a clock in Vienna shows 22:33 today (15th August 2016)? Here is the answer:

```
SELECT CAST('20160815 22:33' AS DATETIME)
AT TIME ZONE 'Central European Standard Time'
AT TIME ZONE 'Pacific Standard Time' AS seattle_time;
```

Note that you must convert the string value to datetime. Usually, a string literal formatted as YYYMMDD HH:ss is interpreted as a valid datetime value, but, in this case, you need to cast it explicitly to datetime data type.

HASHBYTES

The HASHBYTES built-in function is used to hash the string of characters using one of the seven supported hashing algorithms. The function accepts the following two input arguments:

- algorithm: This is a hashing algorithm for hashing the input. The possible values are: MD2, MD4, MD5, SHA, SHA1, SHA2_256, and SHA2_512, but only the last two are recommended in SQL Server 2016.
- input: This is an input variable, column, or expression that needs to be hashed. The data types that are allowed are varchar, nvarchar, and varbinary.

The return type of the function is varbinary (8000).

This function has been available in SQL Server since 2005, but it is enhanced in SQL Server 2016. The most important enhancement is removing the limit for the input size. Prior to SQL Server 2016, the allowed input values were limited to 8.000 bytes; now, no limit is defined. In addition to this significant enhancement, five old algorithms MD2, MD4, MD5, SHA, and SHA1 are marked for deprecation. The SHA2_256 and SHA2_512 algorithms are stronger, require more storage space, and hash calculation is slower, but the collision probability is very low.

To demonstrate the importance of the removed input limit, the former standard sample Adventure Works database will be used. Execute the following code in a SQL Server 2014 instance with this sample database installed to calculate a hash value for the XML representation of the first six orders in the `SalesOrderHeader` table:

```
USE AdventureWorks2014;
SELECT HASHBYTES('SHA2_256',(SELECT TOP (6) * FROM Sales.SalesOrderHeader
FOR XML AUTO)) AS hashed_value;
```

The following hashed value is produced by the previous command:

```
hashed_value
-----------------------------------------------------------------
0x26C8A739DB7BE2B27BCE757105E159647F70E02F45E56C563BBC3669BEF49AAF
```

However, when you want to include the seventh row in the hash calculation, use the following code:

```
USE AdventureWorks2014;
SELECT HASHBYTES('SHA2_256',(SELECT TOP (7) * FROM Sales.SalesOrderHeader
FOR XML AUTO)) AS hashed_value;
```

Instead of the hashed value, this query executed in a SQL Server 2014 instance generates a very well known and very user-unfriendly error message:

```
Msg 8152, Level 16, State 10, Line 2
String or binary data would be truncated.
```

Clearly, the reason for this error is the size of the input string that exceeds the limit of 8,000 bytes. You can confirm this by executing the following query:

```
SELECT DATALENGTH(CAST((SELECT TOP (7) * FROM Sales.SalesOrderHeader FOR
XML AUTO) AS NVARCHAR(MAX))) AS input_length;
```

Indeed, the size of the input argument for the `HASHBYTES` function exceeds 8,000 bytes:

```
input_length
--------------------
8754
```

In SQL Server 2016, this limitation has been removed:

```
USE AdventureWorks2016CTP3;
SELECT HASHBYTES('SHA2_256',(SELECT TOP (7) * FROM Sales.SalesOrderHeader
FOR XML AUTO)) AS hashed_value;
```

The preceding hash query returns the following result:

```
hashed_value
------------------------------------------------------------------
0x864E9FE792E0E99165B46F43DB43E659CDAD56F80369FD6D2C58AD2E8386CBF3
```

Prior to SQL Server 2016, if you wanted to hash more than 8 KB of data, you had to split input data to 8 KB chunks and then combine them to get a final hash for the input entry. Since the limit does not exist anymore, you can use the entire table as an input parameter now. You can slightly modify the initial query to calculate the hash value for the entire order table:

```
USE AdventureWorks2016CTP3;
SELECT HASHBYTES('SHA2_256',(SELECT * FROM Sales.SalesOrderHeader FOR XML
AUTO)) AS hashed_value;
```

This generates the following output:

```
hashed_value
------------------------------------------------------------------
0x2930C226E613EC838F88D821203221344BA93701D39A72813ABC7C936A8BEACA
```

I played around with it and could successfully generate a hash value, even for an expression with a size of 2 GB. It was slow, of course, but it did not break. I just want to check the limit; it does not make much sense to use HASHBYTES to detect changes in a large table.

Note that I have used the old standard SQL Server sample database Adventure Works. The version for SQL Server 2016 is available under the name AdventureWorks2016CTP3 at
https://www.microsoft.com/en-us/download/details.aspx?id=49502. Yes, it contains CTP3 in the name and it seems that it will not be officially presented as a sample database in SQL Server 2016, but in this example, we had to use it to compare two identical queries with different behaviors in the previous and current SQL Server version.

This function can be very useful to check whether relative static tables are changed or to compare them between two instances. With the following query, you can check the status of products in the AdventureWorks database:

```
USE AdventureWorks2016CTP3;
SELECT HASHBYTES('SHA2_256',(SELECT *
 FROM
  Production.Product p
  INNER JOIN Production.ProductSubcategory sc ON p.ProductSubcategoryID =
sc.ProductSubcategoryID
```

```
   INNER JOIN Production.ProductCategory c ON sc.ProductCategoryID =
c.ProductCategoryID
   INNER JOIN Production.ProductListPriceHistory ph ON ph.ProductID =
p.ProductID
   FOR XML AUTO)) AS hashed_value;
```

The following is the output generated by this query:

```
hashed_value
----------------------------------------------------------------
0xAFC05E912DC6742B085AFCC2619F158B823B4FE53ED1ABD500B017D7A899D99D
```

If you want to check whether any of the product attributes defined by the previous statement are different for two or more instances, you can execute the same query against the other instances and compare the values only, without loading and comparing the entire datasets.

With no limit for the input string, you do not need to implement workarounds for large inputs anymore and the fact that you can easily generate a hash value for multiple joined tables can increase the number of use cases for the HASHBYTES function.

JSON functions

SQL Server 2016 introduces JSON data support, and in order to implement this support, four JSON functions have been added to allow manipulation with JSON data:

- ISJSON: This checks whether an input string represents valid JSON data.
- JSON_VALUE: This extracts a scalar value from a JSON string.
- JSON_QUERY: This extracts a JSON fragment from the input JSON string for the specified JSON path.
- JSON_MODIFY: This modifies JSON data: updates the value of an existing property, adds a new element to an existing array, inserts a new property and its value, and deletes a property.
- OPENJSON: This provides a row set view over a JSON document. This table-value function converts JSON text in tabular data.

These functions will be explored in more detail in Chapter 5, *JSON Support in SQL Server*.

Enhanced DML and DDL statements

In this section, you will explore enhancements in **Data Manipulation Language** (**DML**) and **Data Definition Language** (**DDL**) that are not part of new features or improved features from previous SQL Server versions.

The section starts with a small syntax extension that you will use often in the code examples in this book.

The conditional DROP statement (DROP IF EXISTS)

With a conditional DROP statement, you can avoid getting an exception if the object you want to drop does not exist. If, for instance, the T1 table has already been removed or it was not created at all, the following statement will fail:

```
DROP TABLE dbo.T1;
```

Here is the error message:

```
Msg 3701, Level 11, State 5, Line 5
Cannot drop the table 'dbo.T1', because it does not exist or you do not
have permission.
```

SQL Server 2016 introduces the conditional DROP statement for most of the database objects. The conditional DROP statement is a DROP statement extended with the IF EXISTS part. Repeat the preceding command with this extended syntax:

```
DROP TABLE IF EXISTS dbo.T1;
```

You can execute this statement any number of times and you will not get an error. To achieve this prior to SQL Server 2016, you had to check the existence of the object before you removed it, as shown in this code example:

```
IF OBJECT_ID('dbo.T1','U') IS NOT NULL
  DROP TABLE dbo.T1;
```

You had to write one code line more and in addition, it is also error prone—you have to write the name of the object twice. It's not a big deal, but this new form is shorter and is not error prone.

You can use the following code to remove the stored procedure `dbo.P1` from the system:

```
DROP PROCEDURE IF EXISTS dbo.P1;
```

As mentioned earlier, you could use the conditional DROP statement in SQL Server 2016 to remove most of the database objects. The following objects are supported: AGGREGATE, ASSEMBLY, COLUMN, CONSTRAINT, DATABASE, DEFAULT, FUNCTION, INDEX, PROCEDURE, ROLE, RULE, SCHEMA, SECURITY POLICY, SEQUENCE, SYNONYM, TABLE, TRIGGER, TYPE, USER, and VIEW.

If you want, for instance, to remove a partitioned function or schema, DROP IF EXISTS won't work. The following command will fail:

```
DROP PARTITION FUNCTION IF EXISTS PartFunc1;
```

And here is the error message:

```
Msg 156, Level 15, State 1, Line 1
Incorrect syntax near the keyword 'IF'
```

To (conditionally) remove a partitioned function, you still need to write your own code to check the existence of the object.

How does IF EXISTS work? It simply suppresses the error message. This is exactly what you need if the reason for the error is the nonexistence of the object. However, if the user who wants to drop the object does not have appropriate permission, you would expect an error message. The command is executed successfully and the caller does not get an error regardless of the object's existence and user permissions! Here are the results when a user wants to drop an object using the conditional DROP statement:

- **The object exists; user has permissions**: When the object is removed, everything is fine
- **The object does not exist; user has permissions**: There are no error messages displayed
- **The object exists; user does not have permissions**: When the object is not removed, no error messages are displayed. The caller does not get that the object still exists; its DROP command has been executed successfully!
- **The object does not exist; user does not have permissions**: There are no error messages displayed.

You can read more about this inconsistency in the blog post *DROP IF EXISTS aka D.I.E.* at https://milossql.wordpress.com/2016/07/04/drop-if-exists-aka-d-i-e/.

This enhancement is handy; it helps you to abbreviate your code and it is intensively used by consultants, trainers, and conference speakers. They usually create database objects to demonstrate a feature, code technique, or behavior and then drop them from the system. And they do this again and again. However, conditional DROP statements will not be used so often in production systems. How often do you remove database objects from SQL Server? Very rarely, right? When you perform a cleanup or remove some intermediate database objects. In most cases, you add new objects or change the existing ones.

Therefore, I would like to see similar a implementation for the object's creation or updating. To extend Transact-SQL syntax with, for instance, the CREATE OR ALTER or CREATE OR REPLACE command. This would be more important for script deployment than DROP statement extensions. If you want to update a stored procedure with the latest version and you don't know whether the previous version has been installed or not, or you simply execute the same script twice without errors, the following code must be used:

```
IF OBJECT_ID(N'dbo.uspMyStoredProc','P') IS NULL
  EXEC('CREATE PROCEDURE dbo.uspMyStoredProc AS SELECT NULL');
GO
ALTER PROCEDURE dbo.uspMyStoredProc
AS...
```

This piece of code is error prone, awkward and even uses dynamic SQL because CREATE PROC needs to be the first statement in a batch. CREATE or ALTER PROCEDURE would be handy. And some other vendors support it.

More often, you use it to create or alter objects than to remove them from a production system; therefore, it would be more useful to implement this extension. I hope we'll see it in the next SQL Server version.

CREATE OR ALTER

At the time of writing this chapter, SQL Server 2016 RTM has been released. In the meantime, Microsoft came with the SQL Server 2016 Service Pack 1. This package not only includes hotfixes from the RTM version, but also some new features. One of them is exactly described as the CREATE OR ALTER statement. It creates an object if it does not exist, or alters it if it is already there. You can use it with stored procedures, functions, view, and triggers. Here is an example of creating or altering a scalar user-defined function:

```
CREATE OR ALTER FUNCTION dbo.GetWorldsBestCityToLiveIn()
RETURNS NVARCHAR(10)
AS
BEGIN
    RETURN N'Vienna';
```

```
END
```

We were waiting for a long time for this feature and it is most probably the first feature you will adopt in SQL Server 2016.

Online Alter Column

Sometimes you might need to change the attributes of a table column, for instance, to increase the column capacity due to changed requirements, increased data amount, or lack of data capacity planning. Here are the typical actions for altering a column in a SQL Server table:

- **Change the data type**: This is usually when you come close to the maximum value supported by the actual data type (typically from `smallint` to `int`, or from `int` to `bigint`)
- **Change the size**: This is a common case for poorly planned string columns; the current column size cannot accept all the required data
- **Change the precision**: This is when you need to store more precise data; usually due to changed requirements
- **Change the collation**: This is when you have to use a different (usually case sensitive) collation for a column due to changed requirements
- **Change the null-ability**: This is when the requirements are changed

To demonstrate what happens when you perform an alter column action, you first need to create a sample table. Run the following code to accomplish this:

```
USE WideWorldImporters;
DROP TABLE IF EXISTS dbo.Orders;
CREATE TABLE dbo.Orders(
id INT IDENTITY(1,1) NOT NULL,
custid INT NOT NULL,
orderdate DATETIME NOT NULL,
amount MONEY NOT NULL,
rest CHAR(100) NOT NULL DEFAULT 'test',
CONSTRAINT PK_Orders PRIMARY KEY CLUSTERED (id ASC)
);
GO
```

To populate the table efficiently, you can use the `GetNums` function created by Itzik Ben-Gan. The function is available at `http://tsql.solidq.com/SourceCodes/GetNums.txt`. Here is the function definition:

```
------------------------------------------------------------
-- © Itzik Ben-Gan
------------------------------------------------------------
CREATE OR ALTER FUNCTION dbo.GetNums(@low AS BIGINT, @high AS BIGINT)
RETURNS TABLE
AS
RETURN
  WITH
    L0   AS (SELECT c FROM (SELECT 1 UNION ALL SELECT 1) AS D(c)),
    L1   AS (SELECT 1 AS c FROM L0 AS A CROSS JOIN L0 AS B),
    L2   AS (SELECT 1 AS c FROM L1 AS A CROSS JOIN L1 AS B),
    L3   AS (SELECT 1 AS c FROM L2 AS A CROSS JOIN L2 AS B),
    L4   AS (SELECT 1 AS c FROM L3 AS A CROSS JOIN L3 AS B),
    L5   AS (SELECT 1 AS c FROM L4 AS A CROSS JOIN L4 AS B),
    Nums AS (SELECT ROW_NUMBER() OVER(ORDER BY (SELECT NULL)) AS rownum
              FROM L5)
  SELECT TOP(@high - @low + 1) @low + rownum - 1 AS n
  FROM Nums
  ORDER BY rownum;
```

Now you can run the following code to populate the table with 10 million rows:

```
INSERT INTO dbo.Orders(custid,orderdate,amount)
SELECT
  1 + ABS(CHECKSUM(NEWID())) % 1000 AS custid,
  DATEADD(minute,    -ABS(CHECKSUM(NEWID())) % 5000000,  '20160630') AS
orderdate,
  50 + ABS(CHECKSUM(NEWID())) % 1000 AS amount
FROM dbo.GetNums(1,10000000);
```

Now, once you have created and populated the table, suppose you have a requirement to change the data type for the column `amount` to `decimal`. To see what happens during the alter column action, you need to open two connections. In the first connection, you will have the code to change the data type of the column:

```
ALTER TABLE dbo.Orders ALTER COLUMN amount DECIMAL(10,2) NOT NULL;
```

In the second one, you will simply try to return the last two rows from the table just to check whether the table is available for querying. Use the following code for the query in the second connection:

```
USE WideWorldImporters;
SELECT TOP (2) id, custid, orderdate, amount
FROM dbo.Orders ORDER BY id DESC;
```

Now, execute the code from the first connection and then from the second. You can see that both commands are running. Actually, the ALTER COLUMN command is running, while the second query is simply waiting—it is blocked by the ALTER command. During the change of the data type, the table is not available for querying. You can see additional details; you would need to establish a third connection and put the following code there (you need to replace 66 with the session ID from the second connection) and repeat the previous two steps by changing the data type of the column amount to money.

```
SELECT request_mode, request_type, request_status, request_owner_type
FROM sys.dm_tran_locks WHERE request_session_id = 66;
```

The following is the result of this command:

request_mode	request_type	request_status	request_owner_type
S	LOCK	GRANT	SHARED_TRANSACTION_WORKSPACE
IS	LOCK	WAIT	TRANSACTION

You can see that the query could not get IS lock because the ALTER column action is performed as a transaction. Therefore, the table is not available for querying and the query from the second connection has to wait until the ALTER command is done.

You might think that a query with the NOLOCK hint would return results even when an alter column action is performed, because NOLOCK obviously means there is no lock at the table. This is not completely true. It is true that shared lock or intentional shared lock are not acquired, but even with NOLOCK statements we need to acquire a stability schema lock. You can repeat all the three steps with a small modification in the second query to include the NOLOCK hint and the actions will end up with the same results and behavior. The only difference is that in the result set of the third connection, instead of IS the mentioned Sch-S appears.

This behavior is analog to creating nonclustered indexes offline. While creating an index online has been available since 2005, altering column was the only operation that was offline until SQL Server 2016.

When you specify the ONLINE = ON option, SQL Server 2016 creates a new shadow table with the requested change, and when it's finished, it swaps metadata with very short schema locks. This leaves the table available, even for changes, except those which could create a dependency for the altering column.

Now you will repeat the three steps from the preceding example (assuming the column amount has money data type), but this time with the ONLINE = ON option. You need to modify the command from the first connection to the following code:

```
USE WideWorldImporters;
ALTER TABLE dbo.Orders ALTER COLUMN amount DECIMAL(10,2) NOT NULL WITH
(ONLINE = ON);
```

The code in the second connection does not need to be changed:

```
SELECT TOP (2) id, custid, orderdate, amount
FROM dbo.Orders ORDER BY id DESC;
```

Now, execute the command all over again and then run the query from the second connection. You can see that the first command is running, and that the query from the second connection instantly returns results. The table is available for querying although the data type for one column is being changed. This is a very important feature for systems that need to be continually available.

Altering online capabilities does not remove the usual limitations for changing column attributes. If a column is used in an index or expression in a filtered index or filtered statistics, you still cannot change its data type.

However, with the ONLINE = ON option, you can alter a column even if user-created statistics on this column exist. This was not possible prior to SQL Server 2016 (and it is still not possible in the offline mode). To demonstrate this, you will create a user statistic object on the column amount:

```
USE WideWorldImporters;
CREATE STATISTICS MyStat ON dbo.Orders(amount);
```

An attempt to change the data type of the column amount should fail:

```
ALTER TABLE dbo.Orders ALTER COLUMN amount DECIMAL(10,3) NOT NULL;
```

This command immediately generates the following error message:

```
Msg 5074, Level 16, State 1, Line 76
The statistics 'MyStat' is dependent on column 'amount'.
Msg 4922, Level 16, State 9, Line 76
ALTER TABLE ALTER COLUMN amount failed because one or more objects access
this column.
```

However, when you specify the ONLINE = ON option, the same command will work:

```
ALTER TABLE dbo.Orders ALTER COLUMN amount DECIMAL(10,3) NOT NULL WITH
(ONLINE = ON);
```

The statistics are available to the query optimizer during the command execution; it is invalidated after the change is done and it must be updated manually.

Similar to the online index (re)build option, this excellent feature is available in the Enterprise Edition only.

TRUNCATE TABLE

The TRUNCATE TABLE statement is the most efficient way to remove all rows from a table. Logically, this statement is identical to the DELETE statement without the WHERE clause, but unlike the DELETE statement, when the TRUNCATE TABLE has been issued, SQL Server does not log individual row deletion in the transaction log. Therefore, the TRUNCATE TABLE statement is significantly faster. This performance difference can be very important with large tables. However, if you want to enjoy its efficiency, you have to remove all rows from a table. Even if the table is partitioned, you still need to remove all rows from all the partitions. Well, unless you have SQL Server 2016.

In SQL Server 2016, the TRUNCATE TABLE statement has been extended so that you can specify the partitions from which rows have to be removed. You can specify the comma-separated list or the range of partition numbers. Here is a code example showing how to remove all rows from the partitions 1, 2, and 4.

```
TRUNCATE TABLE dbo.T1 WITH (PARTITIONS (1, 2, 4));
```

In the next example, you will see how to specify the range of partition numbers. From a table with the maximum number of supported partitions, you want to remove a lot of data, but not all of it—you want to leave data in partitions 1 and 2. Here is the code that implements this request:

```
TRUNCATE TABLE dbo.T2 WITH (PARTITIONS (3 TO 15000));
```

You can also combine two input formats in one expression. The following code removes all rows from a table with eight partitions, except from the partitions 1 and 3:

```
TRUNCATE TABLE dbo.T1 WITH (PARTITIONS (2, 4 TO 8));
```

Specifying partitions in the TRUNCATE TABLE statement is possible even if the database is not in compatibility level 130.

To simulate truncate table for a specific partition in previous SQL Server versions, you need to perform the following steps:

1. Create a staging table with the same indexes as in a partitioned table.
2. Using the SWITCH PARTITION statement to move data from the partitioned to the staging table.
3. Removing the staging table from the system.

Now, you need a single and very efficient statement—a nice and handy feature.

Maximum key size for nonclustered indexes

In previous SQL Server versions, the total size of all index keys could not exceed the limit of 900 bytes. You were actually allowed to create a nonclustered index, even if the sum of the maximum length of all its key columns exceeded this limit. The limit affects only columns used as index keys; you can use very large columns in a nonclustered index as included columns.

To demonstrate this, we will create a sample table. Note that this code should be executed in a SQL Server 2014/2012/2008 instance:

```
USE tempdb;
CREATE TABLE dbo.T1(id INT NOT NULL PRIMARY KEY CLUSTERED, c1 NVARCHAR(500)
NULL, c2 NVARCHAR(851) NULL);
```

As you can see in the code, the maximal data length of the column c1 is 1000 bytes. Let's now try to create a nonclustered index on this column:

```
CREATE INDEX ix1 ON dbo.T1(c1);
```

Since the table is empty, the command has been executed successfully with no errors, but with the following warning message:

```
Warning! The maximum key length is 900 bytes. The index 'ix1' has maximum
length of 1000 bytes. For some combination of large values, the
insert/update operation will fail
```

As the message says, you can live with the index in harmony if the size of the actual data in the index columns does not exceed the limit of 900 bytes. The query optimizer will even use it in execution plans and it will behave as a *normal* index. Adding a row with data within the maximum key length will be successful, as shown in the following code:

```
INSERT INTO dbo.T1(id,c1, c2) VALUES(1, N'Mila', N'Vasilije');
```

However, when you try to insert or update a row with data longer than the key size limit, the statement will fail:

```
INSERT INTO dbo.T1(id,c1, c2) VALUES(2,REPLICATE('Mila',113), NULL);
```

This action in SQL Server 2014 ends up with an error message and the INSERT statement fails, as follows:

```
Msg 1946, Level 16, State 3, Line 7
Operation failed. The index entry of length 904 bytes for the index 'ix1'
exceeds the maximum length of 900 bytes.
```

In SQL Server 2016, the behavior remains the same with the difference that the maximum index key size for nonclustered indexes has been increased from 900 to 1,700 bytes. Let's repeat the previous steps, but this time in an instance running SQL Server 2016.

```
DROP TABLE IF EXISTS dbo.T1;
CREATE TABLE dbo.T1(id INT NOT NULL PRIMARY KEY CLUSTERED, c1 NVARCHAR(500)
NULL, c2 NVARCHAR(851) NULL);
GO
CREATE INDEX ix1 ON dbo.T1(c1);
```

There is no warning after this action, since the new limit is 1,700 bytes. However, when you add an index on the c2 column using this code:

```
CREATE INDEX ix2 ON dbo.T1(c2);
```

You get the well-known warning message, but with a different limit:

```
Warning! The maximum key length for a nonclustered index is 1700 bytes. The
index 'ix2' has maximum length of 1702 bytes. For some combination of large
values, the insert/update operation will fail.
```

As you can see, the only difference is the different maximum number of bytes.

The maximum key size for clustered indexes remains 900 bytes. For memory-optimized tables, the limit is 2,500 bytes.

Now, you can index wider columns than you could in previous versions. For instance, a text column with 500 Unicode characters can be used as a key in a nonclustered index in SQL Server 2016.

New query hints

The SQL Server Query Optimizer does an amazing job of execution plan generation. Most of the time, for most queries, it generates an optimal execution plan. And this is not easy at all. There is a lot of potential to get a suboptimal plan: wrong server configuration, poorly designed databases, missing and suboptimal indexes, suboptimal written queries, nonscalable solutions, and so on. And the query optimizer should work for all those workloads, all over the world, all the time.

Depending on data constellation, it generates suboptimal execution plans sometimes. If the execution of the queries is very important from a business point of view, you have to do something to try to achieve at least an acceptable execution plan. One of the weapons you have for this is hints to the query optimizer. With hints, which are actually instructions, you instruct the query optimizer how to generate the execution plan. You take responsibility or you take part of the responsibility for the execution plan generation.

There are three types of hints: table, join, and query hints. You use them if you cannot enforce the required execution plan with other actions. Hints should be considered as a last resort in query tuning. You should use them if you don't know another way to get a desired plan, when you have tried all that you know, or when you are under time pressure and have to fix a query as soon as possible. For instance, if you suddenly encounter a problem on the production system on the weekend or during the night, you can use the hint as a temporary solution or a workaround and then look for a definitive solution without time or operative pressures. Literally said, you can use query hints if you know what you are doing. However, you should not forget that the hint and the plan remain forever and you need to periodically evaluate whether the plan is still adequate. In most cases, developers forget about plans with hints as soon as the performance problem is gone.

SQL Server 2016 brings three new query hints to address problems related to memory grants and performance spools:

- `NO_PERFORMANCE_SPOOL`
- `MAX_GRANT_PERCENT`
- `MIN_GRANT_PERCENT`

NO_PERFORMANCE_SPOOL

The new query hint NO_PERFORMANCE_SPOOL has been added to SQL Server 2016 to allow users to enforce an execution plan, which does not contain a spool operator.

A spool operator in an execution plan does not mean that the plan is suboptimal; it is usually a good choice of query optimizer. However, in some cases, it can reduce the overall performance. This happens, for instance, when a query or a stored procedure whose execution plan contains a spool operator is executed by numerous parallel connections. Since the Spool operator uses tempdb, this can lead to tempdb contention when many queries are running at the same time. Using this hint, you can avoid this issue.

To demonstrate the use of this query hint, you will once again use the new WideWorldImporters sample database. Assume that you need to display order details for orders picked up by the sales persons provided in an input list. To ensure that the execution plan contains a spool operator, this example uses a user-defined function and not the new SQL Server 2016 function STRING_SPLIT. Use the following code to create the function and filter orders with the sales persons from the list.

```
USE WideWorldImporters;
GO
CREATE OR ALTER FUNCTION dbo.ParseInt
(
    @List        VARCHAR(MAX),
    @Delimiter  CHAR(1)
)
RETURNS @Items TABLE
(
    Item INT
)
AS
BEGIN
    DECLARE @Item VARCHAR(30), @Pos  INT;
    WHILE LEN(@List)>0
    BEGIN
        SET @Pos = CHARINDEX(@Delimiter, @List);
        IF @Pos = 0 SET @Pos = LEN(@List)+1;
        SET @Item = LEFT(@List, @Pos-1);
        INSERT @Items SELECT CONVERT(INT, LTRIM(RTRIM(@Item)));
        SET @List = SUBSTRING(@List, @Pos + LEN(@Delimiter), LEN(@List));
        IF LEN(@List) = 0 BREAK;
    END
    RETURN;
END
GO
DECLARE @SalesPersonList VARCHAR(MAX) = '3,6,8';
```

```
SELECT o.*
FROM Sales.Orders o
INNER JOIN dbo.ParseInt(@SalesPersonList,',') a ON a.Item =
o.SalespersonPersonID
ORDER BY o.OrderID;
```

When you observe the execution plan for this query, you can see the `Table Spool` operator in it, as *Figure 4.4* shows:

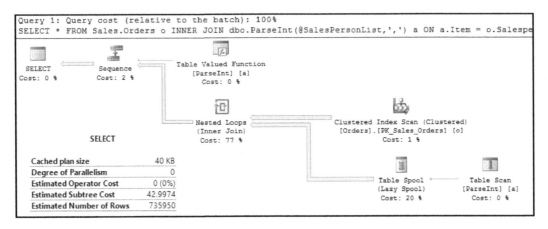

Figure 4.4: Execution plan with the Table Spool operator

When you execute exactly the same query, but with the query hint `OPTION` (`NO_PERFORMANCE_SPOOL`), you get a different execution plan, without the `Spool` operator, as shown in *Figure 4.5*:

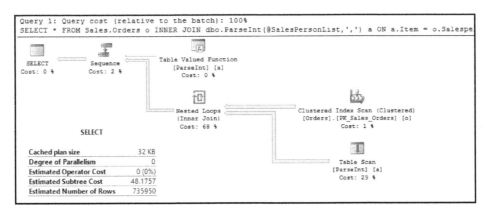

Figure 4.5: Execution plan without the Table Spool operator

By observing the execution plan, you can see that the spool operator has disappeared from it. You can also see that the Estimated Subtree Cost is about 10% higher for the plan without the hint (by comparing the yellow SELECT property boxes); therefore, the query optimizer has chosen the original plan with the Spool operator. Here, you used the hint just for demonstration purposes to show that you can enforce another plan, without the spool operator.

 You have to create a user-defined function in this example because this query with a new STRING_SPLIT function has an execution plan without the Spool operator.

However, if the Spool operator is required in an execution plan to enforce the validity and correctness, the hint will be ignored. To demonstrate this behavior, you will use the next example. First, you need to create a sample table and insert two rows into it:

```
USE WideWorldImporters;
DROP TABLE IF EXISTS dbo.T1
CREATE TABLE dbo.T1(
id INT NOT NULL,
c1 INT NOT NULL,
);
GO
INSERT INTO dbo.T1(id, c1) VALUES(1, 5),(1, 10);
```

Now, assume that you want to add some of the existing rows into the table, say the rows where ID has value less than 10. At this point, only one row qualifies for this insert. The following query implements this requirement:

```
INSERT INTO dbo.T1(id, c1)
SELECT id, c1 FROM dbo.T1
WHERE id < 10;
```

The execution plan for this query is shown in *Figure 4.6*:

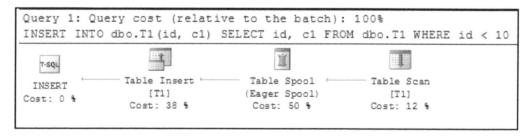

Figure 4.6: Execution plan for INSERT statement with the Table Spool operator

When you observe it, you can see the `Table Spool` operator proudly staying in the middle of the execution plan. However, when you execute the same statement with the `NO_PERFORMANCE_SPOOL` hint, you get an identical execution plan; the query hint is simply ignored. The reason for this decision by the query optimizer is that the spool operator in this plan is used not for optimization, but to guarantee the correctness of the result. To demonstrate this, execute these two statements:

```
INSERT INTO dbo.T1(id, c1)
SELECT id, c1 FROM dbo.T1
WHERE id < 10;

INSERT INTO dbo.T1(id, c1)
SELECT id, c1 FROM dbo.T1
WHERE id < 10
OPTION (NO_PERFORMANCE_SPOOL);
```

Figure 4.7 shows both plans and it is obvious that this is the same execution plan:

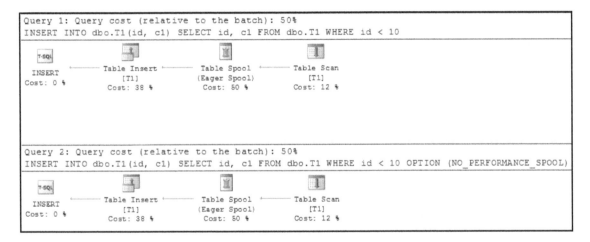

Figure 4.7: Execution plans showing that the hint NO_PERFORMANCE_SPOOL is ignored

Use the query hint `NO_SPOOL_OPERATOR` when:

- You want to avoid the spool operator in the execution object
- You know that this is a good idea (performance issue is caused by the Spool operator)
- You cannot achieve this, with a reasonable effort otherwise

MAX_GRANT_PERCENT

The MIN_GRANT_PERCENT and MAX_GRANT_PERCENT hints were first introduced in the SQL Server 2012 SP3 and now in SQL Server 2016 RTM (they are still not available in SQL Server 2014). They address the problem of inappropriate memory grant for query execution.

Memory grant is a memory associated for the execution of queries whose execution plan contains operators that need to store temporary row data while sorting and joining rows (Sort, Hash Join, and so on). The value for memory grant depends on SQL Server's Estimated Number of Rows that should be processed by memory operators. If the estimated number of rows significantly differs from the actual, the memory grant is overestimated or underestimated.

To demonstrate an overestimated memory grant, use the following code that generates a 10M row large table:

```
USE WideWorldImporters;
DROP TABLE IF EXISTS dbo.T1;
CREATE TABLE dbo.T1(
id INT NOT NULL,
c1 INT NOT NULL,
c2 TINYINT NOT NULL DEFAULT 1,
c3 CHAR(100) NOT NULL DEFAULT 'test',
CONSTRAINT PK_T1 PRIMARY KEY CLUSTERED (id ASC)
);
GO
INSERT INTO dbo.T1(id, c1)
SELECT
  n AS id,
  1 + ABS(CHECKSUM(NEWID())) % 10000 AS c1
FROM dbo.GetNums(10000000);
GO
CREATE INDEX ix1 ON dbo.T1(c2);
GO
```

Note that the c2 column has a value 1 for all the rows in the table. Also, note that the code sample uses the GetNums function introduced at the beginning of this chapter. Assume that your task is to return rows from the T1 table, where the c2 column has value the 0 or 2. The query is very simple:

```
SELECT * FROM dbo.T1 WHERE c2 IN (0, 2) ORDER BY c1;
```

The query returns no rows (as mentioned, c2 = 1 for all rows in the table). The execution plan is simple too: Clustered Index Scan followed by the Sort operator. The plan is shown in *Figure 4.8*:

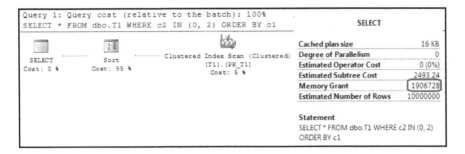

Figure 4.8: Execution plan with an overestimated memory grant

You can see that the query optimizer has significantly overestimated the number of rows for the Sort operator. Therefore, it is the most expensive part of the execution plan, even in concurrency with the Clustered Index Scan of a 10M row table. Actually, the result of the query is an empty set, but SQL Server *thinks* that all rows from the table will be returned. This is a bug with new cardinality in SQL Server 2014 and it is not fixed in SQL Server 2016. Since the Sort operator requires memory, this query needs a memory grant. With the mouse over the Select operator, you can see that the memory granted for this query is 1.9 GB. More details about memory grant are available in the XML representation of the execution plan, as shown in *Figure 4.9*:

```xml
<?xml version="1.0" encoding="utf-16"?>
<ShowPlanXML xmlns:xsi="http://www.w3.org/2001/XMLSchema-instance"
  <BatchSequence>
    <Batch>
      <Statements>
        <StmtSimple StatementCompId="1" StatementEstRows="10000000"
          <StatementSetOptions ANSI_NULLS="true" ANSI_PADDING="true
          <QueryPlan DegreeOfParallelism="0" NonParallelPlanReason=
          <MemoryGrantInfo
                SerialRequiredMemory="512"
                SerialDesiredMemory="1906728"
                RequiredMemory="512"
                DesiredMemory="1906728"
                RequestedMemory="1906728"
                GrantWaitTime="0"
                GrantedMemory="1906728"
                MaxUsedMemory="0" />
```

Figure 4.9: Memory Grant information in the XML representation of the execution plan

For the execution of a single query that returns no rows, about 2 GB memory is granted! If this query was executed by 100 concurrent sessions, almost 200 GB of memory would be granted for its execution.

As mentioned earlier, query hints should be used as a last resort for performance tuning. For demonstration purposes, you will use the MAX_ GRANT_PERCENT query hint to limit the amount of memory granted.

The MAX_GRANT_PERCENT query hint defines the maximum memory grant size as a percentage of available memory. It accepts float values between 0.0 and 100.0. Granted memory cannot exceed this limit, but can be lower if the resource governor setting is lower than this. Since you know that you have no rows in the output, you can use a very low value in the query hint:

```
SELECT * FROM dbo.T1 WHERE c2 IN (0, 2) ORDER BY c1 OPTION
(MAX_GRANT_PERCENT=0.001);
```

When you observe the execution plan shown in *Figure 4.10*, you can see that the plan remains the same, only the memory grant value has dropped to 512 KB!

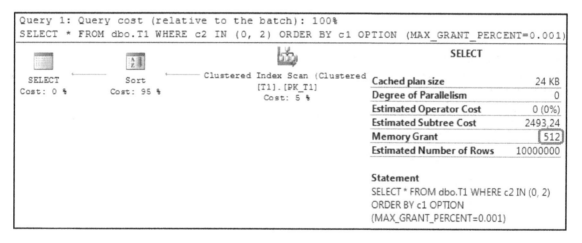

Figure 4.10: Execution plan with the query hint MAX_GRANT_PERCENT

With the memory grant hint, you cannot change the execution plan, but you can significantly reduce the amount of memory granted.

All execution plans shown in this section were generated by a database engine with the SQL Server 2016 RTM installed on it. If you have installed SQL Server 2016 Service Pack 1, you will see a new "Excessive Grant" warning in the `SELECT` property box, indicating a discrepancy between granted and used memory for the query execution. You can find more details about this warning at

`https://support.microsoft.com/en-us/help/3172997`.

You can see that the applied query hint saved 2 GB of memory. The query hint `MAX_GRANT_PERCENT` should be used when:

- You don't know how to trick the optimizer into coming up with the appropriate memory grant
- You want to fix the problem immediately and to buy time to search for a final solution

Here, you have used the query hint just for demonstration purposes, the correct way to fix a query is to understand why the estimated and actual number of rows are so discrepant and to then try to rewrite the query. As mentioned earlier, in this case, the problem is caused by the change in the **Cardinality Estimator (CE)** in the SQL Server 2014 and the query works well under the old CE. Use the following query to force SQL Server to use the old CE using the trace flag `9481`, as shown in the following query:

```
SELECT * FROM dbo.T1 WHERE c2 IN (0, 2) ORDER BY c1 OPTION (QUERYTRACEON
9481);
```

This generates the execution plan displayed in *Figure 4.11*:

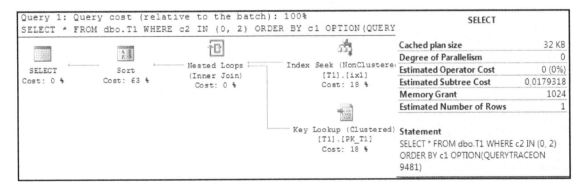

Figure 4.11: Execution plan where the old cardinality estimator is enforced

You can see the expected `Nested Loop Join` operator and a symbolic memory grant of 1 MB. The old CE estimates one row to be returned, while the new CE estimates the whole table. These very different assumptions lead to completely different execution plans and memory grants.

Another option to fix this problem is to rewrite the query to use `UNION ALL` instead of the `IN` operator. Let's rewrite our original query:

```
SELECT * FROM dbo.T1 WHERE c2 = 0
UNION ALL
SELECT * FROM dbo.T1 WHERE c2 = 2
ORDER BY c1;
```

Figure 4.12 shows the execution plan for the preceding query:

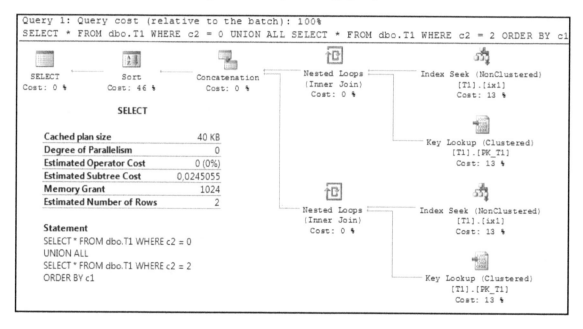

Figure 4.12: Execution plan for the rewritten query

You can see that the plan is a double of the old CE but significantly better than the initial one. With the `MAX_GRANT_PERCENT` query hint, you have successfully reduced the amount of granted memory. However, as demonstrated, you could even improve the initial execution plan by using other techniques. Therefore, use the query hint only when you don't know how to instruct the query optimizer to generate a better estimation.

MIN_GRANT_PERCENT

Similar to the previous example, in the event of a memory underestimation, you can force the optimizer to guarantee a minimum memory grant for a query execution using the MIN_GRANT_PERCENT query hint. It also accepts float values between 0.0 and 100.0. Be very careful with this hint, since if you specify 100 percent as the minimum grant, the whole resource governor memory will be granted to a single query execution. If you specify more memory than is available, the query will simply wait for memory grant.

Summary

This chapter explored new Transact-SQL elements, extensions, and hints. Some of them are small enhancements that make a developer's life easier and increase her/his productivity. There are also significant operational extensions that increase the availability and deployment of solutions. Finally, two newly added query hints address some rare but serious performance problems caused by incorrect query optimizer estimations and assumptions, where it is hard to find a workaround in previous SQL Server versions.

5

JSON Support in SQL Server

In the last few years, JSON has been established as a standard format for data exchange among applications and services. XML is still the exchange standard (and will be), but many applications communicate by exchanging JSON data instead of XML documents. Therefore, the most important relational database management system products need to support JSON.

Two release cycles after the feature was requested by the community, Microsoft has implemented built-in JSON support in SQL Server 2016. The support is not as comprehensive as for XML, but for most databases and workloads, it will be quite fine.

This chapter explores how SQL Server stores and processes JSON data with a comprehensive comparison between JSON and XML support in SQL Server.

The most important actions related to JSON data in SQL Server are demonstrated in detail:

- Formatting and exporting JSON data from SQL Server
- Converting JSON data to a tabular format
- Importing JSON data to SQL Server
- Validating, querying, and modifying JSON data

Finally, you will be made aware of limitations caused by missing JSON data types and indexes, and given advice on how you can improve the performance of JSON queries despite these limitations.

Why JSON?

Microsoft Connect site is the place where you can leave your feedback, suggestions, and wishes for Microsoft products. The most popular feature request for SQL Server is one for JSON support. It was created in June 2011 and got more than 1,100 votes. The request is still open (July 2016) and interestingly it is shown at the very top of the most voted items list, even though the second item in the list has more votes, as you can see in *Figure 5.1*:

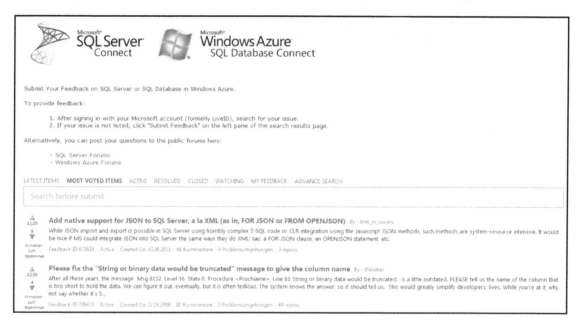

Figure 5.1: Highly ranked requests for SQL Server on the Microsoft Connect site (July 2016)

What arguments are used by community members to justify the request?

- JSON is already standard, and it should be supported, similar to XML
- Other vendors support it (Oracle, PostgreSQL, and so on)
- Due to the lack of JSON support, my customers want to move from SQL Server to other database systems supporting JSON

As always with vox populi, some of the arguments and given examples represent development and business needs. Some of them, however, are very personal, sometimes guided by passion. But there is one thing upon which they agree and which is common in almost all comments: *a serious relational database management system should have significant support for JSON*. Almost 5 years after the item was created, Microsoft added JSON support in SQL Server 2016.

Of course, the number of votes on the Microsoft Connect site is not the only reason for this feature. Other competitors (PostgreSQL, Oracle, DB2, and MySQL) have already introduced support for JSON; some of them, like PostgreSQL, very seriously and robustly. And if you still want to be a respectable vendor, you need to come up with JSON support.

What is JSON?

JavaScript Object Notation (JSON) is an open standard format for data exchange between applications and services. JSON objects are human readable lists of key-value pairs. Although its name suggests differently, JSON is language-independent. It is specified in the ECMA-404 standard

(http://www.ecma-international.org/publications/files/ECMA-ST/ECMA-404.pdf).

 Ecma International is an industry association founded in 1961 and dedicated to the standardization of **Information and Communication Technology (ICT)** and **Consumer Electronics (CE)**. You can find more info about it at https://www.ecma-international.org.

JSON is very simple and very popular. It is commonly used in Ajax applications, configurations, RESTful web services, apps from social media, and NoSQL database management systems such as MongoDB and CouchDB. Many developers prefer JSON to XML because they see JSON as less verbose and easier to read.

Why is it popular?

JSON is a simple data format, but its simplicity is not the only thing that makes it a leading standard for exchanging data among web services and applications. The most important reason for its popularity is the fact that the JSON format is native for many programming languages, such as JavaScript. They can generate and consume JSON data natively, without serialization. One of the biggest problems in software development in recent years is object-relational impedance. The JSON data format is flexible and self-describing and allows you to use it effectively without defining a strict schema for data, which XML might need. This allows the quick integration of data.

JSON versus XML

Both JSON and XML are simple, open, and interoperable. Since JSON usually contains less data, by using JSON, less data traverses through the network. Both formats are human readable; JSON is a bit cleaner, since it contains less text. This is because the number of data formats supported by JSON is much less than with XML.

- JSON is handy for sharing data. Data in JSON is stored in arrays and objects while XML documents form a tree structure. Therefore, data transfer is easier with JSON and native for many programming languages: JavaScript, Python, Perl, Ruby, and so on. On the other hand, XML can store more data types (JSON does not even have a data type for date); it can include photos, videos, and other binary files. XML is more robust and is better suited for complex documents. XML also offers options for data representation, while JSON just transfers data, without suggesting or defining how to display it.
- Generally, JSON is better as a data exchange format, while XML is more convenient as a document exchange format.

JSON objects

According to the ECMA specification, a JSON text is a sequence of tokens formed of Unicode code points that conforms to the JSON value grammar. A JSON value can be:

- **Primitive**: This is a string, number, true/false, or null value
- **Complex:** This is an object or an array

JSON object

A JSON object is a collection of zero or more key-value pairs called object members. The collection is wrapped in a pair of curly brackets. The key and value are separated by a single colon, while object members are separated with a comma character. The key is a string. The value can be any primitive or complex JSON data type. The structure of a JSON object is shown in *Figure 5.2*:

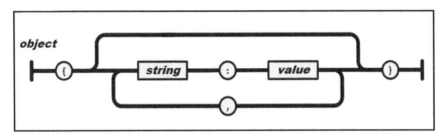

Figure 5.2: JSON object data type

The member name within a JSON object does not need to be unique. The following strings show a JSON text representing an object:

```
{
"Name":"Mila Radivojevic",
"Age":12,
"Instrument": "Flute"
}
{}
{
"Song":"Echoes",
"Group":"Pink Floyd",
"Album":{
"Name":"Meddle",
"Year":1971
}
}
{
"Name":"Tom Waits",
"Name":"Leonard Cohen"
}
```

Since the value can be any data type, including an object or an array, you can have many nested layers. This makes JSON a good choice for even complex data. Note that whitespaces are allowed between the key and the value.

JSON array

A JSON array is an ordered list of zero or more values separated by commas and surrounded by square brackets. The structure is shown in *Figure 5-3*:

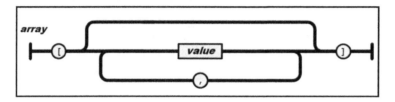

Figure 5.3: JSON array data type

Unlike JSON objects, here, the order of values is significant. Values can have different data types.

The following strings are JSON conform arrays:

```
["Benfica","Juventus","Rapid Vienna","Seattle Seahawks"]
["LYVTA",3, "Käsekrainer", "political correctness", true, null]
```

Primitive JSON data types

JSON is designed to be lightweight and supports only four primitive data types:

- **Numbers**: This is a double-precision float
- **String:** Unicode text surrounded by double quotes
- **True/false**: Boolean values; they must be written in lowercase
- **Null**: This represents a null value

As you can see, there is no date data type. Dates are represented and processed as strings. A JSON string is a sequence of Unicode code points wrapped with quotation marks. All characters may be placed within the quotation marks, except for the characters that must be escaped. *Table 5.1* provides the list of characters that must be escaped according to this specification and their JSON conform representation:

Special character	JSON conform character
Double quote	"
Solidus	/
Reverse solidus	
Backspace	b
Form feed	f
New line	n
Carriage return	r
Tabulation	t

Table 5.1: JSON escaping rules

In addition to this, all control characters with character codes in the range 0-31 need to be escaped too. In JSON output, they are represented in the following format: u<code>. Thus, the control character CHAR(0) is escaped as u0000, while CHAR(31) is represented by u001f.

- The structure of a JSON string is shown in *Figure 5.4*:

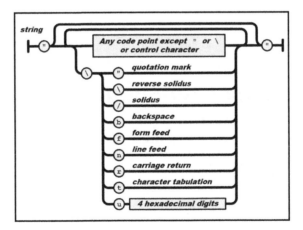

Figure 5.4: JSON string data type

JSON in SQL Server prior to SQL Server 2016

JSON has established itself as a respectable and important data exchange format in the last 5-6 years. You read that JSON support in SQL Server was requested 5 years ago. Since this support was not provided prior to SQL Server 2016, developers had to implement their own solutions. They had to use either CLR or Transact-SQL to process and manipulate JSON data in SQL Server. This section will briefly mention a few solutions.

JSON4SQL

JSON4SQL is a commercial CLR-based solution (with a trial version). It provides a fast, feature-rich binary JSON type for SQL Server. JSON4SQL stores JSON in a binary format ported from the JSONB format used in the PostgreSQL database. It is available at the following web address: http://www.json4sql.com.

JSON.SQL

JSON.SQL is a CLR-based JSON serializer/deserializer for SQL Server written by Bret Lowery, available at this address:
http://www.sqlservercentral.com/articles/SQLCLR/74160/. It uses a popular JSON framework—Json.NET.

Transact-SQL-based solution

There is also a Transact-SQL only solution that does not use .NET functionality at all. It is written by Phil Factor and described in two articles:

- *Consuming JSON Strings in SQL Server*: You can find this article at
  https://www.simple-talk.com/sql/t-sql-programming/consuming-json-strings-in-sql-server/
- *Producing JSON Documents from SQL Server queries via TSQL*: The article is available at
  https://www.simple-talk.com/sql/t-sql-programming/producing-json-documents-from-sql-server-queries-via-tsql/

Since it processes text with Transact-SQL only, the solution is not performant, but it can be used to process small or moderate JSON documents.

Retrieving SQL Server data in the JSON format

This section explores JSON support in SQL Server with a very common action: formatting tabular data as JSON. In SQL Server 2016, the clause FOR JSON can be used with the SELECT statement to accomplish this. It is analogous to formatting relational data as XML by using the FOR XML extension.

When you use the FOR JSON clause, you can choose between two modes:

- FOR JSON AUTO: The JSON output will be formatted by the structure of the SELECT statement automatically.
- FOR JSON PATH: The JSON output will be formatted by the structure explicitly defined by you. With JSON PATH, you can create a more complex output (nested objects and properties).

In both modes, SQL Server extracts relational data defined by the SELECT statement, converts SQL Server data types to appropriate JSON types, implements escaping rules, and finally formats the output according to explicitly or implicitly defined formatting rules.

FOR JSON AUTO

Use FOR JSON AUTO when you want to let SQL Server format query results for you. When you specify this mode, the JSON format is controlled by how the SELECT statement is written.

FOR JSON AUTO requires a table; you cannot use it without a database table or view. For instance, the following query will fail:

```
SELECT GETDATE() AS today FOR JSON AUTO;
```

Here is the error message:

```
Msg 13600, Level 16, State 1, Line 13
FOR JSON AUTO requires at least one table for generating JSON objects. Use
FOR JSON PATH or add a FROM clause with a table name.
```

To demonstrate how SQL Server automatically generates JSON data, use the new SQL Server 2016 sample database `WideWorldImporters`. Consider the following query that returns the first three rows from the `Application.People` table:

```
USE WideWorldImporters;
SELECT TOP (3) PersonID, FullName, EmailAddress, PhoneNumber
FROM Application.People ORDER BY PersonID ASC;
```

Here is the result in tabular format:

PersonID	FullName	EmailAddress	PhoneNumber
1	Data Conversion Only	NULL	NULL
2	Kayla Woodcock	kaylaw@wideworldimporters.com	(415) 555-0102
3	Hudson Onslow	hudsono@wideworldimporters.com	(415) 555-0102

First, you will recall how SQL Server converts this data automatically to XML. To generate an XML, you can use the FOR JSON AUTO extension:

```
SELECT TOP (3) PersonID, FullName, EmailAddress, PhoneNumber
FROM Application.People ORDER BY PersonID ASC FOR XML AUTO;
```

Here is the portion of XML generated by the previous query:

```
<Application.People PersonID="1" FullName="Data Conversion Only" />
<Application.People PersonID="2" FullName="Kayla Woodcock"
EmailAddress="kaylaw@wideworldimporters.com" PhoneNumber="(415) 555-0102"
/>
<Application.People PersonID="3" FullName="Hudson Onslow"
EmailAddress="hudsono@wideworldimporters.com" PhoneNumber="(415) 555-0102"
/>
```

Analogous to this, the simplest way to convert the result in JSON format is to put the FOR JSON AUTO extension at the end of the query:

```
SELECT TOP (3) PersonID, FullName, EmailAddress, PhoneNumber
FROM Application.People ORDER BY PersonID ASC FOR JSON AUTO;
```

The result is an automatically formatted JSON text. By default, it is a JSON array with objects:

```
[{"PersonID":1,"FullName":"Data Conversion
Only"},{"PersonID":2,"FullName":"Kayla
Woodcock","EmailAddress":"kaylaw@wideworldimporters.com","PhoneNumber":"(41
```

```
5) 555-0102"},{"PersonID":3,"FullName":"Hudson
Onslow","EmailAddress":"hudsono@wideworldimporters.com","PhoneNumber":"(415
) 555-0102"}]
```

As you can see, in **SQL Server Management Studio (SSMS)**, the JSON result is prepared in a single line. This is hard to follow and observe from a human-readable point of view. Therefore, you would need a JSON formatter. In this book, JSON output generated in SSMS is formatted by using the JSON formatter and validator that is available at `https://jsonformatter.curiousconcept.com`. The previous result looks better after additional formatting:

```
[
    {
       "PersonID":1,
       "FullName":"Data Conversion Only"
    },
    {
       "PersonID":2,
       "FullName":"Kayla Woodcock",
       "EmailAddress":"kaylaw@wideworldimporters.com",
       "PhoneNumber":"(415) 555-0102"
    },
    {
       "PersonID":3,
       "FullName":"Hudson Onslow",
       "EmailAddress":"hudsono@wideworldimporters.com",
       "PhoneNumber":"(415) 555-0102"
    }
]
```

As you can see, for each row from the original result set, one JSON object with a flat property structure is generated. Compared to XML, you see less text since the table name does not appear in the JSON output.

The difference in size is significant when you compare JSON with XML generated by using the ELEMENTS option instead of default RAW. To illustrate this, you can use the following code; it compares the data length (in bytes) of XML- and JSON-generated output for all rows in the Sales.Orders table:

```
USE WideWorldImporters;
SELECT
  DATALENGTH(CAST((SELECT * FROM Sales.Orders FOR XML AUTO) AS
NVARCHAR(MAX))) AS xml_raw_size,  DATALENGTH(CAST((SELECT * FROM
Sales.Orders FOR XML AUTO,     ELEMENTS) AS NVARCHAR(MAX))) AS
xml_elements_size,  DATALENGTH(CAST((SELECT * FROM Sales.Orders FOR JSON
AUTO) AS     NVARCHAR(MAX))) AS json_size;
```

The preceding query generates the following results:

```
xml_raw_size          xml_elements_size     json_size
-------------------   -------------------   -------------------
49161702              81161852              49149364
```

You can see that the XML representation of data when columns are expressed as XML elements is about 65% larger than the JSON representation. When they are expressed as XML attributes, JSON and XML output have approximately the same size.

The FOR JSON AUTO extension creates a flat structure with single-level properties. If you are not satisfied with the automatically created output and want to create a more complex structure, you should use the FOR JSON PATH extension.

FOR JSON PATH

To maintain full control over the format of the JSON output, you need to specify the PATH option with the FOR JSON clause. The PATH mode lets you create wrapper objects and nest complex properties. The results are formatted as an array of JSON objects.

The FOR JSON PATH clause will use the column alias or column name to determine the key name in the JSON output. If an alias contains dots, the FOR JSON PATH clause will create a nested object.

Assume you want to have more control over the output generated by FOR JSON AUTO in the previous subsection, and instead of a flat list of properties you want to represent EmailAddress and PhoneNumbers as nested properties of a new property named Contact. Here is the required output for the PersonID property with a value of 2:

```
{
        "PersonID":2,
        "FullName":"Kayla Woodcock",
        "Contact":
{
        "EmailAddress":"kaylaw@wideworldimporters.com",
        "PhoneNumber":"(415) 555-0102"
}
    },
```

To achieve this, you simply add an alias to columns that need to be nested. In the alias, you have to use a dot syntax, which defines a JSON path to the property. Here is the code that implements the previous request:

```
SELECT TOP (3) PersonID, FullName,
EmailAddress AS 'Contact.Email', PhoneNumber AS 'Contact.Phone'
FROM Application.People ORDER BY PersonID ASC FOR JSON PATH;
```

Here is the expected result:

```
[
    {
        "PersonID":1,
        "FullName":"Data Conversion Only"
    },
    {
        "PersonID":2,
        "FullName":"Kayla Woodcock",
        "Contact":{
            "Email":"kaylaw@wideworldimporters.com",
            "Phone":"(415) 555-0102"
        }
    },
    {
        "PersonID":3,
        "FullName":"Hudson Onslow",
        "Contact":{
            "Email":"hudsono@wideworldimporters.com",
            "Phone":"(415) 555-0102"
        }
    }
]
```

By default, null values are not included in the output as you can see in the first array element; it does not contain the Contact property.

FOR JSON PATH does not require a database table. The following statement, which was not allowed in the AUTO mode, works in the PATH mode:

```
SELECT GETDATE() AS today FOR JSON PATH;
```

It returns:

```
[{"today":"2016-07-26T09:13:32.007"}]
```

If you reference more than one table in the query, the results are represented as a flat list, and then FOR JSON PATH nests each column using its alias. JSON PATH allows you to control generated JSON data and to create nested documents.

FOR JSON additional options

In both modes of the FOR JSON clause, you can specify additional options to control the output. The following options are available:

- **Adding a root node**: The JSON output will be formatted by the structure of the SELECT statement automatically.
- **Including null values**: The JSON output will be formatted by the structure explicitly defined by you. With JSON PATH, you can create a more complex output (nested objects and properties).
- **Removing array wrapper**: The JSON output will be formatted by the structure explicitly defined by you. With JSON PATH, you can create a more complex output (nested objects and properties).

Adding a root node to the JSON output

By specifying the ROOT option in the FOR JSON query, you can add a single, top-level element to the JSON output. The following code shows this:

```
SELECT TOP (3) PersonID, FullName, EmailAddress, PhoneNumber
FROM Application.People ORDER BY PersonID ASC FOR JSON AUTO,
ROOT('Persons');
```

Here is the result:

```
{
    "Persons":[
        {
            "PersonID":1,
            "FullName":"Data Conversion Only"
        },
        {
            "PersonID":2,
            "FullName":"Kayla Woodcock",
            "EmailAddress":"kaylaw@wideworldimporters.com",
            "PhoneNumber":"(415) 555-0102"
        },
        {
            "PersonID":3,
```

```
            "FullName":"Hudson Onslow",
            "EmailAddress":"hudsono@wideworldimporters.com",
            "PhoneNumber":"(415) 555-0102"
        }
    ]
}
```

By specifying the root element, you have converted the outer array to a single complex property named `Persons`.

Including null values in the JSON output

As you can see in the preceding example, the JSON output does not map a column to a JSON property if the column value is NULL. To include null values in the JSON output, you can specify the INCLUDE_NULL_VALUES option. Let's apply it to our initial example:

```
SELECT TOP (3) PersonID, FullName, EmailAddress, PhoneNumber
FROM Application.People ORDER BY PersonID ASC FOR JSON AUTO,
INCLUDE_NULL_VALUES;
```

Let's observe the result:

```
[
  {
    "PersonID":1,
    "FullName":"Data Conversion Only",
    "EmailAddress":null,
    "PhoneNumber":null
  },
  {
    "PersonID":2,
    "FullName":"Kayla Woodcock",
    "EmailAddress":"kaylaw@wideworldimporters.com",
    "PhoneNumber":"(415) 555-0102"
  },
  {
    "PersonID":3,
    "FullName":"Hudson Onslow",
    "EmailAddress":"hudsono@wideworldimporters.com",
    "PhoneNumber":"(415) 555-0102"
  }
]
```

Now each element has all properties listed even if they don't have a value. This option is similar to the XSINIL option used with the ELEMENTS directive in the case of FOR XML AUTO.

Formatting a JSON output as a single object

The default JSON output is enclosed within square brackets, which means the output is an array. If you want to format it as a single object instead of an array, use the WITHOUT_ARRAY_WRAPPER option.

Even if a query returns only one row, SQL Server will format it by default as a JSON array, as in the following example:

```
SELECT PersonID, FullName, EmailAddress, PhoneNumber
FROM Application.People WHERE PersonID = 2 FOR JSON AUTO;
```

Although only one row is returned, the output is still an array (with a single element):

```
[
  {
    "PersonID":2,
    "FullName":"Kayla Woodcock",
    "EmailAddress":"kaylaw@wideworldimporters.com",
    "PhoneNumber":"(415) 555-0102"
  }
]
```

To return a single object instead of an array, you can specify the WITHOUT_ARRAY_WRAPPER option:

```
SELECT PersonID, FullName, EmailAddress, PhoneNumber
FROM Application.People WHERE PersonID = 2 FOR JSON AUTO,
WITHOUT_ARRAY_WRAPPER;
```

The output looks more convenient now:

```
{
  "PersonID":2,
  "FullName":"Kayla Woodcock",
  "EmailAddress":"kaylaw@wideworldimporters.com",
  "PhoneNumber":"(415) 555-0102"
}
```

Removing square brackets from the output allows us to choose between an object and array in the output JSON. However, only square brackets guarantee that the output is JSON conforming. Without the brackets, JSON text will be valid only if the underlined query returns a single row or no rows at all.

To demonstrate this, include `PersonID` with a value of 3 in your initial query:

```
SELECT PersonID, FullName, EmailAddress, PhoneNumber
FROM Application.People WHERE PersonID IN (2, 3) FOR JSON AUTO,
WITHOUT_ARRAY_WRAPPER;
```

The output is expected, but invalid; there is no parent object or array:

```
{
  "PersonID":2,
  "FullName":"Kayla Woodcock",
  "EmailAddress":"kaylaw@wideworldimporters.com",
  "PhoneNumber":"(415) 555-0102"
},
{
  "PersonID":3,
  "FullName":"Hudson Onslow",
  "EmailAddress":"hudsono@wideworldimporters.com",
  "PhoneNumber":"(415) 555-0102"
}
```

But, wait! By specifying the ROOT option, you can wrap the output in an object, can't you? You saw this demonstrated earlier in this chapter. You can add a no-name root element to the preceding output:

```
SELECT PersonID, FullName, EmailAddress, PhoneNumber
FROM Application.People WHERE PersonID IN (2, 3) FOR JSON AUTO,
WITHOUT_ARRAY_WRAPPER, ROOT('');
```

This should add a top-level element, and with that change, the JSON output should be valid. Check this out in the output:

```
Msg 13620, Level 16, State 1, Line 113
ROOT option and WITHOUT_ARRAY_WRAPPER option cannot be used together in FOR
JSON. Remove one of these options.
```

A bitter disappointment! You cannot combine these two options! Therefore, use this option with caution; be aware that the JSON could be invalid.

Converting data types

As mentioned earlier, JSON does not have the same data types as SQL Server. Therefore, when JSON text is generated from relational data, a data type conversion is performed. The FOR JSON clause uses the following mapping to convert SQL Server data types to JSON types in the JSON output:

SQL Server data type	JSON data type
`Char`, `Varchar`, `Nchar`, `NVarchar`, `Text`, `Ntext`, `Date`, `DateTime`, `DateTime2`, `DateTimeOffset`, `Time`, `UniqueIdentifier`, `Smallmoney`, `Money`, `XML`, `HierarchyId`, `Sql_Variant`	string
`Tinyint`, `Smallint`, `Int`, `Bigint`, `Decimal`, `Float`, `Numeric`	number
`Bit`	`true` or `false`
`Binary`, `Varbinary`, `Image`, `Rowversion`, `Timestamp`	encoded string (BASE 64)

Table 5.2: Conversion between SQL Server and JSON data types

The following data types are not supported: geography, geometry, and CLR-based user-defined data types. Thus, you cannot generate JSON output from tabular data if it includes columns of the aforementioned data types. For instance, the following query will fail:

```
SELECT * FROM Application.Cities FOR JSON AUTO;
```

Instead of returning a JSON output, it will generate an error with the following error message:

```
Msg 13604, Level 16, State 1, Line 282
FOR JSON cannot serialize CLR objects. Cast CLR types explicitly into one
of the supported types in FOR JSON queries.
```

The reason for the error is the `Location` column in the `Cities` table. Its data type is geography.

User-defined data types (UDT) are supported and will be converted following the same rules as underlined data types.

Escaping characters

Another action that is automatically performed when JSON is generated by using FOR
JSON clause is escaping special characters from text columns according to JSON's escaping
rules. The rules are explained in detail in the *Primitive JSON data types* section earlier in this
chapter.

Converting JSON data in a tabular format

Nowadays, JSON is a recognized format for data representation and exchange. However,
most of the existing data still resides in relational databases and you need to combine them
to process and manipulate them together. In order to combine JSON with relational data or
to import it in relational tables, you need to map JSON data to tabular data, that is, convert
it into a tabular format. In SQL Server 2016, you can use the OPENJSON function to
accomplish this.

- OPENJSON is a newly added rowset function. A rowset function is a table-valued
  function and returns an object that can be used as if it were a table or a view. Just
  as OPENXML provides a rowset view over an XML document, OPENJSON gives a
  rowset over JSON data. The OPENJSON function converts JSON objects and
  properties to table rows and columns respectively.
- It accepts two input arguments:
    - **Expression**: JSON text in the Unicode format.
    - **Path**: This is an optional argument. It is a JSON path expression
      and you can use it to specify a fragment of the input expression.

The function returns a table with a default or user-defined schema.

To use the OPENJSON function, the database must be in compatibility level 130. If it is not,
you will get the following error:

```
Msg 208, Level 16, State 1, Line 78
Invalid object name 'OPENJSON'.
```

As mentioned, the returned table can have an implicit (default) schema or an explicit one,
defined by the user. In the next two sections, both schemas will be explored in more detail.

OPENJSON with the default schema

When you don't specify a schema for returned results, the OPENJSON function returns a table with three columns:

- **Key**: This is the name of a JSON property or the index of a JSON element. The data type of the column is nvarchar, the length is 4,000, collation is Latin1_General_BIN2, and the column does not allow null values.
- **Value**: This is the value of the property or index defined by the key column. The data type of the column is nvarchar(max), it inherits collation from the input JSON text, and nulls are allowed.
- **Type**: The JSON data type of the value. The data type of the column is tinyint. *Table 5.3* lists the possible values for this column and appropriate descriptions:

Type column value	JSON data type
0	null
1	string
2	number
3	true/false
4	array
5	object

Table 5.3: OPENJSON mapping of JSON data types

OPENJSON returns only one table; therefore only first-level properties are returned as rows. It returns one row for each JSON property or array element. To demonstrate the different results provided by the OPENJSON function, use the following JSON data with the information about the album *Wish You Were Here* by the British band Pink Floyd. You will provide JSON data as an input string and call the function without specifying an optional path argument:

```
DECLARE @json NVARCHAR(MAX) = N'{
"Album":"Wish You Were Here",
"Year":1975,
"IsVinyl":true,
"Songs":[{"Title":"Shine On You Crazy Diamond","Authors":"Gilmour, Waters,
Wright"},
{"Title":"Have a Cigar","Authors":"Waters"},
{"Title":"Welcome to the Machine","Authors":"Waters"},
```

```
{"Title":"Wish You Were Here","Authors":"Gilmour, Waters"}],
"Members":{"Guitar":"David Gilmour","Bass Guitar":"Roger
Waters","Keyboard":"Richard Wright","Drums":"Nick Mason"}
}';
SELECT * FROM OPENJSON(@json);
```

The function has been invoked without the path expression, simply to convert the whole JSON document into a tabular format. Here is the output of this action:

Key	Value	Type
Album	Wish you Were Here	1
Year	1975	2
IsVinyl	true	3
Songs	[{"Title":"Shine On You Crazy Diamond","Writers":"Gilmour, Waters, Wright" ...]	4
Members	{"Guitar":"David Gilmour","Bass Guitar":"Roger Waters","Keyboard":"Richard Wright","Drums":"Nick Mason"}	5

As you can see, five rows were generated (one row for each JSON property), property names are shown in the key column and their values in the value column.

The input JSON expression must be well formatted; otherwise, an error occurs. In the following code, a leading double quote for the Year property is intentionally omitted:

```
DECLARE @json NVARCHAR(500) = '{
"Album":"Wish You Were Here",
Year":1975,
"IsVinyl":true
}';
SELECT * FROM OPENJSON(@json);
```

Of course, the optimizer does not forgive this small mistake and its reaction is very conservative:

```
Msg 13609, Level 16, State 4, Line 23
JSON text is not properly formatted. Unexpected character 'Y' is found at
position 34.
```

As already mentioned and demonstrated, only first-level properties are returned with the OPENJSON function. To return properties within complex values of a JSON document (arrays and objects), you need to specify the path argument. In this example, assume you want to return the Songs fragment from the initial Wish You Were Here JSON string:

```
DECLARE @json NVARCHAR(MAX) = N'{
"Album":"Wish You Were Here",
"Year":1975,
"IsVinyl":true,
"Songs":[{"Title":"Shine On You Crazy Diamond","Authors":"Gilmour, Waters,
Wright"},
{"Title":"Have a Cigar","Authors":"Waters"},
{"Title":"Welcome to the Machine","Authors":"Waters"},
{"Title":"Wish You Were Here","Authors":"Gilmour, Waters"}],
"Members":{"Guitar":"David Gilmour","Bass Guitar":"Roger
Waters","Keyboard":"Richard Wright","Drums":"Nick Mason"}
}';
SELECT * FROM OPENJSON(@json,'$.Songs');
```

The $ path expression represents the context item and $.Songs refers to the Songs property and actually extracts this fragment from the JSON document. The rest of the document must be valid; otherwise, the path expression cannot be evaluated.

Here is the result:

Key	Value	Type
0	{"Title":"Shine On You Crazy Diamond","Writers":"Gilmour, Waters, Wright"}	5
1	{"Title":"Have a Cigar","Writers":"Waters"}	5
2	{"Title":"Welcome to the Machine","Writers":"Waters"}	5
3	{"Title":"Wish You Were Here","Writers":"Gilmour, Waters"}	5

You can see four entries for four elements in the JSON array representing songs from this album. Since they contain objects, their values are still in the JSON format in the column value.

When you do the same for the Members property, you get a nice list of properties with their names and values:

```
DECLARE @json NVARCHAR(MAX) = N'{
"Album":"Wish You Were Here",
"Year":1975,
"IsVinyl":true,
"Songs":[{"Title":"Shine On You Crazy Diamond","Authors":"Gilmour, Waters,
```

```
Wright"},
{"Title":"Have a Cigar","Authors":"Waters"},
{"Title":"Welcome to the Machine","Authors":"Waters"},
{"Title":"Wish You Were Here","Authors":"Gilmour, Waters"}],
"Members":{"Guitar":"David Gilmour","Bass Guitar":"Roger
Waters","Keyboard":"Richard Wright","Drums":"Nick Mason"}
}';
SELECT * FROM OPENJSON(@json,'$.Members');
```

Here is the result:

key	value	type
Guitar	David Gilmour	1
Bass Guitar	Roger Waters	1
Keyboard	Richard Wright	1
Drums	Nick Mason	1

Note that the returned type this time is 1 (string), while in the previous example it was 5 (object).

The function returns an error if the JSON text is not properly formatted. To demonstrate this, the initial string has been slightly changed: a leading double quote has been omitted for the element Drums (value Nick Mason). Therefore, the string is not JSON valid. Invoke the OPENJSON function for such a string:

```
DECLARE @json NVARCHAR(MAX) = N'{
"Album":"Wish you Were Here",
"Members":{"Guitar":"David Gilmour","Bass Guitar":"Roger
Waters","Keyboard":"Richard Wright","Drums":Nick Mason", "Vocal":"Syd
Barrett"}
}';
SELECT * FROM OPENJSON (@json,'$.Members');
```

Here is the result:

```
Msg 13609, Level 16, State 4, Line 15
JSON text is not properly formatted. Unexpected character 'N' is found at
position 417.
```

key	value	type
Guitar	David Gilmour	1
Bass Guitar	Roger Waters	1
Keyboard	Richard Wright	1

You can see an error message, but also the returned table. The table contains three rows, since the first three properties of the complex `Member` property are JSON conforming. Instead of a fourth row, an error message has been generated and the fifth row is not shown either, although it is well-formatted.

What would happen if the JSON path expression points to a scalar value or to a non-existing property? In the default JSON path mode (lax), the query would return an empty table; and when you specify strict mode, in addition to an empty table, an error message is shown (a batch-level exception is raised), as shown in the following examples:

```
DECLARE @json NVARCHAR(MAX) = N'{
"Album":"Wish you Were Here",
"Year":1975,
"IsVinyl":true,
"Songs" :[{"Title":"Shine On You Crazy Diamond","Writers":"Gilmour, Waters,
Wright"},
{"Title":"Have a Cigar","Writers":"Waters"},
{"Title":"Welcome to the Machine","Writers":"Waters"},
{"Title":"Wish You Were Here","Writers":"Gilmour, Waters"}],
"Members":{"Guitar":"David Gilmour","Bass Guitar":"Roger
Waters","Keyboard":"Richard Wright","Drums":"Nick Mason"}
}';
SELECT * FROM OPENJSON(@json, N'$.Members.Guitar');
SELECT * FROM OPENJSON(@json, N'$.Movies');
```

Both queries return an empty table:

key	value	type

The same calls with the `strict` option end up with error messages:

```
SELECT * FROM OPENJSON(@json, N'strict $.Members.Guitar');
```

The result for the preceding query is the first error message:

```
Msg 13611, Level 16, State 1, Line 12
Value referenced by JSON path is not an array or object and cannot be
opened with OPENJSON.
```

The second query from the preceding example:

```
SELECT * FROM OPENJSON(@json, N'strict $.Movies');
```

The result for the preceding query is the second error message:

```
Msg 13608, Level 16, State 3, Line 13
Property cannot be found on the specified JSON path.
```

You can use OPENJSON not only to convert JSON data into a tabular format but also to implement some non-JSON related tasks.

Processing data from a comma-separated list of values

The following code example demonstrates how to use the OPENJSON rowset function to return the details of orders for IDs provided in a comma-separated list:

```
USE WideWorldImporters;
DECLARE @orderIds AS VARCHAR(100) = '1,3,7,8,9,11';
SELECT o.OrderID, o.CustomerID, o.OrderDate
FROM Sales.Orders o
INNER JOIN (SELECT value FROM OPENJSON('[' + @orderIds + ']' )) x ON
x.value= o.OrderID;
```

Here is the list of orders produced by the preceding query:

```
OrderID      CustomerID  OrderDate
-----------  ----------- -----------
1            832         2013-01-01
3            105         2013-01-01
7            575         2013-01-01
8            964         2013-01-01
9            77          2013-01-01
11           586         2013-01-01
```

In this example, the input argument is wrapped with square brackets to create a proper JSON text and the OPENJSON function is invoked without the path argument. OPENJSON created one row for each element from the JSON array and that is exactly what you needed.

Returning the difference between two table rows

Another example where you can use OPENJSON is to return the difference between two rows in a table. For instance, when you put application settings for different environments in a database table, you might need to know what is different in the settings between the two environments. You can accomplish this task by comparing values in each column, but this can be annoying and error prone if the table has many columns.

The following example returns the difference for database settings in the master and model database in an instance of SQL Server 2016:

```
SELECT
  mst.[key],
  mst.[value] AS mst_val,
  mdl.[value] AS mdl_val
FROM OPENJSON ((SELECT * FROM sys.databases WHERE database_id = 1 FOR JSON
AUTO, WITHOUT_ARRAY_WRAPPER)) mst
INNER JOIN OPENJSON((SELECT * FROM sys.databases WHERE database_id = 3 FOR
JSON AUTO, WITHOUT_ARRAY_WRAPPER)) mdl
ON mst.[key] = mdl.[key] AND mst.[value] <> mdl.[value];
```

Here is the list showing columns that have different values for these two databases:

key	mst_val	mdl_val
name	master	model
database_id	1	3
compatibility_level	120	130
snapshot_isolation_state	1	0
snapshot_isolation_state_desc	ON	OFF
recovery_model	3	1
recovery_model_desc	SIMPLE	FULL
is_db_chaining_on	true	false

This is very handy and efficient; you don't need to know or write a lot of OR statements with column names. For instance, in the system view used in this example (sys.databases), there are 78 columns and you would need to include them all in the WHERE clause in a *relational* Transact-SQL statement.

OPENJSON with an explicit schema

If you need more control over formatting when it is offered by default, you can explicitly specify your own schema. The function will still return a table but with the columns defined by you. To specify the resultant table schema, use the WITH clause of the OPENJSON function. Here is the syntax for the OPENJSON function with an explicit schema:

```
OPENJSON( jsonExpression [ , path ] )
[
    WITH (
        column_name data_type [ column_path ] [ AS JSON ]
    [ , column_name data_type [ column_path ] [ AS JSON ] ]
    [ , . . . n ]
        )
]
```

When you use the WITH clause, you need to specify at least one column. For each column, you can specify the following attributes:

- column_name: This is the name of the output column.
- data_type: This is the data type for the output column.
- column_path: This is the value for the output column specified with the JSON path expression (it can be a JSON property or value of an array element). This argument is optional.
- AS JSON: Use this to specify that the property referenced in the column path represents an object or array. This argument is optional.

The best way to understand how the function works is to look at examples. The following code shows how to extract JSON properties as columns and their values as rows for JSON primitive data types:

```
DECLARE @json NVARCHAR(MAX) = N'{
"Album":"Wish You Were Here",
"Year":1975,
"IsVinyl":true,
"Songs" :[{"Title":"Shine On You Crazy Diamond","Writers":"Gilmour, Waters,
Wright"},
{"Title":"Have a Cigar","Writers":"Waters"},
{"Title":"Welcome to the Machine","Writers":"Waters"},
{"Title":"Wish You Were Here","Writers":"Gilmour, Waters"}],
"Members":{"Guitar":"David Gilmour","Bass Guitar":"Roger
Waters","Keyboard":"Richard Wright","Drums":"Nick Mason"}
}';
SELECT * FROM OPENJSON(@json)
WITH
```

```
(
    AlbumName NVARCHAR(50) '$.Album',
    AlbumYear SMALLINT '$.Year',
    IsVinyl    BIT '$.IsVinyl'
);
```

The result of the previous action is a table defined with the WITH statement:

AlbumName	AlbumYear	IsVinyl
Wish You Were Here	1975	1

You can add a fourth column to show band members. Here is the code:

```
SELECT * FROM OPENJSON(@json)
WITH
(
    AlbumName NVARCHAR(50) '$.Album',
    AlbumYear SMALLINT '$.Year',
    IsVinyl  BIT '$.IsVinyl',
    Members  VARCHAR(200) '$.Members'
);
```

And the resultant table:

AlbumName	AlbumYear	IsVinyl	Members
Wish You Were Here	1975	1	NULL

The result might be unexpected, but the value for the Members property is an object, and therefore the function returns NULL since the JSON path is in default lax mode. If you specified the strict mode, the returned table would be empty and an error would be raised. To solve the problem and show the value of the Members property you need to use the AS JSON option to inform SQL Server that the expected data is properly JSON-formatted:

```
SELECT * FROM OPENJSON(@json)
WITH
(
    AlbumName NVARCHAR(50) '$.Album',
    AlbumYear SMALLINT '$.Year',
    IsVinyl  BIT '$.IsVinyl',
    Members  VARCHAR(MAX) '$.Members' AS JSON

);
```

Now it should return the expected result, but it returns an error:

```
Msg 13618, Level 16, State 1, Line 70
AS JSON option can be specified only for column of nvarchar(max) type in
WITH clause.
```

As the error message clearly says, the AS JSON option requires a column with the nvarchar(max) data type. Finally, here is the code that works and returns the expected result:

```
SELECT * FROM OPENJSON(@json)
WITH
(
  AlbumName NVARCHAR(50) '$.Album',
  AlbumYear SMALLINT '$.Year',
  IsVinyl  BIT '$.IsVinyl',
  Members  NVARCHAR(MAX) '$.Members' AS JSON

);
```

AlbumName	AlbumYear	IsVinyl	Members
Wish You Were Here	1975	1	{"Guitar":"David Gilmour","Bass Guitar":"Roger Waters","Keyboard":"Richard Wright","Drums":"Nick Mason"}

To combine property values from different levels and convert them to a tabular format, you would need to have multiple calls of the OPENJSON function. The following example lists all songs and authors and shows the appropriate album name:

```
DECLARE @json NVARCHAR(MAX) = N'{
"Album":"Wish You Were Here",
"Year":1975,
"IsVinyl":true,
"Songs" :[{"Title":"Shine On You Crazy Diamond","Writers":"Gilmour, Waters,
Wright"},
{"Title":"Have a Cigar","Writers":"Waters"},
{"Title":"Welcome to the Machine","Writers":"Waters"},
{"Title":"Wish You Were Here","Writers":"Gilmour, Waters"}],
"Members":{"Guitar":"David Gilmour","Bass Guitar":"Roger
Waters","Keyboard":"Richard Wright","Drums":"Nick Mason"}
}';
SELECT s.SongTitle, s.SongAuthors, a.AlbumName FROM OPENJSON(@json)
WITH
(
  AlbumName NVARCHAR(50) '$.Album',
```

```
    AlbumYear SMALLINT '$.Year',
    IsVinyl BIT '$.IsVinyl',
    Songs  NVARCHAR(MAX) '$.Songs' AS JSON,
    Members NVARCHAR(MAX) '$.Members' AS JSON

) a
CROSS APPLY OPENJSON(Songs)
WITH
(
    SongTitle NVARCHAR(200) '$.Title',
    SongAuthors NVARCHAR(200) '$.Writers'
) s;
```

This time the result meets expectations. No hidden catch!

SongTitle	SongAuthors	AlbumName
Shine On You Crazy Diamond	Gilmour, Waters, Wright	Wish You Were Here
Have a Cigar	Waters	Wish You Were Here
Welcome to the Machine	Waters	Wish You Were Here
Wish You Were Here	Gilmour, Waters	Wish You Were Here

Import the JSON data from a file

Importing JSON data from a file and converting it into a tabular format is straightforward in SQL Server 2016. To import data from a filesystem (local disk or network location) into SQL Server, you can use the OPENROWSET (BULK) function. It simply imports the entire file content in a single-text value.

To demonstrate this, use your knowledge from the previous section and generate content for a JSON file. Use the following query to create JSON data from the Application.People table:

```
USE WideWorldImporters;
SELECT PersonID, FullName, PhoneNumber, FaxNumber, EmailAddress, LogonName,
IsEmployee, IsSalesperson FROM Application.People FOR JSON AUTO;
```

You then save the resulting JSON text in a file named app.people.json in the C:Temp directory. Now import this JSON file into SQL Server.

By using the OPENROWSET function, the file is imported in a single-text column. Here is the code:

```
SELECT BulkColumn
FROM OPENROWSET (BULK 'C:Tempapp.people.json', SINGLE_CLOB) AS x;
```

Figure 5.5 shows the result of this import action. The entire file content is available in the single-text column named BulkColumn.

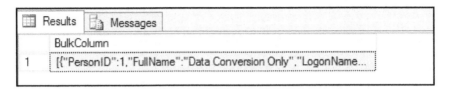

Figure 5.5: Import JSON file into SQL Server by using OPENROWSET function

To represent a JSON file content in a tabular format, you can combine the OPENROWSET function with the OPENJSON function. The following code imports JSON data and displays it with the default schema (columns key, value and type).

```
SELECT [key], [value], [type]
FROM OPENROWSET (BULK 'C:Tempapp.people.json', SINGLE_CLOB) AS x
CROSS APPLY OPENJSON(BulkColumn);
```

The result is shown in *Figure 5.6*. You can see one row for each element of a JSON array in the file.

	key	value	type
1	0	{"PersonID":1,"FullName":"Data Conversion Only","Lo...	5
2	1	{"PersonID":2,"FullName":"Kayla Woodcock","Logon...	5
3	2	{"PersonID":3,"FullName":"Hudson Onslow","LogonNa...	5
4	3	{"PersonID":4,"FullName":"Isabella Rupp","LogonNam...	5
5	4	{"PersonID":5,"FullName":"Eva Muirden","LogonName...	5
6	5	{"PersonID":6,"FullName":"Sophia Hinton","LogonNam...	5
7	6	{"PersonID":7,"FullName":"Amy Trefl","LogonName":"...	5
8	7	{"PersonID":8,"FullName":"Anthony Grosse","LogonNa...	5
9	8	{"PersonID":9,"FullName":"Alica Fatnowna","LogonNa...	5
10	9	{"PersonID":10,"FullName":"Stella Rosenhain","Logon...	5

Figure 5.6: Importing a JSON file into SQL Server and combining with OPENJSON with the default schema

Finally, this code example shows the code that can be used to import a JSON file and represent its content in tabular format, with a user-defined schema:

```
SELECT PersonID, FullName,PhoneNumber, FaxNumber, EmailAddress,LogonName,
IsEmployee, IsSalesperson
FROM OPENROWSET (BULK 'C:Tempapp.people.json', SINGLE_CLOB) as j
CROSS APPLY OPENJSON(BulkColumn)
WITH
(
  PersonID INT '$.PersonID',
  FullName NVARCHAR(50) '$.FullName',
  PhoneNumber NVARCHAR(20) '$.PhoneNumber',
  FaxNumber NVARCHAR(20) '$.FaxNumber',
  EmailAddress NVARCHAR(256) '$.EmailAddress',
  LogonName NVARCHAR(50) '$.LogonName',
  IsEmployee  BIT '$.IsEmployee',
  IsSalesperson BIT '$.IsSalesperson'
);
```

Figure 5.7 shows the result of this import procedure:

	PersonID	FullName	PhoneNumber	FaxNumber	EmailAddress	LogonName	IsEmployee	IsSalesperson
1	1	Data Conversion Only	NULL	NULL	NULL	NO LOGON	0	0
2	2	Kayla Woodcock	(415) 555-0102	(415) 555-0103	kaylaw@wideworldimporters.com	kaylaw@wideworldimporters.com	1	1
3	3	Hudson Onslow	(415) 555-0102	(415) 555-0103	hudsono@wideworldimporters.com	hudsono@wideworldimporters.com	1	1
4	4	Isabella Rupp	(415) 555-0102	(415) 555-0103	isabellar@wideworldimporters.com	isabellar@wideworldimporters.com	1	0
5	5	Eva Muirden	(415) 555-0102	(415) 555-0103	evam@wideworldimporters.com	evam@wideworldimporters.com	1	0
6	6	Sophia Hinton	(415) 555-0102	(415) 555-0103	sophiah@wideworldimporters.com	sophiah@wideworldimporters.com	1	1
7	7	Amy Trefl	(415) 555-0102	(415) 555-0103	amyt@wideworldimporters.com	amyt@wideworldimporters.com	1	1
8	8	Anthony Grosse	(415) 555-0102	(415) 555-0103	anthonyg@wideworldimporters.com	anthonyg@wideworldimporters.com	1	1
9	9	Alica Fatnowna	(415) 555-0102	(415) 555-0103	alicaf@wideworldimporters.com	alicaf@wideworldimporters.com	1	0
10	10	Stella Rosenhain	(415) 555-0102	(415) 555-0103	stellar@wideworldimporters.com	stellar@wideworldimporters.com	1	0

Figure 5.7: Importing a JSON file into SQL Server and combining with OPENJSON with an explicit schema

As expected, the structure is identical to the one generated by the simple SELECT statement against the Application.People table.

JSON storage in SQL Server 2016

As XML support was introduced in SQL Server 2005, the native XML data type has been implemented as well. SQL Server 2016 introduces built-in support for JSON but unlike XML, there is no native JSON data type. Here are the reasons that the Microsoft team exposed for not introducing a new data type:

- **Migration**: Prior to SQL Server 2016, developers already had to deal with JSON data
- **Cross feature compatibility**: The data type `nvarchar` is supported in all SQL Server components, so JSON will also be supported everywhere (memory-optimized tables, temporal tables, and Row-Level Security)
- **Client-side support**: Even if a new data type were introduced, most of the client tools would still represent it outside SQL Server as a string

They also noted that, if you believe that the JSON binary format from PostgreSQL, or a compressed format, such as zipped JSON text is a better option, you can parse JSON text in UDT, store it as JSONB in a binary property of CLR UTD, and create member methods that can use properties from that format. You can find more details about their decision at `https://blogs.msdn.microsoft.com/jocapc/2015/05/16/json-support-in-sql-server-2 016`.

Although these arguments make sense, a native JSON data type would be better, especially from a performance point of view. However, this will require more effort and longer time frames for development and the time between the release of new features is shorter than that. This should also be taken into account when you judge the feature. JSON support in SQL Server 2016 would be complete with a native data type, but built-in support is a respectable implementation and this is a very useful feature.

Since there is no JSON data type, JSON data is stored as text in `NVARCHAR` columns. You can use the newly added `COMPRESS` function to compress JSON data and convert it to a binary format.

Validating JSON data

To validate JSON, you can use the `ISJSON` function. This is a scalar function and checks whether the input string is valid JSON data. The function has one input argument:

- `string`: This is an expression of any string data type, except `text` and `ntext`

The return type of the function is `int`, but only three values are possible:

- `1` if the input string is JSON conforming
- `0` if the input string is not valid JSON data
- `NULL` if the input expression is NULL

The following statement checks whether the input variable is JSON valid:

```
SELECT
   ISJSON ('test'),
   ISJSON (''),
   ISJSON ('{}'),
   ISJSON ('{"a"}'),
   ISJSON ('{"a":1}'),
   ISJSON ('{"a":1"}');
```

Here is the output:

```
------  ------  ------  ------  ------  ------
0       0       1       0       1       0
```

ISJSON does not check the uniqueness of keys at the same level. Therefore, this JSON data is valid:

```
SELECT ISJSON ('{"id":1, "id":"a"}') AS is_json;
```

It returns:

```
is_json
-----------
1
```

Since there is no JSON data type and data must be stored as text, the ISJSON function is important for data validation before the text is saved into a database table. To ensure that a text column stores only JSON conforming data, you can use the ISJSON function in the check constraint. The following code creates a sample table with a JSON column and an appropriate check constraint:

```
USE WideWorldImporters;
DROP TABLE IF EXISTS dbo.Users;
CREATE TABLE dbo.Users(
id INT IDENTITY(1,1) NOT NULL,
username NVARCHAR(50) NOT NULL,
user_settings NVARCHAR(MAX) NULL CONSTRAINT CK_user_settings CHECK
(ISJSON(user_settings) = 1),
CONSTRAINT PK_Users PRIMARY KEY CLUSTERED (id ASC)
);
```

To test the constraint, you will have to insert two rows in the table. The first INSERT statement contains a well-formatted JSON text, while in the second the value for the last property is omitted; thus the JSON text is invalid. Now, execute the statements:

```
INSERT INTO dbo.Users(username, user_settings) VALUES(N'vasilije', '{"team"
: ["Rapid", "Bayern"], "hobby" : ["soccer", "gaming"], "color" : "green"
}');

INSERT INTO dbo.Users(username, user_settings) VALUES(N'mila', '{"team" :
"Liverpool", "hobby" }');
```

The first statement has been executed successfully, but the second, as expected, generated the following error message:

```
Msg 547, Level 16, State 0, Line 12
The INSERT statement conflicted with the CHECK constraint
"CK_user_settings". The conflict occurred in database "WideWorldImporters",
table "dbo.Users", column 'user_settings'.
The statement has been terminated.
```

Ensure that you have dropped the table used in this example:

```
USE WideWorldImporters;
DROP TABLE IF EXISTS dbo.Users;
```

Extracting values from a JSON text

As mentioned earlier in this chapter, JSON has four primitive types (string, number, Boolean, and null) and two complex (structure) types: object and array. SQL Server 2016 offers two functions to extract values from a JSON text:

- JSON_VALUE: This is used to extract values of primitive data types
- JSON_QUERY: This is used to extract a JSON fragment or to get a complex value (object or array)

JSON_VALUE

The JSON_VALUE function extracts a scalar value from a JSON string. It accepts two input arguments:

- **Expression**: This is JSON text in the Unicode format.
- **Path**: This is an optional argument. It is a JSON path expression and you can use it to specify a fragment of the input expression.

The return type of the function is nvarchar(4000), with the same collation as in the input expression. If the extracted value is longer than 4,000 characters, the function returns NULL provided the path is in lax mode or an error message in the case of strict mode.

If either the expression or the path is not valid, the JSON_VALUE function returns an error explaining that the JSON text is not properly formatted.

The following example shows the JSON_VALUE function in action. It is used to return values for properties and an array element:

```
DECLARE @json NVARCHAR(MAX) = N'{
"Album":"Wish You Were Here",
"Year":1975,
"IsVinyl":true,
"Members":["Gilmour","Waters","Wright","Mason"]
}';
SELECT
  JSON_VALUE(@json, '$.Album') AS album,
  JSON_VALUE(@json, '$.Year') AS yr,
  JSON_VALUE(@json, '$.IsVinyl') AS isVinyl,
  JSON_VALUE(@json, '$.Members[0]') AS member1;
```

Here is the result of the previous query:

```
album                    yr     isVinyl  member1
--------------------     -----  ------   --------
Wish You Were Here       1975   true     Gilmour
```

Note that all returned values are strings; as already mentioned, the data type of the returned value is nvarchar.

The aim of the function is to extract scalar values. Therefore, it won't work if the JSON path specifies an array or an object. The following call with the JSON string in the previous example will return a NULL value:

```
DECLARE @json NVARCHAR(MAX) = N'{
"Album":"Wish You Were Here",
```

```
"Year":1975,
"IsVinyl":true,
"Members":["Gilmour","Waters","Wright","Mason"]
}';
SELECT
  JSON_VALUE(@json, '$.Members') AS member;
```

The JSON path `$.members` specifies an array and the function expects a scalar value. A null value will be returned even if the property specified with the path expression does not exist. As mentioned earlier, the JSON path expression has two modes: lax and strict. In the default lax mode, errors are suppressed and functions return NULL values or empty tables, while every unexpected or non-existing path raises a batch-level exception. The same call with the JSON path in strict mode would end up with an error:

```
SELECT
  JSON_VALUE(@json, 'strict $.Members') AS member;
```

Here is the error message:

```
Msg 13623, Level 16, State 1, Line 75
Scalar value cannot be found in the specified JSON path.
```

If the length of a JSON property value or string element is longer than 4,000, the function returns NULL. The next example demonstrates this by using two very long strings as values for two properties. The first one has 4,000 characters and the second is one character longer:

```
DECLARE @json NVARCHAR(MAX) = CONCAT('{"name":"', REPLICATE('A',4000),
'",}'),
@json4001 NVARCHAR(MAX) = CONCAT('{"name":"', REPLICATE('A',4001), '",}')
SELECT
  JSON_VALUE(@json, '$.name') AS name4000,
  JSON_VALUE(@json4001, '$.name') AS name4001;
```

The abbreviated result is here:

```
Name4000              name4001
--------------------  ----------
AAAAAAAAAAAAAAAAA...  NULL
```

You can see that `4001` is too much for `JSON_VALUE`, and the function returns NULL. If you specify strict in the previous example, the function returns an error:

```
DECLARE @json4001 NVARCHAR(MAX) = CONCAT('{"name":"', REPLICATE('A',4001),
'",}')
SELECT
  JSON_VALUE(@json4001, ' strict $.name') AS name4001;
```

Here is the error message:

```
Msg 13625, Level 16, State 1, Line 65
String value in the specified JSON path would be truncated.
```

This is a typical change in function behavior regarding the JSON path mode. Lax mode usually returns NULL and does not break the code, while strict mode raises a batch-level exception.

JSON_VALUE can be used in SELECT, WHERE, and ORDER clauses. In the following example, it is used in all three clauses:

```
SELECT
  PersonID,
  JSON_VALUE(UserPreferences, '$.timeZone') AS TimeZone,
  JSON_VALUE(UserPreferences, '$.table.pageLength') AS PageLength
FROM Application.People
WHERE JSON_VALUE(UserPreferences, '$.dateFormat') = 'yy-mm-dd'
  AND JSON_VALUE(UserPreferences, '$.theme') = 'blitzer'
ORDER BY JSON_VALUE(UserPreferences, '$.theme'), PersonID;
```

One important limitation of the JSON_VALUE function is that a variable as a second argument (JSON path) is not allowed. For instance, the following code won't work:

```
DECLARE @jsonPath NVARCHAR(10) = N'$.Album';
DECLARE @json NVARCHAR(200) = N'{
"Album":"Wish You Were Here",
"Year":1975
}';
SELECT
  JSON_VALUE(@json, @jsonPath) AS album;
```

The query fails with the following error message:

```
Msg 13610, Level 16, State 1, Line 137
The argument 2 of the "JSON_VALUE or JSON_QUERY" must be a string literal
```

This is a significant limitation; you need to provide the JSON path as a static value in advance and you cannot add or change it dynamically. If you think that this function would be more useful without this limitation, then you can vote for the related item *Don't restrict JSON_VALUE and JSON_QUERY to string literals only for the path* at the following web address: https://connect.microsoft.com/SQLServer/Feedback/Details/2235470.

JSON_QUERY

The JSON_QUERY function extracts a JSON fragment from the input JSON string for the specified JSON path. It returns a JSON object or an array; therefore, its output is JSON conforming. This function is complementary to the JSON_VALUE function.

JSON_QUERY always returns JSON conforming text. Thus, if you want to suggest to SQL Server that the string is JSON formatted, you should wrap it with this function.

The function has two input arguments:

- **Expression**: This is a variable or column containing JSON text.
- **Path**: This is a JSON path that specifies the object or the array to extract. This parameter is optional. If it's not specified, the whole input string will be returned.

The return type of the function is nvarchar(max) if the input string is defined as (n)varchar(max); otherwise, it is nvarchar(4000). As already mentioned, the function always returns a JSON conforming string.

If either the expression or the path is not valid, JSON_QUERY returns an error message saying that the JSON text or JSON path is not properly formatted.

In the following self-explanatory examples, how to use this function with different JSON path expressions is demonstrated:

```
DECLARE @json NVARCHAR(MAX) = N'{
"Album":"Wish You Were Here",
"Year":1975,
"IsVinyl":true,
"Songs" :[{"Title":"Shine On You Crazy Diamond","Writers":"Gilmour, Waters,
Wright"},
{"Title":"Have a Cigar","Writers":"Waters"},
{"Title":"Welcome to the Machine","Writers":"Waters"},
{"Title":"Wish You Were Here","Writers":"Gilmour, Waters"}],
"Members":{"Guitar":"David Gilmour","Bass Guitar":"Roger
Waters","Keyboard":"Richard Wright","Drums":"Nick Mason"}
}';
--get Songs JSON fragment (array)
SELECT JSON_QUERY(@json,'$.Songs');
--get Members SON fragment (object)
SELECT JSON_QUERY(@json,'$.Members');
--get fourth Song JSON fragment (object)
SELECT JSON_QUERY(@json,'$.Songs[3]');
```

Here is the result of these invocations:

```
[{"Title":"Shine On You Crazy Diamond","Writers":"Gilmour, Waters,
Wright"},
{"Title":"Have a Cigar","Writers":"Waters"},
{"Title":"Welcome to the Machine","Writers":"Waters"},
{"Title":"Wish You Were Here","Writers":"Gilmour, Waters"}]
{"Guitar":"David Gilmour","Bass Guitar":"Roger Waters","Keyboard":"Richard
Wright","Drums":"Nick Mason"}
{"Title":"Wish You Were Here","Writers":"Gilmour, Waters"}
```

You can see that the returned values are JSON objects and arrays. However, if you specify a value that is not an array or object, the function returns NULL in lax mode and an error in strict mode:

```
--get property value (number)
SELECT JSON_QUERY(@json,'$.Year');
--get property value (string)
SELECT JSON_QUERY(@json,'$.Songs[1].Title');
--get value for non-existing property
SELECT JSON_QUERY(@json,'$.Studios');
```

All three calls return NULL, whereas strict mode raises a batch-level exception:

```
SELECT JSON_QUERY(@json,'strict $.Year');
/*Result:
Msg 13624, Level 16, State 1, Line 54
Object or array cannot be found in the specified JSON path.
*/
--get value for non-existing property
SELECT JSON_QUERY(@json,'strict $.Studios');
/*Result:
Msg 13608, Level 16, State 5, Line 60
Property cannot be found on the specified JSON path
*/
```

You can also use JSON_QUERY to ensure data integrity of JSON data in a table column. For instance, the following check constraint ensures that all persons in the People table have the OtherLanguages property within the CustomFields column if this column has a value:

```
USE WideWorldImporters;
ALTER TABLE Application.People
ADD CONSTRAINT CHK_OtherLanguagesRequired
CHECK (JSON_QUERY(CustomFields, '$.OtherLanguages') IS NOT NULL OR
CustomFields IS NULL);
```

JSON_QUERY has the same restriction for the path argument as JSON_VALUE; only literals are allowed.

Modifying JSON data

You might sometimes need to update only a part of JSON data. In SQL Server 2016, you can modify JSON data using the JSON_MODIFY function. It allows you to:

- Update the value of an existing property
- Add a new element to an existing array
- Insert a new property and its value
- Delete a property based on a combination of modes and provided values

The function accepts three mandatory input arguments:

- **Expression**: This is a variable or column name containing JSON text
- **Path**: This is the JSON path expression with an optional modifier append
- **new_value**: This is the new value for the property specified in the path expression

The JSON_MODIFY function returns the updated JSON string. In the next subsections, you will see this function in action.

Adding a new JSON property

In the following code example, you add a new property named IsVinyl with the value true:

```
DECLARE @json NVARCHAR(MAX) = N'{
"Album":"Wish You Were Here",
"Year":1975
}';
PRINT JSON_MODIFY(@json, '$.IsVinyl', CAST(1 AS BIT));
```

You need to cast the value explicitly to the `BIT` data type; otherwise it will be surrounded by double quotas and interpreted as a string. Here is the result of the modification:

```
{
"Album":"Wish You Were Here",
"Year":1975,
"IsVinyl":true
}
```

Note that the JSON path expression is in default lax mode. By specifying strict mode, the function will return an error:

```
DECLARE @json NVARCHAR(MAX) = N'{
"Album":"Wish You Were Here",
"Year":1975
}';
PRINT JSON_MODIFY(@json, 'strict $.IsVinyl', CAST(1 AS BIT));
```

Strict mode always expects the property specified with the JSON path expression to exist. If it does not exist, it returns the following error message:

```
Msg 13608, Level 16, State 2, Line 34
Property cannot be found on the specified JSON path.
```

Be aware when you add a value that it is already JSON formatted. In the next example, assume you want to add a new property named `Members` and you have already prepared the whole JSON array:

```
DECLARE @json NVARCHAR(MAX) = N'{
"Album":"Wish You Were Here",
"Year":1975,
"IsVinyl":true
}';
DECLARE @members NVARCHAR(500) = N'["Gilmour","Waters","Wright","Mason"]';
PRINT JSON_MODIFY(@json, '$.Members', @members);
```

A new `Members` property has been added to the input JSON data, but our JSON conform value has been interpreted as text and therefore all special characters are escaped. Here is the modified input string:

```
{
"Album":"Wish You Were Here",
"Year":1975,
"IsVinyl":true,
"Members":"["Gilmour","Waters","Wright","Mason"]"
}
```

To avoid the escaping of JSON conforming text, you need to tell the function that the text is already JSON and escaping should not be performed. You can achieve this by wrapping the new value with the JSON_QUERY function:

```
DECLARE @json NVARCHAR(MAX) = N'{
"Album":"Wish You Were Here",
"Year":1975,
"IsVinyl":true
}';
DECLARE @members NVARCHAR(500) = N'["Gilmour","Waters","Wright","Mason"]';
PRINT JSON_MODIFY(@json, '$.Members', JSON_QUERY(@members));
```

As mentioned in the previous section, the JSON_QUERY function returns JSON conforming text and now SQL Server knows that escaping is not required. Here is the expected result:

```
{
"Album":"Wish You Were Here",
"Year":1975,
"IsVinyl":true,
"Members":["Gilmour","Waters","Wright","Mason"]
}
```

This is a drawback of the missing JSON data type. If you had it, it wouldn't be necessary to use JSON_QUERY and SQL Server would distinguish between JSON and string.

Updating the value for a JSON property

In the next examples, you will update the value of an existing property. You will start by updating the Year property from 1973 to 1975. Here is the code:

```
DECLARE @json NVARCHAR(MAX) = N'{
"Album":"Wish You Were Here",
"Year":1973
}';
PRINT JSON_MODIFY(@json, '$.Year', 1975);
PRINT JSON_MODIFY(@json, 'strict $.Year', 1975);
```

You invoked the function twice, to demonstrate using both JSON path modes: lax and strict. Here are the output strings:

```
{
"Album":"Wish You Were Here",
"Year":1975
}
{
"Album":"Wish You Were Here",
```

```
"Year":1975
}
```

You can see that there is no difference between lax and strict mode if the property specified with the path exists.

The following example demonstrates how to update a value of an array element within a JSON text. Assume you want to replace the first element of the Members array (Gilmour) with the value (Barrett):

```
DECLARE @json NVARCHAR(MAX) = N'{
"Album":"Wish You Were Here",
"Year":1975,
"Members":["Gilmour","Waters","Wright","Mason"]
}';
PRINT JSON_MODIFY(@json, '$.Members[0]', 'Barrett');
```

Here is the expected result:

```
{
"Album":"Wish You Were Here",
"Year":1975,
"Members":["Barrett","Waters","Wright","Mason"]
}
```

If you want to add a new element to an array, you have to use append. In the following example, you simply add another element in the Members array:

```
DECLARE @json NVARCHAR(MAX) = N'{
"Album":"Wish You Were Here",
"Year":1975,
"Members":["Gilmour","Waters","Wright","Mason"]
}';
PRINT JSON_MODIFY(@json, 'append $.Members', 'Barrett');
```

Here is the result:

```
{
"Album":"Wish You Were Here",
"Year":1975,
"Members":["Gilmour","Waters","Wright","Mason","Barrett"]
}
```

If you specify an index that is out of range or if the array does not exist, you will get:

- **Strict mode**: This shows an error message and no return value (batch level exception)
- **Lax mode**: This shows no error; the original input string is returned

To update a value of a JSON property to NULL, you have to use a JSON path in strict mode. Use the following code to update the Year property from the input JSON string to a NULL value:

```
DECLARE @json NVARCHAR(MAX) = N'{
"Album":"Wish You Were Here",
"Year":1975,
"Members":["Gilmour","Waters","Wright","Mason"]
}';
PRINT JSON_MODIFY(@json, 'strict $.Year', NULL);
```

Here is the output.

```
{
"Album":"Wish You Were Here",
"Year":null,
"Members":["Gilmour","Waters","Wright","Mason"]
}
```

Removing a JSON property

To remove a property from the input JSON string, you have to use a JSON path expression in lax mode. You will repeat the preceding code, but this time in lax mode:

```
DECLARE @json NVARCHAR(MAX) = N'{
"Album":"Wish You Were Here",
"Year":1975,
"Members":["Gilmour","Waters","Wright","Mason"]
}';
PRINT JSON_MODIFY(@json, '$.Year', NULL);
```

When you observe the result of this action, you can see that the Year property does not exist anymore:

```
{
"Album":"Wish You Were Here",
"Members":["Gilmour","Waters","Wright","Mason"]
}
```

By taking this approach, you can remove only properties and their values. You cannot remove an array element. The following code will not remove the Waters element from the JSON array property Members; it will actually update it to NULL:

```
DECLARE @json NVARCHAR(MAX) = N'{
"Album":"Wish You Were Here",
"Year":1975,
"Members":["Gilmour","Waters","Wright","Mason"]
}';
PRINT JSON_MODIFY(@json, '$.Members[1]', NULL);
```

As you can see in the result:

```
{
"Album":"Wish You Were Here",
"Year":1975,
"Members":["Gilmour",null,"Wright","Mason"]
}
```

If you want to remove the Waters element, you can use the following code:

```
DECLARE @json NVARCHAR(MAX) = N'{
"Album":"Wish You Were Here",
"Year":1975,
"Members":["Gilmour","Waters","Wright","Mason"]
}';
PRINT JSON_MODIFY(@json, '$.Members',
JSON_QUERY('["Gilmour","Wright","Mason"]'));
```

And finally, the expected result:

```
{
"Album":"Wish You Were Here",
"Year":1975,
"Members":["Gilmour","Wright","Mason"]
}
```

Multiple changes

You can change only one property at a time; for multiple changes you need multiple calls. In this example, you want to update the IsVinyl property to false, add a new property Recorded, and add another element called Barrett to the Members property:

```
DECLARE @json NVARCHAR(MAX) = N'{
"Album":"Wish You Were Here",
"Year":1975,
```

```
"IsVinyl":true,
"Members":["Gilmour","Waters","Wright","Mason"]
}';
PRINT JSON_MODIFY(JSON_MODIFY(JSON_MODIFY(@json, '$.IsVinyl', CAST(0 AS
BIT)), '$.Recorded', 'Abbey Road Studios'), 'append $.Members', 'Barrett');
```

Here is the output:

```
{
"Album":"Wish You Were Here",
"Year":1975,
"IsVinyl":false,
"Members":["Gilmour","Waters","Wright","Mason","Barrett"],
"Recorded":"Abbey Road Studios"
}
```

Performance considerations

One of the main concerns about JSON in SQL Server 2016 is performance. As mentioned, unlike XML, JSON is not fully supported; there is no JSON data type. Data in XML columns is stored as **binary large objects (BLOBs)**. SQL Server supports two types of XML indexes that avoid parsing the whole data at runtime to evaluate a query and allow efficient query processing. Without an index, these BLOBs are shredded at runtime to evaluate a query. As mentioned several times, there is no JSON data type; JSON is stored as simple Unicode text and the text has to be interpreted at runtime to evaluate a JSON query. This can lead to slow reading and writing performance for large JSON documents. The primary XML index indexes all tags, values, and paths within the XML instances in an XML column. The primary XML index is a shredded and persisted representation of the XML BLOBs in the XML data type column. For each XML **BLOB** in the column, the index creates several rows of data. The number of rows in the index is approximately equal to the number of nodes in the XML BLOB.

Since JSON is stored as text, it will always be interpreted. On JSON columns that are not larger than 1,700 bytes, you could create a non-clustered index, or use them as an included column without the limit.

Without a dedicated data type and storage, performance and options for JSON query improvements in SQL Server 2016 are limited: you can use computed columns and create indexes on them, or use the benefits of full-text indexes. However, you can expect performance problems during the processing of large amounts of JSON data in SQL Server 2016.

Indexes on computed columns

The following code example creates a sample table with a JSON column and populates it with values from the `Application.People` table:

```
USE WideWorldImporters;
DROP TABLE IF EXISTS dbo.T1;
CREATE TABLE dbo.T1(
id INT NOT NULL,
info NVARCHAR(2000) NOT NULL,
CONSTRAINT PK_T1 PRIMARY KEY CLUSTERED(id)
);

INSERT INTO dbo.T1(id, info)
SELECT PersonID, info FROM Application.People t1
CROSS APPLY(
  SELECT (
    SELECT t2.FullName, t2.EmailAddress, t2.PhoneNumber,      t2.FaxNumber
FROM Application.People t2 WHERE t2.PersonID = t1.PersonID FOR      JSON
AUTO, WITHOUT_ARRAY_WRAPPER
  ) info
  ) x
```

Assume you want to return rows that have the `Vilma Niva` value for the `FullName` property. Since this is a scalar value, you can use the `JSON_VALUE` function. Before you execute the code, ensure that the actual execution plan will be displayed as well (on the **Query** menu, click on **Include Actual Execution Plan**, or click on the **Include Actual Execution Plan** toolbar button). Now execute the following code:

```
SELECT id, info
FROM dbo.T1
WHERE JSON_VALUE(info,'$.FullName') = 'Vilma Niva';
```

The execution plan for the query is shown in *Figure 5.8*:

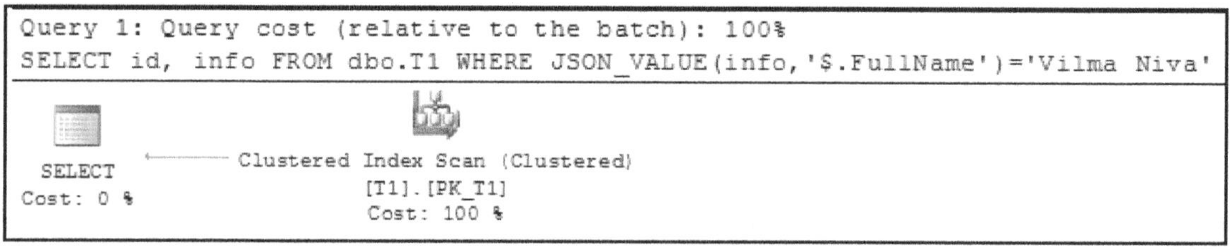

```
Query 1: Query cost (relative to the batch): 100%
SELECT id, info FROM dbo.T1 WHERE JSON_VALUE(info,'$.FullName')='Vilma Niva'
```

SELECT
Cost: 0 %

Clustered Index Scan (Clustered)
[T1].[PK_T1]
Cost: 100 %

Figure 5.8: Execution plan without computed columns

The plan shows that a `Clustered Index Scan` is performed; SQL Server was not able to search for full names within the JSON column in an efficient manner.

To improve the performance of the query, you can create a computed column by using the same expression as in its `WHERE` clause and then a non-clustered index on it:

```
ALTER TABLE dbo.T1 ADD FullName AS  CAST(JSON_VALUE(info, '$.FullName') AS
NVARCHAR(200));
CREATE INDEX IX1 ON dbo.T1(FullName);
```

When you execute the same query again, the execution plan is changed:

```
SELECT id, info
FROM dbo.T1
WHERE JSON_VALUE(info,'$.FullName') = 'Vilma Niva';
```

A newly created index is used and the plan is more efficient, as shown in *Figure 5.9*:

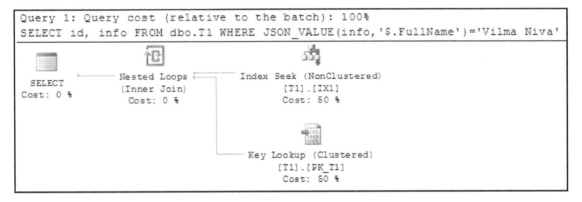

Figure 5.9: Execution plan using the index on the computed column

Of course, this will work only for a particular JSON path, in this case for the `FullName` property only. For the other properties, you would need to create additional computed columns and indexes on them. In the case of XML indexes, all nodes and values are covered; they are not related to particular values.

An important feature of JSON indexes is that they are collation-aware. The result of the `JSON_VALUE` function is a text value that inherits its collation from the input expression. Therefore, values in the index are ordered using the collation rules defined in the source columns.

By using indexes on computed columns, you can improve performance for frequently used queries.

Full-text indexes

One of the advantages of the fact that JSON data is stored as text in SQL Server is that you can use full-text search features. With computed columns, as demonstrated in the previous section, you can index only one property. To index all JSON properties (actually, to simulate this) you can use full-text indexes.

To demonstrate how full-text searching can improve JSON query performance, you first create a full-text catalog and index it in the sample table that you created earlier in this section:

```
USE WideWorldImporters;
CREATE FULLTEXT CATALOG ftc AS DEFAULT;
CREATE FULLTEXT INDEX ON dbo.T1(info) KEY INDEX PK_T1 ON ftc;
```

Now, after you have created a full-text index, you can execute JSON queries to check whether they can use full-text index benefits. You need to use the CONTAINS predicate; it can identify rows where a word is near another word. Here is the query:

```
SELECT id, info
FROM dbo.T1
WHERE CONTAINS(info,'NEAR(FullName,"Vilma")');
```

The execution plan for the query shown in *Figure 5.10* clearly demonstrates that full-text index was helpful for this query.:

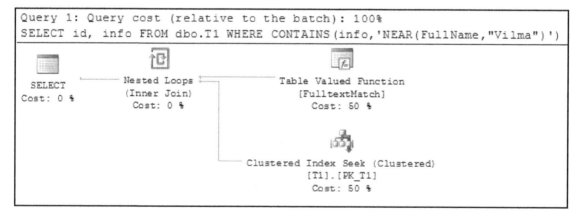

Figure 5.10: Execution plan with full-text index on the FullName property

To ensure that the same index can improve performance for JSON queries searching the other JSON properties and not only `FullName` (as in the case of the index on the computed column), let us execute another query that searches the `PhoneNumber` property:

```
SELECT id, info
FROM dbo.T1
WHERE CONTAINS(info,'NEAR(PhoneNumber,"(209) 555-0103")');
```

The execution plan is the same as for the previous query, as you can see in *Figure 5.11*:

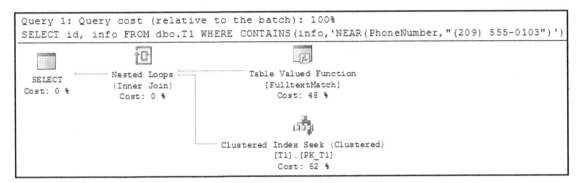

Figure 5.11: Execution plan with full-text index on the PhoneNumber property

The same index covers both queries. Unfortunately, JSON path expressions are not supported in the `CONTAINS` predicate; you can only search for property values, but it is better than scanning the whole table.

You can store and process small and moderate amounts of JSON data within SQL Server with good support of JSON functions and acceptable performance. However, if your JSON documents are large and you need to search them intensively, you should use a NoSQL solution, such as DocumentDB.

Ensure that you have dropped the table used in this example:

```
USE WideWorldImporters;
DROP TABLE IF EXISTS dbo.T1;
```

Summary

This chapter explored JSON support in SQL Server 2016. It is not as robust and deep as is the case with XML—there is no native data type, no optimized storage, and therefore you cannot create JSON indexes to improve performance. Thus, we are talking about built-in and not native JSON support.

However, even with built-in support, it is easy and handy to integrate JSON data in SQL Server. For most of JSON data processing, it would be acceptable. For large JSON documents stored in large database tables, it would be more appropriate to use DocumentDB or other NoSQL based solutions.

In this chapter, you learned the following topics:

- SQL Server 2016 brings built-in support for JSON data; unlike XML, there is no native data type
- Use the FOR JSON extension to generate JSON from data in a tabular format
- Converting JSON data into a tabular format by using the OPENJSON rowset function
- Parsing, querying, and modifying JSON data with a function
- Improving the performance of JSON data processing by using indexes on computed columns and full-text indexes
- Limitations of JSON implementation in SQL Server 2016

6
Stretch Database

Stretch Database (Stretch DB) is a new feature in SQL Server 2016 that allows you to move data or a portion of data transparently and securely from your local database to the cloud (Microsoft Azure). All you need to do is mark the tables that you want to migrate, and the data movement is done transparently and securely. The intention of this feature is to let companies store their old or infrequently used data on the cloud. Companies need to store data locally and operate with active data only, thus reducing the cost and using their resources more effectively. This feature is great and very promising, but there are many limitations that reduce its usability.

In this chapter, we will cover the following points:

- Stretch DB architecture
- How to enable Stretch DB
- How to select tables or part of tables for migration
- Managing and troubleshooting Stretch DB
- When and under what circumstances should you use Stretch DB?

Stretch Database architecture

When you enable Stretch Database for an on-premise SQL Server 2016 database, SQL Server automatically creates a new Stretch Database in MS Azure SQL Database as an external source and a remote endpoint for the database.

When you query the database, the SQL Server database engine runs the query against the local or remote database, depending on the data location. Queries against Stretch-enabled tables return both local and remote data by default. This is completely transparent to the database user. This means that you can use Stretch DB without changing Transact-SQL code in your queries, procedures, or applications. You can stretch an entire table or a portion of table data. The data migration is done asynchronously and transparently. In addition, Stretch Database ensures that no data is lost if a failure occurs during migration. It also has retry logic to handle connection issues that may occur during migration. *Figure 6.1* illustrates the Stretch DB architecture:

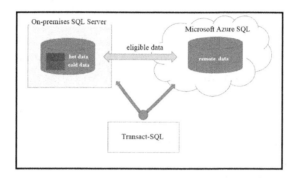

Figure 6.1: Stretch DB architecture

Data can be in three stages:

- **Local data**: Local data is data in the table that remains in the on-premise instance. This is usually frequently used or hot data.
- **Staging (eligible data)**: Eligible data is data marked for migration but not migrated yet.
- **Remote data**: Remote data is data that has already been migrated. This data resides in Microsoft Azure SQL Database and is rarely used.

Stretch Database does not support stretching to another SQL Server instance. You can stretch a SQL Server database only to Azure SQL Database.

Is this for you?

When SQL Server 2016 RTM was released, you could use the tool *Stretch Database Advisor* to identify databases and tables that were candidates for the Stretch DB feature. It was a component of the *SQL Server 2016 Upgrade Advisor,* and by using it, you were also able to identify constraints and blocking issues that prevented the use of the feature.

However, this tool does not exist anymore and it has been replaced by the *Microsoft® Data Migration Assistant*. But why I am mentioning this deprecated tool? The *Stretch Database Advisor* checks all tables in the database and creates a report showing the stretching capabilities of each table. I have used it to check which tables in the Microsoft sample SQL Server database `AdventureWorks` are ready for stretching. The results might look disappointing: there is not a single table that you can stretch! However, as you will see later in this chapter, the Stretch DB feature is not designed for all tables; it is for special ones.

Data Migration Assistant does not have a separate functionality for Stretch DB advises. It analyzes your database and helps you to upgrade it to a new SQL Server version or to Azure SQL Database by detecting compatibility issues that can impact database functionality on your new database version. It also recommends performance and reliability improvements for your target environment. Stretch DB is only one of the storage improvements. You can download **Data Migration Assistant v3.0** from `https://www.micro soft.com/en-us/download/details.aspx?id=53595`.

Using Data Migration Assistant

In this section, you will use **Data Migration Assistant** to see what you should expect for your databases when you migrate them to SQL Server 2016 or Azure SQL Database. This is a standalone program and you can run it by executing the `Dma.exe` file in the default install directory `C:Program FilesMicrosoft Data Migration Assistant`. When you start the tool, you should see an intro screen, as shown in *Figure 6.2*:

Figure 6.2: Data Migration Assistant introduction screen

To start a project, you need to click on the **+** symbol and the new project form appears. On the new project screen, choose **Assessment** as **Project type**, type `AdvWorks_StretchDB` in the **Project name** field, and choose **SQL Server** as **Target server type** (**Source server type** is preselected to **SQL Server**), as displayed in *Figure 6.3*:

Figure 6.3: Data Migration Assistant New Project

After you are done, click on the **Create** button and you will see the next screen, similar to the one shown in *Figure 6.4*:

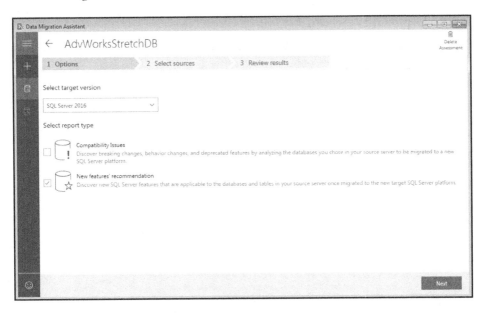

Figure 6.4: Data Migration Assistant Select target version

On this screen, you can choose the target SQL Server version. In the dropdown, all versions from 2012 are available; you should, of course, choose **SQL Server 2016**. In addition to this, you can select the report type. This time you will choose **New features' recommendation** since you want to see which new features Data Migration Assistant recommends to you and not potential compatibility issues.

You then need to click on the **Next** button, connect to a SQL Server 2014 instance, and select the desired databases. In this example, I have selected the Microsoft former standard sample databases `AdventureWorks` and `AdventureWorksDW` that I have restored. If you don't have these two databases, you can choose any other database, but you will most probably end up with different results.

After you have established the connection with the SQL Server 2014 instance, you need to choose the databases that should be analyzed by Data Migration Assistant. As mentioned, choose `AdventureWorks2014` and `AdventureWorksDW2014`. You should see a screen similar to the one shown in *Figure 6.5*:

Figure 6.5: Data Migration Assistant: choose databases for analyzing

When you click on the **Add** button, the selected databases are added to the sources collection. You'll get another screen, where you can start the assessment by clicking on the **Start Assessment** button. The analysis takes less than a minute, and *Figure 6.6* shows its results for the `AdventureWorks2014` database:

Figure 6.6. Data Migration Assistant Review results for the AdventureWorks2014 database

Stretch DB-related recommendations are located under the **Storage** tab. In the case of the `AdventureWorks2014` database, two tables are listed as tables that would benefit from using the Stretch DB feature: `Sales.SalesOrderDetail` and `Production.TransactionHistory`.

However, both of them have properties that prevent the use of Stretch DB, so you can conclude that this feature is irrelevant for the `AdventureWorks2014` database. The result of the analysis for the `AdventureWorksDW2014` looks better. It is shown in *Figure 6.7*:

Figure 6.7: Data Migration Assistant Review results for the AdventureWorksDW2014 database

Data Migration Assistant has found one table (`dbo.FactProductInventory`) that is ready to use the Stretch Database feature. It does not mention the other tables in the report—just three tables from two selected databases. At this point, I need to mention again that the same action with the deprecated tool Stretch Database Advisor reported that not a single table (out of 70 tables) in the `AdventureWorks2014` database is ready for using the Stretch DB feature, although some of them are very simple and have only a few rows. However, in data warehouse databases, tables seem to be more stretch-friendly.

Stretch Database will give you benefits with your data warehouse databases, especially with historical data that is taking up space and is rarely used. On the other hand, this feature might not be eligible for your OLTP system due to the table limitations that your OLTP system has. Now, it is finally time to see in detail what these limitations are.

Limitations of using Stretch Database

As you saw in the previous section, there are many limitations when you work with Stretch Database. You can distinguish between limitations that the prevent usage of Stretch Database and limitations in database tables that are enabled for stretching.

Limitations that prevent you from enabling the Stretch DB feature for a table

In this section, you will see the limitations that prevent you from using Stretch DB. They can be divided into table, column, and index limitations.

Table limitations

You cannot enable the Stretch DB feature for any SQL Server table. A table should have Stretch DB-friendly properties. The following list shows the table properties that prevent the use of the Stretch DB feature:

- It is a memory-optimized table
- It is a file table
- It contains `FILESTREAM` data
- It uses `Change Data Capture` or `Change Tracking` features
- It has more than 1,023 columns or more than 998 indexes
- Tables referenced with a foreign key
- It is referenced by indexed views
- It contains full-text indexes

The list is not so short, but let's see how huge these limitations are in practice. Despite their power and a completely new technology stack behind them, memory-optimized tables are still not in use intensively. From my experience, I can say that most companies still don't use memory-optimized tables in production environments due to the lack of use cases for them, hardware resources, or even the knowledge required for their implementation and configuration. In addition to this, memory-optimized tables usually store hot data, data that is frequently needed and whose content is not intended to be sent to the cloud. Therefore, you cannot say that the first limitation is a huge one. You will spend more time on memory-optimized tables later in this book (in `Chapter 11`, *Introducing SQL Server In-Memory OLTP* and `Chapter 12`, *In-Memory OLTP Improvements in SQL Server 2016*).

File Table and FILESTREAM tables appear frequently in the list of limitations for new SQL Server features. The same is true for tables using Change Data Capture or Change Tracking features. They are simply not compatible with many other features since they address specific use cases. Therefore, I am not surprised to see them in this list. Full-text indexes and indexed views also prevent Stretch DB usage. From my experience, in companies that I have worked with or where I was involved as a consultant, less than 10% of tables belong to these categories. According to all of these limitations, I would say that the potential of Stretch DB is slightly reduced, but not significantly. **However, the most important limitation is that a table cannot be referenced with a foreign key**. This is an implementation of database integrity and many tables are and should be referenced with foreign keys. Therefore, this is a serious limitation for Stretch DB usage and significantly reduces the number of potential tables that can be stretched.

 You should not disable foreign key relationships in order to use the Stretch DB feature! I would never suggest removing any database object or attribute that implements data integrity to gain performance or storage benefits.

However, this is just the beginning; more limitations will come in the next subsection.

Column limitations

Even if your table does not violate constraints from the preceding table of limitations, it is still far away from fulfilling the conditions for stretching. The following properties and characteristics of table columns don't support the Stretch DB feature:

- Unsupported data types: Deprecated large data types (text, ntext, and image), XML, timestamp, sql_variant, spatial data types (geometry and geography), hierarchyId, user-defined CLR data types
- Computed columns
- Default constraints
- Check constraints

Let's repeat a similar analysis of the reduced potential of Stretch DB for the items from this list. I think that Microsoft has a balanced approach with deprecated data types; they are not removed in order to prevent the breaking of changes in legacy code, but all new features don't support them. This is completely correct and it should not be considered a limitation.

The other unsupported data types are used rarely and do not represent a huge limitation.

 You can find user-defined CLR data types in a list of limitations for almost all SQL Server features in recent releases. This is also one of the reasons they are not so popular or frequently used.

However, the most important limitation in this list is that a table column in a Stretch Database cannot have a default or check constraint. **This is a huge limitation and significantly reduces the usage and importance of the Stretch DB feature!**

Also, as mentioned before, you should not remove database objects created to implement database integrity just to enable Stretch DB. Default constraints and foreign keys are the reasons why there is not a single table in the `AdventureWorks2014` database that is ready for stretching.

Limitations for Stretch-enabled tables

If your table survives these limitations and you have enabled it for stretching, you should be aware of these additional constraints:

- Uniqueness is not enforced for `UNIQUE` constraints and `PRIMARY KEY` constraints in the Azure table that contains the migrated data.
- You cannot `UPDATE` or `DELETE` rows that have been migrated or rows that are eligible for migration in a Stretch-enabled table or in a view that includes Stretch-enabled tables.
- You cannot `INSERT` rows into a Stretch-enabled table on a linked server.
- You cannot create an index for a view that includes Stretch-enabled tables.
- Filters on SQL Server indexes are not propagated to the remote table.
- These limitations are not unexpected; the Azure portion of data is automatically managed and it should be protected from direct access and changes. Therefore, these limitations are acceptable, especially compared to all those listed in the previous sections.

Use cases for Stretch Database

With so many limitations, finding use cases for Stretch DB does not seem to be an easy task. You would need tables without constraints and rare data types that are not involved in relations with other tables and that don't use some special SQL Server features. Where to find them? As potential candidates for stretching, you should consider historical or auditing and logging tables.

Archiving of historical data

Historical or auditing data is commonly produced automatically by database systems and does not require constraints to guarantee data integrity. In addition to this, it is usually in large data sets. Therefore, historical and auditing data can be a candidate for using the Stretch DB feature. SQL Server 2016 introduced support for system-versioned temporal tables. They are implemented as a pair of tables: a current and a historical table. One of the requirements for historical tables is that they cannot have any constraints. **Therefore, historical tables used in system-versioned temporal tables are ideal candidates for stretching**. Temporal tables are covered in Chapter 7, *Temporal Tables*.

Archiving of logging tables

Sometimes, developers decide to store application and service logging information in database tables. Such tables usually have no constraints, since writing to log must be as fast as possible. They are also possible candidates for using the Stretch DB feature.

Testing Azure SQL database

Small or medium companies that are considering whether to use the cloud or to move data completely to it can use Stretch DB to start using Azure SQL database. They can learn about data management in Azure and collect experience and then decide whether they need to delegate more or their entire data to the cloud.

Enabling Stretch Database

Before you select some tables for stretching, you need to enable the feature on the instance level. Like many other new features, it is disabled by default. To enable it, you need to execute the following statements:

```
EXEC sys.sp_configure N'remote data archive', '1';
RECONFIGURE;
GO
```

Actually, you have to allow remote data archiving; there is no enabling Stretch Database option. Anyway, after enabling it on the instance level, you can choose a database and enable the feature at the database level.

Enabling Stretch Database at the database level

If the feature is enabled at the instance level and you have enough database permissions (db_owner or CONTROL DATABASE), the next step is to enable Stretch DB at the database level. Of course, before you enable it, you need to have a valid Azure account and subscription. You also need to create and configure firewall rules to allow your Azure database to communicate with your local server. In this section, you will enable the Stretch DB feature for a new database. Use this code to create a database named Mila:

```
DROP DATABASE IF EXISTS Mila; --Ensure that you create a new, empty
database
GO
CREATE DATABASE Mila;
GO
```

Since the database is new and has no tables, it does not violate the limitations listed in the previous section. You can enable the Stretch Database feature at the database level by using wizard or with Transact-SQL.

Enabling Stretch Database by using wizard

You can use the **Enable Database for Stretch** wizard to configure a database for Stretch Database. To launch it, you need to right-click on the newly created Mila database in **SQL Server Management Studio (SSMS)**, and from the right-click context menu, select **Tasks | Stretch | Enable** respectively. When you launch the wizard, you should get the screen shown in *Figure 6.8*:

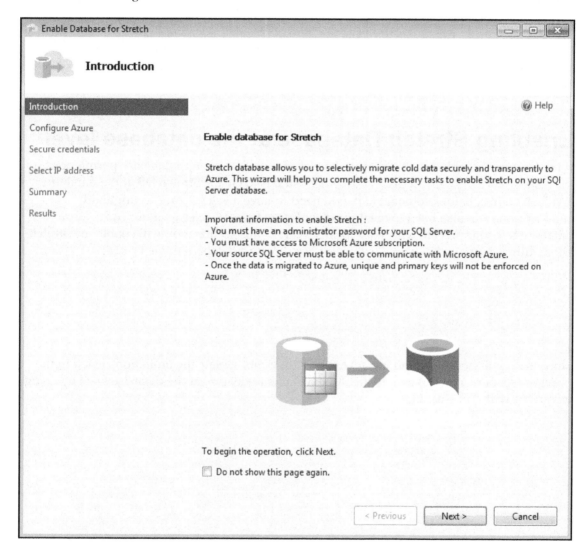

Figure 6.8: Enable Database for Search Wizard – Introduction Page

You can see an intro screen that describes what you can achieve with the Stretch Database feature and what you need to use it. Since your database has no tables, the second section of the wizard is **Configure Azure**. You are asked to enter your Azure credentials and to connect to Azure. The screen is shown in *Figure 6.9*:

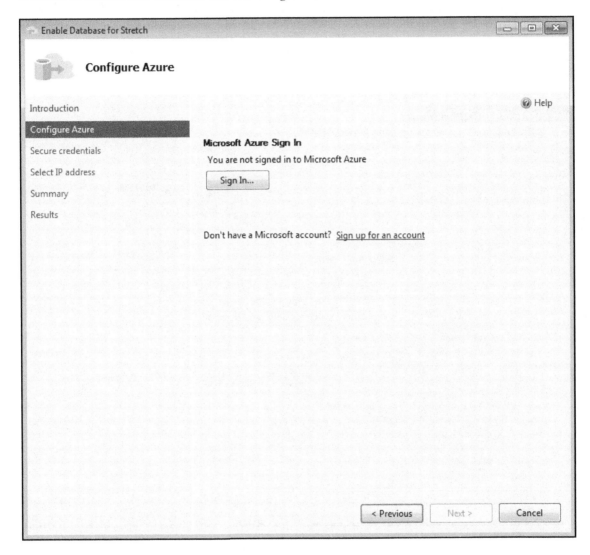

Figure 6.9: Enable Database for Search Wizard – Configure Azure page

After signing in to Azure, you should select one of your Azure subscriptions and an appropriate Azure region. Create a new or choose an existing Azure server, as shown in *Figure 6.10*:

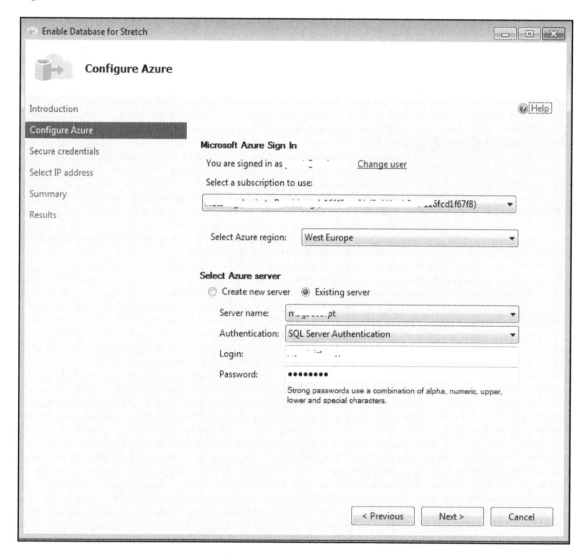

Figure 6.10: Enable Database for Search Wizard – sign in to Azure and select subscription and server

The next part of the wizard is **Secure credentials**. The wizard lets you create a database master key (if your database does not have one) in order to protect the database credentials and connection information stored in your SQL Server database. Database security is covered in detail in Chapter 8, *Tightening the Security*. The appropriate screen is shown in *Figure 6.11*:

Figure 6.11: Enable Database for Search Wizard – Secure credentials

As already mentioned, you need to create Azure firewall rules to let your Azure SQL database communicate with your local SQL Server database. You can define a range of IP addresses with the **Enable Database for Stretch** wizard's page **Select IP address**, as shown in *Figure 6.12*:

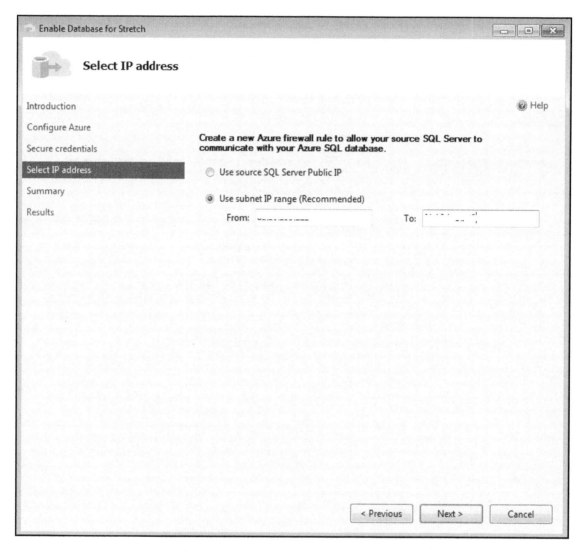

Figure 6.12: Enable Database for Search Wizard – Select IP address

And the tour is almost done. The next screen is **Summary** and it displays what you have already selected and entered, but it also provides an estimated price for the Stretch DB setup. *Figure 6.13* shows the **Summary** screen:

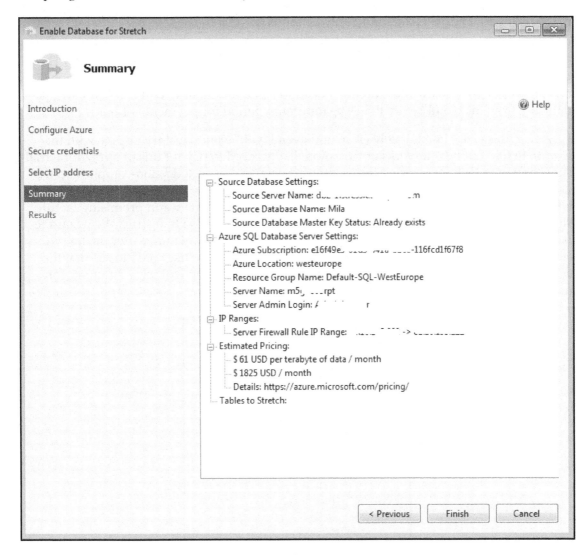

Figure 6.13: Enable Database for Search Wizard – Summary

As you can see, the **Summary** screen brings one very important piece of information to you: the estimated price for enabling the Stretch DB feature. The **Estimated Pricing** section in the summary report is a bit strange: it shows two prices: $61 USD per TB per month and 1,825 USD per month. If you enable Stretch DB for your database with no tables, you would need to pay at least 1,825 USD per month! It does not seem to be cheap at all for an empty database. However, there is also a third piece of information in that section—a link to the pricing page at Microsoft Azure—and you can find more details about pricing there. The pricing is covered later in this chapter, in the *SQL Server Stretch Database pricing* section. For now, it is enough to know that you don't need to pay a full month's cost if you remove your database from the cloud before that. The minimum period for payment is 1 hour.

However, this is not immediately clear, and even if you want to just try or play with the feature to find out how it works or to explore it, you need to pay for this or apply for a trial subscription (which involves giving credit card details). I expected a non-complicated trial version with limited functionalities but without required registration and payment data, where I can check and learn about the feature. Stretch DB as a new and promising feature should be easy to try. Now it is time to click on the **Finish** button to instruct the wizard to perform the final step in the process of enabling the Stretch DB feature. After the last wizard action is done, the stretch database is created in Azure. You can use SSMS to see that the action was successful. When you choose the database Mila, you will see a different icon near to the database name, as displayed in *Figure 6.14*:

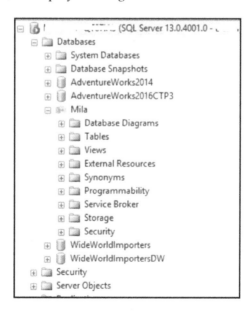

Figure 6.14: Database in SSMS with enabled Stretch DB feature

After the feature is enabled for your sample database, you should not expect anything, since there are no tables in it. You will create a table and continue to play with stretching later in this chapter.

Enabling Stretch Database by using Transact-SQL

You can enable the Stretch DB feature by using Transact-SQL only. As you saw in the previous section, to enable Stretch DB, you need to create and secure communication infrastructure between our local database and the Azure server. Therefore, you need to accomplish the following three tasks:

- Create a database master key to protect server credentials
- Create a database credential
- Define the Azure server

The following code creates a database master key for the sample database *Mila*:

```
USE Mila;
CREATE MASTER KEY ENCRYPTION BY PASSWORD='<very secure password>'; --you
need to put your password here
```

Next, we create a credential. This is saved authentication information that is required to connect to external resources. You need a credential for only one database; therefore you should create a database-scoped credential:

```
CREATE DATABASE SCOPED CREDENTIAL MilaStretchCredential
WITH
IDENTITY = 'Vasilije',
SECRET = '<very secure password>'; --you need to put your password here
```

Now you can finally enable the Stretch DB feature by using the ALTER DATABASE statement. You need to set REMOTE_DATA_ARCHIVE and define two parameters: Azure server and just created database scoped credential. Here is the code that can be used to enable the Stretch DB feature for the database Mila:

```
ALTER DATABASE Mila
    SET REMOTE_DATA_ARCHIVE = ON
        (
            SERVER = '<address of your Azure server>,
            CREDENTIAL = [MilaStretchCredential]
        );
```

With this action, you have created an infrastructure, necessary for communication between your local database and the Azure server that will hold the stretched data. Note that this action can take a few minutes. When I executed the command, it took about 3 minutes, as shown in *Figure 6.15*:

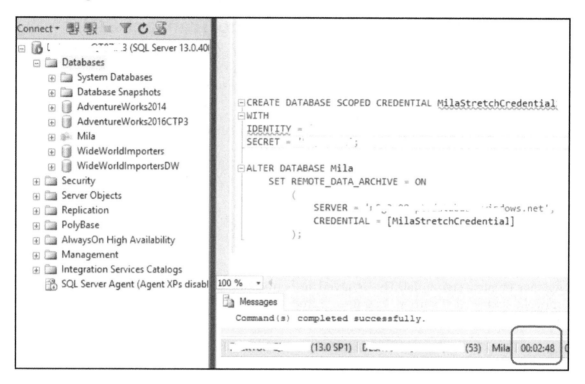

Figure 6.15: Enabling Stretch Database by Using Transact-SQL

The next and final step is to select and enable tables for stretching.

Enabling Stretch Database for a table

To enable Stretch DB for a table, you can also choose between the wizard and Transact-SQL. You can migrate an entire table or just part of a table. If your cold data is stored in a separated table, you can migrate the entire table; otherwise you must specify a filter function to define which rows should be migrated. To enable the Stretch DB feature for a table, you must be a member of the db_owner role. In this section, you will create a new table in the Mila database, populate it with a few rows, and enable it for stretching. Use this code to create and populate the table:

```
USE Mila;
CREATE TABLE dbo.T1 (
id INT NOT NULL,
c1 VARCHAR(20) NOT NULL,
c2 DATETIME NOT NULL,
CONSTRAINT PK_T1 PRIMARY KEY CLUSTERED (id)
);
INSERT INTO dbo.T1 (id, c1, c2) VALUES
    (1, 'Benfica Lisbon','20160515'),
    (2, 'Manchester United','20160602'),
    (3, 'Rapid Vienna','20160528'),
    (4, 'Juventus Torino','20160625'),
    (5, 'Red Star Belgrade','20160625');
```

In the next sections, you will enable and use the Stretch DB feature for the T1 table. Assume that you want to move all rows from this table with a value in the c2 column that is older than 1st June 2016 to the cloud.

Enabling Stretch DB for a table by using wizard

You can create a new table with the Stretch DB feature enabled or enable it for an existing table using the **Enable Table for Stretch** wizard. To launch it, you need to navigate to the T1 table under the database Mila in SQL Server Management Studio (SSMS). Then, after right-clicking, you need to select the option **Tasks/Stretch/Enable** respectively. You should get a screen as shown in *Figure 6.16*:

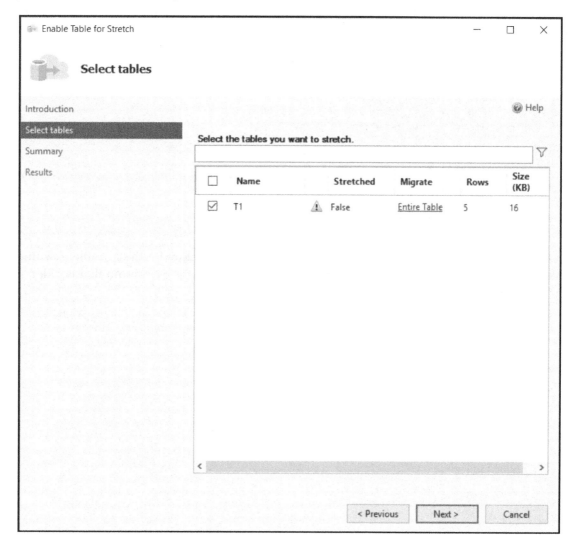

Figure 6.16: Enable Table for Stretch Wizard – Select tables

As you can see, T1 can be selected for stretching, since it meets the Stretch DB requirements discussed in the previous sections. You can choose to migrate the entire table or (by clicking on the link **Entire Table)** only a part of it. When you click on the link, you'll get a screen similar to the one shown in *Figure 6.17*:

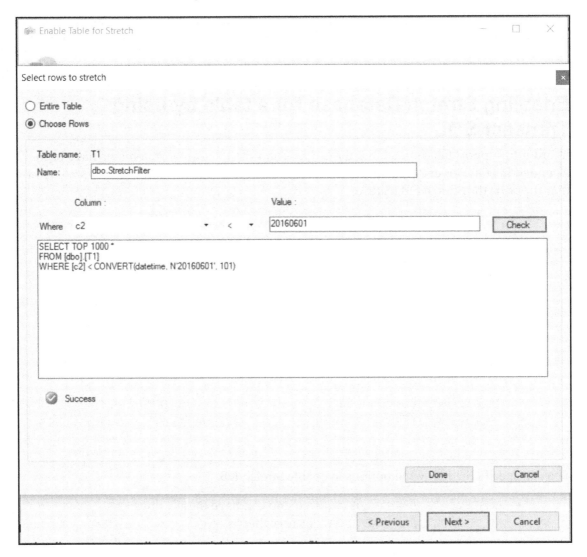

Figure 6.17: Enable Table for Stretch Wizard – Select rows to stretch

You see a query builder that can help you to write the correct filter function. Filter function is used to define which rows have to be migrated to the cloud. In this example, you are going to return all rows from the T1 table, where the value in the c2 column is less than 2016/06/01.

However, developers find query builders a bit clumsy, and most of them prefer to work with Transact-SQL. In the next section, you will see how to use Transact-SQL to configure Stretch DB.

Enabling Stretch Database for a table by using Transact-SQL

In order to support table stretching, the CREATE and ALTER TABLE statements have been extended in SQL Server 2016. Here is the syntax extension for the ALTER TABLE statement that supports the Stretch DB feature:

```
<stretch_configuration> ::=
    {
      SET (
        REMOTE_DATA_ARCHIVE
        {
            = ON (  <table_stretch_options>  )
          | = OFF_WITHOUT_DATA_RECOVERY ( MIGRATION_STATE = PAUSED )
          | ( <table_stretch_options> [, ...n] )
        }
          )
    }
<table_stretch_options> ::=
    {
     [ FILTER_PREDICATE = { null | table_predicate_function } , ]
       MIGRATION_STATE = { OUTBOUND | INBOUND | PAUSED }
    }
```

You can specify the following options to enable Stretch DB:

- REMOTE_DATA_ARCHIVE is required and can have these values: ON, OFF_WITHOUT_DATA_RECOVERY or no value.
- MIGRATION_STATE is also mandatory and can have one of the following values: OUTBOUND, INBOUND, or PAUSED.
- FILTER_PREDICATE is optional and is used to define the part of the data that needs to be migrated. If it's not specified, the entire table will be moved.

If your table contains both hot and cold data, you can specify a filter predicate to select the rows that should be migrated. The filter predicate is an inline table-valued function. Its parameters are identifiers for stretch table columns. At least one parameter is required. Here is the function syntax:

```
CREATE FUNCTION dbo.fn_stretchpredicate(@column1 datatype1, @column2
datatype2 [, ...n])
RETURNS TABLE
WITH SCHEMABINDING
AS
RETURN   SELECT 1 AS is_eligible
         WHERE <predicate>
```

The function returns either a non-empty result or no result set. In the first case, the row is eligible to be migrated, otherwise it remains in the local system.

Note that the function is defined with the SCHEMABINDING option to prevent columns that are used by the filter function from being dropped or altered.

The <predicate> can consist of one condition, or of multiple conditions joined with the AND logical operator.

```
<predicate> ::= <condition> [ AND <condition> ] [ ...n ]
```

Each condition in turn can consist of one primitive condition, or of multiple primitive conditions joined with the OR logical operator. You cannot use subqueries or non-deterministic functions. For a detailed list of limitations, please visit this page in the SQL Server Books Online: https://msdn.microsoft.com/en-us/library/mt613432.aspx.

The following code example shows how to enable the Stretch DB feature for the T1 table in the database Mila:

```
USE Mila;
CREATE FUNCTION dbo.StretchFilter(@col DATETIME)
RETURNS TABLE
WITH SCHEMABINDING
AS
        RETURN SELECT 1 AS is_eligible
WHERE @col < CONVERT(DATETIME, '01.06.2016', 104);
GO
ALTER TABLE dbo.T1
    SET (
    REMOTE_DATA_ARCHIVE = ON (
        FILTER_PREDICATE = dbo.StretchFilter(c2),
```

```
        MIGRATION_STATE = OUTBOUND
    )
);
```

After executing the preceding commands, Stretch DB is enabled for T1 table. *Figure 6.18* shows the SSMS screen immediately after the execution:

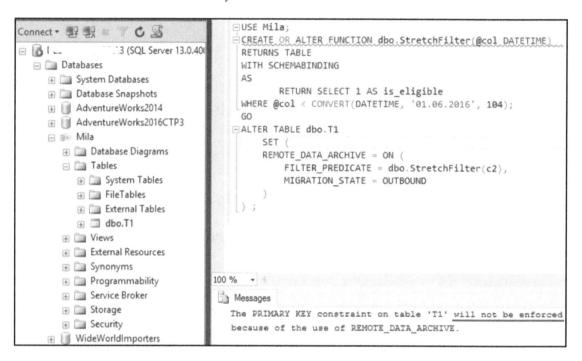

Figure 6.18: Enabling table for stretch by using Transact-SQL

The Stretch DB feature is enabled, but you can also see a warning message that informs you that although your T1 table has a primary key constraint, it will not be enforced! Thus, you can have multiple rows in your table with the same ID, just because you have enabled the Stretch DB. This schema and integrity change silently implemented as part of Stretch DB enabling can be dangerous; some developers will not be aware of it, since the information is delivered through a message warning.

When you ignore this problem, the rest of the action looks correct. After the table is enabled for stretching, you can expect three rows to remain in the local database (they have a value in the c2 column greater than 1 June). Two rows should be moved to the Azure SQL database. You will confirm this by querying stretch tables, but before that you will learn a tip about the creation of a filter predicate with sliding window.

Filter predicate with sliding window

As mentioned earlier, you cannot call a non-deterministic function in a filter predicate. If you, for instance, want to migrate all rows older than 1 month (where a date column has a value older than 1 month), you cannot simply use the DATEADD function in the filter function because DATEADD is a non-deterministic function.

In the previous example, you created the filter function to migrate all rows older than 1 June 2016. Assume that you want to send all rows older than 1 month to the cloud. Since the function must be deterministic and you cannot alter the existing one because it is defined with SCHEMABINDING attribute, you need to create a new function with the literal date again. For instance, on 1 August, you would need a function that instructs the system to migrate rows older than 1 July:

```
CREATE FUNCTION dbo.StretchFilter20160701(@col DATETIME)
RETURNS TABLE
WITH SCHEMABINDING
AS
        RETURN SELECT 1 AS is_eligible
WHERE @col < CONVERT(DATETIME, '01.07.2016', 104);
```

Now you can assign the newly created function to the T1 table:

```
ALTER TABLE dbo.T1
SET (REMOTE_DATA_ARCHIVE = ON
    (FILTER_PREDICATE = dbo.StretchFilter20160701(c2),
     MIGRATION_STATE = OUTBOUND
     )
);
```

Finally, you should remove the old filter function:

```
DROP FUNCTION IF EXISTS dbo.StretchFilter;
```

Querying Stretch Databases

When you query a Stretch Database, the SQL Server Database Engine runs the query against the local or remote database depending on data location. This is completely transparent to the database user. When you run a query that returns both local and remote data, you can see the Remote Query operator in the execution plan. The following query returns all rows from the stretch T1 table:

```
USE Mila;
SELECT * FROM dbo.T1;
```

As expected, it returns five rows:

id	c1	c2
2	Manchester United	2016-06-02 00:00:00.000
4	Juventus Torino	2016-06-25 00:00:00.000
5	Red Star Belgrade	2016-06-25 00:00:00.000
1	Benfica Lisbon	2016-05-15 00:00:00.000
3	Rapid Vienna	2016-05-28 00:00:00.000

You are surely much more interested in how the execution plan looks. It is shown in *Figure 6.19*:

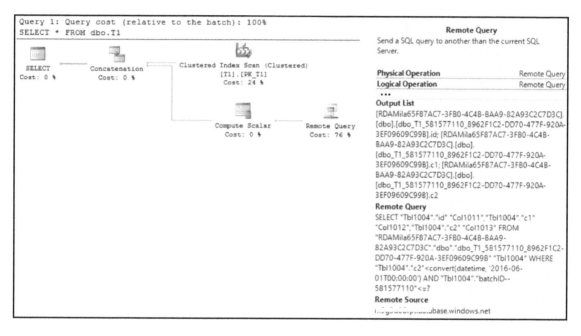

Figure 6.19: Execution plan for query with stretch tables

You can see that the Remote Query operator operates with an Azure database and that its output is concatenated with the output of the Clustered Index Scan that collected data from the local SQL Server instance. Note that the property window for the Remote Query operator has been shortened to show only context-relevant information.

What does SQL Server do when only local rows are returned? To check this, run the following code:

```
SELECT * FROM dbo.T1 WHERE c2 >= '20160601';
```

The query returns three rows, as expected:

```
id            c1                       c2
-----------   ----------------------   ------------------------
2             Manchester United        2016-06-02 00:00:00.000
4             Juventus Torino          2016-06-25 00:00:00.000
5             Red Star Belgrade        2016-06-25 00:00:00.000
```

And the execution plan is shown in *Figure 6.20*:

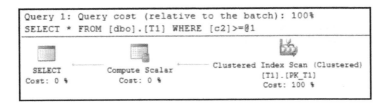

Figure 6.20: Execution plan for query with stretch tables returning local data only

The plan looks good; it checks only the local database and there is no connection to Azure. Finally, you will check the plan for a query that logically returns remote data only. Here is the query:

```
SELECT * FROM dbo.T1 WHERE c2 < '20160601';
```

You will again get the expected result:

```
id            c1                       c2
-----------   ----------------------   ------------------------
1             Benfica Lisbon           2016-05-15 00:00:00.000
3             Rapid Vienna             2016-05-28 00:00:00.000
```

Figure 6.21 shows the execution plan:

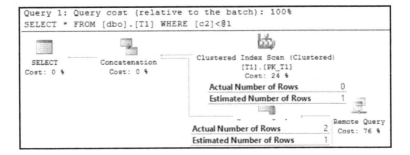

Figure 6.21: Execution plan for query with stretch tables returning remote data only

You probably did not expect both operators here… only Remote Query should be shown.

However, even if the returned data resides in the Azure SQL database only, both operators should be used since data can be in an eligible state, which means that it has not yet been moved to Azure.

Querying stretch tables is straightforward; you don't need to change anything in your queries. One of the most important things about Stretch Databases is that the entire execution is transparent to the user and you don't need to change your code when working with stretch tables.

However, you should not forget that enabling Stretch DB can suspend primary key constraints in your stretched tables. You have defined a primary key constraint in the T1 table; thus you expect that the next statement will fail (T1 already has a row with an ID with a value of 5):

```
INSERT INTO dbo.T1 (id, c1, c2) VALUES (5, Red Star Belgrade,'20170101');
```

However, the statement has been executed successfully even though an entry with the same ID already exists. You can confirm this by checking the rows in the T1 table.

```
SELECT * FROM dbo.T1 WHERE c2 >= '20160601';
```

The query returns four rows, and you can see two rows with the same ID (5):

```
id              c1                      c2
------------    --------------------    ------------------------
2               Manchester United       2016-06-02 00:00:00.000
4               Juventus Torino         2016-06-25 00:00:00.000
5               Red Star Belgrade       2016-06-25 00:00:00.000
5               Red Star Belgrade       2017-01-01 00:00:00.000
```

This is probably something that you would not expect, therefore, you should be aware of it when you enable the Stretch DB feature for a database table.

Querying and updating remote data

As mentioned earlier, queries against Stretch-enabled tables return both local and remote data by default. You can manage the scope of queries by using the system stored procedure `sys.sp_rda_set_query_mode` to specify whether queries against the current Stretch-enabled database and its tables return both local and remote data or local data only. The following modes are available:

- LOCAL_AND_REMOTE (queries against Stretch-enabled tables return both local and remote data). This is the default mode.
- LOCAL_ONLY (queries against Stretch-enabled tables return only local data).

- `DISABLED` (queries against Stretch-enabled tables are not allowed).

When you specify the scope of queries against the Stretch database, this is applied to all queries for all users. However, there are additional options at the single query level for an administrator (member of db_owner group). As administrator, you can add the query hint `WITH ( REMOTE_DATA_ARCHIVE_OVERRIDE = value )` to the `SELECT` statement to specify data location. The option `REMOTE_DATA_ARCHIVE_OVERRIDE` can have one of the following values:

- `LOCAL_ONLY` (query returns only local data)
- `REMOTE_ONLY` (query returns only remote data)
- `STAGE_ONLY` (query returns eligible data)

The following code returns eligible data for the `T1` table:

```
USE Mila;
SELECT * FROM dbo.T1 WITH (REMOTE_DATA_ARCHIVE_OVERRIDE = STAGE_ONLY);
```

Here is the output:

id	c1	c2	batchID--581577110
1	Benfica Lisbon	2016-05-15 00:00:00.000	1
3	Rapid Vienna	2016-05-28 00:00:00.000	1

Run this code to return data from the `T1` table already moved to Azure:

```
SELECT * FROM dbo.T1 WITH (REMOTE_DATA_ARCHIVE_OVERRIDE = REMOTE_ONLY);
```

Here is the output:

id	c1	c2	batchID--581577110
1	Benfica Lisbon	2016-05-15 00:00:00.000	1
3	Rapid Vienna	2016-05-28 00:00:00.000	1

Finally, this code returns data in the `T1` table from the local database server:

```
SELECT * FROM dbo.T1 WITH (REMOTE_DATA_ARCHIVE_OVERRIDE = LOCAL_ONLY);
```

As you expected, three rows are returned:

```
id              c1                      c2
-----------     --------------------    ------------------------
2               Manchester United       2016-06-02 00:00:00.000
4               Juventus Torino         2016-06-25 00:00:00.000
5               Red Star Belgrade       2016-06-25 00:00:00.000
```

By default, you can't update or delete rows that are eligible for migration or rows that have already been migrated in a Stretch-enabled table. When you have to fix a problem, a member of the db_owner role can run an UPDATE or DELETE operation by adding the preceding hint and will be able to update data in all locations.

SQL Server Stretch Database pricing

You can see price details on the https://azure.microsoft.com/en-us/pricing/details /sql-server-stretch-database/ page. Stretch Database bills compute and storage separately. Compute usage is represented by **Database Stretch Unit (DSU)** and customers can scale up and down the level of performance/DSUs they need at any time. The prices given here reflect general availability pricing, which goes into effect on September 1, 2016:

Performance level (DSU)	Price in $ per month
100	1,860
200	3,720
300	5,580
400	7,440
500	9,300
600	11,160
1000	18,600
1200	22,320
1500	27,900
2000	37,200

Table 6.1: StretchDB price list

Database sizes are limited to 240 TB. Monthly price estimates are based on 744 hours per month at constant DSU levels. Stretch DB is generally available in all regions except India South, China North, Brazil South, US North Central, India West, Australia, Japan, and US Gov.

Data storage is charged based on $0.16/GB/month. Data storage includes the size of your Stretch DB and backup snapshots. All Stretch databases have 7 days of incremental backup snapshots.

You can also use the Azure Pricing calculator to estimate expenses for your planned Azure activities. It is available at `https://azure.microsoft.com/en-us/pricing/calculator/?service=sql-server-stretch-database`. You can choose the Azure region and specify the time period, data storage, and DSU, as shown in *Figure 6.22*:

Figure 6.22: Azure Pricing calculator – Calculating price for Stretch DB

This screen shows the price you would pay when you play with the Stretch DB feature for two hours in a database with less than 1 GB of data and with 100 DSU using Azure database in Western Europe.

It is also possible to try the feature for free. You can apply for it at `https://azure.microso ft.com/en-us/free/`. When you do this, you'll see a screen as shown in *Figure 6.23*:

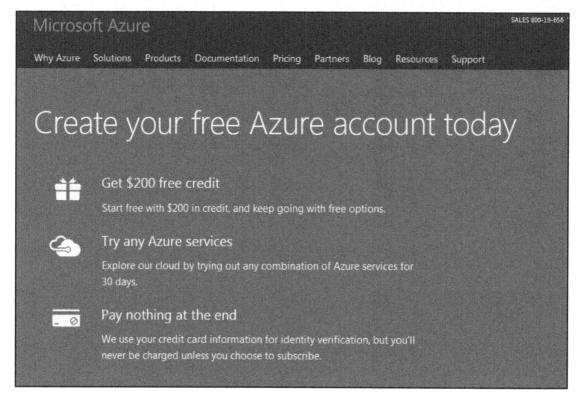

Figure 6.23: Create free Azure account

It is good that you can try the new feature for free, but in this case you must also give your payment details, which could reduce the number of developers who will try the feature.

Stretch DB management and troubleshooting

To monitor stretch-enabled databases and data migration, you can use the Stretch Database Monitor feature, the `sys.remote_data_archive_databases` and `sys.remote_data_archive_tables` catalog views, and the `sys.dm_db_rda_migration_status` dynamic management view.

Monitoring Stretch Database

To monitor stretch-enabled databases and data migration, use the Stretch Database Monitor feature. It is part of SQL Server Management Studio and you open it when you select your database and then choose **Tasks/Stretch/Monitor**, as shown in *Figure 6.24*:

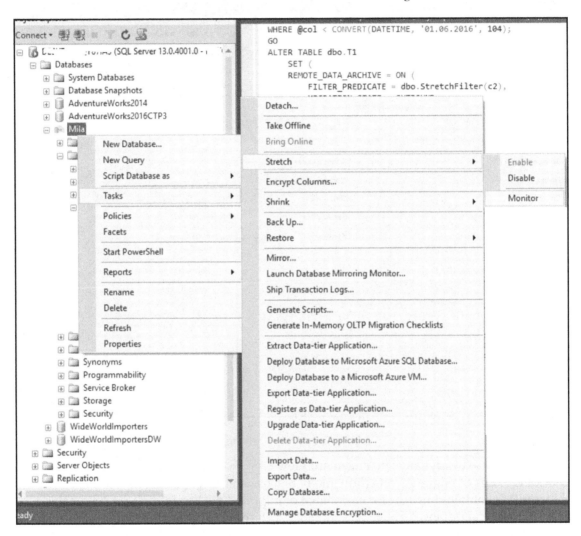

Figure 6.24: Open Stretch Database Monitor in SSMS

The top portion of the monitor displays general information about both the Stretch-enabled SQL Server database and the remote Azure database, while the status of data migration for each Stretch-enabled table in the database is shown in the bottom part of the screen, as shown in *Figure 6.25*:

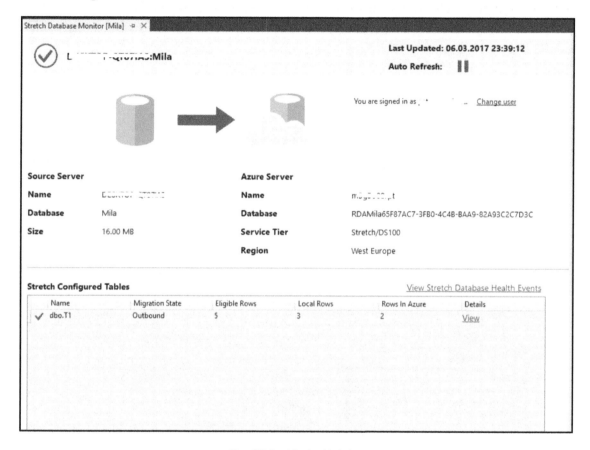

Figure 6.25: Stretch Database Monitoring

You can also use the dynamic management view `sys.dm_db_rda_migration_status` to check the status of migrated data (how many batches and rows of data have been migrated). It contains one row for each batch of migrated data from each Stretch-enabled table on the local instance of SQL Server. *Figure 6.26* shows the result generated by executing this view:

```
USE Mila;
SELECT * FROM sys.dm_db_rda_migration_status;
```

	table_id	database_id	migrated_rows	start_time_utc	end_time_utc	error_number	error_severity	error_state
1	581577110	9	0	2017-03-07 00:27:18.557	2017-03-07 00:27:18.557	NULL	NULL	NULL
2	581577110	9	0	2017-03-07 00:27:18.557	2017-03-07 00:27:20.020	NULL	NULL	NULL
3	581577110	9	0	2017-03-07 00:27:38.560	2017-03-07 00:27:38.560	NULL	NULL	NULL
4	581577110	9	2	2017-03-07 00:27:38.560	2017-03-07 00:27:49.507	NULL	NULL	NULL
5	581577110	9	0	2017-03-07 00:28:03.563	2017-03-07 00:28:03.563	NULL	NULL	NULL
6	581577110	9	0	2017-03-07 00:28:03.563	2017-03-07 00:28:05.060	NULL	NULL	NULL
7	581577110	9	0	2017-03-07 00:28:18.563	2017-03-07 00:28:18.563	NULL	NULL	NULL
8	581577110	9	0	2017-03-07 00:28:18.563	2017-03-07 00:28:20.093	NULL	NULL	NULL
9	581577110	9	0	2017-03-07 00:28:33.570	2017-03-07 00:28:33.570	NULL	NULL	NULL
10	581577110	9	0	2017-03-07 00:28:33.570	2017-03-07 00:28:44.670	NULL	NULL	NULL
11	581577110	9	0	2017-03-07 00:28:58.570	2017-03-07 00:28:58.570	NULL	NULL	NULL

Figure 6.26: Checking migration status by using DMV sys.dm_db_rda_migration_status

The `sys.remote_data_archive_databases` and `sys.remote_data_archive_tables` catalog views give information about the status of migration at the table and database level. *Figures 6.27* shows archive database information:

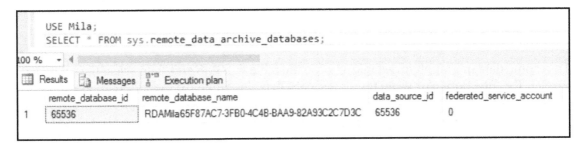

Figure 6.27: Checking archive databases

Details about archive tables on the Azure side are shown in *Figure 6.28*:

Figure 6.28: Checking archive tables

Finally, to see how much space a stretch-enabled table is using in Azure, run the following statement:

```
USE Mila;
EXEC sp_spaceused 'dbo.T1', 'true', 'REMOTE_ONLY';
```

The result of this command is shown in *Figure 6.29*:

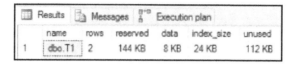

Figure 6.29: Space used by stretch table in Azure SQL Database

In the next sections, you will see how to pause or disable the Stretch DB feature.

Pause and resume data migration

To pause data migration for a table, choose the table in SSMS and then select the option **Stretch | Pause**. You can achieve the same with the following Transact-SQL command; it temporarily breaks the data migration for the T1 table:

```
USE Mila;
ALTER TABLE dbo.T1 SET (REMOTE_DATA_ARCHIVE (MIGRATION_STATE = PAUSED));
```

To resume data migration for a table, choose the table in SSMS and then select the **Stretch/Resume** option or write the Transact-SQL code, similar to the following one:

```
USE Mila;
ALTER TABLE dbo.T1 SET (REMOTE_DATA_ARCHIVE (MIGRATION_STATE = OUTBOUND));
```

To check whether migration is active or paused, you can open Stretch Database Monitor in SQL Server Management Studio and check the value of the Migration State or column check the value of the flag is_migration_paused in the system catalog view sys.remote_data_archive_tables.

Disable Stretch Database

Disabling Stretch Database for a database and tables stops data migration immediately and queries don't include remote data anymore. You can copy the already migrated data back to the local system, or you can leave it in Azure. As with Stretch Database enabling, you can disable it for tables and databases using SSMS and Transact-SQL. In order to disable Stretch Database for a database, you have to disable it for tables involved in stretching.

Disable Stretch Database for tables by using SSMS

To disable Stretch DB for a table, you need to select it in SQL Server Management Studio (SSMS); right-click on it and select the option **Stretch**. Then, go to one of the following options:

- **Disable | Bring data back from Azure** to copy remote data for the table to the local system and then disable the Stretch DB feature
- **Disable | Leave data in Azure** to disable the Stretch DB feature immediately, without transferring it back to the local system (data remains in Azure)

Be aware that the first option includes data transfer costs! When you choose the second option, you don't have transfer costs, but the data remains in Azure and you still need to pay for storage. You can remove it through the Azure management portal. *Figure 6.30* shows the screen after the Stretch DB feature has been disabled for the T1 table:

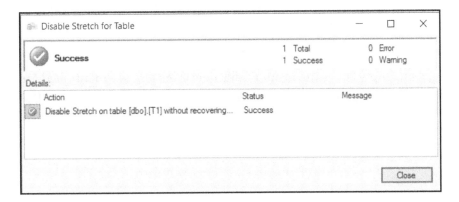

Figure 6.30: Disable Stretch DB for a table

Disable Stretch Database for tables using Transact-SQL

You can use Transact-SQL to perform the same action. The following code example instructs SQL Server to disable Stretch DB for the stretch table T1 but to transfer the already migrated data for the table to the local database first:

```
USE Mila;
ALTER TABLE dbo.T1 SET (REMOTE_DATA_ARCHIVE (MIGRATION_STATE = INBOUND));
```

If you don't need the already migrated data (or you want to avoid data transfer costs), use the following code:

```
USE Mila;
ALTER TABLE dbo.T1 SET (REMOTE_DATA_ARCHIVE = OFF_WITHOUT_DATA_RECOVERY
(MIGRATION_STATE = PAUSED));
```

Disable Stretch Database for a database

After you have disabled Stretch DB for all stretch tables in a database, you can disable it for the database. You can do this by selecting the database in SSMS and choosing the **Task/Stretch/Disable** option in the database context menu.

Alternatively, you can use Transact-SQL to achieve the same:

```
ALTER DATABASE Mila SET (REMOTE_DATA_ARCHIVE = OFF_WITHOUT_DATA_RECOVERY
(MIGRATION_STATE = PAUSED));
```

You can check if the action was successful by using this query:

```
SELECT * FROM sys.remote_data_archive_tables;
```

You should get an empty set as the result of this query. As already mentioned for stretch tables, disabling Stretch DB does not drop a database remotely. You need to drop it by using the Azure management portal.

Backup and restore Stretch-enabled databases

Since you have delegated a part of your database to the remote Azure instance, when you perform a database backup, only local and eligible data will be backed up; remote data is the responsibility of the Azure service. By default, Azure automatically creates storage snapshots at least every 8 hours and retains them for 7 days so that you can restore data to a point in time (by default, 21 points). You can change this behavior and increase the number of hours or backup frequency by using the system stored procedure `sys.sp_rda_set_rpo_duration`. Since the Azure service is not free, this can have additional costs.

As expected, to remotely restore a database you have to log in to the Azure portal. How to restore a live Azure database to an earlier point in time using the Azure portal is shown in *Figure 6.31*.

Figure 6.31: Restore Azure database to an earlier point in time

To restore your Azure database to an earlier point in time, you need to perform the following steps:

1. Log in to the Azure portal.
2. On the left-hand side of the screen, select **BROWSE** and then select **SQL Databases**.
3. Navigate to your database and select it.
4. At the top of the database blade, click on **Restore**.
5. Specify a new **Database name**, select a `Restore Point`, and then click on **Create**.
6. The database restore process will begin and can be monitored using **NOTIFICATIONS**.

After you restore the local SQL Server database, you have to run the `sys.sp_rda_reauthorize_db` stored procedure to re-establish the connection between the Stretch-enabled SQL Server database and the remote Azure database. The same action is required if you restore the Azure database with a different name or in a different region. You can also restore a deleted database up to 7 days after dropping it. The SQL Server Stretch Database service on Azure takes a database snapshot before a database is dropped and retains it for 7 days.

Summary

Stretch DB allows the moving of historical or less frequently needed data dynamically and transparently to Microsoft Azure. Data is always available and online, and you don't need to change queries in your solutions; SQL Server takes care of the location of data and combines retrieving data from the local server and remote Azure location. Therefore, you can completely delegate your cold data to Azure and reduce storage, maintenance, and implementation costs of an on-premise solution for cold data storage and availability. However, there are many limitations of using Stretch DB and most OLTP tables cannot be stretched to the cloud—at least not without schema and constraint changes. Stretch Database brings maximum benefits to tables with historical data that is rarely used. You can calculate the price for data storage and querying against the Azure database and decide whether you would benefit from using the Stretch DB feature.

7

Temporal Tables

Databases that serve business applications often support temporal data. For example, suppose a contract with a supplier is valid for a limited time only. It can be valid from a specific point in time onward, or it can be valid for a specific time interval—from a starting time point to an ending time point. In addition, on many occasions, you need to audit all changes in one or more tables. You might also need to be able to show the state in a specific point in time, or all changes made to a table in a specific period of time. From a data integrity perspective, you might need to implement many additional temporal-specific constraints.

This chapter introduces temporal problems, deals with manual solutions, shows out-of-the-box solutions in SQL Server 2016, and deals with the following topics:

- Defining temporal data
- Using temporal data in SQL Server before version 2016
- System-versioned tables in SQL Server 2016
- What kind of temporal support is still missing in SQL Server 2016?

What is temporal data?

In a table with temporal support, the header represents a predicate with at least one time parameter that represents when the rest of the predicate is valid—the complete predicate is therefore a **timestamped predicate**. Rows represent timestamped propositions, and the valid time period of a row is expressed with one of two attributes: since (for **semi temporal** data), or during (for **fully temporal** data); the latter attribute is usually represented with two values, from and to.

The following shows the original and two additional timestamped versions of an exemplary `Suppliers` table.

Suppliers			Suppliers_Since			Suppliers_FromTo		
PK	**supplierid**		**PK**	**supplierid**		**PK**	**supplierid**	
	companyname			companyname			companyname	
	contactname			contactname			contactname	
	contacttitle			contacttitle			contacttitle	
	address			address			address	
	city			city			city	
	region			region			region	
	postalcode			postalcode			postalcode	
	country			country			country	
	phone			phone			phone	
	fax			fax			fax	
				since			**from**	
							to	

Figure 7.1: Original Suppliers table and two tables with temporal support

From the original table header, you can read a predicate saying that a supplier with identification `supplierid`, named `companyname`, having contact `contactname`, and so on, is currently our supplier, or is currently under contract. You can pretend that this supplier is the supplier forever, from the beginning of time until the end of time. The `Suppliers_Since` table header has this predicate modified with a time parameter: a supplier with the identification `supplierid`, named `companyname`, having contact `contactname`, and so on, is under contract since a specific point in time. In the `Suppliers_FromTo` table, the header has this predicate modified with an even more specific time attribute: a supplier with ID `supplierid`, named `companyname`, having contact `contactname`, and so on, is (or was, or will be, depending on the current time) under contract *from a* specific point in time *to* another point in time.

There is no need to implement semi-temporal tables. You can simply use the maximal possible date and time for the *to* time point. Therefore, the rest of the chapter focuses on fully temporal data only.

In this section, you will learn about:

- Types of temporal tables
- Temporal data algebra
- Temporal constraints
- Temporal data implementation in SQL Server before version 2016
- Optimization of temporal queries

Types of temporal table

You might have noticed during the introduction part at the beginning of this chapter that there are two kinds of temporal issues. The first one is the **validity time** of the proposition—in which period the proposition that a timestamped row in a table represents was actually true. For example, a contract with a supplier was valid only from time point 1 to time point 2. This kind of validity time is meaningful to people, meaningful for the business. The validity time is also called **application time** or **human time**. We can have multiple valid periods for the same entity. For example, the aforementioned contract that was valid from time point 1 to time point 2 might also be valid from time point 7 to time point 9.

The second temporal issue is the **transaction time**. A row for the contract mentioned above was inserted in time point 1 and was the only version of the truth known to the database until somebody changed it, or even till the end of time. When the row is updated at time point 2, the original row is known as being true to the database from time point 1 to time point 2. A new row for the same proposition is inserted with time valid for the database from time point 2 to the end of the time. The transaction time is also known as **system time** or **database time**.

Database management systems can, and should, maintain transaction times automatically. The system has to insert a new row for every update and change the transaction validity period in the original row. The system also needs to allow the querying of the current and historical data, and show the state at any specific point in time. There are not many additional issues with the transaction time. The system has to take care that the start time of the database time period is lower than the end time, and that two periods in two rows for the same entity don't overlap. The database system has to know a single truth at a single point in time. Finally, the database does not care about the future. The end of the database time of the current row is actually the end of time. Database time is about present and past states only.

Implementing the application time might be much more complex. Of course, you might have validity time periods that end, or even begin, in the future. Database management systems can't take care of future times automatically, or check whether they are correct. Therefore, you need to take care of all the constraints you need. The database management system can only help you by implementing time-aware objects, such as declarative constraints. For example, a foreign key from the products to the suppliers table, which ensures that each product has a supplier, could be extended to check not only whether the supplier for the product exists, but also whether the supplier is a valid supplier at the time point when the foreign key is checked.

So far, I've talked about time as though it consists of discrete time points; I used the term time point as if it represented a single, indivisible, infinitely small point in time. Of course, time is continuous. Nevertheless, in common language, we talk about time as though it consists of discrete points. We talk in days, hours, and other time units; the granularity we use depends on what we are talking about. The time points we are talking about are actually intervals of time; a day is an interval of 24 hours, an hour is an interval of 60 minutes, and so on.

So, what is the granularity level of the time points for the system and application intervals? For the system times, the decision is simple: use the lowest granularity level that a system supports. In SQL Server, with the `datetime2` data type, you can support 100 nanoseconds granularity. For the application time, the granularity depends on the business problem. For example, for a contract with a supplier, the day level could work well. For measuring the intervals when somebody is using a service, such as a mobile phone service, granularity of a second may be more appropriate. This looks very complex. However, you can make a generalized solution for the application times. You can translate time points to integers, and then use a lookup table that gives you the context and gives meaning to the integer time points.

Of course, you can also implement both application and system-versioned tables. Such tables are called **bitemporal** tables.

Allen's interval algebra

The theory for the temporal data in a relational model started to evolve more than thirty years ago. I will define quite a few useful Boolean operators and a couple of operators that work on intervals and return an interval. These operators are known as **Allen's operators**, named after J. F. Allen, who defined a number of them in a 1983 research paper on temporal intervals. All of them are still accepted as valid and needed. A database management system could help you when dealing with application times by implementing these operators out-of-the-box.

Let me first introduce the notation I will use. I will work on two intervals, denoted i_1 and i_2. The beginning time point of the first interval is b_1, and the end is e_1; the beginning time point of the second interval is b_2 and the end is e_2. Allen's **Boolean operators** are defined in the following table:

Name	Notation	Definition
Equals	$(i_1 = i_2)$	$(b_1 = b_2)$ AND $(e_1 = e_2)$
Before	$(i_1$ before $i_2)$	$(e_1 < b_2)$
After	$(i_1$ after $i_2)$	$(i_2$ before $i_1)$
Includes	$(i_1 \supseteq i_2)$	$(b_1 \leq b_2)$ AND $(e_1 \geq e_2)$
Properly includes	$(i_1 \supset i_2)$	$(i_1 \supseteq i_2)$ AND $(i_1 \neq i_2)$
Meets	$(i_1$ meets $i_2)$	$(b2 = e1 + 1)$ OR $(b1 = e2 + 1)$
Overlaps	$(i_1$ overlaps $i_2)$	$(b_1 \leq e_2)$ AND $(b_2 \leq e_1)$
Merges	$(i_1$ merges $i_2)$	$(i_1$ overlaps $i_2)$ OR $(i_1$ meets $i_2)$
Begins	$(i_1$ begins $i_2)$	$(b_1 = b_2)$ AND $(e_1 \leq e_2)$
Ends	$(i_1$ ends $i_2)$	$(e_1 = e_2)$ AND $(b_1 \geq b_2)$

In addition to Boolean operators, there are three of Allen's operators that accept intervals as input parameters and return an interval. These operators constitute simple **interval algebra**. Note that those operators have the same name as relational operators you are probably already familiar with: Union, Intersect, and Minus. However, they don't behave exactly like their relational counterparts. In general, using any of the three interval operators, if the operation would result in an empty set of time points or in a set that cannot be described by one interval, then the operator should return NULL. A union of two intervals makes sense only if the intervals meet or overlap. An intersection makes sense only if the intervals overlap. The Minus interval operator makes sense only in some cases. For example, (3:10) Minus (5:7) returns NULL because the result cannot be described by one interval. The following table summarizes the definition of the operators of interval algebra:

Name	Notation	Definition
Union	$(i_1$ union $i_2)$	$(Min(b_1, b_2) : Max(e_1, e_2))$, when $(i_1$ merges $i_2)$; NULL otherwise
Intersect	$(i_1$ intersect $i_2)$	$(Max(b_1, b_2) : Min(e_1, e_2))$, when $(i_1$ overlaps $i_2)$; NULL otherwise

Minus	$(i_1$ minus $i_2)$	$(b_1: Min(b_2 - 1, e_1))$, when $(b_1 < b_2)$ AND $(e_1 \leq e_2)$; $(Max(e_2 + 1, b_1) : e_1)$, when $(b_1 \geq b_2)$ AND $(e_1 > e_2)$; *NULL otherwise*

The following figure shows the interval algebra operators graphically:

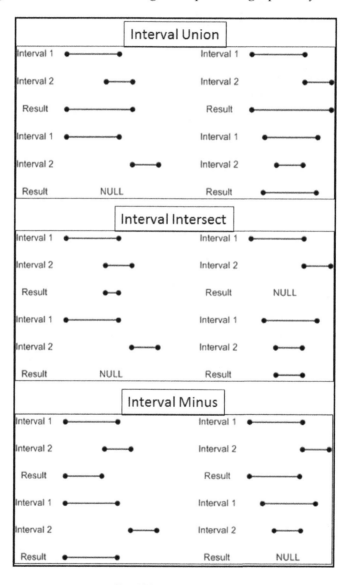

Figure 7.2: Interval algebra operators

Temporal constraints

Depending on the business problem you are solving, you might need to implement many temporal constraints. Remember that for the application time, SQL Server does not help you much. You need to implement the constraints in your code using SQL Server declarative constraints where possible. However, most of the constraints you need to implement through custom code, either in triggers or in stored procedures, or even in the application code.

Imagine the `Suppliers` table example. One supplier can appear multiple times in the table because the same supplier could be under contract for separate periods of time. For example, you could have two tuples like this in the relation with the shortened header **Suppliers** (`supplierid`, `companyname`, `from`, `to`):

```
{2, Supplier VHQZD, d05, d07}
{2, Supplier VHQZD, d12, d27}
```

Here are some possible constraints you might need to implement:

- *To* should never be less than *from*
- Two contracts for the same supplier should not have overlapping time intervals
- Two contracts for the same supplier should not have abutting time intervals
- No supplier can be under two distinct contracts at the same point in time
- There should be no supplies from a supplier at a point in time when the supplier was not under a contract

You might find even more constraints. Anyway, SQL Server 2016 brings support for the system-versioned tables only. To maintain the application validity times, you need to develop code by yourself.

Temporal data in SQL Server before 2016

As mentioned, in SQL Server versions before 2016, you need to take care of temporal data by yourself. Even in SQL Server 2016, you still need to take care of the human, or application times. The following code shows an example of how to create a table with validity intervals expressed with the `b` and `e` columns, where the beginning and the end of an interval are represented as integers. The table is populated with demo data from the `WideWorldImporters.Sales.OrderLines` table. Note that there are multiple versions of the `WideWorldImporters` database, so you might get slightly different results.

I used the `WideWorldImporters-Standard.bak` backup file from
`https://github.com/Microsoft/sql-server-samples/releases/tag/wide-world-importe`
`rs-v1.0` to restore this demo database on my SQL Server instance.

```
USE tempdb;
GO
SELECT OrderLineID AS id,
  StockItemID * (OrderLineID % 5 + 1) AS b,
  LastEditedBy + StockItemID * (OrderLineID % 5 + 1) AS e
INTO dbo.Intervals
FROM WideWorldImporters.Sales.OrderLines;
-- 231412 rows
GO
ALTER TABLE dbo.Intervals ADD CONSTRAINT PK_Intervals PRIMARY KEY(id);
CREATE INDEX idx_b ON dbo.Intervals(b) INCLUDE(e);
CREATE INDEX idx_e ON dbo.Intervals(e) INCLUDE(b);
GO
```

Please also note the indexes created. The two indexes are optimal for searches at the beginning of an interval or at the end of an interval. You can check the minimal begin and maximal end of all intervals with the following code:

```
SELECT MIN(b), MAX(e)
FROM dbo.Intervals;
```

You can see in the results that the minimal beginning time point is 1 and maximal ending time point is 1155. Now you need to give the intervals some time context. In this case, a single time point represents a day. The following code creates a date lookup table and populates it. Note that the starting date is July 1, 2014.

```
CREATE TABLE dbo.DateNums
  (n INT NOT NULL PRIMARY KEY,
   d DATE NOT NULL);
GO
DECLARE @i AS INT = 1,
  @d AS DATE = '20140701';
WHILE @i <= 1200
BEGIN
INSERT INTO dbo.DateNums
  (n, d)
SELECT @i, @d;
SET @i += 1;
SET @d = DATEADD(day,1,@d);
END;
GO
```

Now you can join the `dbo.Intervals` table to the `dbo.DateNums` table twice, to give the context to the integers that represent the beginning and the end of the intervals:

```
SELECT i.id,
  i.b, d1.d AS dateB,
  i.e, d2.d AS dateE
FROM dbo.Intervals AS i
  INNER JOIN dbo.DateNums AS d1
    ON i.b = d1.n
  INNER JOIN dbo.DateNums AS d2
    ON i.e = d2.n
ORDER BY i.id;
```

The abbreviated result from the previous query is:

```
id   b     dateB         e     dateE
--   ---   ----------    ---   ----------
1    328   2015-05-24    332   2015-05-28
2    201   2015-01-17    204   2015-01-20
3    200   2015-01-16    203   2015-01-19
```

Now you can see which day is represented by which integer.

Optimizing temporal queries

The problem with temporal queries is that when reading from a table, SQL Server can use only one index, and successfully eliminate rows that are not candidates for the result from one side only, and then scan the rest of the data. For example, you need to find all intervals in the table which overlap with a given interval. Remember, two intervals overlap when the beginning of the first one is lower or equal to the end of the second one, and the beginning of the second one is lower or equal to the end of the first one, or mathematically, when $(b_1 \le e_2) AND (b_2 \le e_1)$.

The following query searched for all of the intervals that overlap with the interval (10, 30). Note that the second condition $(b_2 \le e_1)$ is turned around to $(e_1 \ge b_2)$ for simpler reading (the beginning and the end of intervals from the table are always on the left side of the condition). The given, or the searched interval, is at the beginning of the timeline for all intervals in the table.

```
SET STATISTICS IO ON;
DECLARE @b AS INT = 10,
  @e AS INT = 30;
SELECT id, b, e
```

```
FROM dbo.Intervals
WHERE b <= @e
  AND e >= @b
OPTION (RECOMPILE);
GO
```

The query used 36 logical reads. If you check the execution plan, you can see that the query used the index seek in the `idx_b` index with the seek predicate `[tempdb].[dbo].[Intervals].b <= Scalar Operator((30))` and then scanned the rows and selected the resulting rows using the residual predicate `[tempdb].[dbo].[Intervals].[e]>=(10)`. Because the searched interval is at the beginning of the timeline, the seek predicate successfully eliminated the majority of the rows; only a few intervals in the table have a beginning point lower than or equal to 30.

You would get a similarly efficient query if the searched interval was at the end of the timeline, just that SQL Server would use the `idx_e` index to seek. However, what happens if the searched interval is in the middle of the timeline, as the following query shows?

```
DECLARE @b AS INT = 570,
  @e AS INT = 590;
SELECT id, b, e
FROM dbo.Intervals
WHERE b <= @e
  AND e >= @b
OPTION (RECOMPILE);
GO
```

This time, the query used 111 logical reads. With a bigger table, the difference from the first query would be even bigger. If you check the execution plan, you will see that SQL Server used the `idx_e` index with the `[tempdb].[dbo].[Intervals].e >= Scalar Operator((570))` seek predicate and `[tempdb].[dbo].[Intervals].[b]<=(590)` residual predicate. The seek predicate excludes approximately half of the rows from one side, while half of the rows from the other side are scanned and the resulting rows are extracted with the residual predicate.

There is a solution which would use that index for elimination of the rows from both sides of the searched interval by using a single index. The following figure shows this logic:

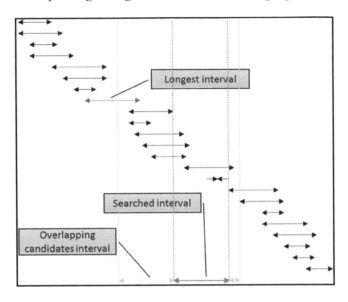

Figure 7.3: Optimizing temporal query

The intervals in the figure are sorted by the lower boundary, representing SQL Server's usage of the `idx_b` index. Eliminating intervals from the right side of the given (searched) interval is simple: just eliminate all intervals where the beginning is at least one unit bigger (more to the right) of the end of the given interval. You can see this boundary in the figure denoted with the rightmost dotted line. However, eliminating from the left is more complex. In order to use the same index, the `idx_b` index for eliminating from the left, I need to use the beginning of the intervals in the table in the WHERE clause of the query. I have to go to the left side, away from the beginning of the given (searched) interval, at least for the length of the longest interval in the table, which is marked with a callout in the figure. The intervals that begin before the left yellow line cannot overlap with the given (blue) interval.

Since I already know that the length of the longest interval is 20, I can write an enhanced query in quite a simple way:

```
DECLARE @b AS INT = 570,
  @e AS INT = 590;
DECLARE @max AS INT = 20;
SELECT id, b, e
FROM dbo.Intervals
WHERE b <= @e AND b >= @b - @max
  AND e >= @b AND e <= @e + @max
OPTION (RECOMPILE);
```

This query retrieves the same rows as the previous one with 20 logical reads only. If you check the execution plan, you can see that the `idx_b` index was used, with the seek predicate `Seek Keys[1]: Start: [tempdb].[dbo].[Intervals].b >= Scalar Operator((550))`, `End: [tempdb].[dbo].[Intervals].b <= Scalar Operator((590))`, which successfully eliminated rows from both sides of the timeline, and then the residual predicate `[tempdb].[dbo].[Intervals].[e]>=(570) AND [tempdb].[dbo].[Intervals].[e]<=(610)` was used to select rows from a very limited partial scan.

Of course, the figure could be turned around to cover cases when the `idx_e` index would be more useful. With this index, the elimination from the left is simple—eliminate all of the intervals which end at least one unit before the beginning of the given interval. This time, the elimination from the right is more complex—the end of the intervals in the table cannot be more to the right than the end of the given interval plus the maximal length of all intervals in the table.

Please note that this performance is the consequence of the specific data in the table. The maximal length of an interval is 20. This way, SQL Server can very efficiently eliminate intervals from both sides. However, if there is only one long interval in the table, the code will become much less efficient, because SQL Server would not be able to eliminate a lot of rows from one side, either left or right, depending on which index it used. Anyway, in real life, interval length does not vary a lot, so this optimization technique might be very useful, especially because it is simple.

After you have finished with temporal queries in this section, you can clean up your tempdb database with the following code:

```
DROP TABLE dbo.DateNums;
DROP TABLE dbo.Intervals;
```

Temporal features in SQL:2011

Temporal data support was introduced in the most recent revision of the SQL standard—SQL:2011. There were also attempts to define the support in previous standard versions, but without success (TSQL2 extensions in 1995). They were not widely accepted and vendors did not implement them.

Finally, the ANSI SQL:2011 standard proposed how temporal data should be supported in relational database management systems. A very important thing is that SQL:2011 did not introduce a new data type to support temporal data, rather it introduced the period.

A period is a table attribute and it's defined by two table columns of date type representing start time and end time respectively. It is defined as follows:

- A period must have a name
- The end time must be greater than the start time
- It is a closed-open period model. The start time is included in the period and the end time is excluded

The SQL:2011 standard recognizes two dimensions of temporal data support:

- Valid or application time tables
- Transaction or system time tables

Application-time period tables are intended for meeting the requirements of applications that capture time periods during which the data is believed to be valid in the real world. A typical example of such an application is an insurance application, where it is necessary to keep track of the specific policy details of a given customer that are in effect at any given point in time.

System-versioned tables are intended for meeting the requirements of applications that must maintain an accurate history of data changes either for business reasons, legal reasons, or both. A typical example of such an application is a banking application, where it is necessary to keep previous states of customer account information so that customers can be provided with a detailed history of their accounts. There are also plenty of examples where certain institutions are required by law to preserve historical data for a specified length of time to meet regulatory and compliance requirements.

Bitemporal tables are tables that implement both application-time and system-versioned time support.

After the standard was published, many vendors came up with the temporal table implementation:

- **IDM DB2 10** added full support for temporal tables (for both application time and system-versioned).
- **Oracle** implemented a feature called the Flashback Data Archive. It automatically tracks all changes made to data in a database and maintains an archive of historical data. Oracle 12c introduced valid time temporal support.
- **PostgreSQL** doesn't support temporal tables natively, but temporal tables approximate them
- **Teradata** implements both valid time and transaction time table types based on the TSQL2 specification.
- All these implementations most probably affected Microsoft's decision to implement temporal tables in SQL Server 2016.

System-versioned tables in SQL Server 2016

SQL Server 2016 introduces support for system-versioned temporal tables. Unfortunately, application-time tables are not implemented in this version. System-versioned temporal tables bring built-in support for providing information about data stored in the table at any point in time rather than only the data that is correct at the current moment in time. They are implemented according to the specification in the ANSI SQL 2011 standard with a few extensions.

How temporal tables work in SQL Server 2016

A system-versioned temporal table is implemented in SQL Server 2016 as a pair of tables: the current table containing the actual data, and the history table where only historical entries are stored. There are many limitations of both current and history tables. Here are limitations and considerations that you must take into account for the current table of a system-versioned temporal table:

- It must have a primary key defined
- It must have one `PERIOD FOR SYSTEM_TIME` defined with two `DATETIME2` columns
- Cannot be `FILETABLE` and cannot contain `FILESTREAM` data type

- INSERT, UPDATE, and MERGE statements cannot reference and modify period columns: start column is always set to system time, end column to max date value
- INSTEAD OF triggers are not allowed
- TRUNCATE TABLE is not supported

The list of limitations for a history table is significantly longer and brings many additional restrictions. The history table of a system-versioned temporal table:

- Cannot have constraints defined (primary or foreign keys, check, table, or column constraints). Only default column constraints are allowed
- You cannot modify data in the history table
- You can neither ALTER nor DROP a history table
- It must have the same schema as the current table (column names, data types, ordinal position)
- Cannot be defined as the current table
- Cannot be FILETABLE and cannot contain FILESTREAM data type
- No triggers are allowed (neither INSTEAD OF nor AFTER)
- Change Data Capture and Change Data Tracking are not supported

You can read more about considerations and limitations when working with temporal tables at https://msdn.microsoft.com/en-us/library/mt604468.aspx.

The list might look long and discouraging, but all these limitations are there to protect data consistency and accuracy in history tables. However, although you cannot change logical attributes, you can still perform actions related to the physical implementations of the history table: you can switch between rowstore and columnstore table storage, you can choose columns for clustered and create additional non-clustered indexes.

Creating temporal tables

To support the creation of temporal tables, the CREATE TABLE and ALTER TABLE Transact-SQL statements have been extended. To create a temporal table, you need to:

- Define a column of DATETIME2 data type for holding the info since when a row is valid from a system point of view
- Define a column of DATETIME2 data type for holding the info until when a row is valid from the same point of view

- Define a period for system time by using previously defined and described columns
- Set the newly-added SYSTEM_VERSIONING table attribute to ON

The following code creates a new temporal table Product in the schema dbo in the database WideWorldImporters:

```
USE WideWorldImporters;
CREATE TABLE dbo.Product
(
    ProductId INT NOT NULL CONSTRAINT PK_Product PRIMARY KEY,
    ProductName NVARCHAR(50) NOT NULL,
    Price MONEY NOT NULL,
    ValidFrom DATETIME2 GENERATED ALWAYS AS ROW START NOT NULL,
    ValidTo DATETIME2 GENERATED ALWAYS AS ROW END NOT NULL,
    PERIOD FOR SYSTEM_TIME (ValidFrom, ValidTo)
)
WITH (SYSTEM_VERSIONING = ON);
```

You can identify all four elements related to temporal table creation from the above list: two period columns, the period, and the SYSTEM_VERSIONING attribute. Note that all elements marked bold are predefined and you must write them exactly like this; data type, nullability, and default values for both period columns are also predefined and you can only choose their names and define data type precision. The data type must be DATETIME2; you can only specify its precision. Furthermore, the period definition itself is predefined too; you must use period column names you chose in the previous step. By defining period columns and the period, you have created the infrastructure required for implementing temporal tables. However, if you create a table with them but without the SYSTEM_VERSIONING attribute, the table will not be temporal. It will contain an additional two columns with values that are maintained by the system, but the table will not be a system-versioned temporal table.

The final, fourth, part is to set the attribute SYSTEM_VERSIONING to ON. When you execute the above code, you implicitly instruct SQL Server to automatically create a history table for the temporal table dbo.Product. The table will be created in the same schema (dbo), and with a name according to the following format MSSQL_TemporalHistoryFor_<current_temporal_table_object_id>_[suffix]. The suffix is optional and it will be added only if the first part of the table name is not unique. *Figure 7.4* shows what you will see when you open SQL Server Management Studio and find the dbo.Product table :

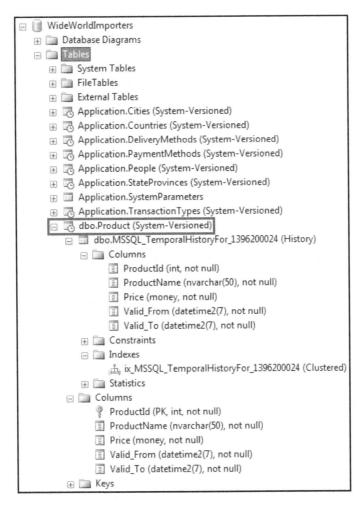

Figure 7.4: Temporal table in SQL Server Management Studio

You can see that all temporal tables have a small clock icon indicating temporality. Under the table name, you can see its history table. Note that columns in both tables are identical (column names, data types, precision, nullability), but also that the history table does not have constraints (primary key).

Period columns must have DATETIME2 as their data type. If you try with DATETIME, you will get an error. Standard does not specify data type precision, so this is not strictly implemented according to standard. This is very important when you migrate your existing temporal solution to new temporal tables in SQL Server 2016. Usually, columns that you were using are DATETIME data type and you have to extend this to DATETIME2.

You can also specify the name of the history table only and let SQL Server create it with the same attributes as described earlier. Use the following code to create a temporal table with a user-defined history table name:

```
USE WideWorldImporters;
CREATE TABLE dbo.Product2
(
    ProductId INT NOT NULL CONSTRAINT PK_Product2 PRIMARY KEY,
    ProductName NVARCHAR(50) NOT NULL,
    Price MONEY NOT NULL,
    ValidFrom DATETIME2 GENERATED ALWAYS AS ROW START NOT NULL,
    ValidTo DATETIME2 GENERATED ALWAYS AS ROW END NOT NULL,
    PERIOD FOR SYSTEM_TIME (ValidFrom, ValidTo)
)
WITH (SYSTEM_VERSIONING = ON (HISTORY_TABLE = dbo.ProductHistory2));
```

What storage type is used for the automatically created history table? By default, it is a rowstore table with the clustered index on the period columns. The table is compressed with PAGE compression, if it can be enabled for compression (has no SPARSE or (B)LOB columns). To find out the storage type, use the following code:

```
SELECT temporal_type_desc, p.data_compression_desc
FROM sys.tables t
INNER JOIN sys.partitions p ON t.object_id = p.object_id
WHERE name = 'ProductHistory2';
```

The result of the above query shows that PAGE compression has been applied:

temporal_type_desc	data_compression_desc
HISTORY_TABLE	PAGE

You can also see that the history table has a clustered index. The following code extracts the index name and the columns used in the index:

```
SELECT i.name, i.type_desc, c.name, ic.index_column_id
FROM sys.indexes i
INNER JOIN sys.index_columns ic on ic.object_id = i.object_id
INNER JOIN sys.columns c on c.object_id = i.object_id AND ic.column_id =
c.column_id
WHERE OBJECT_NAME(i.object_id) = 'ProductHistory2';
```

The output of this query shows that the automatically created history table has a clustered index on the period columns and the name in the following ix_<history_tablename> format:

name	type_desc	name	index_column_id
ix_ProductHistory2	CLUSTERED	ValidFrom	1
ix_ProductHistory2	CLUSTERED	ValidTo	2

However, if the predefined implementation of the history table (rowstore, period columns in clustered index) doesn't meet your criteria for historical data, you can create your own history table. Of course, you need to respect all constraints and limitations listed at the beginning of the chapter. The following code first creates a history table, then a temporal table, and finally assigns the history table to it. Note that, in order to proceed with the code execution, you need to remove the temporal table created in the first example in this chapter:

```
USE WideWorldImporters;
ALTER TABLE dbo.Product SET (SYSTEM_VERSIONING = OFF);
ALTER TABLE dbo.Product DROP PERIOD FOR SYSTEM_TIME;
DROP TABLE IF EXISTS dbo.Product;
DROP TABLE IF EXISTS dbo.ProductHistory;
GO
CREATE TABLE dbo.ProductHistory
(
    ProductId INT NOT NULL,
    ProductName NVARCHAR(50) NOT NULL,
    Price MONEY NOT NULL,
    ValidFrom DATETIME2 NOT NULL,
    ValidTo DATETIME2 NOT NULL
);
CREATE CLUSTERED COLUMNSTORE INDEX IX_ProductHistory ON dbo.ProductHistory;
CREATE NONCLUSTERED INDEX IX_ProductHistory_NC ON
dbo.ProductHistory(ProductId, ValidFrom, ValidTo);
GO
CREATE TABLE dbo.Product
(
```

```
    ProductId INT NOT NULL CONSTRAINT PK_Product PRIMARY KEY,
    ProductName NVARCHAR(50) NOT NULL,
    Price MONEY NOT NULL,
    ValidFrom DATETIME2 GENERATED ALWAYS AS ROW START NOT NULL,
    ValidTo DATETIME2 GENERATED ALWAYS AS ROW END NOT NULL,
    PERIOD FOR SYSTEM_TIME (ValidFrom, ValidTo)
)
WITH (SYSTEM_VERSIONING = ON (HISTORY_TABLE = dbo.ProductHistory));
```

You will learn how to alter and drop system-versioned tables in more detail later in this chapter. Here, you should focus on the fact that you can create your own history table with a clustered columnstore index on it. *Figure 7.5* shows what you will see when you look at SQL Server Management Studio and find the created temporal table:

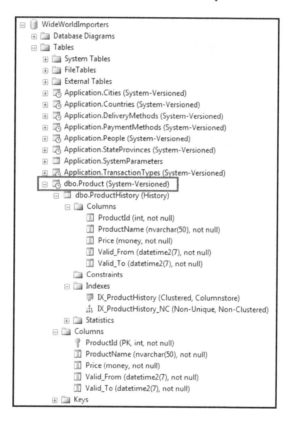

Figure 7.5: Temporal table in SQL Server Management Studio with user-defined history table

You can see that the table created by you acts as a history table and has a clustered columnstore index.

Period columns as hidden attributes

Period columns are used to support temporality of data and do not have business logic value. By using the HIDDEN clause, you can hide the new PERIOD columns to avoid impacting on existing applications that are not designed to handle new columns.

Converting non-temporal to temporal tables

In SQL Server 2016, you can create temporal tables from scratch, but you can also alter an existing table and add attributes to it to convert it to a system-versioned temporal table. All you need is to add period columns, define the SYSTEM_TIME period on them, and set the temporal attribute. The following code example demonstrates how to convert the Department table in the AdventureWorks2016CTP3 database to a temporal table:

```
USE AdventureWorks2016CTP3;
ALTER TABLE HumanResources.Department
ADD ValidFrom DATETIME2 GENERATED ALWAYS AS ROW START HIDDEN NOT NULL
CONSTRAINT DF_Validfrom DEFAULT SYSDATETIME(),
    ValidTo DATETIME2 GENERATED ALWAYS AS ROW END HIDDEN NOT NULL CONSTRAINT
DF_ValidTo DEFAULT '99991231 23:59:59.9999999',
    PERIOD FOR SYSTEM_TIME (ValidFrom, ValidTo);
GO
ALTER TABLE HumanResources.Department SET (SYSTEM_VERSIONING = ON
(HISTORY_TABLE = HumanResources.DepartmentHistory));
```

You have to use two ALTER statements: with the first statement, you define the period columns and the period, while the second statement sets the SYSTEM_VERSIONING attribute to ON and the name of the history table that will be created by the system. You should be aware that you need to provide default constraints for both columns, since they must be non-nullable. You can even use a date value from the past for the default constraint for the first period column; however, you cannot set values in the future.

 Adding a non-nullable column with a default constraint is a metadata operation in the Enterprise Edition only; in all other editions that means a physical operation with the allocation space to update all table rows with newly added columns. For large tables, this can take a long time and be aware that, during this action, the table is locked.

As you can see, it is very easy and straightforward to add temporal functionality to an existing non-temporal table. It works transparently; all your queries and commands will work without changes. But, what if you did not follow best practice and recommendations and used SELECT * in your statements? Since SELECT * includes all columns from tables involved in the FROM clause, two additional columns could lead to exceptions and breaking changes in the application.

To avoid this situation, you are allowed to define period date columns with the HIDDEN attribute, as shown in the above code. That means that these two columns will not be returned as part of the result set for a query that uses the SELECT * operation. Of course, it is still, and will always be, recommended to use a named list of columns (and only required ones) instead of SELECT *.

I need, here, to express my concerns about another implementation which takes care of solutions where SELECT * is implemented. I can understand that the vendor does not want to introduce a feature that can break customers' existing applications, but on the other hand, you cannot expect a developer to stop using SELECT * when new features and solutions don't sanction bad development habits.

Hidden attributes allow you to convert any non-temporal table (which does not violate the temporal table limitations listed in the previous section) to a temporal table without worrying about breaking changes in your solutions.

Migration existing temporal solution to system-versioned tables

Most probably, you have had to deal with historical data in the past. Since there was no out-of-the-box feature in previous SQL Server versions, you had to create a custom temporal data solution. Now that the feature is available, you might think to use it for your existing temporal solutions. You saw earlier in this chapter that you can define your own history table. Therefore, you can also use an existing and populated historical table. If you want to convert your existing solution to use system-versioned temporal tables in SQL Server 2016, you have to prepare both tables so that they fill all requirements for temporal tables. To demonstrate this, you will again use the AdventureWorks2016CTP3 database and create both current and history tables by using tables that exist in this database. Use the following code to create and populate the tables:

```
USE WideWorldImporters;
CREATE TABLE dbo.ProductListPrice
(
    ProductID INT NOT NULL CONSTRAINT PK_ProductListPrice PRIMARY KEY,
    ListPrice MONEY NOT NULL,
);
INSERT INTO dbo.ProductListPrice(ProductID,ListPrice)
SELECT ProductID,ListPrice FROM AdventureWorks2016CTP3.Production.Product;
GO
CREATE TABLE dbo.ProductListPriceHistory
(
    ProductID INT NOT NULL,
    ListPrice MONEY NOT NULL,
    StartDate DATETIME NOT NULL,
```

```
       EndDate DATETIME    NULL,
       CONSTRAINT PK_ProductListPriceHistory PRIMARY KEY CLUSTERED
       (
              ProductID ASC,
              StartDate ASC
       )
);
INSERT INTO
dbo.ProductListPriceHistory(ProductID,ListPrice,StartDate,EndDate)
SELECT ProductID, ListPrice, StartDate, EndDate FROM
AdventureWorks2016CTP3.Production.ProductListPriceHistory;
```

Consider the rows for the product with ID 707 in both tables:

```
SELECT * FROM dbo.ProductListPrice WHERE ProductID = 707;
SELECT * FROM dbo.ProductListPriceHistory WHERE ProductID = 707;
```

Here are the rows in the current and history tables respectively:

ProductID	ListPrice
707	34,99

ProductID	ListPrice	StartDate	EndDate
707	33,6442	2011-05-31 00:00:00.000	2012-05-29 00:00:00.000
707	33,6442	2012-05-30 00:00:00.000	2013-05-29 00:00:00.000
707	34,99	2013-05-30 00:00:00.000	NULL

Assume that this data has been produced by your temporal data solution and that you want to use system-versioned temporal tables in SQL Server 2016 instead of it, but to also use the same tables. The first thing you have to do is align the columns in both tables. Since the current table has no date columns, you need to add two period columns and define the period. The columns should have the same name as the counterpart columns from the history table. Here is the code that creates the temporal infrastructure in the current table:

```
ALTER TABLE dbo.ProductListPrice
ADD StartDate DATETIME2 GENERATED ALWAYS AS ROW START HIDDEN NOT NULL
CONSTRAINT DF_StartDate1 DEFAULT SYSDATETIME(),
    EndDate DATETIME2 GENERATED ALWAYS AS ROW END HIDDEN NOT NULL CONSTRAINT
DF_EndDate1 DEFAULT '99991231 23:59:59.9999999',
    PERIOD FOR SYSTEM_TIME (StartDate, EndDate);
GO
```

The next steps are related to the history table. As you can see from the sample data, your current solution allows gaps in the history table and also contains the current value with the undefined end date. As mentioned earlier in this chapter, the history table only contains historical data and there are no gaps between historical entries (the new start date is equal to the previous end date). Here are the steps you have to implement in order to prepare the dbo.ProductLisPriceHistory table to act as a history table in a system-versioned temporal table in SQL Server 2016:

- Update the non-nullable EndDate column to remove the gap between historical values described earlier and to support the open-closed interval
- Update all rows where the EndDate column is null to the StartDate of the rows in the current table
- Remove the primary key constraint
- Change the data type for both date columns StartDate and EndDate to DATETIME2

Here is the code that implements all these requests:

```
--remove gaps
UPDATE dbo.ProductListPriceHistory SET EndDate = DATEADD(day,1,EndDate);
--update EndDate to StartDate of the actual record
UPDATE dbo.ProductListPriceHistory SET EndDate = (SELECT MAX(StartDate)
FROM dbo.ProductListPrice) WHERE EndDate IS NULL;
--remove constraints
ALTER TABLE dbo.ProductListPriceHistory DROP CONSTRAINT
PK_ProductListPriceHistory;
--change data type to DATETIME2
ALTER TABLE dbo.ProductListPriceHistory ALTER COLUMN StartDate DATETIME2
NOT NULL;
ALTER TABLE dbo.ProductListPriceHistory ALTER COLUMN EndDate DATETIME2 NOT
NULL;
```

Now, both tables are ready to act as a system-versioned temporal table in SQL Server 2016:

```
ALTER TABLE dbo.ProductListPrice SET (SYSTEM_VERSIONING = ON (HISTORY_TABLE
= dbo.ProductListPriceHistory,  DATA_CONSISTENCY_CHECK = ON));
```

The command has been executed successfully and the dbo.ProductListPriceHistory table is now a system-versioned temporal table. Note that the option DATA_CONSISTENCY_CHECK = ON is used to check that all rows in the history table are valid from a temporal data point of view (no gaps, the end date not before the start date). Now, you can check the new functionality by using the UPDATE statement. You will update the price for the product with the ID 707 to 50 and then check the rows in both tables:

```
UPDATE dbo.ProductListPrice SET Price = 50 WHERE ProductID = 707;
SELECT * FROM dbo.ProductListPrice WHERE ProductID = 707;
SELECT * FROM dbo.ProductListPriceHistory WHERE ProductID = 707;
```

Here are the rows for this product in both tables:

```
ProductID    ListPrice
-----------  ----------------

707          50,00
ProductID    ListPrice   StartDate                         EndDate
-----------  ----------  ------------------------------    --------------------

707          33,6442     2011-05-31 00:00:00.000           2012-05-29 00:00:00.000
707          33,6442     2012-05-30 00:00:00.000           2013-05-29 00:00:00.000
707          34,99       2013-05-30 00:00:00.000           2016-08-19 18:14:55.9287816
707          34,99       2016-08-19 18:14:55.9287816       2016-08-19 18:15:12.6947253
```

You can see another row in the history table (compare with previous result). Of course, when you try these examples, you will get different values for the columns StartDate and EndDate since they are managed by the system.

As you can see, it is not so complicated to migrate an existing solution to a system-versioned table in SQL Server 2016, but it is not a single step. You should take into account, that most probably it will take time to update the data type to DATETIME2. However, by using the system-versioned temporal tables feature, your history tables are completely and automatically protected by changes from anyone except the system. This is a great, out-of-the-box, data consistency improvement.

Altering temporal tables

You can use the ALTER TABLE statement to perform schema changes on system-versioned temporal tables. When you use it to add a new data type, change a data type, or remove an existing column, the system will automatically perform the action against both the current and the history table. To check this, run the following code to create a temporal table from the previous section:

```
USE WideWorldImporters;
CREATE TABLE dbo.Product
(
    ProductId INT NOT NULL CONSTRAINT PK_Product PRIMARY KEY,
    ProductName NVARCHAR(50) NOT NULL,
```

```
        Price MONEY NOT NULL,
        ValidFrom DATETIME2 GENERATED ALWAYS AS ROW START NOT NULL,
        ValidTo DATETIME2 GENERATED ALWAYS AS ROW END NOT NULL,
        PERIOD FOR SYSTEM_TIME (ValidFrom, ValidTo)
    )
    WITH (SYSTEM_VERSIONING = ON (HISTORY_TABLE = dbo.ProductHistory));
```

The following code adds a new column named `Color` into both the current and the history table:

```
ALTER TABLE dbo.Product ADD Color NVARCHAR(15);
```

Since the column accepts null values, the action is done instantly.

When you add a non-nullable column, the situation is a bit different. First, you need to provide a default constraint and then you should take into account that this operation is an offline operation in all editions of SQL Server, except in the Enterprise Edition. The following code adds a new column `Category` that requires a value:

```
ALTER TABLE dbo.Product ADD Category SMALLINT NOT NULL CONSTRAINT
DF_Category DEFAULT 1;
```

This action will be online (metadata operation) in the Enterprise Edition only. In all the other editions, all rows in both the current and the history table will be touched to add additional columns with its value.

However, adding LOB and BLOB columns will cause a mass update in both the current and the history table in all SQL Server editions. The next code examples add a new LOB column `Description`:

```
ALTER TABLE dbo.Product ADD Description NVARCHAR(MAX) NOT NULL CONSTRAINT
DF_Description DEFAULT N'N/A';
```

This action will internally update all rows in both tables. For large tables, this can take a long time and during this time, both tables are locked.

You can also use the `ALTER TABLE` statement to add or remove the `HIDDEN` attribute to period columns or to remove it. This code line adds the `HIDDEN` attribute to the columns `ValidFrom` and `ValidTo`:

```
ALTER TABLE dbo.Product ALTER COLUMN ValidFrom ADD HIDDEN;
ALTER TABLE dbo.Product ALTER COLUMN ValidTo ADD HIDDEN;
```

Clearly, you can also remove the `HIDDEN` attribute:

```
ALTER TABLE dbo.Product ALTER COLUMN ValidFrom DROP HIDDEN;
ALTER TABLE dbo.Product ALTER COLUMN ValidTo DROP HIDDEN;
```

However, there are some changes that are not allowed for temporal tables:

- Adding an IDENDITY or computed column
- Adding a ROWGUIDCOL column or changing an existing column to it
- Adding a SPARSE column or changing an existing column to it, when the history table is compressed

When you try to add a SPARSE column, you will get an error, as in the following example:

```
ALTER TABLE dbo.Product ADD Size NVARCHAR(5) SPARSE;
```

The command ends up with the following error message:

```
Msg 11418, Level 16, State 2, Line 20
Cannot alter table 'ProductHistory' because the table either contains
sparse columns or a column set column which are incompatible with
compression.
```

The same happens when you try to add an identity column, as follows:

```
ALTER TABLE dbo.Product ADD ProductNumber INT IDENTITY (1,1);
```

And here is the error message:

```
Msg 13704, Level 16, State 1, Line 26
System-versioned table schema modification failed because history table
'WideWorldImporters.dbo.ProductHistory' has IDENTITY column specification.
Consider dropping all IDENTITY column specifications and trying again.
```

If you need to perform schema changes to a temporal table not supported in the ALTER statement, you have to set its SYSTEM_VERSIONING attribute to false to convert the tables to non-temporal tables, perform the changes, and then convert back to a temporal table. The following code demonstrates how to add the identity column ProductNumber and the sparse column Size into the temporal table dbo.Product:

```
ALTER TABLE dbo.ProductHistory REBUILD PARTITION = ALL WITH
(DATA_COMPRESSION=NONE);
GO
BEGIN TRAN
ALTER TABLE dbo.Product SET (SYSTEM_VERSIONING = OFF);
ALTER TABLE dbo.Product ADD Size NVARCHAR(5) SPARSE;
ALTER TABLE dbo.ProductHistory ADD Size NVARCHAR(5) SPARSE;
ALTER TABLE dbo.Product ADD ProductNumber INT IDENTITY (1,1);
ALTER TABLE dbo.ProductHistory ADD ProductNumber INT NOT NULL DEFAULT 0;
ALTER TABLE dbo.Product SET(SYSTEM_VERSIONING = ON (HISTORY_TABLE = dbo.
ProductHistory));
```

```
COMMIT;
```

To perform ALTER TABLE operations, you need to have CONTROL permission on the current and history tables. During the changes, both tables are locked with schema locks.

Dropping temporal tables

You cannot drop a system-versioned temporal table. Both current and history tables are protected until the SYSTEM_VERSIONING attribute of the current table is set to ON. When you set it to OFF, both tables automatically become non-temporal tables and are fully independent of each other. Therefore, you can perform all operations against them that are allowed according to your permissions. You can also drop period if you definitely want to convert a temporal table to a non-temporal one. The following code converts the Product table into a non-temporal table and removes the defined SYSTEM_TIME period:

```
ALTER TABLE dbo.Product SET (SYSTEM_VERSIONING = OFF);
ALTER TABLE dbo.Product DROP PERIOD FOR SYSTEM_TIME;
```

Note that the period columns ValidFrom and ValidTo remain in the table and will be further updated by the system. However, the history table will not be updated when data in the current table is changed.

Data manipulation in temporal tables

In this section, what happens when temporal data is inserted, updated, or deleted will be demonstrated. Note that the history table is protected; only the system can write into it. Even members of the sysadmin server role cannot insert, update, or delete rows from a history table of a system-versioned temporal table in SQL Server 2016.

In this section, you will insert into, and manipulate data from, the dbo.Product temporal table created in the previous section. Assume you have added the Fog product with the 150 price into the table on *21st November 2016*. Here is the code for this action and the state of the current and history tables after the statement's execution:

```
INSERT INTO dbo.Product(ProductId, ProductName, Price)
VALUES(1, N'Fog', 150.00) ;-- on 21st November
```

CURRENT TABLE

ProductId	ProductName	Price	ValidFrom	ValidTo
1	Fog	150	21.11.2016	31.12.9999

HISTORY TABLE

ProductId	ProductName	Price	ValidFrom	ValidTo
-				

Note that the dates in the `ValidFrom` and `ValidTo` columns are displayed in short format for clarity: their actual value is of `DATETIME2` data type.

As you can see after an `INSERT` into a temporal table:

- In the current table, a new row has been added with attributes from the `INSERT` statement, the period start date column is set to the system date, the period end date column is set to the max date
- The history table is not affected at all

Now, assume that the price for the product has been changed to `200` and that this change was entered into the database on 28th November 2016. Here is the code for this action and the state of the current and history tables after the statement's execution:

```
UPDATE dbo.Product SET Price = 200.00 WHERE ProductId = 1;-- on 28th
November
```

CURRENT TABLE

ProductId	ProductName	Price	ValidFrom	ValidTo
1	Fog	200	28.11.2016	31.12.9999

HISTORY TABLE

ProductId	ProductName	Price	ValidFrom	ValidTo
1	Fog	150	21.11.2016	28.11.2016

We remind you again that values in the `ValidFrom` and `ValidTo` columns are displayed in short format for clarity. The value in the `ValidTo` column in the history table is identical to the `ValidFrom` value in the current table: there are no gaps.

Now, assume that you have reduced the price the next day to `180`. Here is the code for this action and the state of the current and history tables after the statement's execution:

```
UPDATE dbo.Product SET Price = 180.00 WHERE ProductId = 1;-- on 29th
November
```

CURRENT TABLE

ProductId	ProductName	Price	ValidFrom	ValidTo
1	Fog	180	29.11.2016	31.12.9999

HISTORY TABLE

ProductId	ProductName	Price	ValidFrom	ValidTo
1	Fog	150	21.11.2016	28.11.2016
1	Fog	200	28.11.2016	29.11.2016

You can see another entry in the history table indicating that the price `200` was valid for one day. What would happen if you execute the same statement again, say, on 30th November? There is no real change; no business logic attributes are changed, but what does it mean for temporal tables? Here is the code for this action and the state of the current and history tables after the statement's execution:

```
UPDATE dbo.Product SET Price = 180.00 WHERE ProductId = 1;-- on 30th
November
```

CURRENT TABLE

ProductId	ProductName	Price	ValidFrom	ValidTo
1	Fog	180	30.11.2016	31.12.9999

HISTORY TABLE

ProductId	ProductName	Price	ValidFrom	ValidTo
1	Fog	150	21.11.2016	28.11.2016
1	Fog	200	28.11.2016	29.11.2016
1	Fog	180	29.11.2016	30.11.2016

As you can see in the history table, even if there is no real change to the attributes in the current table, an entry in the history table is created and period date columns are updated.

You can think about this as a bug, but although no attributes have been changed, if you use temporal tables for auditing you probably want to see all attempts of data manipulation in the main table.

Here is how an UPDATE of a single row in a temporal table affects the current and history tables:

- Values in the row of the current table are updates to those provided by the UPDATE statement, the period start date column is set to system date, the period end date column is set to max date
- From the current table before updating is copied to the history table, only the period end date column is set to the system date (exactly the same value as in the period start date column of the current row after the update)
- Every UPDATE statement issued against a single row in the current table will generate an entry in the history table

You can also see that there are no gaps in the dates in the same row in the history table. Even duplicates are possible: the history table does not have constraints to prevent them! Therefore, it is possible to have multiple records for the same row with the same values in period columns. Moreover, even values in period columns can be identical! The only constraint that is enforced is that the date representing the period end date column cannot be before the date representing the period start date (therefore, it is guaranteed that ValidFrom <= ValidTo).

You will finally remove the row from the current table in order to demonstrate how the DELETE statement affects temporal tables. Here is the code for this action and the state of the current and history tables after the statement's execution:

```
DELETE FROM dbo.Product WHERE ProductId = 1;-- on 1st December
```

CURRENT TABLE

ProductId	ProductName	Price	ValidFrom	ValidTo
		-		

HISTORY TABLE

ProductId	ProductName	Price	ValidFrom	ValidTo
1	Fog	150	21.11.2016	21.11.2016
1	Fog	200	28.11.2016	29.11.2016
1	Fog	180	29.11.2016	30.11.2016
1	Fog	180	30.11.2016	01.12.2016

As you expected, there is no row in the current table, but another row has been added into the history table. After executing the DELETE statement against a single row in a temporal table:

- **Current table**: The row has been removed
- **History table**: The row from the current table before deleting is copied to the history table, only the period end date column is set to the system date

Querying temporal data in SQL Server 2016

System-versioned tables are primarily intended for tracking historical data changes. Queries on system-versioned tables often tend to be concerned with retrieving table content as of a given point in time or between any two given points in time. As you saw, Microsoft has implemented them according to SQL:2011 standard, which means that two physical tables exist: a table with actual data and a history table. In order to simplify queries against temporal tables, SQL:2011 standard introduced a new SQL clause; FOR SYSTEM_TIME. In addition to it, some new temporal-specific sub-clauses have been added too. SQL Server 2016 has not only implemented these extensions, but added two more extensions. Here is the complete list of clauses and extensions you can use to query temporal data in SQL Server 2016:

- FOR SYSTEM_TIME AS OF
- FOR SYSTEM_TIME FROM TO
- FOR SYSTEM_TIME BETWEEN AND
- FOR SYSTEM TIME CONTAINED_IN
- FOR SYSTEM_TIME ALL

Retrieving temporal data at a specific point in time

When you want to retrieve temporal data that was valid at a given point in time, the resulting set could contain both actual and historical data. For instance, the following query would return all rows from the People temporal table in the WideWorldImporters sample database that were valid at 20th March 2016 at 8 A.M.:

```
SELECT PersonID, FullName, OtherLanguages, ValidFrom, ValidTo
FROM Application.People WHERE ValidFrom <= '2016-03-20 08:00:00' AND
ValidTo > '2016-03-20 08:00:00'
UNION ALL
SELECT PersonID, FullName, OtherLanguages, ValidFrom, ValidTo
FROM Application.People_Archive WHERE ValidFrom <= '2016-03-20 08:00:00'
```

```
AND ValidTo > '2016-03-20 08:00:00';
```

The query returns 1,109 rows. For a single person, only one row is returned: either the actual or a historical record. A record is valid if its start date was before or exactly on the given date and its end date is greater than the given date.

The new FOR SYSTEM_TIME clause with the AS OF sub-clause can be used to simplify the preceding query. Here is the same query with temporal Transact-SQL extensions:

```
SELECT PersonID, FullName, OtherLanguages, ValidFrom, ValidTo
FROM Application.People FOR SYSTEM_TIME AS OF '2016-03-20 08:00:00';
```

Of course, it returns the same result set and the execution plans are identical, as shown in *Figure 7.6*:

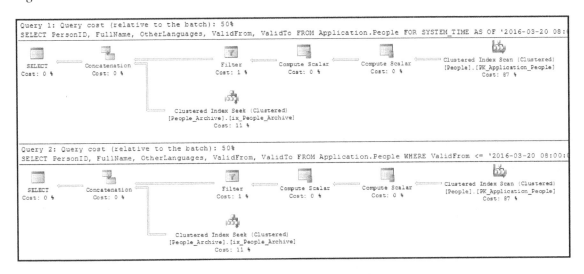

Figure 7.6. Execution plans for point in time queries against temporal tables

Under the hood, the query processor touches both tables and retrieves data, but the query looks simpler.

A special case of a point-in-time query against a temporal table is a query where you specify the actual date as the point in time. The following query returns actual data from the same temporal table:

```
DECLARE @Now AS DATETIME = CURRENT_TIMESTAMP;
SELECT PersonID, FullName, OtherLanguages, ValidFrom, ValidTo
FROM Application.People FOR SYSTEM_TIME AS OF @Now;
```

The query is logically equivalent to this one:

```
SELECT PersonID, FullName, OtherLanguages, ValidFrom, ValidTo
FROM Application.People;
```

However, when you look at the execution plans (see *Figure 7.7*), for the execution of the first query, both tables have been processed, while the non-temporal query had to retrieve data from the current table only:

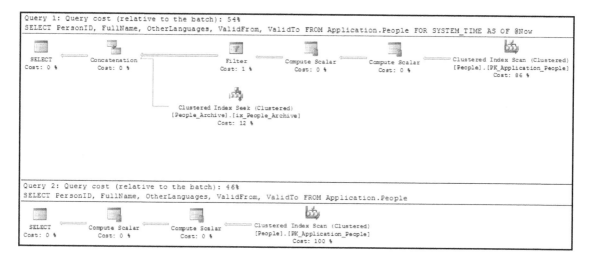

Figure 7.7: Compare execution plans for temporal and non-temporal queries that retrieve current data only

Therefore, you should not use temporal queries with the FOR SYSTEM_TIME AS clause to return data from the current table.

Retrieving temporal data from a specific period

You can use a new FOR SYSTEM_TIME clause to retrieve temporal data that was or is valid between two points in time. These queries are typically used for getting changes to specific rows over time. To achieve this, you could use one of two SQL:2011 standard specified sub-clauses:

- FROM...TO returns all data that started before or at the beginning of a given period and ended after the end of the period (closed-open interval)
- BETWEEN...AND returns all data that started before or at the beginning of a given period and ended after or at the end of the period (closed-closed interval)

As you can see, the only difference between these two sub-clauses is how data with a starting date to the right side of the given period is interpreted: BETWEEN includes this data, FROM...TO does not.

The following queries demonstrate usage and the difference between them:

```
--example using FROM/TO
SELECT PersonID, FullName, OtherLanguages, ValidFrom, ValidTo
FROM Application.People FOR SYSTEM_TIME FROM '2016-03-20 08:00:00' TO
'2016-05-31 23:14:00' WHERE PersonID = 7;

--example using BETWEEN
SELECT PersonID, FullName, OtherLanguages, ValidFrom, ValidTo
FROM Application.People FOR SYSTEM_TIME BETWEEN '2016-03-20 08:00:01' AND
'2016-05-31 23:14:00' WHERE PersonID = 7;
```

Here are the result sets generated by the preceding queries:

```
PersonID  FullName    OtherLanguages                  ValidFrom         ValidTo
--------- ----------  ------------------------------  ---------------   ---------------
7         Amy Trefl   NULL                            2016-03-20 08:00  2016-05-31 23:13
7         Amy Trefl   ["Slovak","Spanish","Polish"]   2016-05-31 23:13  2016-05-31 23:14


PersonID  FullName    OtherLanguages                  ValidFrom         ValidTo
--------- ----------  ------------------------------  ---------------   ---------------
7         Amy Trefl   ["Slovak","Spanish","Polish"]   2016-05-31 23:14  9999-12-31 23:59
7         Amy Trefl   NULL                            2016-03-20 08:00  2016-05-31 23:13
7         Amy Trefl   ["Slovak","Spanish","Polish"]   2016-05-31 23:13  2016-05-31 23:14
```

As you can see, the second query returns three rows: it includes the row where the start date is equal to the value of the right boundary of the given period.

These two sub-clauses return row versions that overlap with a specified period. If you need to return rows that existed within specified period boundaries, you need to use another extension CONTAINED IN. This extension (an implementation of one of the Allen's Operators) is not defined in the SQL:2011 standard, it is implemented in SQL Server 2016. Rows that either start or end outside a given interval will not be part of a result set when the CONTAINED IN sub-clause is used. When you replace the sub-clause BETWEEN with it in the above example, only rows whose whole life belongs to the given interval will survive:

```
SELECT PersonID, FullName, OtherLanguages, ValidFrom, ValidTo
FROM Application.People FOR SYSTEM_TIME CONTAINED IN ('2016-03-20
08:00:01','2016-05-31 23:14:00') WHERE PersonID = 7;
```

Instead of three rows by using BETWEEN or two with FROM...TO sub-clauses, this time only one row is returned:

```
PersonID   FullName      OtherLanguages                  ValidFrom          ValidTo
--------   ----------    ---------------------------     ----------------   ----------------
7          Amy Trefl     ["Slovak","Spanish","Polish"]   2016-05-31 23:13   2016-05-31 23:14
```

Although this extension is not standard, its implementation in SQL Server 2016 is welcomed: it covers a reasonable and not-so-rare use case and simplifies the development of database solutions based on temporal tables.

Retrieving all temporal data

Since temporal data is separated into two tables, to get all temporal data you need to combine data from both tables. However, there is no sub-clause defined in SQL:2011 standard for that purpose. However, the SQL Server team has introduced the extension (sub-clause) ALL to simplify such queries.

Here is a temporal query that returns both actual and historical data for the person with the ID 7:

```
SELECT PersonID, FullName, OtherLanguages, ValidFrom, ValidTo
FROM Application.People FOR SYSTEM_TIME ALL
WHERE PersonID = 7;
```

The query returns 14 rows, since there are 13 historical rows and one entry in the current table. Here is the logically equivalent, standard query but it's a bit more complex:

```
SELECT PersonID, FullName, OtherLanguages, ValidFrom, ValidTo
FROM Application.People
WHERE PersonID = 7
UNION ALL
SELECT PersonID, FullName, OtherLanguages, ValidFrom, ValidTo
FROM Application.People_Archive
WHERE PersonID = 7;
```

The only purpose of this sub-clause is to simplify queries against temporal tables. New extensions for querying temporal tables do not bring performance benefits, but they significantly simplify queries against them.

Performance and storage considerations with temporal tables

Introducing temporal tables and especially adding this functionality to existing tables can significantly increase the storage used for data in your system. Since there is no out-of-the-box solution for managing the retention of history tables, if you don't do something, data will remain there forever. This can be painful in terms of storage costs, maintenance, and the performance of queries on temporal tables, especially if rows in your current tables are heavily updated.

History data retention

Unfortunately, you cannot configure a history table to automatically remove data according to a user-defined retention policy. That means that you have to implement data retention manually. This is not very complicated, but it is not a trivial action. I had expected it as a part of the implementation and will be disappointed if it is not delivered in the next SQL Server version. As mentioned, you can use some other SQL Server features to implement data retention for history tables:

- **Stretch databases** allows you to move an entire part of historical data transparently to Azure.
- **Partitioning** of history tables allows you to easily truncate the oldest historical data by implementing a sliding window approach.
- **Custom Cleanup** doesn't require any other features. You use Transact-SQL scripts to convert a temporal table to non-temporal, delete old data, and convert the table back to a temporal table.

More details about data retention can be found in Books Online at the following address: `https://msdn.microsoft.com/en-us/library/mt 637341.aspx`.

History table physical implementation

You saw in one of the previous sections that you can create your own history table and associate it with a current table or you can let SQL Server do it for you. When SQL Server creates a history table, by default it creates a row stored clustered table with a clustered index on period columns. If the current table does not contain data types that prevents the usage of data compression, the table is created with PAGE compression. Is this OK? Well, it depends on the use case. This approach is good, if dominant temporal queries are based on date range that is, return a snapshot for all rows that were valid at the given point in time. However, if your temporal queries usually look for historical records for individual items, a clustered index on primary key columns followed by period columns would be a better solution.

Finally, if you plan to process a lot of data in temporal queries or to aggregate them, the best approach is to create your own history table with a clustered columnstore index and eventual additional non-clustered normal B-tree indexes.

History table overhead

Converting a non-temporal table into a temporal table is very easy. With two ALTER TABLE statements, you get the full temporal table functionality. However, this cannot be completely free; adding a temporal feature to a table brings a performance overhead in data modification operations. According to my measurements, a single update operation against a row in a temporal table is about 30% slower than it would be when the table is non-temporal. I performed a simple test where I updated a different number of rows in a table before it was converted to a temporal table and after that. *Figure 7.8* displays the results of this test. For a small amount of rows (<1000) locking, calculating, and inserting data into the history table slows down the update about two times. Updating 50,000 rows in a temporal table takes about 8 times longer than the same operation against the same table when it is implemented as a non-temporal table.

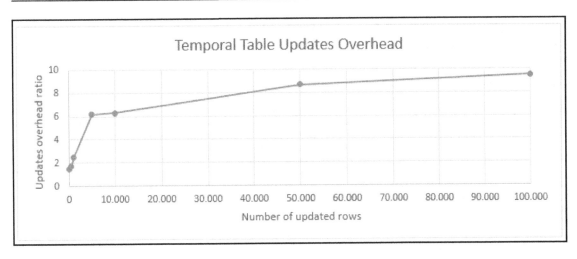

Figure 7.8: Temporal table updates overhead

Finally, massive updates (>100K rows) are 10 times slower for temporal tables compared to those against their non-temporal counterparts.

Temporal tables with memory-optimized tables

System-versioned temporal tables are also supported for memory-optimized tables. You can assign or let SQL Server create a history table for your memory-optimized table. The history table must be a disk table, but this is exactly what you want: frequently used (hot) data remains in memory, while cold data can reside in disk tables. By taking this approach, you can use all the benefits provided by memory-optimized tables (high transactional throughput, lock-free concurrency) and save their historical data on disk-based tables and leave memory for active datasets only.

Figure 7.9 shows the architecture of system-versioned memory-optimized tables. It is taken from the Books Online page at `https://msdn.microsoft.com/en-us/library/mt590207.a spx`.

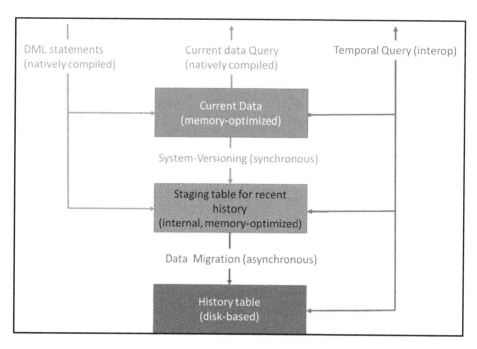

Figure 7.9: System-Versioned Temporal Tables with Memory-Optimized Tables Architecture

As you can see, system-versioned temporal tables are implemented with three tables:

- **Current table** is a memory-optimized table and all native compiled operations are supported
- **Recent history table** is an internal memory-optimized table that handles changes in the current table synchronously and enables DMLs to be executed from natively compiled code
- **History table** is a disk table that contains changes in the current table and manages them asynchronously

Historical data is a union of data in the recent history and history tables. A history row is either in the staging memory table or in the disk table: it cannot be in both tables. The following code example creates a new memory-optimized temporal table:

```
USE WideWorldImporters;
CREATE TABLE dbo.Product
(
    ProductId INT NOT NULL PRIMARY KEY NONCLUSTERED,
    ProductName NVARCHAR(50) NOT NULL,
    Price MONEY NOT NULL,
    ValidFrom DATETIME2 GENERATED ALWAYS AS ROW START HIDDEN NOT NULL,
    ValidTo DATETIME2 GENERATED ALWAYS AS ROW END HIDDEN NOT NULL,
    PERIOD FOR SYSTEM_TIME (ValidFrom, ValidTo)
)
WITH (MEMORY_OPTIMIZED = ON, DURABILITY = SCHEMA_AND_DATA,
SYSTEM_VERSIONING = ON (HISTORY_TABLE = dbo.ProductHistory));
```

After the execution of this query, you can see that one memory-optimized table is:

```
SELECT CONCAT(SCHEMA_NAME(schema_id),'.', name) AS table_name,
is_memory_optimized, temporal_type_desc FROM sys.tables WHERE name IN
('Product',
 'ProductHistory');
```

The result of the preceding query is as follows:

table_name	is_memory_optimized	temporal_type_desc
dbo.Product	1	SYSTEM_VERSIONED_TEMPORAL_TABLE
dbo.ProductHistory	0	HISTORY_TABLE

As mentioned earlier, SQL Server creates a third table automatically: an internal memory-optimized table. Here is the code that you can use to find its name and properties:

```
SELECT CONCAT(SCHEMA_NAME(schema_id),'.', name) AS table_name,
internal_type_desc FROM  sys.internal_tables WHERE name =
CONCAT('memory_optimized_history_table_', OBJECT_ID('dbo.Product'));
```

And here is its output:

table_name	internal_type_desc
sys.memory_optimized_history_table_608721221	INTERNAL_TEMPORAL_HISTORY_TABLE

Only durable, memory-optimized tables can be system-versioned temporal tables and history tables must be disk-based. Since all current rows are in memory, you can use natively compiled modules to access this data. Use the following code to create a native compiled stored procedure that handles the inserting and updating of products:

```
CREATE OR ALTER PROCEDURE dbo.SaveProduct
(
@ProductId INT,
@ProductName NVARCHAR(50),
@Price MONEY
)
WITH NATIVE_COMPILATION, SCHEMABINDING, EXECUTE AS OWNER
AS
    BEGIN ATOMIC WITH
    (TRANSACTION ISOLATION LEVEL = SNAPSHOT, LANGUAGE = N'English')
    UPDATE dbo.Product SET ProductName = @ProductName, Price = @Price
    WHERE ProductId = @ProductId
    IF @@ROWCOUNT = 0
        INSERT INTO dbo.Product(ProductId,ProductName,Price) VALUES
(@ProductId, @ProductName, @Price);
END
GO
```

Now you can, for instance, add two rows and update one of them by using the above procedure:

```
EXEC dbo.SaveProduct 1, N'Home Jersey Benfica', 89.95;
EXEC dbo.SaveProduct 2, N'Away Jersey Juventus', 89.95;
EXEC dbo.SaveProduct 1, N'Home Jersey Benfica', 79.95;
```

Under the hood, everything works perfectly: both the current and history tables are updated. Here are the resulting datasets:

ProductId	ProductName	Price
2	Away Jersey Juventus	89.95
1	Home Jersey Benfica	79.95

ProductId	ProductName	Price	ValidFrom	ValidTo
1	Home Jersey Benfica	89.95	2016-08-20 10:29:52	2016-08-20 10:29:53

Note that values in the column ValidFrom and ValidTo are shortened to fit in a single line.

The querying of historical data is effectively under the SNAPSHOT isolation level and always returns a union between the in-memory staging buffer and the disk based table without duplicates. Since temporal queries (queries that use the FOR SYSTEM_TIME clause) are touching memory-optimized and disk tables, they can be used only in the interop mode; it is not possible to use them in native compiled procedures.

Data from the internal memory-optimized staging table is regularly moved to the disk-based history table by the asynchronous data flush task. This data flush mechanism has the goal of keeping the internal memory buffers at less than 10% of the memory consumption of their parent objects.

When you add system-versioning to an existing non-temporal table, expect a performance impact on update and delete operations because history table is updated automatically. Every update and delete is recorded into the internal memory-optimized history table, so you may experience unexpected memory consumption if your workload uses those two operations massively.

What is missing in SQL Server 2016?

SQL Server 2016 is the first SQL Server version that has some built-in support for temporal data. However, the support is still quite basic. SQL Server 2016 supports system-versioned tables only. You saw at the beginning of this chapter that application-versioned tables, and of course bitemporal tables, add much more to the complexity of temporal problems. Unfortunately, in order to deal with application validity times, you need to develop your own solution, including your own implementation of all the constraints you need to enforce data integrity. In addition, you need to deal with the optimization of temporal queries by yourself as well.

It would also be nice if you were able to define the **retention period** for the historical rows, like you can define for the Query Store. Currently, you have to do the history data cleanup by yourself.

If you are familiar with analytical applications and data warehouses, you might think that system-versioned temporal tables could help you in analytical scenarios. However, as you will learn in the next section, which briefly introduces data warehouses and slowly changing dimension problems, analytical applications typically have different granularity requests and system-versioned temporal tables don't help here.

SQL Server 2016 temporal tables and data warehouses

For analytical purposes, **data warehouses** (DW) evolved. Data warehouses support historical data. You should not confuse data warehouse (historical) data with temporal data, the subject of this chapter. In a data warehouse, historical data just means archived non-temporal data from the past; a typical data warehouse holds from 5 to 10 years of data for analytical purposes. Data warehouses are not suitable for business applications because a data warehouse typically has no constraints.

Data warehouses have a simplified data model that consists of multiple **star schemas**. You can see a typical star schema in the following screenshot:

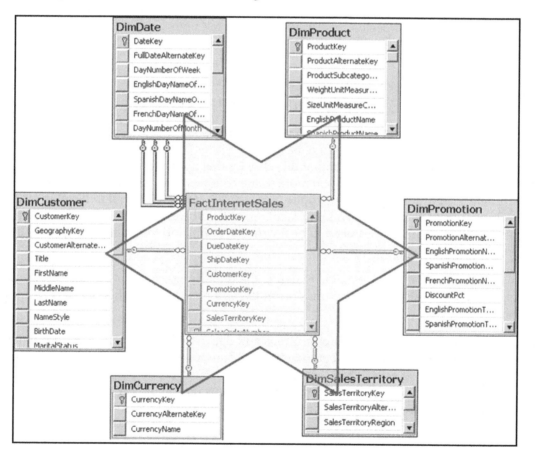

Figure 7.10: Star schema

One schema covers one business area. It consists of a single central table, called the **fact table**, and multiple surrounding tables, called **dimensions**. The fact table is always on the many side in every single relationship. The star schema is deliberately denormalized. The fact table includes measures, while dimensions give context to those measures. Shared dimensions connect star schemas in a data warehouse.

Dimensions can change over time. The pace of changes is usually slow compared to the pace of changes in fact tables. Transactional systems show the current state only, and don't preserve the history. In a DW, you might need to preserve the history. This is known as the **slowly changing dimensions (SCD)** problem. Type 1 solution means not preserving the history in the DW by simply overwriting the values when the values in the sources change. Type 2 means adding a new row for a change, and marking which row is the current. You can also mix both types—for some attributes, like City in the example, you use type 2; while for some, like Occupation, you use type 1. Note the additional problem—when you update the Occupation attribute, you need to decide whether to update the current row only, or also the historical rows (that come from the type 2 changes). You can see these possibilities in the following figure:

- **OLTP data**

CUSTID	FULLNAME	CITY	OCCUPATION
17	Bostjan Strazar	Vienna	Professional

- **OLTP data and DW SCD Type 1 after change**

CUSTID	FULLNAME	CITY	OCCUPATION
17	Bostjan Strazar	Ljubljana	Professional

- **DW SCD Type 2 after change**

DWCID	CUSTID	FULLNAME	CITY	OCCUPATION	CURRENT
17	17	Bostjan Strazar	Vienna	Professional	0
289	17	Bostjan Strazar	Ljubljana	Professional	1

- **DW SCD Type 1 & 2 after change**

DWCID	CUSTID	FULLNAME	CITY	OCCUPATION	CURRENT
17	17	Bostjan Strazar	Vienna	Professional	0
289	17	Bostjan Strazar	Ljubljana	Management	1

Figure 7.11: Slowly changing dimension

At first glimpse, SQL Server system-versioned tables might be the solution for the SCD problem when using the type 2 implementation. However, this is typically not true. In a data warehouse, more often than not, you need to implement a mixed solution, type 1 for some attributes and type 2 for others. The granularity of the time points in system-versioned tables is one hundred nanoseconds; in a data warehouse, typical granularity is one day. In the source system, the same entity, such as customer, can be updated multiple times per day. You can have multiple historical rows for the same entity in a single day. Therefore, when transferring the data from a transactional database to a data warehouse, you need to take care to transfer the last state for each day. The following query illustrates the problem:

```
USE WideWorldImporters;
SELECT PersonID, FullName,
 ValidFrom, ValidTo
FROM Application.People
 FOR SYSTEM_TIME ALL
WHERE IsEmployee = 1
  AND PersonID = 14;
```

In the `WideWorldImporters` database, the `Application.People` is a system-versioned table. The previous query returns all rows for an employee called `Lily Code`. Here is the abbreviated result:

PersonID	FullName	ValidFrom	ValidTo
14	Lily Code	2016-05-31 23:14:00.0000000	9999-12-31 23:59:59.9999999
14	Lily Code	2013-01-01 00:00:00.0000000	2013-01-01 08:00:00.0000000
14	Lily Code	2013-01-01 08:00:00.0000000	2013-01-19 08:00:00.0000000
14	Lily Code	2013-01-19 08:00:00.0000000	2013-02-14 08:00:00.0000000

You can see that this person has multiple rows for a single date. For example, there are two rows for `Lily` where the `ValidTo` date (just the date part) equals to `2013-01-01`. You need to select only the last row per employee per day. This is done by the following query. You can run it and check the results.

```
WITH PersonCTE AS
(
SELECT PersonID, FullName,
 CAST(ValidFrom AS DATE) AS ValidFrom,
 CAST(ValidTo AS DATE) AS ValidTo,
 ROW_NUMBER() OVER(PARTITION BY PersonID, CAST(ValidFrom AS Date)
                ORDER BY ValidFrom DESC) AS rn
FROM Application.People
 FOR SYSTEM_TIME ALL
WHERE IsEmployee = 1
)
```

```
SELECT PersonID, FullName,
 ValidFrom, ValidTo
FROM PersonCTE
WHERE rn = 1;
```

Summary

SQL Server 2016 system-versioned temporal tables are a very nice feature you can start using immediately, without changes to applications. You can use them for auditing all changes in specific tables. You can retrieve the state of those tables at any point in time in history. You can find all states and changes in a specific period. SQL Server automatically updates the period in the current row and inserts the old version of the row in the history table as soon as you update the current row.

Nevertheless, there is still a lot to do in future versions of SQL Server. We still need better support for application validity times, including support for constraints and the optimization of temporal queries.

8
Tightening the Security

Developers like to forget about security and simply leave the security issues to the database administrators. However, it is much harder for a DBA to tighten the security for a database where developers did not plan and design for security. To secure your data, you must understand the potential threats as well as the security mechanisms provided by SQL Server and the other components your application is using, including the operating system and programming language.

When talking about securing SQL Server, we are actually talking about defending data access to the database platform and guaranteeing the integrity of that access. In addition, you have to protect all SQL Server components included in your solution. Remember that your system is only as secure as the least secure component. As a defender, you have to close all holes, while an attacker only has to find a single hole. However, dealing with all aspects of security would be out of the scope of this chapter. Therefore, this chapter will cover only the most important security features of the SQL Server Database Engine, and introduce the three new SQL Server 2016 security features.

With **Always Encrypted**, SQL Server 2016 finally enables full data encryption, so that no tools or persons, regardless of their database and server permissions, can read encrypted data except the client application with an appropriate key. **Row-level security**, on the other hand, restricts which data in a table can be seen by a specific user. This is very useful in multi-tenant environments where you usually want to avoid a data-reading intersection between different customers. **Dynamic data masking** is a soft feature that limits sensitive data exposure by masking it to non-privileged users.

This chapter will cover the following points:

- SQL Server security basics
- Data encryption
- Row-level security
- Dynamic data masking

SQL Server security basics

The structure of secure systems generally consists of three parts: authentication, authorization, and enforcement of rules. **Authentication** is the process of checking the identity of a principal by examining the credentials and validating those credentials against some authority. **Authorization** is the process of determining whether a principal is allowed to perform a requested action. Authorization occurs after authentication, and uses information about the principal's identity and roles to determine what resources the principal can access. The **enforcement of** rules provides the mechanism to block direct access to resources. Blocking access is essential to securing any system. The following figure shows the structure of a secure system:

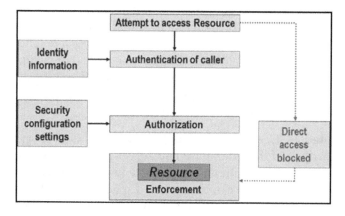

Structure of secure systems

You will learn how SQL Server implements the logic of a secure system, including:

- Principals
- Securables
- Schemas
- Object permissions
- Statement permissions

Defining principals and securables

SQL Server supports two authentication modes: Windows mode and mixed mode. In Windows mode, when a user connects through a Windows user account, SQL Server validates the account name and password by using information from the operating system. In mixed mode, in addition to the Windows authentication, a user can provide a SQL login and password to connect to SQL Server. SQL Server can use and enforce the Windows password policy mechanisms.

SQL Server defines two fundamental terms for security: principals and securables. **Principals** are entities that can request SQL Server resources. They are arranged in a hierarchy in the principal's scope: you can have Windows, server, and database-level principals. A principal can be a Windows domain login, a Windows local login, a Windows group, a SQL Server login, a server role, a database user, a database role, or an application role in a database. In addition to having regular users, you can create a SQL Server login or a database user from a certificate or an asymmetric key.

Securables are the resources you are protecting. Some securables can be contained within others in nested hierarchies (scopes). You can secure a complete scope, and the objects in the scope inherit permissions from the upper level of the hierarchy. The securable scopes are server, database, and schema.

After authentication, in the authorization phase, SQL Server checks whether a principal has appropriate permissions to use the securables. The following figure shows the most important principals, securables, and permissions in SQL Server, including the level where they are defined.

Principals	Permissions	Securables
Windows level		
• Groups • Domain user accounts • Local user accounts		
SQL Server level		

• Fixed server roles
• SQL Server logins
	• Grant – Deny – Revoke
	  – Control
	  – Create
		• SQL Server logins and roles
		• Endpoints
		• Databases

Database level	– Alter – Drop	

• Fixed database roles
• Database users
• Application roles
	– Select
	– Insert
	– Update
	– Delete
	– Execute
	– Connect
	– Reference
	– Take ownership
	– View definition
		• Users and roles
		• Assemblies
		• Keys and certificates
		• Full-text catalogs and stoplists
		• Service Broker services, bindings, contracts, routes, and message types
		• Schemas
		  – Tables
		  – Views
		  – Functions
		  – Procedures
		  – Types
		  – XML schema collections
		  – Service Broker queues
		  – Synonyms

Principals, securables, and permissions

You manage principals with **data definition language** (**DDL**) statements. You maintain permissions with **data control language** (**DCL**) statements. You create a principal as you do any other objects—by using the CREATE statement. You modify them by using the ALTER statement and delete them by using the DROP statement.

You can create SQL Server logins, which are security principals, or you can create logins from different sources, such as from Windows, certificates, or asymmetric keys. When you create SQL Server logins, you can specify that you want to bypass the password expiration and account policies. However, these policies help to secure your system, for example, preventing brute-force password attacks, and therefore this option is not recommended.

Database users are still part of the authentication. SQL Server supports two models: **traditional login and user model** and **contained database user model**.

- In the traditional model, a login is created in the master database and then mapped to a user in some other database. The end user connects to SQL Server with a login, and, through the mapping to one or more databases, the user gets access to the database(s).
- In the contained model, a database user is either mapped to a Windows user directly or one is created with a password. The end user connects to a single database directly, without having a login in the master database.

The following code shows how to create an SQL Server login with a weak password. If you execute this code, you get an error because the password does not meet Window's password policy requirements.

```
USE master;
CREATE LOGIN LoginA WITH password='LoginA';
GO
```

However, the following code succeeds. It creates an SQL Server login with a weak password, this time bypassing the Windows password policy, and creates a login from a built-in Windows group.

```
CREATE LOGIN LoginA WITH password='LoginA',
CHECK_POLICY=OFF;
CREATE LOGIN [BuiltinPower Users] FROM WINDOWS;
```

Bypassing password expiration and complexity policies is definitely not recommended. The SQL Server login just created is now very prone to brute-force attacks. You can check the `sys.sql_logins` catalog view to see which SQL logins do not enforce the policies mentioned, as the following code shows:

```
SELECT name,
type_desc,
is_disabled,
is_policy_checked,
is_expiration_checked
FROM sys.sql_logins
WHERE name LIKE 'L%';
```

The result shows the login that was just created:

```
name    type_desc    is_disabled  is_policy_checked  is_expiration_checked
------  -----------  -----------  ----------------   --------------------
LoginA  SQL_LOGIN    0            0                  0
```

In SQL Server, you have some special principals. On the server level, you have the sa SQL Server login, which is created when you install SQL Server. The default database for this login is master. This login has all permissions on the server and you cannot revoke any permissions from this login. You should protect the sa login with a strong password. If you use Windows authentication only, this login cannot be used to connect to SQL Server.

In every database, you get the public fixed role and the guest user account. You cannot drop them. You can only disable the guest user account. Any login without a directly mapped user in a database can access the database through the guest account. Application roles can also use this account to access the data in databases other than the database in the context for which they were invoked. Before you give any permission to the guest user account, make sure you consider all the ramifications. Every database user and every database role is a member of the public role. Therefore, any user or role—including an application role—inherits all permissions given to the public role. You should be careful when giving any permission to the public role; the best practice is to never give any permission to it.

The privileged database user dbo still exists in SQL Server. This user is a member of the db_owner role and, therefore, has all permissions on the database. You cannot drop dbo from the db_owner role.

Every database includes two additional principals: INFORMATION_SCHEMA and sys. You cannot drop these principals because SQL Server needs them. They serve like schemas (namespaces) for ANSI-standard information schema views and for SQL Server catalog views. Finally, SQL Server provides some special logins based on certificates, where their name starts and ends with two hash characters, such as ##MS_dqs_db_owner_login##. These logins are for SQL Server internal use only.

The principals are securables by themselves. You can control who can modify logins via membership in the **sysadmin** and **securityadmin** server-level roles, and the ALTER ANY LOGIN server-level permission. You can control who can modify database users and roles by memberships in the db_owner and db_securityadmin roles, and the ALTER ANY USER and ALTER ANY ROLE permissions.

In SQL Server, the metadata of the objects is not visible to the public role (that is, everyone) by default. You can control the metadata visibility by using two permissions: VIEW ANY DATABASE and VIEW DEFINITION.

The VIEW ANY DATABASE permission is granted to the public role by default, so all logins can still see the list of all databases on an SQL Server instance unless you revoke this permission from the public role. You can check this server-level permission by querying the sys.server_permissions catalog view:

```
SELECT pr.name,
pe.state_desc,
pe.permission_name
FROM sys.server_principals AS pr
INNER JOIN sys.server_permissions AS pe
ON pr.principal_id = pe.grantee_principal_id
WHERE permission_name = 'VIEW ANY DATABASE';
```

The result of this query is as follows:

```
name        state_desc permission_name
------      ---------- -----------------
public      GRANT       VIEW ANY DATABASE
```

The VIEW DEFINITION permission lets a user see the definition of the securable for which this permission is granted. However, this permission does not give the user access to the securable; you have to give other permissions to the user if the user must work with database objects. If the user has any other permission on an object, the user can see the metadata of the object as well.

Managing schemas

The complete name of a relational database management system (RDBMS) object consists of four parts. In SQL Server, the complete name form is **server.database.schema.object**. Objects also have owners, and owners are database users and roles. However, the owners are hidden; you typically never refer to an object owner in the code that deals with data, while you intensively use the schemas. **Schemas** are more than just namespaces for database objects; they are securables as well. Instead of giving permissions to specific database objects, a DBA can give users permissions to schemas. For example, granting the Execute permission to schema Sales gives the grantees the Execute permission on all objects in this schema for which this permission makes sense, such as stored procedures and functions. Therefore, you should plan your schemas carefully.

When you refer to database objects in your code, you should always use a two-part name, in form **schema.object**. You don't want to use more than two parts because you don't want to make your application dependent on a specific server or database name. However, because of the way SQL Server does the name resolution, you should not use a single-part name either.

In SQL Server, every user has a default schema. You can specify the default schema for a user when you create the user. You can change the default schema of a user at any later time. If you do not specify an explicit default schema for a user, the default schema is dbo. This schema exists in all SQL Server databases and is owned by the dbo user. Thus, SQL Server first checks for a partially specified object name if the object exists in the user's default schema and then checks the dbo schema. To fully understand this behavior, work through the following code; note that this code assumes you are working in the dbo database user context because it uses the EXECUTE AS command to impersonate a database user and you must have the correct permission to use this command.

The first part of the code creates a demo database and another login called LoginB. Note that the login called LoginA should already exist at this point:

```
USE master;
IF DB_ID(N'SQLDevGuideDemoDb') IS NULL
CREATE DATABASE SQLDevGuideDemoDb;
CREATE LOGIN LoginB WITH password='LB_ComplexPassword';
GO
```

The next part of the code creates a new schema called Sales in the SQLDevGuideDemoDb demo database, and then two tables with the same name and structure, one in the dbo schema and one in the new Sales schema:

```
USE SQLDevGuideDemoDb;
GO
CREATE SCHEMA Sales;
GO
CREATE TABLE dbo.Table1
(id INT, tableContainer CHAR(5));
CREATE TABLE Sales.Table1
(id INT, tableContainer CHAR(5));
GO
```

The following two insert statements insert one row into each table. The value of the character column shows the name of the table schema:

```
INSERT INTO dbo.Table1(id, tableContainer)
VALUES(1,'dbo');
INSERT INTO Sales.Table1(id, tableContainer)
VALUES(1,'Sales');
GO
```

The next part of the code creates two database users, one for LoginA and one for LoginB, with the same name as their respective login name. Note that the default schema for user LoginA is dbo, while for LoginB it is Sales. Both users are also granted the permission to select the data from both demo tables:

```
CREATE USER LoginA FOR LOGIN LoginA;
GO
CREATE USER LoginB FOR LOGIN LoginB
 WITH DEFAULT_SCHEMA = Sales;
GO
GRANT SELECT ON dbo.Table1 TO LoginA;
GRANT SELECT ON Sales.Table1 TO LoginA;
GRANT SELECT ON dbo.Table1 TO LoginB;
GRANT SELECT ON Sales.Table1 TO LoginB;
GO
```

Next, you impersonate LoginA. In a query, you refer to the table you are reading with a single-part name only (that is, with table name only):

```
EXECUTE AS USER='LoginA';
SELECT USER_NAME() AS WhoAmI,
id,
tableContainer
FROM Table1;
REVERT;
GO
```

Here are the results:

```
WhoAmI  id  tableContainer
------  --  --------------
LoginA  1   dbo
```

You can see that you read from the dbo.Table1 table. Repeat the same thing for the database user LoginB:

```
EXECUTE AS USER='LoginB';
SELECT USER_NAME() AS WhoAmI,
id,
tableContainer
FROM Table1;
REVERT;
GO
```

This time the results show that you read the data from the `Sale.Table1` table:

```
WhoAmI   id   tableContainer
------   --   --------------
LoginB   1    Sales
```

Now you drop the `Sales.Table1` table. Then you impersonate the user `LoginB` again, and read from the table using the table name only:

```
DROP TABLE Sales.table1;
GO
EXECUTE AS USER='LoginB';
SELECT USER_NAME() AS WhoAmI,
id,
tableContainer
FROM Table1;
REVERT;
GO
```

Here are the results:

```
WhoAmI   id   tableContainer
------   --   --------------
LoginA   1    dbo
```

After gaining the knowledge of how schemas work, you should be able to understand the following guidelines for managing schemas:

- You should group objects in schemas based on application-access requirements. Classify applications by access requirements and then create appropriate schemas. For example, if an application module deals with sales data, create a `Sales` schema to serve as a container for all database objects that pertain to sales.

- Typically, you can map end users to application modules. You should specify appropriate default schemas for database users and roles. For example, you should specify `Sales` as the default schema for users in the `sales` department.

- Because SQL Server uses a permissions hierarchy, you can manage permissions efficiently if you set up appropriate schemas. For example, you can give permissions on data to sales-department users quickly by giving them appropriate permissions on the `Sales` schema. Later, you can define exceptions by denying permissions to some users on the objects contained in the `Sales` schema.

- You should use either the dbo user or database roles as the owners of schemas and objects. This way, you can drop a database user without worrying about orphaned objects.

- Although you set appropriate default schemas for users, you should still always refer to database objects by using two-part names. With this strategy, you can avoid confusion in your application if the default schema for a user changes, or if an object from the user's default schema is dropped and an object with the same name exists in the dbo schema (as you saw in the code example).

- You can use schemas to control development environments as well. You can identify different developer groups based on application requirements and then map those groups to schemas.

- In SQL Server, you can control permissions on schemas and objects with a lot of precision. For example, giving developers permission to create objects does not imply that they can create objects in all schemas. On the contrary, the developers must have an ALTER or CONTROL schema permission on every schema they want to modify by creating, altering, or dropping objects contained in that schema.

- You can move objects between schemas by using the ALTER SCHEMA command.

- Your documentation should include schema information.

Object and statement permissions

All the demo code so far has supposed that you are authorized inside a database as the dbo user. This user has all possible permissions inside a database. However, in real life, it might be necessary for other users to create and modify objects. These users could be developers or other database administrators. To modify objects, they need statement permissions. Statement permissions are on the server, database, schema, or at object level, depending on which level you work at. In addition, end users must use objects, and thus need object permissions. Object permissions depend on the type of the object you are working with.

The statement permissions include permissions to use any **Data Definition Language (DDL)** statements (that is, to create, alter, and drop objects). The object permissions include permissions to use the objects (that is, to use the **Data Modification Language (DML)** statements). However, the two permissions' classes slightly overlap, and you can treat a couple of permissions as both statement and object permissions.

You control permissions by using the **Data Control Language** (DCL) elements: the GRANT, REVOKE, and DENY statements. You already know that without explicitly granted permission, a user cannot use an object. You give the permissions by using the GRANT statement. You explicitly prohibit the usage of an object by using the DENY statement. You clear an explicit GRANT or an explicit DENY permission by using the REVOKE statement. You might wonder why you need an explicit DENY statement when, without an explicit GRANT, a user cannot use an object. The DENY statement exists because all grants are cumulative. For example, if a user gets a GRANT permission to select from table1 and the role that the user is a member of is granted permission to select from table2, the user can select from both tables. If you want to be sure that the user can never select from table2, you should deny the select permission from table2 to this user. A DENY for an ordinary user always supersedes all GRANTs.

You cannot grant, deny, or revoke permissions to or from special roles at the server or database level. For example, you cannot deny anything inside a database to the db_owner role. You cannot grant, deny, or revoke permissions to special logins and database users (that is, to sa, dbo, INFORMATION_SCHEMA, and sys). Finally, you cannot grant, deny, or revoke permissions to yourself.

Statement permissions let users create and alter objects, or back up a database and transaction log. Permissions granted on a higher level include implicit permissions on a lower level. For example, permissions granted at the schema level are implicitly granted on all objects in the schema. In addition, there is a hierarchy between permissions on the same level; some are stronger and implicitly include weaker permissions. The CONTROL permission is the strongest. For example, the CONTROL permission on the database level implies all other permissions on the same database. Therefore, you have two different kinds of hierarchy: hierarchy between securables and hierarchy between permissions. You can treat high-level permissions as covering the more detailed, low-level permissions that they imply. For example, if a user needs to alter an object, the user needs either the ALTER OBJECT permission or any other higher permission, such as the ALTER ANY SCHEMA permission.

The types of permissions depend on the types of database objects. You can get a list of permissions applicable for an object or objects by using the sys.fn_builtin_permissions system function. For example, you can check which permissions are applicable for user-defined types, or check the objects for which the SELECT permission is applicable, like the following two queries do:

```
SELECT * FROM sys.fn_builtin_permissions(N'TYPE');
SELECT * FROM sys.fn_builtin_permissions(DEFAULT)
WHERE permission_name = N'SELECT';
GO
```

In SQL Server, you can specify very detailed permissions. For example, you can specify that a user can select or update only some columns of a table. Specifying permissions on such a granular level means a lot of administrative work, and is nearly impossible to do in a limited time with graphical tools such as SQL Server Management Studio. You should rarely go that far.

 You should specify permissions on the higher levels of the object hierarchy, namely on the schema level, and then handle exceptions. If you need column-level permissions, you should use programmable objects such as views and stored procedures. You should keep permissions as simple as possible.

The GRANT statement includes the WITH GRANT OPTION. This option indicates that the principal to whom you grant permission on an object can grant this permission on the same object to other principals.

The DENY statement comes with the CASCADE option. When you use this option with the DENY statement, you indicate that the permission you are denying is also denied to other principals to which it has been granted by this principal.

The REVOKE statement has the GRANT OPTION FOR and the CACSCADE options. GRANT OPTION FOR means you are revoking permission to grant the same permission to other principals (that is, you are revoking the WITH GRANT OPTION permission you gave to this principal by using the GRANT statement). The CASCADE option means you are revoking permission not just from the principal you mention in the statement but also from other principals to which permission has been granted by this principal. Note that such a cascading revocation revokes both the GRANT and DENY of that permission.

The following code shows how to use the object permissions. First, the code grants the CONTROL permission on dbo.Table1 to LoginB. LoginB can read the table.

```
GRANT CONTROL ON dbo.Table1 TO LoginB;
GO
EXECUTE AS USER = 'LoginB';
SELECT *
FROM dbo.Table1;
REVERT;
GO
```

Next, you deny the SELECT permission on dbo.Table1 to LoginB. Note that LoginB still has the CONTROL permission on this table, so this user can insert into the table.

```
DENY SELECT ON dbo.Table1 TO LoginB;
GO
EXECUTE AS USER = 'LoginB';
INSERT INTO dbo.Table1(id, tableContainer)
VALUES (2, 'dbo');
REVERT;
GO
```

However, you denied the SELECT permission to LoginB. An explicit DENY for an ordinary user always supersedes all explicit GRANT. Therefore, the following code produces an error, stating that the SELECT permission is denied:

```
EXECUTE AS USER = 'LoginB';
SELECT *
FROM dbo.Table1;
REVERT;
GO
```

Finally, security would not worth much if a user could change their own settings. The following code impersonates LoginB and tries to change the permissions to the same database user:

```
EXECUTE AS USER = 'LoginB';
REVOKE SELECT ON dbo.Table1 FROM LoginB;
REVERT;
GO
```

Of course, the previous code produced an error. However, you as the dbo database users, can change the permissions for the user LoginB, and therefore the following code succeeds:

```
REVOKE SELECT ON dbo.Table1 FROM LoginB;
GO
```

Encrypting the data

If you need to store confidential data in your database, you can use **data encryption**. SQL Server supports encryption with symmetric keys, asymmetric keys, certificates, and password phrases. Let's first have a theoretical look at each of these encryption techniques.

When you use **symmetric key** encryption, the party that encrypts the data shares the same key with the party that decrypts the data. Because the same key is used for encryption and decryption, this is called symmetric key encryption. This encryption is very fast. However, if an unauthorized party somehow acquires the key, that party can decrypt the data. Protecting symmetric keys is a challenge. The symmetric key must remain secret. Symmetric encryption is also called **secret key** encryption.

In **asymmetric key** encryption, you use two different keys that are mathematically linked. You must keep one key secret and prevent unauthorized access to it; this is the **private key**. You make the other key public to anyone; this is the **public key**. If you encrypt the data with the public key, you can decrypt the data with the private key; if you encrypt the data with the private key, you can decrypt it with the public key. Asymmetric encryption is very strong; however, it is much slower than symmetric encryption. Asymmetric encryption is useful for digital signatures. A developer applies a **hash algorithm** to the code to create a **message digest**, which is a compact and unique representation of data. Then the developer encrypts the digest with the private key. Anybody with a public key from the same pair can decrypt the digest and use the same hash algorithm to calculate the digest from the code again. If the re-calculated and decrypted digests match, you can identify who created the code.

A **certificate** is a digitally signed statement that binds the value of a public key to the identity of the person, device, or service that holds the corresponding private key. It identifies the owner of the public/private keys. You can use certificates for authentication. A certificate can be issued by a trusted authority or by SQL Server. You can create a certificate from a file (if the certificate was issued by a trusted authority) or a digitally signed executable file (assembly), or you can create a self-signed certificate in SQL Server directly. You can use certificates to encrypt the data; of course, this way you are actually using asymmetric encryption.

You should use symmetric keys to encrypt the data because secret key encryption is much faster than public-key encryption. You can then use asymmetric encryption to protect symmetric keys and use certificates for authentication. You combine certificates and keys to encrypt data in the following manner:

1. The server sends a certificate and public key to a client. The certificate identifies the server to the client.
2. The client creates two symmetric keys. The client encrypts one symmetric key with the public key and sends it to the server.
3. The server's private key can decrypt the symmetric key. The server and client encrypt and decrypt data with symmetric keys.

When encrypting data, you should consider all possible surface areas for an attack. For example, if you encrypt the data in SQL Server, but send clear text over the network, an attacker could use a network monitor to intercept the clear text. You should use on-the-wire encryption, such as **Internet Protocol Security (IPSec)**, a framework of open source standards for network security, or **Secure Sockets Layer / Transport Layer Security (SSL/TLS)**, which are protocols based on public key cryptography. An attacker can even sniff client computer memory to retrieve clear text. Therefore, you should use .NET encryption in client applications in addition to or instead of server encryption.

Consider the following trade-offs when you design a solution that uses data encryption:

- Encrypted data is typically stored in a binary data type column; space is not allocated according to the original data type like it is with unencrypted data. This means you need to change your database schema to support data encryption.
- Sorting encrypted data is different from sorting unencrypted data and, of course, makes no sense from a business point of view.
- Similarly, indexing and filtering operations on encrypted data are useless from a business point of view.
- You might need to change applications to support data encryption.
- Encryption is a processor-intensive process.
- Longer keys mean stronger encryption. However, the stronger the encryption, the higher the consumption of CPU resources.
- When the length of the keys is the same, then asymmetric encryption is weaker than symmetric encryption. However, asymmetric key encryption is slower than symmetric encription.
- Although you probably already know this, it is still worth mentioning that long and complex passwords are stronger than short and simple ones.

Instead of storing all keys in SQL Server, you can also use an external cryptographic provider to store the asymmetric keys used to encrypt and decrypt the symmetric keys stored in SQL Server, or to store both asymmetric and symmetric keys outside SQL Server. This is called **Extensible Key Management (EKM)**. For example, you can use the Azure Key Vault service as the external cryptographic provider.

As already mentioned, you can protect symmetric keys with asymmetric keys or certificates. In addition, you can protect them with passwords or even other symmetric keys. You can protect certificates and asymmetric keys stored in SQL Server with the **Database Master Key (DMK)** and passwords. You protect the DMK when you create it with the **Service Master Key (SMK)** and password. The SMK is created by SQL Server Setup, and is protected by the Windows system **Data Protection Application Programming Interface (DPAPI)**. This whole encryption hierarchy looks quite complex. The following figure shows the encryption hierarchy in a condensed way. It shows all components and a couple of possible paths to the encrypted data.

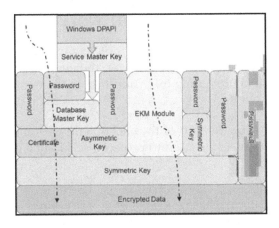

Encryption hierarchy

SQL Server supports many encryption algorithms. You can choose from DES, Triple DES, TRIPLE_DES_3KEY, RC2, RC4, 128-bit RC4, DESX, 128-bit AES, 192-bit AES, and 256-bit AES. However, from SQL Server 2016 onwards, you should use only the AES_128, AES_192, and AES_256 algorithms; all other algorithms have been deprecated.

You don't need to encrypt all of the data all of the time. SQL Server provides many encryption options, and you should choose the one that suits you the best. In addition, you should also consider encrypting and decrypting the data in the client application. In this section, you will learn about the different encryption options in SQL Server, including the strengths and weaknesses of each option. These options include:

- Backup encryption
- Column-level encryption
- Transparent data encryption
- Always encrypted

Leveraging SQL Server data encryption options

SQL Server encryption options start with **backup encryption**. This encryption was introduced in version 2014. You can encrypt the data while creating a backup. You need to specify an **encryptor**, which can be either a certificate or an asymmetric key, and define which algorithm to use for the encryption. The supported algorithms are AES_128, AES_192, AES_256, and Triple DES. Of course, you also need to back up the encryptor, and store it in a different, probably even off-site, location from the backup files. Without the encryptor, you can't restore an encrypted backup. You can also use EKM providers for storing your encryptor safely outside SQL Server. Actually, if you are using an asymmetric key as an encryptor instead of a certificate, then this key must reside in an EKM provider.

The restore process of an encrypted backup is completely transparent. You don't need to specify any particular encryption options. However, the encryptor must be available on the instance of SQL Server you are restoring to. In addition to the regular restore permissions, you also need to have at least the VIEW DEFINITION permission on the encryptor.

In the following code, showing the start of the backup encryption process, first a master database DMK is created. This key is used to protect a self-issued certificate, also created in the master database.

```
USE master;
CREATE MASTER KEY ENCRYPTION BY PASSWORD = 'Pa$$w0rd';
CREATE CERTIFICATE DemoBackupEncryptCert
WITH SUBJECT = 'SQLDevGuideDemoDb Backup Certificate';
GO
```

The master DMK is encrypted using the SMK created during the setup. You can check both keys with the following query:

```
SELECT name, key_length, algorithm_desc
FROM sys.symmetric_keys;
```

The query returns the following result set:

```
Name                         key_length    algorithm_desc
-------------------------    -----------   ---------------
##MS_DatabaseMasterKey##     256           AES_256
##MS_ServiceMasterKey##      256           AES_256
```

For a test, the following code creates an unencrypted backup in the C:SQL2016DevGuide folder, which should be created in advance:

```
BACKUP DATABASE SQLDevGuideDemoDb
TO DISK = N'C:SQL2016DevGuideSQLDevGuideDemoDb_Backup.bak'
WITH INIT;
```

Next, you can create an encrypted backup:

```
BACKUP DATABASE SQLDevGuideDemoDb
TO DISK = N'C:SQL2016DevGuideSQLDevGuideDemoDb_BackupEncrypted.bak'
WITH INIT,
ENCRYPTION
  (
   ALGORITHM = AES_256,
   SERVER CERTIFICATE = DemoBackupEncryptCert
  );
```

Note that this time you get a warning telling you that the certificate used for encrypting the database encryption key has not been backed up. Therefore, you should back up the certificate used for the backup encryption, and, in addition, the master DMK used to protect the certificate and the SQL Server SMK used to protect the master DMK, as the following code shows:

```
-- Backup SMK
BACKUP SERVICE MASTER KEY
  TO FILE = N'C:SQL2016DevGuideSMK.key'
  ENCRYPTION BY PASSWORD = 'Pa$$w0rd';
-- Backup master DMK
BACKUP MASTER KEY
  TO FILE = N'C:SQL2016DevGuidemasterDMK.key'
  ENCRYPTION BY PASSWORD = 'Pa$$w0rd';
-- Backup certificate
BACKUP CERTIFICATE DemoBackupEncryptCert
  TO FILE = N'C:SQL2016DevGuideDemoBackupEncryptCert.cer'
  WITH PRIVATE KEY
  (
    FILE = N'C:SQL2016DevGuideDemoBackupEncryptCert.key',
    ENCRYPTION BY PASSWORD = 'Pa$$w0rd'
  );
GO
```

Now you are ready to simulate a failure. Drop the demo database, the certificate used for the encryption, and the master DMK:

```
DROP DATABASE SQLDevGuideDemoDb;
DROP CERTIFICATE DemoBackupEncryptCert;
DROP MASTER KEY;
```

Try to restore the encrypted backup. You should get error 33111, telling you that SQL Server cannot find server certificate.

```
RESTORE DATABASE SQLDevGuideDemoDb
FROM  DISK = N'C:SQL2016DevGuideSQLDevGuideDemoDb_BackupEncrypted.bak'
WITH  FILE = 1;
```

You have to start the restore process by restoring the master DMK:

```
RESTORE MASTER KEY
FROM FILE = N'C:SQL2016DevGuidemasterDMK.key'
DECRYPTION BY PASSWORD = 'Pa$$w0rd'
ENCRYPTION BY PASSWORD = 'Pa$$w0rd';
```

Next, you open the master DMK and restore the certificate:

```
OPEN MASTER KEY DECRYPTION BY PASSWORD = 'Pa$$w0rd';
CREATE CERTIFICATE DemoBackupEncryptCert
 FROM FILE = N'C:SQL2016DevGuideDemoBackupEncryptCert.cer'
 WITH PRIVATE KEY (FILE = N'C:SQL2016DevGuideDemoBackupEncryptCert.key',
  DECRYPTION BY PASSWORD = 'Pa$$w0rd');
```

Now you are ready to restore the encrypted backup. The following code should restore the demo database successfully:

```
RESTORE DATABASE SQLDevGuideDemoDb
FROM  DISK = N'C:SQL2016DevGuideSQLDevGuideDemoDb_BackupEncrypted.bak'
WITH  FILE = 1, RECOVERY;
```

Finally, you can check which backups are encrypted by querying the `msdb.dbo.backupset` table:

```
SELECT b.database_name,
 c.name,
 b.encryptor_type,
 b.encryptor_thumbprint
FROM sys.certificates AS c
 INNER JOIN msdb.dbo.backupset AS b
  ON c.thumbprint = b.encryptor_thumbprint;
```

Backup encryption encrypts backups only. It does not encrypt the data in the data files. You can encrypt data in tables with T-SQL using **column-level encryption**. Column-level encryption is present in SQL Server from version 2008 onwards. You encrypt the data in a specific column by using a symmetric key. You protect the symmetric key with an asymmetric key or a certificate. The keys and the certificate are stored inside your database where the tables with the encrypted columns are. You protect the asymmetric key or the certificate with the database master key. The following code, which created the DMK in the demo database, issues an SQL Server certificate and then creates the symmetric key used for the column encryption:

```
USE SQLDevGuideDemoDb;
-- Create the SQLDevGuideDemoDb database DMK
CREATE MASTER KEY ENCRYPTION BY PASSWORD = 'Pa$$w0rd';
-- Create the column certificate in SQLDevGuideDemoDb
```

```
CREATE CERTIFICATE DemoColumnEncryptCert
 WITH SUBJECT = 'SQLDevGuideDemoDb Column Certificate';
-- Create the symmetric key
CREATE SYMMETRIC KEY DemoColumnEncryptSimKey
 WITH ALGORITHM = AES_256
 ENCRYPTION BY CERTIFICATE DemoColumnEncryptCert;
GO
```

Next, you can prepare an additional column to store the encrypted data. The dbo.Table1 should already exist from the demo code earlier in this chapter.

```
ALTER TABLE dbo.Table1
ADD tableContainer_Encrypted VARBINARY(128);
GO
```

Now you are ready to encrypt the data in the new column. You need to open the symmetric key and decrypt it with the certificate used for the encryption. The following code opens the symmetric key and then updates the new column in the table with the values from an unencrypted column. The code uses the ENCRYPTBYKEY() T-SQL function to encrypt the data with a symmetric key:

```
OPEN SYMMETRIC KEY DemoColumnEncryptSimKey
 DECRYPTION BY CERTIFICATE DemoColumnEncryptCert;
UPDATE dbo.Table1
SET tableContainer_Encrypted =
    ENCRYPTBYKEY(Key_GUID('DemoColumnEncryptSimKey'), tableContainer);
GO
```

You can check the data with the following query, which uses the DECRYPTBYKEY() T-SQL function for the decryption:

```
OPEN SYMMETRIC KEY DemoColumnEncryptSimKey
 DECRYPTION BY CERTIFICATE DemoColumnEncryptCert;
-- All columns
SELECT id, tableContainer,
 tableContainer_Encrypted,
 CAST(DECRYPTBYKEY(tableContainer_Encrypted) AS CHAR(5))
  AS tableContainer_Decrypted
FROM dbo.Table1;
GO
```

Here are the results, with the encrypted value abbreviated for simpler reading:

Id	tableContainer	tableContainer_Encrypted	tableContainer_Decrypted
1	dbo	0x003D10428AE86248A44F70	dbo
2	dbo	0x003D10428AE86248A44F70	dbo

You can use the following code to clean up your SQL Server instance. The code also deletes the backups in the demo folder. You need to run SSMS as administrator and turn on the SQLCMD mode in SSMS to successfully execute the clean-up code (go to Query menu and select the SQLCMD mode option).

```
USE master;
!!del C:SQL2016DevGuideDemoBackupEncryptCert.cer
!!del C:SQL2016DevGuideDemoBackupEncryptCert.key
!!del C:SQL2016DevGuidemasterDMK.key
!!del C:SQL2016DevGuideSMK.key
!!del C:SQL2016DevGuideSQLDevGuideDemoDb_Backup.bak
!!del C:SQL2016DevGuideSQLDevGuideDemoDb_BackupEncrypted.bak
GO
IF DB_ID(N'SQLDevGuideDemoDb') IS NOT NULL
   DROP DATABASE SQLDevGuideDemoDb;
DROP LOGIN LoginA;
DROP LOGIN [BuiltinPower Users];
DROP LOGIN LoginB;
DROP CERTIFICATE DemoBackupEncryptCert;
DROP MASTER KEY;
GO
```

Column-level encryption protects the data in the database, not just backups. However, it protects data at rest only. When the data is used by an application, the data is decrypted. If you don't use network encryption, the data travels over the network in an unencrypted way. All the keys are in a SQL Server database, and therefore a DBA can always decrypt the data. End users who don't have access to the certificates and keys can't decrypt the encrypted data. In addition, the implementation of the column-level encryption might be quite complex because you might need to modify a lot of T-SQL code. The column-level encryption is available in all editions of SQL Server.

Another option to protect data at rest is **Transparent Data Encryption (TDE).** You can use the TDE for the real-time encryption and decryption of the data and log files. You encrypt the data with the **database encryption key (DEK),** which is a symmetric key. It is stored in the database boot record and is therefore already available during the database recovery process. You protect the DEK with a certificate in the master database. You can also use an asymmetric key instead of the certificate; however, the asymmetric key must be stored in an EKM module. TDE uses the AES and Triple DES encryptions only. TDE was first implemented in SQL Server with version 2012.

You can use TDE on user databases only. You cannot export the database encryption key. This key is used by the SQL Server database engine only. End users never use it. Even if you change the database owner, you don't need to regenerate the DEK.

TDE encrypts data on a page level. In addition, it also encrypts the transaction log. You should backup the certificate used to protect the DEK and the private key used to protect the certificate immediately after you enable TDE. If you need to restore or attach the encrypted database to another SQL Server instance, you need to restore both the certificate and the private key, or you are not able to open the database. Note again that you don't export the DEK as it is a part of the database itself. You need to keep and maintain the certificate used to protect the DEK even after you disable the TDE on the database. This is because parts of the transaction log might still be encrypted. The certificate is needed until you perform a full database backup.

The following code starts the process of enabling the TDE by creating a DMK in the master database:

```
USE master;
CREATE MASTER KEY ENCRYPTION BY PASSWORD = 'Pa$$w0rd';
GO
```

You can check whether the master DMK was created successfully with the following code:

```
SELECT name, key_length, algorithm_desc
FROM sys.symmetric_keys;
```

Let's backup the SMK and the master DMK immediately, as the next part of the code shows:

```
BACKUP SERVICE MASTER KEY
  TO FILE = N'C:SQL2016DevGuideSMK.key'
  ENCRYPTION BY PASSWORD = 'Pa$$w0rd';
-- Backup master DMK
BACKUP MASTER KEY
  TO FILE = N'C:SQL2016DevGuidemasterDMK.key'
  ENCRYPTION BY PASSWORD = 'Pa$$w0rd';
GO
```

The next portion of the code creates a demo database:

```
IF DB_ID(N'TDEDemo') IS NULL
CREATE DATABASE TDEDemo;
GO
```

While still in the context of the master database, use the following code to create the certificate you will use to protect the DEK:

```
CREATE CERTIFICATE DemoTDEEncryptCert
WITH SUBJECT = 'TDEDemo TDE Certificate';
GO
```

Of course, you need to backup this certificate immediately:

```
BACKUP CERTIFICATE DemoTDEEncryptCert
 TO FILE = N'C:SQL2016DevGuideDemoTDEEncryptCert.cer'
 WITH PRIVATE KEY
  (
   FILE = N'C:SQL2016DevGuideDemoTDEEncryptCert.key',
   ENCRYPTION BY PASSWORD = 'Pa$$w0rd'
  );
GO
```

You create the database encryption key in the demo user database:

```
USE TDEDemo;
CREATE DATABASE ENCRYPTION KEY
 WITH ALGORITHM = AES_128
 ENCRYPTION BY SERVER CERTIFICATE DemoTDEEncryptCert;
GO
```

The final step of this process is to actually turn the TDE on:

```
ALTER DATABASE TDEDemo
SET ENCRYPTION ON;
GO
```

You can check which databases are encrypted by querying the sys. dm_database_encryption_keys dynamic management view. This view exposes the information about the encryption keys and the state of encryption of a database.

```
SELECT DB_NAME(database_id) AS DatabaseName,
    key_algorithm AS [Algorithm],
    key_length AS KeyLength,
   encryption_state AS EncryptionState,
   CASE encryption_state
        WHEN 0 THEN 'No database encryption key present, no encryption'
        WHEN 1 THEN 'Unencrypted'
        WHEN 2 THEN 'Encryption in progress'
        WHEN 3 THEN 'Encrypted'
        WHEN 4 THEN 'Key change in progress'
        WHEN 5 THEN 'Decryption in progress'
    END AS EncryptionStateDesc,
    percent_complete AS PercentComplete
 FROM sys.dm_database_encryption_keys;
```

The results of this query are as follows.

DatabaseName	Algorithm	KeyLength	EncryptionState	EncryptionStateDesc	PercentComplete
Tempdb	AES	256	3	Encrypted	0
TDEDemo	AES	128	3	Encrypted	0

Note that the Tempdb system database also inherited the encryption. The demo database is empty and thus very small. The encryption process on such a small database is very fast. However, in a production database, you would be able to monitor the percentage complete rising from zero to one hundred, while the encryption state would be "Encryption in progress." SQL Server needs to scan all of the data files and log files to finish the encryption.

Now let's turn the encryption off for the demo database:

```
ALTER DATABASE TDEDemo
SET ENCRYPTION OFF;
GO
```

Using the same query, you can check the encryption status again:

```
SELECT DB_NAME(database_id) AS DatabaseName,
    key_algorithm AS [Algorithm],
    key_length AS KeyLength,
  encryption_state AS EncryptionState,
    CASE encryption_state
        WHEN 0 THEN 'No database encryption key present, no encryption'
        WHEN 1 THEN 'Unencrypted'
        WHEN 2 THEN 'Encryption in progress'
        WHEN 3 THEN 'Encrypted'
        WHEN 4 THEN 'Key change in progress'
        WHEN 5 THEN 'Decryption in progress'
    END AS EncryptionStateDesc,
    percent_complete AS PercentComplete
FROM sys.dm_database_encryption_keys;
```

Please note the result. The tempdb system database is still encrypted.

DatabaseName	Algorithm	KeyLength	EncryptionState	EncryptionStateDesc	PercentComplete
Tempdb	AES	256	3	Encrypted	0
TDEDemo	AES	128	1	Unencrypted	0

Restart your SQL Server instance and execute the previous query again. This time, the tempdb system database is unencrypted.

You can use the following code to clean up your SQL Server instance. Again, use the SQLCMD mode to execute it.

```
USE master;
!!del C:SQL2016DevGuideDemoTDEEncryptCert.cer
!!del C:SQL2016DevGuideDemoTDEEncryptCert.key
!!del C:SQL2016DevGuidemasterDMK.key
!!del C:SQL2016DevGuideSMK.key
IF DB_ID(N'TDEDemo') IS NOT NULL
    DROP DATABASE TDEDemo;
DROP CERTIFICATE DemoTDEEncryptCert;
DROP MASTER KEY;
GO
```

Always Encrypted

SQL Server 2016 Enterprise Edition introduces a new level of encryption, namely the **Always Encrypted (AE)** feature. This feature enables the same level of data protection as encrypting the data in the client application. Actually, although this is an SQL Server feature, the data is encrypted and decrypted on the client side. The encryption keys are never revealed to the SQL Server Database Engine. This way, a DBA can't also see sensitive data without the encryption keys, just by having sysadmin permissions on the SQL Server instance with the encrypted data. This way, AE makes a separation between the administrators who manage the data and the users who own the data.

You need two keys for AE. First you create the **column master key (CMK)**. Then you create the **column encryption key (CEK)** and protect it with the CMK. An application uses the CEK to encrypt the data. SQL Server stores only encrypted data, and can't decrypt it. This is possible because the column master keys aren't really stored in a SQL Server database. In the database, SQL Server stores only the link to those keys. The column master keys are stored outside SQL Server, in one of the following possible places:

- Windows Certificate Store for the current user
- Windows Certificate Store for the local machine
- Azure Key Vault service
- **A hardware security module (HSM)** that supports Microsoft CryptoAPI or Cryptography API: Next Generation

The column encryption keys are stored in the database. Inside an SQL Server database, only the encrypted part of the values of the column encryption keys are stored, together with the information about the location of the column master keys. CEKs are never stored as plain text in a database. CMKs are, as mentioned, actually stored in external trusted key stores.

An application can use the AE keys and encryption by using an AE-enabled driver, such as .NET Framework Data Provider for SQL Server version 4.6 or higher, Microsoft JDBC Driver for SQL Server 6.0 or higher, or Windows ODBC driver for SQL Server version 13.1 or higher. The application must send parameterized queries to SQL Server. The AE-enabled driver works together with the SQL Server Database Engine to determine which parameters should be encrypted or decrypted. For each parameter that needs to be encrypted or decrypted, the driver obtains the metadata needed for the encryption from the Database Engine, including the encryption algorithm, the location of the corresponding CMK, and the encrypted value for the corresponding CEK. Then the driver contacts the CMK store, retrieves the CMK, decrypts the CEK, and uses the CEK to encrypt or decrypt the parameter. Next the driver caches the CEK in order to speed up the next usage of the same CEK. The following figure shows the process graphically:

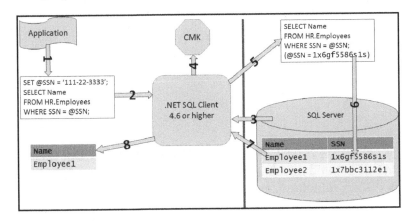

Always Encrypted process

The figure represents the whole process in these steps:

1. The client application creates a parameterized query.
2. The client application sends the parameterized query to the AE-enabled driver.
3. The AE-enabled driver contacts SQL Server to determine which parameters need encryption or decryption, the location of the CMK, and the encrypted value of the CEK.
4. The AE-enabled driver retrieves the CMK and decrypts the CEK.
5. The AE-enabled driver encrypts the parameter(s).

6. The driver sends the query to the Database Engine.
7. The Database Engine retrieves the data and sends the result set to the driver.
8. The driver performs decryption, if needed, and sends the result set to the client application.

The Database Engine never operates on the plain text data stored in the encrypted columns. However, some queries on the encrypted data are possible, depending on the encryption type. There are two types of encryption:

- **Deterministic encryption**, which always generates the same encrypted value for the same input value. With this encryption, you can index the encrypted column and use point lookups, equality joins, and grouping expressions on the encrypted column. However, a malicious user could try to guess the values by analyzing the patterns of the encrypted values. This is especially dangerous when the set of possible values for a column is discrete, with a small number of distinct values.
- **Randomized encryption**, which encrypts data in an unpredictable manner.

It is time to show how AE works through some demo code. First, let's create and use a demo database:

```
USE master;
IF DB_ID(N'AEDemo') IS NULL
    CREATE DATABASE AEDemo;
GO
USE AEDemo;
GO
```

Next, create the CMK in SSMS GUI. In Object Explorer, refresh the Databases folder to see the AEDemo database. Expand this database folder, expand the Security subfolder and the Always Encrypted Keys subfolder, and right-click on the Column Master Key subfolder and select the New Column Master Key option from the pop-up menu. In the Name text box, write AE_ColumnMasterKey, and make sure you select the Windows Certificate Store–Local Machine option in the Key Store drop-down list, as shown in the following screenshot. Then click **OK**.

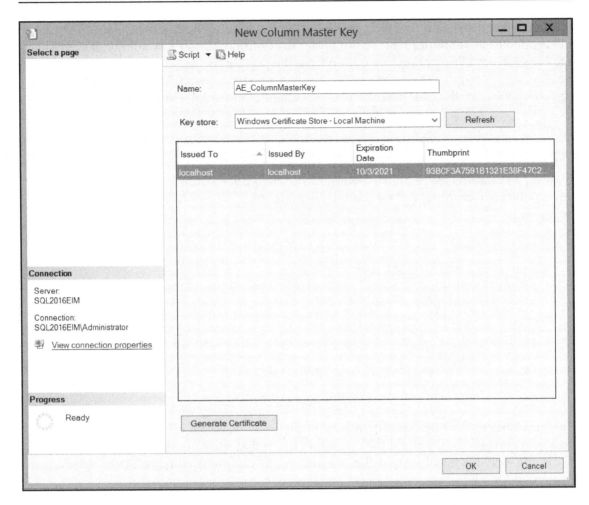

Creating a CMK

You can check if the CMK was created successfully with the following query:

```
SELECT *
FROM sys.column_master_keys;
```

Next, you create the CEK. In SSMS, in Object Explorer, right-click on the Column Encryption Keys subfolder that is right under the Column Master Key subfolder, and select the New Column Encryption Key option from the pop-up menu. Name the CEK `AE_ColumnEncryptionKey` and use the `AE_ColumnMasterKey` CMK to encrypt it. You can check whether the CEK creation was successful with the following query:

```
SELECT *
FROM sys.column_encryption_keys;
GO
```

Now try to create a table with one deterministic encryption column and one randomized encryption column. My database used the default `SQL_Latin1_General_CP1_CI_AS` collation.

```
CREATE TABLE dbo.Table1
(id INT,
 SecretDeterministic NVARCHAR(10)
  ENCRYPTED WITH (COLUMN_ENCRYPTION_KEY = AE_ColumnEncryptionKey,
   ENCRYPTION_TYPE = DETERMINISTIC,
   ALGORITHM = 'AEAD_AES_256_CBC_HMAC_SHA_256') NULL,
 SecretRandomized NVARCHAR(10)
  ENCRYPTED WITH (COLUMN_ENCRYPTION_KEY = AE_ColumnEncryptionKey,
   ENCRYPTION_TYPE = RANDOMIZED,
   ALGORITHM = 'AEAD_AES_256_CBC_HMAC_SHA_256') NULL
);
GO
```

The previous statement produced an error number 33289, which tells me that I cannot create an encrypted column for the character strings that use a non-BIN2 collation. Currently, only the new binary collations (that is, the collations with the BIN2 suffix) are supported for AE.

So let's try to create the table again, this time with correct collations for the character columns:

```
CREATE TABLE dbo.Table1
(id INT,
 SecretDeterministic NVARCHAR(10) COLLATE Latin1_General_BIN2
  ENCRYPTED WITH (COLUMN_ENCRYPTION_KEY = AE_ColumnEncryptionKey,
   ENCRYPTION_TYPE = DETERMINISTIC,
   ALGORITHM = 'AEAD_AES_256_CBC_HMAC_SHA_256') NULL,
 SecretRandomized NVARCHAR(10) COLLATE Latin1_General_BIN2
  ENCRYPTED WITH (COLUMN_ENCRYPTION_KEY = AE_ColumnEncryptionKey,
   ENCRYPTION_TYPE = RANDOMIZED,
   ALGORITHM = 'AEAD_AES_256_CBC_HMAC_SHA_256') NULL
);
GO
```

This time, table creation succeeds. Now you can try to insert a row of data with the following statement:

```
INSERT INTO dbo.Table1
(id, SecretDeterministic, SecretRandomized)
VALUES (1, N'DeterSec01', N'RandomSec1');
```

You get the error 206 with error text "Operand type clash: nvarchar is incompatible with nvarchar(4000) encrypted with (encryption_type = 'DETERMINISTIC', encryption_algorithm_name = 'AEAD_AES_256_CBC_HMAC_SHA_256', column_encryption_key_name = 'AE_ColumnEncryptionKey', column_encryption_key_database_name = 'AEDemo')." SQL Server cannot encrypt or decrypt the data. You need to modify the data from a client application. You can do a limited set of operations on the table from SQL Server. For example, you can use the TRUNCATE TABLE statement on a table with AE columns.

I created a very simple client Windows Console application in Visual C#. The application actually just retrieves the keys and inserts a single row into the table that was created with the code above. Here is the C# code. The first part of the code just defines the namespaces used in the application or added by default in a new project in Visual Studio 2015.

```
using System;
using System.Collections.Generic;
using System.Data;
using System.Data.SqlClient;
using System.Linq;
using System.Text;
using System.Threading.Tasks;
```

The next part of the code defines the connection string to my local SQL Server. Please note the new connection string property in .NET 4.6 and above, the Column Encryption Setting=enabled property. Then the application opens the connection:

```
namespace AEDemo
{
    class Program
    {
        static void Main(string[] args)
        {
            string connectionString = "Data Source=localhost; " +
                "Initial Catalog=AEDemo; Integrated Security=true; " +
                "Column Encryption Setting=enabled";
            SqlConnection connection = new SqlConnection(connectionString);
            connection.Open();
```

The next part is just a simple check whether three arguments were passed. Please note that in a real application you should use a try-catch block when parsing the first argument to an integral number.

```
if (args.Length != 3)
    {
        Console.WriteLine("Please enter a numeric " +
          "and two string arguments.");
        return;
    }
int id = Int32.Parse(args[0]);
```

The next part of the code defines the parameterized INSERT statement and executes it:

```
{
    using (SqlCommand cmd = onnection.CreateCommand())
    {
     cmd.CommandText = @"INSERT INTO dbo.Table1 " +
      "(id, SecretDeterministic, SecretRandomized)" +
        " VALUES (@id, @SecretDeterministic,
            @SecretRandomized);";

    SqlParameter paramid= cmd.CreateParameter();
    paramid.ParameterName = @"@id";
    paramid.DbType = DbType.Int32;
    paramid.Direction = ParameterDirection.Input;
    paramid.Value = id;
    cmd.Parameters.Add(paramid);

    SqlParameter paramSecretDeterministic =
        cmd.CreateParameter();
                    paramSecretDeterministic.ParameterName =
      @"@SecretDeterministic";
    paramSecretDeterministic.DbType = DbType.String;
    paramSecretDeterministic.Direction =
      ParameterDirection.Input;
    paramSecretDeterministic.Value = "DeterSec1";
    paramSecretDeterministic.Size = 10;
cmd.Parameters.Add(paramSecretDeterministic);

    SqlParameter paramSecretRandomized = cmd.CreateParameter();
    paramSecretRandomized.ParameterName =
@"@SecretRandomized";
paramSecretRandomized.DbType = DbType.String;
paramSecretRandomized.Direction = ParameterDirection.Input;
paramSecretRandomized.Value = "RandomSec1";
paramSecretRandomized.Size = 10;
                    cmd.Parameters.Add(paramSecretRandomized);
```

```
cmd.ExecuteNonQuery();
    }
}
```

Finally, the code closes the connection and informs you that a row was inserted successfully:

```
connection.Close();
Console.WriteLine("Row inserted successfully");
        }
    }
}
```

If you don't have Visual Studio installed, you can just run the AEDemo.exe application provided with the code examples associated with this book. As mentioned, the application inserts a single row into the previously created table with two AE-enabled columns. Please run the application from SSMS in SQLCMD mode, as the following example shows; there is no prompting for values in the application:

```
!!C:SQL2016DevGuideAEDemo 1 DeterSec01 RandomSec1
!!C:SQL2016DevGuideAEDemo 2 DeterSec02 RandomSec2
```

Now try to read the data from the same session in SSMS that you used to create the table:

```
SELECT *
FROM dbo.Table1;
```

You can see only encrypted data. Now open a second query window in SSMS. Right-click in this window and choose Connection, then Change Connection. In the connection dialog, click the Options button at the bottom. Type in AEDemo for the database name and then click the Additional Connection Parameters tab. In the text box, enter Column Encryption Setting=enabled (without the double quotes). Then click on **Connect**.

Try again to insert a row from SSMS. Use the following query:

```
INSERT INTO dbo.Table1
(id, SecretDeterministic, SecretRandomized)
VALUES (2, N'DeterSec2', N'RandomSec2');
```

When I ran this when writing this book, I got the same error 206 again. At the time of writing, I used SSMS version 13.0.15700.28. This SSMS version still can't parametrize ad hoc inserts. However, let's try to read the data with the following query:

```
SELECT *
FROM dbo.Table1;
```

This time, the query works and you get the following result:

```
Id   SecretDeterministic   SecretRandomized
---  --------------------  ----------------
1    DeterSec1             RandomSec1
2    DeterSec2             RandomSec2
```

You can now close this query window and continue in the first one. Try to index the column with deterministic encryption. The following code creates a nonclustered index on the dbo.Table1 with the SecretDeterministic column used as the key:

```
CREATE NONCLUSTERED INDEX NCI_Table1_SecretDeterministic
ON dbo.Table1(SecretDeterministic);
GO
```

The creation succeeds. Now try to also create an index on the column with randomized encryption:

```
CREATE NONCLUSTERED INDEX NCI_Table1_SecretRandomized
ON dbo.Table1(SecretRandomized);
GO
```

This time you get an error message telling you that you cannot index a column with randomized encryption. Finally, execute the following code to clean up your SQL Server instance:

```
USE master;
IF DB_ID(N'AEDemo') IS NOT NULL
DROP DATABASE AEDemo;
GO
```

You have already seen some of the limitations of AE, including:

- Only BIN2 collations are supported for strings
- You can only index columns with deterministic encryption, and use a limited set of T-SQL operations on those columns
- You cannot index columns with randomized encryption
- AE is limited to the Enterprise and Developer editions only
- Working with AE in SSMS can be painful

Refer to Books Online for a more detailed list of AE's limitations. However, please also note the strengths of AE. It is simple to implement because it does not need modifications in an application, except the modification for connection strings. Data is encrypted end-to-end, from client memory, through network to database storage. Even DBAs can't view the data within SQL Server only; they need access to the key storage outside SQL Server to read the CMK. AE and other encryption options in SQL Server provide a complete set of possibilities, and it is up to you to select the appropriate method for the business problem you are solving.

Row-Level security

In the first part of this chapter, you learned about the permissions on database objects, including objects with data, namely tables, views, and table-valued, user-defined functions. Sometimes you need to give permissions to end users in a more granular way. For example, you might need to give permissions to a specific user to read and update only a subset of columns in the table, and to see only a subset of rows in a table.

You can use programmable objects, such as stored procedures, to achieve these granular permission needs. You can use declarative permissions with the DCL statements GRANT, REVOKE, and DENY on the column level already available in previous versions of SQL Server. However, SQL Server 2016 also offers **declarative row-level security**, abbreviated as RLS. In this section, you will learn how to:

- Use programmable objects to maintain security
- Use SQL Server 2016 row-level security

Using programmable objects to maintain security

In Transact-SQL, you can write views, stored procedures, scalar and table-valued user-defined functions, and triggers. Views serve best as a layer for selecting data, although you can modify data through views as well. Views are especially useful for column and row-level security. You can grant column permissions directly; however, doing this means a lot of administrative work. You can create a view as a projection on the base table with selected columns only, and then maintain permissions on a higher granularity level (that is, on the view instead of on the columns). In addition, you cannot give row-level permissions through a predicate in the GRANT statement. Of course, you can use the same predicate in the WHERE clause of the SELECT statement of the view you are using as a security layer. You can use table-valued functions as parameterized views.

Stored procedures are appropriate for all update activity, and also for querying data. Maintaining security through stored procedures is the easiest method of administration; with stored procedures, you typically need to grant the EXECUTE permission only. You can use triggers and scalar functions for advanced security checking; for example, for validating users' input.

Programmable objects refer to base tables and to each other in a kind of chain. For example, a stored procedure can use a view that selects from a base table. All the objects in SQL Server have owners. As long as there is a single owner for all the objects in the chain, you can manage permissions on the highest level only. Using the previous example, if the stored procedure, view, and base table have the same owner, you can manage permissions for the stored procedure only. SQL Server trusts that the owner of the procedure knows what the procedure is doing. This works for any DML statement (SELECT, INSERT, UPDATE, DELETE, and MERGE).

If the chain of owners between dependent objects is broken, SQL Server must check the permissions for any objects where the chain is broken. For example, if the owner of the procedure from the previous example is different from the owner of the view, SQL Server will check the permissions on the view as well. If the owner of the table was different from the owner of the view, SQL Server will also check permissions on the base table. In addition, if you use dynamic T-SQL code, concatenate a T-SQL statement as a string, and then use the EXECUTE command to execute them, SQL Server checks the permissions on all the objects the dynamic code is using. This is logical because SQL Server cannot know which objects the dynamic code is going to use until it actually executes the code, especially if you concatenate a part of the dynamic code from user input. Besides the threat of code injection, this extra checking is another reason why you should not use dynamic string concatenation in T-SQL code in production.

To start testing the programmable-objects-based row-level security, let's create a new demo database and change the context to this database:

```
USE master;
IF DB_ID(N'RLSDemo') IS NULL
CREATE DATABASE RLSDemo;
GO
USE RLSDemo;
```

The next step is to create four database users without logins. Three of them represent regular users from the Sales department, and the fourth one represents the Sales department manager.

```
CREATE USER SalesUser1 WITHOUT LOGIN;
CREATE USER SalesUser2 WITHOUT LOGIN;
CREATE USER SalesUser3 WITHOUT LOGIN;
CREATE USER SalesManager WITHOUT LOGIN;
GO
```

The next piece of code creates a table for the employee data. This table needs row-level security.

```
CREATE TABLE dbo.Employees
(
 EmployeeId    INT           NOT NULL PRIMARY KEY,
 EmployeeName  NVARCHAR(10)  NOT NULL,
 SalesRegion   NVARCHAR(3)   NOT NULL,
 SalaryRank    INT           NOT NULL
);
GO
```

Now let's insert some data into the dbo.Employees table. The three rows inserted represent the three regular users from the Sales department. You can check the inserted rows immediately with a query. Note that the sales region for the first two users is USA, and for the third one it is EU.

```
INSERT INTO dbo.Employees
(EmployeeId, EmployeeName, SalesRegion, SalaryRank)
VALUES
  (1, N'SalesUser1', N'USA', 5),
  (2, N'SalesUser2', N'USA', 4),
  (3, N'SalesUser3', N'EU', 6);
-- Check the data
SELECT *
FROM dbo.Employees;
GO
```

The dbo.Customers table, created with the following code, will also need row-level security:

```
CREATE TABLE dbo.Customers
(
 CustomerId    INT           NOT NULL PRIMARY KEY,
 CustomerName NVARCHAR(10) NOT NULL,
 SalesRegion  NVARCHAR(3)  NOT NULL
);
GO
```

Again, let's insert some rows into this table and check them. There are two customers from the USA and two from the EU.

```
INSERT INTO dbo.Customers
(CustomerId, CustomerName, SalesRegion)
VALUES
 (1, N'Customer01', N'USA'),
 (2, N'Customer02', N'USA'),
 (3, N'Customer03', N'EU'),
 (4, N'Customer04', N'EU');
-- Check the data
SELECT *
FROM dbo.Customers;
GO
```

None of the users have been given any permissions yet. Therefore, you can read the data only as the dbo user. If you execute the following five lines of code, only the first SELECT succeeds. For the other four EXECUTE commands, you get an error.

```
SELECT * FROM dbo.Employees;
EXECUTE (N'SELECT * FROM dbo.Employees') AS USER = N'SalesUser1';
EXECUTE (N'SELECT * FROM dbo.Employees') AS USER = N'SalesUser2';
EXECUTE (N'SELECT * FROM dbo.Employees') AS USER = N'SalesUser3';
EXECUTE (N'SELECT * FROM dbo.Employees') AS USER = N'SalesManager';
```

In the next step, the code creates a stored procedure that reads the data from the dbo.Employees table. It filters the rows for regular users and returns all rows for the Sales department manager.

```
CREATE PROCEDURE dbo.SelectEmployees
AS
SELECT *
FROM dbo.Employees
WHERE EmployeeName = USER_NAME()
OR USER_NAME() = N'SalesManager';
GO
```

You must give the permission to execute this procedure to the database users:

```
GRANT EXECUTE ON dbo.SelectEmployees
TO SalesUser1, SalesUser2, SalesUser3, SalesManager;
GO
```

Users still cannot see the data by querying the tables directly. You can test this fact by executing the following code again. You can read the data as the dbo user, but will get errors when you impersonate other database users.

```
SELECT * FROM dbo.Employees;
EXECUTE (N'SELECT * FROM dbo.Employees') AS USER = N'SalesUser1';
EXECUTE (N'SELECT * FROM dbo.Employees') AS USER = N'SalesUser2';
EXECUTE (N'SELECT * FROM dbo.Employees') AS USER = N'SalesUser3';
EXECUTE (N'SELECT * FROM dbo.Employees') AS USER = N'SalesManager';
GO
```

Try to execute the stored procedure, once as dbo and once by impersonating each database user:

```
EXEC dbo.SelectEmployees;
EXECUTE AS USER = N'SalesUser1' EXEC dbo.SelectEmployees;
REVERT;
EXECUTE AS USER = N'SalesUser2' EXEC dbo.SelectEmployees;
REVERT;
EXECUTE AS USER = N'SalesUser3' EXEC dbo.SelectEmployees;
REVERT;
EXECUTE AS USER = N'SalesManager' EXEC dbo.SelectEmployees;
REVERT;
GO
```

As the dbo user, you can execute the procedure; however, you don't see any rows because the filter in the query in the procedure did not take the dbo user into consideration. Of course, the dbo user can still query the table directly. The regular users see their rows only. The Sales department manager sees all of the rows in the table.

The next procedure uses dynamic SQL to read the data from the table for a single user. By using dynamic SQL, the procedure creates a broken ownership chain.

```
CREATE PROCEDURE dbo.SelectEmployeesDynamic
AS
DECLARE @sqlStatement AS NVARCHAR(4000);
SET @sqlStatement = N'
SELECT *
FROM dbo.Employees
WHERE EmployeeName = USER_NAME();'
EXEC(@sqlStatement);
```

```
GO
```

Give the users permission to execute this procedure:

```
GRANT EXECUTE ON dbo.SelectEmployeesDynamic
TO SalesUser1, SalesUser2, SalesUser3, SalesManager;
GO
```

Try to execute the procedure by impersonating different users:

```
EXEC dbo.SelectEmployeesDynamic;
EXECUTE AS USER = N'SalesUser1' EXEC dbo.SelectEmployeesDynamic;
REVERT;
EXECUTE AS USER = N'SalesUser2' EXEC dbo.SelectEmployeesDynamic;
REVERT;
EXECUTE AS USER = N'SalesUser3' EXEC dbo.SelectEmployeesDynamic;
REVERT;
EXECUTE AS USER = N'SalesManager' EXEC dbo.SelectEmployeesDynamic;
REVERT;
```

When you execute it as the dbo users, the execution succeeds, but you don't get any data returned. However, when you execute the procedure when impersonating other users, you get an error because other users don't have permission to read the underlying table.

Predicate-based Row-Level Security

Using programmable objects for row-level security protects the sensitive data very well because users don't have direct access to the tables. However, implementation of such security might be very complex for existing applications that don't use stored procedures, and other programmable objects. This is why SQL Server 2016 includes predicate-based **Row-Level Security (RLS)**. A DBA creates the security filters and policies. The new security policies are transparent to the application. RLS is available in Standard, Enterprise, and Developer editions. There are two types of RLS security predicates:

- **Filter predicates** that silently filter the rows the application reads. For these predicates, no application change is needed. Note that, besides reading, filter predicates also filter the rows when an application updates or deletes the rows; this is because the application again simply does not see the filtered rows.

- **Block predicates** that explicitly block write operations. You can define them for after-insert and after-update operations, when the predicates block such inserts or updates that would move a row out of the scope of the block predicate. The after-insert block predicates also apply to minimally logged or bulk inserts. You can also define the block predicates for before-update and delete operations, when they serve as the filter predicates for the updates and deletes. Note that if you already use filter predicates, the before-update and before-delete predicates are not needed. You might want to change the affected applications to catch the additional errors produced by the block predicates.

You define the predicates through a `predicate` function. In the body of this function, you can use other tables with the `JOIN` or `APPLY` operators. If the function is schema bound, no additional permission checks are needed. If the function is not schema bound, users need permissions to read the data from the joined tables. When a `predicate` function is schema bound, you cannot modify the objects it refers to.

A security policy adds an RLS predicate to a table using a `predicate` function. The policy can be disabled. If it is disabled, users see all of the rows. A security policy also filters and/or blocks the rows for the database owners (`dbo user`, `db_owner` database role, and `sysadmin` server role).

Before testing the SQL Server 2016 RLS, the users need permissions to read the data. The following code gives the users permissions to read data from both tables in the demo database:

```
GRANT SELECT ON dbo.Employees
TO SalesUser1, SalesUser2, SalesUser3, SalesManager;
GRANT SELECT ON dbo.Customers
TO SalesUser1, SalesUser2, SalesUser3, SalesManager;
GO
```

To check the permissions, you can try to read from the `dbo.Employees` table by impersonating each of the users again. All of the users see all of the rows.

```
SELECT * FROM dbo.Employees;
EXECUTE (N'SELECT * FROM dbo.Employees') AS USER = N'SalesUser1';
EXECUTE (N'SELECT * FROM dbo.Employees') AS USER = N'SalesUser2';
EXECUTE (N'SELECT * FROM dbo.Employees') AS USER = N'SalesUser3';
EXECUTE (N'SELECT * FROM dbo.Employees') AS USER = N'SalesManager';
GO
```

The following command creates a separate schema for security objects. It is good practice to move the security objects into a separate schema. If they are in a regular schema, a DBA might inadvertently give permission to modify the security objects when giving the ALTER SCHEMA permission to users for some other reason, such as allowing them to alter the procedures in that schema.

```
CREATE SCHEMA Security;
GO
```

The following predicate function limits the users to seeing only their own rows in a table. The Sales department manager role can see all rows. In addition, the predicate also takes care of the dbo users, enabling these users to see all of the rows as well.

```
CREATE FUNCTION Security.EmployeesRLS(@UserName AS NVARCHAR(10))
RETURNS TABLE
WITH SCHEMABINDING
AS
RETURN SELECT 1 AS SecurityPredicateResult
 WHERE @UserName = USER_NAME()
    OR USER_NAME() IN (N'SalesManager', N'dbo');
GO
```

The next step is to create the security policy. The security policy created with the following code adds a filter predicate for the dbo.Employees table. Note that the EmployeeName column is used as the argument for the predicate function.

```
CREATE SECURITY POLICY EmployeesFilter
ADD FILTER PREDICATE Security.EmployeesRLS(EmployeeName)
ON dbo.Employees
WITH (STATE = ON);
GO
```

You can test the filter predicate by querying the dbo.Employees table again. This time, each regular user gets their own row only, while the Sales department manager and the dbo users see all of the rows.

```
SELECT * FROM dbo.Employees;
EXECUTE (N'SELECT * FROM dbo.Employees') AS USER = N'SalesUser1';
EXECUTE (N'SELECT * FROM dbo.Employees') AS USER = N'SalesUser2';
EXECUTE (N'SELECT * FROM dbo.Employees') AS USER = N'SalesUser3';
EXECUTE (N'SELECT * FROM dbo.Employees') AS USER = N'SalesManager';
GO
```

Note that the users can still gain access to the sensitive data if they can write queries. With carefully crafted queries, they can conclude that a specific row exists, for example. The salary rank for the SalesUser1 user is 5. This user might be interested if another user with salary rank 6 exists. The user can execute the following query:

```
EXECUTE (N'SELECT * FROM dbo.Employees
WHERE SalaryRank = 6')
AS USER = N'SalesUser1';
```

The query returns zero rows. The SalesUser1 did not get any information yet. However, when a query is executed, the WHERE predicate is evaluated before the security policy filter predicate. Imagine that the SalesUser1 tries to execute the following query:

```
EXECUTE (N'SELECT * FROM dbo.Employees
WHERE SalaryRank / (SalaryRank - 6) = 0')
AS USER = N'SalesUser1';
```

When you execute this code, you get error 8134, divide by zero error encountered. Now SalesUser1 knows that an employee with salary rank equal to 6 exists.

Now let's create another predicate function that will be used to filter the rows in the dbo.Customers table. It applies a tabular expression to each row of the dbo.Customers table to include the rows with the same sales region as the sales region value for the user that is querying the tables. It does not filter the data for the Sales department manager and the dbo database user.

```
CREATE FUNCTION Security.CustomersRLS(@CustomerId AS INT)
RETURNS TABLE
WITH SCHEMABINDING
AS
RETURN
SELECT 1 AS SecurityPredicateResult
FROM dbo.Customers AS c
 CROSS APPLY(
  SELECT TOP 1 1
  FROM dbo.Employees AS e
  WHERE c.SalesRegion = e.SalesRegion
    AND (e.EmployeeName = USER_NAME()
         OR USER_NAME() IN (N'SalesManager', N'dbo')))
 AS E(EmployeesResult)
WHERE c.CustomerId = @CustomerId;
GO
```

The next step is, of course, to add a security policy. Note that you need to use a column from the dbo.Customers table for the argument of the predicate function. This argument is a dummy one, it does not filter the rows; the actual filter i is implemented in the body of the function.

```
CREATE SECURITY POLICY CustomersFilter
ADD FILTER PREDICATE Security.CustomersRLS(CustomerId)
ON dbo.Customers
WITH (STATE = ON);
GO
```

The following queries test the filter predicate:

```
SELECT * FROM dbo.Customers;
EXECUTE (N'SELECT * FROM dbo.Customers') AS USER = N'SalesUser1';
EXECUTE (N'SELECT * FROM dbo.Customers') AS USER = N'SalesUser2';
EXECUTE (N'SELECT * FROM dbo.Customers') AS USER = N'SalesUser3';
EXECUTE (N'SELECT * FROM dbo.Customers') AS USER = N'SalesManager';
GO
```

The rows from the dbo.Customers table are filtered for the regular users. However, note that SalesUser1 and SalesUser2 see the same rows—the rows for the customers from the USA—because the sales territory for both of them is USA. Now let's give the users permissions to modify the data in the dbo.Customers table.

```
GRANT INSERT, UPDATE, DELETE ON dbo.Customers
TO SalesUser1, SalesUser2, SalesUser3, SalesManager;
```

Try to impersonate the SalesUser1 user, and delete or update a row that SalesUser1 does not see because of the filter predicate. In both cases, zero rows are affected.

```
EXECUTE (N'DELETE FROM dbo.Customers WHERE CustomerId = 3')
 AS USER = N'SalesUser1';
EXECUTE (N'UPDATE dbo.Customers
 SET CustomerName =' + '''' + 'Updated' + '''' +
  'WHERE CustomerId = 3')
 AS USER = N'SalesUser1';
```

However, SalesUser1 can insert a row that is filtered out when the same user queries the data. In addition, the user can also update a row in such a way that the row would disappear from the user's scope. Check the following code:

```
EXECUTE (N'INSERT INTO dbo.Customers
(CustomerId, CustomerName, SalesRegion)
 VALUES(5, ' + '''' + 'Customer05' + '''' + ',' +
  '''' + 'EU' + '''' + ');'
 ) AS USER = N'SalesUser1';
```

```
EXECUTE (N'UPDATE dbo.Customers
 SET SalesRegion =' + '''' + 'EU' + '''' +
 'WHERE CustomerId = 2')
 AS USER = N'SalesUser1';
```

Now try to read the data. The `dbo` user sees all of the rows, while `SalesUser1` sees neither the row (s)he just inserted nor the row (s)he just updated.

```
SELECT * FROM dbo.Customers;
EXECUTE (N'SELECT * FROM dbo.Customers') AS USER = N'SalesUser1';
```

You need to add a block predicate to block the inserts and updates that would move a row outside the scope of the user performing the write operation:

```
ALTER SECURITY POLICY CustomersFilter
ADD BLOCK PREDICATE Security.CustomersRLS(CustomerId)
ON dbo.Customers AFTER INSERT,
ADD BLOCK PREDICATE Security.CustomersRLS(CustomerId)
ON dbo.Customers AFTER UPDATE;
GO
```

Try to do similar data modifications while impersonating the `SalesUser1` user again:

```
EXECUTE (N'INSERT INTO dbo.Customers
(CustomerId, CustomerName, SalesRegion)
 VALUES(6, ' + '''' + 'Customer06' + '''' + ',' +
 '''' + 'EU' + '''' + ');'
) AS USER = N'SalesUser1';
EXECUTE (N'UPDATE dbo.Customers
SET SalesRegion =' + '''' + 'EU' + '''' +
'WHERE CustomerId = 1')
 AS USER = N'SalesUser1';
```

This time, you get an error for both commands. You can see that the block predicate works. Finally, you can clean up your SQL Server instance:

```
USE master;
IF DB_ID(N'RLSDemo') IS NOT NULL
    ALTER DATABASE RLSDemo SET SINGLE_USER WITH ROLLBACK IMMEDIATE;
    DROP DATABASE RLSDemo;
GO
```

Exploring dynamic data masking

With the new SQL Server 2016 **Dynamic Data Masking (DDM)**, you have an additional tool that helps you limit the exposure of sensitive data by masking it to non-privileged users. The masking is done on the SQL Server side, and thus you don't need to implement any changes to applications to start using it. DDM is available in Standard, Enterprise, and Developer editions.

This section introduces DDM, including:

- Defining masked columns
- DDM limitations

Defining masked columns

You define DDM at the column level. You can obfuscate values from a column in a table by using four different masking functions:

- The `default` function implements full masking. The mask depends on the data type of the column. A string is masked by changing each character of a string to `X`. Numeric values are masked to zero. Date and time data type values are masked to "01.01.2000 00:00:00.0000000" (without double quotes). Binary data is masked to a single byte of ASCII value 0.
- The `email` function masks strings that represent e-mail addresses in the form `aXXX@XXXX.com`.
- The `random` function masks numeric values to a random value in a specified range.
- The `partial` function uses a custom string for masking character data. You can skip masking some characters at the beginning of the string (prefix) or at the end of the string (suffix).

You must give the users the `UNMASK` database level permission if you want them to see unmasked data.

Let's start testing the DDM feature by creating a new demo database and changing the context to the newly created database:

```
USE master;
IF DB_ID(N'DDMDemo') IS NULL
CREATE DATABASE DDMDemo;
GO
USE DDMDemo;
```

Next, you need a couple of database users for the test:

```
CREATE USER SalesUser1 WITHOUT LOGIN;
CREATE USER SalesUser2 WITHOUT LOGIN;
```

The following code creates and populates a demo table using the SELECT INTO statement. It uses the employees from the WideWorldImporters demo database, and adds a randomized salary.

```
SELECT PersonID, FullName, EmailAddress,
 CAST(JSON_VALUE(CustomFields, '$.HireDate') AS DATE)
  AS HireDate,
 CAST(RAND(CHECKSUM(NEWID()) % 100000 + PersonID) * 50000 AS INT) + 20000
  AS Salary
INTO dbo.Employees
FROM WideWorldImporters.Application.People
WHERE IsEmployee = 1;
```

You must grant the SELECT permission on this table to the two database users:

```
GRANT SELECT ON dbo.Employees
TO SalesUser1, SalesUser2;
```

If you execute the following queries, you can see that you, as the dbo user, and both database users you created, can see all of the data:

```
SELECT * FROM dbo.Employees;
EXECUTE (N'SELECT * FROM dbo.Employees') AS USER = N'SalesUser1';
EXECUTE (N'SELECT * FROM dbo.Employees') AS USER = N'SalesUser2';
```

Here is the partial result of one of the three previous queries:

```
PersonID FullName      EmailAddress                       HireDate    Salary
-------- ------------- ---------------------------------- ----------- ------
2        Kayla Woodcock kaylaw@wideworldimporters.com     2008-04-19 45823
3        Hudson Onslow  hudsono@wideworldimporters.com    2012-03-05 39344
```

The following code adds masking:

```
ALTER TABLE dbo.Employees ALTER COLUMN EmailAddress
  ADD MASKED WITH (FUNCTION = 'email()');
ALTER TABLE dbo.Employees ALTER COLUMN HireDate
  ADD MASKED WITH (FUNCTION = 'default()');
ALTER TABLE dbo.Employees ALTER COLUMN FullName
  ADD MASKED WITH (FUNCTION = 'partial(1, "&&&&&", 3)');
ALTER TABLE dbo.Employees ALTER COLUMN Salary
  ADD MASKED WITH (FUNCTION = 'random(1, 100000)');
GO
```

Try to read the data as one of the regular users:

```
EXECUTE (N'SELECT * FROM dbo.Employees') AS USER = N'SalesUser1';
```

The result for this user is masked:

PersonID	FullName	EmailAddress	HireDate	Salary
2	K&&&&&ock	kXXX@XXXX.com	1900-01-01	57709
3	H&&&&&low	hXXX@XXXX.com	1900-01-01	44627

Note that you might get different values for the salary because this column uses the random masking function. Now you can grant the UNMASK permission to the SalesUser1 user, and try to read the data again. This time, the result is unmasked.

```
GRANT UNMASK TO SalesUser1;
EXECUTE (N'SELECT * FROM dbo.Employees') AS USER = N'SalesUser1';
```

Dynamic data masking limitations

You might have already noticed the first DDM limitation. The UNMASK permission currently works at the database level only. You also cannot mask the columns encrypted with the AE feature. FILESTREAM and COLUMN_SET (sparse) columns don't support masking either. A masked column cannot be used in a full-text index. You cannot define a mask on a computed column. If a user who does not have permission to unmask the columns creates a copy of the data with the SELECT INTO statements, then the data in the destination is converted to masked values and the original data is lost. For example, the following code gives the CREATE TABLE and ALTER SCHEMA permissions to both test users, while only the first user has the UNMASK permission. Both users execute the SELECT INTO statement.

```
GRANT CREATE TABLE TO SalesUser1, SalesUser2;
GRANT ALTER ON SCHEMA::dbo TO  SalesUser1, SalesUser2;
EXECUTE (N'SELECT * INTO dbo.SU1 FROM dbo.Employees') AS USER =
```

```
N'SalesUser1';
EXECUTE (N'SELECT * INTO dbo.SU2 FROM dbo.Employees') AS USER =
N'SalesUser2';
GO
```

You can query the two new tables as the dbo user. The values in the table created by the SalesUser2 user are converted into the masked values.

Carefully crafted queries can also bypass DDM. Some numeric system functions automatically unmask the data in order to perform the calculation. The following query is executed in the context of the SalesUser2 user, who does not have permission to unmask the data.

```
EXECUTE AS USER = 'SalesUser2';
SELECT Salary AS SalaryMaskedRandom,
 EXP(LOG(Salary)) AS SalaryExpLog,
 SQRT(SQUARE(salary)) AS SalarySqrtSquare
FROM dbo.Employees
WHERE PersonID = 2;
REVERT;
```

Here are the results:

SalaryMaskedRandom	SalaryExpLog	SalarySqrtSquare
70618	45822.96875	45823

Filtering in a query also works on the unmasked value. For example, the SalesUser2 user can check which employees have a salary greater than 50,000 with the following query:

```
EXECUTE AS USER = 'SalesUser2';
SELECT *
FROM dbo.Employees
WHERE Salary > 50000;
REVERT;
```

Here are the abbreviated results.

PersonID	FullName	EmailAddress	HireDate	Salary
4	I&&&&upp	iXXX@XXXX.com	1900-01-01	8347
8	A&&&&sse	aXXX@XXXX.com	1900-01-01	60993

Please note that you might get different results because the `Salary` column is masked with the random masking function. Finally, you can clean up your SQL Server instance:

```
USE master;
DROP DATABASE DDMDemo;
GO
```

Summary

In this chapter, you have learned about SQL Server security. You have learned about principals and securables. When designing a database, you should carefully implement schemas. You give object and statement permissions to database users. To enhance data protection, SQL Server implements encryption in many different ways. The new SQL Server 2016 Always Encrypted feature might be extremely useful because you don't need to change existing applications (except for the connection string) to use it. You can filter the rows the users can see and modify these with the help of programmable objects or SQL Server 2016 predicate-based row level security. Finally, in SQL Server 2016, you can also mask the data with dynamic data masking for the non-privileged users.

9
Query Store

Query Store is a new performance troubleshooting tool, fully integrated into the database engine. In my opinion, it is one of the best database engine features since 2005 and the introduction of `OPTION (RECOMPILE)`. Query Store helps you to troubleshoot query performance by collecting information about queries, resource utilization, execution plans, and the other execution parameters. It is stored in a database and therefore it survives server crashes, restarts, and failovers.

Query Store does not only help you to identify issues with query executions, but also lets you easily and quickly fix or workaround problems caused by poorly chosen execution plans.

In this chapter, you will learn about the following points:

- Why Query Store has been introduced
- What Query Store is intended for and what it is not
- Query Store Architecture
- How Query Store can help you to quickly identify and solve some performance issues

Why Query Store?

I am sure that everyone who reads this book had to deal with a situation where a stored procedure or query suddenly started to perform poorly. That means, performance was good in the past, and it was working regularly up to some point in time, but the same procedure or query does not perform well anymore: either you got a timeout when you executed it, or the execution time has been significantly increased. Usually you need to fix it as soon as possible, especially when this happens in an important application module and/or during non-working or peak hours.

How do you proceed with this? What is the first step you take when you start such troubleshooting? By gathering information such as system information, query stats and plans, execution parameters, and so on, right? When a query or stored procedure is slow, you want to see its execution plan. Therefore, the first thing is to check the execution plan in the server cache. You can use this query to return the execution plan for a given stored procedure:

```
SELECT c.usecounts, c.cacheobjtype, c.objtype, q.text AS query_text,
p.query_plan
FROM
sys.dm_exec_cached_plans c
CROSS APPLY sys.dm_exec_sql_text(c.plan_handle) q
CROSS APPLY sys.dm_exec_query_plan(c.plan_handle) p
WHERE
c.objtype = 'Proc' AND q.text LIKE '%<SlowProcedureName>%';
```

By observing the execution plan of a poorly performed query you could find the reason why the execution is slow: you could see Scan, Hash Join, and Sort operators, and at least make some assumptions about the slow execution. You can also find out when the plan was generated. In addition to the plan info, you can also use the execution statistics. The following query returns info about the execution time and logical reads for the execution of a given stored procedure:

```
SELECT p.name, s.execution_count,
ISNULL(s.execution_count*60/(DATEDIFF(second, s.cached_time, GETDATE())),
0) AS calls_per_minute,
(s.total_elapsed_time/(1000*s.execution_count)) AS avg_elapsed_time_ms,
s.total_logical_reads/s.execution_count AS avg_logical_reads,
s.last_execution_time,
s.last_elapsed_time/1000 AS last_elapsed_time_ms,
s.last_logical_reads
FROM sys.procedures p
INNER JOIN sys.dm_exec_procedure_stats AS s ON p.object_id = s.object_id
AND s.database_id = DB_ID()
WHERE p.name LIKE '%<SlowProcedureName>%';
```

By using the results of this query, you can compare current and average execution parameters, and also discover if only occasional executions are slow or if each execution under current circumstances runs longer. These two queries can help you to find out how the execution looks now and to see how it differs from the execution in the past from the response time and used resources point of view. You can also include a third query that returns current waiting tasks on the server within your database, to see if bad performance is caused by blocking issues.

However, there are some limitations in the set of information in the server cache. First, dynamic management views reflect particular or aggregated information from the last server restart only. When a server crashes, is restarted, or fails over, all cache information disappears. This could be a huge limitation in the query troubleshooting process. In the server cache, only the actual execution plan for a query is available and even this is not guaranteed. Sometimes, the plan is not in the cache due to memory pressure or infrequent usage. For queries with the OPTION (RECOMPILE), for instance, only the latest version of the execution plan is in the cache, although the plan is generated by every execution. Since only the latest execution plan for a query is available, you don't know if and how the execution plan changed over time.

Every upgrade to a new SQL Server version, every failover, patch, and installation of a new version of an application or service could lead to new execution plans. In most of the cases, these plans look the same after the mentioned action, sometimes they are even better (new versions and installing of cumulative updates and service packs usually improve overall performance), but in some cases newly-generated plans could be significantly slower than before the change. However, in server cache, the old, good plan cannot be found.

What do we do in such cases? For the most critical stored procedures, I collect execution plans and statistics from dynamic management views mentioned at the beginning of this chapter and save them regularly into a database table by using a SQL job. The job runs every five minutes, data is persistent, belongs to the database, and is not lost when the server is restarted. On the top of the tables, I created a few PowerPivot reports and notifications. I check them immediately after a failover, patch, or installation of a new application version and use them to confirm that the action was successful or to quickly identify performance degradations. A typical report is shown in the following screenshot.

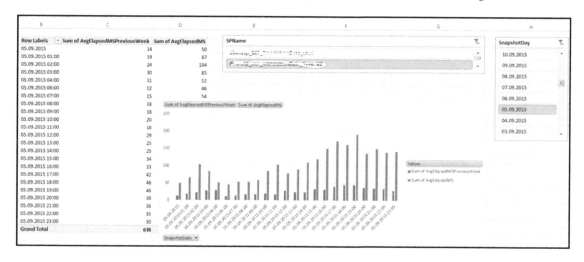

Figure9.1: Report using previously collected execution data

It clearly shows one regressed stored procedure after an application release.

This approach works very well and I have good experience with it. It helped me many times not only to identify performance issues, but also to confirm that an update action was successful and learn more about my workload and how it behaves over time. However, I had to write, maintain, and deploy this custom solution to every database, and ensure that the mentioned SQL job will run on all servers for all databases, regardless of failover or restart. It also requires consideration for, and even negotiations with, database administrators to ensure that server performance will not be significantly affected with the SQL job that collects my statistics. I would prefer an out-of-box solution for this, but such a solution did not exist. Until SQL Server 2016.

What is Query Store?

Query Store is the answer to the challenges described above. It collects the most relevant information about the executed queries: query text, parameters, query optimization and compilation details, execution plans, and execution statistics (execution time, CPU and memory usage, I/O execution details) and stores them in a database so that they are available after server restarts, failovers, or crashes.

You can use Query Store not only to identify performance issues, but also to fix some of them. Query Store offers a solution for issues caused by changed execution plans. By using Query Store, you can easily enforce the old plan; it is not required to rewrite the query or to write any code. You don't affect the business logic, therefore there is no need for testing, there is neither code deployment nor application restart. By taking this approach you can quickly implement a solution or at least a workaround, and save time and money.

 In addition to this, stored information can be used (they are exposed through catalog views) outside of SQL Server, usually in reports and notifications, to let you to get a better or more complete picture about your workload and help you to be more familiar with it.

Query Store also captures some information that is not available in server cache such as unfinished queries or queries with broken execution, either by the caller or by an exception. You can easy find out how many executions of a single query were successful and how many executions ended with exceptions. This was not possible prior to SQL Server 2016 with querying server cache.

Query Store architecture

Query Store is integrated with the query processor of the database engine. The simplified architecture diagram is shown in the following diagram:

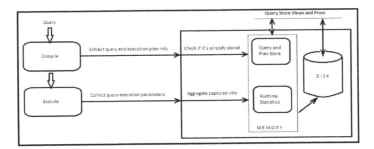

Figure 9.2: Query Store architecture

Query Store actually has two stores:

- **Query and PlanStore**: Stored information about executed queries and execution plans used for their execution
- **Runtime Statistics Store**: This store holds aggregated execution parameters (execution time, logical reads, and so on) for executed queries within a specified time

Both stores have instances in memory and persisted representation through disk tables. Due to performance reasons, captured info is not immediately written to disk, it is rather written asynchronously. Query Store physically stores this info into the database primary file group.

When a query is submitted to the database engine and Query Store is enabled for the database, during query compilation, Query Store captures information about the query and execution plan. This is then sent into the Query and Plan store, if the information is not already there. Information about a single query is stored only once in Query Store; the same for execution plans. For every execution plan we have only one row (up to 200 different execution plans are supported by default).

When the query is executed, execution parameters Query Store captures the most relevant execution parameters (duration, logical reads, CPU time, used memory, and so on), uses them in aggregated calculations, and sends them into the Runtime Stats Store only at configured time intervals. Therefore, Query Store does not store info about every single execution. If the time interval is 10 minutes, for instance, it stores runtime stats for a single execution plan every 10 minutes.

Captured data is persistently stored in internal database tables. It is not directly available for reading and manipulation. Instead of that, Query Store functionalities are exposed through Query Store catalog views and stored procedures. There are seven query store catalog views:

- `sys.database_query_store_options`
- `sys.query_context_settings`
- `sys.query_store_plan`
- `sys.query_store_query`
- `sys.query_store_query_text`
- `sys.query_store_runtime_stats`
- `sys.query_store_runtime_stats_interval`

Detailed info about query store catalog views can be found in SQL Server Books Online at `https://msdn.microsoft.com/en-us/library/dn 818149.aspx`.

You can also interact and perform some actions with Query Store by using six query store stored procedures:

- `sp_query_store_flush_db`
- `sp_query_store_force_plan`
- `sp_query_store_remove_plan`
- `sp_query_store_remove_query`
- `sp_query_store_reset_exec_stats`
- `sp_query_store_unforce_plan`

Of course, SQL Server Books Online describes query store stored procedure in detail at `http s://msdn.microsoft.com/en-us/library/dn818153.aspx`.

Enabling and configuring Query Store

As with all new features, Query Store is not active for a database by default. You can enable and configure it in **SQL Server Management Studio** (**SSMS**) by using the database properties (Query Store Page) or by using Transact-SQL. To enable Query Store, your account must be `db_owner` of the database or a member of the sysadmin fixed server role.

Enabling Query Store with SSMS

To enable Query Store for a database, you need to select it and click on **Properties**. You can find a new **Query Store** property page at the bottom of the list. As mentioned at the beginning of the section, it is disabled by default, which is indicated by the values **Off** for both **Operation Mode (Actual)** and **Operation Mode (Requested)**. To enable it, you need to change the value for the parameter **Operation Mode (Requested)** to **Read Write**, as shown in the following screenshot:

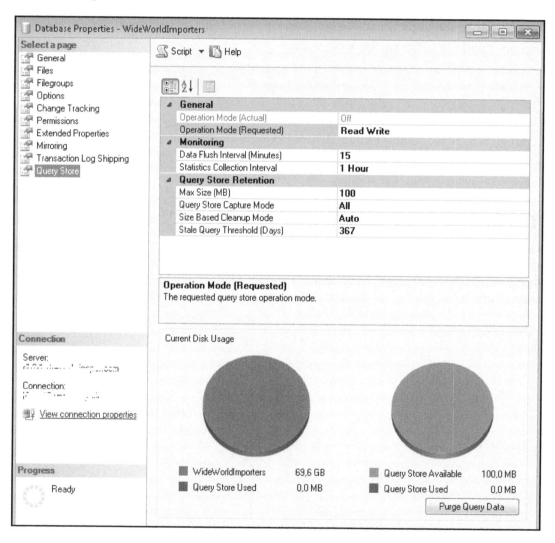

Figure 9-3: Enabling Query Store in SQL Server Management Studio

Enabling Query Store with Transact-SQL

The same action can be done by using Transact-SQL. Use the following statement to enable Query Store in the database `WideWorldImporters`:

```
ALTER DATABASE WideWorldImporters SET QUERY_STORE = ON;
```

Configuring Query Store

As shown in the above section, to enable Query Store you need to set only one parameter or click once. When you do this, you have enabled it with default values for all of its parameters. There is a collection of query store options that can be configured. Again, you can set them through SSMS or Transact-SQL. However, some of them have different names and even metrics in both tools. Here is the list of configurable Query Store parameters:

- **Operation Mode** defines the operation mode of the query store. Only two modes are supported: `READ_WRITE` and `READ_ONLY`. Default value is `READ_WRITE`, which means that Query Store collects query plans and runtime statistics and writes them to the disk. `READ_ONLY` mode makes sense only when the collected info in the query store exceeds the maximum allocated space for it. In this case, the mode is set to `READ_ONLY` automatically. The name of the parameter in the `ALTER DATABASE` Transact-SQL statement is `OPERATION_MODE`.

- **Max Size (MB)** determines the space in megabytes allocated to the query store. The parameter data type is `bigint`, default value is `100`. The name of the parameter in the `ALTER DATABASE` Transact-SQL statement is `STORAGE_SIZE_MB`.

- **Statistics Collection Interval** defines a fixed time window at which runtime execution statistics data is aggregated into the query store. The parameter data type is `bigint`, default value is `60`. The name of the parameter in the `ALTER DATABASE` Transact-SQL statement is `INTERVAL_LENGTH_MINUTES`.

- **Data Flush Interval (Minutes)** determines the frequency at which data written to the query store is persisted to disk. The parameter data type is `bigint`, default value is `15`. The minimum value is 1 minute. If you want to use it in the `ALTER DATABASE` Transact-SQL statement its name is `DATA_FLUSH_INTERVAL_SECONDS`. As you can see, in the Transact-SQL you need to use seconds, and in SSMS, minutes as parameter metric. It seems that consistency is lost somewhere between these two configuration modes.

- **Query Store Capture Mode** defines the scope of queries that will be captured. The parameter data type is `nvarchar`, and has the following values: `AUTO` (only relevant queries based on execution count and resource consumption are captured), `ALL` (all queries are captured) and `NONE` (new queries are not captured, only info about already captured queries). Default value is `ALL`. The name of the parameter in the ALTER DATABASE Transact-SQL statement is `QUERY_CAPTURE_MODE`.

- **Stale Query Threshold (Days)** controls the retention period of persisted runtime statistics and inactive queries. The parameter data type is `bigint`, default value is `30` days. When you use Transact-SQL you need to know that this parameter is a part of another parameter called `CLEANUP_POLICY`. The following Transact-SQL code configures the Stale Query Threshold parameter for the Query Store in the database `WideWorldImporters` to `60` days:

```
ALTER DATABASE WideWorldImporters
SET QUERY_STORE (CLEANUP_POLICY = (STALE_QUERY_THRESHOLD_DAYS =
60));
```

- **Size Based Cleanup Mode** controls whether cleanup will be automatically activated when the total amount of data gets close to maximum size. The parameter data type is `nvarchar`, and has the following values: `AUTO` (size based cleanup will be automatically activated when size on disk reaches 90% of `max_storage_size_mb`. Size-based cleanup removes the least expensive and oldest queries first. It stops at approximately 80% of `max_storage_size_mb`), `ALL` (all queries are captured) and `OFF` (size based cleanup won't be automatically activated). Default value is *OFF*. The name of the parameter in the ALTER DATABASE Transact-SQL statement is `SIZE_BASED_CLEANUP_MODE`.

- `MAX_PLANS_PER_QUERY` determines the maximum number of plans maintained for a single query. The parameter data type is `int`, default value is *200*. This parameter is inconsistently implemented, too. It is not even shown on the Query Store property page and can be set only via Transact-SQL.

Query Store default configuration

Enabling Query Store with default values is equivalent to this Transact-SQL statement:

```
ALTER DATABASE WideWorldImporters
SET QUERY_STORE = ON
  (
   OPERATION_MODE = READ_WRITE,
   MAX_STORAGE_SIZE_MB = 100,
```

```
    DATA_FLUSH_INTERVAL_SECONDS = 900,
    INTERVAL_LENGTH_MINUTES = 60,
    CLEANUP_POLICY = (STALE_QUERY_THRESHOLD_DAYS = 367),
    QUERY_CAPTURE_MODE = ALL,
    SIZE_BASED_CLEANUP_MODE = OFF,
    MAX_PLANS_PER_QUERY = 200
);
```

Default configuration is good for small databases or when you want to enable the feature and learn about it with the real query workload. However, for large databases and volatile database workloads you might need to change values for some Query Store options.

Query Store Recommended Configuration

What are the most important settings, and are default values a good starting point for using Query Store in your database? The most important values are Max Size, Size Based Cleanup Mode, Statistics Collection Interval, and Query Capture Mode.

- **Max Size**: When maximum storage size allocated for Query Store is reached, then Query Store switches to *Read Only* operation mode and no info is captured anymore: you can only read already captured data. In most of the cases, this is not what you want—you are usually interested in the recent data. To leave the most recent data in Query Store, you would need to set Size Based Cleanup Mode to *Auto*, which instructs a background process to remove the oldest data from the store, when the data size approaches the max size, keeping the most recent data in Query Store, similar to flight recorders in aircrafts. However, even for a moderate workload, *100 MB* for storage is not enough: I've seen moderate databases, where Query Store contains queries from the last 24 hours only. Therefore, I would suggest you to increase this value at least to *1 GB* and set Size Based Cleanup Mode to *Auto* to ensure that the most recent data is available and to avoid switching to *Read Only* operation mode.

- **Statistics Collection Interval**: You can leave this on its default value (1 hour) if you don't need to track queries over time in less granular intervals. If your database workload is volatile and depends on time patterns, you can consider using a smaller value. However, bear in mind that this will increase the amount of runtime statistics data.

- **Query Store Capture Mode**: Should be set to auto to instruct Query Store to capture info about only relevant queries based on execution count and resource consumption. This will exclude some queries and captured info would not reflect the whole workload, but the most relevant and important information will be there.

Disabling and cleaning Query Store

You might need to remove collected data from Query Store sometimes. For instance, when you use it for demo purposes or when you fixed queries that were a long time in regression and will be shown in Query Store reports in the next period too, because of their significant regression. You can remove captured information by clicking on the **Purge Query Data** button in the Query Store properties page inside SQL Server Management Studio (see *Figure 9.3*).

In addition to this, you can use the following Transact-SQL command:

```
ALTER DATABASE WideWorldImporters SET QUERY_STORE CLEAR;
```

To disable Query Store, you would need to set operation mode property to *Off* either through SQL Server management studio (Query Store page within database properties) or Transact-SQL command:

```
ALTER DATABASE WideWorldImporters SET QUERY_STORE = OFF;
```

Query Store in action

In this section, you will see how Query Store collects information about queries and query plans and how it can identify and fix regressed queries. It will be demonstrated how Query Store supports and facilitates an upgrade to SQL Server 2016.

First, you will create a new database with a single table and populate it with two million rows. This database will simulate a database that is created and used in SQL Server 2012 and that you restored in SQL Server 2016 but left in the old compatibility mode. Use the following code to accomplish this task:

```
IF DB_ID('Mila') IS NULL CREATE DATABASE Mila;
GO
USE Mila;
GO
--help function GetNums created by Itzik Ben-Gan (http://tsql.solidq.com)
CREATE OR ALTER FUNCTION dbo.GetNums(@n AS BIGINT) RETURNS TABLE
AS
RETURN
  WITH
  L0    AS(SELECT 1 AS c UNION ALL SELECT 1),
  L1    AS(SELECT 1 AS c FROM L0 AS A CROSS JOIN L0 AS B),
  L2    AS(SELECT 1 AS c FROM L1 AS A CROSS JOIN L1 AS B),
  L3    AS(SELECT 1 AS c FROM L2 AS A CROSS JOIN L2 AS B),
  L4    AS(SELECT 1 AS c FROM L3 AS A CROSS JOIN L3 AS B),
```

```
L5    AS(SELECT 1 AS c FROM L4 AS A CROSS JOIN L4 AS B),
  Nums AS(SELECT ROW_NUMBER() OVER(ORDER BY (SELECT NULL)) AS n FROM L5)
  SELECT n FROM Nums WHERE n <= @n;
GO
--Create sample table
DROP TABLE IF EXISTS dbo.Order;
CREATE TABLE dbo.Order(
id INT IDENTITY(1,1) NOT NULL,
custid INT NOT NULL,
details NVARCHAR(200) NOT NULL,
status TINYINT NOT NULL DEFAULT (1) INDEX ix1 NONCLUSTERED,
CONSTRAINT PK_Order PRIMARY KEY CLUSTERED (id ASC)
);
GO
-- Populate the table with 2M rows
INSERT INTO dbo. Ord (custid, details)
SELECT 1 + ABS(CHECKSUM(NEWID())) % 1111100 AS custid, REPLICATE(N'X', 200)
AS details
FROM dbo.GetNums(2000000);
```

To simulate a database created with SQL Server 2012, set the compatibility level to 110:

```
ALTER DATABASE Mila SET COMPATIBILITY_LEVEL = 110;
```

Now, you will enable and configure Query Store for the database. It will accompany you in your migration adventure. The following statement enables and configures Query Store for the sample database:

```
ALTER DATABASE Mila
SET QUERY_STORE = ON
    (
       OPERATION_MODE = READ_WRITE,
       INTERVAL_LENGTH_MINUTES = 1
    );
```

You can check the status and configured parameters of your query store by using the following view:

```
SELECT * FROM sys.database_query_store_options;
```

The following screenshots shows Query Store configuration, done by the previous command.

desired_state	desired_state_desc	actual_state	actual_state_desc	readonly_reason	current_storage_size_mb	flush_interval_seconds	interval_length_minutes	max_storage_size_mb
2	READ_WRITE	2	READ_WRITE	0	0	2000	1	100

Figure 9.4: Check Query Store Configuration

As you noticed, in this example you have used minimal value (one minute) for the parameter INTERVAL_LENGTH_MINUTES. This is done for demonstration purposes; you want to see collected data immediately. On the production system, this action can generate a lot of runtime statistics rows and could mean, for instance, that data is available for the last few hours only.

After you have enabled and configured Query Store, it immediately starts to collect information about executed queries. You can now simulate a workload by executing a sample query against the table you have created at the beginning of this section.

Capturing Query info

To simulate a database workload, you will execute one simple query. Ensure that the database is in the compatibility mode *110*, and that the Query Store is clean in order to track your queries easily:

```
ALTER DATABASE Mila SET COMPATIBILITY_LEVEL = 110;
ALTER DATABASE Mila SET QUERY_STORE CLEAR;
```

Run this code to execute one statement 100 times, as shown in the following command:

```
SET NOCOUNT ON;
SELECT id, custid, details, status FROM dbo.Orders WHERE status IN (0, 2);
GO 100
```

The above query returns no rows; all rows in your table have *1* as value in the *status* column. After executing this single query 100 times, you can check what has been captured by Query Store by using the following query:

```
SELECT * FROM sys.query_store_query;
```

The query repository contains a single row for each compiled query. You can see in the following screenshot one row representing the query you have executed in the previous step.

query_id	query_text_id	context_settings_id	object_id	batch_sql_handle	query_hash	is_internal_query	query_parameterization_type
1	1	1	0	NULL	0x3400C010AC4BA0F0	0	0

Figure 9.5: Check captured queries in Query Store

You have cleared the Query Store before executing the above query, and since you have executed a single query only, Query Store captured only one query. However, you could still get more rows from this catalog view if you run this code when you try code examples from this chapter, because some system queries such as updated statistics could also run at this time. Use the following query to return the `query_text` beside the `query_id` for all captured queries in the Query Store so that you can identify your query:

```
SELECT q.query_id, qt.query_sql_text FROM sys.query_store_query q
INNER JOIN sys.query_store_query_text AS qt ON q.query_text_id =
qt.query_text_id;
```

The preceding query produces the following output:

query_id	query_sql_text
1	SELECT id, custid, details, status FROM dbo.Orders WHERE status IN (0, 2)
2	SELECT * FROM sys.query_store_query

 As you can see, the `query_id` of your initial query has a value of 1, and you will use it for further queries. If you get some other value when you run these examples, use it later instead of *1*. In this section, the initial query will be tracked by using `query_id =1`.

The catalog view `sys.query_store_query` contains information about query hash, query compilation details, binding and optimizing, and also parametrization. The full list and description of all attributes of the catalog view you can find in the Books Online at `https://msdn.microsoft.com/en-us/library/dn818156.aspx`.

The catalog view `sys.query_store_query_text` contains query text and statement SQL handle for all queries captured in the Query Store. It has only five attributes and is linked to the `sys.query_store_query` catalog view via the attribute `query_id`. The full list and description of all attributes of the catalog view you can find in the Books Online at `https://msdn.microsoft.com/en-us/library/dn818159.aspx`.

Capturing plan info

For each query, you can have at least one execution plan. Therefore, in the plan repository, at least one entry exists for each query from the query repository. The following query returns rows from the plan repository:

```
SELECT * FROM sys.query_store_plan;
```

You can see four plans for four executed queries in the database `Mila`. The first query is your initial query; the rest are queries against the catalog views as shown in the following screenshot. As mentioned earlier in this section, you can see more entries if you execute the code examples from this chapter.

plan_id	query_id	plan_group_id	engine_version	compatibility_level	query_plan_hash	query_plan
1	1	0	13.0.4001.0	110	0x63A52BF104A38D3B	\<ShowPlanXML xmlns="http:/
2	2	0	13.0.4001.0	110	0xC63CA0FA9CC60C73	\<ShowPlanXML xmlns="http:/
3	3	0	13.0.4001.0	110	0xE2E1199F3FE566C6	\<ShowPlanXML xmlns="http:/
4	4	0	13.0.4001.0	110	0xA2F4083B141DD93F	\<ShowPlanXML xmlns="http:/

Figure 9.6: Check captured query plans in Query Store

The catalog view `sys.query_store_plan` contains information about query plan generation, including the plan in XML format. The full list and description of all attributes of the catalog view can be found in the Books Online at `https://msdn.microsoft.com/en-us/library/dn818155.aspx`.

Retuning query text beside IDs is always a good idea. Run the following code to show query text info, too:

```
SELECT qs.query_id, q.query_sql_text, p.query_plan
FROM sys.query_store_query AS qs
INNER JOIN sys.query_store_plan AS p ON p.query_id = qs.query_id
INNER JOIN sys.query_store_query_text AS q ON qs.query_text_id =
q.query_text_id;
```

The output is more user friendly as the following screenshot clearly shows:

query_id	query_sql_text	query_plan
1	SELECT id, custid, details, status FROM dbo.Order WHERE status IN (0, 2)	\<ShowPlanXML xmlns="http://schemas.microsoft.com...
2	SELECT * FROM sys.query_store_query	\<ShowPlanXML xmlns="http://schemas.microsoft.com...
3	SELECT q.query_id, qt.query_sql_text FROM sys.query_store_query q INNER JOIN ...	\<ShowPlanXML xmlns="http://schemas.microsoft.com...
4	SELECT * FROM sys.query_store_plan	\<ShowPlanXML xmlns="http://schemas.microsoft.com...
5	SELECT StatMan([SC0], [SC1]) FROM (SELECT TOP 100 PERCENT [query_id] AS [...	\<ShowPlanXML xmlns="http://schemas.microsoft.com...
6	SELECT qs.query_id, q.query_sql_text, p.query_plan FROM sys.query_store_query ...	\<ShowPlanXML xmlns="http://schemas.microsoft.com...

Figure 9-7. Check captured queries and query plans in Query Store

As you can see, queries against catalog views are also there, but you are interested in user queries only. For the initial query, you can see that all its executions were done with the same execution plan.

Already here, you can see the first great thing about Query Store. You can identify all queries that are executed with more than one execution plan. Use the following query to identify `query_id` for queries that have at least two different plans:

```
SELECT query_id, COUNT(*) AS cnt
FROM sys.query_store_plan p
GROUP BY query_id
HAVING COUNT(*) > 1 ORDER BY cnt DESC;
```

The query returns no rows in this case, you have simply executed only one query, but this is very useful information: you can instantly identify unstable queries in your system.

Collecting runtime statistics

In the previous two subsections, you saw two kinds of information: query details and execution plan. Now, it is time for execution statistics parameters. You will query a new catalog view:

```
SELECT * FROM sys.query_store_runtime_stats;
```

The output is shown in the following screenshot:

runtime_stats_id	plan_id	runtime_stats_interval_id	execution_type_desc	count_executions	avg_duration	last_duration	avg_logical_io_reads	last_logical_io_reads
1	1	1	Regular	100	47,42	49	6	6
2	2	1	Regular	1	259	259	4	4
3	3	1	Regular	1	182	182	6	6
4	4	1	Regular	1	7549	7549	42	42
5	5	2	Regular	1	311	311	2	2
6	6	2	Regular	1	8894	8894	98	98

Figure 9.8: Check collected runtime statistics in Query Store

Again, the output generated when you execute the above query can differ from the one shown in *Figure 9.8*. The catalog view `sys.query_store_runtime_stats` contains information about the runtime execution statistics information for the query. The full list and description of all attributes of the catalog view can be found in the Books Online at `https://msdn.microsoft.com/en-us/library/dn818158.aspx`.

Every minute (you have so configured Query Store), one entry per query plan will be entered in this store.

Actually, for each execution plan, you can have more than one entry in the runtime statistics store per unit defined with Statistics Collection Interval option. If all queries were successfully executed, one row will be added to the store. However, if some executions with the same plan were aborted by the client or ended with an exception, you can have more rows representing each execution type. Three execution types are supported: Regular, Aborted, and Exception which means that for each execution plan you can have up to three rows in the runtime statistics store per unit defined with Statistics Collection Interval option.

If you execute the initial query again, say, 200 times:

```
SET NOCOUNT ON;
SELECT id, custid, details, status FROM dbo.Orders WHERE status IN (0, 2);
GO 200
```

When you check the runtime statistics, you can see two entries for the same execution plan. In this example, it is plan_id = 1, because it is identified as the plan for the initial query. If you run this code later, your plan_id can be different.

```
SELECT * FROM sys.query_store_runtime_stats WHERE plan_id = 1;
```

The following screenshot shows these three entries:

runtime_stats_id	plan_id	runtime_stats_interval_id	execution_type_desc	count_executions	avg_duration	last_duration	avg_logical_io_reads	last_logical_io_reads
1	1	1	Regular	100	47,42	49	6	6
17	1	13	Regular	42	44,5952380952381	46	6	6
16	1	12	Regular	158	46,3607594936709	45	6	6

Figure 9-9. Check multiple runtime statistics entries for an execution plan in Query Store

You can see two additional entries with 200 executions and their aggregated statistic relevant execution parameters. You can use this query to see how execution parameters are changing over time.

Query Store and migration

In previous sections, you saw how Query Store captures and stores data about queries and their execution plans. It is now time to see how Query Store can help you with migration.

To simulate migration to SQL Server 2016, you will now change the compatibility level to 130.

```
ALTER DATABASE Mila SET COMPATIBILITY_LEVEL = 130;
```

And execute the initial query:

```
SET NOCOUNT ON;
SELECT id, custid, details, status FROM dbo.Orders WHERE status IN (0, 2);
GO 100
```

This time, it will take much longer than the execution under the old compatibility mode; you will see why later. It is clear that a new plan has been created for the query and it is also clear that the old one was better. After the execution is done, you can check query and plan repositories. Since you already know the `query_id` for the query, you can check the plan repository to confirm that the plan has been changed under the new compatibility mode.

```
SELECT * FROM sys.query_store_plan WHERE query_id = 1;
```

The following screenshot shows two entries in the plan repository. You can also see that two plans have been generated with different compatibility modes: **110** and **130** respectively.

plan_id	query_id	plan_group_id	engine_version	compatibility_level	query_plan_hash	query_plan
1	1	0	13.0.4001.0	110	0x63A52BF104A38D3B	<ShowPlanXML xmlns="http://schemas.microsoft.com...
14	1	0	13.0.4001.0	130	0x019EE823702337E8	<ShowPlanXML xmlns="http://schemas.microsoft.com...

Figure 9.10: Check multiple plans for a single query in Query Store

Setting the compatibility mode for the sample database to 130 triggers the generation of new execution plans for queries against this database. Most of them will probably be the same as they were before, but some of them will change. You can expect small or big improvements for most of them, but the upgrade to the latest compatibility mode will introduce significant regression for some queries, as in the sample query in this section. In the next section, you will see how Query Store can help you to solve these issues.

Query Store – identifying regressed queries

To see how Query Store represents regression, you will use new Query Store node within SQL Server management studio. From four integrated reports, you will choose **Tracked Queries** as shown in the following screenshot:

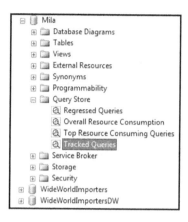

Figure 9.11: Tracked Queries report in Query Store section of SQL Server Management Studio

When you click to **Tracked Queries**, a new window will be opened in SSMS. In the text field `Tracking query`, enter 1 and click on the button with the small play icon. As mentioned earlier, assume that the ID of your initial query is 1. You will see a screen similar to the one displayed in the following screenshot:

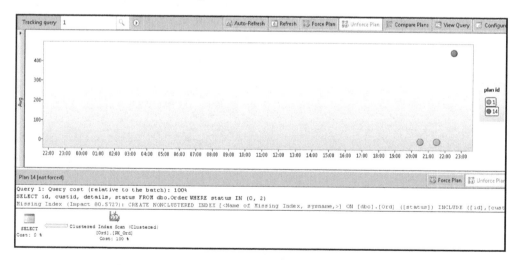

Figure 9.12: Tracked Queries report showing the new execution plan (compatibility level 130)

You can see two different colors for bullets, representing two execution plans used for the execution of the query with the ID 1. The vertical axis shows the average execution time for the plans in milliseconds. It is clear that the yellow plan performs better and that average execution time for the blue plan is significantly increased. In the bottom pane, you can see the execution plan for the selected circle (in this case, this is a plan with the ID 14, which represents the execution plan under the compatibility level 130). The plan uses clustered index scan operator and performs the full scan of the sample table.

When you click on the pink circle in the screen, you get the window shown in the following screenshot:

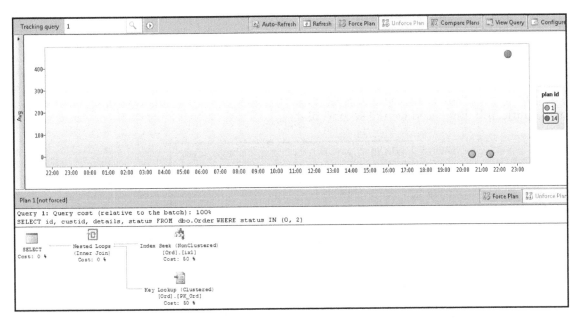

Figure 9.13: Tracked Queries report showing the old execution plan (compatibility level 110)

You can see the old execution plan that uses nested loop join operator, while the new one has clustered index scan as the main operator, which explains why the old execution plan is better for this high selective query (no rows are returned).

Changes in the cardinality estimator introduced in SQL Server 2014 are responsible for new execution plans in this example. The old CE estimates only one row, while the new CE expects all rows to be returned, which of course, leads to an execution plan with a scan operator. Since the query returns no rows, the estimation done by the old CE is more suitable in this case. The same plan (clustered index scan) would be generated under the compatibility level 120.

Of course, you can get this info by querying catalog views, too. The following query returns rows from the collected runtime statistics for two plans in the Query Store:

```
SELECT plan_id, CAST(avg_duration AS INT) AS avg_duration,
avg_logical_io_reads FROM sys.query_store_runtime_stats WHERE plan_id = 1
UNION ALL
SELECT plan_id, CAST(avg_duration AS INT) AS avg_duration,
avg_logical_io_reads FROM sys.query_store_runtime_stats WHERE plan_id = 14;
```

The output is shown in the following screenshot. You can see that all execution parameters are significantly increased for the second plan:

plan_id	avg_duration	avg_logical_io_reads
1	47	6
1	46	6
1	44	6
14	451180	105657
14	450968	105657

Figure 9-14. Comparing multiple runtime statistics for two different execution plans

Query Store – fixing regressed queries

Of course, after migration, you need to fix the regression as soon as possible. It is obvious in this case that the old plan is better: both average execution time and number of logical reads are significantly increased. What can you do with this information? All you want is to have the same or similar execution parameters as you had before the migration. How can you get them back? Here are the steps you usually need to perform prior to SQL Server 2016 when an important query suddenly starts to run slow:

- You need to understand why SQL Server decided to change the plan
- You can try to rewrite the query and hope that the optimizer will choose a better plan or the old plan

- You can apply a query hint to enforce a better plan or the old execution plan
- If you have saved the old plan, you can try to enforce it by using plan guides

All these tasks require time and knowledge for the implementation, and since they include code changes, there is risk that the change will break the application functionality. Therefore, it introduced testing efforts, which means additional time, resources, and money. You usually don't have a lot of time, and company management is not happy when an action requires more money.

As you can guess, Query Store will save you time and money. It allows you to instruct the optimizer to use the old plan. All you have to do is to choose the plan you want to be applied and to click the button **Force Plan**, and then confirm the decision by clicking on **Yes** in the **Confirmation** dialog box as shown in the following screenshot:

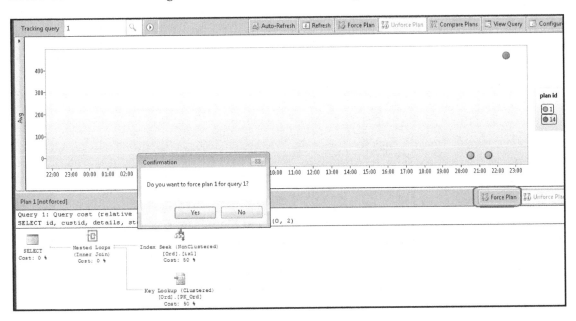

Figure 9.15: Query Store plan forcing

Now, when you execute the query again, you will see the third color with the circle representing the third execution plan as shown in the following screenshot:

```
SET NOCOUNT ON;
SELECT id, custid, details, status FROM dbo.Orders WHERE status IN (0, 2);
```

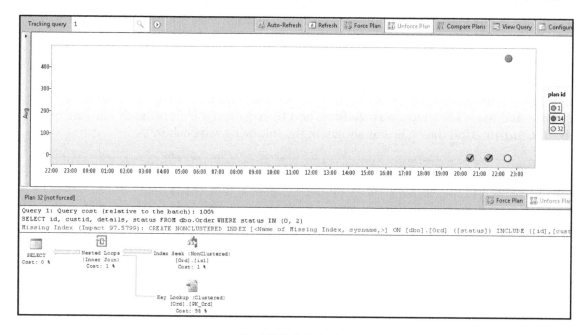

Figure 9-16. Plan forcing in action

The execution is faster, you get the old plan again and there is no risk of a breaking change. And also, you did not spend much time fixing the issue!

You can also force and unforce a plan by using Query Store stored procedures. The following command unforces the execution plan that you forced in the previous step:

```
EXEC sp_query_store_unforce_plan @query_id = 1, @plan_id = 1;
```

When you execute the query again, you will see that the plan is not forced anymore and that the execution is slow again as shown in the following screenshot.

```
SET NOCOUNT ON;
SELECT id, custid, details, status FROM dbo.Orders WHERE status IN (0, 2);
```

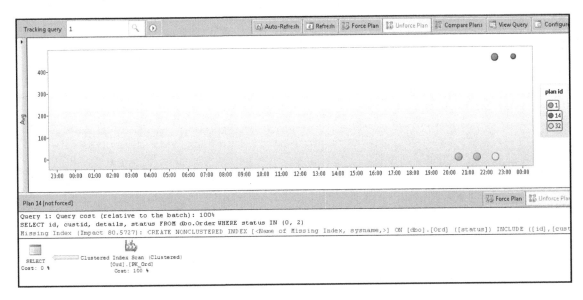

Figure 9-17. Query Store plan un-forcing

Now you can use Transact-SQL to force the old plan again:

```
EXEC sp_query_store_force_plan @query_id = 1, @plan_id = 1;
```

When you execute the query again, you will see that the plan is forced again and another circle came to the main pane as you can see in the following screenshot:

```
SET NOCOUNT ON;
SELECT id, custid, details, status FROM dbo.Orders WHERE status IN (0, 2);
```

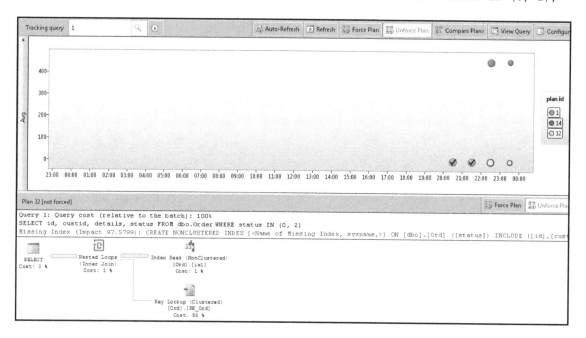

Figure 9-18. Query Store plan forcing

In this section, you saw that Query Store can not only help you to identify performance regressions, but also to solve them quickly, elegantly, and with almost no effort. However, bear in mind that forcing an old plan is a "forever decision"; the plan will always be applied whenever the query is executed. You have to be absolutely sure that you want this when you force the plan.

Forcing a plan will instruct SQL Server to use one plan whenever the query is executed regardless of its costs or improvement in the database engine. However, if the execution plan requires database objects that don't exist anymore (for instance, an index used in the plan is dropped), the query execution will not fail, but a new plan will be generated. The forced plan will be saved and set in the "hold on" mode and will be applied again when the missing object is available.

You should also notice that forcing an old, good looking execution plan in a Query Store report does not guarantee that the execution with it will be better. A typical example would be issues with parameter sniffing, where different parameter combinations require different plans. Forcing an old plan in that case can be good for some parameter combinations only, but for others, it could be even worse than the actual, bad execution plan. Generally, Query Store helps you to solve problems with queries whose execution plans have changed over time but that have stable input parameters. You should not force the old plan for all queries when you see that the old execution parameters look better!

I am using Query Store intensively, and it is an excellent tool and great help for me during query troubleshooting. I have forced an old execution plan several times in the production system to solve or mitigate a significant performance degradation. In my company, the massive workload and peaks happen on a weekend, and if you have an issue on a weekend, you usually want to solve it or find a workaround as quickly as possible. Query Store allows me to force a well-known and good plan and solve the issue temporarily. I review and evaluate it later, during regular working time, without pressure and risk of breaking some applications. Sometimes, I rewrite the code and unforce the plan, sometimes, when I am completely sure that I want exactly the plan that I have forced, I leave it in the production database. When you know what are you doing, you can use all Query Store features. Query Store can save time and money.

Query Store reports in SQL Server management studio

In the previous section, you saw that migration to SQL Server 2016 can lead to performance regressions for some database queries. In this example, you had only one query and since the regression was significant, you could immediately detect it; you did not need help from Query Store. However, in the production system, you could have hundreds or thousands of queries, and you will not be able to check them to see if they perform well after migration. To find regressed queries or queries that are consuming most server resources, you can use the Query Store reports.

When Query Store is enabled for a database, in the Object Explorer of the SQL Server management studio you can find a new node Query Store for this database. When you expand the node, you can find four reports under it:

- Regressed queries
- Top resource consuming queries
- Overall resource consumption
- Tracked queries

You have already seen the report Tracked Queries in action; here we will describe the other three reports.

Regressed queries

The report page Regressed queries shows queries where performance is regressed over time. Query Store analyzes database workload and extracts the 25 most regressed queries according to the chosen metrics. You can choose between the following metrics: CPU time, Duration, Logical reads, Logical writes, Memory consumptions, and Physical reads. You can also decide whether you want to see total numbers or maybe average, max, min, or standard deviation of the value chosen in the first step. The following screenshot shows regressed queries in a moderate database in a chart format:

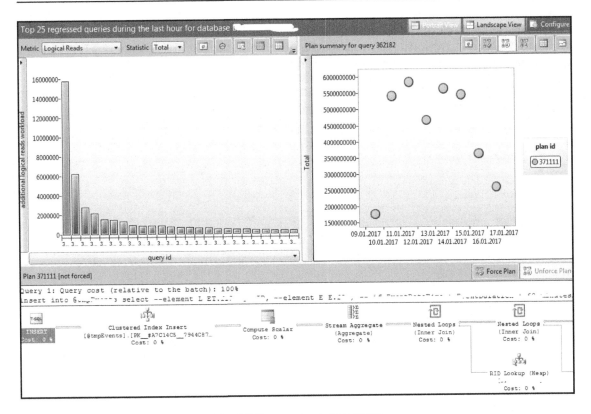

Figure 9-19. View regressed queries in a chart format

Chart format allows you to focus on the most regressed queries. As you can see, there are three panes on the page. In the first pane, you can see up to 25 of the most regressed queries. The pane on the right side shows the execution plans over time for the query chosen in the left pane. Finally, the bottom pane shows the graphical representation of the plan chosen in the second pane.

In the top-right corner in the left pane, you can find an option which allows you to choose between chart and grid format of regressed queries. The same regressed queries but in a grid format are shown in the following screenshot:

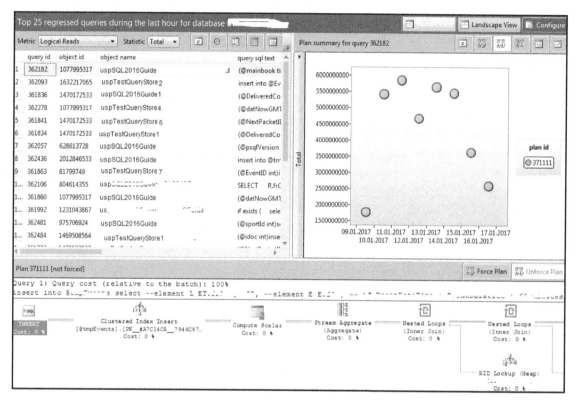

Figure 9-20. View regressed queries in a grid format

Compared to the other display mode, only the left pane is different. It contains textual information such as query text and procedure name and numerical values for many metrics with significantly more information than chart view.

In the top-right corner in the right pane, you can configure time intervals for query executions. In *Figure 9-20*, the time interval is set to one week (last week).

Top resource consuming queries tab

The report top resource consuming queries shows you the most expensive queries (25), based on your chosen metric, analog to the previous report type. The displayed panes are the same as in the regressed queries report. The only difference between them is extracted queries: top resource consumers can also see queries that did not regress, but just use a lot of server resources. A sample report is shown in Figure 9-21.

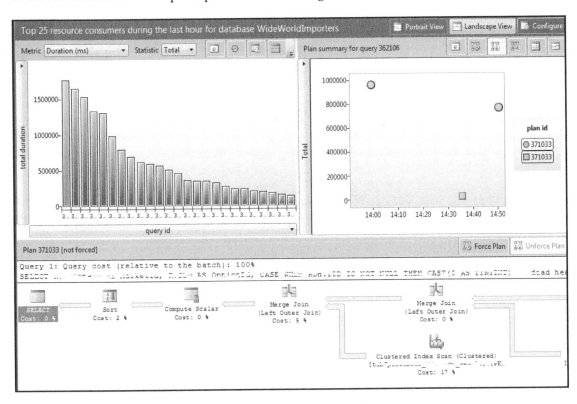

Figure 9-21. Top Resource Consuming Queries

This Query Store report will not find plan regressions, but can help you to quickly identify the most expensive queries in a database in a given time interval.

Overall resource consumption

The report overall resource consumption can be used to determine the impact of particular queries to all database resources. The report has predefined panes where you can see the impact of queries for overall duration, execution count, CPU time, and logical reads. You can define an additional three parameters (logical writes, memory consumption, and physical reads) and you can also show this info in a grid format. A common report with default windows is shown in the following screenshot:

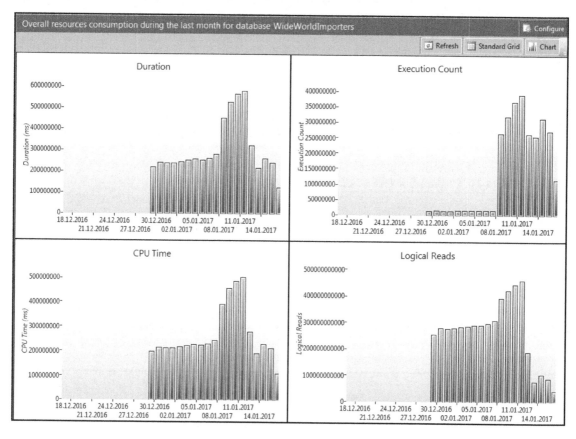

Figure 9.22: Overall Resource Consumption

Query Store use cases

Query Store is a very useful feature and can help you to identify and solve some performance problems, but also help you to learn about your workload and to be more familiar with it.

The main use cases are related to issues caused by a changed execution plan. Complex queries can have many potential execution plans and some of them can be performant, while some others lead to serious performance problems. The Query Optimizer does a great job when it generates execution plans but sometimes it comes up with a suboptimal plan. It is possible that two, totally different execution plans have similar costs. When a complex query has a good plan, the next plan for the same query can perform badly. The next plan might be generated when the old plan is not in the cache anymore. This happens when SQL Server is upgrading to a new version, when cumulative update or Service Pack is installed, when patching is performed, when a failover happens, and also when a new application or service version is deployed. In all these cases, when a new plan performs badly, Query Store can help not only for identifying but also to find a solution or a workaround for the problem.

SQL Server version upgrades and patching

The main use case, and most probably the one that triggered introducing of this feature, is upgrading to a new SQL Server version. An upgrade is never a trivial action, and it brings improvements (that's the reason why we upgrade, right?), but sometimes also brings regressions. These regressions are not always predictable and it happens often that companies do not perform a full upgrade to the latest SQL Server version, but leave the most important or most volatile database in the old compatibility mode. This means execution plans will use the logic, rules, and algorithms from the previous database version. By taking this approach, you can reduce the risk of performance regression, but you will not be able to use some of the new features because they are available only in the latest compatibility mode. In my experience, after changes in the Cardinality Estimator in SQL Server 2014, more than 50% of companies did not upgrade all large and volatile databases to its compatibility mode 120 because of significant regressions. Most of the queries perform well, but some of them got different, sub-optimal execution plans and fixing them on production systems would be too expensive and risky.

Query Store can help you to perform upgrades without worrying about issues with different plans in the new version. It can easily and quickly identify issues with execution plans and offer you an option to force the old plan in case of regression, without a big impact to the production workload.

In measurements and tests that I have performed, I could not detect a significant impact of Query Store activities to the database workload. I would estimate that the Query Store impact is roughly 3-5% of server resources.

A typical scenario for SQL Server version upgrade follows:

- Upgrade SQL Server to the latest version (SQL Server 2016 Service Pack 1), but leave all user databases in the old compatibility mode.
- Enable and configure Query Store.
- Let Query Store work and collect information about your representative workload.
- Change compatibility level to the latest one (130).
- Check Regressed Queries report in Query Store.
- Force old plans for regressed queries.
- Query Store will let you fix the problems by choosing the old plan. However, as mentioned earlier, this might not be a final solution and it is good idea to analyze why regression happened and to try to tune the query. Of course, this could be time and resource consuming and it is better to do this later, when you have enough time, than when under pressure, at the time when problems occur on the production system.

Application and service releases, patching, failovers, and cumulative updates

In all these cases, Query Store can help you to identify issues after the actions and to fix problems caused by changed execution plans very quickly, efficiently, and without risking business applications. A typical scenario is:

- Ensure that Query Store is enabled and configured.
- Let Query Store work and capture information about your representative workload.
- Perform the install action. This can be one of these actions.
- Server failover.
- Installing SQL Server Service Pack.
- Installing SQL Server Cumulative Update.
- Upgrade hardware configuration.
- Operating system and network patching.

- Application and service deployment.
- Let Query Store collect information about queries and plans.
- Run Regressed Queries and Top Resources Consuming Query reports
- Query Store will let you fix the problems by choosing the old plan. It is good idea to analyze why regression happened, but it is better to do this later, when you have enough time.

Identifying ad hoc queries

You can use Query Store to identify ad hoc workloads, which are typically characterized by a relatively large number of different queries executed very rarely, and usually only once. Use the following query to identify all queries that are executed exactly once:

```
SELECT p.query_id
FROM sys.query_store_plan p
INNER JOIN sys.query_store_runtime_stats s ON p.plan_id = s.plan_id
GROUP BY p.query_id
HAVING SUM(s.count_executions) = 1;
```

Identifying unfinished queries

In the section, Query Store in Action, you saw that Query Store does not capture runtime statistics only for successfully executed queries. When query execution is aborted by the caller or end with an exception, this info is not stored to server cache, but Query Store collects that info too. This can help you to easily identify queries with an incomplete execution process.

To see an example, you first need to clean-up info that was captured in the previous sections of this chapter:

```
ALTER DATABASE Mila SET QUERY_STORE CLEAR ALL;
ALTER DATABASE Mila SET QUERY_STORE = OFF;
ALTER DATABASE Mila
SET QUERY_STORE = ON
    (
      OPERATION_MODE = READ_WRITE
    , DATA_FLUSH_INTERVAL_SECONDS = 2000
    , INTERVAL_LENGTH_MINUTES = 1
    );
```

You should also ensure that the latest compatibility mode is applied:

```
ALTER DATABASE Mila SET COMPATIBILITY_LEVEL = 130;
```

Now, you can execute the same query as you did in the section Query Store in Action:

```
SELECT * FROM dbo.Orders WHERE status IN (0,2);
GO 100
```

You should execute the query, then click the cancel executing query button in the SQL Server management studio, then click again to execute it in order to simulate the execution and query abortion.

In addition to this you should execute the following query, too:

```
SELECT Status/ (SELECT COUNT(*) FROM dbo.Orders WHERE Status IN (0, 2))
FROM dbo.Orders WHERE id = 1;
```

This query will not be successfully executed; it will raise a *Divide by zero* exception. Now, you can check what Query Store has captured. To do this run the following code:

```
SELECT * FROM sys.query_store_runtime_stats;
```

In the following screenshot you can see two entries for your initial query (regular executed and aborted) and also an entry for the query with the *Divide by zero* exception:

runtime_stats_id	plan_id	runtime_stats_interval_id	execution_type	execution_type_desc	count_executions	avg_duration
4	3	2	0	Regular	1	4272
3	2	1	4	Exception	1	365
2	1	1	3	Aborted	1	93051
1	1	1	0	Regular	6	432375,333333333

Figure 9-23. Identifying unfinished queries by using Query Store

As you can see, by using Query Store you can easily identify started but not executed queries in your database.

Summary

Query Store is a great troubleshooting tool which captures all execution relevant parameters for database queries: query details, execution plans, and runtime statistics and stores them in the same database so that they can survive after server failures. All that is done out-of-the-box, with minimal impact on the database workload.

By using Query Store, you can not only quickly identify performance regressions, but also mitigate them by forcing a well-known and previously used execution plan. Query Store will save you time and money. It also helps you to learn how your database workload changes over time and to identify queries that did not execute successfully.

10
Columnstore Indexes

Analytical queries that scan huge amounts of data were always problematic in a relational database. Nonclustered balanced tree indexes are efficient for transactional queries seeks; however, they rarely help with analytical queries. A great idea occurred nearly 30 years ago: why do we need to store data physically in the same way we work with it logically—row by row? Why don't we store it column by column and transform columns back to rows when we interact with the data? Microsoft was playing with this idea for a long time and finally implemented it in SQL Server.

Columnar storage was first added to SQL Server in version 2012. It included **nonclustered columnstore indexes (NCCI)** only. **Clustered columnstore indexes (CCI)** were added in version 2014. In this chapter, the readers revise the columnar storage and then explore huge improvements for columnstore indexes in SQL Server 2016: updatable nonclustered columnstore indexes, columnstore indexes on in-memory tables, and many other new features for operational analytics.

In the first section, you will learn about the SQL Server support for analytical queries without using the columnar storage. The next section of this chapter jumps directly to the columnar storage and explains the internals about it, with the main focus on columnar storage compression. In addition, the batch execution mode is introduced.

Then it is time to show columnar storage in action. The chapter starts with a section that introduces the nonclustered columnstore indexes. The demo code shows the compression you can get with this storage and also how to create a filtered nonclustered columnstore index.

The clustered columnstore indexes can have even better compression. You will learn how much these clustered and nonclustered columnstore indexes compress data and improve the performance of your queries. You can also combine columnar indexes with regular B-tree indexes. In addition, you will learn how to update data in a clustered columnstore index, especially how to insert new data efficiently. Finally, the chapter introduces the way to use columnar indexes together with regular B-tree indexes to implement a solution for operational analytics.

This chapter will cover the following points:

- Data compression in SQL Server
- Indexing for analytical queries
- T-SQL support for analytical queries
- Columnar storage basics
- Nonclustered columnstore indexes
- Using clustered columnstore indexes
- Creating regular B-tree indexes for tables with CCI
- Discovering support for primary and foreign keys for tables with CCI
- Discovering additional performance improvements with batch mode
- Columnstore indexes query performance
- Columnstore for real time operational analytics
- Data loading for columnstore indexes

Analytical queries in SQL Server

Supporting analytical applications in SQL Server differs quite a lot from supporting transactional applications. The typical schema for reporting queries is the star schema. In a star schema, there is one central table called **fact table** and multiple surrounding tables called **dimensions.** The fact table is always on the many side of every relationship with every dimension. The database that supports analytical queries and uses the star schema design is called **Data Warehouse** (**DW**). Dealing with data warehousing design in detail is out of the scope of this book. Nevertheless, there is a lot of literature available. For a quick start, you can read the data warehouse concepts MSDN blog at `https://blogs.msdn.microsoft.com/syedab/2010/06/01/data-warehouse-concepts/`. The `WideWorldImportersDW` demo database implements multiple star schemas. The following screenshot shows a subset of tables from this database that supports analytical queries for sales:

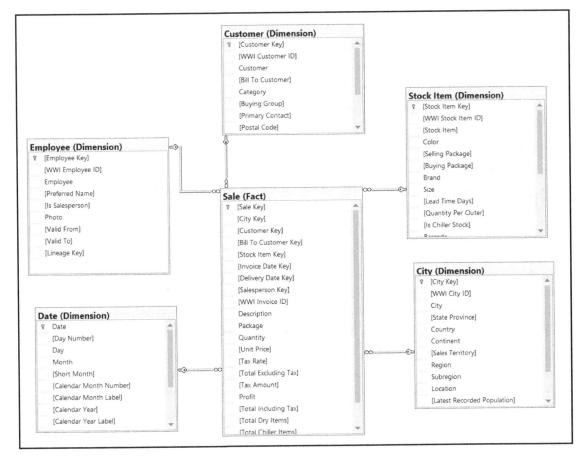

Figure 10-1: Sales Star schema

Typical analytical queries require huge amounts of data, for example, sales data for two years, which is then aggregated. Therefore, index seeks are quite rare. Most of the times, you need to optimize the number of IO reads using different techniques than you would use in a transactional environment, where you have mostly selective queries that benefit a lot from index seeks. **Columnstore indexes** are the latest and probably the most important optimization for analytical queries in SQL Server. However, before going to the columnar storage, you should be familiar with other techniques and possibilities for optimizing data warehousing scenarios. All you will learn about in this section will help you understand the need for and the implementation of columnstore indexes. You will learn about the following:

- Join types
- Bitmap filtered hash joins

- B-tree indexes for analytical queries
- Filtered nonclustered indexes
- Table partitioning
- Indexed views
- Row compression
- Page compression
- Appropriate query techniques

Joins and indexes

SQL Server executes a query by a set of physical **operators**. Because these operators iterate through rowsets, they are also called **iterators**. There are different join operators, because when performing joins, SQL Server uses different algorithms. SQL Server supports three basic algorithms: **nested loops joins**, **merge joins**, and **hash joins**. A hash join can be further optimized by using **bitmap filtering**; a **bitmap filtered hash join** could be treated as the fourth algorithm or as an enhancement of the third, the hash algorithm. The last one, the bitmap filtered hash join, is an example of SQL Server's optimization for analytical queries.

The nested loops algorithm is a very simple and, in many cases, efficient algorithm. SQL Server uses one table for the outer loop, typically the table with fewer rows. For each row in this outer input, SQL Server seeks matching rows in the second table, which is the inner table. SQL Server uses the join condition to find the matching rows. The join can be a **non-equijoin**, meaning that the equality operator does not need to be part of the join predicate. If the inner table has no supporting index to perform seeks, then SQL Server scans the inner input for each row of the outer input. This is not an efficient scenario. A nested loops join is efficient when SQL Server can perform an index seek in the inner input.

Merge join is a very efficient join algorithm. However, it has its own limitations. It needs at least one **equijoin** predicate and sorted inputs from both sides. This means that the merge join should be supported by indexes on both tables involved in the join. In addition, if one input is much smaller than another, then the nested loops join could be more efficient than a merge join.

In a one-to-one or one-to-many scenario, the merge join scans both inputs only once. It starts by finding the first rows on both sides. If the end of the input is not reached, the merge join checks the join predicate to determine whether the rows match. If the rows match, they are added to the output. Then the algorithm checks the next rows from the other side and adds them to the output until they match the predicate. If the rows from the inputs do not match, then the algorithm reads the next row from the side with the lower value from the other side. It reads from this side and compares the row to the row from the other side until the value is bigger than the value from the other side. Then it continues reading from the other side, and so on. In a many-to-many scenario, the merge join algorithm uses a worktable to put the rows from one input side aside for reusage when duplicate matching rows from the other input exist.

If none of the inputs is supported by an index and an equijoin predicate is used, then the hash join algorithm might be the most efficient one. It uses a searching structure named **hash table**. This is not a searching structure you can build like a balanced tree used for indexes. SQL Server builds the hash table internally. It uses a **hash function** to split the rows from the smaller input into **buckets**. This is the build phase. SQL Server uses the smaller input for building the hash table because SQL Server wants to keep the hash table in memory. If it needs to get spilled out to tempdb on disk, then the algorithm might become much slower. The hash function creates buckets of approximately equal size.

After the hash table is built, SQL Server applies the hash function on each of the rows from the other input. It checks to see which bucket the row fits. Then it scans through all rows from the bucket. This phase is called the probe phase.

A hash join is a kind of compromise between creating a full balanced tree index and then using a different join algorithm and performing a full scan of one side input for each row of the other input. At least in the first phase, a seek of the appropriate bucket is used. You might think that the hash join algorithm is not efficient. It is true that in a single-thread mode, it is usually slower than merge and nested loops join algorithms that are supported by existing indexes. However, SQL Server can split rows from the probe input in advance. It can push the filtering of the rows that are candidates for a match with a specific hash bucket down to the storage engine. This kind of optimization of a hash join is called a bitmap filtered hash join. It is typically used in a data warehousing scenario, where you can have large inputs for a query, which might not be supported by indexes. In addition, SQL Server can parallelize query execution and perform partial joins in multiple threads. In data warehousing scenarios, it is not uncommon to have only a few concurrent users, so SQL Server can execute a query in parallel. Although a regular hash join can be executed in parallel as well, the bitmap filtered hash join is even more efficient because SQL Server can use bitmaps for early elimination of rows not used in the join from the bigger table involved in the join.

In the bitmap filtered hash join, SQL Server first creates a bitmap representation of a set of values from a dimension table to prefilter rows to join from a fact table. A bitmap filter is a bit array of m bits. Initially, all bits are set to 0. Then SQL Server defines k different hash functions. Each one maps some set element to one of the m positions with a uniform random distribution. The number of hash functions k must be smaller than the number of bits in array m. SQL Server feeds each of the k hash functions to get k array positions with values from dimension keys. It set the bits at all these positions to 1. Then SQL Server tests the foreign keys from the fact table. To test whether any element is in the set, SQL Server feeds it to each of the k hash functions to get k array positions. If any of the bits at these positions are 0, the element is not in the set. If all are 1, then either the element is in the set, or the bits have been set to 1 during the insertion of other elements. The following diagram shows the bitmap filtering process:

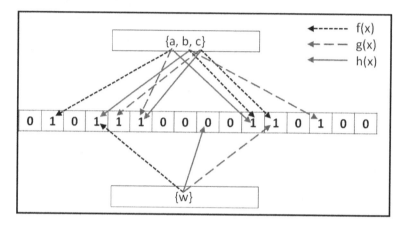

Figure 10.2: Bitmap filtering

In the preceding diagram, the length m of the bit array is 16. The number k of hash functions is 3. When feeding the hash functions with the values from the set {a, b, c}, which represents dimension keys, SQL Server sets bits at positions 2, 4, 5, 6, 11, 12, and 14 to 1 (starting numbering positions with 1). Then SQL Server feeds the same hash functions with the value w from the smaller set at the bottom {w}, which represents a key from a fact table. The functions would set bits at positions 4, 9, and 12 to 1. However, the bit at position 9 is set to 0. Therefore, the value w is not in the set {a, b, c}.

 If all of the bits for the value w would be set to 1, this could mean either that the value w is in the set {a, b, v} or that this is a coincidence.

Bitmap filters return so-called false positives. They never return false negatives. This means that when you declare that a probe value might be in the set, you still need to scan the set and compare it to each value from the set. The more false positive values a bitmap filter returns, the less efficient it is. Note that if the values in the probe side in the fact table are sorted, it will be quite easy to avoid the majority of false positives.

The following query reads the data from the tables introduced earlier in this section and implements star schema optimized bitmap filtered hash joins:

```
USE WideWorldImportersDW;
SELECT cu.[Customer Key] AS CustomerKey, cu.Customer,
  ci.[City Key] AS CityKey, ci.City,
  ci.[State Province] AS StateProvince, ci.[Sales Territory] AS
SalesTeritory,
  d.Date, d.[Calendar Month Label] AS CalendarMonth,
  d.[Calendar Year] AS CalendarYear,
  s.[Stock Item Key] AS StockItemKey, s.[Stock Item] AS Product, s.Color,
  e.[Employee Key] AS EmployeeKey, e.Employee,
  f.Quantity, f.[Total Excluding Tax] AS TotalAmount, f.Profit
FROM Fact.Sale AS f
  INNER JOIN Dimension.Customer AS cu
    ON f.[Customer Key] = cu.[Customer Key]
  INNER JOIN Dimension.City AS ci
    ON f.[City Key] = ci.[City Key]
  INNER JOIN Dimension.[Stock Item] AS s
    ON f.[Stock Item Key] = s.[Stock Item Key]
  INNER JOIN Dimension.Employee AS e
    ON f.[Salesperson Key] = e.[Employee Key]
  INNER JOIN Dimension.Date AS d
    ON f.[Delivery Date Key] = d.Date;
```

The following diagram shows a part of the execution plan. You can see the **Bitmap Create** operator that is fed with values from the dimension date table. The filtering of the fact table is done in the Hash Match operator:

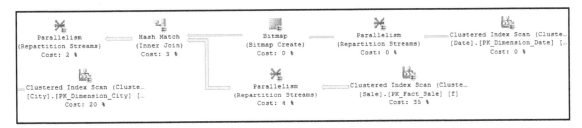

Figure 10-3: Bitmap Create operator in the execution plan

Benefits of clustered indexes

SQL Server stores a table as a **heap** or as a **balanced tree (B-tree)**. If you create a clustered index, a table is stored as a B-tree. As a general best practice, you should store every table with a clustered index because storing a table as a B-tree has many advantages, as listed here:

- You can control table fragmentation with the ALTER INDEX command using the REBUILD or REORGANIZE option.
- A clustered index is useful for range queries because the data is logically sorted on the key.
- You can move a table to another filegroup by recreating the clustered index on a different filegroup. You do not have to drop the table as you would to move a heap.
- A clustering key is a part of all nonclustered indexes. If a table is stored as a heap, then the row identifier is stored in nonclustered indexes instead. A short integer-clustering key is shorter than a row identifier, thus making nonclustered indexes more efficient.
- You cannot refer to a row identifier in queries, but clustering keys are often part of queries. This raises the probability for covered queries. Covered queries are queries that read all data from one or more nonclustered indexes without going to the base table. This means that there are fewer reads and less disk IO.

Clustered indexes are particularly efficient when the clustering key is short. Creating a clustering index with a long key makes all nonclustered indexes less efficient. In addition, the clustering key should be unique. If it is not unique, SQL Server makes it unique by adding a 4-byte sequential number called **uniquifier** to duplicate keys. Uniquifier becomes a part of the clustering key, which is duplicated in every nonclustered index. This makes keys longer and all indexes less efficient. Clustering keys could be useful if they are ever-increasing. With ever-increasing keys, minimally logged bulk inserts are possible even if a table already contains data, as long as the table does not have additional nonclustered indexes.

Data warehouse surrogate keys are often ideal for clustered indexes. Because you are the one who defines them, you can define them as efficiently as possible. Use integers with autonumbering options. The primary key constraint creates a clustered index by default. In addition, clustered indexes can be very useful for **partial scans**. Remember that analytical queries typically involve a lot of data and, therefore, don't use seeks a lot. However, instead of scanning the whole table, you can find the first value with a seek and then perform a partial scan until you reach the last value needed for the query result. Many times, analytical queries use date filters; therefore, a clustering key over a date column might be ideal for such queries.

You need to decide whether to optimize your tables for data load or for querying. However, with partitioning, you can get both—efficient data load without a clustered key on an ever-increasing column, and more efficient queries with partial scans. In order to show the efficiency of partial scans, let's first create a new table organized as a heap with the following query:

```
SELECT 1 * 1000000 + f.[Sale Key] AS SaleKey,
  cu.[Customer Key] AS CustomerKey, cu.Customer,
  ci.[City Key] AS CityKey, ci.City,
  f.[Delivery Date Key] AS DateKey,
  s.[Stock Item Key] AS StockItemKey, s.[Stock Item] AS Product,
  f.Quantity, f.[Total Excluding Tax] AS TotalAmount, f.Profit
INTO dbo.FactTest
FROM Fact.Sale AS f
  INNER JOIN Dimension.Customer AS cu
    ON f.[Customer Key] = cu.[Customer Key]
  INNER JOIN Dimension.City AS ci
    ON f.[City Key] = ci.[City Key]
  INNER JOIN Dimension.[Stock Item] AS s
    ON f.[Stock Item Key] = s.[Stock Item Key]
  INNER JOIN Dimension.Date AS d
    ON f.[Delivery Date Key] = d.Date;
```

Now you can turn the STATISTICS IO on to show the number of logical reads in the following two queries:

```
SET STATISTICS IO ON;
-- All rows
SELECT *
FROM dbo.FactTest;
-- Date range
SELECT *
FROM dbo.FactTest
WHERE DateKey BETWEEN '20130201' AND '20130331';
SET STATISTICS IO OFF;
```

SQL Server used a `Table Scan` operator for executing both queries. For both of them, even though the second one used a filter on the delivery date column, SQL Server performed 5,893 logical IOs.

 Note that your results for the logical IOs might vary slightly for every query in this chapter. However, you should be able to notice which query is more efficient and which is less.

Now let's create a clustered index in the delivery date column:

```
CREATE CLUSTERED INDEX CL_FactTest_DateKey
ON dbo.FactTest(DateKey);
GO
```

If you execute the aforementioned same two queries, you get around 6,091 reads and the `Clustered Index Scan` operator for the first query, and 253 logical reads for the second query, with `Clustered Index Seek` operator that finds the first value needed for the query and performs a partial scan after.

Leveraging table partitioning

Loading even very large fact tables is not a problem if you can perform incremental loads. However, this means that data in the source should never be updated or deleted; data should only be inserted. This is rarely the case with LOB applications. In addition, even if you have the possibility of performing an incremental load, you should have a parameterized ETL procedure in place so you can reload portions of data loaded already in earlier loads. There is always a possibility that something might go wrong in the source system, which means that you will have to reload historical data. This reloading will require you to delete part of the data from your data warehouse.

Deleting large portions of fact tables might consume too much time unless you perform a minimally logged deletion. A minimally logged deletion operation can be done using the `TRUNCATE TABLE` command; however, this command deletes all the data from a table, and deleting all the data is usually not acceptable. More commonly, you need to delete only portions of the data.

Inserting huge amounts of data could consume too much time as well. You can do a minimally logged insert, but as you already know, minimally logged inserts have some limitations. Among other limitations, a table must either be empty, have no indexes, or use a clustered index only on an ever-increasing (or ever-decreasing) key so that all inserts occur on one end of the index.

You can resolve all of these problems by *partitioning a table*. You can even achieve better query performance using a partitioned table because you can create partitions in different filegroups on different drives, thus parallelizing reads. In addition, SQL Server query optimizer can do early partition elimination, so SQL Server does not even touch a partition with data excluded from the result set of a query. You can also perform maintenance procedures on a subset of filegroups and thus on a subset of partitions only. That way, you can also speed up regular maintenance tasks. Altogether, partitions have many benefits.

Although you can partition a table on any attribute, partitioning over dates is most common in data warehousing scenarios. You can use any time interval for a partition. Depending on your needs, the interval could be a day, a month, a year, or any other interval.

In addition to partitioning tables, you can also partition indexes. If indexes are partitioned in the same way as the base tables, they are called **aligned indexes**. Partitioned table and index concepts include the following:

- **Partition function**: This is an object that maps rows to partitions by using values from specific columns. The columns used for the function are called **partitioning columns**. A partition function performs logical mapping.

- **Partition scheme**: A partition scheme maps partitions to filegroups. A partition scheme performs physical mapping.

- **Aligned index**: This is an index built on the same partition scheme as its base table. If all indexes are aligned with their base table, switching a partition is a metadata operation only, so it is very fast. Columnstore indexes have to be aligned with their base tables. Nonaligned indexes are, of course, indexes that are partitioned differently than their base tables.

- **Partition switching**: This is a process that switches a block of data from one table or partition to another table or partition. You switch the data by using the `ALTER TABLE` T-SQL command. You can perform the following types of switches:

  - Reassign all data from a nonpartitioned table to an empty existing partition of a partitioned table

  - Switch a partition of a one-partitioned table to a partition of another partitioned table

  - Reassign all data from a partition of a partitioned table to an existing empty nonpartitioned table

- **Partition elimination**: This is a query optimizer process in which SQL Server accesses only those partitions needed to satisfy query filters.

For more information about table and index partitioning, refer to the MSDN Partitioned Tables and Indexes article at `https://msdn.microsoft.com/en-us/library/ms190787.aspx`.

Nonclustered indexes in analytical scenarios

As mentioned, data warehouse queries typically involve large scans of data and aggregation. Very selective seeks are not common for reports from a DW. Therefore, nonclustered indexes generally don't help DW queries much. However, this does not mean that you shouldn't create any nonclustered indexes in your DW.

An attribute of a dimension is not a good candidate for a nonclustered index key. Attributes are used for pivoting and typically contain only a few distinct values. Therefore, queries that filter based on attribute values are usually not very selective. Nonclustered indexes on dimension attributes are not a good practice.

DW reports can be parameterized. For example, a DW report could show sales for all customers or for only a single customer, based perhaps on parameter selection by an end user. For a single-customer report, the user would choose the customer by selecting that customer's name. Customer names are selective, meaning that you retrieve only a small number of rows when you filter by customer name. Company names, for example, are typically unique, so by filtering by a company name, you typically retrieve a single row. For reports like these, having a nonclustered index on a name column or columns could lead to better performance.

You can create a filtered nonclustered index. A filtered index spans a subset of column values only and thus applies to a subset of table rows. Filtered nonclustered indexes are useful when some values in a column occur rarely, whereas other values occur frequently. In such cases, you would create a filtered index over the rare values only. SQL Server uses this index for seeks of rare values but performs scans for frequent values. Filtered nonclustered indexes can be useful not only for name columns and member properties but also for attributes of a dimension, and even foreign keys of a fact table. For example, in our demo fact table, the customer with ID equal to 378 has only 242 rows. You can execute the following code to show that even if you select data for this customer only, SQL Server performs a full scan:

```
SET STATISTICS IO ON;
-- All rows
SELECT *
FROM dbo.FactTest;
-- Customer 378 only
SELECT *
FROM dbo.FactTest
WHERE CustomerKey = 378;
SET STATISTICS IO OFF;
```

Both queries needed 6,091 logical reads. Now you can add a filtered nonclustered index to the table:

```
CREATE INDEX NCLF_FactTest_C378
 ON dbo.FactTest (CustomerKey)
 WHERE CustomerKey = 378;
GO
```

If you execute the same two queries again, you get much less IO for the second query. It needed 752 logical reads in my case and used the Index Seek and Key Lookup operators.

You can drop the filtered index when you don't need it anymore with the following code:

```
DROP INDEX NCLF_FactTest_C378
 ON dbo.FactTest;
GO
```

Using indexed views

You can optimize queries that aggregate data and perform multiple joins by permanently storing the aggregated and joined data. For example, you could create a new table with joined and aggregated data and then maintain that table during your ETL process.

However, creating additional tables for joined and aggregated data is not best practice because using these tables means you have to change queries used in your reports. Fortunately, there is another option for storing joined and aggregated tables. You can create a view with a query that joins and aggregates data. Then you can create a clustered index on the view to get an **indexed view**. With indexing, you are materializing a view; you are storing physically the data the view is returning when you query it. In the Enterprise or Developer Edition of SQL Server, SQL Server Query Optimizer uses the indexed view automatically—without changing the query. SQL Server also maintains indexed views automatically. However, to speed up data loads, you can drop or disable the index before load and then recreate or rebuild it after the load.

For example, note the following query that aggregates the data from the test fact table:

```
SET STATISTICS IO ON;
SELECT StockItemKey,
 SUM(TotalAmount) AS Sales,
 COUNT_BIG(*) AS NumberOfRows
FROM dbo.FactTest
GROUP BY StockItemKey;
SET STATISTICS IO OFF;
```

In my case, this query used 6,685 logical IOs. It used the clustered Index scan operator on the fact table to retrieve the whole dataset. Now let's create a view with the same query used for the definition:

```
CREATE VIEW dbo.SalesByProduct
WITH SCHEMABINDING AS
SELECT StockItemKey,
 SUM(TotalAmount) AS Sales,
 COUNT_BIG(*) AS NumberOfRows
FROM dbo.FactTest
GROUP BY StockItemKey;
GO
```

Indexed views have many limitations. One of them is that they have to be created with the SCHEMABINDING option if you want to index them, as you can see in the previous code. Now let's index the view:

```
CREATE UNIQUE CLUSTERED INDEX CLU_SalesByProduct
 ON dbo.SalesByProduct (StockItemKey);
GO
```

Try to execute the last query before creating the view again. Make sure you notice that the query refers to the base table and not the view. This time, the query needed only four logical reads. If you check the execution plan, you should see that SQL Server used the Clustered Index Scan operator on the indexed view. If your indexed view was not used automatically, please check which edition of SQL Server you use. When you finish with testing, you can drop the view with the following code:

```
DROP VIEW dbo.SalesByProduct;
GO
```

Data compression and query techniques

SQL Server supports data compression. Data compression reduces the size of the database, which helps improve query performance because queries on compressed data read fewer pages from disk and thus use less IO. However, data compression requires extra CPU resources for updates, because data must be decompressed before and compressed after the update. Data compression is therefore suitable for data warehousing scenarios in which data is mostly read and only occasionally updated.

SQL Server supports three compression implementations:

- **Row compression**: Row compression reduces metadata overhead by storing fixed data type columns in a variable-length format. This includes strings and numeric data. Row compression has only a small impact on CPU resources and is often appropriate for OLTP applications as well.
- **Page compression**: Page compression includes row compression, but also adds prefix and dictionary compressions. **Prefix compression** stores repeated prefixes of values from a single column in a special compression information structure that immediately follows the page header, replacing the repeated prefix values with a reference to the corresponding prefix. **Dictionary compression** stores repeated values anywhere in a page in the compression information area. Dictionary compression is not restricted to a single column.
- **Unicode compression**: In SQL Server, Unicode characters occupy an average of two bytes. Unicode compression substitutes single-byte storage for Unicode characters that don't truly require two bytes. Depending on collation, Unicode compression can save up to 50 per cent of the space otherwise required for Unicode strings. Unicode compression is very cheap and is applied automatically when you apply either row or page compression.

You can gain quite a lot from data compression in a data warehouse. Foreign keys are often repeated many times in a fact table. Large dimensions that have Unicode strings in name columns, member properties, and attributes can benefit from Unicode compression.

The following diagram explains dictionary compression:

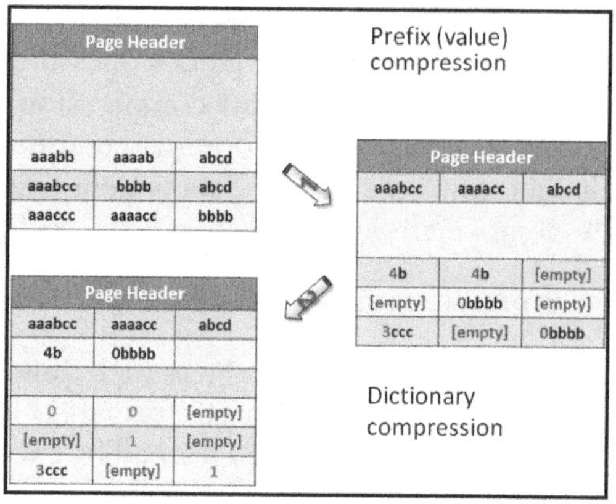

Figure 10.4: Dictionary compression

As you can see from the diagram, the dictionary compression (corresponding to the first arrow) starts with prefix compression. In the compression information space on the page right after the page header, you can find stored prefixes for each column. If you look at the top left cell, the value in the first row, first column, is **aaabb**. The next value in this column is **aaabcc**. A prefix value **aaabcc** is stored for this column in the first column of the row for the prefix compression information. Instead of the original value in the top left cell, a value **4b** is stored. This means use four characters from the prefix for this column and add the letter *b* to get back the original value. The value in the second row for the first column is empty because the prefix for this column is equal to the whole original value in that position. The value in the last row for the first column after the prefix compression is **3ccc**, meaning that in order to get the original value, you need to take the first three characters from the column prefix and add a string **ccc**, thus getting the value **aaaccc**, which is, of course, equal to the original value. Check also the prefix compression for other two columns.

After the prefix compression, dictionary compression is applied (corresponding to the second arrow in the *Figure 10.4*). It checks all strings across all columns to find common substrings. For example, the value in the first two columns of the first row after the prefix compression was applied is **4b**. SQL Server stores this value in the dictionary compression information area as the first value in this area, with index 0. In the cells, it stores just the index value 0 instead of the value **4b**. The same happens for the value **0bbbb**, which you can find in the second row, second column, and third row, third column, after prefix compression is applied. This value is stored in the dictionary compression information area in the second position with index 1; in the cells, the value 1 is left.

You might wonder why prefix compression is needed. For strings, a prefix is just another substring, so the dictionary compression could cover the prefixes as well. However, prefix compression can work on nonstring data types as well. For example, instead of storing integers 900, 901, 902, 903, and 904 in the original data, you can store a prefix 900 and leave values 0, 1, 2, 3, and 4 in the original cells.

Now it's time to test SQL Server compression. First of all, let's check the space occupied by the test fact table:

```
EXEC sys.sp_spaceused N'dbo.FactTest', @updateusage = N'TRUE';
GO
```

The result is as follows:

Name	rows	reserved	data	index_size	unused
dbo.FactTest	227981	49672 KB	48528 KB	200 KB	944 KB

The following code enables row compression on the table and checks the space used again:

```
ALTER TABLE dbo.FactTest
  REBUILD WITH (DATA_COMPRESSION = ROW);
EXEC sys.sp_spaceused N'dbo.FactTest', @updateusage = N'TRUE';
```

This time the result is as follows:

Name	rows	reserved	data	index_size	unused
dbo.FactTest	227981	25864 KB	24944 KB	80 KB	840 KB

You can see that a lot of space was saved. Let's also check the page compression:

```
ALTER TABLE dbo.FactTest
  REBUILD WITH (DATA_COMPRESSION = PAGE);
EXEC sys.sp_spaceused N'dbo.FactTest', @updateusage = N'TRUE';
```

Now the table occupies even less space, as the following result shows:

Name	rows	reserved	data	index_size	unused
dbo.FactTest	227981	18888 KB	18048 KB	80 KB	760 KB

If these space savings are impressive for you, wait for the columnstore compression! Anyway, before continuing, you can remove the compression from the test fact table with the following code:

```
ALTER TABLE dbo.FactTest
  REBUILD WITH (DATA_COMPRESSION = NONE);
```

Before continuing with other SQL Server features that support analytics, I want to explain another compression algorithm because this algorithm is also used in columnstore compression. The algorithm is called **LZ77 compression**. It was published by Abraham Lempel and Jacob Ziv in 1977; the name of the algorithm comes from the first letters of the author's last names plus the publishing year. The algorithm uses sliding window dictionary encoding, meaning it encodes chunks of an input stream with dictionary encoding. The following are the steps of the process:

1. Set the coding position to the beginning of the input stream.
2. Find the longest match in the window for the look ahead buffer.
3. If a match is found, output the pointer P and move the coding position (and the window) L bytes forward.
4. If a match is not found, output a null pointer and the first byte in the look ahead buffer and move the coding position (and the window) one byte forward.
5. If the look ahead buffer is not empty, return to step 2.

The following figure explains this process in an example:

Input stream	Position	1	2	3	4	5	6	7	8	9
	Byte	A	A	B	C	B	B	A	B	C

Step	Position	Match	Byte	Output
1.	1	~	A	(0, 0) A
2.	2	A	~	(1, 1)
3.	3	~	B	(0, 0) B
4.	4	A	C	(0, 0) C
5.	5	B	~	(2, 1)
6.	6	B	~	(1, 1)
7.	7	A B C	~	(5, 3)

Figure 10.5: LZ77 compression

The input stream chunk that is compressed in the figure is **AABCBBABC**:

- The algorithm starts encoding from the beginning of the window of the input stream. It stores the first byte (the **A** value) in the result, together with the pointer **(0,0)**, meaning this is a new value in this chunk.
- The second byte is equal to the first one. The algorithm stores just the pointer **(1,1)** to the output. This means that in order to recreate this value, you need to move one byte back and read one byte.
- The next two values, **B** and **C**, are new and are stored to the output together with the pointer **(0,0)**.

- Then the **B** value repeats. Therefore, the pointer **(2,1)** is stored, meaning that in order to find this value, you need to move two bytes back and read one byte.
- Then the **B** value repeats again. This time, you need to move one byte back and read one byte to get the value, so the value is replaced with the pointer **(1,1)**. You can see that when you move back and read the value, you get another pointer. You can have a chain of pointers.
- Finally, the substring **ABC** is found in the stream. This substring can be also found in the positions 2-4. Therefore, in order to recreate the substring, you need to move five bytes back and read three bytes, and the pointer **(5,3)** is stored in the compressed output.

Writing efficient queries

Before finishing this section, I also need to mention that no join or compression algorithm, or any other feature that SQL Server offers can help you if you write inefficient queries. A good example of a typical DW query is one that involves running totals. You can use non-equi self joins for such queries, which is a very good example of an inefficient query. The following code calculates the running total for the profit ordered over the sale key with a self join. The code also measures IO and time needed for executing the query. Note that the query uses a CTE first to select only 12,000 rows from the fact table. A non-equi self join is a quadratic algorithm; with double the amount of the rows, the time needed increases four times. You can play with different amount of rows to prove that:

```
SET STATISTICS IO ON;
SET STATISTICS TIME ON;
WITH SalesCTE AS
(
SELECT [Sale Key] AS SaleKey, Profit
FROM Fact.Sale
WHERE [Sale Key] <= 12000
)
SELECT S1.SaleKey,
 MIN(S1.Profit) AS CurrentProfit,
 SUM(S2.Profit) AS RunningTotal
FROM SalesCTE AS S1
 INNER JOIN SalesCTE AS S2
  ON S1.SaleKey >= S2.SaleKey
GROUP BY S1.SaleKey
ORDER BY S1.SaleKey;
SET STATISTICS IO OFF;
SET STATISTICS TIME OFF;
```

With 12,000 rows, the query needed 817,584 logical reads in a worktable, which is a temporary representation of the test fact table on the right side of the self join, and on the top of it, more than 3,000 logical reads for the left representation of the fact table. On my computer, it took more than 12 seconds (elapsed time) to execute this query, with more than 72 seconds of CPU time, as the query was executed with a parallel execution plan. With 6,000 rows, the query would need approximately four times less IO and time.

You can calculate running totals very efficiently with window aggregate functions. The following example shows the query rewritten. The new query uses the window aggregate functions:

```
SET STATISTICS IO ON;
SET STATISTICS TIME ON;
WITH SalesCTE AS
(
SELECT [Sale Key] AS SaleKey, Profit
FROM Fact.Sale
WHERE [Sale Key] <= 12000
)
SELECT SaleKey,
 Profit AS CurrentProfit,
 SUM(Profit)
   OVER(ORDER BY SaleKey
        ROWS BETWEEN UNBOUNDED PRECEDING
                AND CURRENT ROW) AS RunningTotal
FROM SalesCTE
ORDER BY SaleKey;
SET STATISTICS IO OFF;
SET STATISTICS TIME OFF;
```

This time, the query used 331 reads in the fact table, 0 (zero) reads in the worktable, 0.15 second elapsed time, and 0.02 second CPU time. SQL Server didn't even bother to find a parallel plan.

Columnar storage and batch processing

Various researchers started to think about **columnar storage** already in the 80's. The main idea is that a **relational database management system (RDBMS)** does not need to store the data in exactly the same way we understand it and work with it. In a relational model, a tuple represents an entity and is stored as a row of a table, which is an entity set. Traditionally, database management systems store entities row by row. However, as long as we get rows back to the client application, we do not care how an RDBMS stores the data.

This is actually one of the main premises of the relational model—we work with data on the logical level, which is independent of the physical level of the physical storage. However, it was not until approximately the year 2000 when the first attempts to create columnar storage came to life. SQL Server added columnar storage first in version 2012.

Columnar storage is highly compressed. Higher compression means more CPU usage because the data must be decompressed when you want to work with it and recompressed when you store it. In addition, SQL Server has to transform columns back to rows when you work with data and vice versa when you store the data. Add to this picture parallelized query execution, and suddenly CPU becomes a bottleneck. CPU is rarely a bottleneck in a transactional application. However, analytical applications have different requests. SQL Server solves the CPU problem by introducing **batch processing**.

In this section, you will learn about SQL Server columnar storage and batch processing, including the following:

- How SQL Server creates columnar storage
- Columnstore compression
- Nonclustered columnstore indexes
- Clustered columnstore indexes
- Limitations of columnar storage in different versions of SQL Server
- Batch processing
- Limitations of batch processing in different versions of SQL Server

Columnar storage and compression

Storing the data column by column instead of row by row gives the opportunity to store each column in a sorted way. Imagine that you have every column totally sorted. Then for every equijoin, the merge join algorithm could be used, which is, as you already know, a very efficient algorithm. In addition, with sorted data, you get one more type of compression nearly for free—the **run-length encoding (RLE)** compression.

The following figure explains the idea graphically:

Row / Col	1	2	3
	Name	Color	City
1	Nut	Red	London
2	Bolt	Green	Paris
3	Screw	Blue	Oslo
4	Screw	Red	London
5	Cam	Blue	Paris
6	Cog	Red	London

Row / Col	1	2	3
	Name	Color	City
1	Bolt [1:1]	Blue [1:2]	London [1:3]
2	Cam [2:2]	Green [3:3]	Oslo [4:4]
3	Cog [3:3]	Red [4:6]	Paris [5:6]
4	Nut [4:4]		
5	Screw [5:6]		
6			

Row / Col	1	2	3
	Name	Color	City
1	Bolt	Blue	London
2	Cam	Blue	London
3	Cog	Green	London
4	Nut	Red	Oslo
5	Screw	Red	Paris
6	Screw	Red	Paris

Figure 10-6: Sorted columnar storage and RLE

An RDBMS in the first step reorders every single column. Then the RLE compression is implemented. For example, if you look at the **Color** column, you don't need to repeat the value **Red** three times; you can store it only once and store either the frequency of the value or the index in form from position to position, as shown in the figure.

Note that SQL Server does not implement total sorting. Total sorting of every single column would simply be too expensive. Creating such storage would take too much time and resources. SQL Server uses its own patented **row-rearranging algorithm**, which rearranges the rows in the most optimal way for ordering all columns as best as possible, with a single pass through the data. This means that SQL Server does not totally sort any column; however, all columns are at least partially sorted. Therefore, SQL Server does not target merge join algorithm; hash join algorithm is preferred. Partial sort still optimizes the usage of the bitmap filters because fewer false positives are returned from a bitmap filter when compared with randomly organized values. The RLE compression can still reduce the size of the data substantially.

Recreating rows from columnar storage

Of course, there is still the question of how to recreate rows from the columnar storage. In 1999, Stephen Tarin patented the Tarin Transform Method that uses a **row reconstruction table** to regenerate the rows. Mr. Tarin called columnar storage the Trans-Relational Model. This does not mean the model is beyond relational; this was more a marketing term, short for "Transform Relational Model".

SQL Server documentation does not publish the row recreation algorithm it uses. I am presenting the Tarin's method here. It should still be good enough for a better understanding of the amount of work SQL Server has to do when it recreates rows from columns.

The following figure explains the Tarin Transform Method:

Row / Col	1	2	3
	Name	Color	City
1	3	6	4
2	1	4	6
3	6	5	3
4	4	1	5
5	2	2	1
6	5	3	2

Row / Col	1	2	3
	Name	Color	City
1	Bolt [1:1]	Blue [1:2]	London [1:3]
2	Cam [2:2]	Green [3:3]	Oslo [4:4]
3	Cog [3:3]	Red [4:6]	Paris [5:6]
4	Nut [4:4]		
5	Screw [5:6]		
6			

Figure 10.7: Tarin transform Method

In the figure, the top table is the row reconstruction table. You start reconstructing the rows in the top left corner. For the first column of the first row value, take the top left value in the columnar storage table at the bottom, in this case the value **Bolt**. In the first cell of the row reconstruction table is the pointer to the row number of the second column in this table. In addition, it is an index for the value of the second column in the columnar storage table. In the figure, this value is **3**. This means that you need to find the value in the second column of the columnar storage table with index **3**, which is **Green**. In the row reconstruction table, you read the value **5** in the second column, third row. You use this value as an index for the value of the third column in the columnar storage table, which, in the example, is **Paris**. In the row reconstruction table, you read the value **1**. Because this is the last column in the table, this value is used for a cyclic redundancy check, checking whether you correctly get to the starting point of the row reconstruction process. The row **Bolt**, **Green**, and **Paris**, the second row from the original table from the previous figure, was successfully reconstructed.

As mentioned, it is not published how SQL Server reconstructs the rows. Nevertheless, you can imagine this is quite an intensive process. You can also imagine changes in the original data. Just a small update of the original values might cause the complete recreation of the row reconstruction table. This would simply be too expensive. This is why columnar storage, once it is created, is actually read only. In SQL Server 2014 and 2016, columnstore indexes are updateable; however, SQL Server does not update the columnar storage online. SQL Server uses additional row storage for the updates. You will learn further details later in this section.

Columnar storage creation process

SQL Server starts creating the columnar storage by first splitting the data into **rowgroups**. The maximum number of rows per rowgroup is 1,048,576. The idea here is that the time-consuming row rearranging is done on smaller datasets, just as how the hash join algorithm splits the data into buckets and then performs smaller joins on portions of the data. SQL Server performs row rearranging in each of the groups separately. Then SQL Server encodes and compresses each column. Each column data in each rowgroup is called a **segment**. Then SQL Server stores the segments in blobs in database files. Therefore, SQL Server leverages the existing storage for columnar storage. The following figure shows the process:

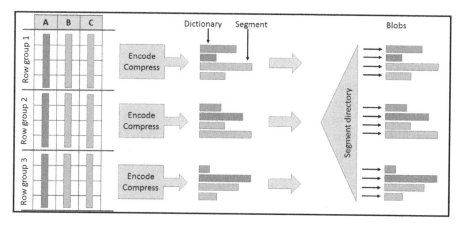

Figure 10-8: How SQL Server creates columnar storage

SQL Server implements different compressing algorithms:

- SQL Server does bit-packing. Bit-packing is similar to row compression, just pushed one level further. Instead of storing the minimal number of bytes, SQL Server stores the minimal number of bits that can represent the value. For example, with row compression, you would get one byte instead of four bytes for value 5, if this value is an integer. With bit-packing, SQL Server would store this value using three bits only *(101)*.
- Then SQL Server encodes the values to integers with **value encoding** and **dictionary encoding**. The value encoding is similar to the prefix encoding in the page compression, and the dictionary encoding is the same. Therefore, this part of the compression uses the ideas of the page compression. However, dictionaries for the columnar storage are much more efficient because they are built on more values than dictionaries in the page compression. With page compression, you get a separate dictionary for each 8 KB page. With columnar storage, you get one dictionary per rowgroup plus one global dictionary over all rowgroups.
- Because of the partial ordering, the run-length encoding algorithm is also used.
- Finally, SQL Server can also use the LZ77 algorithm to compress the columnar data.

All of these compression algorithms except the LZ77 one are implemented automatically when you create a columnstore index. This is called COLUMNSTORE compression. You must turn the LZ77 compression on manually to get so-called the COLUMNSTORE_ARCHIVE compression.

With all of these compression algorithms implemented, you can count on at least 10 times compression compared to the original, non-compressed row storage. In reality, you can get much better compression levels, especially when you also implement the archive compression with the LZ77 algorithm.

However, compression is not the only advantage with large scans. Because each column is stored separately, SQL Server can retrieve only the columns a query is referring to. This is like having a covering nonclustered index. Each segment also has additional metadata associated with it. This metadata includes the minimal and the maximal value in the segment. SQL Server query optimizer can use this metadata for early segment elimination, just as SQL Server can do early partition elimination if a table is partitioned. Finally, you can combine partitioning with columnstore indexes to maintain even very large tables.

Development of columnar storage in SQL Server

SQL Server introduced columnar storage in version 2012. Only **nonclustered columnstore indexes (NCCI)** were supported. This means that you still need to have the original row storage, either organized as a heap or as a **clustered index (CI)**. There were many other limitations, including the following:

- Nonclustered columnstore index only
- One per table
- Must be partition-aligned
- Table becomes read-only (partition switching allowed)
- Unsupported types
    - Decimal > 18 digits
    - Binary, Image, CLR (including Spatial, HierarchyId)
    - (n)varchar(max), XML, Text, Ntext
    - Uniqueidentifier, Rowversion, SQL_Variant
    - Date/time types > 8 bytes

SQL Server 2014 introduced **clustered columnstore indexes (CCI)**. This means that the original row storage does not exist anymore; the CCI is the only storage you need. Just like in a regular clustered index, SQL Server needs to identify each row in a clustered columnstore index as well. Note that SQL Server 2014 does not support constraints on the columnar storage. Therefore, SQL Server 2014 adds a **bookmark**, which is a unique tuple id inside a rowgroup, stored as a simple sequence number. SQL Server 2014 has still many data types unsupported for the columnar storage, including the following:

- Varbinary(MAX), Image, CLR (including Spatial, HierarchyId)
- (N)Varchar(max), XML, Text, Ntext
- Rowversion, SQL_Variant

SQL Server 2014 also optimizes columnstore index build. For example, SQL Server 2012 used a fixed number of threads to build the index. This number was estimated in advance. If, for some reason, the operating system took some threads away from SQL Server while SQL Server was building a columnstore index, the build might have failed. In SQL Server 2014, the degree of parallelism or the number of threads can be adjusted dynamically while SQL Server builds the columnstore index.

The CCI in SQL 2014 is updateable. However, the columnar storage is immutable. The following figure explains the update process:

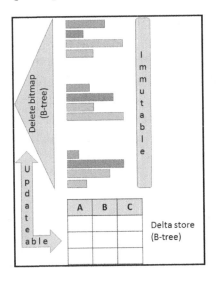

Figure 10.9: How SQL Server updates columnar storage

The data modification is implemented as follows:

- **Insert**: The new rows are inserted into a delta store
- **Delete**: If the row to be deleted is in a column store row group, a record containing its row ID is inserted into the B-tree storing the delete bitmap; if it is in a delta store, the row is simply deleted
- **Update**: Split into a delete and an insert
- **Merge**: Split into a delete, an insert, and an update

A delta store can be either open or closed. When a new delta store is created, it is open. After you insert the maximum number of rows for a rowgroup in an open delta store, SQL Server changes the status of this delta store to closed. If you remember, this means a bit more than one million rows. Then a background process called **tuple-mover** converts the closed delta stores to column segments. This process starts by default every five minutes. You can run it manually with the ALTER INDEX ... REORGANIZE or ALTER INDEX ... REBUILD commands.

Non-bulk (trickle) inserts go to an open delta store. Bulk inserts up to 102,400 rows; smaller go to an open delta store, and larger go directly to column segments. More delta stores mean less compression. Therefore, when using bulk insert, you should try to optimize the batches to contain close to 1,000,000 rows. You can also rebuild the index occasionally.

SQL Server 2016 brings many additional features to the columnstore indexes. The most important features in version 2016 include the following:

- CCI supports additional NCI (B-tree) indexes
- CCI supports through NCIs primary and foreign key constraints
- CCI supports snapshot and read committed snapshot isolation levels
- NCCI on a heap or B-tree updateable and filtered
- Columnstore indices on in-memory tables
- Defined when you create the table
- Must include all columns and all rows (not filtered)
- NCI indexes can be filtered

Batch processing

With columnar storage, the CPU can become a bottleneck. SQL Server solves these problems with **batch mode processing**. In batch mode processing, SQL Server processes data in batches rather than processing one row at a time. A batch represents roughly 900 rows of data. Each column within a batch is stored as a vector in a separate memory area, meaning that batch mode processing is vector-based. Batch mode processing interrupts a processor with metadata only once per batch rather than once per row, as in row mode processing, which lowers the CPU burden substantially. This means that the batch mode spreads the metadata access costs over all of the 900 rows in a batch.

Batch mode processing is orthogonal to columnar storage. This means SQL Server could use it with many different operators, no matter whether the data is stored in row or column storage. However, batch mode processing gives the best result when combined with columnar storage. DML operations, such as insert, update, or delete work in row mode. Of course, SQL Server can mix batch and row mode operators in a single query.

SQL Server introduced batch mode also in version 2012. The batch mode operators in this version include the following:

- Filter
- Project
- Scan
- Local hash (partial) aggregation
- Hash inner join

- Batch hash table build, but only in-memory, no spilling
- Bitmap filters limited to a single column, data types represented with a 64-bit integer

In SQL Server 2014, the following batch mode operators were added:

- All join types
- Union all
- Scalar aggregation
- Spilling support
- Complex bitmap filters, all data types supported

SQL Server 2016 added the following improvements to the batch mode processing:

- Single-threaded queries
- Sort operator
- Multiple distinct count operations
- Left anti-semi join operators
- Window aggregate functions
- Window analytical functions
- String predicate and aggregate pushdown to the storage engine
- Row-level locking on index seeks against a nonclustered index and rowgroup-level locking on full table scans against the columnstore

The following table summarizes the most important features and limitations of columnar storage and batch mode processing in SQL Server versions 2012-2106:

Columnstore Index / Batch Mode Feature	SQL 2012	SQL 2014	SQL 2016
Batch execution for multi-threaded queries	yes	yes	yes
Batch execution for single-threaded queries			yes
Archival compression		yes	yes
Snapshot isolation and read-committed snapshot isolation			yes
Specify CI when creating a table			yes
AlwaysOn supports CIs	yes	yes	yes
AlwaysOn readable secondary supports read-only NCCI	yes	yes	yes
AlwaysOn readable secondary supports updateable CIs			yes

Read-only NCCI on heap or B-tree	yes	yes	yes
Updateable NCCI on heap or B-tree			yes
B-tree indexes allowed on a table that has a NCCI	yes	yes	yes
Updateable CCI		yes	yes
B-tree index on a CCI			yes
CI on a memory-optimized table			yes
Filtered NCCI			yes

You can check whether SQL Server uses row or batch mode for an operator by analyzing the properties of the operator in the execution plan. Before checking the batch mode, the following code adds nine time more rows to the test fact table:

```
DECLARE @i AS INT = 1;
WHILE @i < 10
BEGIN
SET @i += 1;
INSERT INTO dbo.FactTest
(SaleKey, CustomerKey,
 Customer, CityKey, City,
 DateKey, StockItemKey,
 Product, Quantity,
 TotalAmount, Profit)
SELECT @i * 1000000 + f.[Sale Key] AS SaleKey,
  cu.[Customer Key] AS CustomerKey, cu.Customer,
  ci.[City Key] AS CityKey, ci.City,
  f.[Delivery Date Key] AS DateKey,
  s.[Stock Item Key] AS StockItemKey, s.[Stock Item] AS Product,
  f.Quantity, f.[Total Excluding Tax] AS TotalAmount, f.Profit
FROM Fact.Sale AS f
  INNER JOIN Dimension.Customer AS cu
    ON f.[Customer Key] = cu.[Customer Key]
  INNER JOIN Dimension.City AS ci
    ON f.[City Key] = ci.[City Key]
  INNER JOIN Dimension.[Stock Item] AS s
    ON f.[Stock Item Key] = s.[Stock Item Key]
  INNER JOIN Dimension.Date AS d
    ON f.[Delivery Date Key] = d.Date;
END;
```

Let's check how much space this table uses now:

```
EXEC sys.sp_spaceused N'dbo.FactTest', @updateusage = N'TRUE';
GO
```

The result is as follows:

Name	rows	reserved	data	index_size	unused
dbo.FactTest	2279810	502152 KB	498528 KB	2072 KB	1552 KB

Now let's start querying this table. Before executing the following query, make sure you turn the actual execution plan on:

```
SELECT f.StockItemKey,
  SUM(f.TotalAmount) AS Sales
FROM dbo.FactTest AS f
WHERE f.StockItemKey < 30
GROUP BY f.StockItemKey
ORDER BY f.StockItemKey;
```

You can hover the mouse over any of the operators. For example, the following screenshot shows the details of the Hash Match (Partial Aggregate) operator:

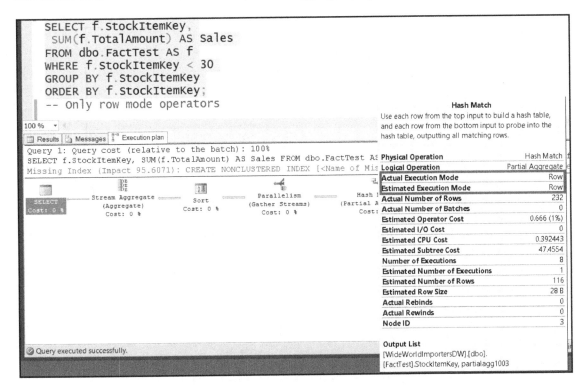

Figure 10-10: Row mode operators

You can see that SQL Server used the row mode processing. As mentioned, the batch mode is not strictly bound to the columnar storage; however, it is much more likely that SQL Server would use it as you use the columnar storage. The following code creates a filtered nonclustered columnstore index. It is actually empty:

```
CREATE NONCLUSTERED COLUMNSTORE INDEX NCCI_FactTest
ON dbo.FactTest
(SaleKey, CustomerKey,
 Customer, CityKey, City,
 DateKey, StockItemKey,
 Product, Quantity,
 TotalAmount, Profit)
WHERE SaleKey = 0;
GO
```

Now, execute the same query as the aforementioned again. As you can see from the following screenshot, this time the batch mode is used for the `Hash Match` (Partial Aggregate) operator:

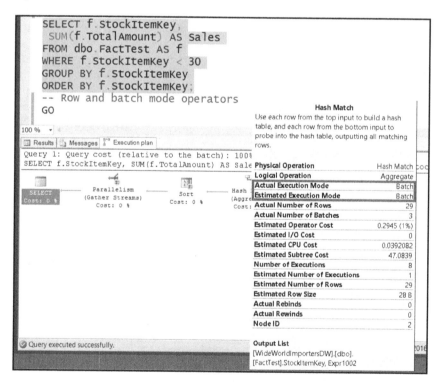

Figure 10.11: Batch mode operators

Nonclustered columnstore indexes

After all of the theoretical introduction, it is time to start using the columnar storage. You will start by learning how to create and use nonclustered **columnstore indexes** (**NCCI**). You already know from the previous section that a NCCI can be filtered. Now you will learn how to create, use, and ignore a NCCI. In addition, you will measure the compression rate of the columnar storage.

Because of the different burdens on SQL Server when a transactional application uses it compared to analytical applications usage, traditionally, companies split these applications and created data warehouses. Analytical queries are diverted to the data warehouse database. This means that you have a copy of data in your data warehouse, of course with a different schema. You also need to implement the **Extract Transform Load** (**ETL**) process for scheduled loading of the data warehouse. This means that the data you analyze is somehow stall. Frequently, the data is loaded overnight and is thus one day old when you analyze it. For many analytical purposes, this is good enough. However, in some cases, users would like to analyze the current data together with the archive data. This is called **operational analytics**. SQL Server 2016 with columnar storage and in-memory tables makes operational analytics realistically possible.

In this section, you will learn how to do the following:

- Create nonclustered columnstore indexes
- Ignore an NCCI in a query
- Use NCCI in a query
- Architecture an operational analytics solution

Compression and query performance

Without any further hesitation, let's start with the code. The first thing is to drop the filtered (empty) NCCI created in the previous section:

```
DROP INDEX NCCI_FactTest
ON dbo.FactTest;
GO
```

The test fact table is organized as a B-tree with no additional nonclustered index, neither a rowstore nor columnstore one. The clustering key is the date. In order to make a comparison with NCCIs, let's set a baseline. First, recheck the space used by the test fact table:

```
EXEC sys.sp_spaceused N'dbo.FactTest', @updateusage = N'TRUE';
GO
```

The result is as follows:

Name	rows	reserved	data	index_size	unused
dbo.FactTest	2279810	502152 KB	498528 KB	2072 KB	1552 KB

You can measure IO with the SET STATISTICS IO ON command. In addition, you can turn on the actual execution plan. Here is the first exemplary query; let's call it the *simple* query:

```
SET STATISTICS IO ON;
SELECT f.StockItemKey,
  SUM(f.TotalAmount) AS Sales
FROM dbo.FactTest AS f
WHERE f.StockItemKey < 30
GROUP BY f.StockItemKey
ORDER BY f.StockItemKey;
```

The query did a full clustered index scan, and there were 63,601 logical reads. You can also notice in the execution plan that only row mode operators were used.

 You can get slightly different results for the IO. The exact number of pages used by the table might vary slightly based on your dataset files organization, parallel operations when you load the data or change the table from a heap to a B-tree, and other possibilities. Nevertheless, your numbers should be very similar, and the point is to show how much less space will be used by the columnar storage because of the compression.

The next query involves multiple joins; let's call it the *complex* query:

```
SELECT f.SaleKey,
  f.CustomerKey, f.Customer, cu.[Buying Group],
  f.CityKey, f.City, ci.Country,
  f.DateKey, d.[Calendar Year],
  f.StockItemKey, f.Product,
  f.Quantity, f.TotalAmount, f.Profit
FROM dbo.FactTest AS f
  INNER JOIN Dimension.Customer AS cu
    ON f.CustomerKey = cu.[Customer Key]
```

```
INNER JOIN Dimension.City AS ci
  ON f.CityKey = ci.[City Key]
INNER JOIN Dimension.[Stock Item] AS s
  ON f.StockItemKey = s.[Stock Item Key]
INNER JOIN Dimension.Date AS d
  ON f.DateKey = d.Date;
```

This time, SQL Server created a much more complex execution plan. Yet, SQL Server used the full clustered index scan to read the data from the test fact table. SQL Server used 62,575 logical reads in this table.

The third test query is very selective—it selects only the rows for the customer 378. If you remember, this customer has only 242 rows in the fact table. Let's call the third query the *point* query:

```
SELECT CustomerKey, Profit
FROM dbo.FactTest
WHERE CustomerKey = 378;
SET STATISTICS IO OFF;
```

The query again did a full clustered index scan, and there were 63,601 logical reads.

Testing the nonclustered columnstore Index

The following code creates an NCCI on the fact table, this time without a filter, so all data is included in the NCCI:

```
CREATE NONCLUSTERED COLUMNSTORE INDEX NCCI_FactTest
ON dbo.FactTest
(SaleKey, CustomerKey,
 Customer, CityKey, City,
 DateKey, StockItemKey,
 Product, Quantity,
 TotalAmount, Profit);
GO
```

So how much space is used by the test fact table now?

```
EXEC sys.sp_spaceused N'dbo.FactTest', @updateusage = N'TRUE';
GO
```

The result is as follows:

Name	rows	reserved	data	index_size	unused
dbo.FactTest	2279810	529680 KB	498528 KB	29432 KB	1720 KB

Note the numbers. The index size is about 17 times less than the data size! And remember, in this size are also the non-leaf levels of the clustered index, so the actual compression rate was even more than 17 times. This is impressive. So what does this mean for the queries? Before measuring the improvements in queries, I want to show how you can ignore the NCCI you just created with a specific option in the `OPTION` clause of the `SELECT` statement. So here is the *simple* query that ignores the NCCI:

```
SET STATISTICS IO ON;
SELECT f.StockItemKey,
 SUM(f.TotalAmount) AS Sales
FROM dbo.FactTest AS f
WHERE f.StockItemKey < 30
GROUP BY f.StockItemKey
ORDER BY f.StockItemKey
OPTION (ignore_nonclustered_columnstore_index);
```

Because the NCCI was ignored, the query still did the full-clustered index scan with 63,301 logical reads. However, you can see from the execution plan that this time row mode operators were used, as shown in the following screenshot:

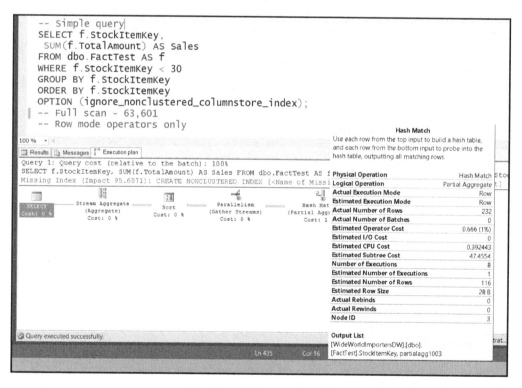

Figure 10-12: Row mode processing operators

This is different compared to the execution plan SQL Server used for the same query when the NCCI was empty, when SQL Server used batch mode operators. The ignore option really means that SQL Server completely ignores the NCCI. You can check that this is also true for the other two queries, the *complex* and the *point* one. You can also check the execution plans when ignoring the NCCI with the *complex* and *point* queries:

```
-- Complex query
SELECT f.SaleKey,
   f.CustomerKey, f.Customer, cu.[Buying Group],
   f.CityKey, f.City, ci.Country,
   f.DateKey, d.[Calendar Year],
   f.StockItemKey, f.Product,
   f.Quantity, f.TotalAmount, f.Profit
FROM dbo.FactTest AS f
   INNER JOIN Dimension.Customer AS cu
     ON f.CustomerKey = cu.[Customer Key]
   INNER JOIN Dimension.City AS ci
     ON f.CityKey = ci.[City Key]
   INNER JOIN Dimension.[Stock Item] AS s
     ON f.StockItemKey = s.[Stock Item Key]
   INNER JOIN Dimension.Date AS d
     ON f.DateKey = d.Date
OPTION (ignore_nonclustered_columnstore_index);
-- Point query
SELECT CustomerKey, Profit
FROM dbo.FactTest
WHERE CustomerKey = 378
OPTION (ignore_nonclustered_columnstore_index);
SET STATISTICS IO OFF;
```

For both queries, SQL Server did a full table scan on the fact table, with around 63,000 logical reads in this table. Now let's finally see how the queries can benefit from the NCCI. The first query is the *simple* query again:

```
SET STATISTICS IO ON;
SELECT f.StockItemKey,
 SUM(f.TotalAmount) AS Sales
FROM dbo.FactTest AS f
WHERE f.StockItemKey < 30
GROUP BY f.StockItemKey
ORDER BY f.StockItemKey;
```

As you can see from the following figure, the columnstore index scan was used, and only four segments were read, with 2,001 LOB reads. Remember that the columnstore indexes are stored in blobs in SQL Server. Compare this to the number of logical reads when the NCCI was ignored. Of course, batch mode operators were used:

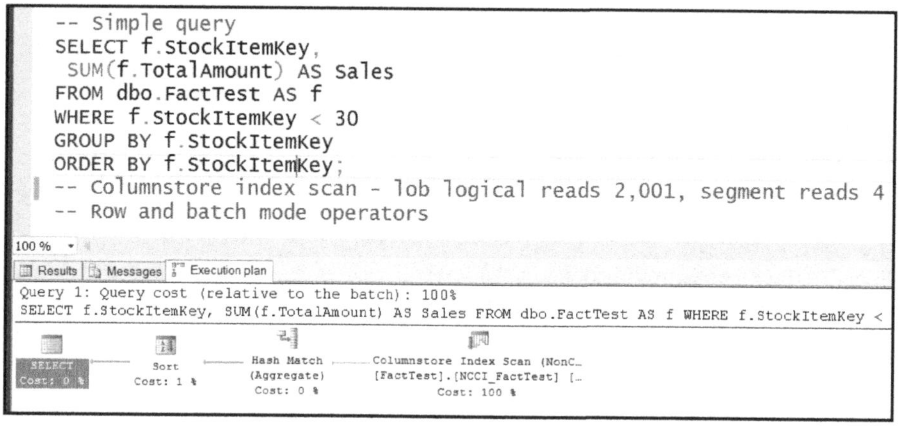

```
-- Simple query
SELECT f.StockItemKey,
  SUM(f.TotalAmount) AS Sales
FROM dbo.FactTest AS f
WHERE f.StockItemKey < 30
GROUP BY f.StockItemKey
ORDER BY f.StockItemKey;
-- Columnstore index scan - lob logical reads 2,001, segment reads 4
-- Row and batch mode operators
```

100 %

| Results | Messages | Execution plan |

```
Query 1: Query cost (relative to the batch): 100%
SELECT f.StockItemKey, SUM(f.TotalAmount) AS Sales FROM dbo.FactTest AS f WHERE f.StockItemKey <
```

SELECT	Sort	Hash Match	Columnstore Index Scan (NonC...
Cost: 0 %	Cost: 1 %	(Aggregate)	[FactTest].[NCCI_FactTest] [...
		Cost: 0 %	Cost: 100 %

Figure 10.13: Row mode processing operators

You can check how many segments in total are occupied by the NCCI with the following query that uses the `sys.column_store_segments` catalog view:

```
SELECT ROW_NUMBER()
       OVER (ORDER BY s.column_id, s.segment_id) AS rn,
  COL_NAME(p.object_id, s.column_id) AS column_name,
  S.segment_id, s.row_count,
  s.min_data_id, s.max_data_id,
  s.on_disk_size AS disk_size
FROM sys.column_store_segments AS s
INNER JOIN sys.partitions AS p
    ON s.hobt_id = p.hobt_id
INNER JOIN sys.indexes AS i
    ON p.object_id = i.object_id
WHERE i.name = N'NCCI_FactTest'
ORDER BY s.column_id, s.segment_id;
```

Here is the abbreviated result of this query:

rn	column_name	segment_id	row_count	min_data_id	max_data_id	disk_size
1	SaleKey	0	1048576	1000001	10106307	4194888
2	SaleKey	1	336457	1001951	10185925	1346560
3	SaleKey	2	441851	1106610	10227981	1768336
4	SaleKey	3	452926	1001228	10213964	1812656

5	CustomerKey	0	1048576	0	402	773392
...	...					
44	Profit	3	452926	−64500	920000	25624
45	NULL	0	1048576	0	3539	1678312
...	...					
48	NULL	3	452926	0	3879	725640

The total number of segments used is 48. SQL Server created four rowgroups and then one segment per column inside each rowgroup, plus one segment per rowgroup for the rowgroup dictionary. You can also see the number of rows and disk space used per segment. In addition, the `min_data_id` and `max_data_id` columns point to the minimal and the maximal value in each segment. SQL Server query optimizer uses this information for early segment elimination.

You can also execute the other two queries:

```
-- Complex query
SELECT f.SaleKey,
    f.CustomerKey, f.Customer, cu.[Buying Group],
    f.CityKey, f.City, ci.Country,
    f.DateKey, d.[Calendar Year],
    f.StockItemKey, f.Product,
    f.Quantity, f.TotalAmount, f.Profit
FROM dbo.FactTest AS f
    INNER JOIN Dimension.Customer AS cu
        ON f.CustomerKey = cu.[Customer Key]
    INNER JOIN Dimension.City AS ci
        ON f.CityKey = ci.[City Key]
    INNER JOIN Dimension.[Stock Item] AS s
        ON f.StockItemKey = s.[Stock Item Key]
    INNER JOIN Dimension.Date AS d
        ON f.DateKey = d.Date;
-- Point query
SELECT CustomerKey, Profit
FROM dbo.FactTest
WHERE CustomerKey = 378;
SET STATISTICS IO OFF;
```

For the *complex* query, the number of LOB reads is 7,128. For the *point* query, the number of LOB reads is 2,351. In both cases, the columnstore index scan was used to read the data from the fact table. The *point* query used less LOB reads than the *complex* query because the query refers to less columns, and SQL Server retrieves only the columns needed to satisfy the query. Still, the results for the *point* query are not overexciting. You should be able to get much less IO with a B-tree nonclustered index, especially with a covering one.

In my case, the *complex* query used a serial plan. Note that depending on the hardware resources and concurrent work, you might get a different execution plan. SQL Server sees eight logical processors in my virtual machine, so you might have expected a parallel plan. SQL Server 2016 is much more conservative about using a parallel plan compared to previous versions. This is better for the majority of queries. If you really need to get a parallel execution plan, you could change the compatibility level to the version 2014, as the following code shows:

```
USE master;
GO
ALTER DATABASE WideWorldImportersDW SET COMPATIBILITY_LEVEL = 120;
GO
```

Now you can try to execute the *complex* query again:

```
USE WideWorldImportersDW;
SET STATISTICS IO ON;
SELECT f.SaleKey,
    f.CustomerKey, f.Customer, cu.[Buying Group],
    f.CityKey, f.City, ci.Country,
    f.DateKey, d.[Calendar Year],
    f.StockItemKey, f.Product,
    f.Quantity, f.TotalAmount, f.Profit
FROM dbo.FactTest AS f
  INNER JOIN Dimension.Customer AS cu
    ON f.CustomerKey = cu.[Customer Key]
  INNER JOIN Dimension.City AS ci
    ON f.CityKey = ci.[City Key]
  INNER JOIN Dimension.[Stock Item] AS s
    ON f.StockItemKey = s.[Stock Item Key]
  INNER JOIN Dimension.Date AS d
    ON f.DateKey = d.Date;
SET STATISTICS IO OFF;
```

This time, SQL Server used a parallel plan on my computer. Before continuing, reset the compatibility level to 2016:

```
USE master;
GO
ALTER DATABASE WideWorldImportersDW SET COMPATIBILITY_LEVEL = 130;
GO
```

Operational analytics

Real-time operational analytics has become a viable option in SQL Server 2016, especially if you combine columnar storage together with in-memory tables. Here is just a brief overview of two possible solutions for operational analytics—one with on-disk and another with in-memory storage. You will learn more about in-memory tables in `Chapter 11`, *Introducing SQL Server In-Memory OLTP* and `Chapter 12`, *In-Memory OLTP Improvements in SQL Server 2016*.

The following figure shows an architecture of an operational analytics solution with on-disk tables:

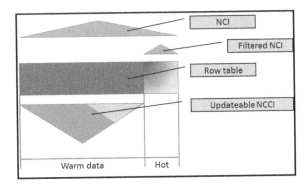

Figure 10-14: On-disk operational analytics

The majority of the data does not change much (so-called **warm data**), or is maybe even historical, immutable data (so-called **cold data**). You use a filtered nonclustered columnstore index over this warm or cold data. For the **hot data**—data that is changed frequently—you can use a regular filtered nonclustered index. You can also use additional nonclustered indexes over the whole table. The table can be organized as a heap or as B-tree.

For in-memory tables, you can implement a slightly different architecture. You have to take into account that nonclustered columnstore indexes on an in-memory table cannot be filtered. Therefore, they must cover both warm and hot data areas. However, they are updateable, and in-memory updates are much faster than on-disk updates.

You can combine columnstore index with other in-memory index types, namely with hash indexes and nonclustered indexes.

The in-memory operational analytics solution is shown in the following figure:

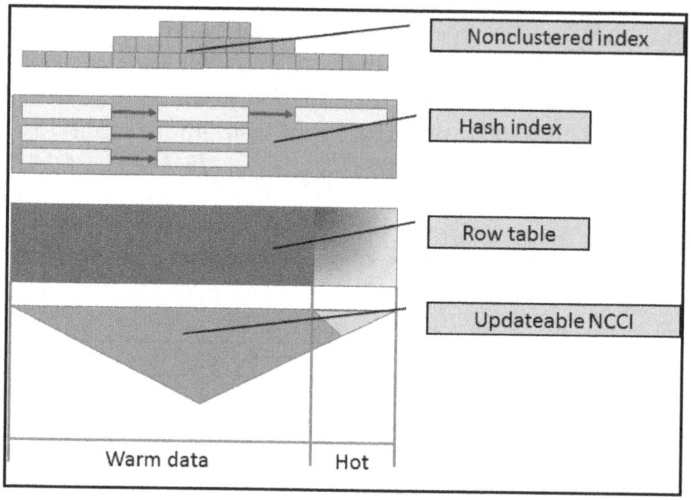

Figure 10-15: In-memory operational analytics

Clustered columnstore indexes

In the last section of this chapter, you will learn how to manage a clustered columnstore index (CCI). Besides optimizing query performance, you will also learn how to add a regular B-tree **nonclustered index** (**NCI**) to a CCI and use it instead of the primary key or unique constraints. When creating the NCCI in the previous section, the LZ77 or the archive compression has not been used yet. You will use it with a CCI in this section. Altogether, you will learn how to do the following:

- Create clustered columnstore indexes
- Use archive compression
- Add B-tree NCI to a CCI
- Use B-tree NCI for a constraint
- Update data in a CCI

Compression and query performance

Let's start by dropping both indexes from the demo fact table, the NCCI and the CI, to make a heap again:

```
USE WideWorldImportersDW;
-- Drop the NCCI
DROP INDEX NCCI_FactTest
  ON dbo.FactTest;
-- Drop the CI
DROP INDEX CL_FactTest_DateKey
  ON dbo.FactTest;
GO
```

Now let's create the **clustered columnstore index (CCI)**:

```
CREATE CLUSTERED COLUMNSTORE INDEX CCI_FactTest
  ON dbo.FactTest;
GO
```

And, of course, the next step is to recheck the space used by the test fact table:

```
EXEC sys.sp_spaceused N'dbo.FactTest', @updateusage = N'TRUE';
GO
```

The result is as follows:

Name	rows	reserved	data	index_size	unused
dbo.FactTest	2279810	23560 KB	23392 KB	0 KB	168 KB

The CCI even uses slightly less space than the NCCI. You can check the number of segments with the following query:

```
SELECT ROW_NUMBER() OVER (ORDER BY s.column_id, s.segment_id) AS rn,
  COL_NAME(p.object_id, s.column_id) AS column_name,
  S.segment_id, s.row_count,
  s.min_data_id, s.max_data_id,
  s.on_disk_size
FROM sys.column_store_segments AS s
INNER JOIN sys.partitions AS p
    ON s.hobt_id = p.hobt_id
INNER JOIN sys.indexes AS i
    ON p.object_id = i.object_id
WHERE i.name = N'CCI_FactTest'
ORDER BY s.column_id, s.segment_id;
```

This time, the number of segments is 44. The CCI does not show a dictionary segment per row group; it has a global dictionary that apparently covers the whole table. How does that influence the queries?

Testing the clustered columnstore Index

Again, the first test is with the *simple* query:

```
SET STATISTICS IO ON;
SELECT f.StockItemKey,
  SUM(f.TotalAmount) AS Sales
FROM dbo.FactTest AS f
WHERE f.StockItemKey < 30
GROUP BY f.StockItemKey
ORDER BY f.StockItemKey;
```

From the statistics IO output, you can see that SQL Server used only 82 logical reads. This time, this is really impressive. Note that the execution plan again used the `Columnstore Index Scan` operator, only this time scanning the CCI and selecting only the rowgroups and segments needed to satisfy the query. You can see the execution plan in the following figure:

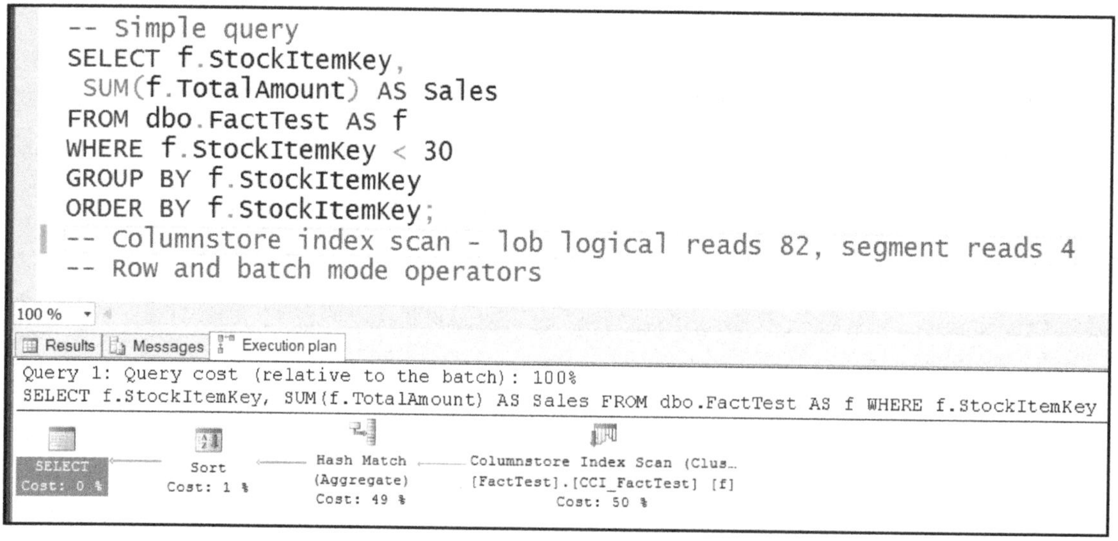

Figure 10-16: CCI scan execution plan

The next query to test is the *complex* query:

```
SELECT f.SaleKey,
   f.CustomerKey, f.Customer, cu.[Buying Group],
   f.CityKey, f.City, ci.Country,
   f.DateKey, d.[Calendar Year],
   f.StockItemKey, f.Product,
   f.Quantity, f.TotalAmount, f.Profit
FROM dbo.FactTest AS f
   INNER JOIN Dimension.Customer AS cu
     ON f.CustomerKey = cu.[Customer Key]
   INNER JOIN Dimension.City AS ci
     ON f.CityKey = ci.[City Key]
   INNER JOIN Dimension.[Stock Item] AS s
     ON f.StockItemKey = s.[Stock Item Key]
   INNER JOIN Dimension.Date AS d
     ON f.DateKey = d.Date;
```

This time, SQL Server needed 6,101 LOB logical reads. SQL Server used a serial plan on my virtual machine and mixed batch (for CCI scan and for hash joins) and row mode operators (for other index scans). This is only slightly better than when using an NCCI. How about the *point* query?

```
SELECT CustomerKey, Profit
FROM dbo.FactTest
WHERE CustomerKey = 378;
SET STATISTICS IO OFF;
```

The *point* query this time used 484 LOB logical reads. Better, but still not the best possible.

Using archive compression

You might remember that there is still one option left for the columnar storage compression—the archive compression. Let's turn it on with the following code:

```
ALTER INDEX CCI_FactTest
 ON dbo.FactTest
 REBUILD WITH (DATA_COMPRESSION = COLUMNSTORE_ARCHIVE);
GO
```

You can imagine what comes next: recheck the space used by the test fact table:

```
EXEC sys.sp_spaceused N'dbo.FactTest', @updateusage = N'TRUE';
GO
```

The result is as follows:

```
Name            rows      reserved   data       index_size  unused
-------------   -------   ---------  ---------   ----------  -------
dbo.FactTest    2279810   19528 KB   19336 KB         0 KB   192 KB
```

The LZ77 algorithm added some additional compression. Compare the data size now with the initial data size when the data size was 498,528 KB; now, it is only 19,336 KB; the compression rate is more than 25 times! This is really impressive. Of course, you can expect that the test queries are even more efficient now. For example, here is the *simple* query:

```
SET STATISTICS IO ON;
SELECT f.StockItemKey,
 SUM(f.TotalAmount) AS Sales
FROM dbo.FactTest AS f
WHERE f.StockItemKey < 30
GROUP BY f.StockItemKey
ORDER BY f.StockItemKey;
```

This time, SQL Server needed only 23 LOB logical reads. The next query to test is the *complex* query:

```
SELECT f.SaleKey,
   f.CustomerKey, f.Customer, cu.[Buying Group],
   f.CityKey, f.City, ci.Country,
   f.DateKey, d.[Calendar Year],
   f.StockItemKey, f.Product,
   f.Quantity, f.TotalAmount, f.Profit
FROM dbo.FactTest AS f
   INNER JOIN Dimension.Customer AS cu
     ON f.CustomerKey = cu.[Customer Key]
   INNER JOIN Dimension.City AS ci
     ON f.CityKey = ci.[City Key]
   INNER JOIN Dimension.[Stock Item] AS s
     ON f.StockItemKey = s.[Stock Item Key]
   INNER JOIN Dimension.Date AS d
     ON f.DateKey = d.Date;
```

This time, SQL Server needed 4,820 LOB logical reads in the test fact table. It can't get much better than this for scanning all of the data. And what about the *point* query?

```
SELECT CustomerKey, Profit
FROM dbo.FactTest
WHERE CustomerKey = 378;
```

This time, it used 410 LOB logical reads. This number can still be improved.

Adding B-Tree indexes and constraints

There is still one query, the *point* query, which needs additional optimization. In SQL Server 2016, you can create regular, rowstore B-tree nonclustered indexes on a clustered columnstore index, on the table that is organized as columnar storage. The following code adds a nonclustered index with included column, an index that is going to cover the *point* query:

```
CREATE NONCLUSTERED INDEX NCI_FactTest_CustomerKey
 ON dbo.FactTest(CustomerKey)
 INCLUDE(Profit);
GO
```

Before executing the queries, let's check the space used by the demo fact table:

```
EXEC sys.sp_spaceused N'dbo.FactTest', @updateusage = N'TRUE';
GO
```

The result is as follows:

Name	rows	reserved	data	index_size	unused
dbo.FactTest	2279810	90256 KB	19344 KB	70192 KB	720 KB

You can see that the row storage uses much more space than the columnar storage. However, a regular NCI is very efficient for seeks. Let's test the queries, starting with the *simple* query:

```
SET STATISTICS IO ON;
SELECT f.StockItemKey,
 SUM(f.TotalAmount) AS Sales
FROM dbo.FactTest AS f
WHERE f.StockItemKey < 30
GROUP BY f.StockItemKey
ORDER BY f.StockItemKey;
```

This query still needed 23 LOB logical reads. If you check the execution plan, you can see that SQL Server is still using the columnstore index scan. Of course, the NCI is not very useful for this query. How about the *complex* query?

```
SELECT f.SaleKey,
   f.CustomerKey, f.Customer, cu.[Buying Group],
   f.CityKey, f.City, ci.Country,
   f.DateKey, d.[Calendar Year],
   f.StockItemKey, f.Product,
   f.Quantity, f.TotalAmount, f.Profit
FROM dbo.FactTest AS f
```

```
INNER JOIN Dimension.Customer AS cu
  ON f.CustomerKey = cu.[Customer Key]
INNER JOIN Dimension.City AS ci
  ON f.CityKey = ci.[City Key]
INNER JOIN Dimension.[Stock Item] AS s
  ON f.StockItemKey = s.[Stock Item Key]
INNER JOIN Dimension.Date AS d
  ON f.DateKey = d.Date;
```

Again, SQL Server needed 4,820 LOB logical reads in the test fact table. The NCI didn't improve this query; it is already optimized. Finally, let's check the *point* query:

```
SELECT CustomerKey, Profit
FROM dbo.FactTest
WHERE CustomerKey = 378;
SET STATISTICS IO OFF;
```

This time, the query needed only 13 logical reads. SQL Server query optimizer decided to use the covering NCI index, as you can see from the following figure, showing the execution plan for the *point* query for this execution:

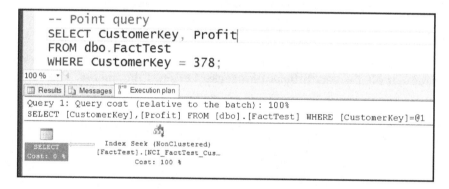

Figure 10-17: Execution plan for the *point* query that uses the nonclustered covering index

We don't need the nonclustered index anymore, so let's drop it:

```
DROP INDEX NCI_FactTest_CustomerKey
 ON dbo.FactTest;
GO
```

You can check the physical status of the rowgroups of the CCI using the `sys.dm_db_column_store_row_group_physical_stats` dynamic management view, like the following query shows:

```
SELECT OBJECT_NAME(object_id) AS table_name,
 row_group_id, state, state_desc,
 total_rows, deleted_rows
FROM sys.dm_db_column_store_row_group_physical_stats
WHERE object_id = OBJECT_ID(N'dbo.FactTest')
ORDER BY row_group_id;
```

Here is the result:

table_name	row_group_id	state	state_desc	total_rows	deleted_rows
FactTest	0	3	COMPRESSED	1048576	0
FactTest	1	3	COMPRESSED	343592	0
FactTest	2	3	COMPRESSED	444768	0
FactTest	3	3	COMPRESSED	442874	0

You can see that all rowgroups are closed and compressed.

In SQL 2016, you can also add primary key and unique constraints to a CCI table. The following code adds a unique constraint to the test fact table. Note that you cannot add a primary key constraint because the `SaleKey` column is nullable:

```
ALTER TABLE dbo.FactTest
 ADD CONSTRAINT U_SaleKey UNIQUE (SaleKey);
GO
```

You can check in **Object Explorer** that the Unique constraint is enforced with help from unique rowstore nonclustered index. The following screenshot of the **Object Explorer** window shows that the `SaleKey` column is nullable as well:

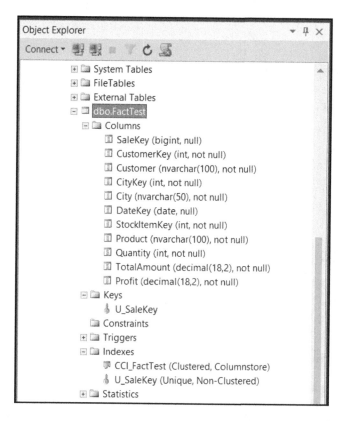

Figure 10-18: Unique constraint on a CCI table

Let's test the constraint. The following command tries to insert 75,993 rows into the test fact table that already exist in the table:

```
INSERT INTO dbo.FactTest
(SaleKey, CustomerKey,
 Customer, CityKey, City,
 DateKey, StockItemKey,
 Product, Quantity,
 TotalAmount, Profit)
SELECT 10 * 1000000 + f.[Sale Key] AS SaleKey,
  cu.[Customer Key] AS CustomerKey, cu.Customer,
  ci.[City Key] AS CityKey, ci.City,
  f.[Delivery Date Key] AS DateKey,
```

```
    s.[Stock Item Key] AS StockItemKey, s.[Stock Item] AS Product,
    f.Quantity, f.[Total Excluding Tax] AS TotalAmount, f.Profit
FROM Fact.Sale AS f
  INNER JOIN Dimension.Customer AS cu
    ON f.[Customer Key] = cu.[Customer Key]
  INNER JOIN Dimension.City AS ci
    ON f.[City Key] = ci.[City Key]
  INNER JOIN Dimension.[Stock Item] AS s
    ON f.[Stock Item Key] = s.[Stock Item Key]
  INNER JOIN Dimension.Date AS d
    ON f.[Delivery Date Key] = d.Date
WHERE f.[Sale Key] % 3 = 0;
```

If you execute the code, you get the error 2627, violating the Unique constraint. Let's recheck the status of the rowgroups:

```
SELECT OBJECT_NAME(object_id) AS table_name,
  row_group_id, state, state_desc,
  total_rows, deleted_rows
FROM sys.dm_db_column_store_row_group_physical_stats
WHERE object_id = OBJECT_ID(N'dbo.FactTest')
ORDER BY row_group_id;
```

This time, the result differs slightly:

table_name	row_group_id	state	state_desc	total_rows	deleted_rows
FactTest	0	3	COMPRESSED	1048576	0
FactTest	1	3	COMPRESSED	343592	0
FactTest	2	3	COMPRESSED	444768	0
FactTest	3	3	COMPRESSED	442874	0
FactTest	4	1	OPEN	0	0

Although the insert was rejected, SQL Server did not close or delete the delta storage. Of course, this makes sense since this storage might become useful pretty soon for next updates of the data. You can rebuild the index to get rid of this delta storage. The following command rebuilds the CCI, this time without archive compression:

```
ALTER INDEX CCI_FactTest
  ON dbo.FactTest
  REBUILD WITH (DATA_COMPRESSION = COLUMNSTORE);
GO
```

You can check the rowgroup's status again:

```
SELECT OBJECT_NAME(object_id) AS table_name,
  row_group_id, state, state_desc,
  total_rows, deleted_rows
FROM sys.dm_db_column_store_row_group_physical_stats
WHERE object_id = OBJECT_ID(N'dbo.FactTest')
ORDER BY row_group_id;
```

Here is the result:

table_name	row_group_id	state	state_desc	total_rows	deleted_rows
FactTest	0	3	COMPRESSED	1048576	0
FactTest	1	3	COMPRESSED	343592	0
FactTest	2	3	COMPRESSED	444768	0
FactTest	3	3	COMPRESSED	442874	0

 Note that your results for the number of rows in each row group can vary slightly.

Updating a clustered columnstore index

So far, only an unsuccessful insert was tested. Of course, you can also try to insert some valid data. Before that, let's drop the constraint since it is not needed for further explanation anymore:

```
ALTER TABLE dbo.FactTest
  DROP CONSTRAINT U_SaleKey;
GO
```

Next, you can insert some valid rows. The following statement inserts 113,990 rows to the test fact table. Note that this is more than the 102,400 rows limit for the trickle inserts; therefore, you should expect that this is treated as a bulk insert:

```
INSERT INTO dbo.FactTest
(SaleKey, CustomerKey,
 Customer, CityKey, City,
 DateKey, StockItemKey,
 Product, Quantity,
 TotalAmount, Profit)
SELECT 11 * 1000000 + f.[Sale Key] AS SaleKey,
  cu.[Customer Key] AS CustomerKey, cu.Customer,
  ci.[City Key] AS CityKey, ci.City,
```

```
      f.[Delivery Date Key] AS DateKey,
      s.[Stock Item Key] AS StockItemKey, s.[Stock Item] AS Product,
      f.Quantity, f.[Total Excluding Tax] AS TotalAmount, f.Profit
FROM Fact.Sale AS f
  INNER JOIN Dimension.Customer AS cu
    ON f.[Customer Key] = cu.[Customer Key]
  INNER JOIN Dimension.City AS ci
    ON f.[City Key] = ci.[City Key]
  INNER JOIN Dimension.[Stock Item] AS s
    ON f.[Stock Item Key] = s.[Stock Item Key]
  INNER JOIN Dimension.Date AS d
    ON f.[Delivery Date Key] = d.Date
WHERE f.[Sale Key] % 2 = 0;
```

You can check whether this was a bulk insert by checking the rowgroups again:

```
SELECT OBJECT_NAME(object_id) AS table_name,
  row_group_id, state, state_desc,
  total_rows, deleted_rows
FROM sys.dm_db_column_store_row_group_physical_stats
WHERE object_id = OBJECT_ID(N'dbo.FactTest')
ORDER BY row_group_id;
```

The result shows you that you have only compressed rowgroups:

table_name	row_group_id	state	state_desc	total_rows	deleted_rows
FactTest	0	3	COMPRESSED	1048576	0
FactTest	1	3	COMPRESSED	343592	0
FactTest	2	3	COMPRESSED	444768	0
FactTest	3	3	COMPRESSED	442874	0
FactTest	4	3	COMPRESSED	113990	0

Although all rowgroups are compressed, you will notice that the last rowgroups have less rows than the other rowgroups. It would be more efficient if you could use bulk inserts with more rows, closer to 1,000,000 rows. Now let's try to insert a smaller amount of rows. This time, you can also turn on the graphical execution plan:

```
INSERT INTO dbo.FactTest
(SaleKey, CustomerKey,
 Customer, CityKey, City,
 DateKey, StockItemKey,
 Product, Quantity,
 TotalAmount, Profit)
SELECT 12 * 1000000 + f.[Sale Key] AS SaleKey,
  cu.[Customer Key] AS CustomerKey, cu.Customer,
  ci.[City Key] AS CityKey, ci.City,
  f.[Delivery Date Key] AS DateKey,
```

```
    s.[Stock Item Key] AS StockItemKey, s.[Stock Item] AS Product,
    f.Quantity, f.[Total Excluding Tax] AS TotalAmount, f.Profit
FROM Fact.Sale AS f
  INNER JOIN Dimension.Customer AS cu
    ON f.[Customer Key] = cu.[Customer Key]
  INNER JOIN Dimension.City AS ci
    ON f.[City Key] = ci.[City Key]
  INNER JOIN Dimension.[Stock Item] AS s
    ON f.[Stock Item Key] = s.[Stock Item Key]
  INNER JOIN Dimension.Date AS d
    ON f.[Delivery Date Key] = d.Date
WHERE f.[Sale Key] % 3 = 0;
```

In the plan, you can see that only row mode operators were used. SQL Server does not use batch mode operators for DDL operations. The following screenshot shows a portion of the execution plan, with one `Hash Match` operator highlighted, to show that the row mode processing was used:

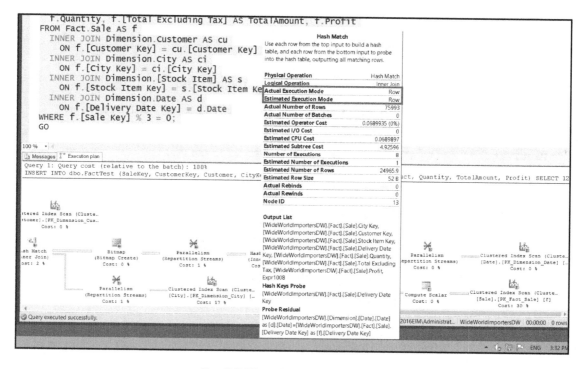

Figure 10.19: DDL operations are processed in row mode

Let's recheck the status of the rowgroups:

```
SELECT OBJECT_NAME(object_id) AS table_name,
  row_group_id, state, state_desc,
  total_rows, deleted_rows
FROM sys.dm_db_column_store_row_group_physical_stats
WHERE object_id = OBJECT_ID(N'dbo.FactTest')
ORDER BY row_group_id;
```

This time, another open rowgroup is in the result:

table_name	row_group_id	state	state_desc	total_rows	deleted_rows
FactTest	0	3	COMPRESSED	1048576	0
FactTest	1	3	COMPRESSED	343592	0
FactTest	2	3	COMPRESSED	444768	0
FactTest	3	3	COMPRESSED	442874	0
FactTest	4	3	COMPRESSED	113990	0
FactTest	5	1	OPEN	75993	0

Let's rebuild the index to get only compressed rowgroups again:

```
ALTER INDEX CCI_FactTest
  ON dbo.FactTest REBUILD;
GO
```

After the rebuild, let's see what happened to the rowgroups.

```
SELECT OBJECT_NAME(object_id) AS table_name,
  row_group_id, state, state_desc,
  total_rows, deleted_rows
FROM sys.dm_db_column_store_row_group_physical_stats
WHERE object_id = OBJECT_ID(N'dbo.FactTest')
ORDER BY row_group_id;
```

The result shows you that you have only compressed rowgroups:

table_name	row_group_id	state	state_desc	total_rows	deleted_rows
FactTest	0	3	COMPRESSED	1048576	0
FactTest	1	3	COMPRESSED	428566	0
FactTest	2	3	COMPRESSED	495276	0
FactTest	3	3	COMPRESSED	497375	0

SQL Server has added the rows from the trickle insert to other rowgroups. Let's now select the rows from the last trickle insert:

```
SELECT *
FROM dbo.FactTest
WHERE SaleKey >= 12000000
ORDER BY SaleKey;
```

Deleting from a clustered columnstore index

Let's test what happens when you delete rows from a CCI with the following `DELETE` command. Before executing the command, you can check the estimated execution plan. Therefore, don't execute the following command yet:

```
DELETE
FROM dbo.FactTest
WHERE SaleKey >= 12000000;
```

The following screenshot shows the execution plan. Again, you can see that the DDL operations use row mode processing operators only:

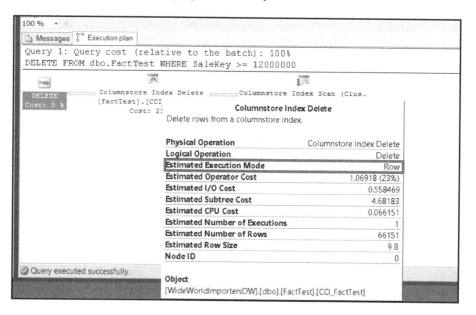

Figure 10-20: Estimated execution plan for a DELETE

And here is the final check of the state of the rowgroups:

```
SELECT OBJECT_NAME(object_id) AS table_name,
 row_group_id, state, state_desc,
 total_rows, deleted_rows
FROM sys.dm_db_column_store_row_group_physical_stats
WHERE object_id = OBJECT_ID(N'dbo.FactTest')
ORDER BY row_group_id;
```

The result shows you that you have only compressed rowgroups:

table_name	row_group_id	state	state_desc	total_rows	deleted_rows
FactTest	0	3	COMPRESSED	1048576	0
FactTest	1	3	COMPRESSED	428566	0
FactTest	2	3	COMPRESSED	495276	0
FactTest	3	3	COMPRESSED	497375	75993

You can see that one of the rowgroups has deleted rows. Although the total number of rows in this rowgroup did not change, you cannot access the deleted rows; the delete bitmap B-tree structure for this rowgroup defines which rows are deleted. You can try to retrieve the deleted rows:

```
SELECT *
FROM dbo.FactTest
WHERE SaleKey >= 12000000
ORDER BY SaleKey;
```

This time, no rows are returned.

Finally, let's clean the WideWorldImporters database with the following code:

```
USE WideWorldImportersDW;
GO
DROP TABLE dbo.FactTest;
GO
```

Before finishing this chapter, the following table summarizes the space needed for different versions of row and columnar storage:

Storage	Rows	Reserved	Data	Index
CI	227,981	49,672 KB	48,528 KB	200 KB
CI row compression	227,981	25,864 KB	24,944 KB	80 KB
CI page compression	227,981	18,888 KB	18,048 KB	80 KB
CI (10 times more rows)	2,279,810	502,152 KB	498,528 KB	2,072 KB
CI with NCCI	2,279,810	529,680 KB	498,528 KB	29,432 KB
CCI	2,279,810	23,560 KB	23,392 KB	0 KB
CCI archive compression	2,279,810	19,528 KB	19,336 KB	0 KB
CCI archive compression and NCI	2,279,810	90,256 KB	19,344 KB	70,192 KB

Summary

Columnar storage brings a completely new set of possibilities in SQL Server. You can get lightning performance of analytical queries right from your data warehouse, without a special analytical database management system. This chapter started by describing features that support analytical queries in SQL Server other that columnar storage. You can use row or page data compression levels, bitmap filtered hash joins, filtered indexes, indexed views, window analytical and aggregate functions, table partitioning, and more. However, columnar storage adds an additional level of compression and performance boost. You learned about the algorithms behind the fantastic compression with columnar storage. This chapter also includes a lot of code, showing you how to create and use the nonclustered and the clustered columnstore indexes, including updating the data, creating constraints, and adding additional B-tree nonclustered indexes.

In the next two chapters, you are going to learn about a completely different way of improving the performance of your databases: memory-optimized tables. In addition, this chapter only started with analytics in SQL Server; the last two chapters introduce R, a whole analytical language supported by SQL Server 2016.

11

Introducing SQL Server In-Memory OLTP

IT systems today are required to deliver maximum performance with zero downtime and maximum flexibility for developers and administrators. As developers, we all know that if the performance of our applications is somehow lacking, then the cause of the slowdown *must* be in the database!

Major causes of performance problems inside database projects can be followed back to database design mistakes or to the limitations built into the database engine to ensure data consistency for concurrent connections, or a mixture of both of these aspects.

Microsoft SQL Server adheres to the ACID theory. A simplified explanation of the ACID theory is that it describes how changes made to a database are required to fulfil four properties: Atomicity, Consistency, Isolation, and Durability:

- **Atomicity** states that the contents of each transaction are either processed successfully and completely or fail in their entirety. "Half-transactions" are not possible.
- **Consistency** states that a transaction brings a database from one valid state to another. This includes the adherence to the logical model inside the database (constraints, rules, triggers, and so on). A transaction may not change a database from a logically valid state to a logically invalid state, for example, performing a data change that violates a unique constraint.
- **Isolation** states that the changes made inside a transaction are isolated from and unaffected by other concurrent operations/transactions.
- **Durability** states that the changes made inside a transaction remain inside the database permanently, even a system goes offline immediately after the transaction has completed.

To adhere to the ACID theory, Microsoft SQL Server employs the pessimistic concurrency model. Pessimistic concurrency assumes there will be conflicting concurrent transactions attempting to change the same data simultaneously. Therefore, transactions must (temporarily) lock the data they are changing to prevent other transactions from interfering with the isolation of those changes.

However, a system with enough concurrent users will eventually reach a logical limitation for transactional throughput through the design of the pessimistic concurrency model. Assuming unlimited hardware resources, the locking of data through pessimistic concurrency will become the bottleneck for transaction processing inside SQL Server.

Microsoft has developed a solution to this logical limitation, by implementing a method for employing the optimistic concurrency model. This model uses row versioning to avoid the need to lock and block data changes between concurrent users. Their implementation was made available in SQL Server 2014 under the code name **Hekaton** (Greek for 100-fold, hinting at the possible performance increases) and the official feature name **In-Memory OLTP**.

This chapter will introduce the In-Memory OLTP feature as it was initially made available in SQL Server 2014. We will discuss the feature's implementation and limitations before the specific additions and improvements in SQL Server 2016 are expanded upon in Chapter 12, *In-Memory OLTP Improvements in SQL Server 2016*.

 For the examples in this chapter, we will be working with SQL Server 2014. Chapter 12, *In-Memory OLTP Improvements in SQL Server 2016* will cover the improvements and enhancements of In-Memory OLTP for SQL Server 2016.

In-Memory OLTP architecture

In-Memory OLTP is the name of the optimistic concurrency model implementation offered from SQL Server 2014 onwards. The challenge that In-Memory OLTP is designed to solve is the ability to process massively concurrent transaction workloads while removing the logical limitations of the pessimistic concurrency model present in the traditional transaction processing engine in SQL Server. Microsoft also wanted to introduce In-Memory OLTP as an *additional* transaction processing engine and *not* as a replacement for the standard transaction processing engine. This decision was made to ensure that existing applications running on SQL Server would be compatible with newer SQL Server versions, but offer the ability to allow newer applications to take advantage of the new engine without separating the two systems.

In this section, we will take a look at the architecture of the In-Memory OLTP engine and see how data is stored and processed.

Row and index storage

The first major difference in In-Memory OLTP is the storage structure of both tables and indexes. The traditional storage engine in SQL Server was optimized for disk storage, especially for the block storage of hard disk subsystems. However, In-Memory OLTP was designed from the ground up to be memory resident, or memory-optimized. This small, but important difference allowed a design with byte storage in mind. This means that memory-optimized tables avoid the needs of data pages and extents that we know from the normal, disk-optimized tables in SQL Server. Through this change, a significant overhead in page and extent management is removed. This reduction in overhead provides a major performance increase in itself.

Row structure

Rows in memory-optimized tables are stored as heaps. These heaps are not to be confused with heaps in the traditional storage engine, but are memory structures storing the row data itself. These rows have no specific physical ordering and no requirement or expectation of being located *near* to other rows in memory. They also have no *knowledge* of connected rows themselves; they are solely created to store row data. The connection of these rows is controlled via the indexes created on memory-optimized tables. Knowing that the index stores and controls the connection of the memory-optimized row data heaps, we can infer that a table must have at least one index. This index (or indexes) must be defined during table creation.

In the introduction to the chapter, we discussed that the In-Memory OLTP system is an implementation of the optimistic concurrency model. This model uses row versioning to allow concurrent connections to change data and still provide the necessary isolation. Row versioning is an important portion of how memory-optimized tables are structured. Let's look at how a row is structured for a memory-optimized table.

In *Figure 11.1*, we can see a depiction of a memory-optimized table, which is split into a row header (information about the row) and payload (the actual row data). The row header structure is expanded in the lower part of the diagram:

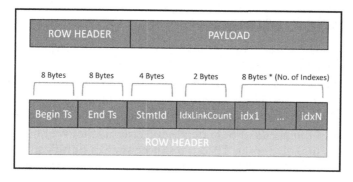

Figure 11.1: Memory-optimized table row structure - Header and Payload

Row header

The row header is split into five sections:

- **Begin Ts**: This is the timestamp of the transaction that inserted the row into the database.

- **End Ts**: This is the timestamp of the transaction that deleted the row from the database. For rows that have not yet been deleted, this field contains the value "infinity".

- **StmtId**: This field stores a unique statement ID corresponding to the statement inside the transaction that created this row.

- **IdxLinkCount**: This field is a counter for the number of indexes that reference this row. An in-memory table stores data only and has no reference to other rows in the table. The indexes that are linked to the table control which rows belong together.

- Finally, we have a set of pointers that reference the indexes connected to this row. The number of pointers stored here corresponds directly to the number of indexes that reference this row.

Row payload

The row payload is where the actual row data is stored. The key columns and all other columns are stored here. The structure of the payload depends upon the columns and data types that make up the table from the CREATE TABLE command.

Index structure

All memory-optimized tables must have at least one index. The indexes on a memory-optimized table store the connections between the rows. It is also important to remember that, as the name suggests, In-Memory OLTP indexes reside inside non-permanent memory (RAM) and are not written to disk. The only portions written to disk are the data rows of the base memory-optimized table and data changes, which are written to the transaction log (which is a requirement to fulfill the Durability part of the ACID concept).

There are two types of index available for memory-optimized tables: non-clustered index and hash index.

Non-clustered Index

To be able to discuss the structure of a non-clustered index itself, we first need to understand how the storage engine creates, references, and processes these indexes. The name of this type of index should be well known to all SQL Server developers. A non-clustered index for a memory-optimized table is widely similar to a non-clustered index in the traditional storage engine. This type of index uses a variation of the B-tree structure called a Bw-tree and is very useful for searching on ranges of data in a memory-optimized table. A Bw-tree is essentially a B-tree structure, without the locking and latching used to maintain a traditional B-tree. The index contains ordered key-values which themselves store pointers to the data rows. With the Bw-tree, these pointers do not point to a physical page number (these data page structures don't exist for memory-optimized tables); the pointers direct to a logical **Page ID (PID)**, which directs to an entry in a Page Mapping Table. This Page Mapping Table stores the physical memory address of the row data. This behavior mimics a covering index from the traditional disk-based non-clustered indexes, containing the columns of the key columns of the index. As mentioned, memory-optimized tables run in optimistic concurrency and use versioning to avoid the need for locks and latches. The memory-optimized non-clustered index never updates a page when a change occurs; updated pages are simply replaced by adding a new page to the index and adding the physical memory address to the Page Mapping Table.

In *Figure 11.2*, we see an example of a memory-optimized non-clustered index:

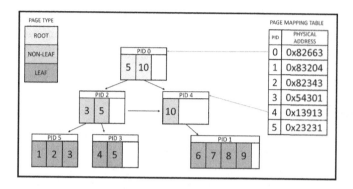

Figure 11.2: Memory-optimized non-clustered index – Bw-tree structure

The Bw-tree looks a lot like a B-tree except that we have a connection with the Page Mapping Table (instead of an Index Allocation Map for disk-based tables), which translates the index to the physical memory location of the row data. The root page and the non-leaf pages store key value information and a PID of the page "below" themselves in the tree. Particularly noteworthy here, is that the key value stored is the highest value on the page on the next level down and not, as with a traditional B-tree, the lowest value. The leaf level also stores the PID to the memory address of the row that the index references. If multiple data rows have the same key, they will be stored as a "chain of rows", where the rows reference the same physical address for the value. Data changes in a memory-optimized non-clustered index are processed through a delta record process. The value that was originally referenced is then no longer referenced by the index and can be physically removed via the **Garbage Collector (GC)**.

A memory-optimized non-clustered index page follows a familiar pattern, with each page having a header which carries uniform control information:

- **PID**: The Page ID pointer which references the Page Mapping Table
- **Page Type**: This indicates the type of the page—leaf, internal, or delta
- **Right PID**: The PID of the page to the right of the current page in the Bw-tree
- **Height**: The distance of the current page to the leaf
- **Page statistics**: The count of records on the page, including the delta records
- **Max Key**: The maximum key value on the page

For pages lower down the Bw-tree structure, that is, internal and leaf, there are additional fields containing more detailed information required for deeper traversal than the root page:

- **Values**: This is an array of pointers that directs to either (for internal pages) the PID of the page on the next level down, or (for leaf pages) the memory location for the first row in a chain of rows with the same key values
- **Keys**: This represents the first value on the page (for internal pages) or the value in a chain of rows (for leaf pages)
- **Offsets**: This stores the key value start offset for indexes with variable length keys

Hash indexes

The second type of index for memory-optimized tables is the hash index. An array of pointers is created, with each element in the array representing a single value—this element is known as a hash bucket. The index key column of a table that should have a hash index created on it has a hashing function applied to it and the resulting hash value is used to "bucketize" rows. Values that generate the same hash value are stored in the same hash bucket as a linked chain of values. To access this data, we pass in the key value we wish to search for; this value is also hashed to determine which hash bucket should be accessed. The hash index translates the hash value to the pointer and allows us to retrieve all the duplicate values in a chain.

In *Figure 11.3*, we can see a very simplified representation of the hashing and retrieval of data. The row header has been removed for clarity's sake.

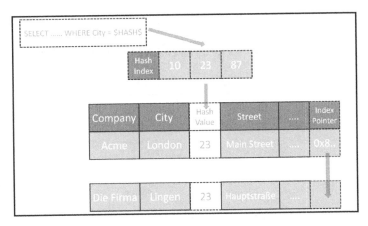

Figure 11.3

In *Figure 11.3*, we can see a table storing company address information. We are interested in the *city* column, which is the key for a hash index. If we were to insert a value of **London** into this hash index, we will get a value **23** (the hash function is simplified here for illustration purposes). This stores the key value **London** and the memory address of the table row of the memory-optimized table. If we then insert the second row with a city value of **Lingen** and our hash function hashes **Lingen** to **23** too, then this will be added to the hash index in the hash bucket for the value **23** and added to the chain started with **London**. Each hash index on a memory-optimized table adds an index pointer column (shown here with a dashed outline). This is an internal column that is used to store the pointer information for the next row in the chain. Every row of a chain has a pointer to the next row, barring the last row, which can have no following chain row. When no pointer is in this column, the retrieval routine knows it has reached the end of the chain and can stop loading rows.

The creation of a hash index requires some thought. We have seen that we can have multiple values that hash to the same hash value, which creates chains of records. However, the idea of a hashing function is to try and keep these chains as short as possible. An optimal hash index will have enough hash buckets to store as many unique values as possible, but has as few buckets as possible to reduce the overhead of maintaining these buckets (more buckets equal more memory consumption for the index). Having more buckets than is necessary will not improve performance either but rather hinder it, as each additional bucket makes a scan of the buckets slower. We must decide how many buckets to create when we initially create the index, which we will see with a sample script shortly. It is also important to realize that the hash index and hashing function consider *all* key columns of an index we create. So a multi-column index raises the chances that hash values will be unique and can require more hash buckets to assist with keeping those buckets emptier.

Creating memory-optimized tables and indexes

Now that we have looked at the theory behind the storage of memory-optimized tables, we want to get to the real fun and create some of these objects.

Laying the foundation

Before we can start creating our memory-optimized objects, we need to create a database with a filegroup designed for memory-optimized objects. This can be achieved as follows:

```
CREATE DATABASE InMemoryTest
    ON
    PRIMARY(NAME = [InMemoryTest_disk],
                FILENAME = 'C:\temp\InMemoryTest_disk.mdf', size=100MB),
    FILEGROUP [InMemoryTest_inmem] CONTAINS MEMORY_OPTIMIZED_DATA
                (NAME = [InMemoryTest_inmem],
                FILENAME = 'C:\temp\InMemoryTest_inmem')
    LOG ON (name = [InMemoryTest_log],
Filename='c:\temp\InMemoryTest_log.ldf', size=100MB)
    COLLATE Latin1_General_100_BIN2;
```

The first main thing to note is that we have a separate filegroup dedicated to the memory-optimized objects, with the keywords CONTAINS MEMORY_OPTIMIZED_DATA. This filegroup is used to persist the memory-optimized objects between server restarts (if required). The filestream APIs are used for this; you can observe which objects are created by navigating to the folder location and accessing the folder (with administrator permissions).

Also of note is that the database has been created with the windows BIN2 collation. This is an initial implementation limitation of In-Memory OLTP with SQL Server 2014 and limited the support for comparisons, grouping and sorting with memory-optimized objects.

It is equally possible to add a filegroup to an existing database using the ALTER DATABASE command, specifying the filegroup and then the location for the filestream folder:

```
ALTER DATABASE AdventureWorks2014
        ADD FILEGROUP InMemTest CONTAINS MEMORY_OPTIMIZED_DATA;
GO
ALTER DATABASE AdventureWorks2014
        ADD FILE (NAME='InMemTest', FILENAME='c:\temp\InMemTest')
    TO FILEGROUP InMemTest;
GO
```

As we can see, Microsoft has tried to keep the integration of the In-Memory OLTP engine as seamless as possible. A simple filegroup addition is all it takes to be able to start creating memory-optimized objects. We are one step closer to a faster database, let's keep going.

Creating a table

Now that we have a filegroup/database that is ready for high-performance workloads, we need to take a moment and consider what limitations there are with the In-Memory OLTP engine.

The following data types are supported:

- All integer types: `tinyint`, `smallint`, `int`, and `bigint`
- All float types: `float` and `real`
- All money types: `smallmoney` and `money`
- Numeric and decimal
- All non-LOB string types: `char(n)`, `varchar(n)`, `nchar(n)`, `nvarchar(n)`, and `sysname`
- Non-LOB binary types: `binary(n)` and `varbinary(n)`
- Date/time types: `smalldatetime`, `datetime`, `date`, `time`, and `datetime2`
- Uniqueidentifier

This leaves out the LOB data types, that is, XML, max types (for example, `varchar(max)`) and CLR types (remembering that this is valid for the initial implementation in SQL Server 2014). This also includes row lengths of more than 8,060 bytes. This limit is generally not recommended, as it will cause issues even in regular tables. However, with memory-optimized tables we cannot even create a table whose row length is more than 8,060 bytes.

Other than the data type limitations, the following restrictions also apply:

- No `FOREIGN KEY` or `CHECK` constraints
- No `UNIQUE` constraints (except for `PRIMARY KEY`)
- No DML Triggers
- A maximum of eight indexes (including the `PRIMARY KEY` index)
- No schema changes after table creation

More specifically to the last restriction, absolutely no DDL commands can be issued on a memory-optimized table: No `ALTER TABLE`, `CREATE INDEX`, `ALTER INDEX`, and `DROP INDEX`. Effectively, once you create a memory-optimized table, it is unchangeable.

So, with the bad news out of the way, let's create our first memory-optimized table. But before we do, we must note that memory-optimized tables cannot be created in system databases (including `tempdb`). If we attempt to do so, we will receive an error message:

```
Msg 41326, Level 16, State 1, Line 43
```

```
Memory optimized tables cannot be created in system databases.
```

The following code will therefore change the connection into the previously created
InMemoryTest database and then create a test memory-optimized table:

```
USE InMemoryTest
GO
CREATE TABLE InMemoryTable
(
    UserId INT NOT NULL PRIMARY KEY NONCLUSTERED,
    UserName VARCHAR(255) NOT NULL,
    LoginTime DATETIME2 NOT NULL,
    LoginCount INT NOT NULL,
CONSTRAINT PK_UserId PRIMARY KEY NONCLUSTERED (UserId),  INDEX NCL_IDX HASH
(UserName) WITH (BUCKET_COUNT=10000)
) WITH (MEMORY_OPTIMIZED = ON, DURABILITY=SCHEMA_AND_DATA)
GO
```

Let us consider a few of the lines of code above. Firstly, the table creation command
resembles that of many other tables that can be created in SQL Server. We are not
confronted with anything unfamiliar. Only in the last two lines of code do we notice
anything peculiar. We have the previously mentioned hash index, with a bucket count of
10000 on the UserName column. The last line of code has two new keywords:
MEMORY_OPTIMIZED=ON is simple enough. We are informing SQL Server that this table
should be created as a memory-optimized table. However, the DURABILITY keyword is
something that we have only tangentially mentioned so far.

The durability options available to us are either SCHEMA_AND_DATA or SCHEMA_ONLY. These
keyword options are clear enough to understand. Either the schema *and* the data will be
recovered after a server restart, or only the schema. With SCHEMA_ONLY, we have the ability
to completely bypass writing data changes to the transaction log, because our memory-
optimized table has no requirements in terms of data recovery. This has a major positive
performance impact if the data in a SCHEMA_ONLY table meets those requirements of not
needing recovery.

After making our decisions about columns, indexes, and the durability of our table, we
issue the CREATE TABLE command. At this point, SQL Server receives the command and
generates the table as a memory-optimized object. This results in a compiled DLL being
created for the memory-optimized table including the compiled access methods for the
memory-resident object. This compilation process is the main factor in the limitations listed
previously, especially the reason for alterations of the table and indexes *after* creation.

Querying and data manipulation

Now that we have a memory-optimized table, the next logical step is to start querying the table and manipulating the data stored inside it.

We have two methods of interacting with these memory-optimized objects. Firstly, we can issue standard T-SQL queries and allow the SQL Server Query Optimizer to deal with accessing this new type of table. The second method is to use Natively Compiled Stored Procedures.

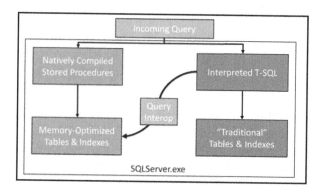

Figure 11.4: Overview of the SQL Server engine illustrating Query Interop between In-Memory OLTP and "normal" OLTP

In *Figure 11.4*, we can see a simplified diagram of a query that is either querying "normal" tables or memory-optimized tables. In the center of the diagram is a node titled **Query Interop**. This is a mechanism that is responsible for enabling "normal" interpreted T-SQL statements to access memory optimized tables. Note that this is a one-way mechanism and that the natively compiled stored procedures are *not* able to access traditional objects, only memory-optimized objects.

Back to querying memory-optimized tables!

```
SELECT *
FROM dbo.InMemoryTable;
```

The above select statement is standard T-SQL and has no special syntax to query the memory-optimized table we created earlier. At this point, we are unaware that this table is a memory-optimized table and that is a good thing. This is further proof of Microsoft's commitment to integrating this high-performance feature as a seamless extension of the storage engine. Essentially, it should not be of major interest whether we are using In-Memory OLTP or the traditional storage engine for our table—it should just be fast. We could even extrapolate that in the future, it may be possible that the entire SQL Server storage engine becomes purely memory-optimized.

If we can select data without any syntax changes, then we can expect that inserting data is equally simple:

```
INSERT INTO dbo.InMemoryTable
        ( UserId ,
          UserName ,
          LoginTime ,
          LoginCount
        )
VALUES  ( 1 ,
          'John Smith' ,
          SYSDATETIME() ,
          1
        )
;
SELECT *
FROM dbo.InMemoryTable
;
```

Of course, this insert works flawlessly and the final select returns a single row:

UserId	UserName	LoginTime	LoginCount
1	John Smith	2016-12-09 20:27:04.3424133	1

The important thing to realize here is that we are using "normal" T-SQL. This may sound rather uninteresting; however, this means that if we want to start migrating some of our tables to be memory-optimized, then we are free to do so without needing to refactor our code (provided we adhere to the limitations of the engine). This makes the possibilities of using this feature much more attractive, especially in legacy projects where logical design limitations lead to locking and latching issues.

Due to the way that this interoperability works and the lock-free nature of memory-optimized tables, there are some further limitations with the T-SQL language and querying itself that we need to consider. Luckily, the large majority of T-SQL language features are available to us, so the list of unsupported commands is mercifully short:

- The MERGE statement when a memory-optimized table is the target of the MERGE
- Dynamic cursors (to adhere to memory-optimized rules, these are automatically changed to static cursors)
- TRUNCATE TABLE
- Cross-database transactions
- Cross-database queries
- Linked Servers

- Locking hints: XLOCK, TABLOCK, PAGLOCK, and so on
- READUNCOMMITTED, READCOMMITTED, and READCOMMITTEDLOCK isolation level hints

If we consider how each of these unsupported features work, it becomes clear that these limitations exist. Many, if not all, of these limitations are linked to how locking and latching is controlled in one way or another with those features. The only way to continue our high-performance adventure is to accept these limitations and adjust our system design accordingly.

There is a similar list of limitations for natively compiled stored procedures. This list is unfortunately quite long, and if we look back at Figure 4 with the diagram of the SQL Server engine, we see that natively compiled stored procedures are only able to access memory-optimized tables and *not* the traditional storage engine objects. This main limitation causes the list of unsupported features to be quite a lot longer. You can find an exhaustive list of which features are supported and which aren't by visiting Microsoft's Books Online site and reading the list. You will also be able to change the documentation website to a different version of SQL Server to see that newer versions support an increasing number of features inside the In-Memory OLTP engine. For more details, visit https://msdn.microsoft.com/en-us/library/dn246937(v=sql.120).aspx#Anchor_4.

Performance comparisons

We have seen the lists of limitations at both the table structure level and at the T-SQL language level. It is not all doom and gloom, but these restrictions may cause some readers to re-think their enthusiasm for memory-optimized objects.

In this section, we will take a look at how traditional disk-based tables compare to their younger brothers, memory-optimized tables. According to the codename of the In-Memory OLTP feature, *Hekaton (Greek for 100-fold)*, the new feature should be in the order of one hundred times faster.

We begin our test by creating a comparable disk-based table and inserting one row into it:

```
USE InMemoryTest
GO
CREATE TABLE DiskBasedTable
(
    UserId INT NOT NULL PRIMARY KEY NONCLUSTERED,
    UserName VARCHAR(255) NOT NULL,
    LoginTime DATETIME2 NOT NULL,
    LoginCount INT NOT NULL,
```

```
        INDEX NCL_IDX NONCLUSTERED (UserName)
)
GO
INSERT INTO dbo.DiskBasedTable
         ( UserId ,
           UserName ,
           LoginTime ,
           LoginCount
         )
VALUES   ( 1 ,
           'John Smith' ,
           SYSDATETIME() ,
           1
         )
  ;
```

We have an identical table structure, with the only difference being that the disk based table doesn't have a hash index but rather a normal non-clustered index.

We will now run a test, inserting 500,000 rows of data into each table and measuring solely the execution time of each run. We begin by creating a stored procedure that will insert one row into the disk based table:

```
CREATE PROCEDURE dbo.DiskBasedInsert
    @UserId INT,
    @UserName VARCHAR(255),
    @LoginTime DATETIME2,
    @LoginCount INT
AS
BEGIN

    INSERT dbo.DiskBasedTable
    (UserId, UserName, LoginTime, LoginCount)
    VALUES
    (@UserId, @UserName, @LoginTime, @LoginCount);

END;
```

This stored procedure is then called 500,000 times in a simple loop and the time difference between start and finish is recorded:

```
USE InMemoryTest
GO
TRUNCATE TABLE dbo.DiskBasedTable
GO

DECLARE @start DATETIME2;
SET @start = SYSDATETIME();
```

```
DECLARE @Counter int = 0,
        @_LoginTime DATETIME2 = SYSDATETIME(),
        @_UserName VARCHAR(255);
    WHILE @Counter < 50000
    BEGIN
        SET @_UserName = 'UserName ' + CAST(@Counter AS varchar(6))

        EXECUTE dbo.DiskBasedInsert
            @UserId = @Counter,
            @UserName = @_UserName,
            @LoginTime = @_LoginTime,
            @LoginCount = @Counter
        SET @Counter += 1;
    END;

SELECT DATEDIFF(ms, @start, SYSDATETIME()) AS 'insert into disk-based table
(in ms)';
GO

insert into disk-based table (in ms)
----------- -------------- ------------------------------- ------------
6230
```

The execution on my machine was repeatable with an average execution time of between 6 and 7 seconds for 50,000 rows with a disk-based table.

The first step of optimizing this insert is to move from a disk-based table to a memory-optimized table:

```
USE InMemoryTest
GO
SET NOCOUNT ON
GO
CREATE PROCEDURE dbo.InMemoryInsert
    @UserId INT,
    @UserName VARCHAR(255),
    @LoginTime DATETIME2,
    @LoginCount INT
AS
BEGIN

    INSERT dbo.InMemoryTable
    (UserId, UserName, LoginTime, LoginCount)
    VALUES
    (@UserId, @UserName, @LoginTime, @LoginCount);

END;
GO
```

```
USE InMemoryTest
GO
DELETE FROM dbo.InMemoryTable
GO


DECLARE @start DATETIME2;
SET @start = SYSDATETIME();

DECLARE @Counter int = 0,
        @_LoginTime DATETIME2 = SYSDATETIME(),
        @_UserName VARCHAR(255);
   WHILE @Counter < 50000
   BEGIN
        SET @_UserName = 'UserName ' + CAST(@Counter AS varchar(6))

        EXECUTE dbo.InMemoryInsert
             @UserId = @Counter,
             @UserName = @_UserName,
             @LoginTime = @_LoginTime,
             @LoginCount = @Counter
        SET @Counter += 1;
   END;

SELECT DATEDIFF(ms, @start, SYSDATETIME()) AS 'insert into memory-optimized
table (in ms)';
GO

insert into memory-optimized table (in ms)
----------- -------------- -------------------------- -----------
1399
```

Okay. We have made a massive leap in terms of execution time. We are down from ~6 seconds to a quite respectable ~1.4 seconds. That improvement is purely down to the difference in the locking and latching of our two tables. We swapped the disk-based table for a memory-optimized table.

Natively compiled stored procedures

When we issue T-SQL commands to SQL Server, the commands are parsed and compiled into machine code, which is then executed. This parsing and compiling becomes a major bottleneck when the locking and latching caused by pessimistic concurrency is removed. This is where natively compiled stored procedures come into play. They are effectively T-SQL code that is compiled into machine code once, and then instead of the parse and compile of a standard T-SQL command, the compiled DLL for the stored procedure is called. The improvements in execution time can be phenomenal.

Our next possibility for improvement is to reduce our parse and compile time of the insert command (the Query Interop mentioned earlier in this chapter). This can be achieved by natively compiling the insert stored procedure. Let's do just that, and run the same test with our memory-optimized table also using a natively compiled stored procedure:

```
USE InMemoryTest
GO
CREATE PROCEDURE dbo.InMemoryInsertOptimized
    @UserId INT,
    @UserName VARCHAR(255),
    @LoginTime DATETIME2,
    @LoginCount INT
WITH NATIVE_COMPILATION, SCHEMABINDING
AS
BEGIN ATOMIC WITH
(
    TRANSACTION ISOLATION LEVEL = SNAPSHOT,
    LANGUAGE = N'English'
)

    INSERT dbo.InMemoryTable
    (UserId, UserName, LoginTime, LoginCount)
     VALUES
     (@UserId, @UserName, @LoginTime, @LoginCount);
    RETURN 0;
END;
GO


USE InMemoryTest
GO
DELETE FROM dbo.InMemoryTable
GO

DECLARE @start DATETIME2;
SET @start = SYSDATETIME();
```

```
DECLARE @Counter int = 0,
        @_LoginTime DATETIME2 = SYSDATETIME(),
        @_UserName VARCHAR(255);
    WHILE @Counter < 50000
    BEGIN
        SET @_UserName = 'UserName ' + CAST(@Counter AS varchar(6))

        EXECUTE dbo.InMemoryInsertOptimized
            @UserId = @Counter,
            @UserName = @_UserName,
            @LoginTime = @_LoginTime,
            @LoginCount = @Counter
        SET @Counter += 1;
    END;

SELECT DATEDIFF(ms, @start, SYSDATETIME()) AS 'insert into memory-optimized
table & native stored procedure (in ms)';
GO
```

```
insert into memory-optimized table & native stored procedure (in ms)
----------- -------------- ---------------------------- -----------
631
```

We can see from the results that the execution time has been reduced from ~1.4 seconds down to ~600 milliseconds. This is an impressive improvement, considering we have again only made minimal changes.

However, there is *still* room for improvement here. At present, we have created a native compiled stored procedure, which allows us to save on compile time for the insert statement itself. With this solution, we are still using non-compiled T-SQL for the loop. This optimization is easily achieved and we can run the final test to see how fast we can get:

```
USE InMemoryTest
GOCREATE PROCEDURE dbo.FullyNativeInMemoryInsertOptimized
WITH NATIVE_COMPILATION, SCHEMABINDING
AS
BEGIN ATOMIC WITH
(
    TRANSACTION ISOLATION LEVEL = SNAPSHOT,
    LANGUAGE = N'English'
)

    DECLARE @Counter int = 0,
    @_LoginTime DATETIME2 = SYSDATETIME(),
    @_UserName VARCHAR(255)
    ;
    WHILE @Counter < 50000
```

```
    BEGIN
                SET  @_UserName = 'UserName ' + CAST(@Counter AS varchar(6))

                INSERT dbo.InMemoryTable
                (UserId, UserName, LoginTime, LoginCount)
                VALUES
                (@Counter, @_UserName, @_LoginTime, @Counter);

        SET @Counter += 1;
    END;
    RETURN 0;
END;
GO


USE InMemoryTest
GO
DELETE FROM dbo.InMemoryTable
GO


DECLARE @start DATETIME2;
SET @start = SYSDATETIME();

EXEC dbo.FullyNativeInMemoryInsertOptimized

SELECT DATEDIFF(ms, @start, SYSDATETIME()) AS 'insert into fully native
memory-optimized table (in ms)';
GO
```

insert into fully native memory-optimized table (in ms)
```
----------- -------------- ---------------------------- -----------
155
```

With a fully optimized workflow, taking advantage of both memory-optimized tables as well as natively compiled stored procedures, the execution time has dropped from 6.2 seconds to 155 milliseconds. With just a few simple steps, the execution time of the example insert has been reduced by 40 times; while not quite the 100-fold improvement that the codename suggests, this is a serious improvement by any measure.

Looking behind the curtain of concurrency

So far, we have seen that we can easily create a table with indexes, query and insert data into that table and do so with our traditional T-SQL knowledge. It is now also clear that we are able to change an existing implementation of disk-based tables into memory-optimized tables with some simple changes. If we want to push performance to the max, we can also consider natively compiled stored procedures to further improve upon some quite large performance gains. We have also seen how the two types of index: hash index and non-clustered index are implemented in the storage engine. However, to better understand how the magic happens, we need to have a closer look at what is happening to our sample table and indexes while we are manipulating them.

We already mentioned at the beginning of this chapter that SQL Server uses a pessimistic concurrency model in the disk-based storage engine and an optimistic concurrency model for memory-optimized objects. The implementation of this optimistic concurrency model is achieved via **multi-version concurrency control** (**MVCC**), or to describe it another way, snapshotting the data. MVCC is not a new technology; it has been around in one form or another since the early 1980s and has been an optional isolation level in SQL Server since SQL Server 2005 (READ COMMITTED SNAPSHOT). This technology has been repurposed in the In-Memory OLTP engine to allow for lock and latch-free optimistic concurrency. Read-committed snapshot isolation level provides row-versioning for disk-based tables by redirecting write operations into the row-version store inside `tempdb`. However, In-Memory OLTP works entirely inside memory and cannot push row-versions into `tempdb`.

If we take a look at our row header from the beginning of the chapter again, we can investigate the two fields—**Begin Ts** and **End Ts**:

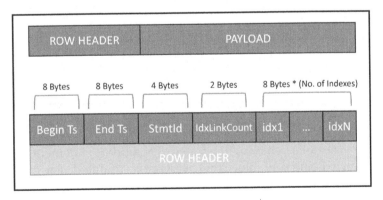

Figure 11.5: Memory-optimized table row structure – Header and Payload

When a row is inserted, the **Begin Ts** timestamp is filled. This timestamp is constructed from two pieces of information: A transaction ID, which is a globally unique value on the instance. This value increments whenever a transaction starts on the instance and is reset when the server restarts. The second portion of this generated timestamp is created from the Global Transaction Timestamp. This is equally unique across the instance, but is *not* reset at server restart and increments whenever a transaction completes.

In order to avoid the requirements of locking records to update them, memory-optimized tables only ever add new records to a table. Whenever an insert occurs (the simplest change operation), a new row is added to a table, with a **Begin Ts** at the transaction start time. The **End Ts** is left empty, allowing SQL Server to know that this row exists inside the database from the **Begin Ts** and is valid until **End Ts** (or in the case of the row not being deleted it is valid until "infinite").

The interesting changes occur when we wish to update or delete an existing row. To avoid having to lock the row and perform a delete (for a pure delete) or a delete and insert (for an update), a memory-optimized table will simply insert the "updated" version of the row with a **Begin Ts** of the transaction timestamp and insert the same timestamp in the **End Ts** of the newly "deleted" row.

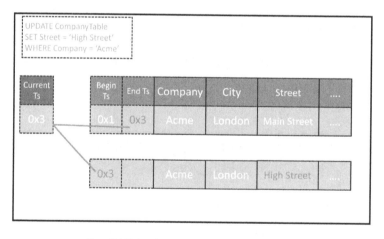

Figure 11.5: Update of a memory-optimized table – row versioning

In *Figure 11.5*, we can see this behavior illustrated. The update statement in the top-left corner shows that an existing row (blue row) needs to be updated. The concurrency model then creates a new copy of the row (green) while noting the current transaction timestamp (orange). At this point, we have a new row which is valid from timestamp **0x3** and an old row that was valid from timestamp **0x1** until **0x3**. Any transaction that started at timestamp **0x2** would see the original row (blue), while any transaction from **0x3** onwards would see the new row (green).

As you may realize, the action of continually appending new versions of a row will cause this linked list of row-versions to grow over time. This is where the **Garbage Collector** (**GC**) comes into play. The GC is a background process which periodically traverses the tables, indexes in the In-Memory storage engine, and removes the old and invalidated rows. In order to further accelerate this clean-up process, user processes also assist with identifying entries that can be cleaned up. When a user process scans across a table or index which has stale row-version data, it will remove their links from the row chains as it passes them.

As with many features inside SQL Server, we can gain insight into the inner workings of this row-version mechanism using **Dynamic Management Objects** (**DMOs**).

To take a look at the table we created above and to see the row version information, we query sys.dm_db_xtp_index_stats joining to sys.indexes to retrieve the corresponding object information:

```
SELECT i.name AS 'index_name',
    s.rows_returned,
    s.rows_expired,
    s.rows_expired_removed
FROM sys.dm_db_xtp_index_stats s
    JOIN sys.indexes i
        ON s.object_id = i.object_id
            AND s.index_id = i.index_id
WHERE OBJECT_ID('InMemoryTable') = s.object_id;
GO
```

index_name	rows_returned	rows_expired	rows_expired_removed
NULL	594115	0	0
NCL_IDX	0	0	0
PK_UserId	0	649901	399368

Here, after our data wrangling using different methods, we can see that the table has had rows added and also "expired" (detected as stale) or "expired removed" (how many rows have been unlinked from the index).

Data durability concerns

Now that we have a better understanding of how data moves inside a memory-optimized table, we need to also dive a little deeper into the durability of memory-optimized tables. Earlier in the chapter, we saw that we can choose between SCHEMA_AND_DATA or SCHEMA_ONLY for durability of these objects. The succinct description for SCHEMA_ONLY durability is that any data (or changes) inside a memory-optimized table that has SCHEMA_ONLY durability will be lost when the server restarts. The reason for the server restart is irrelevant; when the server is brought back online, the table (and any associated indexes) is recreated and will be empty.

The SCHEMA_AND_DATA option informs SQL Server that you wish the data inside the memory-optimized table to be permanently stored on non-volatile storage. This will ensure that the data is available even after a server restart. This initially sounds like it would be a problem for a high-performance data processing system, especially when we consider the speed differences between mass storage (HDDs/SSDs) versus main system memory (DIMMs). However, the type and amount of data required to be stored on durable storage is kept to a minimum, so that the chances of a bottleneck in making the data durable are greatly reduced.

The data that gets written to disk contains only the data that has changed, only the row data of the memory-optimized table, and *not* the index data. Only the index definitions are stored durably, the index content is recreated every time the server is restarted. This recreation is rapid, because SQL Server can create the index based on the data that is already in main memory, which is extremely low latency and high throughput.

There are two streams of data processed and written to disk: *checkpoint streams* and *log streams*.

A checkpoint stream is itself split into two files known as **checkpoint file pairs** (**CFPs**). These CFPs utilize the filestream API which we addressed when creating our test In-Memory OLTP database. The two file types in this file pair are *data streams* (containing all row versions inserted in a timestamp interval) and *delta streams* (containing a list of deleted row versions matching the data stream file pair).

The *log streams* contain the changes made by committed transactions, and like normal transactions, they are stored in the SQL Server transaction log. This allows SQL Server to use the entries in the transaction log to reconstruct information during the redo phase of crash recovery.

We can investigate the behavior of durability by running our insert stored procedures for the disk-based table and then our SCHEMA_ONLY memory-optimized table. After running each stored procedure, we can investigate the contents of the transaction log using the undocumented and unsupported (but on a test machine perfectly usable) fn_dblog() to view how these two processes affect the transaction log.

	Current LSN	Operation	Context	Transaction ID	Log Record Fixed Length	Log Record Length	Previous LSN	Flag Bits	Log Reserve	AllocUnitId	AllocUnitName
1	00000058:00001a35:0005	LOP_COMMIT_XACT	LCX_NULL	0000:002700d3	80	84	00000058:00001a35:0001	0x0002	90	NULL	NULL
2	00000058:00001a35:0004	LOP_INSERT_ROWS	LCX_INDEX_LEAF	0000:002700d3	62	116	00000058:00001a35:0003	0x0002	74	72057594048544768	dbo.DiskBasedTable.PK_
3	00000058:00001a35:0003	LOP_INSERT_ROWS	LCX_INDEX_LEAF	0000:002700d3	62	128	00000058:00001a35:0002	0x0002	74	72057594048479232	dbo.DiskBasedTable.NCL
4	00000058:00001a35:0002	LOP_INSERT_ROWS	LCX_HEAP	0000:002700d3	62	132	00000058:00001a35:0001	0x0002	178	72057594048413696	dbo.DiskBasedTable
5	00000058:00001a35:0001	LOP_BEGIN_XACT	LCX_NULL	0000:002700d3	76	124	00000000:00000000:0000	0x0002	9436	NULL	NULL
6	00000058:00001a33:0005	LOP_COMMIT_XACT	LCX_NULL	0000:002700d2	80	84	00000058:00001a33:0001	0x0002	90	NULL	NULL
7	00000058:00001a33:0004	LOP_INSERT_ROWS	LCX_INDEX_LEAF	0000:002700d2	62	116	00000058:00001a33:0003	0x0002	74	72057594048544768	dbo.DiskBasedTable.PK_
8	00000058:00001a33:0003	LOP_INSERT_ROWS	LCX_INDEX_LEAF	0000:002700d2	62	128	00000058:00001a33:0002	0x0002	74	72057594048479232	dbo.DiskBasedTable.NCL
9	00000058:00001a33:0002	LOP_INSERT_ROWS	LCX_HEAP	0000:002700d2	62	132	00000058:00001a33:0001	0x0002	178	72057594048413696	dbo.DiskBasedTable
10	00000058:00001a33:0001	LOP_BEGIN_XACT	LCX_NULL	0000:002700d2	76	124	00000000:00000000:0000	0x0002	9436	NULL	NULL
11	00000058:00001a31:0005	LOP_COMMIT_XACT	LCX_NULL	0000:002700d1	80	84	00000058:00001a31:0001	0x0002	90	NULL	NULL
12	00000058:00001a31:0004	LOP_INSERT_ROWS	LCX_INDEX_LEAF	0000:002700d1	62	116	00000058:00001a31:0003	0x0002	74	72057594048544768	dbo.DiskBasedTable.PK_
13	00000058:00001a31:0003	LOP_INSERT_ROWS	LCX_INDEX_LEAF	0000:002700d1	62	128	00000058:00001a31:0002	0x0002	74	72057594048479232	dbo.DiskBasedTable.NCL
14	00000058:00001a31:0002	LOP_INSERT_ROWS	LCX_HEAP	0000:002700d1	62	132	00000058:00001a31:0001	0x0002	178	72057594048413696	dbo.DiskBasedTable
15	00000058:00001a31:0001	LOP_BEGIN_XACT	LCX_NULL	0000:002700d1	76	124	00000000:00000000:0000	0x0002	9436	NULL	NULL
16	00000058:00001a2f:0005	LOP_COMMIT_XACT	LCX_NULL	0000:002700d0	80	84	00000058:00001a2f:0001	0x0002	90	NULL	NULL
17	00000058:00001a2f:0004	LOP_INSERT_ROWS	LCX_INDEX_LEAF	0000:002700d0	62	116	00000058:00001a2f:0003	0x0002	74	72057594048544768	dbo.DiskBasedTable.PK_

Figure 11.6: fn_dblog() output after disk-based insert run

	Current LSN	Operation	Context	Transaction ID	Log Record Fixed Length	Log Record Length	Previous LSN	Flag Bits	Log Reserve	AllocUnitId	AllocUnitName
1	00000058:00001a4f:0002	LOP_HK	LCX_NULL	0000:00000000	28	152	00000000:00000000:0000	0x0000	0	NULL	NULL
2	00000058:00001a4f:0001	LOP_HK	LCX_NULL	0000:00000000	28	88	00000000:00000000:0000	0x0000	0	NULL	NULL
3	00000058:00001a4e:0001	LOP_END_CKPT	LCX_NULL	0000:00000000	136	136	00000058:00001a4c:0001	0x0000	0	NULL	NULL
4	00000058:00001a4d:0001	LOP_XACT_CKPT	LCX_BOOT_PAGE_CKPT	0000:00000000	24	28	00000000:00000000:0000	0x0000	0	NULL	NULL
5	00000058:00001a4c:0001	LOP_BEGIN_CKPT	LCX_NULL	0000:00000000	96	96	00000058:00001a37:002c	0x0000	0	NULL	NULL
6	00000058:00001a4b:0002	LOP_HK	LCX_NULL	0000:00000000	28	152	00000000:00000000:0000	0x0000	0	NULL	NULL

Figure 11.7

In figures 11.6 and 11.77, we see a snapshot of the data retrieved immediately after running first the disk-based insert (*Figure 11.6*) and the memory-optimized insert (*Figure 11.7*).

The disk-based insert created thousands of log record entries for each iteration of the loop; this takes time to process and inflates the transaction log unnecessarily. The memory-optimized insert causes zero entries in the transaction log, because the table was defined as SCHEMA_ONLY and as such has no requirement for log redo or crash recovery. The schema will be loaded at server startup and is immediately ready for normal operations.

We can now take a look at our filestream folder, where the checkpoint stream is directed. We will find multiple checkpoint files in this folder, Each checkpoint file will contain either data or delta streams, as described earlier in this section of the chapter. The checkpoint files are created and filled with an append-only mechanism, adding data to the end of the file. A single checkpoint file pair will continue to be used until either a manual CHECKPOINT command is used, or 512 MB of transaction information has accumulated since the last automatic checkpoint.

When this occurs, the checkpoint process generates a checkpoint file inventory of multiple data and delta files; this inventory file catalogues the data and delta files and writes this information to the transaction log. These files are used in a recovery scenario to be able to reconstruct data for the SCHEMA_AND_DATA defined memory-optimized tables.

> This PC > OS (C:) > Temp > InMemoryTest_inmem > $HKv2		
Name	Type	Size
{659C3B5A-93DD-4036-B9CB-198916371D65}.hckckp	HKCKP File	65,536 KB
{45078208-9E87-46E1-844C-ABE566F1B42E}.hckckp	HKCKP File	65,536 KB
{BB5D2943-DED2-474A-9B27-8F891BDA9B56}.hckckp	HKCKP File	65,536 KB
{BCBB7428-00DE-4E07-921C-64EC96557BDB}.hckckp	HKCKP File	16,384 KB
{23EB0035-BF08-43D8-8A64-853A385045A9}.hckckp	HKCKP File	16,384 KB
{025CFA00-4A01-43E1-8E8F-B84228B081C5}.hckckp	HKCKP File	131,072 KB
{EE7C6290-8A4D-4E1E-96E1-28E3A0FE8E1F}.hckckp	HKCKP File	16,384 KB
{4B3A1792-7CDB-4CBD-AC02-EC31E23DC8BF}.hckckp	HKCKP File	131,072 KB
{717E9794-AECB-48C8-B8E1-137C5370F0F8}.hckckp	HKCKP File	131,072 KB
{B7BBE7E7-3D17-4C6F-8CEE-F5502FAE2171}.hckckp	HKCKP File	8,192 KB
{B823B4A2-D634-4977-ACD9-63E14806CE89}.hckckp	HKCKP File	8,192 KB

Figure 11.8: Filestream folder used for storing memory-optimized checkpoint file pairs

Database startup and recovery

Recovery of memory-optimized tables is performed in an optimized manner compared to disk-based tables.

The In-Memory OLTP engine gathers information on which checkpoints are currently valid and their locations. Each checkpoint file pair (delta and data) is identified and the delta file is used to filter out rows from the data file (deleted data doesn't need to be recovered). The In-Memory OLTP engine creates one recovery thread per CPU core, allowing for parallel recovery of memory-optimized tables. These recovery threads load the data from the data and delta files, creating the schema and all indexes. Once the checkpoint files have been processed, the tail of the transaction log is replayed from the timestamp of the latest valid checkpoint.

The ability to process recovery in parallel is a huge performance gain and allows objects that are memory-optimized to be recovered in a much shorter time than if only serial recovery was available.

Management of in-memory objects

Managing memory-optimized tables is similar to disk-based tables. SQL Server Management Studio provides full syntax and GUI support for memory-optimized tables. There is a long list of **Dynamic Management Objects (DMOs)** that provide detailed insights into each aspect of the feature, but the legacy management objects such as `sys.tables` or `sys.indexes` have also received some updates to include pertinent memory-optimized information.

Dynamic management objects

The DMOs concerned with the In-Memory OLTP engine all have **XTP (eXtreme Transaction Processing)** in their name:

- `sys.dm_db_xtp_checkpoint`
- `sys.dm_db_xtp_checkpoint_files`
- `sys.dm_db_xtp_gc_cycles_stats`
- `sys.dm_xtp_gc_stats`
- `sys.dm_xtp_system_memory_consumers`
- `sys.dm_xtp_threads`
- `sys.dm_xtp_transaction_stats`
- `sys.dm_db_xtp_index_stats`
- `sys.dm_db_xtp_memory_consumers`
- `sys.dm_db_xtp_object_stats`
- `sys.dm_db_xtp_transactions`
- `sys.dm_db_xtp_table_memory_stats`

Full details of the columns and meanings for each DMO can be found in Microsoft Books Online (`https://msdn.microsoft.com/library/dn133203(SQL.130).aspx`).

Extended Events

As with all new features inside SQL Server, In-Memory OLTP also provides Extended Events session details. There is an extensive set of events that can be captured by Extended Events. Using the Extended Events Wizard will allow you to easily choose which events you wish to collect. Extended Events is the preferred method for collecting internal system information on any feature of SQL Server (where possible). Extended Events is a lightweight collection framework that allows you to collect system runtime statistics while keeping resource usage to a minimum.

A T-SQL query to return a list of the Extended Events that are available for the In-Memory OLTP engine would be:

```
SELECT p.name,
    o.name,
    o.description
FROM sys.dm_xe_objects o
    JOIN sys.dm_xe_packages p
        ON o.package_guid = p.guid
WHERE p.name = 'XtpEngine';
```

Perfmon counters

SQL Server also provides perfmon counters for the In-Memory OLTP engine. However, perfmon is a much older technology than Extended Events and has certain limitations that prevent it from exposing all the details that Extended Events can. Be as it may, it is still possible to collect certain information on the In-Memory OLTP engine.

A T-SQL query to return a list of the perfmon counters that are available for the In-Memory OLTP engine would be:

```
SELECT object_name,
    counter_name
FROM sys.dm_os_performance_counters
WHERE object_name LIKE '%XTP%';
```

Assistance in migrating to In-memory OLTP

Now that we have explored the possibilities that memory-optimized tables offer, it would be fantastic to be able to somehow evaluate our existing databases. Ideally, this evaluation would show how many tables or stored procedures could potentially be converted from traditional disk-based objects into ultra-fast memory-optimized objects.

Luckily for us, Microsoft has also provided us with some help here. Inside SQL Server Management Studio are two interesting standard reports that help us to analyze our databases and see how we can benefit from memory-optimized objects.

The first report is the **Transaction Performance Analysis Overview**. This report allows us to quickly identify possible candidates for a move from disk-based to memory-optimized. We can reach this report by navigating through SQL Server Management Studio, as shown in *Figure 11.9*:

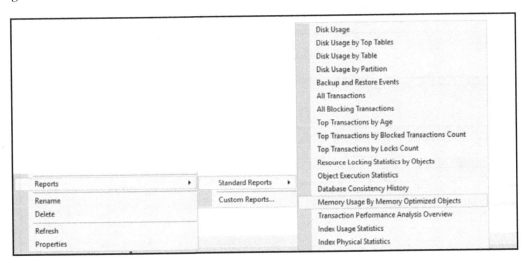

Figure 11.9: Transaction Performance Analysis Overview Report in SQL Server Management Studio

Once we select the standard report **Transaction Performance Analysis Overview**, we are greeted with a start page asking if we want to evaluate tables or stored procedures. Our example queries are focused on tables, so choosing **Tables Analysis** will give us a little sample data for illustration purposes:

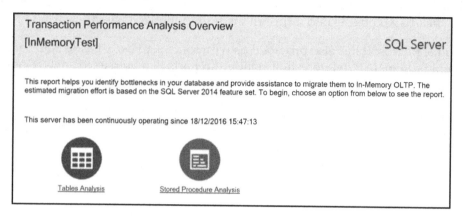

Figure 11.10: Transaction Performance Analysis Overview Report

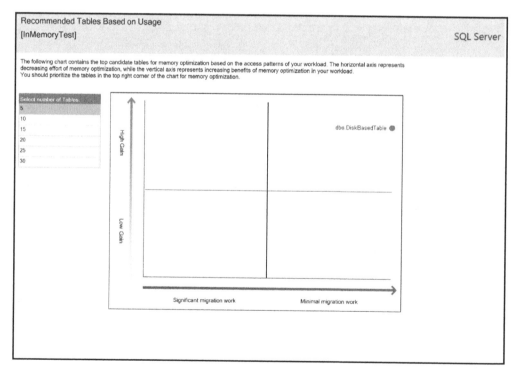

Figure 11.11

A click on **Tables Analysis** brings up a detailed report of all tables in the database that are eligible candidates for a migration to memory-optimized tables.

As the report states, eligible candidate tables are shown on this report. An entry higher up and further to the right of the table means a higher recommendation for conversion to a memory-optimized table. Based on our sample queries, it should be no surprise that the table called `DiskBasedTable` is an ideal candidate for memory-optimized storage. The data types are perfect, the behavior of the data movement is ideal. There is pretty much no reason at this point to *not* migrate this table to the In-Memory OLTP engine.

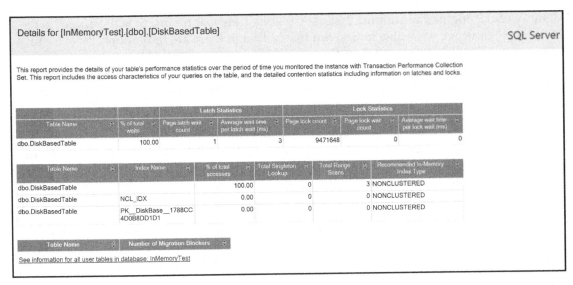

Figure 11.12: Table level report for the Transaction Performance Analysis Overview

A further click on the table name pulls up a report based on the table itself, providing details on lock and latch statistics for the table, along with recommendations on what indexes are currently available and what index these should be migrated into (either hash or non-clustered).

Summary

In this chapter, we took a look at the In-Memory OLTP engine as it was introduced in SQL Server 2014. Along the way, we investigated how the In-Memory OLTP differs from the traditional SQL Server storage engine with respect to the concurrency model. The main difference is the ability to allow multiple concurrent users to access the data structure without relying on the pessimistic concurrency model of using locking and latching to uphold data isolation within transactions.

We continued our journey by exploring what T-SQL constructs and data types the In-Memory OLTP engine can support the first version of the feature inside SQL Server 2014. At the same time, we were able to find out that although there are limitations, there is still a wide range of available data types and programming approaches that can be used immediately. Especially exciting is the fact that the T-SQL language receives (almost) transparent support for powerful new capabilities. Memory-optimized tables appear at first glance to be just normal tables that somehow process data at a much higher rate than normal.

The chapter then discussed how memory-optimized tables can take advantage of different data durability options and how this can affect both performance and recoverability of data. The new storage engine provides solutions that were previously impossible in the traditional storage engine.

We rounded off the first encounter with the In-Memory OLTP engine with a discussion around how the internals of the storage engine work. We also saw how to interrogate the system using different methods to explore how data flows through the In-Memory OLTP engine.

Finally, we had a glimpse of a useful migration assistant that can help in the preparation or identification of objects in existing databases that are possible candidates for a migration to the In-Memory OLTP engine.

12

In-Memory OLTP Improvements in SQL Server 2016

When In-Memory OLTP was introduced in SQL Server 2014, many developers were initially excited. The hope of a new, ultra-high-performance data processing engine, coupled with a leading relational database engine, offered a potentially massive improvement for many SQL Server developers. However, this excitement quickly turned into mild disappointment at the number of restrictions assigned to In-Memory OLTP. Many of these restrictions prevented wide adoption of the technology and forced it into a niche set of very tight implementation scenarios. Some of these restrictions, such as lacking support for **large data object types** (**LOBs**) or the missing support for ALTER commands, dampened many people's enthusiasm for the technology.

As with previous features inside SQL Server, In-Memory OLTP has followed a similar pattern. SQL Server 2014 saw the introduction of the In-Memory OLTP Engine. With SQL Server 2016, the feature has experienced an evolution: many of the restrictions that were present in SQL Server 2014 have been removed and existing functionality has been extended. In this chapter, we will take a look at the improvements that should now make In-Memory OLTP really attractive to almost all developers out there.

This chapter will demonstrate these improvements and additions, including: Altering existing memory-optimized objects, expanded data type support, expanded functionality/reduced limitations, and integration of In-Memory OLTP into other areas of the database engine.

Ch-Ch-Changes

It's not only the legend himself, Mr. David Bowie, who could sing about changes. In SQL Server 2014, we were destined to create In-Memory OLTP objects that were unchangeable after creation. If we needed to change the structure of a memory-optimized table, we had to resort to dropping and recreating the object with the new, updated structure.

For many developers/customers, this was a deal breaker. Being able to add and remove columns or indexes is something that every SQL Server developer is used to without any such restrictions. Especially, with the advent of agile software development and similar development strategies such as continuous integration, making changes to software applications is something many developers strive towards.

Now, with SQL Server 2016, it *is* possible to do just that. We will be continuing this chapter using the same database as in Chapter 11, *Introducing SQL Server In-Memory OLTP*, creating a simple memory-optimized table:

```
USE master
GO
CREATE DATABASE InMemoryTest
    ON
    PRIMARY(NAME = [InMemoryTest_disk],
                FILENAME = 'C:tempInMemoryTest_disk.mdf', size=100MB),
    FILEGROUP [InMemoryTest_inmem] CONTAINS MEMORY_OPTIMIZED_DATA
                (NAME = [InMemoryTest_inmem],
                FILENAME = 'C:tempInMemoryTest_inmem')
    LOG ON (name = [InMemoryTest_log],
Filename='c:tempInMemoryTest_log.ldf', size=100MB)
    COLLATE Latin1_General_100_BIN2;
GO
USE InMemoryTest
GO
CREATE TABLE InMemoryTable
(
    UserId INT NOT NULL,
    UserName VARCHAR(20) COLLATE Latin1_General_CI_AI NOT NULL,
    LoginTime DATETIME2 NOT NULL,
    LoginCount INT NOT NULL,
    CONSTRAINT PK_UserId  PRIMARY KEY NONCLUSTERED (UserId),
    INDEX HSH_UserName HASH (UserName) WITH (BUCKET_COUNT=10000)
) WITH (MEMORY_OPTIMIZED = ON, DURABILITY=SCHEMA_AND_DATA);
GO
INSERT INTO dbo.InMemoryTable
        ( UserId, UserName , LoginTime, LoginCount )
VALUES ( 1, 'Mickey Mouse', '2016-01-01', 1 );
GO
```

The list of supported ALTER statements for a table in SQL Server 2016 is as follows:

- Changing, adding, and removing a column
- Adding and removing an index
- Adding and removing a constraint
- Changing the bucket count

First up, we will add a column to the demo table. Note how the DDL statement is no different from adding a column to a disk-based table:

```
USE InMemoryTest;
GO
ALTER TABLE dbo.InMemoryTable ADD NewColumn INT NULL;
GO
```

We can also remove columns. Here, the DDL has also not changed:

```
USE InMemoryTest;
GO
ALTER TABLE dbo.InMemoryTable DROP COLUMN NewColumn;
GO
```

We are also able to add indexes after a table has already been created:

```
USE InMemoryTest;
GO
ALTER TABLE dbo.InMemoryTable ADD INDEX HSH_LoginTime NONCLUSTERED HASH
(LoginTime) WITH (BUCKET_COUNT = 250);
GO
```

Until now, the DDL statements looked normal. However, adding an index to a memory-optimized table is done using ALTER TABLE rather than CREATE INDEX. The same can be said for dropping or altering an index:

```
USE InMemoryTest;
GO
ALTER TABLE dbo.InMemoryTable ALTER INDEX HSH_LoginTime REBUILD WITH
(BUCKET_COUNT=10000);
GO
ALTER TABLE dbo.InMemoryTable DROP INDEX HSH_LoginTime;
GO
```

In the previous chapter, we discovered how the indexes on a memory-optimized table are the Bw-tree linked lists, which actually provide us with an access path to the memory pages of the *actual* data in a memory-optimized table. As such, they are more an extension of the table definition (similar to constraints) than an index on a disk-based table can be considered. This is reflected in the requirement for issuing an `ALTER TABLE` command to add, remove, or alter an index on a memory-optimized table.

Altering the bucket count of an index (as shown in the previous listing) is quite interesting. We always strive to implement new code with the plan of ensuring it is fit for purpose *before* we deploy to production. We also know that the first implementation of code rarely survives the first encounter with production usage. Predicting the correct bucket count is like predicting the future; the more information we have, the better our predictions can be. But who has full knowledge of how a new feature will be used? It is rarely possible to get a 1:1 comparison of production into a development environment. As such, changing the bucket count is likely something that we will need to do. Later in this chapter, we will be looking at the internals of indexing memory-optimized tables and will cover bucket counts in more detail.

A further interesting addition to SQL Server 2016 is the ability to bundle multiple changes (specifically, multiple change types—columns and indexes) together in one `ALTER` statement:

```
USE InMemoryTest
GO
ALTER TABLE dbo.InMemoryTable
ADD ANewColumn INT NULL,
    AnotherColumn TINYINT NULL,
INDEX HSH_ANewColumn NONCLUSTERED HASH (ANewColumn) WITH (BUCKET_COUNT =
250);
```

Adding multiple columns was possible in previous versions of SQL Server, but the ability to add an index in the same statement is new. This has to do with how the In-Memory OLTP Engine creates and manages memory-optimized objects in general. In Chapter 11, *Introducing SQL Server In-Memory OLTP*, we saw that memory-optimized objects are memory-resident objects with matching access methods (in fact, compiled C code). Indexes for memory-optimized tables are part of the memory-optimized table insofar as they require the C constructs and access methods to ensure SQL Server can work with them. Because these objects require compilation into machine code, they are somewhat static, even with the new ability to issue `ALTER` commands to them.

To overcome this logical limitation of compiled code being unchangeable, SQL Server receives the desired changes inside the ALTER statement and proceeds to create a new version of the existing object. Upon creation of this copy, the desired changes are incorporated into the new version. If the object being changed is a table, the rows from the old version are copied to the new version. The background process then compiles the access methods (including the changed columns) and the new version is ready for use. At this point, SQL Server dereferences the old version and redirects future calls to the new version.

As the ALTER of a table requires that the entire contents of a table be copied from the old version to the new version, we must be mindful of the fact that we are doubling the memory requirements for the table for the duration of the ALTER transaction (and until the background garbage collection cleans up the old structure). Equally, ALTER commands for memory-optimized tables are *offline* operations. This means that the memory-optimized table is blocked for the duration of the ALTER transaction.

As such, if we are manipulating a large table, we must ensure that we have enough memory available for the operation to succeed and understand that the table will be blocked for the duration of the transaction. It may, therefore, be prudent to consider emptying extremely large tables *before* issuing the ALTER command, to allow the change to complete quicker.

Many ALTER statements are metadata changes only. These types of change can be processed in parallel and have a greatly reduced impact on the transaction log. When only the metadata changes need to be processed, only these metadata changes are processed through the transaction log. Coupled with parallel processing, we can expect the execution of these changes to be extremely fast.

However, parallel processing is *excluded* for a few operations that require more than simple metadata changes; these are:

- Altering or adding a column to use a **large object (LOB)** type: nvarchar(max), varchar(max), or varbinary(max)
- Adding or dropping a COLUMNSTORE index
- Almost anything that affects an off-row column:
    - Causing an on-row column to move off-row
    - Causing an off-row column to move on-row
    - Creating a new off-row column
    - Exception: Lengthening an already off-row column is logged in the optimized way

As well as serial processing being forced for these operations, making changes to these data types causes a complete copy of the table being processed to be copied into the transaction log. This can cause the transaction log to fill up and also produce extra load on the storage subsystem.

The removal of restrictions on altering tables extends to altering natively compiled stored procedures. The well-known ALTER PROCEDURE command can now be used to make changes to previously created natively compiled stored procedures (the following demo code creates the stored procedure with no content to allow the ALTER statement to then be run):

```
USE InMemoryTest
GO
CREATE PROCEDURE dbo.InMemoryInsertOptimized
    @UserId INT,
    @UserName VARCHAR(255),
    @LoginTime DATETIME2,
    @LoginCount INT
WITH NATIVE_COMPILATION, SCHEMABINDING
AS
BEGIN ATOMIC WITH
(
    TRANSACTION ISOLATION LEVEL = SNAPSHOT,
    LANGUAGE = N'English'
)
    RETURN 0;
END;
GO

ALTER PROCEDURE dbo.InMemoryInsertOptimized
    @UserId INT,
    @UserName VARCHAR(255),
    @LoginTime DATETIME2,
    @LoginCount INT
WITH NATIVE_COMPILATION, SCHEMABINDING, EXECUTE AS OWNER
AS
BEGIN ATOMIC WITH
(
    TRANSACTION ISOLATION LEVEL = SNAPSHOT,
    LANGUAGE = N'English'
)
    -- Add an Insert
    INSERT dbo.InMemoryTable
    (UserId, UserName, LoginTime, LoginCount)
    VALUES
    (@UserId, @UserName, @LoginTime, @LoginCount);
    RETURN 0;
```

```
END;
GO
```

The following aspects of an existing natively compiled stored procedure *can* be changed using the ALTER PROCEDURE syntax:

- Parameters
- EXECUTE AS
- TRANSACTION ISOLATION LEVEL
- LANGUAGE
- DATEFIRST
- DATEFORMAT
- DELAYED_DURABILITY

 However, it is important to note that it is not possible to ALTER a natively compiled stored procedure to become non-native compiled, and the reverse is equally *not supported*.

If we wish to make such a change, we are required to perform a DROP PROCEDURE and CREATE PROCEDURE. This should make sense, as we are moving from the In-Memory into the normal Relational Engine (respectively). As such, we are recreating these objects in their entirety to achieve the desired change. This also means that we have to consider that any permissions assigned to such an object need to be re-assigned at (re)creation time.

During the recompile process, when an ALTER command is issued, the old version of the natively compiled stored procedure can still be executed. Upon compilation of the altered stored procedure, the old version will be destroyed and all subsequent calls of the stored procedure will use the new definition. This allows an ALTER command to be issued without causing long waiting periods, but may allow transactions to execute using potentially old code.

Feature improvements

While it is welcome that we can now alter existing objects without having to drop them first, many developers are more interested in finally being able to use data types and T-SQL syntax in the In-Memory OLTP engine that go beyond just the basics. In SQL Server 2016, we have been presented with a great deal of extra support, as is typical with version 2 of a product. In this section of the chapter, we will take a look at what areas of the database engine are now supported in the In-Memory OLTP engine.

Collations

The first major addition is the fact that both memory-optimized tables and natively compiled stored procedures support all code pages and collations that SQL Server supports. The previous limitation of only supporting a subset of collations otherwise available in SQL Server has been completely removed from the product (a newly supported collation has been used in the test table in the demo scripts in this chapter).

This improvement allows us to incorporate tables and stored procedures using the collations that we are used to or already using in our database designs.

Data types and types of data

SQL Server 2016 now supports the vast majority of data types in the In-Memory OLTP engine. In fact, the list of supported data types is now so long that it is easier to list the *unsupported* types instead. The data types that are currently *unsupported* are as follows:

- Datetimeoffset
- Geography
- Geometry
- Hierarchyid
- Rowversion
- Xml
- Sql_variant

This means that (except for XML), Large Binary Objects (LOBs) *are* supported; this covers the max datatypes varchar(max), nvarchar(max), and varbinary(max). This is great news, as there are many cases where disk-based tables that had only one LOB column but multiple supported columns were barred from the In-Memory OLTP engine.

LOB data type support is not limited to tables and indexes; it is now also possible to use LOB data types in memory-optimized stored procedures. This will allow parameters to be passed into and out of natively compiled stored procedures.

An exhaustive list of current In-Memory OLTP limitations can be found in Microsoft Books Online: https://msdn.microsoft.com/en-us/library/dn246937.aspx

Microsoft Books Online also has indications of which commands or DDL/data types will be made available to the In-Memory OLTP engine in the next version of SQL Server. One such example is the upcoming support of Computed Columns.

What's new with indexes?

Indexing memory-optimized tables was quite restrictive in the initial version of the In-Memory OLTP engine. So far in the chapter, we have seen that there have been a number of improvements (adding, removing, and rebuilding indexes), but that is not all!

It is now possible to define non-unique indexes with NULLable key columns for memory-optimized tables. NULLability is something that is widely used and the move toward parity between memory-optimized and disk-based indexes is continued here.

Similarly, it is possible to declare UNIQUE indexes (other than the primary key) for memory-optimized tables.

We will take a deeper look at indexing later in this chapter, in the section titled Down the index rabbit-hole.

Unconstrained integrity

Referential integrity and data integrity are important foundational rules inside relational databases. The In-Memory OLTP Engine introduced an extremely limited set of constraints that could be used in SQL Server 2014. This meant that solutions had to widely forego many expectations of assigning referential and data integrity to memory-optimized tables.

With SQL Server 2016, it is now possible to implement the following referential and data integrity rules for memory-optimized tables:

- FOREIGN KEY constraints (between memory-optimized tables).
- CHECK constraints.
- DEFAULT constraints.
- UNIQUE constraints.
- AFTER triggers for INSERT, UPDATE, and DELETE operations. Triggers for memory-optimized tables must be created using WITH NATIVE_COMPILATION so that the trigger is natively compiled at creation time.

This will now allow developers to create tables with some semblance of sane referential and data integrity rules (as they are used to with disk-based tables).

Not all operators are created equal

While the number of commands that are supported for natively compiled T-SQL in SQL Server 2016 has expanded, unfortunately a wide range of the most powerful T-SQL commands are still not available for In-Memory OLTP solutions.

The following notable operators are *unsupported* in SQL Server 2016:

- LIKE
- CASE
- INTERSECT
- EXCEPT
- APPLY

Attempting to use these operators inside a natively compiled stored procedure or scalar function will result in an error message explaining that the syntax is not supported:

`The operator 'LIKE' is not supported with natively compiled modules.`

We can expect these and other currently unsupported operators to be added to future releases of SQL Server.

A full list of unsupported operators can be found on the Microsoft Books Online page: `https://msdn.microsoft.com/en-us/library/dn246937.aspx#Anchor_4`

It is important to understand that these T-SQL limitations are for *natively compiled T-SQL* (stored procedures and scalar functions). You are still able to write interpreted T-SQL (non-natively compiled T-SQL) using these commands. For example, it is perfectly fine to query a memory-optimized table and issue a LIKE operator to search in a character column.

Size is everything!

When the In-Memory OLTP engine was initially introduced in SQL Server 2014 Microsoft announced that the maximum size of any memory-optimized table was 256 GB. This limit was reached via internal testing at Microsoft and named to ensure stability and reliability of the feature in production environments. The main decision here was the design of the storage subsystem, particularly around the checkpoint file pairs. There was a hard limit of 8,192 checkpoint file pairs, each capable of storing 128 MB of data. The limit of 256 GB was not a hard limit but rather a suggested maximum. The memory requirements for a memory-optimized table are dynamic. This dynamism is grounded in the memory requirements for merging data changes into the memory-optimized tables (insert, deletes, updates) and the follow-on redundancies of versioned rows and rows waiting for garbage collection.

When SQL Server 2016 was released, Microsoft quoted a maximum size of 2 TB for a memory-optimized table. Again, this was due to testing and reliability measurements inside the development team at Microsoft. The development team has re-architected the storage subsystem for the checkpoint file pairs, removing the 8,192-pair limit, effectively allowing a memory-optimized table to have no upper size limit (as long as you have memory available, the table can grow). This *does not* mean that any and all tables should be memory-optimized, but it *does* mean that we are now able to consider using the In-Memory OLTP Engine to store any size of table that we can design.

Improvements in the In-Memory OLTP Engine

Further to the above-mentioned size limitation removal, there are a number of improvements under the hood of the In-Memory OLTP Engine that may not be immediately apparent, but can drastically improve performance and scalability.

First up is a range of improvements to the storage subsystem: not only the previously mentioned removal of the checkpoint file pair limit, but also the introduction of multi-threaded checkpointing. In SQL Server 2014, the offline checkpoint process was a single-threaded system. This thread would scan the transaction log for changes to memory-optimized tables and write those changes to the checkpoint file pairs. This meant that a potentially multi-core system would have a "busy" core for the checkpointing process. With SQL Server 2016, this checkpointing system has now been redesigned to run on multiple threads, thereby increasing throughput to the checkpoint file pairs and thus increasing overall performance and scalability of the In-Memory OLTP Engine.

Similar improvements have been made to the recovery process. When the server is performing crash recovery, or bringing a database online after a server was taken offline, the log apply operations are now also processed using multiple threads.

The theme of multi-threading or parallel processing has also been continued in the query processing portion of the In-Memory OLTP Engine. Here we can expect performance improvements for a range of queries, both interpreted and natively compiled. The query processing engine is now able to process the MERGE statement using multiple threads (as long as your server/database MAXDOP settings allow for this). This allows the query optimizer to use parallelism where it deems parallel processing to be more efficient than serial processing.

Equally, in SQL Server 2014, hash indexes could only be scanned using a single-thread/serial scan rather than a parallel scan. SQL Server 2016 has now implemented a parallel scan method to provide a significant performance gain when scanning a hash index. This helps to mitigate the inherent performance pain that is experienced when performing an index scan over a hash index.

Down the index rabbit-hole

So far in this chapter, we have seen the additions of features and functionalities that were available in disk-based objects, into the In-Memory OLTP Engine. The improvements in indexing and the ability to alter your indexing strategy with memory-optimized tables without dropping the table are particularly attractive. With that in mind, we will spend some time investigating how the indexes are treated inside the storage engine. This will include a journey through the system catalogs and **Dynamic Management Views (DMVs)**, to allow us to see how index information can be queried.

We will now take this opportunity to explore what the alteration of a bucket count can have on the data in our demonstration table.

Let us begin by rolling back two of our changes from earlier in the chapter by dropping the hash index `HSH_ANewColumn`, dropping the two columns `ANewColumn` and `AnotherColumn` and finally, recreating a hash index `HSH_LoginTime` using an extremely irregular and sub-optimal value of 2:

```
USE InMemoryTest
GO
ALTER TABLE dbo.InMemoryTable DROP INDEX NCL_ANewColumn
GO
ALTER TABLE dbo.InMemoryTable DROP COLUMN ANewColumn
GO
ALTER TABLE dbo.InMemoryTable DROP COLUMN AnotherColumn
GO
ALTER TABLE dbo.InMemoryTable ADD INDEX HSH_LoginTime NONCLUSTERED HASH
(LoginTime) WITH (BUCKET_COUNT=2);
GO
```

We will begin by taking a look into the system catalog views that we have used in past versions of SQL Server to inspect the table and indexes we have created so far:

```
USE InMemoryTest
GO
SELECT OBJECT_NAME(i.object_id) AS [table_name],
    COALESCE(i.name,'--HEAP--') AS [index_name],
    i.index_id,
    i.type,
    i.type_desc
FROM sys.indexes AS i
WHERE i.object_id = OBJECT_ID('InMemoryTable');
```

table_name	index_name	index_id	type	type_desc

InMemoryTable	--HEAP--	0	0	HEAP
InMemoryTable	HSH_UserName	2	7	NONCLUSTERED HASH
InMemoryTable	PK_InMemory	3	2	NONCLUSTERED
InMemoryTable	HSH_LoginTime	4	7	NONCLUSTERED HASH

The results of this first query against `sys.indexes` shows us that we have a `HEAP` (the data pages of the memory-optimized table) and three additional indexes that we have created so far. Particularly noteworthy here are the two non-clustered hash indexes that we created: `HSH_UserName` and `HSH_LoginTime`. Both appear as index type `7` and index description `NONCLUSTERED HASH`. This should come as no great surprise, but shows us that the old system views have been extended to include information regarding memory-optimized tables and indexes. The listing above may be executed without the `WHERE` clause to see that the details for both memory-optimized and disk-based tables and indexes can be queried simultaneously.

We already know that hash indexes are exclusive to memory-optimized tables. However, if we go through the demo code so far, we also know that the primary key of this table is also memory-optimized. The query referencing `sys.indexes`, however, only shows us that the primary key is a non-clustered index. So, we have no way of knowing if this non-clustered index is a memory-optimized or a disk-based index.

The information about whether a table is a memory-optimized or disk-based table is stored in the newly extended `sys.tables` catalog view:

```
SELECT COALESCE(i.name,'--HEAP--') AS [index_name],
    i.index_id,
    i.type,
    t.is_memory_optimized,
    t.durability,
    t.durability_desc
FROM sys.tables t
    INNER JOIN sys.indexes AS i
        ON i.object_id = t.object_id
WHERE t.name = 'InMemoryTable'
```

index_name	index_id	type	is_memory_optimized	durability	durability_desc
--HEAP--	0	0	1	0	SCHEMA_AND_DATA
HSH_UserName	2	7	1	0	SCHEMA_AND_DATA
PK_InMemory	3	2	1	0	SCHEMA_AND_DATA
HSH_LoginTime	4	7	1	0	SCHEMA_AND_DATA

As the results of the query show, the table and all indexes are memory-optimized (`is_memory_optimized = 1`). We are also able to determine which durability option has been chosen for the table.

With these two queries, we are able to take our first look at the index information for memory-optimized tables. However, we are not able to see any particular information regarding our hash index (bucket counts or chain lengths). To access that information, we leave the general system catalog views `sys.indexes` and `sys.tables` behind and venture forwards into more feature specific catalog views.

Our first port of call is the obviously named `sys.hash_indexes`, which displays information on any hash indexes in a database. The catalog view `sys.hash_indexes` has the same columns as the catalog view `sys.indexes`, with the exception of the column `bucket_count`. This column displays the bucket count for the index from the creation time / last rebuild, with the option `BUCKET_COUNT` supplied:

```
USE InMemoryTest
GO
SELECT hi.name AS [index_name],
    hi.index_id,
    hi.type,
    hi.bucket_count
FROM sys.hash_indexes AS hi;
```

index_name	index_id	type	bucket_count
HSH_UserName	2	7	16384
HSH_LoginTime	4	7	2

This catalog view only provides us with information about the index structure from the time of creation; it does *not* provide us with any details on chain length inside each bucket (the number of rows that are assigned to each bucket via the hashing algorithm).

To access this much more important and relevant information, we must access another catalog view specifically created for the memory-optimized indexes—`sys.dm_db_xtp_hash_index_stats`:

```
SELECT COALESCE(i.name, '--HEAP--') AS [index_name],
    i.index_id,
    i.type,
    ddxhis.total_bucket_count AS [total_buckets],
    ddxhis.empty_bucket_count AS [empty_buckets],
    ddxhis.avg_chain_length,
    ddxhis.max_chain_length
FROM sys.indexes AS i
    LEFT JOIN sys.dm_db_xtp_hash_index_stats AS ddxhis
        ON ddxhis.index_id = i.index_id
            AND ddxhis.object_id = i.object_id
WHERE i.object_id = OBJECT_ID('InMemoryTable');
```

index_name max_chain_length	index_id	type	total_buckets	empty_buckets	avg_chain_length
--HEAP-- NULL	0	0	NULL	NULL	NULL
HSH_UserName 1	2	7	16384	16383	1
PK_UserId NULL	3	2	NULL	NULL	NULL
HSH_LoginTime 1	4	7	2	1	1

By joining the system catalog view `sys.dm_db_xtp_hash_index_stats` to `sys.indexes` (or even directly to `sys.hash_indexes`), we are able to finally see our bucket count and our usage statistics. We see how many buckets are empty, the average chain length, and max chain length for each hash index.

We will want to monitor the statistics of our hash indexes to see if the bucket count is optimal or not. As each bucket takes up 8 bytes of memory, the higher the bucket count, the more memory we will use for the index. A higher bucket count also results in slower traversal of the index when performing index scans. So, if we note a high number of empty buckets, we may consider reducing the bucket count to improve potential scan speeds. In general, it is best to avoid performing index scans on a hash index, as the scan must first scan the hash buckets and then the chains of rows for each bucket. This has considerable overhead versus scanning a non-clustered index, which doesn't have the added complexity of the bucket structure to traverse.

Equally, if we see a high average or maximum chain length, this could indicate that there are not enough buckets available for the data coming into the index. Higher chain lengths can also impact performance when performing seeks or inserts.

The general idea of a hash index is to have just enough buckets to cover all possible unique values going into the index (or as near to this as possible), so that when a query seeks for a single hash value, the storage engine can retrieve the one (or very few) row(s) that belong to that hash value.

The recommendation from Microsoft is to aim for an empty bucket percentage of 33% or above. If the bucket count matches the number of unique values for the index, the hashing algorithm's distribution will cause around 33% of buckets to remain empty.

The recommendation from Microsoft is to aim for a chain length of less than 10, with the ideal value being 1 (one row per hash value and therefore bucket).

If you have wildly non-unique values with many duplicates, a non-clustered index would more likely be a better choice versus a hash index.

We can see how the empty buckets and chain lengths are affected by inserting a handful of rows into the test table and re-running the previous query to show how the chain length and bucket "fullness" has changed:

```
USE InMemoryTest
GO
INSERT INTO dbo.InMemoryTable
        ( UserId, UserName , LoginTime, LoginCount )
VALUES
            (2,  'Donald Duck'     , '2016-01-02', 1),
            (3,  'Steve Jobs'      , '2016-01-03', 1),
            (4,  'Steve Ballmer'   , '2016-01-04', 1),
            (5,  'Bill Gates'      , '2016-01-05', 1),
            (6,  'Ted Codd'        , '2016-01-06', 1),
            (7,  'Brian Kernighan', '2016-01-07', 1),
            (8,  'Dennis Ritchie' , '2016-01-08', 1);
GO
SELECT COALESCE(i.name, '--HEAP--') AS [index_name],
    i.index_id,
    i.type,
    ddxhis.total_bucket_count AS [total_buckets],
    ddxhis.empty_bucket_count AS [empty_buckets],
    ddxhis.avg_chain_length,
    ddxhis.max_chain_length
FROM sys.indexes AS i
    LEFT JOIN sys.dm_db_xtp_hash_index_stats AS ddxhis
        ON ddxhis.index_id = i.index_id
            AND ddxhis.object_id = i.object_id
WHERE i.object_id = OBJECT_ID('InMemoryTable');
```

index_name	index_id	type	total_buckets	empty_buckets	avg_chain_length	max_chain_length
--HEAP--	0	0	NULL	NULL	NULL	NULL
HSH_UserName	2	7	16384	16376	1	1
PK_UserId	3	2	NULL	NULL	NULL	NULL
HSH_LoginTime	4	7	2	0	4	5

Here we can see that the two hash indexes now have slightly different information in them. We now have a total of eight rows in the table (and the indexes). HSH_UserName has 16376 buckets with a hash function applied to the UserName column. As we inserted seven new rows, each with a unique value for UserName, they will all be stored in an empty bucket. This leaves the average and max chain lengths at 1. The data inserted into LoginTime was also unique for each of the 7 rows. However, there are only 2 buckets assigned to the HSH_LoginTime. This results in the 7 rows hashing to one of two possible values and being placed in one of the two available buckets. The average and max chain lengths are then no longer 1.

This example is very simplified, but would allow us to recognize that the implementation of the hash index on LoginTime requires attention. Either the bucket count needs raising or the choice of a hash index is possibly incorrect. Equally, the hash index on UserName is providing ideal chain lengths, but has an excessive empty bucket count. The index is using more memory than is necessary and may need the bucket count reducing to release memory for other memory-optimized objects. Now that we know that the bucket counts and chain lengths can affect the amount of memory required to store our memory-optimized tables and indexes, we should also take a quick look at how the two hash indexes in the example can differ:

```
USE InMemoryTest
GO
SELECT COALESCE(i.name, '--HEAP--') AS [index_name],
    i.index_id,
    i.type,
    c.allocated_bytes,
    c.used_bytes
FROM sys.dm_db_xtp_memory_consumers c
    JOIN sys.memory_optimized_tables_internal_attributes a
        ON a.object_id = c.object_id
            AND a.xtp_object_id = c.xtp_object_id
    LEFT JOIN sys.indexes i
        ON c.object_id = i.object_id
            AND c.index_id = i.index_id
WHERE c.object_id = OBJECT_ID('InMemoryTable')
    AND a.type = 1
ORDER BY i.index_id;
```

index_name	index_id	type	allocated_bytes	used_bytes
--HEAP--	NULL	NULL	131072	696
HSH_UserName	2	7	131072	131072
PK_UserId	3	2	196608	1368
HSH_LoginTime	4	7	16	16

The results show an interesting fact. The `HSH_LoginTime` index was created with two buckets and has 16 bytes allocated and used. This makes sense when we think about how each bucket takes up 8 bytes of memory. However, `HSH_UserName` takes up 128 MB of memory, although the index has 10,000 buckets. We would expect ~78 MB (10,000 * 8 bytes = 80,000 bytes); however, the memory allocation follows base—2 size allocations. As the size is larger than 64 MB, the next largest size in base—2 is 128 therefore 128 MB are allocated. We can test this theory by altering the number of buckets to a value low enough for the size to be below 64 (the next step down the base—2 scale):

```
USE InMemoryTest
GO
ALTER TABLE dbo.InMemoryTable ALTER INDEX HSH_UserName REBUILD WITH
(BUCKET_COUNT=8000);
GO
SELECT COALESCE(i.name, '--HEAP--') AS [index_name],
    i.index_id,
    i.type,
    c.allocated_bytes,
    c.used_bytes
FROM sys.dm_db_xtp_memory_consumers c
    JOIN sys.memory_optimized_tables_internal_attributes a
        ON a.object_id = c.object_id
            AND a.xtp_object_id = c.xtp_object_id
    LEFT JOIN sys.indexes i
        ON c.object_id = i.object_id
            AND c.index_id = i.index_id
WHERE c.object_id = OBJECT_ID('InMemoryTable')
        AND a.type = 1
ORDER BY i.index_id;
```

index_name	index_id	type	allocated_bytes	used_bytes
--HEAP--	NULL	NULL	131072	760
HSH_UserName	2	7	65536	65536
PK_InMemory	3	2	196608	1368
HSH_LoginTime	4	7	16	16

We now see that the `HSH_UserName` index has 64 MB allocated, although 8,000 buckets equate to ~62.5 MB. This gives us further information regarding memory use for indexing memory-optimized tables and that we have a certain amount of overhead for the storage of indexes in relation to the number of buckets we assign to a hash index.

Large object support

We will now take a look at exactly what LOB data types are supported in SQL Server 2016 and what aspects of these data types need to be considered when using them with memory-optimized objects.

Let's begin by adding a LOB column to our test table:

```
USE InMemoryTest
GO
ALTER TABLE dbo.InMemoryTable Add NewColumnMax VARCHAR(MAX) NULL
GO
```

This follows the same scheme as the previous code examples; adding a LOB column is no different with a memory-optimized table than a disk-based table. At least on the surface!

Let's take another look into our index metadata to see how exactly LOB columns are handled by the storage engine:

```
USE InMemoryTest
GO
SELECT COALESCE(i.name, '--HEAP--') AS [index_name],
    c.allocated_bytes AS allocated,
    c.used_bytes AS used,
    c.memory_consumer_desc AS memory_consumer,
    a.type_desc
FROM sys.dm_db_xtp_memory_consumers c
    JOIN sys.memory_optimized_tables_internal_attributes a
        ON a.object_id = c.object_id
            AND a.xtp_object_id = c.xtp_object_id
    LEFT JOIN sys.indexes i
        ON c.object_id = i.object_id
            AND c.index_id = i.index_id
WHERE c.object_id = OBJECT_ID('InMemoryTable')
        AND i.index_id IS NULL;
GO
```

index_name	allocated	used	memory_consumer	type_desc
--HEAP--	131072	760	Table Heap	USER_TABLE
--HEAP--	0	0	LOB Page Allocator	INTERNAL OFF-ROW DATA TABLE
--HEAP--	0	0	Table heap	INTERNAL OFF-ROW DATA TABLE

There are a number of things to note here:

- We are filtering on the table/heap only (AND i.index_id IS NULL). This will allow us to concentrate on the base table only.
- Two additional columns have been added, showing what type of memory consumer each row represents.
- We now see two additional rows displayed.

The preceding listing returns two additional rows, one marked LOB Page Allocator and one marked Table heap, and both with an internal table attribute of Internal off row data table. These are references to how the LOB data is stored for memory-optimized tables.

LOB data is not stored along with the other data pages for a memory-optimized table. Rather, the LOB data is stored in a separate data structure that is optimized for LOB style data. The LOB Page Allocator stores the actual LOB data, while the Table heap stores the references to the LOB data and references back to the original data pages. This arrangement has been designed so that the row-versioning mechanism, which is the foundation of the multi-version concurrency control inside the In-Memory OLTP engine (described in Chapter 11, *Introducing SQL Server In-Memory OLTP*) doesn't need to keep multiple versions of the LOB data in the same way it must do for the regular columns. By decoupling the two data storage classes, SQL Server can be much more efficient with the storage of these two quite different data types. In particular, LOB data has been regarded as a data type that is likely to be modified less often compared to non-LOB columns. As such, processing the LOB data separately will greatly reduce the memory resource usage and this reduces the overhead of storing LOB data in a memory-optimized table while still affording the ability of processing the data types through one interface.

At the moment, the LOB column is empty (allocated = 0 and used = 0); if we now run a simple update to copy the UserName column data into the LOB column, we can run the same query and investigate how the data is stored in the LOB data structures:

```
USE InMemoryTest
GO
UPDATE dbo.InMemoryTable
SET NewColumnMax = UserName
GO
SELECT COALESCE(i.name, '--HEAP--') AS [index_name],
    c.allocated_bytes AS allocated,
    c.used_bytes AS used,
    c.memory_consumer_desc AS memory_consumer,
    a.type_desc
FROM sys.dm_db_xtp_memory_consumers c
```

```
      JOIN sys.memory_optimized_tables_internal_attributes a
          ON a.object_id = c.object_id
              AND a.xtp_object_id = c.xtp_object_id
      LEFT JOIN sys.indexes i
          ON c.object_id = i.object_id
              AND c.index_id = i.index_id
  WHERE c.object_id = OBJECT_ID('InMemoryTable')
        AND i.index_id IS NULL;
GO
```

index_name	allocated	used	memory_consumer	type_desc
--HEAP--	131072	1520	Table Heap	USER_TABLE
--HEAP--	131072	376	LOB Page Allocator	INTERNAL OFF-ROW DATA TABLE
--HEAP--	65536	512	Table heap	INTERNAL OFF-ROW DATA TABLE

We are observing a similar behavior as earlier in the chapter, where allocation is occurring in base-2 steps. The LOB Page Allocator has allocated 128 MB and the supporting Table heap has allocated 64 MB, although both are using much less space. This is a pure efficiency step to avoid having to perform unnecessary additional allocations too often. However, we notice a behavior that could cause memory resource contention if large amounts of LOB data were to be processed in this way.

If you run the index metadata queries shortly after modifying the table structure, you may notice that the memory allocations of the table are larger than shown in the example results here. This has to do with how ALTER statements are processed by the In-Memory OLTP Engine. Earlier in the chapter, this mechanism was described and it was stated that an ALTER makes a copy of the original table, incorporating the desired changes into the new copy. This leads to a doubling of the memory allocation until the ghost record cleanup can remove the old copy of the data from memory.

When SQL Server processes LOB data in the In-Memory OLTP Engine, the decision on whether or not to push the data from in-row to off-row storage is made according to the table schema. This is a different mechanism than the disk-based storage engine, which bases the decision on the data being processed at execution time. Disk-based storage only places data off-row when it won't fit on a data page, while memory-optimized tables place data off-row when the table schema describes a column as being either a max data type or that the row can store more than 8,060 bytes when completely full. When LOB data is stored off-row for a memory-optimized table, there is a significant overhead associated with that storage. A reference must be stored for the in-row data (the base memory-optimized table), the off-row data (the LOB data itself in the LOB Page Allocator), and the leaf level of the range index (the intermediary heap referencing between the on-row and off-row data).

In addition to this, the actual data must be stored in the `LOB Page Allocator`. This overhead can go beyond 50 bytes per row. This additional overhead is created and must be maintained for each and every LOB column that a memory-optimized table has. The more LOB columns, the more overhead and bloated referencing required. As you may see, writing an additional 50+ bytes for each row with a LOB column (or multiples of this) can quickly cause significant resource and performance issues.

Storage differences of on-row and off-row data

Let's now take a look at the difference in storage and processing between two tables with variable length character columns. One table has `varchar(5)` columns, which will be small enough to fit in the in-row storage. The other table will have a series of `varchar(max)` columns, which will automatically be stored in the off-row storage. These tables will be created and filled with 100,000 rows each to demonstrate both the storage and also performance differences between the two storage types:

```
USE InMemoryTest
GO
DROP TABLE IF EXISTS dbo.InMemoryTableMax
DROP TABLE IF EXISTS dbo.InMemoryTableNotMax
GO

CREATE TABLE dbo.InMemoryTableMax
(
    UserId INT NOT NULL IDENTITY (1,1),
    MaxCol1 VARCHAR(max) COLLATE Latin1_General_CI_AI NOT NULL ,
    MaxCol2 VARCHAR(max) COLLATE Latin1_General_CI_AI NOT NULL ,
    MaxCol3 VARCHAR(max) COLLATE Latin1_General_CI_AI NOT NULL ,
    MaxCol4 VARCHAR(max) COLLATE Latin1_General_CI_AI NOT NULL ,
    MaxCol5 VARCHAR(max) COLLATE Latin1_General_CI_AI NOT NULL ,
    CONSTRAINT PK_InMemoryTableMax  PRIMARY KEY NONCLUSTERED (UserId),

) WITH (MEMORY_OPTIMIZED = ON, DURABILITY=SCHEMA_AND_DATA)
GO

CREATE TABLE dbo.InMemoryTableNotMax
(
    UserId INT NOT NULL IDENTITY (1,1),
    Col1 VARCHAR(5) COLLATE Latin1_General_CI_AI NOT NULL ,
    Col2 VARCHAR(5) COLLATE Latin1_General_CI_AI NOT NULL ,
    Col3 VARCHAR(5) COLLATE Latin1_General_CI_AI NOT NULL ,
    Col4 VARCHAR(5) COLLATE Latin1_General_CI_AI NOT NULL ,
    Col5 VARCHAR(5) COLLATE Latin1_General_CI_AI NOT NULL ,
    CONSTRAINT PK_InMemoryTableNotMax  PRIMARY KEY NONCLUSTERED (UserId),
```

```
) WITH (MEMORY_OPTIMIZED = ON, DURABILITY=SCHEMA_AND_DATA)
GO
```

The only difference between these two tables are the column data types; one uses the `varchar(max)`, while the other uses a `varchar(5)` data type. We are leaving the tables with only a primary key and no other indexes, because we only want to investigate the on-row and off-row storage differences.

If we now run our memory consumers query from earlier in this section, we can investigate how the `LOB Page Allocator` and matching Table heap objects are created for each table:

```
SELECT OBJECT_NAME(c.object_id) AS [table_name],
    c.allocated_bytes AS allocated,
    c.used_bytes AS used,
    c.memory_consumer_desc AS memory_consumer,
    a.type_desc
FROM sys.dm_db_xtp_memory_consumers c
    JOIN sys.memory_optimized_tables_internal_attributes a
        ON a.object_id = c.object_id
            AND a.xtp_object_id = c.xtp_object_id
    LEFT JOIN sys.indexes i
        ON c.object_id = i.object_id
            AND c.index_id = i.index_id
WHERE
(
    c.object_id = OBJECT_ID('InMemoryTableNotMax')
    OR c.object_id = OBJECT_ID('InMemoryTableMax')
)
AND i.index_id IS NULL
```

table_name	allocated	used	memory_consumer	type_desc
InMemoryTableNotMax	0	0	Table heap	USER_TABLE
InMemoryTableMax	0	0	Table heap	USER_TABLE
InMemoryTableMax	0	0	LOB Page Allocator	INTERNAL OFF-ROW DATA TABLE
InMemoryTableMax	0	0	Table heap	INTERNAL OFF-ROW DATA TABLE
InMemoryTableMax	0	0	LOB Page Allocator	INTERNAL OFF-ROW DATA TABLE
InMemoryTableMax	0	0	Table heap	INTERNAL OFF-ROW DATA TABLE
InMemoryTableMax	0	0	LOB Page Allocator	INTERNAL OFF-ROW DATA TABLE
InMemoryTableMax	0	0	Table heap	INTERNAL OFF-ROW DATA TABLE
InMemoryTableMax	0	0	LOB Page Allocator	INTERNAL OFF-ROW DATA TABLE
InMemoryTableMax	0	0	Table heap	INTERNAL OFF-ROW DATA TABLE
InMemoryTableMax	0	0	LOB Page Allocator	INTERNAL OFF-ROW DATA TABLE
InMemoryTableMax	0	0	Table heap	INTERNAL OFF-ROW DATA TABLE;

The results of the memory consumer query show that we have a single `Table heap` for the table `InMemoryTableNotMax` (the table with the `varchar(5)` columns) and we have several internal off-row data tables for the `InMemoryTableMax` table. In fact, we have a `LOB Page Allocator` and a matching `Table heap` for each `varchar(max)` column in the table.

We then fill each table with 100,000 rows of data while running a basic timing comparison to see what performance overhead the `LOB Page Allocator` and `Table heap` maintenance causes:

```
SET NOCOUNT ON
GO

SET STATISTICS TIME ON
GO

INSERT INTO dbo.InMemoryTableMax
        ( MaxCol1 ,
          MaxCol2 ,
          MaxCol3 ,
          MaxCol4 ,
          MaxCol5
        )
SELECT TOP 100000
    'Col1',
    'Col2',
    'Col3',
    'Col4',
    'Col5'
FROM sys.columns a
    CROSS JOIN sys.columns;
GO

INSERT INTO dbo.InMemoryTableNotMax
        ( Col1 ,
          Col2 ,
          Col3 ,
          Col4 ,
          Col5
        )
SELECT TOP 100000
    'Col1',
    'Col2',
    'Col3',
    'Col4',
    'Col5'
FROM sys.columns a
```

```
    CROSS JOIN sys.columns
GO

SET STATISTICS TIME OFF
GO

SQL Server Execution Times:
   CPU time = 1797 ms,  elapsed time = 1821 ms.

SQL Server Execution Times:
   CPU time = 281 ms,  elapsed time = 382 ms.
```

The results at the end of this listing show that the elapsed time for inserting 100,000 rows into the table with varchar(max) columns took roughly five times longer than inserting the same rows into the table with varchar(5) columns. This timing difference is down to the overhead of inserting the data into the off-row storage (the LOB Page Allocator and matching Heap table).

If we also take another look into the memory consumption statistics, we can see that there is also a significant difference in memory consumption between the two tables:

```
SELECT OBJECT_NAME(c.object_id) AS [table_name],
    SUM(c.allocated_bytes) / 1024. AS allocated,
    SUM(c.used_bytes) / 1024. AS used
FROM sys.dm_db_xtp_memory_consumers c
    JOIN sys.memory_optimized_tables_internal_attributes a
        ON a.object_id = c.object_id
            AND a.xtp_object_id = c.xtp_object_id
    LEFT JOIN sys.indexes i
        ON c.object_id = i.object_id
            AND c.index_id = i.index_id
WHERE
(
    c.object_id = OBJECT_ID('InMemoryTableNotMax')
    OR c.object_id = OBJECT_ID('InMemoryTableMax')
)
AND i.index_id IS NULL
GROUP BY c.object_id;
```

table_name	allocated	used
InMemoryTableMax	59392.000000	58593.750000
InMemoryTableNotMax	7104.000000	7031.250000

We can see that we should very carefully consider the use of LOB data types for memory-optimized tables. If LOB data types are required, then the performance and resource consumption overhead should be noted, especially where high performance is the driving factor for adoption of a memory-optimized solution.

Cross-feature support

We have seen that the In-Memory OLTP Engine has increasingly added support for features outside the engine itself, allowing interoperability between disk-based and memory-optimized objects with increasing parity with each new release. However, developers need to also be aware of how the feature support of In-Memory OLTP is also expanding into the more administrator focused areas of SQL Server.

Security

The first important feature we will discuss under the subtitle cross-feature support is the ability to use Transparent Data Encryption (TDE) on memory-optimized objects. TDE, as the name suggests, allows a database administrator to apply an encryption mechanism to an entire database. This encryption will protect all the data stored inside the database. The encryption is designed in such a way that should the database fall into the wrong hands (the data and log files are copied or a backup is misplaced), then the data inside those files is completely encrypted and useless without the encryption key(s) and certificate(s), which are stored separately from the database files themselves. The scope of this chapter/book does not allow for a full excursion into the inner workings of TDE. However, it is enough to know that should you wish to use this simple, but effective encryption solution, you are now able to also use memory-optimized objects in such a database without any restrictions.

For developers wishing to implement In-Memory OLTP using the newest security features introduced in SQL Server 2016—Always Encrypted, Row-Level Security, and Dynamic Data Masking (all explained in detail in Chapter 8, *Tightening the Security)*—can also rest assured that Microsoft was paying attention during the design of these features and memory-optimized tables can also take advantage of these improved security features.

Programmability

We are also able to take full advantage of the extremely useful Query Store feature, which was also introduced in SQL Server 2016 and has a chapter dedicated to it: Chapter 9, *Query Store*. There is no additional configuration required to include memory-optimized tables or natively compiled code; when Query Store is activated, the memory-optimized objects will be collected in the Query Store analysis along with disk-based objects and queries.

The focus on feature inclusion continues to also cover Temporal Tables, a chapter explaining what Temporal Tables are and how they can be implemented is available: Chapter 7, *Temporal Tables*. Similar to the other cross-feature support items, Temporal Tables allows for a transparent implementation of memory-optimized tables versus disk-based tables. There are no special requirements to accommodate memory-optimized tables with this feature.

High availability

High availability support is of great importance for systems that are processing large volumes of data requiring the performance of the In-Memory OLTP Engine.

SQL Server 2016 fully supports the use of memory-optimized objects in conjunction with Always On Availability Groups. Any memory-optimized table will be replicated to the secondary server(s) in the same way that disk-based tables are. For SCHEMA_ONLY tables, the table schema will be replicated to the secondary server(s), but not the data (because the data is never logged for schema only tables). As such, if SCHEMA_ONLY tables are replicated, a mechanism to refill these tables must be included for a failover scenario. If the memory-optimized tables are defined as SCHEMA_AND_DATA, the data will be replicated to the secondary server(s) and will be available to any readable secondary connections that may be reading from the secondary server(s).

Failover Cluster Instances are also fully supported for high availability with the In-Memory OLTP Engine. The memory-optimized tables behave in exactly the same way as with a standalone instance, meaning that tables defined with the SCHEMA_AND_DATA property will be instantiated at server startup, which means that they are created and filled using the checkpoint file pairs at startup. Depending on how large these tables are, this initialization can take some time. This is *not* unique to Failover Cluster Instances, but rather for any SQL Server that uses the In-Memory OLTP Engine.

It is now also possible to use replication in conjunction with memory-optimized tables. The initial implementation inside SQL Server 2016 allows for a transactional or snapshot replication publisher to publish tables to a subscriber and for the subscriber tables to be created as memory-optimized tables. This means that the memory-optimized tables are in fact available on the subscriber side of the replication topology. Using this topology removes the bottleneck of locking and blocking on the subscriber side and would allow the subscriber to easily keep up with the replication data flow.

Tools and wizards

As with many of the features in SQL Server, In-Memory OLTP also has some useful tools to assist in working with the technology.

The main desire for many developers is to take their existing database solutions and to convert them to memory-optimized solutions (ideally automatically). Microsoft has provided a few options to investigate a database and deliver feedback on the database design with suggestions where memory-optimized solutions would be possible and feasible.

We can begin with the simplest of these tools: the In-Memory OLTP Migration Checklist. This is a wizard provided inside **SQL Server Management Studio** (**SSMS**), which will perform a variety of checks against an entire database and provide a set of checklists/reports that inform exactly what objects inside a database are candidates for conversion into memory-optimized objects. An overview of the work required is also provided (for example, supported and unsupported data types). The checklist wizard can be found by right-clicking a database and choosing **Tasks** and then **Generate In-Memory OLTP Migration Checklists**:

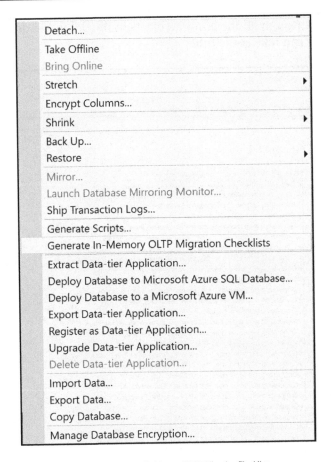

Figure 12.1: Generating In-Memory OLTP Migration Checklists

This will then launch the wizard for the chosen database, which guides us through the process of evaluating a database for compatibility with the In-Memory OLTP Engine. After choosing the objects to be processed by the wizard and where to store the resulting report, the wizard can be started.

The wizard then runs through all the chosen objects in the database; depending on the number of objects, this can take some time:

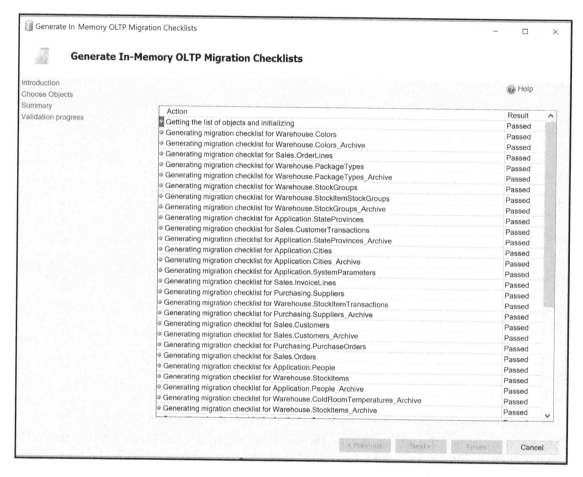

Figure 12.2: In-Memory OLTP Migration Checklist progress

Upon completion, the wizard can be closed and the reports found in the location specified before running the analysis. The resulting report files are HTML files, one per database object that has been analyzed, showing what changes (if any) are required to make the object compatible with the In-Memory OLTP Engine:

Memory optimization checklist for [WideWorldImporters].[BuyingGroups]

Description	Validation Result
No unsupported data types are defined on this table.	Succeeded
No sparse columns are defined for this table.	Succeeded
No identity columns with unsupported seed and increment are defined for this table.	Succeeded
Supported foreign key relationships are defined on this table but the table cannot be migrated through the memory-optimization wizard. To migrate this table as well as the other tables involved in the FOREIGN KEY references, first remove the FOREIGN KEYs, then migrate the tables using the memory-optimization wizard, and finally add the FOREIGN KEY references to the migrated memory-optimized tables.	Failed: More information
- FK_Sales_BuyingGroups_Application_People: Foreign Key on this table (referencing Application.People)	
- FK_Sales_Customers_BuyingGroupID_Sales_BuyingGroups: Foreign Key as primary table (referenced by Sales.Customers)	
- FK_Sales_SpecialDeals_BuyingGroupID_Sales_BuyingGroups: Foreign Key as primary table (referenced by Sales.SpecialDeals)	
No unsupported constraints are defined on this table.	Succeeded
No unsupported indexes are defined on this table.	Succeeded
No unsupported triggers are defined on this table.	Succeeded
Post migration row size does not exceed the row size limit of memory-optimized tables.	Succeeded
Table is not partitioned or replicated.	Succeeded

Figure 12.3: Example Migration Checklist Report for a table

As we can see in *Figure 12.3*, the report files generated by the wizard provide an overview of what properties of an object are or are not supported by the In-Memory OLTP Engine. Where appropriate, a link is supplied that loads a Books Online support page, describing the issue found and possible solutions.

The next tool to assist in evaluating a database for a possible migration of objects into the In-Memory OLTP Engine is a standard report delivered with SSMS, the **Transaction Performance Analysis Overview**. This report requires no pre-configuration of a database, except for the database being hosted on a SQL Server 2016 instance. The report collects execution statistics for queries in the database and shows which tables or stored procedures are possible candidates for a migration to the In-Memory OLTP Engine. This means that the report will only have meaningful data in it *after* the database has been in use for a few hours or days:

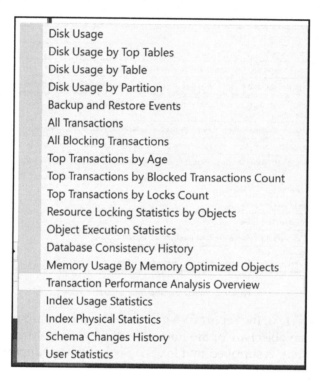

Figure 12.4: Transaction Performance Analysis Overview report

The report loads inside SSMS and offers the choice of table or stored procedure analysis. Both options deliver a similar report, displaying the objects that have been recently accessed. These objects are plotted on a graph showing the potential performance impact of a migration to the In-Memory OLTP Engine versus the estimated work required to make the change. The best candidates are objects plotted toward the top-right of the graph (high impact, minimal migration work).

These two analysis options allow us to get an idea of how much impact and how much work would be involved in migrating to the In-Memory OLTP Engine. The results should be considered a basic indication and by no means offer a guarantee of accuracy:

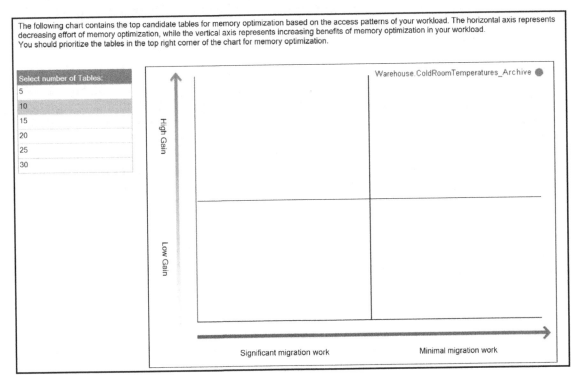

Figure 12.5: Transaction Performance Analysis Overview result

Summary

In this chapter, we covered how the In-Memory OLTP Engine has evolved from the first version released with SQL Server 2014 to the latest version in SQL Server 2016.

Many of the restrictions around data types, constraints, large binary objects, and collations, along with the ability to alter objects without having to drop and recreate them, provide us all with huge improvements for developers. However, we have also seen that there are still limitations and areas where the use of In-Memory OLTP is not the best choice, or must at least be carefully considered before being chosen for a particular implementation.

A vastly more efficient processing engine allows us to consider scenarios where current implementations may benefit from the reduced overhead of the In-Memory OLTP Engine. The ability to seamlessly interact between memory-optimized and disk-based objects makes for a very compelling programming experience. The tooling that Microsoft provides allows us to quickly create an overview of how/where time and resources need investing to take a disk-based implementation and convert it to a memory-optimized solution.

The In-Memory OLTP Engine has made good progress from its initial incarnation in SQL Server 2014 and it is clear that the feature is here to stay. Future versions of SQL Server will no doubt build on the evolution of the engine and provide further integration and support for the remaining data types and programming constructs that are currently unsupported. I for one look forward to seeing this evolution take place and am excited to see developers adopting this fantastic technology in their projects. Now, go forth and see where you can accelerate your SQL Server database projects, by removing those locks and blocks!

13

Supporting R in SQL Server

SQL Server R Services combines the power and flexibility of the open source R language with enterprise-level tools for data storage and management, workflow development, and reporting and visualization. This chapter introduces R Services and the R language. R is developing quite fast, so it is worth mentioning that the R version used in this book is 3.2.2 (2015-08-14).

In the first section, you will learn about the free version of the R language and engine. You will also become familiar with the basic concepts of programming in R.

When developing an advanced analytical solution, you spend the vast majority of time with data. Typically, data is not in a shape useful for statistical and other algorithms. Data preparation is not really glorious but is an essential part of analytical projects. You will learn how to create a new or use an existing dataset and learn about basic data manipulation with R in the second section of this chapter.

The data preparation part of an analytical project is interleaved with the data understanding part. You need to gather in-depth knowledge of your data and data values before you can analyze it. Showing data graphically is a very efficient and popular method of data understanding. Fortunately, R support for data visualization is really comprehensive. However, sometimes numbers tell us more or in a more condensed way than graphs. Introductory statistics, like descriptive statistics, provide you with the numbers you need to understand your data. Again, R support for introductory statistics is astonishing.

Open source products also have some disadvantages. For example, scalability might be an issue. SQL Server 2016 brings R support inside the database engine. With this support, many of your problems are solved. You get many scalable procedures and enhanced security for your R applications.

This chapter will cover the following points:

- R: basics and concepts
- Core elements of the R language
- R data structures
- Basic data management
- Simple visualizations
- Introductory statistics
- SQL Server R Services architecture
- Creating and using scalable R solutions in SQL Server

Introducing R

R is the most widely used language for statistics, data mining, and machine learning. Besides the language, R is also the environment and the engine that executes the R code. You need to learn how to develop R programs, just as you need to learn any other programming language you intend to use.

Before going deeper into the R language, let's explain what the terms **statistics**, **data mining**, and **machine learning** mean. Statistics is the study and analysis of data collections, and interpretation and presentation of the results of the analysis. Typically, you don't have all population data, or *census* data, collected. You have to use **samples**—often survey samples. Data mining is again a set of powerful analysis techniques used on your data in order to discover patterns and rules that might improve your business. Machine learning is programming to use data to solve a given problem automatically. You can immediately see that all three definitions overlap. There is not a big distinction between them; you can even use them as synonyms. Small differences are visible when you think of the users of each method. Statistics is a science, and the users are scientists. Data mining users are typically business people. Machine learning users are, as the name suggests, often machines. Nevertheless, in many cases, the same algorithms are used, so there is really a lot of overlapping among the three branches of applied mathematics in analytical applications.

Let's not get lost in these formal definitions and start with R immediately. You will learn about:

- Parts of open source R
- Basic description of the R language
- Obtaining help
- R core syntax elements

- R variables
- R vectors
- R packages

This chapter assumes that you are already familiar with the SQL Server and R tools, including SQL Server Management Studio, RStudio, or R Tools for Visual Studio, so you can start to write the code immediately.

Starting with R

You can download R from the **Comprehensive R Archive Network (CRAN)** site at http://cran.r-project.org. You can get the R engine for Windows, Linux, or Mac OS X. Microsoft also maintains its own R portal, the **Microsoft R Application Network (MRAN)** site at https://mran.revolutionanalytics.com/. You can use this site to download Microsoft R Open, the enhanced distribution of open source R from Microsoft. After installation, you start working in an interactive mode. You can use the R console client tool to write code line by line. As you already know, there are many additional tools. Let's just repeat here that the most widely used free tool for writing and executing R code is RStudio. It is free and you can download it from https://www.rstudio.com/. This section assumes you use RStudio for the code examples.

R is a **case-sensitive, functional**, and **interpreted language**. The R engine interprets your commands one by one. You don't type commands but rather call functions to achieve results, even a function called q() to quit an R session. As in any programming language, it is good practice to comment the code well. You can start a comment with a hash mark (#) anywhere in the line; any text after the hash mark is not executed and is treated as a comment. You end a command with a semicolon (;) or a new line. Commands finished by a semicolon can be combined in a single line. Similarly, as in T-SQL, the explicit end of a command with a semicolon is a better practice than just entering a new command on a new line. Here is the first example of the R code, showing a comment and using the contributors() function to list the authors and other contributors to the language:

```
# R Contributors
contributors();
```

The abbreviated results are:

```
R is a project which is attempting to provide a modern piece of
statistical software for the GNU suite of software.
The current R is the result of a collaborative effort with
contributions from all over the world.
Authors of R.
R was initially written by Robert Gentleman and Ross Ihaka-also known as "R
& R"
of the Statistics Department of the University of Auckland.
Since mid-1997 there has been a core group with write access to the R
source, currently consisting of
...
```

In R, help is always at your fingertips. With the `help()` function, you can get onto help first, and then search for the details you need. Using `help.start()` gives you the links to the free documentation about R. With `help("options")`, you can examine the global options that are used to affect the way in which R computes and displays the results. You can get help for a specific function. For example, `help("exp")` displays the help for the exponential function. You can use the shorter version of the help function—just the question mark. For example, `?"exp"` also displays help for the exponential function. With `example("exp")`, you can get examples of usage of the exponential function. You can also search in help using a command—either `help.search("topic")` or `??"topic"`. With `RSiteSearch("exp")`, you can perform an online search for documentation about exponential functions over multiple R sites. The following code summarizes these help options:

```
# Getting help on help
help();
# General help
help.start();
# Help about global options
help("options");
# Help on the function exp()
help("exp");
# Examples for the function exp()
example("exp");
# Search
help.search("constants");
??"constants";
# Online search
RSiteSearch("exp");
```

Finally, there is also the `demo()` function. This function runs some more advanced demo scripts, showing you the capabilities of R code. For example, the following call to this function shows you some graphic capabilities:

```
demo("graphics");
```

In RStudio, you get the code to execute in the **Console** window (bottom-left window by default). You need to move the cursor to that window and hit the *Enter* key to execute the first part of the code. You get the first graph in the bottom-right window. Then you hit the *Enter* key a couple of times more to scroll through all demo graphs. One part of the code that creates a nice pie chart is shown here:

```
pie.sales <- c(0.12, 0.3, 0.26, 0.16, 0.04, 0.12);
names(pie.sales) <- c("Blueberry", "Cherry", "Apple",
                "Boston Cream", "Other", "Vanilla Cream");
pie(pie.sales,
    col = c("purple","violetred1","green3","cornsilk","cyan","white"));

title(main = "January Pie Sales", cex.main = 1.8, font.main = 1);
title(xlab = "(Don't try this at home kids)", cex.lab = 0.8, font.lab = 3);
```

The graphical results are shown in the following figure:

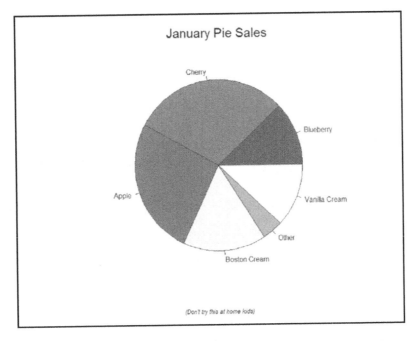

Figure 13.1: Demo pie chart

All of the objects created exist in memory. Each session has its own **workspace**. When you finish a session, you can save the workspace or the objects from memory to disk in an .RData file and load them in the next session. The workspace is saved in the folder from which R reads the source code files, or in a default folder. You can check the objects in the current workspace with the objects() function or with the ls() function. You can check the working folder, or directory, with the getwd() call. You can change it interactively with the setwd(dir) function, where the dir parameter is a string representing the new working directory. You can remove single objects from the workspace and memory with the rm(objectname) function, or a full list of objects using the same function with the list of objects as a parameter (you will learn about lists and other data structures later in this chapter). There are many more possibilities, including saving images, getting the history of last commands, saving the history, reloading the history, and even saving a specific object to a specific file. You will learn about some of them later in this chapter.

R language Basics

You can start investigating R by writing simple expressions that include literals and operators. Here are some examples:

```
1 + 1;
2 + 3 * 4;
3 ^ 3;
sqrt(81);
pi;
```

This code evaluates three mathematical expressions first using the basic operators. Check the results and note that R, as expected, evaluates the expressions using operator precedence as we know from mathematics. Then it calls the sqrt() function to calculate the square root of 81. Finally, the code checks the value of the base package built-in constant for the number pi (π). R has some built-in constants. Check them by searching help for them with ??"constants".

It is easy to generate **sequences**. The following code shows some examples:

```
rep(1,10);
3:7;
seq(3,7);
seq(5,17,by=3);
```

The first command replicates number 1 ten times using the `rep()` function. The second line generates the sequence of numbers between three and seven. The third line does exactly the same, just this time using the `seq()` function. This function gives you additional possibilities, as the fourth line shows. This command generates a sequence of numbers between 5 and 17, but this time with an increment of 3.

Writing ad hoc expressions means you need to rewrite them whenever you need them. To reuse the values, you need to store them in variables. You assign a value to a variable with an assignment operator. R supports multiple assignment operators. You can use the left assignment operator (<-), where the variable name is on the left side, or right assignment operator (->), where the variable name is on the right side. You can also use the equals (=) operator. The left assignment operator is the one you will see most commonly in R code. The following code stores the numbers 2, 3, and 4 in variables and then performs a calculation using the variables:

```
x <- 2;
y <- 3;
z <- 4;
x + y * z;
```

The result is 14. Note again that R is case sensitive. For example, the following line of code produces an error, because variables X, Y, and Z are not defined:

```
X + Y + Z;
```

You can separate part of a variable name with a dot. This way, you can organize your objects into namespaces, just as you can in .NET languages. Here is an example:

```
This.Year <- 2016;
This.Year;
```

You can check whether the equals assignment operator really works:

```
x = 2;
y = 3;
z = 4;
x + y * z;
```

If you executed the last code, you would get the same result as with the code that used the left assignment operator instead of the equals operator.

Besides mathematical operators, R supports logical operators as well. To test the exact equality, use the double equals (==) operator. Other logical operators include <, <=, >, >=, and != to test the inequality. In addition, you can combine two logical expressions into a third one using the logical AND (&) and logical OR (|) operators. The following code checks a variable for exact equality with a number literal:

```
x <- 2;
x == 2;
```

The result is TRUE.

Every variable in R is actually an object. A simple scalar variable is a **vector** of length one. A vector is a one-dimensional array of scalars of the same **type**, or **mode**: numeric, character, logical, complex (imaginary numbers), and raw (bytes). You use the combine function c() to define the vectors. Here are the ways to assign variable values as vectors. Note that the variables with the same names will be overwritten:

```
x <- c(2,0,0,4);
assign("y", c(1,9,9,9));
c(5,4,3,2) -> z;
q = c(1,2,3,4);
```

The first line uses the left assignment operator. The second assigns the second vector to the variable y using the assign() function. The third line uses the right assignment operator, and the fourth line the equals operator.

You can perform operations on vectors just like you would perform them on scalars (remember, after all, a scalar is just a vector of length one). Here are some examples of vector operations:

```
x + y;
x * 4;
sqrt(x);
```

The results of the previous three lines of code are:

```
3  9  9 13
8  0  0 16
1.414214 0.000000 0.000000 2.000000
```

You can see that the operations were performed element by element. You can operate on a selected element only as well. You use numerical index values to select specific elements. Here are some examples:

```
x <- c(2,0,0,4);
x[1];
```

```
x[-1];
x[1] <- 3; x;
x[-1] = 5; x;
```

First, the code assigns a vector to a variable. The second line selects the first element of the vector. The third line selects all elements except the first one and returns a vector of three elements. The fourth line of the code assigns a new value to the first element and then shows the vector. The last line assigns new values to all elements but the first one, and then shows the vector. The results are, therefore:

```
2
0  0  4
3  0  0  4
3  5  5  5
```

You can also use logical operators on vectors. Here are some examples:

```
y <- c(1,9,9,9);
y < 8;
y[4] = 1;
y < 8;
y[y<8] = 2; y;
```

The first line assigns a vector to variable y. The second line compares each vector value to a numeric constant 8 and returns TRUE for those elements where the value is lower than the given value. The third line assigns a new value to the fourth element of the vector. The fourth line performs the same comparison of the vector elements to number 8 again and returns TRUE for the first and fourth element. The last line edits the elements of vector y that satisfy the condition in the parenthesis—those elements where the value is less than 8. The result is:

```
TRUE FALSE FALSE FALSE
TRUE FALSE FALSE  TRUE
2  9  9  2
```

Vectors and scalars are very basic data structures. You will learn about more advanced data structures in the next section of this chapter. Before that, it is high time to mention a very important concept in R: packages.

> The R code shown in this chapter has used only core capabilities so far; capabilities that you get when you install the R engine. Although these capabilities are already very extensive, the real power of R comes with additional packages.

Packages are optional modules you can download and install. Each package brings additional functions, or demo data, in a well-defined format. The number of available packages is growing year by year. At the time of writing this book, in summer 2016, the number of downloadable packages was already nearly 9,000. A small set of standard packages is already included when you install the core engine. You can check out installed packages with the `installed.packages()` command. Packages are stored in the folder called `library`. You can get the path to the library with the `.libPaths()` function (note the dot in the name). You can use the `library()` function to list the packages in your library.

The most important command to learn is the `install.packages("packagename")`. This command searches the CRAN sites for the package, downloads it, unzips it, and installs it. Of course, you need a web connection in order to execute it successfully. You can imagine that such a simplistic approach is not very welcome in highly secure environments. Of course, in order to use R Services in SQL Server, the package installation is more secure and more complex, as you will learn later in this chapter.

Once a package is installed, you load it into memory with the `library(packagename)` command. You can get help on the content of the package with the `help(package = "packagename")` command. For example, if you want to read the data from a SQL Server database, you need to install the RODBC library. The following code installs this library, loads it, and gets the help for functions and methods available in it:

```
install.packages("RODBC");
library(RODBC);
help(package = "RODBC");
```

Before reading the data from SQL Server, you need to perform two additional tasks. First, you need to create a login and a database user for the R session and give the user the permission to read the data. Then, you need to create an ODB **data source name (DSN)** that points to this database. In SQL Server Management Studio, connect to your SQL Server, and then in **Object Explorer**, expand the `Security` folder. Right-click on the `Logins` subfolder. Create a new login and a database user in the `WideWorldImportersDW` database, and add this user to the `db_datareader` role.

I created a SQL Server login called RUser with password Pa$$w0rd, and a user with the same name, as the following screenshot shows:

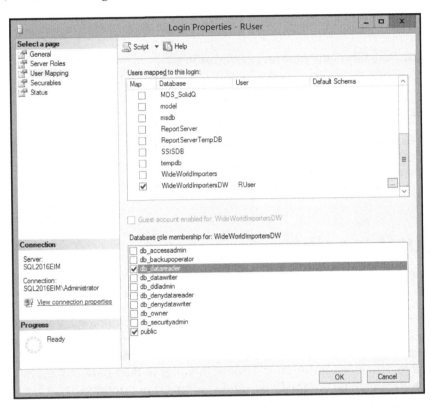

Figure 13.2: Generating the RUser login and database user

After that, I used the ODBC Data Sources tool to create a system DSN called WWIDW. I configured the DSN to connect to my local SQL Server with the RUser SQL Server login and appropriate password, and change the context to the WideWorldImportersDW database. If you've successfully finished both steps, you can execute this R code to read the data from SQL Server:

```
con <- odbcConnect("WWIDW", uid="RUser", pwd="Pa$$w0rd");
sqlQuery(con,
        "SELECT c.Customer,
            SUM(f.Quantity) AS TotalQuantity,
            SUM(f.[Total Excluding Tax]) AS TotalAmount,
            COUNT(*) AS SalesCount
        FROM Fact.Sale AS f
          INNER JOIN Dimension.Customer AS c
          ON f.[Customer Key] = c.[Customer Key]
```

```
         WHERE c.[Customer Key] <> 0
         GROUP BY c.Customer
         HAVING COUNT(*) > 400
         ORDER BY SalesCount DESC;");
close(con);
```

The code returns the following (abbreviated) result:

	Customer	TotalQuantity	TotalAmount	SalesCount
1	Tailspin Toys (Vidrine, LA)	18899	340163.8	455
2	Tailspin Toys (North Crows Nest, IN)	17684	313999.5	443
3	Tailspin Toys (Tolna, ND)	16240	294759.1	443
4	Wingtip Toys (Key Biscayne, FL)	18658	335053.5	441
5	Tailspin Toys (Peeples Valley, AZ)	15874	307461.0	437
6	Wingtip Toys (West Frostproof, FL)	18564	346621.5	436
7	Tailspin Toys (Maypearl, TX)	18219	339721.9	436

Manipulating data

Before you can extract some information from your data, you need to understand how the data is stored. First, you need to understand data structures in R.

Scalars and vectors are the most basic data structures. In R terminology, you analyze a dataset. A dataset consists of rows with *cases* or observations to analyze and columns representing the variables or attributes of the cases. This definition of a dataset looks like a SQL Server table. However, R does not work with tables in the relational sense. For example, in a relational, the order of rows and columns is not defined. In order to get a value, you need the column name and the key of the row. However, in R, you can use the position of a cell for most of the data structures. You have already seen this position reference for vectors.

In this section, you will learn about the data structures in R and the basic manipulation of datasets, including:

- Arrays and matrices
- Factors
- Data frames
- Lists
- Creating new variables
- Recoding variables
- Dealing with missing values
- Type conversions
- Merging datasets

Introducing data structures in R

A **matrix** is a two-dimensional array of values of the same type, or mode. You generate matrices from vectors with the `matrix()` function. Columns and rows can have labels. You can generate a matrix from a vector by rows or by columns (default). The following code shows some matrices and the difference of generation by rows or by columns:

```
x = c(1,2,3,4,5,6); x;
Y = array(x, dim=c(2,3)); Y;
Z = matrix(x,2,3,byrow=F); Z
U = matrix(x,2,3,byrow=T); U;   # A matrix - fill by rows
rnames = c("Row1", "Row2");
cnames = c("Col1", "Col2", "Col3");
V = matrix(x,2,3,byrow=T, dimnames = list(rnames, cnames)); V;
```

The first line generates and shows a one-dimensional vector. The second line creates a two-dimensional array, which is the same as a matrix, with two rows and three columns. The matrix is filled from a vector column by column. The third row actually uses the `matrix()` function to create a matrix, and fill it by columns. The matrix is equivalent to the previous one. The fourth row fills the matrix by rows. The fifth and sixth rows define row and column names. The last row again creates a matrix filled by rows; however, this time it adds row and column names in a list of two vectors. Here are the results:

```
[1] 1 2 3 4 5 6
     [,1] [,2] [,3]
[1,]    1    3    5
[2,]    2    4    6
     [,1] [,2] [,3]
[1,]    1    3    5
```

```
[2,]    2    4    6
       [,1] [,2] [,3]
[1,]    1    2    3
[2,]    4    5    6
       Col1 Col2 Col3
Row1    1    2    3
Row2    4    5    6
```

You can see the difference between filling by rows or by columns. The following code shows how you can refer to matrix elements by position, or even by name, if you've named columns and rows:

```
U[1,];
U[1,c(2,3)];
U[,c(2,3)];
V[,c("Col2", "Col3")];
```

The results are:

```
[1] 1 2 3
[1] 2 3
       [,1] [,2]
[1,]    2    3
[2,]    5    6
       Col2 Col3
Row1    2    3
Row2    5    6
```

As you can see from the matrix examples, a matrix is just a two-dimensional array. You generate arrays with the array() function. This function again accepts a vector of values as the first input parameter, then a vector specifying the number of elements on dimensions, and then a list of vectors for the names of the dimensions' elements. An array is filled by columns, then by rows, then by the third dimension (let's call it pages), and so on. Here is an example that generates a three-dimensional array:

```
rnames = c("Row1", "Row2");
cnames = c("Col1", "Col2", "Col3");
pnames = c("Page1", "Page2", "Page3");
Y = array(1:18, dim=c(2,3,3), dimnames = list(rnames, cnames,  pnames)); Y;
```

The result is as follows:

```
, , Page1
     Col1 Col2 Col3
Row1    1    3    5
Row2    2    4    6
, , Page2
     Col1 Col2 Col3
Row1    7    9   11
Row2    8   10   12
, , Page3
     Col1 Col2 Col3
Row1   13   15   17
Row2   14   16   18
```

Variables can store **discrete** or **continuous** values. Discrete values can be **nominal**, or **categorical**, where they represent labels only, or **ordinal**, where there is an intrinsic order in the values. In R, **factors** represent nominal and ordinal variables. **Levels** of a factor represent distinct values. You create factors from vectors with the factor() function. It is important to properly determine the factors because advanced data mining and machine learning algorithms treat discrete and continuous variables differently. Here are some examples of factors:

```
x = c("good", "moderate", "good", "bad", "bad", "good");
y = factor(x); y;
z = factor(x, order=TRUE); z;
w = factor(x, order=TRUE,
          levels=c("bad", "moderate","good")); w;
```

The first line defines a vector of six values denoting whether the observed person was in a good, moderate or bad mood. The second line generates a factor from the vector and shows it. The third line generates an ordinal variable. Note the results—the order is defined alphabetically. The last commands in the last two lines generate another ordinal variable from the same vector, just this time specifying the order explicitly. Here are the results:

```
[1] good       moderate good     bad       bad       good
Levels: bad good moderate
[1] good       moderate good     bad       bad       good
Levels: bad < good < moderate
[1] good       moderate good     bad       bad       good
Levels: bad < moderate < good
```

Lists are the most complex data structures in R. Lists are ordered collections of different data structures. You typically do not work with them a lot. You need to know them because some functions return multiple results, or complex results, packed in a list, and you need to extract specific parts. You create lists with the `list()` function. You refer to objects of a list by position, using the index number enclosed in double parentheses. If an element is a vector or a matrix, you can additionally use the position of a value in a vector enclosed in single parentheses. Here is an example:

```
L = list(name1="ABC", name2="DEF",
         no.children=2, children.ages=c(3,6));
L;
L[[1]];
L[[4]];
L[[4]][2];
```

The example produces the following result:

```
$name1
[1] "ABC"
$name2
[1] "DEF"
$no.children
[1] 2
$children.ages
[1] 3 6
[1] "ABC"
[1] 3 6
[1] 6
```

Finally, the most important data structure is a **data frame**. Most of the time, you analyze data stored in a data frame. Data frames are matrices where each variable can be of a different type. Remember, a variable is stored in a column, and all values of a single variable must be of the same type. Data frames are very similar to SQL Server tables. However, they are still matrices, meaning that you can refer to the elements by position, and that they are ordered. You create a data frame with the `data.frame()` function from multiple vectors of the same length. Here is an example of generating a data frame:

```
CategoryId = c(1,2,3,4);
CategoryName = c("Bikes", "Components", "Clothing", "Accessories");
ProductCategories = data.frame(CategoryId, CategoryName);
ProductCategories;
```

The result is:

```
     CategoryId CategoryName
1         1            Bikes
2         2       Components
3         3         Clothing
4         4      Accessories
```

Most of the time, you get a data frame from your data source, for example from a SQL Server database. The results of the earlier example that was reading from SQL Server can be actually stored in a data frame. You can also enter the data manually, or read it from many other sources, including text files, Excel, and many more. The following code retrieves the data from a **comma-separated values** (CSV) file in a data frame, and then displays the first four columns for the first five rows of the data frame. The CSV file is provided in the download for the accompanying code for this book, as described in the preface of the book:

```
TM = read.table("C:\\SQL2016DevGuide\\Chapter13_TM.csv",
                sep=",", header=TRUE, row.names = "CustomerKey",
                stringsAsFactors = TRUE);
TM[1:5,1:4];
```

The code specifies that the first row of the file holds column names (header), and that the CustomerKey column represents the row names (or row identifications). If you are interested, the data comes from the dbo.vTargetMail view from the AdventureWorksDW2014 demo SQL Server database you can download from Microsoft CodePlex at https://msftdbprodsamples.codeplex.com/. The first five rows are presented here:

```
      MaritalStatus Gender TotalChildren NumberChildrenAtHome
11000           M       M             2                    0
11001           S       M             3                    3
11002           M       M             3                    3
11003           S       F             0                    0
11004           S       F             5                    5
```

Getting sorted with data management

After you've imported the data to analyze in a data frame, you need to prepare it for further analysis. There are quite a few possibilities of how to retrieve values from a data frame. You can refer to the data by position, or by using the subscript notation. However, if you use a single subscript only, then you retrieve columns defined by the subscript and all rows. The same is true if you use a vector of column names only, without specifying the rows. If you specify two indexes or index ranges, then the first one is used for rows and the second one for columns. The following code shows these options:

```
TM[1:2];                                # Two columns
TM[c("MaritalStatus", "Gender")];       # Two columns
TM[1:3,1:2];                            # Three rows, two columns
TM[1:3,c("MaritalStatus", "Gender")];
```

The first command returns all rows and two columns only. The second command produces the same result. The third command returns three rows, again for the MaritalStatus and Gender columns only. The fourth row produces the same result as the third one.

The most common notation is using the data frame name and column name, separated by the dollar ($) sign, like TM$Gender. You can also avoid excessive writing of the data frame name by using the attach() or with() functions. With the attach() function, you add the data frame to the search path that R uses to find the objects. You can refer to a variable name directly without the data frame name if the variable name is unique in the search path. The detach() function removes the data frame from the search path, to avoid possible ambiguity with duplicate variable names later. The with() function allows you to name the data frame only once, and then use the variables in a set of statements enclosed in { } brackets inside the body of the function. The following code shows these approaches:

```
table(TM$MaritalStatus, TM$Gender);
attach(TM);
table(MaritalStatus, Gender);
detach(TM);
with(TM,
     {table(MaritalStatus, Gender)});
```

The first line produces a cross-tabulation of the `MaritalStatus` and `Gender`. Please note the `dataframe$variable` notation. The second line adds the data frame to the search path. The third command produces the same cross-tabulation as the first one, however, this time referring to variable names only. The fourth command removes the data frame from the search path. The last command uses the `with()` function to allow you to define the data frame name only once and then use only variable names in the commands inside the function. Note that, because there is only one command in the function, the brackets `{ }` can be omitted. All three cross-tabulations return the same result:

```
                Gender
MaritalStatus   F     M
            M 4745 5266
            S 4388 4085
```

Sometimes, you get numeric categorical variable values and you want to use character labels. The `factor()` function can help you here. For example, in the TM data frame, there is the `BikeBuyer` variable. For this variable, 0 means the person never purchased a bike and 1 means this person is a bike buyer. The following code shows you how to add labels to the numerical values:

```
table(TM$BikeBuyer, TM$Gender);
TM$BikeBuyer <- factor(TM$BikeBuyer,
                    levels = c(0,1),
                    labels = c("No","Yes"));
table(TM$BikeBuyer, TM$Gender);
```

The results are shown here. Note that, the second time, the labels for the values of the `BikeBuyer` variable are used:

```
      F    M
0  4536 4816
1  4597 4535
          F    M
No   4536 4816
Yes  4597 4535
```

You can easily get the metadata about your objects. Some useful functions that give you information about your objects include the following:

- `class()`: This function returns the type of object
- `names()`: This function returns the names of the components, such as variable names in a data frame
- `length()`: This function returns the number of elements, for example, the number of variables in a data frame

- `dim()`: This function returns the dimensionality of an object, for example, the number of rows and columns in a data frame
- `str()`: This function gives details about the structure of an object

Here are examples of using these metadata functions:

```
class(TM);
names(TM);
length(TM);
dim(TM);
str(TM);
```

The results are as follows:

```
[1] "data.frame"
[1] "MaritalStatus"          "Gender"            "TotalChildren"
[4] "NumberChildrenAtHome"   "Education"         "Occupation"
[7] "HouseOwnerFlag"         "NumberCarsOwned"   "CommuteDistance"
[10] "Region"                "BikeBuyer"         "YearlyIncome"
[13] "Age"
[1] 13
[1] 18484       13
'data.frame':        18484 obs. of  13 variables:
$ MaritalStatus : Factor w/ 2 levels "M","S": 1 2 1 2 2 2 2 1 2 2 ...
$ Gender        : Factor w/ 2 levels "F","M": 2 2 2 1 1 2 1 2 1 2 ...
$ TotalChildren : int  2 3 3 0 5 0 0 3 4 0 ...
```

Note that the `CustomerKey` column is not listed among the thirteen columns of the data frame, because when the data was imported, this column was set to row names. In addition, only string variables were converted to factors. In the abbreviated result of the last command, you can see that the `TotalChildren` is an integer and not a factor, although it can occupy only values from zero to five.

Many times, calculated variables are much more meaningful for an analysis than just the base ones you read from your data source. For example, in medicine, the **body mass index (BMI)**, defined as weight divided by the square of the height, is much more meaningful than the base variables of height and weight it is derived from. You can add new variables to a data frame, recode continuous values to a list of discrete values, change the data type of variable values, and more. The following example uses the `within()` function, which is similar to the `with()` function. It's just that it allows updates of a data frame, to add a new variable `MartitalStatusInt`, derived from the `MaritalStatus` as an integer. This variable tells us the number of additional people in the household of the case observed:

```
TM <- within(TM, {
  MaritalStatusInt <- NA
```

```
    MaritalStatusInt[MaritalStatus == "S"] <- 0
    MaritalStatusInt[MaritalStatus == "M"] <- 1
});
str(TM);
```

In the body of the function, firstly the new variable is defined as missing. Then, the MaritalStatus values are used to define the number of additional persons in the household; if the person in the case observed is married, then the value is 1, if the person is single, then 0. The last line of the code shows the new structure of the data frame. The abbreviated structure is:

```
'data.frame':    18484 obs. of  14 variables:
$ MaritalStatus       : Factor w/ 2 levels "M","S": 1 2 1 2 2 2 1 2 2 ...
...
$ MaritalStatusInt    : num  1 0 1 0 0 0 0 1 0 0 ...
```

You can see that the new variable values are correct; however, the mode is defined as numeric. You can change the data type with one of the as.targettype() functions, where targettype() is a placeholder for the actual target type function, as the following example shows:

```
TM$MaritalStatusInt <- as.integer(TM$MaritalStatusInt);
str(TM);
```

Now, the abbreviated structure of the TM data frame shows that the mode of the new column is integer.

In the next example, a new variable is added to the data frame, just as a simple calculation. The new variable, HouseholdNumber, is used to define the total number of people in the household of the person in the case observed. The calculation summarizes the number of children at home plus one if the person is married plus one for the person herself/himself. Finally, the mode is changed to an integer:

```
TM$HouseholdNumber = as.integer(
    1 + TM$MaritalStatusInt + TM$NumberChildrenAtHome);
str(TM);
```

The structure of the data frame shows that the calculation is correct:

```
'data.frame':    18484 obs. of  15 variables:
$ MaritalStatus       : Factor w/ 2 levels "M","S": 1 2 1 2 2 2 1 2 2 ...
...
$ MaritalStatusInt    : int  1 0 1 0 0 0 0 1 0 0 ...
$ HouseholdNumber     : int  2 4 5 1 6 1 1 5 5 1 ...
```

On many occasions, you have to deal with missing values, denoted with a literal NA. R treats missing values as completely unknown. This influences the results of the calculations. For example, adding a missing value to a known integer produces a missing value. You have to decide how to deal with missing data. You can exclude the rows with missing data completely, you can recode the missing values to a predefined value, or you can exclude the missing values from a single calculation. The following code defines a vector of six values; however, the last value is missing. You can use the is.na() function to check for each value, whether it is missing or not. Then, the code tries to calculate the mean value for all values of the vector. The last line of code tries to calculate the mean again, just this time by disregarding the missing value by using the na.rm = TRUE option. This option is available in most numeric functions and simply removes the missing values from the calculation:

```
x <- c(1,2,3,4,5,NA);
is.na(x);
mean(x);
mean(x, na.rm = TRUE);
```

The results of the previous code are here:

```
[1] FALSE FALSE FALSE FALSE FALSE  TRUE
[1] NA
[1] 3
```

You can see that the is.na() function evaluated each element separately, and returned a vector of the same dimensionality as the vector checked for the missing values. The mean() function returned a missing value when in the calculation a missing value was present, and the result you might have expected when the missing values were removed.

Frequently, you need to merge two datasets, or to define a new dataset as a projection of an existing one. Merging is similar to joining two tables in SQL Server, and a projection means selecting a subset of variables only. The merge() function joins two data frames based on a common identification of each case. Of course, the identification must be unique. The following code shows how to do the projection:

```
TM = read.table("C:\\SQL2016DevGuide\\Chapter13_TM.csv",
                sep=",", header=TRUE,
                stringsAsFactors = TRUE);
TM[1:3,1:3];
cols1 <- c("CustomerKey", "MaritalStatus");
TM1 <- TM[cols1];
cols2 <- c("CustomerKey", "Gender");
TM2 <- TM[cols2];
TM1[1:3, 1:2];
TM2[1:3, 1:2];
```

The code first re-reads the TM data frame, just this time without using the CustomerKey column for the row names. This column must be available in the data frame, because this is the unique identification of each case. Then the code defines the columns for the two projection data frames and shows the first three rows of each new data frame, as you can see in the results of the last two commands:

```
  CustomerKey MaritalStatus
1       11000             M
2       11001             S
3       11002             M
  CustomerKey Gender
1       11000      M
2       11001      M
3       11002      M
```

Now, let's join the two new datasets.

```
TM3 <- merge(TM1, TM2, by = "CustomerKey");
TM3[1:3, 1:3];
```

The results show that the join was done correctly:

```
  CustomerKey MaritalStatus Gender
1       11000             M      M
2       11001             S      M
3       11002             M      M
```

A data frame is a matrix. Sort order is important. Instead of merging two data frames by columns, you can bind them by columns. However, you need to be sure that both data frames are sorted in the same way; otherwise you might bind variables from one case with variables from another case. The following code binds two data frames by columns:

```
TM4 <- cbind(TM1, TM2);
TM4[1:3, 1:4];
```

The results show that, unlike the merge() function, the cbind() function did not use the CustomerKey for a common identification. It has blindly bound columns case by case, and preserved all variables from both source data frames. That's why the CustomerKey column appears twice in the result:

```
  CustomerKey MaritalStatus CustomerKey.1 Gender
1       11000             M         11000      M
2       11001             S         11001      M
3       11002             M         11002      M
```

You can also use the `rbind()` function to bind two data frames by rows. This is equal to the union of two rowsets in SQL Server. The following code shows how to filter a dataset by creating two new datasets, each one with two rows and two columns only. Then the code uses the `rbind()` function to union both data frames:

```
TM1 <- TM[TM$CustomerKey < 11002, cols1];
TM2 <- TM[TM$CustomerKey > 29481, cols1];
TM5 <- rbind(TM1, TM2);
TM5;
```

The results are here:

```
      CustomerKey MaritalStatus
1          11000            M
2          11001            S
18483      29482            M
18484      29483            M
```

Finally, what happens if you want to bind two data frames by columns but you are not sure about the ordering? Of course, you can sort the data. The following code shows how to create a new data frame from the TM data frame, this time sorted by the Age column descending. Note the usage of the minus (–) sign in the `order()` function to achieve the descending sort:

```
TMSortedByAge <- TM[order(-TM$Age),c("CustomerKey", "Age")];
TMSortedByAge[1:5,1:2];
```

The result is shown here:

```
      CustomerKey Age
1726        12725  99
5456        16455  98
3842        14841  97
3993        14992  97
7035        18034  97
```

Understanding the data

As already mentioned, understanding data is interleaved with data preparation. In order to know what to do, which variables need recoding, which variables have missing values, and how to combine variables into a new one, you need to deeply understand the data you are dealing with. You can get this understanding with a simple overview of the data, which might be a method good enough for small datasets, or a method for checking just a small subset of a large dataset.

You can get more information about the distribution of the variables by showing the distributions graphically. Basic statistical methods are also useful for data overview. Finally, sometimes these basic statistical results and graphs are already exactly what you need for a report.

R is an extremely powerful language and environment for both visualizations and statistics. You will learn how to:

- Create simple graphs
- Show plots and histograms
- Calculate frequencies distribution
- Use descriptive statistics methods

Basic visualizations

In R, you build a graph step-by-step. You start with a simple graph, and then add features to it with additional commands. You can even combine multiple plots and other graphs into a single graph. Besides viewing the graph interactively, you can save it to a file. There are many functions for drawing graphs. Let's start with the most basic one, the plot() function. Note that, if you removed the TM dataset from memory or didn't save the workspace when you exited the last session, you need to re-read the dataset. Here is the code that uses it to draw a graph for the Education variable of the TM dataset, which is also added to the search path to simplify further addressing to the variables:

```
TM = read.table("C:\\SQL2016DevGuide\\Chapter13_TM.csv",
                sep=",", header=TRUE,
                stringsAsFactors = TRUE);
attach(TM);

# A simple distribution
plot(Education);
```

The following screenshot shows the graph:

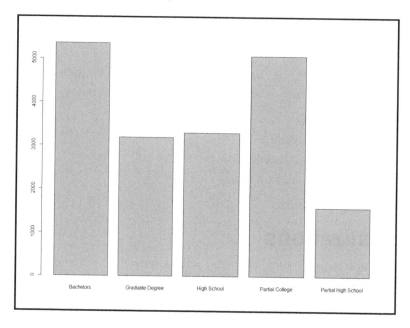

Figure 13.3: Basic plot for Education

The plot does not look too good. The Education variable is correctly identified as a factor; however, the variable is ordinal, so the levels should be defined. You can see the problem in the graph in the previous figure, where the values are sorted alphabetically. In addition, the graph and axes could also have titles, and a different color might look better. The plot() function accepts many parameters. In the following code, the parameters main for the main title, xlab for the x axis label, ylab for the y axis label, and col for the fill color are introduced:

```
Education = factor(Education, order=TRUE,
                levels=c("Partial High School",
                      "High School","Partial College",
                      "Bachelors", "Graduate Degree"));
plot(Education, main = 'Education',
     xlab='Education', ylab ='Number of Cases',
     col="purple");
```

This code produces a nicer graph, as you can see in the following screenshot:

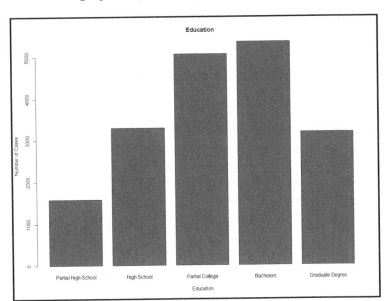

Figure 13.4: Enhanced plot for Education

Now, let's make some more complex visualizations with multiple lines of code! For a start, the following code generates a new data frame TM1 as a subset of the TM data frame, selecting only ten rows and three columns. This data frame will be used for line plots, where each case is plotted. The code also renames the variables to get unique names and adds the data frame to the search path:

```
cols1 <- c("CustomerKey", "NumberCarsOwned", "TotalChildren");
TM1 <- TM[TM$CustomerKey < 11010, cols1];
names(TM1) <- c("CustomerKey1", "NumberCarsOwned1", "TotalChildren1");
attach(TM1);
```

The next code cross-tabulates the NumberCarsOwned and the BikeBuyer variables and stores the result in an object. This cross-tabulation is used later for a bar plot:

```
nofcases <- table(NumberCarsOwned, BikeBuyer);
nofcases;
```

The cross-tabulation result is shown here:

```
                   BikeBuyer
NumberCarsOwned     0    1
              0 1551 2687
              1 2187 2696
              2 3868 2589
              3  951  694
              4  795  466
```

You can specify graphical parameters directly or through the `par()` function. When you set parameters with this function, these parameters are valid for all subsequent graphs until you reset them. You can get a list of parameters by simply calling the function without any arguments. The following line of code saves all modifiable parameters to an object by using the `no.readonly = TRUE` argument when calling the `par()` function. This way, it is possible to restore the default parameters later, without exiting the session:

```
oldpar <- par(no.readonly = TRUE);
```

The next line defines that the next four graphs will be combined in a single graph in a 2 x 2 invisible grid, filled by rows:

```
par(mfrow=c(2,2));
```

Now let's start filling the grid with smaller graphs. The next command creates a stacked bar showing marital status distribution in different education levels. It also adds a title and *x* and *y* axes labels. It changes the default colors used for different marital statuses to blue and yellow. This graph appears in the top-left corner of the invisible grid:

```
plot(Education, MaritalStatus,
     main='Education and marital status',
     xlab='Education', ylab ='Marital Status',
     col=c("blue", "yellow"));
```

The `hist()` function produces a histogram for numeric variables. Histograms are especially useful if they don't have too many bars. You can define breakpoints for continuous variables with many distinct values. However, the `NumberCarsOwned` variable has only five distinct values, and therefore defining breakpoints is not necessary. This graph fills the top-right cell of the grid:

```
hist(NumberCarsOwned, main = 'Number of cars owned',
     xlab='Number of Cars Owned', ylab ='Number of Cases',
     col="blue");
```

The next part of the code is slightly longer. It produces a line chart with two lines: one for the `TotalChildren1` and one for the `NumberCarsOwned1` variable. Note that the limited dataset is used, in order to get just a small number of plotting points. Firstly, a vector of colors is defined. This vector is used to define the colors for the legend. Then, the `plot()` function generates a line chart for the `TotalChildren1` variable. Here, two new parameters are introduced: the `type="o"` parameter defines the over-plotted points and lines, and the `lwd=2` parameter defines the line width. Then, the `lines()` function is used to add a line for the `NumberCarsOwned1` variable to the current graph, to the current cell of the grid. Then, a legend is added with the `legend()` function to the same graph. The `cex=1.4` parameter defines the character expansion factor relative to the current character size in the graph. The `bty="n"` parameter defines that there is no box drawn around the legend. The `lty` and `lwd` parameters define the line type and the line width for the legend. Finally, a title is added. This graph is positioned in the bottom-left cell of the grid:

```
plot_colors=c("blue", "red");
plot(TotalChildren1,
     type="o",col='blue', lwd=2,
     xlab="Key",ylab="Number");
lines(NumberCarsOwned1,
      type="o",col='red', lwd=2);
legend("topleft",
       c("TotalChildren", "NumberCarsOwned"),
       cex=1.4,col=plot_colors,lty=1:2,lwd=1, bty="n");
title(main="Total children and number of cars owned line chart",
      col.main="DarkGreen", font.main=4);
```

There is one more cell in the grid to fill. The `barplot()` function generates the histogram of the `NumberCarsOwned` variable in groups of the `BikeBuyer` variable and shows the histograms side by side. Note that the input for this function is the cross-tabulation object generated with the `table()` function. The `legend()` function adds a legend in the top-right corner of the chart. This chart fills the bottom-right cell of the grid:

```
barplot(nofcases,
        main='Number of cars owned and bike buyer gruped',
        xlab='BikeBuyer', ylab ='NumberCarsOwned',
        col=c("black", "blue", "red", "orange", "yellow"),
        beside=TRUE);
legend("topright",legend=rownames(nofcases),
       fill = c("black", "blue", "red", "orange", "yellow"),
       ncol = 1, cex = 0.75);
```

The following figure shows the big results, all four graphs combined into one:

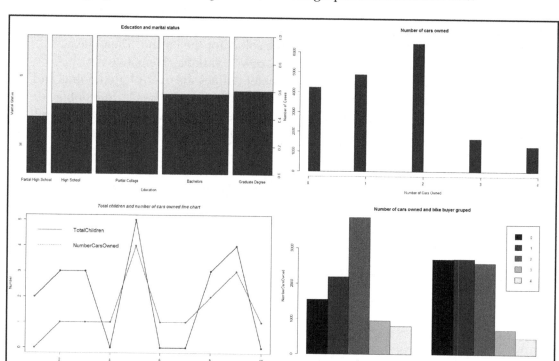

Figure 13.5: Four graphs in an invisible grid

The last part of the code is the cleanup part. It restores the old graphics parameters and removes both data frames from the search path:

```
par(oldpar);
detach(TM);
detach(TM1);
```

Introductory statistics

Sometimes, numbers tell us more than pictures. After all, the name "descriptive statistics" tells you it is about describing something. Descriptive statistics describes a distribution of a variable. Inferential statistics tells you about the associations between variables. There are a plethora of possibilities for introductory statistics in R. However, before calculating the statistical values, let's quickly define some of the most popular measures of descriptive statistics.

The **mean** is the most common measure for determining the center of a distribution. It is also probably the most abused statistical measure. The mean does not mean anything without the standard deviation or some other measure, and it should never be used alone. Let me give you an example. Imagine there are two pairs of people. In the first pair, both people earn the same—let's say, $80,000 per year. In the second pair, one person earns $30,000 per year, while the other earns $270,000 per year. The mean salary for the first pair is $80,000, while the mean for the second pair is $150,000 per year. By just listing the mean, you could conclude that each person from the second pair earns more than either of the people in the first pair. However, you can clearly see that this would be a seriously incorrect conclusion.

The definition of the mean is simple; it is the sum of all values of a continuous variable divided by the number of cases, as shown in the following formula:

$$\mu = \frac{1}{n} * \sum_{i=1}^{n} v_i$$

The **median** is the value that splits the distribution into two halves. The number of rows with a value lower than the median must be equal to the number of rows with a value greater than the median for a selected variable. If there are an odd number of rows, the median is the middle row. If the number of rows is even, the median can be defined as the average value of the two middle rows (the financial median), the smaller of them (the lower statistical median), or the larger of them (the upper statistical median).

The **range** is the simplest measure of the spread; it is the plain distance between the maximum value and the minimum value that the variable takes.

A quick review: a variable is an attribute of an observation represented as a column in a table.

The first formula for the range is:

$$R = v_{max} - v_{min}$$

The median is the value that splits the distribution into two halves. You can split the distribution more—for example, you can split each half into two halves. This way, you get quartiles as three values that split the distribution into quarters. Let's generalize this splitting process. You start with sorting rows (cases, observations) on selected columns (attributes, variables). You define the rank as the absolute position of a row in your sequence of sorted rows. The percentile rank of a value is a relative measure that tells you how many percent of all (*n*) observations have a lower value than the selected value.

By splitting the observations into quarters, you get three percentiles (at 25%, 50%, and 75% of all rows), and you can read the values at those positions that are important enough to have their own names: the quartiles. The second quartile is, of course, the median. The first one is called the **lower quartile** and the third one is known as the **upper quartile**. If you subtract the lower quartile (the first one) from the upper quartile (the third one), you get the formula for the **inter-quartile range (IQR)**:

$$IQR = Q_3 - Q_1$$

Let's suppose for a moment you have only one observation ($n=1$). This observation is also your sample mean, but there is no spread at all. You can calculate the spread only if n exceeds 1. Only the ($n-1$) pieces of information help you calculate the spread, considering that the first observation is your mean. These pieces of information are called **degrees of freedom**. You can also think of degrees of freedom as the number of pieces of information that can vary. For example, imagine a variable that can take five different discrete states. You need to calculate the frequencies of four states only to know the distribution of the variable; the frequency of the last state is determined by the frequencies of the first four states you calculated, and they cannot vary because the cumulative percentage of all states must equal 100.

You can measure the distance between each value and the mean value and call it the **deviation**. The sum of all distances gives you a measure of how spread out your population is. But you must consider that some of the distances are positive, while others are negative; actually, they mutually cancel themselves out, so the total gives you exactly zero. So there are only (n–1) deviations free; the last one is strictly determined by the requirement just stated. In order to avoid negative deviation, you can square them. So, here is the formula for **variance**:

$$Var = \frac{1}{n-1} * \sum_{i=1}^{n}(v_i - \mu)^2$$

This is the formula for the variance of a sample, used as an estimator for the variance of the population. Now, imagine that your data represents the complete population, and the mean value is unknown. Then, all the observations contribute to the variance calculation equally, and the degrees of freedom make no sense. The **variance for a population** is defined in a similar way as the variance for a sample. You just use all n cases instead of $n-1$ degrees of freedom.

$$Var = \frac{1}{n} * \sum_{i=1}^{n} (v_i - \mu)^2$$

Of course, with large samples, both formulas return practically the same number. To compensate for having the deviations squared, you can take the square root of the variance. This is the definition of **standard deviation** (σ):

$$\sigma = \sqrt{Var}$$

Of course, you can use the same formula to calculate the **standard deviation for the population**, and the standard deviation of a sample as an estimator of the standard deviation for the population; just use the appropriate variance in the formula.

You probably remember **skewness** and **kurtosis** from `Chapter 2`, *Review of SQL Server Features for Developers*. These two measures measure the skew and the peakedness of a distribution. The formulas for skewness and kurtosis are:

$$Skewness = \frac{n}{(n-1)*(n-2)} * \sum_{i=1}^{n} \left(\frac{v_i - \mu}{\sigma}\right)^3$$

$$Kurtosis = \frac{n*(n+1)}{(n-1)*(n-2)*(n-3)} * \sum_{i=1}^{n} \left(\frac{v_i - \mu}{\sigma}\right)^4 - \frac{3*(n-1)^2}{(n-2)*(n-3)}$$

$$n = number\ of\ cases$$
$$v_i = ith\ value$$
$$\mu = mean$$
$$\sigma = standard\ deviation$$

These are the descriptive statistics measures for continuous variables. Note that some statisticians calculate kurtosis without the last subtraction, which is approximating 3 for large samples; therefore, a kurtosis around 3 means a normal distribution, neither significantly peaked nor flattened.

For a quick overview of discrete variables, you use frequency tables. In a frequency table, you can show values, the absolute frequency of those values, absolute percentage, cumulative percentage, and a histogram of the absolute percentage.

One very simple way to calculate most of the measures introduced so far is by using the `summary()` function. You can feed it with a single variable or with a whole data frame. For a start, the following code re-reads the CSV file in a data frame and correctly orders the values of the Education variable. In addition, the code attaches the data frame to the search path:

```
TM = read.table("C:\\SQL2016DevGuide\\Chapter13_TM.csv",
                sep=",", header=TRUE,
                stringsAsFactors = TRUE);
attach(TM);
Education = factor(Education, order=TRUE,
                   levels=c("Partial High School",
                            "High School","Partial College",
                            "Bachelors", "Graduate Degree"));
```

Note that you might get a warning, `"The following object is masked _by_ .GlobalEnv: Education"`. You get this warning if you didn't start a new session with this section. Remember, the Education variable was already ordered earlier in the code, and is already part of the global search path, and therefore hides or masks the newly read column Education. You can safely disregard this message and continue with defining the order of the Education values again.

The following code shows the simplest way to get a quick overview of descriptive statistics for the whole data frame:

```
summary(TM);
```

The partial results are here:

```
  CustomerKey      MaritalStatus  Gender      TotalChildren      NumberChildrenAtHome
 Min.   :11000     M:10011        F:9133     Min.   :0.000      Min.   :0.000
 1st Qu.:15621     S: 8473        M:9351     1st Qu.:0.000      1st Qu.:0.000
 Median :20242                               Median :2.000      Median :0.000
 Mean   :20242                               Mean   :1.844      Mean   :1.004
 3rd Qu.:24862                               3rd Qu.:3.000      3rd Qu.:2.000
 Max.   :29483                               Max.   :5.000      Max.   :5.000
```

As mentioned, you can get a quick summary for a single variable as well. In addition, there are many functions that calculate a single statistic, for example, `sd()` to calculate the standard deviation. The following code calculates the summary for the Age variable, and then calls different functions to get the details. Note that the dataset was added to the search path. You should be able to recognize which statistic is calculated by which function from the function names and the results:

```
summary(Age);
mean(Age);
```

```
median(Age);
min(Age);
max(Age);
range(Age);
quantile(Age, 1/4);
quantile(Age, 3/4);
IQR(Age);
var(Age);
sd(Age);
```

Here are the results, with added labels for better readability:

```
    Min. 1st Qu.  Median   Mean 3rd Qu.   Max.
   28.00   36.00   43.00  45.41   53.00  99.00
Mean   45.40981
Median       43
Min    28
Max    99
Range  28 99
25%    36
75%    53
IQR    17
Var    132.9251
StDev  11.52931
```

To calculate the skewness and kurtosis, you need to install an additional package. One possibility is the moments package. The following code installs the package, loads it in memory, and then calls the skewness() and kurtosis() functions from the package:

```
install.packages("moments");
library(moments);
skewness(Age);
kurtosis(Age);
```

The kurtosis() function from this package does not perform the last subtraction in the formula and therefore kurtosis of 3 means no peakedness. Here are the results:

```
0.7072522
2.973118
```

Another possibility to calculate the skewness and the kurtosis is to create a custom function. Creating your own function is really simple in R. Here is an example, together with a call:

```
skewkurt <- function(p){
  avg <- mean(p)
  cnt <- length(p)
  stdev <- sd(p)
  skew <- sum((p-avg)^3/stdev^3)/cnt
  kurt <- sum((p-avg)^4/stdev^4)/cnt-3
  return(c(skewness=skew, kurtosis=kurt))
};
skewkurt(Age);
```

Note that this is a simple example, not taking into account all the details of the formulas, and not checking for missing values. Nevertheless, here is the result. Note that, in this function, the kurtosis was calculated with the last subtraction in the formula and is therefore different from the kurtosis from the package moments for approximately 3:

```
  skewness      kurtosis
0.70719483 -0.02720354
```

Before finishing with these introductory statistics, let's calculate some additional details for the discrete variables. The summary() function returns absolute frequencies only. The table() function can be used for the same task. However, it is more powerful, as it can also do cross-tabulation of two variables. You can also store the results in an object and pass this object to the prop.table() function, which calculates the proportions. The following code shows how to call the last two functions:

```
edt <- table(Education);
edt;
prop.table(edt);
```

Here are the results:

```
Partial High School    High School    Partial College       Bachelors
               1581           3294               5064            5356
   Graduate Degree
              3189
Partial High School    High School    Partial College       Bachelors
         0.08553343     0.17820818         0.27396667      0.28976412
   Graduate Degree
         0.17252759
```

Of course, there is a package that includes a function that gives you a more condensed analysis of a discrete variable. The following code installs the `descr` package, loads it to memory, and calls the `freq()` function:

```
install.packages("descr");
library(descr);
freq(Education);
```

Here are the results.

	Frequency	Percent	Cum Percent
Partial High School	1581	8.553	8.553
High School	3294	17.821	26.374
Partial College	5064	27.397	53.771
Bachelors	5356	28.976	82.747
Graduate Degree	3189	17.253	100.000
Total	18484	100.000	

SQL Server R services

In SQL Server suite, **SQL Server Analysis Services (SSAS)** supports data mining from version 2000. SSAS has included some of the most popular algorithms with very explanatory visualizations. SSAS data mining is very simple to use. However, the number of algorithms is limited, and the whole statistical analysis is missing in the SQL Server suite. By introducing R in SQL Server, Microsoft made a quantum leap forward in statistics, data mining and machine learning.

Of course, the R language and engine have their own issues. For example, installing packages directly from code might not be in accordance with the security policies of an enterprise. In addition, most of the calculations are not scalable. Scalability might not be an issue for statistical and data mining analyses, because you typically work with samples. However, machine learning algorithms can consume huge amounts of data.

With SQL Server 2016, you get a highly scalable R engine. Not every function and algorithm is rewritten as a scalable one. Nevertheless, you will probably find the one you need for your analysis of a big dataset. You can store an R data mining or machine learning model in a SQL Server table and use it for predictions on new data. You can even store graphs in a binary column and use it in **SQL Server Reporting Services (SSRS)** reports. Finally, R support is not limited to SQL Server only. You can use R code also in **Power BI** Desktop and Power BI Service, and in **Azure Machine Learning (Azure ML)** experiments.

Installing packages is not that simple, and must be done by a DBA. In SQL Server, you call R code through a stored procedure. This way, a DBA can apply all SQL Server security to R code as well. In addition, you need a SQL Server, a Windows login, or Windows to run the code that uses SQL Server R Services. This login must also have enough permissions on SQL Server objects. It needs to access the database where you run the R code, permissions to read SQL Server data, and potentially, if you need to store the results in a SQL Server table, permissions to write data.

This section introduces R support in SQL Server, including:

- Architecture
- Using R code in T-SQL
- Scalable solutions
- Security
- Deploying R models in SQL Server

Discovering SQL Server R services

Microsoft provides the highly scalable R engine in two flavors:

- **R Services (In-Database)**: This is the installation that integrates R into SQL Server. It includes a database service that runs outside the SQL Server Database Engine and provides a communication channel between the Database Engine and R runtime. You install it with SQL Server setup. The R engine includes the open source R components and in addition a set of scalable R packages.
- **Microsoft R Server**: This is a standalone R server with the same open and scalable packages that runs on multiple platforms.

For development, you prepare a client installation. You can download Microsoft R Client from http://aka.ms/rclient/download. This installation includes the open R engine and the scalable packages as well. In addition to the engine, you probably want to also install a development IDE, either RStudio or R Tools for Visual Studio. Of course, you can also download and install the Developer Edition of SQL Server 2016 instead. This way, you get both the R runtime with the scalable packages and the database engine.

Some of the scalable packages shipped with SQL Server R Services are:

- **RevoScaleR**: This is a set of parallelized scalable R functions for processing data, data overview and preliminary analysis, and machine learning models. The procedures in this package can work with chunks of data at a time, so they don't need to load all of the data in memory immediately.

- **RevoPemaR**: This package allows you to write custom parallel external algorithms.
- **MicrosoftML**: This is a new package from December 2016, with many additional scalable machine learning algorithms implemented.

The following figure shows how the communication process between SQL Server and R engine works:

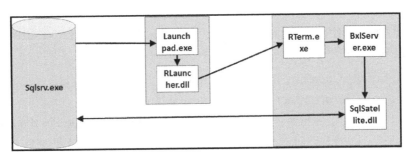

Figure 13.6: The communication between SQL Server and R runtime

The components involved and their communications are as follows:

- In SQL Server Database Engine, you run R script with the `sys.sp_execute_external_script` system stored procedure. SQL Server sends the request to the **Launchpad** service, a new service that supports the execution of external scripts.
- The Launchpad service starts the launcher appropriate for the language of your script. Currently, the only launcher available is the RLauncher, and therefore you can launch an external script from SQL Server using the R language only. However, you can see that the infrastructure is prepared to enable the execution of scripts in additional programming languages.
- The RLauncher starts **RTerm**, the R terminal application for executing R scripts.
- The RTerm sends the script to **BxlServer.** This is a new executable used for communication between SQL Server and the R engine. The scalable R functions are implemented in this executable as well.
- The BxlServer uses **SQL Satellite**, a new extensibility API that provides a fast data transfer between SQL Server and external runtime. Again, currently only R runtime is supported.

Time to test the execution of R script in SQL Server! First, you need to use the sys.sp_configure system stored procedure to enable external scripts. You can do this with the following code:

```
USE master;
EXEC sys.sp_configure 'show advanced options', 1;
RECONFIGURE
EXEC sys.sp_configure 'external scripts enabled', 1;
RECONFIGURE;
```

After that, you can call the sys.sp_execute_external_script system stored procedure. The most important parameters of this procedure include:

- @language: Currently limited to value R
- @script: The actual script in the external language
- @input_data_1_name: The name of the data frame, as seen in the R code in the @script parameter for the first input dataset; the default name is InputDataSet
- @input_data_1: The T-SQL query that specifies the first input dataset
- @output_data_1_name: The name of the R object, most probably a data frame, with the output dataset; the default name is OutputDataSet
- WITH RESULT SETS: The option where you specify the column names and data types of the output of the R script, as seen in SQL Server

In the following example, the R script called from SQL Server retrieves the list of installed packages:

```
EXECUTE sys.sp_execute_external_script
  @language=N'R',
  @script =
  N'str(OutputDataSet);
    packagematrix <- installed.packages();
    NameOnly <- packagematrix[,1];
    OutputDataSet <- as.data.frame(NameOnly);'
WITH RESULT SETS ( ( PackageName nvarchar(20) ) );
```

The shortened results are:

```
PackageName
--------------------
base
boot
class
...
RevoIOQ
revoIpe
```

```
RevoMods
RevoPemaR
RevoRpeConnector
RevoRsrConnector
RevoScaleR
RevoTreeView
RevoUtils
RevoUtilsMath
...
spatial
splines
stats
...
```

You can see that besides some base packages, there is a set of packages where the name starts with the string RevoScaleR and RevoPemaR packages. These are two packages with scalable functions and their associated packages.

Creating scalable solutions

You can use the scalable server resources from the client. You start development in RStudio or R Tools for Visual Studio by setting the execution context to the server. Of course, you must do it with a function from the RevoScaleR package, which is loaded in memory at the beginning of the following R code. The code defines the execution context on SQL Server, in the context of the AdventureWorksDW2014 database. Remember, the dbo.vTargetMail view comes from this database. Also note that the RUser used to connect to SQL Server needs permission to use the sys.sp_execute_external_script procedure. For the sake of simplicity, I just added the RUser database user in the AdventureWorksDW2014 database on my local SQL Server instance to the db_owner database role. The following code changes the execution context to SQL Server:

```
library(RevoScaleR);
sqlConnStr <- "Driver=SQL Server;Server=SQL2016EIM;
 Database=AdventureWorksDW2014;Uid=RUser;Pwd=Pa$$w0rd";
sqlShare <- "C:\\SQL2016DevGuide";
chunkSize = 1000;
srvEx <- RxInSqlServer(connectionString = sqlConnStr, shareDir = sqlShare,
                       wait = TRUE, consoleOutput = FALSE);
rxSetComputeContext(srvEx);
```

The parameters define the connection string to my SQL Server instance, the shared folder used to exchange the data between SQL Server and R engine, and the chunk size, which is actually used later when reading the data. Please note that you need to change the name of the SQL Server to your SQL Server instance. The `RxInSqlServer()` object creates the compute context in SQL Server. The `wait` parameter defines whether the execution in SQL Server is blocking and the control does not return to the client until the execution is finished or the execution is not blocking. The `consoleOutput` parameter defines whether the output of the R code started by SQL Server should be returned to the user console. The `rxSetComputeContext()` function actually sets the execution context to SQL Server.

After the execution context has been set to SQL Server, you can try to use other scalable functions. For example, `rxImport()` can be used to import comma-separated value file data to a data frame. The `rowsPerRead` parameter reads in batches, using the chunk size defined earlier in the code. The batch size of 1,000 rows is quite small, just to show how this import in chunks works. For larger datasets, you should use much larger batches. You should test what the best size is for your datasets and the processing power you have:

```
TMCSV = rxImport(inData = "C:\\SQL2016DevGuide\\Chapter13_TM.csv",
              stringsAsFactors = TRUE, type = "auto",
              rowsPerRead = chunkSize, reportProgress = 3);
```

The `reportProgress` parameter defines a detailed output. The abbreviated result of the previous code is here:

```
ReadNum=1, StartRowNum=1, CurrentNumRows=1000, TotalRowsProcessed=1000,
ReadTime=0.01, ProcessDataTime = 0, LoopTime = 0.01
ReadNum=2, StartRowNum=1001, CurrentNumRows=1000, TotalRowsProcessed=2000,
ReadTime=0.007, ProcessDataTime = 0.002, LoopTime = 0.007
. . .
Overall compute summaries time: 0.133 secs.
Total loop time: 0.132
Total read time for 19 reads: 0.115
Total process data time: 0.041
Average read time per read: 0.00605263
Average process data time per read: 0.00215789
Number of threads used: 2
```

You can see that the chunk size was really 1,000 rows, how much time was needed for each chunk, the total time, the number of threads used, and more. This confirms that `RevoScaleR` functions use parallelism.

The next code reads the same data again, this time from SQL Server. Note that an ODBC connection is not needed; the code is already executed on the server side in the context of the `AdventureWorksDW2014` database. The `RxSqlServerData()` function generates a SQL Server data source object. You can think of it as a proxy object to the SQL Server rowset, which is the result of the query:

```
TMquery <-
"SELECT CustomerKey, MaritalStatus, Gender,
  TotalChildren, NumberChildrenAtHome,
  EnglishEducation AS Education,
  EnglishOccupation AS Occupation,
  HouseOwnerFlag, NumberCarsOwned, CommuteDistance,
  Region, BikeBuyer,
  YearlyIncome, Age
 FROM dbo.vTargetMail";
sqlTM <- RxSqlServerData(sqlQuery = TMquery,
                         connectionString = sqlConnStr,
                         stringsAsFactors = TRUE,
                         rowsPerRead = chunkSize);
TMSQL <- rxImport(inData = sqlTM, reportProgress = 3);
```

The `sqlTM` object is the pointer to the SQL Server data, and exposes the metadata of the result set of the query to the client R code. Note that the last line creates a new data frame and physically transfers data to the client. Therefore, if you executed the code in this section step-by-step, you should have two data frames—TMCSV and TMSQL—with data in local client memory, and the `sqlTM` data source connection, which you can use as a data frame. You can see the difference if you try to get the info about all three objects with the `rxGetInfo()` function:

```
rxGetInfo(TMCSV);
rxGetInfo(sqlTM);
```

The previous code returns the following result:

```
Data frame: TMCSV
Number of observations: 18484
Number of variables: 14
Connection string: Driver=SQL Server;Server=localhost;
 Database=AdventureWorksDW2014;Uid=RUser;Pwd=Pa$$w0rd
Data Source: SQLSERVER
```

You get the details about the metadata of the SQL data source connection object with the rxGetVarInfo() function. You can get summary statistics and different cross-tabulations of the SQL Server data with the rxSummary(), rxCrossTabs(), and rxCube() functions. You can create histograms with the rxHistogram() function. All these functions use the SQL Server execution context. The following code shows how to use the functions mentioned:

```
sumOut <- rxSummary(
    formula = ~ NumberCarsOwned + Occupation + F(BikeBuyer),
    data = sqlTM);
sumOut;
cTabs <- rxCrossTabs(formula = BikeBuyer ~
                    Occupation : F(HouseOwnerFlag),
                    data = sqlTM);
print(cTabs, output = "counts");
print(cTabs, output = "sums");
print(cTabs, output = "means");
summary(cTabs, output = "sums");
summary(cTabs, output = "counts");
summary(cTabs, output = "means");
cCube <- rxCube(formula = BikeBuyer ~
              Occupation : F(HouseOwnerFlag),
              data = sqlTM);
cCube;
rxHistogram(formula = ~ BikeBuyer | MaritalStatus,
          data = sqlTM);
```

Note that all of these scalable functions accept data from the SQL Server data source connection object. Because they execute on SQL Server, you cannot use the local data frames to feed them. If you would use a local data frame, you would get an error. If you want to use the scalable functions with the local datasets, you need to switch the execution context back to local.

The following code shows how to set the execution context back to the client machine:

```
rxSetComputeContext("local");
```

The RevoScaleR package includes a function to calculate clusters of similar cases based on the values of the input variables. It uses the **K-means clustering** algorithm. The rxKmeans() function in the following code uses a local data frame. It defines two clusters and then assigns each case to one of the clusters. The summary() function gives you the details of the clustering model:

```
TwoClust <- rxKmeans(formula = ~ BikeBuyer + TotalChildren +
NumberCarsOwned,
                    data = TMSQL,
```

```
                              numClusters = 2);
    summary(TwoClust);
```

You can add the cluster membership to the original data frame and rename the variable to a friendlier name:

```
TMClust <- cbind(TMSQL, TwoClust$cluster);
names(TMClust)[15] <- "ClusterID";
```

In order to understand the meaning of the clusters, you need to analyze them. The following code creates a nice graph that consists of three individual small graphs showing the distribution of each input variable in each cluster:

```
attach(TMClust);
oldpar <- par(no.readonly = TRUE);
par(mfrow=c(1,3));

# NumberCarsOwned and clusters
nofcases <- table(NumberCarsOwned, ClusterID);
nofcases;
barplot(nofcases,
        main='Number of cars owned and cluster ID',
        xlab='Cluster Id', ylab ='Number of Cars',
        legend=rownames(nofcases),
        col=c("black", "blue", "red", "orange", "yellow"),
        beside=TRUE);
# BikeBuyer and clusters
nofcases <- table(BikeBuyer, ClusterID);
nofcases;
barplot(nofcases,
        main='Bike buyer and cluster ID',
        xlab='Cluster Id', ylab ='BikeBuyer',
        legend=rownames(nofcases),
        col=c("blue", "yellow"),
        beside=TRUE);
# TotalChildren and clusters
nofcases <- table(TotalChildren, ClusterID);
nofcases;
barplot(nofcases,
        main='Total children and cluster ID',
        xlab='Cluster Id', ylab ='Total Children',
        legend=rownames(nofcases),
        col=c("black", "blue", "green", "red", "orange", "yellow"),
        beside=TRUE);

# Clean up
par(oldpar);
detach(TMClust);
```

You should already be familiar with this code from the examples earlier in this chapter. The next screenshot shows the results:

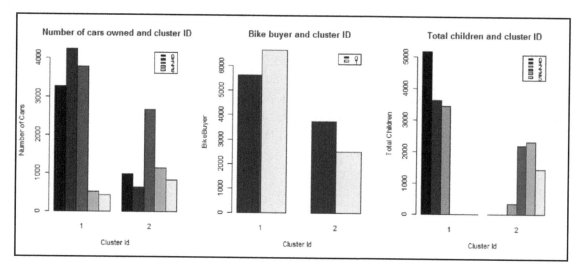

Figure 13.7: The analysis of the clusters

Deploying R models

Once you have created a model, you can deploy it to a SQL Server table and use it later for predictions. You can also do the predictions in R and store just the results in a SQL Server table.

Let's start by creating another model in R. This time, the model uses the **Logistic Regression** algorithm. The model uses the SQL Server data and the dbo.vTargetMail view to learn how the values of the NumberCarsOwned, TotalChildren, Age, and YearlyIncome input variables influence the value of the BikeBuyer target variable. The following code sets the execution context back to SQL Server, creates the model with the RevoScale RrxLogit() function, and shows the summary of the model:

```
rxSetComputeContext(srvEx);
bbLogR <- rxLogit(BikeBuyer ~
        NumberCarsOwned + TotalChildren + Age + YearlyIncome,
        data = sqlTM);
summary(bbLogR);
```

You can use the model to perform predictions. In the following example, the model is used to make predictions on the same dataset that was used for training the model. In a real-life situation, you would perform predictions on a new dataset. The code stores the predictions, together with the input values used, in a SQL Server table. The `RxSqlServerData()` function prepares the connection to the SQL Server database and the target table name. The `rxPredict()` function performs the predictions and physically creates the SQL Server table and inserts the data. Of course, the database user used to connect to SQL Server must have appropriate permissions to create a table:

```
bbLogRPredict <- RxSqlServerData(connectionString = sqlConnStr,
                                 table = "dbo.TargetMailLogR");
rxPredict(modelObject = bbLogR,
          data = sqlTM, outData = bbLogRPredict,
          predVarNames = "BikeBuyerPredict",
          type = "response", writeModelVars = TRUE);
```

You can use a T-SQL query to check the results, as shown here:

```
USE AdventureWorksDW2014;
SELECT *
FROM dbo.TargetMailLogR;
```

The partial results are shown here. Values above 0.5 mean positive predictions:

BikeBuyerPredict	BikeBuyer	NumberCarsOwned	TotalChildren	Age	YearlyIncome
0.733910292274223	1	0	2	44	90000
0.540550204813772	1	1	3	40	60000
0.529196837245225	1	1	3	45	60000

As mentioned, you can store a model in a SQL Server table. The following T-SQL code creates a table where the models are going to be stored and a stored procedure that actually inserts a model:

```
CREATE TABLE dbo.RModels
(Id INT NOT NULL IDENTITY(1,1) PRIMARY KEY,
 ModelName NVARCHAR(50) NOT NULL,
 Model VARBINARY(MAX) NOT NULL);
GO
CREATE PROCEDURE dbo.InsertModel
(@modelname NVARCHAR(50),
 @model NVARCHAR(MAX))
AS
BEGIN
    SET NOCOUNT ON;
    INSERT INTO dbo.RModels (ModelName, Model)
    VALUES (@modelname, CONVERT(VARBINARY(MAX), @model, 2));
```

```
    END;
```

The infrastructure is created. Now you can store the model in a SQL Server table from R. However, in order to call a stored procedure, you need to use an ODBC connection. Therefore, the following code first loads the RODBC library to memory, and creates a connection to the SQL Server database. Then it serializes the model to a binary variable, and creates a string from the binary variable using the `paste()` function. The same function is used to prepare a string with the T-SQL code to insert the model in the table. Finally, the `sqlQuery()` function sends the T-SQL command to SQL Server. Again, the R user used to execute this code must have permission to execute the stored procedure:

```
library(RODBC);
conn <- odbcDriverConnect(sqlConnStr);
modelbin <- serialize(bbLogR, NULL);
modelbinstr=paste(modelbin, collapse="");
sqlQ <- paste("EXEC dbo.InsertModel @modelname='bbLogR', @model='",
              modelbinstr,"'", sep="");
sqlQuery(conn, sqlQ);
close(conn);
```

The final step is to use the model from T-SQL. The following code uses the `sys.sp_execute_external_script` system procedure to use the model and perform a prediction on a single case. First, it creates an input dataset that consists of a single row with four input variables. Then, it retrieves the stored model. Then the R code is executed, which un-serializes the model and uses the `rxPredict()` function again to generate the output dataset, which includes the input variables and the prediction:

```
DECLARE @input AS NVARCHAR(MAX)
SET @input = N'
    SELECT *
    FROM (VALUES
          (0, 2, 44, 90000)) AS
          inpQ(NumberCarsOwned, TotalChildren, Age, YearlyIncome);'
DECLARE @mod VARBINARY(max) =
 (SELECT Model
  FROM DBO.RModels
  WHERE ModelName = N'bbLogR');
EXEC sys.sp_execute_external_script
 @language = N'R',
 @script = N'
 mod <- unserialize(as.raw(model));
 OutputDataSet<-rxPredict(modelObject = mod, data = InputDataSet,
 outData =  NULL,
         predVarNames = "BikeBuyerPredict", type = "response",
           checkFactorLevels=FALSE,
           writeModelVars = TRUE, overwrite = TRUE);
```

```
',
  @input_data_1 = @input,
  @params = N'@model VARBINARY(MAX)',
  @model = @mod
WITH RESULT SETS ((
  BikeBuyerPredict FLOAT,
  NumberCarsOwned INT,
  TotalChildren INT,
  Age INT,
  YearlyIncome FLOAT));
```

The results are:

BikeBuyerPredict	NumberCarsOwned	TotalChildren	Age	YearlyIncome
0.733910292274223	0	2	44	90000

The input values used were the same as the values in the first row of the batch predictions from the `dbo.vTargetMail` view used in the previous prediction example. You can see that the predicted value is also the same.

Summary

In this chapter, you learned the basics of the R language. You learned data structures in R (especially the most important one, the data frame) and how to do simple data manipulation. Then you saw some of the capabilities of R by creating graphical visualizations and calculating descriptive statistics in order to get a deeper understanding of your data. Finally, you got a comprehensive view of R integration in SQL Server. The next chapter, `Chapter 14`, *Data Exploration and Predictive Modeling with R in SQL Server*, continues the story and gives you more in-depth knowledge about some of the most important data mining and machine learning algorithms and tasks.

14

Data Exploration and Predictive Modeling with R in SQL Server

Using the R language inside SQL Server gives us the opportunity to get knowledge out of data. We introduced R and R support in SQL Server in the previous chapter, and this chapter demonstrates how you can use R for advanced data exploration and for statistical analysis and predictive modeling, way beyond the possibilities offered by using T-SQL language only.

You will start with intermediate statistics: exploring associations between two discrete, two continuous, and one discrete and one continuous variable. You will also learn about linear regression, where you explain the values of the dependent continuous variable with a linear regression formula using one or more continuous input variables.

The second section of this chapter starts with introducing advanced multivariate data mining and machine learning methods. You will learn about methods that do not use a target variable, or so-called undirected methods.

In the third part, you will learn about the most popular directed methods.

Finally, to finish the chapter and the book in a slightly lighter way, you will play with graphs again. The last section introduces ggplot2, the most popular package for visualizing data in R.

 The target audience of this book is database developers and solution architects who plan to use new SQL Server 2016 features or simply want to know what is now available and which limitations from previous versions have been removed.

Most of the readers deal daily with simple statistics only, and less often with data mining and machine learning. Because of that, this chapter does not only show how to write the code for advanced analysis in R, it also gives you an introduction to the mathematics behind the code, and explains when you want to use which method.

This chapter will cover the following points:

- Associations between two or more variables
- Undirected data mining and machine learning methods
- Directed data mining and machine learning methods
- Advanced graphing in R
- Mathematics behind the advanced methods explained
- A mapping between problems and algorithms to use

Intermediate statistics – associations

In the previous chapter, you learned about the discrete statistics methods for getting the information about the distribution of discrete and continuous variables. In a data science project, the next typical step is to check for the **associations** between pairs of variables.

When checking for the associations between pairs of variables, you have three possibilities:

- Both variables are discrete
- Both variables are continuous
- One discrete and one continuous variable

Besides dealing with two variables only, this section also introduces **linear regression**, one of the most important statistical methods, where you model a single **response** (or **dependent**) variable with a regression formula that includes one or more **predictor** (or **independent**) variables.

Altogether, you will learn about the following in this section:

- Chi-squared test of independence of two discrete variables
- Phi coefficient, contingency coefficient, and Cramer's V coefficient that measures the association of two discrete variables
- Covariance and correlations between two continuous variables
- T-Test and one-way ANOVA that measure associations between one continuous and one discrete variable
- Simple and polynomial linear regression

Exploring discrete variables

Contingency tables are used to examine the relationship between subject's scores on two qualitative or categorical variables. They show the actual and expected distribution of cases in a **cross-tabulated** (pivoted) format for the two variables. The following table is an example of the **actual** (or **observed**) and **expected** distribution of cases over the Occupation column (on rows) and the MaritalStatus column (on columns).

Occupation \ MaritalStatus	Married	Single	Total
Clerical Actual	4,745	4,388	**9,133**
Expected	4,946	4,187	**9,133**
Professional Actual	5,266	4,085	**9,351**
Expected	5,065	4,286	**9,351**
Total Actual	**10,011**	**8,473**	**18,484**
Expected	**10,111**	**8,473**	**18,484**

If the two variables are independent, then the actual distribution in every single cell should be approximately equal to the expected distribution in that cell. Expected distribution is used by calculating the marginal probability. For example, the marginal probability for value "Married" is 10,111 / 18,484 = 0.5416: There are more than 54% of married people in the sample. If the two variables are independent, then you would expect to have approximately 54% of married people among clericals and 54% among professionals. You might notice dependency between two discrete variables by just viewing the contingency table for the two. However, a solid numerical measure is preferred.

If the columns are not contingent on the rows, then the rows and column frequencies are independent. The test of whether the columns are contingent on the rows is called the **chi-squared test of independence**. The **null hypothesis** is that there is no relationship between row and column frequencies. Therefore, there should be no difference between the observed (*O*) and expected (*E*) frequencies.

Chi-squared is simply a sum of normalized squared frequency's deviations (that is, the sum of squares of differences between observed and expected frequencies divided by expected frequencies). This formula is also called the Pearson chi-squared formula.

$$\chi^2 = \frac{1}{n} * \sum_{i=1}^{n} \frac{(O - E)^2}{E}$$

There are already prepared tables with critical points for the chi-squared distribution. If the calculated chi-squared value is greater than a critical value in the table for the defined degrees of freedom and for a specific confidence level, you can reject the null hypothesis with that confidence (which means the variables are interdependent). The degrees of freedom, explained for a single variable in the previous chapter, is the product of the degrees of freedom for columns (C) and rows (R), as the following formula shows.

$$DF = (C - 1) * (R - 1)$$

The following table is the **chi-squared critical points** table for the first ten degrees of freedom. Greater differences between expected and actual data produce a larger chi-squared value. The larger the chi-squared value, the greater the probability that there really is a significant difference. The Probability row in the table shows you what is the maximal probability that the null hypothesis holds when the chi-squared value is greater than or equal to the value in the table for the specific degrees of freedom.

DF	Chi-squared Value									
1	0.004	0.02	0.15	0.46	1.07	1.64	2.71	3.84	6.64	10.83
2	0.10	0.21	0.71	1.39	2.41	3.22	4.60	5.99	9.21	13.82
3	0.35	0.58	1.42	2.37	3.66	4.64	6.25	7.82	11.34	16.27
4	0.71	1.06	2.20	3.36	4.88	5.99	7.78	9.49	13.28	18.47
5	1.14	1.61	3.00	4.35	6.06	7.29	9.24	11.07	15.09	20.52
6	1.63	2.20	3.83	5.35	7.23	8.56	10.64	12.59	16.81	22.46
7	2.17	2.83	4.67	6.35	8.38	9.80	12.02	14.07	18.48	24.32
8	2.73	3.49	5.53	7.34	9.52	11.03	13.56	15.51	20.09	26.12
9	3.32	4.17	6.39	8.34	10.66	12.24	14.68	16.92	21.67	27.88
10	3.94	4.86	7.27	9.34	11.78	13.44	15.99	18.31	23.21	29.59
Probability	0.95	0.90	0.70	0.50	0.30	0.20	0.10	0.05	0.01	0.001
	Not significant							Significant		

For example, you have calculated chi-squared for two discrete variables. The value is 16, and the degrees of freedom are 7. Search for the first smaller and first bigger value for the chi-squared in the row for degrees of freedom 7 in the *Table 8.6*. The values are 14.07 and 18.48. Check the appropriate probability for these two values, which are 0.05 and 0.01. This means that there is less than 5% probability that the two variables are independent from each other, and more than 1% that they are independent. This is a significant percentage, meaning that you can say the variables are dependent with more than 95% probability.

The following core re-reads the target mail data from a CSV file, adds the new data frame to the search path, and defines the levels for the Education factor variable.

```
TM = read.table("C:\\SQL2016DevGuide\\Chapter14_TM.csv",
    sep=",", header=TRUE,
    stringsAsFactors = TRUE);
attach(TM);
Education = factor(Education, order=TRUE,
    levels=c("Partial High School",
        "High School","Partial College",
        "Bachelors", "Graduate Degree"));
```

You can create pivot tables with the `table()` or the `xtabs()` R functions, as the following code shows:

```
table(Education, Gender, BikeBuyer);
table(NumberCarsOwned, BikeBuyer);
xtabs(~Education + Gender + BikeBuyer);
xtabs(~NumberCarsOwned + BikeBuyer);
```

You can check the results yourself. Nevertheless, in order to test for independence, you need to store the pivot table in a variable. The following code checks for independence between two pairs of variables—`Education` and `Gender` and `NumberCarsOwned` and `BikeBuyer`:

```
tEduGen <- xtabs(~ Education + Gender);
tNcaBik <- xtabs(~ NumberCarsOwned + BikeBuyer);
chisq.test(tEduGen);
chisq.test(tNcaBik);
```

Here are the results.

```
data:    tEduGen
X-squared = 5.8402, df = 4, p-value = 0.2114
data:    tNcaBik
X-squared = 734.38, df = 4, p-value < 2.2e-16
```

From the chi-squared critical points table, you can see that you can confirm the null hypothesis for the first pair of variables, while you need to reject it for the second pair. The p-value tells you the probability that the null hypothesis is correct. Therefore, you can conclude that the variables `NumberCarsOwned` and `BikeBuyer` are associated.

You can measure the association by calculating one of the following coefficients: **phi coefficient**, **contingency coefficient**, or **Cramer's V coefficient**. You can use the phi coefficient for two binary variables only. The formulas for the three coefficients are:

$$\Phi = \sqrt{\frac{\chi^2}{n}}, \quad C = \sqrt{\frac{\chi^2}{n + \chi^2}}, \quad V = \sqrt{\frac{\chi^2}{n * (k - 1)}},$$

$$where \; k = \min(n \; of \; rows, n \; of \; columns)$$

Contingency coefficient is not scaled between 0 and 1; for example, the highest possible value for a 2×2 table is 0.707. Anyway, the function `assocstats()` from the **vcd** package calculates all three of them; since the phi coefficient can be calculated for two binary variables only, it is not useful here. The following code installs the package and calls the function:

```
install.packages("vcd");
library(vcd);
assocstats(tEduGen);
assocstats(tNcaBik);
```

In addition, the vcd package includes the `strucplot()` function, which visualizes the contingency tables very nicely. The following code calls this function to visualize expected and observed frequencies for the two associated variables:

```
strucplot(tNcaBik, shade = TRUE, type = "expected", main = "Expected");
strucplot(tNcaBik, shade = TRUE, type = "observed", main = "Observed");
```

You can see the graphical representation of the observed frequencies in the following figure.

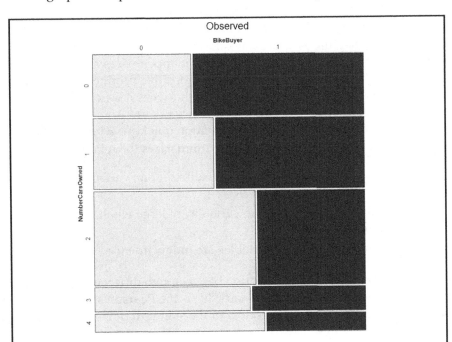

Figure 14-1: Contingency tables visualization

Finding associations between continuous variables

The first measure for the association of two continuous variables is the **covariance**. Here is the formula.

$$cov(X, Y) = \sum_{i=1}^{n} (X_i - \mu(X)) * (Y_i - \mu(Y)) * P(X, Y)$$

Covariance indicates how two variables, X and Y, are related to each other. When large values of both variables occur together, the deviations are both positive (because $X_i -$ *Mean(X) > 0 and* $Y_i -$ *Mean(Y) > 0)*, and their product is therefore positive. Similarly, when small values occur together, the product is positive as well. When one deviation is negative and one is positive, the product is negative. This can happen when a small value of X occurs with a large value of Y and the other way around. If positive products are absolutely larger than negative products, the covariance is positive; otherwise, it is negative. If negative and positive products cancel each other out, the covariance is zero. And when do they cancel each other out? Well, you can imagine such a situation quickly—when two variables are really independent. So the covariance evidently summarizes the relation between variables:

- If the covariance is positive, when the values of one variable are large, the values of the other one tend to be large as well
- When negative, the values of one variable are large when the values of the other one tend to be small
- If the covariance is zero, the variables are independent

In order to compare the strength of association between two different pairs of variables, a relative measure is better than an absolute one. This is the **Pearson's correlation coefficient**, which divides the covariance with the product of the standard deviations of both variables:

$$\rho(X,Y) = \frac{cov(X,Y)}{\sigma(X) * \sigma(Y)}$$

The reason that the correlation coefficient is a useful measure of the relation between two variables is that it is always bounded: -1 <= correlation coefficient <= 1. Of course, if the variables are independent, the correlation is zero, because the covariance is zero. The correlation can take the value 1 if the variables have a perfect positive linear relation (if you correlate a variable with itself, for example). Similarly, the correlation would be -1 for the perfect negative linear relation. The larger the absolute value of the coefficient is, the more the variables are related. But the significance depends on the size of the sample. The following code creates a data frame that is a subset of the TM data frame used so far. The new data frame includes only continuous variables. Then the code calculates the covariance and the correlation coefficient between all possible pairs of variables.

```
x <- TM[,c("YearlyIncome", "Age", "NumberCarsOwned")];
cov(x);
cor(x);
```

Here are the correlation coefficients shown in a correlation matrix.

```
                  YearlyIncome       Age NumberCarsOwned
YearlyIncome         1.0000000 0.1446627       0.4666472
Age                  0.1446627 1.0000000       0.1836616
NumberCarsOwned      0.4666472 0.1836616       1.0000000
```

You can see that the income and number of cars owned are correlated better than other pairs of variables.

Pearson's coefficient is not so suitable for ordinal variables so you can calculate the Spearman's coefficient instead. The following code shows you how to calculate the Spearman's coefficient on ordinal variables:

```
y <- TM[,c("TotalChildren", "NumberChildrenAtHome", "HouseOwnerFlag",
"BikeBuyer")];
cor(y);
cor(y, method = "spearman");
```

Finally, you can also visualize the correlation matrix. A nice visualization is provided by the `corrgram()` function in the `corrgram` package, as the following code shows:

```
install.packages("corrgram");
library(corrgram);
corrgram(y, order = TRUE, lower.panel = panel.shade,
        upper.panel = panel.shade, text.panel = panel.txt,
        cor.method = "spearman", main = "Corrgram");
```

In the following figure, you can see the Spearman's correlation coefficient between pairs of four ordered variables graphically.

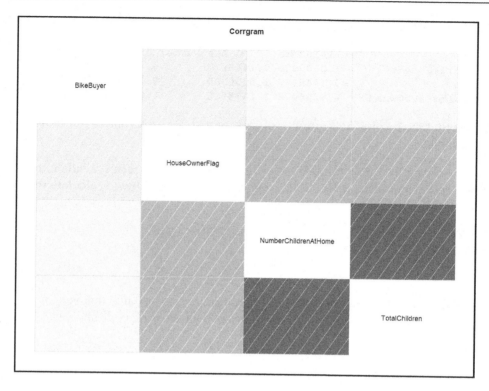

Figure 14-2: Correlation matrix visualization

The darker the shading in the preceding figure, the stronger the association; right-oriented texture means a positive association, and left-oriented texture means a negative association.

Continuous and discrete variables

Finally, it is time to check for linear dependencies between a continuous and a discrete variable. You can do this by measuring the variance between means of the continuous variable in different groups of the discrete variable, for example measuring the difference in salary (continuous variable) between different genders (discrete variable). The null hypothesis here is that all variance between means is a result of the variance within each group, for example there is one woman with a very large salary, which raises the mean salary in the female group and makes a difference to the male group. If you reject it, this means that there is some significant variance of the means between groups. This is also known as the residual, or unexplained, variance. You are analyzing the variance of the means, so this analysis is called the **analysis of variance**, or **ANOVA**. A simpler test is **Student's t-test**, which you can use to test for the differences between means in two groups only.

For a simple **one-way** ANOVA, testing means (averages) of a continuous variable for one independent discrete variable, you calculate the variance between groups MSA as the sum of squares of deviations of the group mean from the total mean multiplied by the number of cases in each group, with the degrees of freedom equal to the number of groups minus one. The formula is:

$$MS_A = \frac{SS_A}{DF_A}, where\ SS_A = \sum_{i=1}^{a} n_i * (\mu_i - \mu), and\ DF_A = (a - 1)$$

The discrete variable has discrete states, μ is the overall mean of the continuous variable, and μ_i is the mean in the continuous variable in the ith group of the discrete variable.

You calculate the variance within groups MSE as the sum over groups of the sum of squares of deviations of individual values from the group mean, with the degrees of freedom equal to the sum of the number of rows in each group minus one:

$$MS_E = \frac{SS_E}{DF_E}, where\ SS_E = \sum_{i=1}^{a}\sum_{j=1}^{ni} (v_{ij} - \mu_i), and\ DF_E = \sum_{i=1}^{a} (n_i - 1)$$

The individual value of the continuous variable is denoted as v_{ij}, μ_i is the mean in the continuous variable in the ith group of the discrete variable, and n_i is the number of cases in the ith group of the discrete variable.

Once you have both variances, you calculate the so-called F ratio as the ratio between the variance between groups and the variance within groups:

$$F = \frac{MS_A}{MS_E}$$

A large F value means you can reject the null hypothesis. Tables for the cumulative distribution under the tails of F distributions for different degrees of freedom are already calculated. For a specific F value with degrees of freedom between groups and degrees of freedom within groups, you can get critical points where there is, for example, less than a 5% of distribution under the F distribution curve up to the F point. This means that there is less than a 5% probability that the null hypothesis is correct (that is, there is an association between the means and the groups).

The following code checks for the differences in mean between two groups: checks the YearlyIncome mean in the groups of Gender and HouseOwnerFlag variables. Note that the last line, after the comment, produces an error, because you can't use t-test for more than two groups.

```
t.test(YearlyIncome ~ Gender);
t.test(YearlyIncome ~ HouseOwnerFlag);
# Error - t-test supports only two groups
t.test(YearlyIncome ~ Education);
```

Instead of using the t.test() function, you can use the aov() function to check for the variance of the YearlyIncome means in the five groups of Education, as the following code shows. Note that the code first correctly orders the Education variable:

```
Education = factor(Education, order=TRUE,
levels=c("Partial High School",
"High School","Partial College",
"Bachelors", "Graduate Degree"));
AssocTest <- aov(YearlyIncome ~ Education);
summary(AssocTest);
```

If you execute the code above and check the results, you can conclude that yearly income is associated with the level of the education. You can see that the *F* value (324.7) is quite high and the probability for such high F value to be accidental is very low (<2e-16). You can also visualize the differences of the distribution of a continuous variable in groups of a discrete variable with the boxplot() function.

```
boxplot(YearlyIncome ~ Education,
        main = "Yearly Income in Groups",
        notch = TRUE,
        varwidth = TRUE,
        col = "orange",
        ylab = "Yearly Income",
        xlab = "Education");
```

The results of the box plot are shown in the following screenshot:

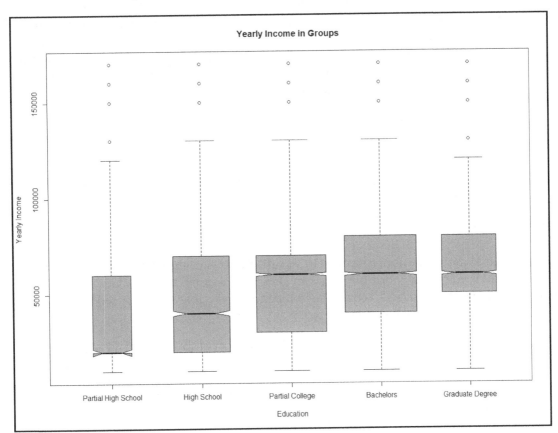

Figure 14-3: Variability of means in groups

Getting deeper into linear regression

When you get a high correlation between two continuous variables, you might want to express the relation between them in a functional way; that is, one variable as a function of the other one. The **linear function** between two variables is a line determined by its **slope** and its **intercept**. Here is the formula for the linear function.

$$Y' = a + b * X$$

You can imagine that the two variables you are analyzing form a two-dimensional plane.

Their values define coordinates of the points in the plane. You are searching for a line that fits all the points best. Actually, it means that you want the points to fall as close to the line as possible. You need the deviations from the line—that is, the difference between actual value for the Y_i and the line value Y'. If you use simple deviations, some are going to be positive and others negative, so the sum of all deviations is going to be zero for the best-fit line. A simple sum of deviations, therefore, is not a good measure. You can square the deviations, like they are squared to calculate the mean squared deviation. To find the best-fit line, you have to find the minimal possible sum of squared deviations. Here are the formulas for the slope and the intercept.

$$\text{Slope}(Y) = \frac{\sum_{i=1}^{n}(X_i - \mu(X)) * (Y_i - \mu(Y))}{\sum_{i=1}^{n}(X_i - \mu(X))^2}$$

$$\text{Intercept}(Y) = \mu(Y) - Slope(Y) * \mu(X)$$

Linear regression can be more complex. In a **multiple linear regression**, you use multiple independent variables in a formula. You can also try to express the association with a **polynomial regression** model, where the independent variable is introduced in the equation as an nth order polynomial.

The following code creates another data frame as a subset of the original data frame, this time keeping only the first one hundred rows. The sole purpose of this action is the visualization at the end of this section, where you will see every single point in the graph. The code also removes the TM data frame from the search path and adds the new TMLM data frame to it:

```
TMLM <- TM[1:100, c("YearlyIncome", "Age")];
detach(TM);
attach(TMLM);
```

The following code uses the `lm()` function to create a simple linear regression model, where `YearlyIncome` is modelled as a linear function of `Age`:

```
LinReg1 <- lm(YearlyIncome ~ Age);
summary(LinReg1);
```

If you check the `summary` results for the model, you can see that there is some association between the two variables; however, the association is not that strong. You can try to express the association with polynomial regression, including squared `Age` in the formula:

```
LinReg2 <- lm(YearlyIncome ~ Age + I(Age ^ 2));
summary(LinReg2);
```

If you plot the values for the two variables in a graph, you can see that there is a non-linear dependency between them. The following code plots the cases as points in the plane, and then adds a linear and a **lowess** line to the graph. A lowess line calculation is more complex; it is used here to represent the polynomial relationship between two variables:

```
plot(Age, YearlyIncome,
    cex = 2, col = "orange", lwd = 2);
abline(LinReg1,
    col = "red", lwd = 2);
lines(lowess(Age, YearlyIncome),
    col = "blue", lwd = 2);
```

The following screenshot shows the results:

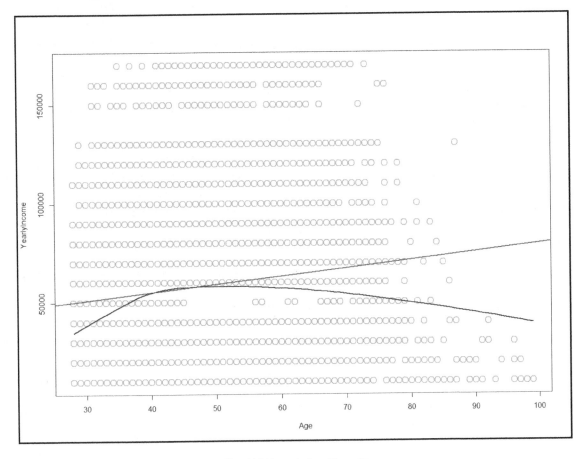

Figure 14-4: Linear and polynomial regression

You can see that the polynomial line (the curve) fits the data slightly better. The polynomial model is also more logical: you earn less when you are young, then you earn more and more, until at some age your income goes down again, probably after you retire. Finally, you can remove the TMLM data frame from the search path:

```
detach(TMLM);
```

Advanced analysis – undirected methods

Data mining and machine learning techniques are divided into two main classes:

- The **directed**, or **supervised** approach: You use known examples and apply information to unknown examples to predict selected target variable(s)
- The **undirected**, or **unsupervised** approach: You discover new patterns inside the dataset as a whole

The most common undirected techniques are **clustering, dimensionality reduction**, and **affinity grouping**, also known as **basket analysis** or **association rules**. An example of clustering is looking through a large number of initially undifferentiated customers and trying to see if they fall into natural groupings based on similarities or dissimilarities of their features. This is a pure example of "undirected data mining" where the user has no preordained agenda and hopes that the data mining tool will reveal some meaningful structure. Affinity grouping is a special kind of clustering that identifies events or transactions that occur simultaneously. A well-known example of affinity grouping is market basket analysis, which attempts to understand what items are sold together at the same time.

In this section, you will learn about four very popular undirected methods:

- Principal components analysis (PCA)
- Exploratory factor analysis (EFA)
- Hierarchical clustering
- K-mean clustering

Principal components and exploratory factor analysis

The **Principal Component Analysis (PCA)** is a **data-reduction** technique. You use it as an intermediate step in a more complex analytical session. Imagine that you need to use hundreds of input variables, which can be correlated. With PCA, you convert a collection of possibly correlated variables into a new collection of linearly uncorrelated variables called principal components. The transformation is defined in such a way that the first principal component has the largest possible dataset overall variance, and each succeeding component in turn has the highest variance possible under the constraint that it is **orthogonal** to (uncorrelated with) the preceding components. The principal components are orthogonal because they are the **eigenvectors** of the covariance matrix, which is symmetric. The first principal component is the eigenvector with the highest **eigenvalue**, the second with the second highest, and so on. In short, an eigenvector is a direction of an eigenvalue with explained variance for this point, for this direction. In further analysis, you keep only few principal components instead of the plethora of original variables. Of course, you lose some variability; nevertheless, the first few principal components should retain the majority of overall dataset variability.

The following figure explains the process of defining the principal components graphically. Initially, variables used in the analysis form a multidimensional space, or matrix, of dimensionality m, if you use m variables. The following picture shows a two-dimensional space. Values of the variables v1 and v2 define cases in this 2-D space. Variability of the cases is spread across both source variables approximately equally. Finding principal components means finding new m axes, where m is exactly equal to the number of the source variables. However, these new axes are selected in such a way that most of the variability of the cases is spread over a single new variable, or over a principal component, like shown in the figure.

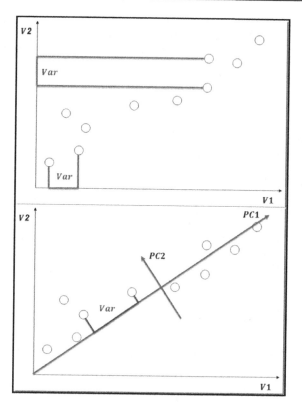

Figure 14-5: Principal components analysis

You use the PCA analysis, as mentioned, to reduce the number of variables in further analysis. In addition, you can use PCA for **anomaly detection**, for finding cases that are somehow different from the majority of cases. You use the residual variability not explained by the couple of first principal components for this task.

Similar to PCA is the **Exploratory Factor Analysis** (EFA), which is used to uncover the latent structure in the input variables collection. A smaller set of calculated variables called **factors** is used to explain the relations between the input variables.

For a start, the following code creates a subset of the TM data frame by extracting the numerical variables only:

```
TMPCAEFA <- TM[, c("TotalChildren", "NumberChildrenAtHome",
                "HouseOwnerFlag", "NumberCarsOwned",
                "BikeBuyer", "YearlyIncome", "Age")];
```

You can use the `princomp()` function from the base R installation to calculate the principal components. However, the following code uses the `principal()` function from the `psych` package, which returns results that are easier to understand. The following code installs the package, loads it in memory, and calculates two principal components from the seven input variables. Note the comment—the components are not rotated. You will learn about the rotation very soon.

```
install.packages("psych");
library(psych);
# PCA not rotated
pcaTM_unrotated <- principal(TMPCAEFA, nfactors = 2, rotate = "none");
pcaTM_unrotated;
```

Here are some partial results:

```
Standardized loadings (pattern matrix) based upon correlation matrix
                         PC1    PC2    h2     u2  com
TotalChildren            0.73   0.43 0.712 0.29 1.6
NumberChildrenAtHome     0.74  -0.30 0.636 0.36 1.3
HouseOwnerFlag           0.20   0.44 0.234 0.77 1.4
NumberCarsOwned          0.70  -0.34 0.615 0.39 1.5
BikeBuyer               -0.23  -0.21 0.097 0.90 2.0
YearlyIncome             0.67  -0.43 0.628 0.37 1.7
Age                      0.46   0.65 0.635 0.36 1.8
                         PC1    PC2
SS loadings              2.32  1.23
Proportion Var           0.33  0.18
Cumulative Var           0.33  0.51
```

In the pattern matrix part, you can see the two **Principal Components (PC) loadings**, in the `PC1` and `PC2` columns. These loadings are correlations of the observed variables with the two PCs. You can use the component loading to interpret the meaning of the PCs. The h2 column tells you the amount of the variance explained by the two components. In the SS loadings row, you can see the eigenvalues of the first two PCs, and how much variability is explained by each of them and cumulatively by both of them.

From the pattern matrix, you can see that all of the input variables highly correlate with `PC1`. For most of them, the correlation is higher than with `PC2`. This is logical, because this is how the components were calculated. However, it is hard to interpret the meaning of the two components. Note that for pure machine learning you might not even be interested in the interpretation; you might just continue with further analysis using the two principal components only instead of the original variables.

You can improve the understanding of the PCs by rotating them. This means you are rotating the axes of the multidimensional hyperspace. The **rotation** is done in such a way that it maximizes associations of PCs with different subsets of input variables each. The rotation can be **orthogonal**, where the rotated components are still uncorrelated, or **oblique**, where correlation between PCs is allowed. In principal component analysis, you typically use orthogonal rotation, because you probably want to use uncorrelated components in further analysis. The following code recalculates the two PCAs using the `varimax`, the most popular orthogonal rotation:

```
pcaTM_varimax <- principal(TMPCAEFA, nfactors = 2, rotate = "varimax");
pcaTM_varimax;
```

The abbreviated results are now slightly different, and definitely more interpretable:

```
Standardized loadings (pattern matrix) based upon correlation matrix
                        PC1    PC2    h2    u2  com
    TotalChildren        0.38   0.76 0.712 0.29 1.5
    NumberChildrenAtHome 0.78   0.15 0.636 0.36 1.1
    HouseOwnerFlag      -0.07   0.48 0.234 0.77 1.0
    NumberCarsOwned      0.78   0.09 0.615 0.39 1.0
    BikeBuyer           -0.08  -0.30 0.097 0.90 1.1
    YearlyIncome         0.79   0.01 0.628 0.37 1.0
    Age                  0.04   0.80 0.635 0.36 1.0
                        PC1    PC2
    SS loadings          2.00  1.56
    Proportion Var       0.29  0.22
    Cumulative Var       0.29  0.51
```

Now you can easily see that the `PC1` has high loadings, or highly correlates with the number of children at home, the number of cars owned, yearly income, and also with the total number of children. The second one correlates more with total children and age, quite well with house ownership flag as well, and negatively with the bike buyer flag.

When you do the EFA, you definitely want to understand the results. The factors are the underlying combined variables that help you understand your data. This is similar to adding computed variables, just in a more complex way, with many input variables. For example, the obesity index could be interpreted as a very simple factor that includes height and weight, and gives you much more information about a person's health than the base two variables do. Therefore, you typically rotate the factors, and also allow correlations between them. The following code extracts two factors from the same dataset as used for the PCA, this time with the `promax` rotation, which is an oblique rotation:

```
efaTM_promax <- fa(TMPCAEFA, nfactors = 2, rotate = "promax");
efaTM_promax;
```

Here are the abbreviated results:

```
Standardized loadings (pattern matrix) based upon correlation matrix
                         MR1    MR2    h2    u2   com
TotalChildren            0.23   0.72 0.684 0.32 1.2
NumberChildrenAtHome     0.77   0.04 0.618 0.38 1.0
HouseOwnerFlag           0.03   0.19 0.040 0.96 1.1
NumberCarsOwned          0.55   0.07 0.332 0.67 1.0
BikeBuyer               -0.05  -0.14 0.027 0.97 1.2
YearlyIncome             0.60  -0.02 0.354 0.65 1.0
Age                     -0.18   0.72 0.459 0.54 1.1
                         MR1    MR2
SS loadings              1.38  1.13
Proportion Var           0.20  0.16
Cumulative Var           0.20  0.36
With factor correlations of
        MR1   MR2
MR1  1.00  0.36
MR2  0.36  1.00
```

Note that this time the results include the correlation between the two factors. In order to interpret the results even more easily, you can use the `fa.diagram()` function, as the following code shows:

```
fa.diagram(efaTM_promax, simple = FALSE,
           main = "EFA Promax");
```

The code produces the following diagram:

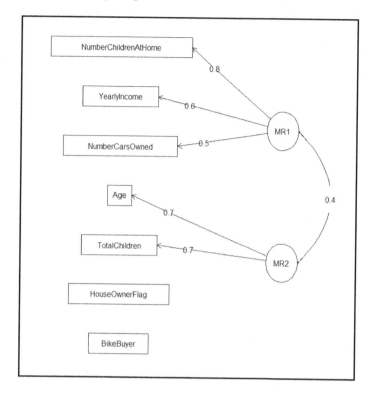

Figure 14-6: Exploratory factor analysis

You can now easily see which variables correlate with which of the two factors, and also the correlation between the two factors.

Finding groups with clustering

Clustering is the process of grouping the data into classes or clusters so that objects within a cluster have high **similarity** in comparison to one another, but are very dissimilar to objects in other clusters. Dissimilarities are assessed based on the attribute values describing the objects.

There are a large number of clustering algorithms. The major methods can be classified into the following categories.

- **Partitioning methods**: A partitioning method constructs K partitions of the data, which satisfy the following requirements: (1) each group must contain at least one object, and (2) each object must belong to exactly one group. Given the initial K number of partitions to construct, the method creates initial partitions. It then uses an iterative relocation technique that attempts to improve the partitioning by moving objects from one group to another. There are various kinds of criteria for judging the quality of the partitions. Some of the most popular include the **k-means** algorithm, where each cluster is represented by the mean value of the objects in the cluster, and the **k-medoids** algorithm, where each cluster is represented by one of the objects located near the center of the cluster. You can see an example of the k-means clustering in the previous chapter. The example used the scalable `rxKmeans()` function from the `RevoScaleR` package. You can use this function on very large datasets as well.

- **Hierarchical methods**: A hierarchical method creates a hierarchical decomposition of the given set of data objects. These methods are agglomerative or divisive. The agglomerative (bottom-up) approach starts with each object forming a separate group. It successively merges the objects or groups close to one another, until all groups are merged into one. The divisive (top-down) approach starts with all the objects in the same cluster. In each successive iteration, a cluster is split up into smaller clusters, until eventually each object is in one cluster or until a termination condition holds.

- **Density-based methods**: Methods based on the distance between objects can find only spherical-shaped clusters and encounter difficulty in discovering clusters of arbitrary shapes. So other methods have been developed based on the notion of density. The general idea is to continue growing the given cluster as long as the density (number of objects or data points) in the "neighborhood" exceeds some threshold; that is, for each data point within a given cluster, the neighborhood of a given radius has to contain at least a minimum number of points.

- **Model-based methods**: Model-based methods hypothesize a model for each of the clusters and find the best fit of the data to the given model. A model-based technique might locate clusters by constructing a density function that reflects the spatial distribution of the data points. Unlike conventional clustering, which primarily identifies groups of like objects, this conceptual clustering goes one step further by also finding characteristic descriptions for each group, where each group represents a concept or a class.

A hierarchical clustering model training typically starts by calculating a **distance matrix**–a matrix with distances between data points in a multidimensional hyperspace, where each input variable defines one dimension of that hyperspace. Distance measure can be a geometrical distance or some other, more complex measure. A **dendrogram** is a tree diagram frequently used to illustrate the arrangement of the clusters produced by hierarchical clustering. Dendrograms are also often used in computational biology to illustrate the clustering of genes or samples. The following figure shows the process of building an agglomerative hierarchical clustering dendrogram from six cases in a two-dimensional space (two input variables) in six steps:

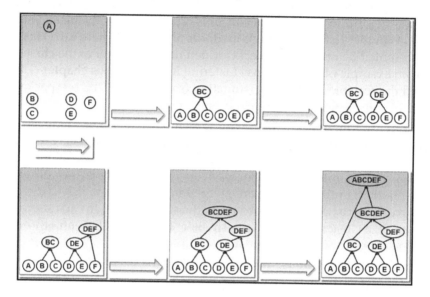

Figure 14-7: Hierarchical clustering process

The following code creates a subset of the data with 50 randomly selected rows and numerical columns only. You cannot show a dendrogram with thousands of cases. Hierarchical clustering is suitable for small datasets only:

```
TM50 <- TM[sample(1:nrow(TM), 50, replace=FALSE),
          c("TotalChildren", "NumberChildrenAtHome",
            "HouseOwnerFlag", "NumberCarsOwned",
            "BikeBuyer", "YearlyIncome", "Age")];
```

Then you can calculate the distance matrix with the `dist()` function and create a hierarchical clustering model with the `hclust()` function:

```
ds <- dist(TM50, method = "euclidean") ;
TMCL <- hclust(ds, method="ward.D2");
```

In a dendrogram, you can easily see how many clusters you should use. You make a cut where the difference in the distance is the highest. You can plot the model to see the dendrogram. The following code plots the model, and then uses the `cutree()` function to define two clusters, and the `rect.hclust()` function to draw two rectangles around the two clusters:

```
plot(TMCL, xlab = NULL, ylab = NULL);
groups <- cutree(TMCL, k = 2);
rect.hclust(TMCL, k = 2, border = "red");
```

You can see the final result in the following screenshot:

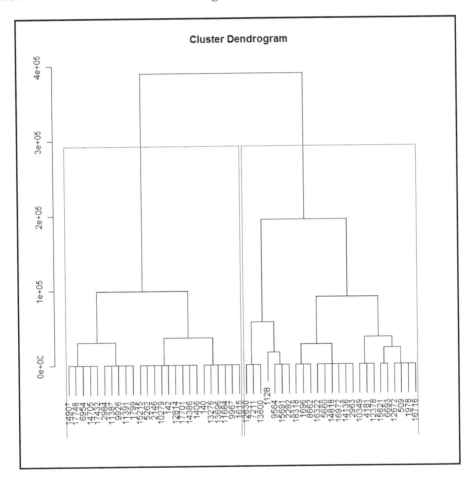

Figure 14-8: A dendrogram with two clusters

The dendrogram shows the growth of the clusters, and how the cases were associated together. Please note that the decision to cut the population into two clusters is arbitrary: a cut into three or five clusters would work as well. You would decide how many clusters to use based on your business perspective, because the clusters must be meaningful for you.

Advanced analysis – directed methods

Some of the most important directed techniques include **classification**, **estimation**, and **forecasting**. Classification means to examine a new case and assign it to a predefined discrete class. For example, assigning keywords to articles and assigning customers to known segments. Next is estimation, where you are trying to estimate the value of a continuous variable of a new case. You can, for example, estimate the number of children or the family income. Forecasting is somewhat similar to classification and estimation. The main difference is that you can't check the forecasted value at the time of the forecast. Of course, you can evaluate it if you just wait long enough. Examples include forecasting which customers will leave in the future, which customers will order additional services, and the sales amount in a specific region at a specific time in the future.

After you train the models, you use them to perform predictions. In most of the classification and other directed approach projects, you build multiple models, using different algorithms, different parameters of the algorithms, different independent variables, additional calculated independent variables, and more. The question arises which model is the best. You need to test the accuracy of the predictions of different models. To do so, you simply split the original dataset into training and test sets. You use the training set to train the model. A common practice is to use 70 percent of the data for the **training set**. The remaining 30 percent of the data goes into the **test set**, which is used for predictions. When you know the value of the predicted variable, you can measure the quality of the predictions.

In R, there is a plethora of directed algorithms. This section is limited to three only: The logistic regression from the base installation, **decision trees** from the base installation, and **conditional inference trees** from the `party` package .

In this section, you will learn how to:

- Prepare the training and the test dataset
- Use the logistic regression algorithm
- Create decision trees models
- Evaluate predictive models

Predicting with logistic regression

A **logistic regression** model consists of **input units** and an **output unit**, which is the predicted value. Input units are combined into a single transformed output value. This calculation uses the unit's **activation function**. An activation function has two parts: The first part is the **combination function** that merges all of the inputs into a single value (weighted sum, for example); the second part is the **transfer function**, which transfers the value of the combination function to the output value of the unit. The transfer function is called **sigmoid** or **logistic function** and is S-shaped. Training a logistic regression model is the process of setting the best weights on the inputs of each of the units to maximize the quality of the predicted output. The formula for the logistic function is:

$$S(x) = \frac{1}{1 + e^{-x}}$$

The following figure shows the logistic regression algorithm graphically.

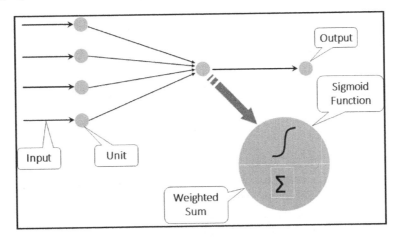

Figure 14-9: The logistic regression algorithm

In the previous module, you have already seen the `rxLogit()` function from the `RevoScaleR` package in action. Now you are going to learn how to use the `glm()` function from the base installation. In addition, you will see how you can improve the quality of the predictions by improving the data and selecting different algorithms.

Let's start the advanced analytics session with re-reading the target mail data. In addition, the following code defines the ordered levels of the `Education factor` variables and changes the `BikeBuyer` variable to a labeled factor.

```
TM = read.table("C:\\SQL2016DevGuide\\Chapter14_TM.csv",
                sep=",", header=TRUE,
                stringsAsFactors = TRUE);
TM$Education = factor(TM$Education, order=TRUE,
                levels=c("Partial High School",
                         "High School","Partial College",
                         "Bachelors", "Graduate Degree"));
TM$BikeBuyer <- factor(TM$BikeBuyer,
                levels = c(0,1),
                labels = c("No","Yes"));
```

Next, you need to prepare the training and the test sets. The split must be random. However, by defining the seed, you can reproduce the same split later, meaning you can get the same cases in the test and in the training set again.

```
set.seed(1234);
train <- sample(nrow(TM), 0.7 * nrow(TM));
TM.train <- TM[train,];
TM.test <- TM[-train,];
```

Now it's time to create the first logistic regression model. For the sake of simplicity, the first model uses three input variables only.

```
TMLogR <- glm(BikeBuyer ~
              YearlyIncome + Age + NumberCarsOwned,
              data=TM.train, family=binomial());
```

You test the model by performing predictions on the test dataset. Logistic regression returns the output as a continuous value between zero and 1. The following code recodes the output value to a factor where a value greater than 0.5 is transformed to "Yes", meaning this is a predicted bike buyer, and otherwise to "No", meaning this is not a predicted bike buyer. The results are shown in a pivot table together with the actual values:

```
probLR <- predict(TMLogR, TM.test, type = "response");
predLR <- factor(probLR > 0.5,
                 levels = c(FALSE, TRUE),
                 labels = c("No","Yes"));
perfLR <- table(TM.test$BikeBuyer, predLR,
                dnn = c("Actual", "Predicted"));
perfLR;
```

The pivot table created is called the classification (or confusion) matrix. Here is the result:

```
         Predicted
Actual   No   Yes
    No  1753 1084
   Yes  1105 1604
```

You can compare the predicted and the actual numbers to find the following results to check **true positives** (the values that were predicted correctly as Yes), true negatives (the values that were predicted correctly as No), **false positives** (the values that were predicted incorrectly as Yes), and **false negatives** (the values that were predicted incorrectly as No). The result is not over-exciting. So let's continue the session by creating and testing a new logistic regression model, this time with all possible input variables, to see whether we can get a better result:

```
TMLogR <- glm(BikeBuyer ~
              MaritalStatus + Gender +
              TotalChildren + NumberChildrenAtHome +
              Education + Occupation +
              HouseOwnerFlag + NumberCarsOwned +
              CommuteDistance + Region +
              YearlyIncome + Age,
              data=TM.train, family=binomial());
probLR <- predict(TMLogR, TM.test, type = "response");
predLR <- factor(probLR > 0.5,
                 levels = c(FALSE, TRUE),
                 labels = c("No","Yes"));
perfLR <- table(TM.test$BikeBuyer, predLR,
                dnn = c("Actual", "Predicted"));
perfLR;
```

This time, the results are slightly better, as you can see from the following classification matrix. Still, the results are not very exciting:

```
         Predicted
Actual   No   Yes
    No  1798 1039
   Yes   928 1781
```

In the target mail dataset, there are many variables that are integers, although they actually are factors (nominal or ordinal variables). Let's try to help the algorithm by explicitly defining them as factors. All of them are also ordered. Of course, after changing the original data set, you need to recreate the training and test sets. The following code does all the aforementioned tasks:

```
TM$TotalChildren = factor(TM$TotalChildren, order=TRUE);
TM$NumberChildrenAtHome = factor(TM$NumberChildrenAtHome, order=TRUE);
```

```
TM$NumberCarsOwned = factor(TM$NumberCarsOwned, order=TRUE);
TM$HouseOwnerFlag = factor(TM$HouseOwnerFlag, order=TRUE);
set.seed(1234);
train <- sample(nrow(TM), 0.7 * nrow(TM));
TM.train <- TM[train,];
TM.test <- TM[-train,];
```

Now let's rebuild and test the model with all possible independent variables:

```
TMLogR <- glm(BikeBuyer ~
                MaritalStatus + Gender +
                TotalChildren + NumberChildrenAtHome +
                Education + Occupation +
                HouseOwnerFlag + NumberCarsOwned +
                CommuteDistance + Region +
                YearlyIncome + Age,
              data=TM.train, family=binomial());
probLR <- predict(TMLogR, TM.test, type = "response");
predLR <- factor(probLR > 0.5,
                 levels = c(FALSE, TRUE),
                 labels = c("No","Yes"));
perfLR <- table(TM.test$BikeBuyer, predLR,
                dnn = c("Actual", "Predicted"));
perfLR;
```

The results have improved again:

```
         Predicted
Actual    No  Yes
    No  1850  987
   Yes   841 1868
```

Still, there is room for improving the predictions. However, this time we are going to use a different algorithm.

Classifying and predicting with decision trees

Decision trees are one of the most frequently used data mining algorithms. The algorithm is not very complex, yet it gives very good results in many cases. In addition, you can easily understand the result. You use decision trees for classification and prediction. Typical usage scenarios include:

- Predicting which customers will leave
- Targeting the audience for mailings and promotional campaigns
- Explaining reasons for a decision

Decision trees is a directed technique. Your target variable is the one that holds information about a particular decision, divided into a few discrete and broad categories (yes / no; liked / partially liked / disliked, and so on). You are trying to explain this decision using other gleaned information saved in other variables (demographic data, purchasing habits, and so on). With limited statistical significance, you are going to predict the target variable for a new case using its known values of the input variables based on the results of your trained model.

You use **recursive partitioning** to build the tree. The data is split into partitions using a certain value of one of the explaining variables. The partitions are then split again and again. Initially the data is in one big box. The algorithm tries all possible breaks of both input (explaining) variables for the initial split. The goal is to get purer partitions considering the classes of the target variable. The tree continues to grow using the two new partitions as separate starting points and splitting them more. You have to stop the process somewhere. Otherwise, you could get a completely fitted tree that has only one case in each class. The class would be, of course, absolutely pure and this would not make any sense; you could not use the results for any meaningful prediction, because the prediction would be 100% accurate, but for this case only. This phenomenon is called **overfitting**.

The following code uses the `rpart()` function from the base installation to build a decision tree using all possible independent variables, with factors properly defined, as used in the last logistic regression model:

```
TMDTree <- rpart(BikeBuyer ~ MaritalStatus + Gender +
                 TotalChildren + NumberChildrenAtHome +
                 Education + Occupation +
                 HouseOwnerFlag + NumberCarsOwned +
                 CommuteDistance + Region +
                 YearlyIncome + Age,
                 method="class", data=TM.train);
```

You can plot the tree to understand how the splits were made. The following code uses the `prp()` function from the `rpart.plot` package to plot the tree:

```
install.packages("rpart.plot");
library(rpart.plot);
prp(TMDTree, type = 2, extra = 104, fallen.leaves = FALSE);
```

You can see the plot of the decision tree in the following figure. You can easily read the rules from the tree, for example if the number of cars owned is two, three, or four, and yearly income is not lower than 65,000, then you have approximately 67% of non-buyers (in the following figure, just follow the path to the leftmost node):

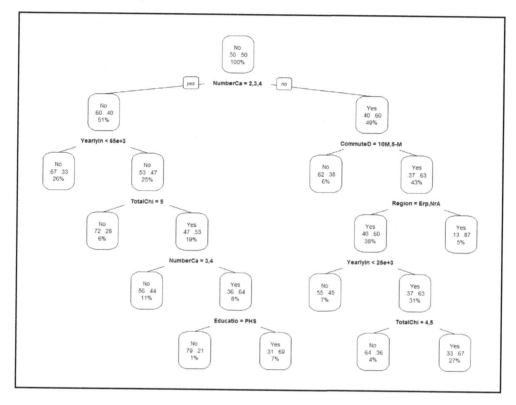

Figure 14-10: Decision tree plot

So how does this model perform? The following code creates the classification matrix for this model:

```
predDT <- predict(TMDTree, TM.test, type = "class");
perfDT <- table(TM.test$BikeBuyer, predDT,
           dnn = c("Actual", "Predicted"));
perfDT;
```

Here are the results:

```
            Predicted
Actual    No   Yes
    No  2119   718
   Yes  1232  1477
```

The predictions are better in some cells and worse in other cells, comparing to the last logistic regression model. The number of false negatives (predicted "No", actual "Yes") is especially disappointing. So let's try it with another model. This time, the following code uses the `ctree()` function from the `party` package:

```
install.packages("party", dependencies = TRUE);
library("party");
TMDT <- ctree(BikeBuyer ~ MaritalStatus + Gender +
              TotalChildren + NumberChildrenAtHome +
              Education + Occupation +
              HouseOwnerFlag + NumberCarsOwned +
              CommuteDistance + Region +
              YearlyIncome + Age,
              data=TM.train);
predDT <- predict(TMDT, TM.test, type = "response");
perfDT <- table(TM.test$BikeBuyer, predDT,
              dnn = c("Actual", "Predicted"));
perfDT;
```

The results are:

```
            Predicted
Actual    No   Yes
    No  2190   647
   Yes   685  2024
```

Now you can finally see some big improvements. The version of the decision trees algorithm used by the `ctree()` function is called the **conditional inference trees**. This version uses a different method for deciding how to make the splits. The function accepts many parameters. For example, the following code creates a new model, this time lowering the condition for a split, thus forcing more splits:

```
TMDT <- ctree(BikeBuyer ~ MaritalStatus + Gender +
              TotalChildren + NumberChildrenAtHome +
              Education + Occupation +
              HouseOwnerFlag + NumberCarsOwned +
              CommuteDistance + Region +
              YearlyIncome + Age,
              data=TM.train,
              controls = ctree_control(mincriterion = 0.70));
```

```
predDT <- predict(TMDT, TM.test, type = "response");
perfDT <- table(TM.test$BikeBuyer, predDT,
                dnn = c("Actual", "Predicted"));
perfDT;
```

The classification matrix for this model is shown below:

```
          Predicted
Actual   No   Yes
    No  2200   637
   Yes   603  2106
```

The predictions have slightly improved again. You could continue with the process until you reach the desired quality of the predictions.

Advanced graphing

Now is the time when we head towards the final section of this chapter. This section is a bit lighter. We will finish the chapter and the book with additional visualizations of the data. This section discusses advanced graphing with the help of the ggplot2 package.

This section introduces the following:

- Basic ggplot() function
- Advanced plot types
- Trellis charts

Introducing ggplot2

The ggplot2 package is a frequently used graphical package among the R community. The package provides comprehensive and coherent grammar for graphical functions. The grammar is also consistent, and you can create nice graphs with this package. The ggplot2 package enhances the built-in graphical capabilities and gives a layer-oriented approach to plotting graphs.

The following command installs the package and loads it to memory:

```
install.packages("ggplot2");
library("ggplot2");
```

Here is the code for the first graph that uses the `ggplot()` function. The data used is the TM data frame, as created and modified in the previous section, with all of the factors properly defined:

```
ggplot (TM, aes(Region, fill=Education)) +
    geom_bar(position="stack");
```

The `ggplot()` function defines the dataset used (TM in this case) and initializes the plot. Inside this function, the `aes()` (short for aesthetics) function defines the roles of the variables for the graph. In this case, the graph shows the frequencies of the `Region` variable, where the `Region` bars are filled with the `Education` variable, to show the number of cases with each level of education in each region. The `geom_bar()` function defines the plot type, in this case a bar plot. There are many other `geom_xxx()` functions for other plot types. The following screenshot shows the results:

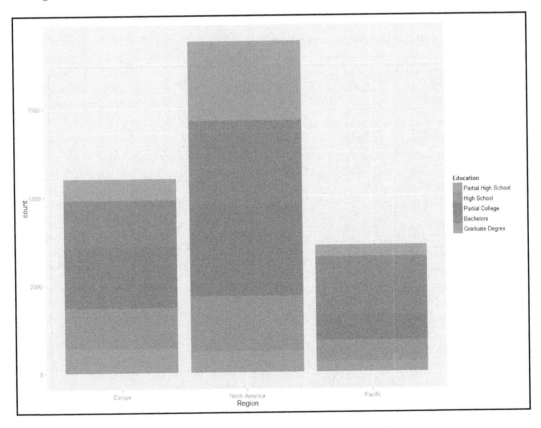

Figure 14-11: Education in regions

You should also try to create graphs with different a position parameter—you can use position = "fill" to create stacked bars, where you can easily see the relative distribution of education inside each region, and position = "dodge" to show the distribution of education for each region side by side.

Remember the graph from the *Linear Regression* section, the fourth graph in this chapter, the graph that shows the data points for the first 100 cases for the YearlyIncome and Age variables, together with the linear regression and the lowess line? The following code creates the same graph, this time with the ggplot() function, with multiple geom_xxx() functions:

```
TMLM <- TM[1:100, c("YearlyIncome", "Age")];
ggplot(data = TMLM, aes(x=Age, y=YearlyIncome)) +
  geom_point() +
  geom_smooth(method = "lm", color = "red") +
  geom_smooth(color = "blue");
```

The result is shown in the following screenshot:

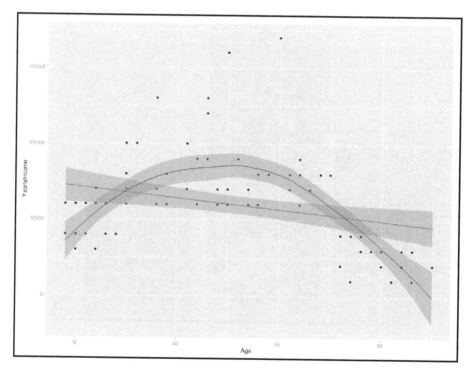

Figure 14.12: Linear and polynomial regression with ggplot

Advanced graphs with ggplot2

The third figure in this chapter is a box plot showing the `YearlyIncome` variable distribution in classes of the `Education` variable. Again, it is possible to make this graph even prettier with ggplot. Besides box plots, ggplot can add violin plots as well. A violin plot shows the kernel density for a continuous variable. This is an effective way to see the distribution of a continuous variable in classes of a discrete variable. The following code produces a combination of a violin and a box plot in order to show the distribution of yearly income in classes of education:

```
ggplot(TM, aes (x = Education, y = YearlyIncome)) +
  geom_violin(fill = "lightgreen") +
  geom_boxplot(fill = "orange",
               width = 0.2);
```

The graph produced is not just nice, it is really informative, as you can see in the following screenshot:

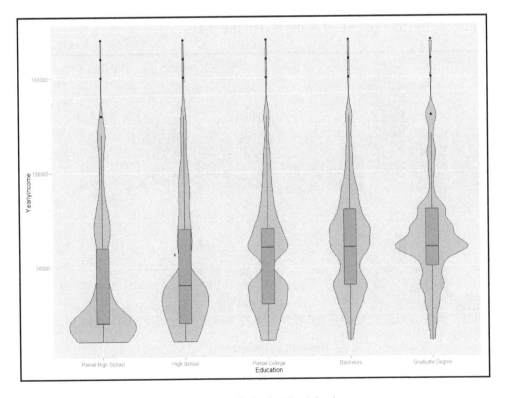

Figure 14-13: A combination of a violin and a box plot

For the last graph in this book, I selected a **trellis chart**. A trellis chart is a multi-panel chart of small, similar charts, which use the same axes and same scale. This way you can easily compare them. Trellis graphs are called faceted graphs in the `ggplot` semantics. The `facet_grid()` function defines the discrete variables to be used for splitting the chart in small multiples over rows and columns. The following code creates an example of a trellis chart:

```
ggplot(TM, aes(x = NumberCarsOwned, fill = Region)) +
    geom_bar(stat = "bin") +
    facet_grid(MaritalStatus ~ BikeBuyer) +
    theme(text = element_text(size=30));
```

You can see the results in the next figure. The values of the `MaritalStatus` variable are used to split the chart in two rows, while the values of the `BikeBuyer` column are used to split the chart in two columns. The chart has four small multiples, one for each combination of `MaritalStatus` and `BikeBuyer`. Inside each of the four small charts you can see the distribution of the `NumberCarsOwned` variable, and inside each bar you can see the distribution of the Region variable for that specific number of cars. The `theme()` function is used to increase the font size of all of the text in the chart:

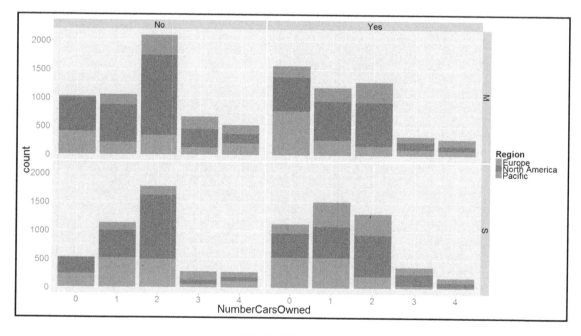

Figure 14-14: A trellis chart

This is not the end of capabilities of the `ggplot2` package. There are many more additional graphs and visualizations in the package, and the visualization does not stop here. With additional packages, you can plot maps, Google maps, heat maps, areas, circulars, word clouds, networks, tree maps, funnels, and more.

Summary

For an SQL Server developer, this must have been quite an exhaustive chapter. Of course, the whole chapter is not about the T-SQL language, it is about the R language, and about statistics and advanced analytics. Of course, developers can also profit from the capabilities that the new language has to offer. You learned how to measure the associations between discrete, continuous, and the combination of discrete and continuous variables. You learned about directed and undirected data mining and machine learning methods. Finally, you saw how to produce quite advanced graphs in R.

Please be aware that if you want to become a real data scientist, you need to learn more about statistics, data mining and machine learning algorithms, and practice programming in R. Data science is a long learning process, just like programming and development. Therefore, when you start using R, you should have your code double-checked by a senior data scientist for all the tricks and tips that I haven't covered in this chapter. Nevertheless, this and the previous chapter should give you enough knowledge to start your data science learning journey, and even kick off a real-life data science project.

Index